VOICES FROM THE MOUNTAIN

ŚATA-PIṬAKA SERIES

INDO-ASIAN LITERATURES

Volume 648

Reproduced in original scripts and languages
Translated, annotated and critically evaluated by
specialists of the East and the West

Founded by
Prof. RAGHUVIRA *M.A., Ph.D., D.Litt. et Phil.*
Continued by his son
Prof. LOKESH CHANDRA

आचार्य—रघुवीर—समुपक्रान्तं

जम्बुद्वीप-राष्ट्राणां
(भारत-नेपाल-गान्धार-शूलिक-तुरुष्क-पारस-ताजक-भोट-चीन-मोंगोल-मञ्जु-
उदयवर्ष-सिंहल-सुवर्णभू-श्याम-कम्बुज-चम्पा-द्वीपान्तरादीनां)

एकैकेषां समस्रोतसां संस्कृति—साहित्य—समुच्चय—
सरितां सागरभूतं

शतपिटकम्

VOICES FROM THE MOUNTAIN:

THE ŚAILENDRA INSCRIPTIONS DISCOVERED IN CENTRAL JAVA AND ON THE MALAY PENINSULA

translations and commentaries by

MARK E. LONG

INTERNATIONAL ACADEMY OF INDIAN CULTURE
and ADITYA PRAKASHAN, NEW DELHI

First published: 2014

ISBN 978-81-7742-141-5

Published by Aditya Prakashan, 2/18 Ansari Road, New Delhi – 110 002.

email: contact@adityaprakashan.com
website: www.adityaprakashan.com
Printed at : Thomson Press (India) Ltd.

This publication is dedicated to Prof. Lokesh Chandra out of gratitude for his extensive guidance, patience, sagacity, ingenuity, vigilance, generosity, equanimity, and clear-minded compassion.

Table of Contents

List of Illustrations

Chapter VIII

Appendices

Homage to Mañjuśrī!

Wearing the dress of a Buddhist monk bearing the dark-blue color of a swarm of bees, carrying a chaplet of various fragrant and beautiful flowers,

Traversing a multitude of Buddha fields in all the directions at the same time, taking away every obstacle by means of a mighty and invincible performance,

Causing the cessation of the fires of ghostly existences and hells by means of an unrestrained rain, along with pursuing the advantage of good beings by abiding in proximity to the abyss of transmigration,

Bearing the ornament of strength for producing the opening of the eyes of the people, wise, strong in body, effecting the astonishment of the world,

He who is bestowed and heaped upon the people, whose splendor is to be acknowledged as the 'sweet glory' (*mañjuśrī*), again and again with my body, completely as it were, adoration unto Him,

A great lake of acts of joy for those tormented by various sorrows, a mighty cloud for satiating the hells of thirst in the three worlds,

A wishing-tree cherished by the earth with fruit abounding in the ten directions that is venerated by the lotus-eyes of people delighted by the attainment of their desires,

Who is praised by hundreds of bodhisattvas with their horripilations from bewilderment being gone, I pay homage to Mañjuśrī with ever-increasing reverential salutations,

To the physician who completely destroys suffering for the sake of effecting happiness and munificence, honor to thee, Mañjughoṣa, for that on which one depends in every way.

Dedication of merit

Thus, after having written of the sons of the Conqueror, and of their extraordinary marvels in every respect, by whatever has been acquired, practiced, and a benefit to me, let there be happiness without end for living beings thereby until the condition of the one gone to bliss is the governing influence to the furthest extent of the boundless sky.

— From the *Śikṣā-samuccaya* by Śāntideva (XIX.64-XIX.73).

Introduction

The inscriptions, architecture and art objects produced during Central Java's so-called Classic Age are the primary references at our disposal for gaining an understanding of the historical evolution of this splendid civilization during the eighth and ninth centuries of the Common Era (CE)—particularly with respect to the relatively abrupt flowering of Mahāyāna Buddhism under the royal patronage of the enigmatic Śailendra ('Lord of the mountain') dynasty. It is therefore entirely surprising that the Sanskrit inscriptions attributed to members of the Śailendra dynasty (*śailendravaṅśa*) have not heretofore been the subject of a systematic and thoroughly comprehensive review.

The majority of all Javanese *praśasti* were intended to proclaim and delineate the legal rights obtained by religious foundations over villages, irrigated rice fields and other properties that were donated to support Buddhist and Hindu temples. Known as freeholds (*sīma*), the annual output of these donations were not subject to the same rules of taxation as would have been the case at other institutions in the kingdom. These charters often include lists of the state officials and local dignitaries, including the kingdom's tax officials, who had acted as witnesses. In some cases, these charters also delineate obligations to be honored periodically by the local community at specific intervals goings forward.

Several of the Śailendra charters to be discussed in this book likewise refer to the establishment of legal rights for Buddhist religious foundations. However, the greater part of their contents is devoted to paying homage to the Buddhist divinity or divinities enshrined at the religious institution to which each charter pertains as well as to honor the Śailendra family member or members responsible for promulgating these inscriptions. Furthermore, some of the Śailendra charters to be discussed below also refer to specific members of the Buddhist clergy as well as visitors from abroad. In all of these respects, the Śailendra inscriptions provide us with a wealth of additional information about the fostering of Buddhism on the island as well as Central Java's participation in Asia's Buddhistic community at large.

As Pollock (2006: 115-161) has incitefully observed, beginning quite suddenly in the fourth and fifth centuries CE, depending on locale, *praśasti* composers right across South and Southeast Asia began harnessing the power of Sanskrit's unique communicative capabilities[1] to conceive of and articulate the very nature of political power in terms that transcend time, space and ethnicity, and with the ruler's fame, as opposed to historical fact, constituting the core value of the monarch's nature to be promoted. Their principle aim was "to lift the lord they celebrate out of the flux of time and emancipate him from the constraints of place." Indeed, royal claims "to universal sovereignty would have been unintelligible if asserted in a *deśabhāsa*, a language of place; those languages were to become the medium of an altogether different—a regional—political conception" (Pollock 2006: 147). Yet another closely related feature is Sanskrit's trans-ethnicity, "whereby such claims were not only intelligible but in a sense rational, since they comprised a view from everywhere in general and nowhere in particular" (Pollock 2006: 259).

---

[1]For example, Pollock (2006: 136) has characterized *śleṣa*, or "the capacity to express two significations simultaneously" as being "one of the grandeurs of the *praśasti* style and a unique achievement of Sanskrit culture...." Moreover, "Sanskrit alone was authorized for figures of sound, and more important, for complex meters which were one of the great cultural exports of Indian antiquity.... These semantic and phonic capacities radically separated the object of Sanskrit political discourse from the world of the everyday."

Pollock (2006: 133) cautions against viewing either military conquest or religious revolution as having been responsible for Sanskrit's rise to prominence as the exclusive language for expressing this "cosmopolitan way of political being".

> "What transpired seems to have happened according to some cultural process of imitation and borrowing less familiar to us as causative than conquest or conversion, some impulse toward transculturation that made it sensible, even desirable, to adopt the new Sanskrit cultural-political style as an act of pure free will. Second, the development of this style occurred at the cost of retarding or even arresting local literary traditions..... When Sanskrit was superseded, it was precisely in combination with a new assertion of local literary language and local kinds of polity.... Third, the cosmopolitan cultural gestalt generated by these transregional developments consisted of not just a shared language but a set of shared expressive practices and political representations, which points toward something like an aestheticization of power. If political will—in the form of a declaration of qualification to rule in consequence of history, identity, piety, valor, intelligence, culture, civility, beauty, and an account of what that rule meant in terms of good works and heroic deeds—was to be expressed in a public text, it would henceforth and invariably have to be expressed in Sanskrit" (Pollock 2006: 133-134).

By contrast, the straightforward materiality of land boundaries and tax exemptions increasingly became expressed over time in local languages rather than Sanskrit throughout South and Southeast Asia, though Pollock (2006: 131) noted that the use of non-Sanskritic official titles in Central Java's Kalasan (Chapter II) and Abhayagirivihāra (Chapter IV) charters "suggests a more complex negotiation between local and cosmopolitan political styles than was typical elsewhere". Furthermore, the Kayuwaṅan charter (Chapter V) represents yet another attempt to bridge the language divide by presenting both Sanskrit and Old Javanese text segments. Additionally, the Old Javanese Śivagṛha inscription (856 CE) is a unique example of an attempt to supplant Sanskrit as the preferred language for promulgating political poetry on the island, "but it has been remodeled for a smaller, regional world, that of Java alone" (Pollock 2006: 390). Indeed, the abandonment of Sanskrit shortly thereafter as the preferred language for promulgating royal charters in Central Java strongly suggests that a major change had taken place with respect to the Javanese conception of kingship, given that the vast majority of the Old Javanese *praśasti* records issued thereafter typically focus on recording the transfer of tax-exempt status to religious institutions or otherwise documenting additional legal decisions.

The need for greater transparency

All of the inscriptions discussed in this book have already been described, transcribed, translated and analyzed, in whole and in part, by numerous Java scholars over the past 150 years and we are deeply indebted to them for the progress made to date. Nevertheless, the growth over time in our knowledge about Central Java's Classic Age civilization provides us with further opportunities to broaden our understanding of these historical documents as well as resolve certain outstanding issues that have been the subject of scholarly debate. The principal problem faced by most historians and students, however, is their lack of expertise in the Sanskrit language.

In my quest to further my own research into the history of Central Java I was most fortunate to have been able to enlist the close collaboration of the Sanskrit scholar Prof. Lokesh Chandra. Over a five-year period, our frequent correspondence about each and every stanza contained in the six inscriptions analyzed in this book made it possible for me to gain many valuable insights into the plethora of nuances presented in the charters to be discussed herein. In the final analysis, however, the present work is my own interpretation for which I bear total responsibility. In those instances in which I have disagreed with new, previously unpublished translations proposed by Prof. Chandra for selected verses I have presented his alternate interpretations in the footnotes.

In the following chapters discussing the six 'Śailendra' inscriptions discovered in maritime Southeast Asia, several basic assumptions have guided my efforts. First and foremost, it is to be presumed that the Śailendra inscriptions were meant to be read by Sanskrit-literate people in general and with the inscriptions' composers having intended to communicate to their audiences through their eloquent composition of verses.

All translations are compromises that attempt to balance the requirements of grammar with the poet's pursuit of elegance. Hence, no single translation can be considered the final word on message content. For this reason, the present publication should be viewed more as a workbook than a definitive, polished set of English-language equivalents. Moreover, the potential poetic merit of the compositions to be presented below strongly suggests that certain strophes were intended to simultaneously convey multiple layers of meaning, which makes it all but impossible for a single literal translation to capture all of the nuances that their composers had intended to convey.

The translations to be presented below are broken down into parts that identify the overall grammatical structure without being encumbered by the wide variety of structural text changes that become imposed at word boundaries according the rules of *sandhi* ('joining'), which have been formulated to forestall any sound combinations that are hard to pronounce. Moreover, the transcriptions for verses, or fragments thereof, are accompanied by diagrams that clarify the requirements imposed by the specific Sanskrit meter selected for use in a strophe or a series of stanzas. And for a number of reasons, I have also presumed that the composers of the individual inscriptions to be analyzed below had selected a specific meter for a single verse or contiguous set of strophes on the basis of the moods conveyed by cadence. In my opinion, there are plenty of instances in which the name that has been assigned to a specific Sanskrit meter potentially underlines the central theme of each stanza as well as communicates additional nuances that may shed further light on the composer's overall message.

The Sanskrit experts who have previously translated the Śailendra inscriptions have invariably presented their works in much the same form. First, a transcription of the complete Sanskrit text is provided in its entirety. Next, the translator presents an English-only translation for the entire text. For the general reader, this format is cumbersome because of the need to flip back and forth between the two discrete segments. Though the prior translators have also included comments on a specific word or compositum, by and large there had been no attempt to otherwise explain the innumerable choices that they had to make in order to arrive at a final draft.

Consequently, the conventional format imposed by virtually all prior translators appears to be directed at an audience composed primarily of Sanskrit specialists. In my opinion, this lack of transparency is a major obstacle to historical research because it fails to give historians, students and enthusiasts the tools they need to more closely evaluate content and context. The end result is akin to a Javanese *wayang* performance during which the audience is presented with a monochrome experience consisting of a series of shadow shapes, which are cast upon a opaque screen. Moreover, most audience members are unfamiliar with the ancient language in which these shadow casting performances are uttered. It is only occasionally that specific characters appear that speak directly to the audience in a familiar vernacular. It is only when we view the *wayang* from behind the screen that we actually can see the original hand-held attributes in all their glorious colors as well as view the various activities performed by the narrator and puppeteer (*dalang*) guiding the performance.

The Sanskrit meter employed for each and every verse also receives a higher level of scrutiny herein than in prior translation works. Among other things, a Sanskrit poet may select a particular meter for a verse to convey a specific mood, to indicate a change in topic or to make a verse or series of stanzas stand out from the remainder of the composition (Morgan 2011: 29). Furthermore, the cadences selected by the inscriptions' composers are comparable to the *gamelan* music accompanying Javanese *wayang* performances.

One major goal of the translation method presented in this book is to eliminate the opaque screen so that a wider audience can ascertain just how each stanza's translation has been accomplished. Moreover, the plethora of additional nuances potentially conveyed by each Sanskrit term, which no single stock translation simply can convey, are evaluated. Whenever an English-language synonym is used in a translation, the closest Sanskrit dictionary match is provided in quotation marks within the parentheses that also enclose the original Sanskrit word.

Another important goal of the translation method presented in this book is to place less emphasis on the many emendations proposed by other translators by placing most of them in the footnotes rather than in-line with the main text. This avoids potentially misleading translations such as de Casparis' English-language rendering of v.1 from the Plaosan inscription (1956), which is a Śailendra charter in theory only. His emendation of *pratima<modayah>* ('as an incomparable sunrise') is not the only possibility, as the reader shall see in Chapter VI and Chapter VII.

When offering speculative translations for fragmentary verses, however, those emendations which are entirely hypothetical are placed in square brackets. Moreover, when dealing with fragmentary strophes, the present work seeks to avoid mixing and matching content from two different half verses. This is an interpretive technique frequently used by Chandra in volume IV of his *Cultural Horizons of India* (1995) series.

A third goal of the present publication is to correct the mistakes and oversights of prior translators such as Sarkar (I: 1971/2), whose incomplete research pertaining to the comments of other scholars with respect to their various interpretations of specific strophes has led many scholars astray, particularly with respect to several important points that previously had been discussed by de Casparis and Damais. One example is his perpetuation (Sarkar I: 1971/2: 48xv) of the Dharmmatuṅgadeva identification of the promulgator of the so-called Ratu Boko charter, despite de Casparis' (1961) subsequent correction of the king's name to Samaratuṅgadeva. Moreover, at times we are presented with nonsensical translations without any attempt on the translator's part to provide any explanation (see, for example, Sarkar I: 1971/2: 48vi and 48xii: "again gave birth to a son this day having parts of eight hands").

Though this book contains a considerable number of critical comments concerning the efforts of prior translators, the present work would not have been possible without their many contributions to our understanding of the Śailendra inscriptions. In particular, the many works by J. G. de Casparis are critical source materials and therefore our debt of gratitude to him is great indeed.

Context and theories

Another obvious shortcoming of all prior translations of the Śailendra inscriptions pertains to the cursory discussions they offer with respect to context, of which three different types are directly relevant. The Isthmus of Kra (the so-called Ligor) stele, for example, requires a systematic analysis of the context based on contemporary historical events, geography and temple architecture developments, which can potentially provide further insights concerning the inscription's original resting place as well as the contents and relationship between the texts incised on sides A and side B. Moreover, any discussion of the Abhayagirivihāra charter cannot be considered complete unless the analysis also evaluates the specific architectural details pertaining to the site on the western prominence of the Ratu Boko Plateau. Furthermore, a comparison of the many toponyms cited in the Old Javanese segment of the Kayumwuṅan charter with those mentioned in other charters from the Temanggung Regency supports the earliest reports concerning the provenance of this inscription as opposed to the theories proposed by de Casparis and Kandahjaya concerning the charter's potential relationship with Barabuḍur.

No discussion of the Śailendra inscriptions can be considered complete without a thorough evaluation of the many theories that prior translators have proposed based on the content of one or more of the charters discussed herein. For example, de Casparis (1950) sought to identify the daughter of King Samaratuṅga mentioned in the Kayumwuṅan inscription with the Plaosan subsidiary temple donor Śrī Kahulunnan, who he wrongfully regarded as the consort of Rakai Pikatan. Moreover, Chandra (1995) maintained that the image of Śrī Ghananātha mentioned in the Kayumwuṅan charter had represented the deceased husband of Samaratuṅga's daughter. These and other hypotheses are evaluated in the present work in order to determine to what extent such speculations ought to influence our evaluation of the Śailendra charters.

This book concludes with a chapter devoted to suggestions for future research as well as to some longstanding hypotheses in need of further evaluation. Among other things, the final chapter examines a number of outdated theories put forward by J. G. de Casparis and other researchers that have heavily influenced the historical reconstructions subsequently put forward by Java scholars. Additionally, the concluding segment of this book proposes new hypotheses in need of scrutiny and analysis by the reader.

Acknowledgments

This book would have proven to have been an impossible undertaking for me were it not for the huge amount of time and resources that Prof. Lokesh Chandra devoted to furthering my knowledge of the Sanskrit texts. This publication is dedicated to him.

Thanks is also due to Nicolas Revire for his generous contribution of photographs, including several that he shot specifically for my use in this book, as well as his vetting of the French-language translations that have been incorporated into the present work. Likewise I would like to express my gratitude to Roy Jordaan for reviewing my Dutch and Indonesian translations as well as providing me with his valuable insights and research concerning temple construction developments on the Prambanan Plain. Andrea Acri reviewed and commented upon the Sanskrit translations and other compositional elements in five of the chapters, which led to superior final drafts, whilst Jeffrey Sundberg provided me with helpful epigraphical materials and observations as well as critical comments about two of the chapters.

I deeply appreciate having received permission to use the photographs of selected inscriptions taken by Shigehisa Taguchi while visiting the National Museum at Jakarta. John Huntington granted his permission for the use of his photograph of the *harmikā* from Shotorak, Kapisa, Afghanistan, Véronique Degroot kindly provided me with her sketch of the three miniature *caṇḍi*-s next to the Abhayagirivihāra *pĕṇḍapa* on the Ratu Boko Plateau and Rolf Giebel helped me track down the early use of the Sanskrit term *sugatapada* in the *Śikṣāsamuccaya* by Śāntideva. Last but not least, I would like to thank the many contributors to the WikiCommons web site who have made their photographs and artwork available for publication under the GNU General Public License.

I: The Isthmus of Kra stele dating from 775 CE

Inscribed on both sides with Sanskrit verses carved in the same style of script, this eighth century stele from South Thailand is about 1.0 m. in height, 9 cm. in depth and with a width that tapers from 50 cm. at the top to 40 cm. at the base. Cœdès (1918) initially reported the stone as having come from Wieng Sra—a small archeological site located on a tributary of the Tapi (Luong) River south of Bandon Bay.[1] After conducting a survey at Wieng Sra in 1926, however, Cœdès (1927a: 462, n. 1) concluded that the stele could not have originated from such a small archaeological site where all the surviving images he encountered depicted Brahmanic divinities.[2] He proposed the alternative site of Wat Semā Müang in Nakhon Si Thammarat (the peninsular port formerly known as 'Ligor' among foreign maritime traders).[3] While passing through Bangkok, a monk hailing from Nakhon Si Thammarat believed to recognize in this stele a stone that had at one time stood at Wat Semā Müang (Cœdès 1950: 60). Accordingly, the authors of historical works subsequently began citing the inscription cataloged as no. 23 in Bangkok as the 'stele of Ligor'.

Nai Thammatas Panij—a resident of Chaiya with an interest in local history—was the first person to suggest that the stele had come from Chaiya (Rajani 1974: 292-293 and note at the bottom of 289). According to his theory, when government antiquities authorities sent the region's inscriptions to Bangkok at the beginning of the twentieth century they had taken insufficient precautions to preserve precise knowledge about the provenance of two stones (nos. 23 and 24). Quaritch Wales (1935: 30) also thought it more likely that the so-called Ligor stele had come from Chaiya and Griswold (1951: 27) believed a re-examination of the two inscriptions in the light of the theory cited above concerning "the transfer of labels might produce useful results".

The other Sanskrit inscription (no. 24), which was initially thought to come from Wat Hua Wieng in Chaiya, refers to the monarch Candrabhānu—the 'Lord of Tāmbraliṅga' (*tāmbraliṅgeśvaraḥ*) also known as Śrī Dharmarāja (Cœdès 1918: 32; 1927a: 462). Nakhon Si Thammarat is a Thai-language derivation of the Sanskrit *nagara śrī dharmarāja* ('city of

[1]Cœdès based his initial site identification on an article published by Finot (1910) that referred to a communiqué from Lunet de Lajonquière concerning the stone, which had arrived in Bangkok prior to Lajonquière's tour of South Thailand and the Malay states.

[2]Cœdès' survey of the Wieng Sra site had overlooked a standing Buddha carved in relief that Quaritch Wales subsequently discovered in 1935. "[S]o far as was known, the only ancient foundation was at the centre. There we found on excavation an enclosure, regularly oriented, measuring about 250 metres each side.... The only distinguishable break in the enclosure is at the centre of the east side, where a gap may represent the position of an ancient gateway. The interior was filled with jungle, and, [insofar] as was known, the only ancient foundation was at the centre. There we found on excavation the base of a small brick shrine, only one brick thick, of a shape, which could not be determined since the bricks were very old and rotten. Only a few sherds of domestic pottery were found; but it was in the roots of a tree at the edge of this brick structure that we found the nearly Gupta sandstone Buddha relief" (Quaritch Wales 1976: 56; see also plate 2B).

[3]Wiang Sak locality, Mueang District, Nakhon Si Thammarat: 8° 25' 29.36" north latitude; 99° 57' 48.30" east longitude.

Śrī Dharmarāja'). Thus, the site of Wat Semā Müang would seem to provide a better match for the inscription promulgated by Candrabhānu in 1230 CE. Though the Sichon district of Nakhon Si Thammarat is rich in archaeological remains from the seventh century or perhaps even earlier, the religious icons from this early period depict Hindu divinities for the most part (Woodward 2003: 48-49).

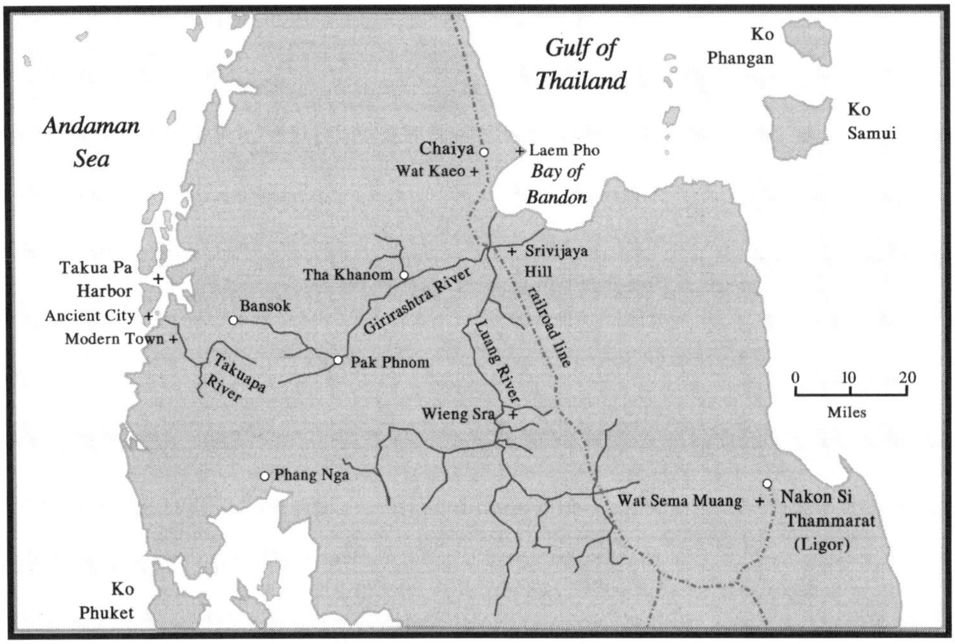

Fig. 1-1. The Isthmus of Kra (after Quaritch Wales, 1935).[4]

Jacq-Hergoualc'h (2004: 16-18) attributes the rise of Tāmbraliṅga as a major peninsular trading emporium to a gradual shifting of the shoreline of Bandon Bay, which had made it far more difficult for foreign ships to access the port-emporium of Laem Pho to the east of Chaiya. During the tenth century, the region's political center shifted from Chaiya to Phra Wiang on the south side of Nakhon Si Thammarat, and Tha Rua gradually became the more important trading emporium on the east coast of the isthmus.[5] This is why a growing number of scholars believe that the so-called 'Chaiya inscription' (1230 CE) actually hails from Nakhon Si Thammarat and that the 'stele of Ligor' originally had stood in the ancient city of Chaiya, which sent trade missions to China in the fifth, sixth and seventh centuries that Chinese court officials recorded under the designation P'an-P'an. Still, it is uncertain whether either stone had ever been installed near the specific temple attributed to it, as the following observation by Quaritch Wales indicates:

[4]Quaritch Wales (1937) observed that the principal river south of Chaiya flowing roughly from west to east across the Isthmus of Kra is the Girirāṣṭra ('Kingdom of the mountain'). The river's source is near Bansok, a mere twenty miles from the ancient port city of Takuapa on the west coast (see figure 1-1). From Bansok, the Girirāṣṭra flowed eastward across the isthmus until joining the Luong River, which flows from south to north. The confluence of these two rivers subsequently forms the delta that empties into the Bay of Bandon on the east coast. Hence, the Girirāṣṭra could have served as a means of transport with respect to the overland transshipment of goods across the Isthmus of Kra during ancient times.

[5]The naval prowess of Tāmbraliṅga reached its apogee in the thirteenth century, when King Candrabhānu invaded Sri Lanka on two separate occasions (Cœdès 1927a: 460-461; Sumio 2006: 4-5).

"[I]t was the custom in capitals and larger towns in Siam to collect up (and not destroy as in the Malay country) old sculptures and inscriptions, affording them a measure of protection in later monasteries. That was before collectors and the trade entered into competition, at least for the sculptures. The point is that such an object preserved in a Nak'on *wat* may in fact have originated from a shrine less than five or more than fifty miles away" (Quaritch Wales 1976: 32).

To avoid perpetuating yet another potentially misleading label, the present publication shall refer to inscription no. 23 as the 'Isthmus of Kra stele' hereunder.[6]

Script style considerations

One face of the stele presents a short Sanskrit text that refers to the Śailendra dynasty of kings mentioned in several inscriptions from Central Java that date from the late eighth and early ninth centuries. Cœdès (1918) designated this face of the stone as 'side B' and referred to the reverse face, which presents 29 lines of Sanskrit text, as 'side A'. According to de Casparis (1975: 29-32), the variety of script displayed on both sides of the stone is comparable to what Krom had dubbed the 'Old Javanese script', but which de Casparis preferred to call an archaic form of 'Early Kawi' since the 'Ligor' stele hails from beyond Java's shores.

Fig. 1-2. Side 'A' (Cœdès 1918: plate I).

"What distinguishes this script from the Later Pallava style is not only the use of some new shapes of *akṣaras* such as *ra* and the different form of the *virāma* . . . but above all the style of the script. Instead of the upright, elongated, and decorative shapes of the Canggal inscription [promulgated by king Sañjaya in Central Java during 732 CE], we here find an essentially cursive hand, such as that which is the result of writing with a pen or stylus on palm leaf or other material. The letters are all moderately sloping with all angles rounded off. There is also a pronounced tendency towards squareness as the *akṣaras* of medium width (*pa, sa, ma, ka,* etc.) are given a width equal to their height. Serifs, almost absent from the letters of the Canggal inscription, are clearly indicated and linear in shape" (de Casparis 1975: 29-30).

[6]Damais (1968: 353) referred to this stone as the *Trisamayacaitya* stele based on the name of the religious foundation cited on side A. Given the uncertainty over whether the contents constitutes a single text or two separate inscriptions, however, the stone is designated herein as the Isthmus of Kra stele.

Two early Javanese inscriptions likewise display variations of the same style of Indic script. Damais (1952: 20-23) noted that the Hampran (Plumpungan) charter dating from 750 CE displays a script that is quite distinct from the Pallava-Grantha type appearing on the Canggal stele. He also remarked that the Kañjuruhan inscription (760 CE) from East Java displays a variety of the same script. Unable to recommend the designation 'Kawi', Damais preferred to call this script Palaeojavanese and the present work will adopt the same designation hereunder except when directly quoting the comments of other researchers.

Despite the inevitable analogies, the most important point for Damais was that such varieties of Palaeojavanese script are clearly distinct from the Pallava type. Besides, even if epigraphy experts were ever able to demonstrate that Palaeojavanese represents a development of Pallava, he believed the differentiation of the two types must have taken place during very ancient times and with Palaeojavanese having subsequently led an independent existence. Therefore, he thought it clearly impossible to view the script variations displayed by the Hampran and Kañjuruhan charters as local derivatives of the Pallava-Grantha script displayed by the stele promulgated by Sañjaya in 732 CE.

Initially dubbed the Plumpungan inscription by de Casparis (1950: 1-11), the Hampran charter appears on the top of a boulder located near the town Salatiga to the south of Semarang, Central Java.

"All letters [from the Hampran charter] are of precisely the same height with generous interlinear space. They are well aligned with clear, but unobtrusive, serifs. The *virāma* is, as in Dinoyo and Ligor, expressed by a concave horizontal stroke over the letters of about the width of the average letter. The *akṣaras* are moderately sloping" (de Casparis 1975: 32).

Fig. 1-3. The Hampran charter (photo credit: Andi Widhibrata).

The Sanskrit text on the stone of Hampran appears within three rectangular segments (A, B & C), delineated by double horizontal lines:

- 75 x 10 cm., which contains two lines of Sanskrit text pertaining to the inscription's date;
- 70 x 23 cm., which encompasses a single strophe in the Sragdharā ('decorated with a garland') meter, and with each of the four lines of the text displayed comprising a single quarter-verse or *pāda* (Damais 1952: 21); and
- 76 x 22 cm., which displays five elaborate drawings, each accompanied by a short text that is only readable in some cases. Furthermore, de Casparis (1950) saw something inscribed within each leaf-like shape, perhaps an *akṣara.*

Voices from the mountain: the Śailendra inscriptions

De Casparis (1950: 10) remarked that the Hampran charter (750 CE) displays a striking example of the syllable *yo*, and that side B of the stele from the Isthmus of Kra presents a parallel example: 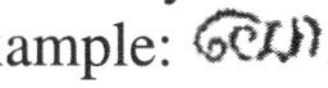. Furthermore, the Sanskrit salutation *svasti* on side B is comparable in form to the *svasti* from the Hampran charter (D.113, National Museum in Jakarta).

The lapicide's use of double lines to subdivide the text of the Hampran charter suggests a possible explanation for the vertical double-line margins on side A of the Isthmus of Kra stele (see figure 1-2). By contrast, Cœdès (1950: 62) noted that side B only exhibits a single line that hugs the top of the stele pediment. Consequently, the purpose of the double-line margins on side A may have been to segregate the longer text from the incomplete short composition that appears on the reverse face of the stone.

Archaeologists discovered the four fragments of the Kañjuruhan (Dinoyo, 760 CE) charter[7] in pairs in the small villages of Dinoyo and Merjosari to the northwest of Malang, East Java. "[T]he cursive style of the Dinoyo inscription creates the impression of a script primarily used for writing on palm-leaf..." (de Casparis 1975: 31). With respect to the basic *akṣara* forms, the Palaeojavanese script exhibited by the Kañjuruhan charter provides the closest match overall for the those depicted on both sides of the so-called 'stele of Ligor'.

> "The Sanskrit inscription of Ligor, dated 775, presents a number of curious features, most of which appear to have been of no consequence. The serifs are very distinct and linear but often detached from the letter to which they belong. The *-ā* usually extends to below the base line. In the case of *ja* the *ā* is, as usual in older script, attached to the middle bar of the *ja*, then runs upwards turning left and goes in a full circle around the letter ending at the right top level in a little outward bending hook. [In addition] the *cakra* goes in a wide bend but, as usual, turning clockwise round the base of the *akṣara*. The *akṣaras* are generally roundish and slightly tilted—less than those of the Dinoyo inscription" (de Casparis 1975: 31-32).

According to de Casparis, certain Palaeojavanese elements are also discernible in several other inscriptions from Central Java, including the Old Javanese segment of the Kayumwuṅan (also known as the Karangtĕngah) charter dating from 824 CE as well as the undated short inscriptions on the base of Barabuḍur. To his list of examples, we can add the inscribed stone from Caṇḍi Mendut (OD-305)[8] that presents the traditional testimony of the Buddhist faith. "The character of the Mendut writing is very old Kawi; the *virāma* is still given by a stroke above the letter" (Krom 1927: I: 16). By contrast, the short inscriptions on the small shrines at Caṇḍi Plaosan Lor apparently mark "a transitional phase leading to the standard form of Early Kawi..." (de Casparis 1975: 33; see also de Casparis 1958).

---

[7]The earlier literature refers to this inscription under the name of the village from whence the first pair of fragments came, written as Dinoyo (de Casparis 1975), Dinojo (de Casparis 1941) or Dinaja (Bosch 1916, 1923, 1924).

[8]It is possible that this stone had originally come from another location, as the special niche provided for its enshrinement over the doorway suggests (see the photo in Long 2010: 61).

Chapter I: The Isthmus of Kra stele dating from 775 CE

Points of contention

A rubbing of what was then cataloged in Bangkok as the 'Wieng Sra' stele was brought to France by Lunet de Lajonquière[9] and a partial translation subsequently published by Finot (1910: 153): "The record is 697 Śaka (775 A.D.). It begins by praising a king..who founded a shrine of Buddha...and then instructed his chaplain (*rājasthavira*) Jayanta to raise three *stūpas*; upon Jayanta's death, his disciple...built two brick *caityas* near the first three". Cœdès (1918) interpreted the compounds *śrīvijayendrarājā* (line A14), *śrīvijayeśvarabhūpati* (line A16) and *śrīvijayanṛpati* (line A28) as royal titles meaning the king of the country of Śrīvijaya, which is presumed to have had its capital in South Sumatra as attested by a number of late seventh-century inscriptions, including several discovered in the vicinity of modern-day Palembang. Other inscriptions were found upstream from Jambi on the bank of the river Batang Hari, in southeastern Sumatra near the Sunda Strait and on the island of Bangka (Kulke 1993: 160, map on 161). Though these seventh century inscriptions were composed in Old Malay, a number of Sanskrit terms were also used, such as in the undated Sabokingking (Tĕlaga Batu) *praśasti*, which displays the Sanskrit titles for a number of the kingdom's functionaries and occupations (de Casparis 1956: 15-46).

One hotly debated issue has been whether one should consider the two sides of the Isthmus of Kra stele as two segments of a single text or as entirely separate records. According to Majumdar (1933), the king of Śrīvijaya had promulgated side A, and a king of the Śailendra dynasty had issued side B at a somewhat later, but roughly contemporary, date. By contrast, Chhabra (1935)[10] believed that the stele displays a single text of which only four of the lines on side B have survived and with the reverse side of the stone containing the remainder of the text.

> "Evidently the writing on both the faces must have originally formed one continuous inscription. But its first half was on the face which M. Cœdès indicates as B. This is clear from the very first word *svasti*, which is the appropriate beginning of a Hindu record. The other part indicated as A is obviously the continuation of the former" (Chhabra 1965: 27).

Bosch (1941) observed that the king's own name and dynasty became recorded on side B without any mention of his empire whereas the empire of the king is expressly mentioned on side A but the king's personal name is not. According to Bosch, reading the stele as a single inscription, which began with side B and ended with side A, provides us with a *praśasti* of a normal form and no less sane content.

> "The composition would start with *svasti* and then follow with the glorification of the royal promulgator of the inscription, stating his name and dynasty first then the kingdom over which he ruled, [and] finishing with the foundations and the date. The only thing

[9]In 1908, having completed an inventory of the monuments in the region of Angkor at the request of l'École française d'Extrême-Orient (EFEO), Lunet de Lajonquière (1909, 1912) began his archaeological exploration of Siam and the Malay Peninsula. In July-August 1908, he followed the eastern coastline from Chumphon on the Isthmus of Kra to Terengganu and in October-November he toured the Malay Federated States as well as the ports of the peninsula's west coast (see BEFEO 1921: 319).

[10]All later references to Chhabra's original 1935 dissertation presented herein come from the 1965 reprint.

abnormal in the text thus read would be the absence of the middle section of the glorification. For the meaning this made no difference" (Bosch 1941: 32).[11]

	Side A: lines 5, 24	Side B: line 1		Side A: line 22	Side B: line 4		Side A: lines 3, 9, 13, 14, 26	Side B: lines 3, 4
dhi			*nāmā*			*sa*		
	Side A: line 3	Side B: line 3		Side A: line 10	Side B: line 4		Side A: line 23	Side B: lines 1, 3
di			*ni*			*sva*		
	Side A: line 25	Side B: line 3		Side A: line 14	Side B: line 4		Side A: line 3	Side B: line 3
dvi			*ndra*			*śara*		
	Side A: line 26	Side B: line 2		Side A: line 22	Side B: lines 1, 2		Side A: line 28	Side B: line 4
kā			*nta*			*śrī*		
	Side A: line 6	Side B: line 4		Side A: line 22	Side B: lines 1, 4		Side A: lines 10, 10, 11, 27	Side B: line 4
mā			*pu*			*ta*		
	Side A: line 6	Side B: line 4		Side A: Lines 22, 14	Side B: lines 1, 1		Side A: lines, 1, 3	Side B: line 3
mahā			*rājā/ rāja*			*vi*		
	Side A: line 23	Side B: line 3		Side A: line 1, 4, 23	Side B: line 1, 3		Side A: line 2	Side B: line 4
n			*ri*			*ya*		

Fig. 1-4. Comparing *akṣara*-s and character groups common to both stele faces.[12]

Bosch thought that the same hand had incised both faces. However, several major differences are discernible between the two sides. Among other things, the four lines

[11]Zakharov (2012: 7) has likewise embraced the single text theory proposed by Chhabra and Bosch.

[12]The *akṣara*-s and character groups presented in figure 1-4 have been isolated from the surrounding text and processed using a variety of digital enhancement techniques such as high contrast and gamma adjustments and other modes of digital filtering.

incised on side B are missing two *akṣara*-s[13] as well as the *-ṃ* for *yaṃ* (or *-ḥ* for *yaḥ*) in line four. Side B also fails to display a double *daṇḍa* (||) between the salutation and the initial verse or between the end of the first strophe and the initial character of the incomplete stanza that follows. By contrast, side A presents a double *daṇḍa* at the end of each of its ten verses and only contains a couple of abnormalities in 29 lines.

Figure 1-4 provides readers with the ability to make their own side-by-side comparisons of the identical *akṣara*-s incised on the two faces of the stele. A visual inspection confirms the conclusion reached by Majumdar (1933: 126): the same hand did not carve the *akṣara*-s on both sides of the stone, but the two faces do appear to be roughly contemporary.[14]

Overall, the Sanskrit syllables and words from the A-side exhibit a smoother, more iconic form than on side B, where the *akṣara*-s are less elegantly shaped and in some instances even have a somewhat disjointed appearance. Whether these noticeable differences are an indication that the *akṣara*-s on side B represent a more archaic form of Palaeojavanese, or that the lapicide working on side A was simply the superior artisan, remains a debatable point.[15] Among other things, the *virāma*—the concave horizontal stroke over the letter—carved on side B is downward facing, which is likewise the case on the earlier Kañjuruhan and Hampran charters. This is clearly different from those carved on side A, which face upward (for example, see the 'n' in figure 1-4). "The inscription is definitely engraved by two persons. The first side is incomplete and the stanzas [that the composer had wished to have] engraved on it were lost. The second side was engraved by a more conscientious person who avoided misspellings" (Chandra, pc 1 Oct. 2011).

According to Bosch (1941: 29), the fabrication of a charter required the participation of two different individuals: a handwriting expert whose task was to trace the characters onto the copperplate or stone using *krüt* or charcoal and a potentially illiterate mason whose task was to incise the characters into the heated metal or to chisel them onto the stone. As an example, Bosch cited a report by F. E. Pargiter concerning an incomplete copperplate discovered at the great *stūpa* behind the Nirvana Temple in Kasiñ (Gorakhpur, United Prov.) on which only one line of characters had actually been etched but the remainder of the text was nevertheless readable.

> "One most interesting feature in the plate is that it reveals how copper-plates were inscribed. The inscription was first written out in ink on the plate, and when the ink had dried, the plate was given to the engraver to cut the written letters into the metal.... [The engraver of the Kasiñ-copperplate] was manifestly inexperienced and did not know how to incise them aright.... In fact his work was so unsatisfactory, that the incision of the rest

---

[13]Throughout this publication, Sanskrit and Old Javanese words are presented in italics followed by the plain face ending -s to express the plural in English-language sentences, except when quoting other authors.

[14]One more point of contention is worth briefly mentioning. In response to the statement by Bosch (1941) concerning the absence of any Indonesian inscriptions featuring discrete texts promulgated by two different kings, Cœdès (1950: 61) replied: "there are many examples, at least in Cambodia and Campā, of stones inscribed with a number of major texts at different times".

[15]Cœdès (1950: 62) maintained that the *akṣara* '*sa*' on the B-side represents a posterior development, a claim for which he did not provide any epigraphical evidence. Given that only two examples of *sa* appear on side B, however, Cœdès' assertion is debatable (see fig. 1-4).

of the inscription was given up and the plate was accepted as it was, written only in ink" (as cited in Bosch 1941: 29, n. 1).[16]

According to Chaiya resident Nai Thammatas Panij, additional writing—presumably in chalk or charcoal—on the uninscribed portion of the stele's B-side had been washed off the stone by the people of Chaiya prior to the stone's shipment to Bangkok (Rajani 1974: 293).

Side A refers to two generations of royal chaplains (*rājasthavira*), which suggested to K. Sastri (1940: 257) the existence of a complex *saṅgha* organization on the Isthmus of Kra at that time. The reference to the death of the royal chaplain Jayanta on side A suggests a plausible explanation for side B's previously noted eccentricities. "The scribe naturally drafted his text in the script current in his time, while the stone-cutter reproduced this draft as accurately as possible on the stone" (de Casparis 1975: 30, n. 3).

Jayanta could have traced a complete text on the B-side of the stele during the weeks prior his death, in which case it is hypothetically possible to attribute the outright mistakes and other eccentricities to his infirmities and/or advanced age. Alternatively, perhaps the lapicide had been solely responsible for the errors. In either case, Jayanta's successor Dhīmukti may have elected to suspend the stone cutter's work on the characters already traced by his predecessor. Then after completing the two additional *caitya* structures attributed to him in the inscription, Dhīmukti could have initiated his own composition on the reverse face of the stele, which ends with the commemoration of the king's consecration of the entire site in the spring of 775.

The ancient city of Chaiya

Lunet de Lajonquière was the first western visitor to Chaiya to describe some of the archaeological remains found at the center of the ancient archeological site.

> "The Wat Wieng, the pagoda within the enclosure wall 1 km further to the east, probably occupied the central part of the ancient city. Two inscriptions have been found nearby the ruins of this Thai temple that have not yet been studied. One is engraved on a stone hewed into a *liṅga*, the other on a stele. These two documents were taken away to Bangkok, but there are still fragments of statues of which the style remains remarkable and which, moreover, are clearly distinguishable from those of the Indo-Cambodian [style] by means of many details of costume" (Lajonquière 909: 228).

Wat Kaeo.[17] While conducting a survey of the Chaiya area in 1929, Claeys (1931: 380-387) observed that the three brick constructions of Wat Hua Wieng, Wat Long and Wat Kaeo[18] were situated along an axis that roughly runs north-south and were separated from one another by relatively equal distances (about 400 m). After having the opportunity to examine Wat Kaeo in 1934-1935, Quaritch Wales agreed with Cœdès (1927b) about several

---

[16]See *Archaeological Survey of India: Annual Report*, 1910-1911: 74.

[17]A summary of the Thai Fine Arts Department's excavation and reconstruction activities at Wat Kaeo in 1976 and 1979, including photos of the principal artifacts unearthed, is presented in Diskul 1980: 1-4 & figs. 1-18.

[18]The GPS coordinates are 9° 22' 41.41" north latitude; 99° 11' 24.97" east longitude.

basic features in evidence at Wat Kaeo being similar to those exhibited by other ancient temples located in mainland Southeast Asia and on the island of Java.

Fig. 1-5. Wat Kaeo, southwest view (photo credit: Nicolas Revire).

> "So far as Java is concerned the building reminds us by reason of its cruciform plan of Chandi Kalasan (A.D. 778), the earliest Buddhist temple in Java, the porches (real and false) of the earlier type of Indian tower having been developed to form chapels at the cardinal points. The architecture, however, suggests that of the early Primitive Khmer temples, and still more, [because] of the excellence of its brickwork, the presence of pilasters and the rounded brick pillars beside the doors, the earlier temples of Champa." (Quaritch Wales 1937: 153-154).[19]

Quaritch Wales believed that the combination in a single temple of basic features from temples found in Java, Cambodia, and Campā provides a good indication of the dissemination of art influences from a cultural center located in the vicinity of the Bay of Bandon. However, Boisselier (1969: 60-61) viewed in an entirely different manner the relationships between the elevation plan and method of construction in evidence at Wat Kaeo and the comparable architectural components from Cam temples (particularly those

[19]Quaritch Wales pointed out that Wat Kaeo was not an isolated example; other ancient temples in Chaiya as well as in Nakhon Sri Thammarat featured the same type of composite design. "And at the latter place the Brahmans have in their custody a couple of old ruined brick temples the architecture of which, in its extreme simplicity, is more reminiscent of the little stone, cell-like Hindu buildings of the Dieng Plateau, in Java" (Quaritch Wales 1937: 154).

of the Hobnail type) as well as Khmer monuments constructed in the Cam-influenced Kulen style, such as the central sanctuary of Prasat Damrei Krap. As all of these comparable structures are datable to between the end of the eight century and the first half of the ninth century, Boisselier said he could date Wat Kaeo to no earlier than the ninth century. He also remarked about the similarities between the cruciform foundation for Wat Kaeo and that of Caṇḍi Kalasan[20] from Central Java, which reflects a later construction phase that may not have occurred until the early ninth century. Boisselier (1979: 43-44) subsequently affirmed a mid-ninth century building date for Wat Kaeo based on construction similarities found at Dong Duang, Hoà-lai and other temple sites on the mainland of Southeast Asia. Jacq-Hergoualc'h (2001: 50-55) generally concurred with this estimate but did not rule out the possibility that earlier stages of construction had occurred at Wat Kaeo.

Fig. 1-6. Wat Kaeo, north view (photo credit: Nicolas Revire).

"We may add here that this date, which we find acceptable, does not compromise the date of the foundation or of the first state of the building, which could have been much

[20]The original structure at Caṇḍi Kalasan appears to have consisted of a simple square plan that subsequently was cleared from the foundation to make way for a more elaborate construction (Bernet Kempers & Soekmono 1954; Dumarçay 2007: 211). The Kalasan inscription of 778 CE refers to the donation of the hamlet Kālasa (a Sanskritization of the Old Javanese toponym Kalasan) to a Buddhist religious foundation dedicated to the goddess Tārā—presumably Caṇḍi Kalasan, which is located on the outskirts of modern-day Yogyakarta. Quaritch Wales (1937: 194) reported the discovery of an eight-armed bronze depicting Tārā with a height of 18.5 cm. (ninth century; see fig. 111 in Jacq-Hergoualc'h 2002) at the same banana garden in the Chaiya District where the owners had previously unearthed a wealth of Song dynasty ceramics.

earlier.... In the same way, certain monuments still standing (votive *stūpas*), integrated into the enclosures of contemporary temples in the region of Chaiya, reveal in their design and their general appearance an ancient origin belied by decorations that were continually 'updated' through the years (in Wat Palelăi and Wat To, for example). The situation was probably similar at Wat Kaeo, which may have been altered, at least in its decoration, in the middle of the ninth century...." (Jacq-Hergoualc'h 2002: 304).

Fig. 1-7 Wat Long (photo credit: Nicolas Revire).

Brick constructions also arose in Central Java during the late eighth century. Brandes (1902: 141-143) discovered that Caṇḍi Mendut contains within its stone mantle a building constructed entirely from red brick that was all-but-complete except for the final decorative elements. Given the colossal size of the image triad in the building's interior, with each sculpture carved from a single block of stone, the three images must have been present within the original brick building. Unfortunately with respect to the discussion at hand, Brandes did not discern the existence of the original brick structure until a later stage of the building's restoration, which prohibited further study of the first phase of construction (see Long 2010: xxxi-xxxiii). Other red-brick constructions were found in the environs of Caṇḍi Mendut such as the brick foundation of Caṇḍi Banon, where archeologists recovered five classic Brahmanic images dating from the eighth century, the earthen terrace faced in red bricks at Caṇḍi Pawon (Long 2010: 72) and the brick *stūpa* foundations unearthed at the foot of the Barabuḍur hill (Bernet Kempers 1976: 17). The brick foundation for the so-called 'audience hall' discovered on the south side of Caṇḍi Kalasan—the entrances of which were protected by pairs of *dvārapāla* images—also arose during late eighth century in all probability (Long 2011: 7, n. 9). However, none of these brick structures are still standing today.

Wat Long. Claeys (1931: 386) encountered the vestiges of the podium of Wat Long, which was about 12 m. square in size and roughly oriented to the points of the compass. However, local notables told Claeys that the restorers of Wat Phra Borommathat were using most of the bricks from Wat Long for making repairs. Hence, the historical accuracy of the restored base of Wat Long depicted in figure 1-7 is questionable. Besides, archeologists discovered an earlier structure measuring 30 m. square underneath the podium at Wat Long during excavations conducted in 1946 (Chihara 1996: 213).

Wat Hua Wieng. Unfortunately, no one has excavated the original construction at Hua Wieng (Thai for 'Heart of the city') because the Thais had already built a modern *vihāra* on top of the old site. "[B]ut the abbot stated that it stood on a brick terrace larger than that of the new building, and having the same measurements as that discovered at Wat Long" (Quaritch Wales 1976: 107). Claeys (1931: 387) also observed the traces of an edifice with a square plan located about 100 m. to the west of the Wat as well as the remains of a tank for ablutions with a broken waterspout lying next to it. Boisselier (1969: 61) likewise only encountered vague traces of constructions near Wat Hua Wieng but thought the terrace and various substructures he had encountered deserved further investigation because of the possibility they had formed a contemporary ensemble with Wat Kaeo.

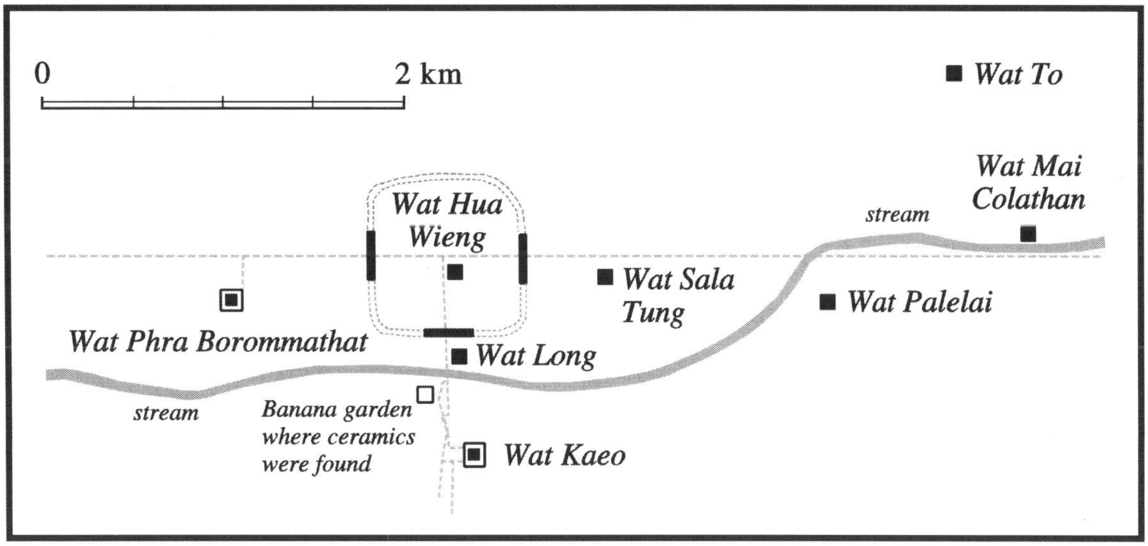

Fig. 1-8. The heart of the ancient city at Chaiya (after Quaritch Wales, 1976).

Within the immediate environs of Wat Hua Wieng, Quaritch Wales discovered the remnants of a moat and an earthwork fortification of quadrangular form, which according to Jacq-Hergoualc'h and Hobson (2002: 302) had measured about 800 m. at its widest extent. The enclosure surrounding Wat Hua Wieng suggests the possibility that the enclosed area may have been the site of a royal residence. "It will be seen that Wat Hua Wieng is situated at the centre of the city, Wat Long is at about the same distance south of Wat Hua Wieng, on a north-south axis, as Wat Keu is from Wat Long. So at first sight the three readily lent themselves to identification with the three brick buildings whose foundation is recorded in the inscription [but] it must be admitted that the remains...gave little enough support for any such identification" (Quaritch Wales 1976: 106).

Quaritch Wales (1976: 112) also mentioned the discovery a huge number of Song Dynasty (960—1279 CE) ceramics in a banana garden to the south of Wat Hua Wieng. To him this suggested that the site might have formerly been a habitation for traders. His trial excavation in the banana garden during 1935 uncovered the old riverbed of a nearby stream (see figure 1-8) that had formerly run through this site (Quaritch Wales 1937: 194). The Song Dynasty ceramics also demonstrate that Chaiya had continued as a trade emporium even after the aforementioned rise in status of Tāmbraliṅga.

Figs. 1-9 & 1-10: Four-armed Viṣṇu with ornate miter (left) **and the bodhisattva Avalokiteśvara** (right) **from Wat Sala Tung** (photo credits: Nicolas Revire).

Wat Sala Tung. The three images discovered at this small porch temple to the east of Wat Hua Wieng include a four-armed Viṣṇu featuring an ornate miter (67 cm. in height, *circa* fourth century CE). The image of the bodhisattva Avalokiteśvara (114 cm. in height, *circa* sixth century CE), which has a small figure of Amitābha in the coiffure, reminded Claeys (1931: 392) of similar examples from Cam art as well as the narrative reliefs at Barabuḍur. The third image depicted the sun god Sūrya (71 cm. in height, *circa* ninth to tenth centuries CE; see Jacq-Hergoualc'h and Hobson 2002: Fig. 186).

It is perhaps significant that the Isthmus of Kra stele mentions all three of these divinities—Viṣṇu and Sūrya on side B and Avalokiteśvara (*kaja-kara*, 'lotus-handed', e.g. Padmapāṇi) on side A. According to Bernet Kempers (1933: 9, 36-38), images of the Hindu divinities Viṣṇu and Sūrya as well as Avalokiteśvara were represented within the large cache of Mahāyāna Buddhist bronze figures recovered from the fire-decimated ruins of the monastery at Nālandā founded by the Śailendra monarch Śrī Bālaputradeva. Still, there is no way to ascertain whether Wat Sala Tung had been the original emplacement location for any of the stone images recovered from this site.

Figs. 1-11 & 2-12: Head of the male image found at Khao Nam Ron and a map (photo credits: Nicolas Revire).

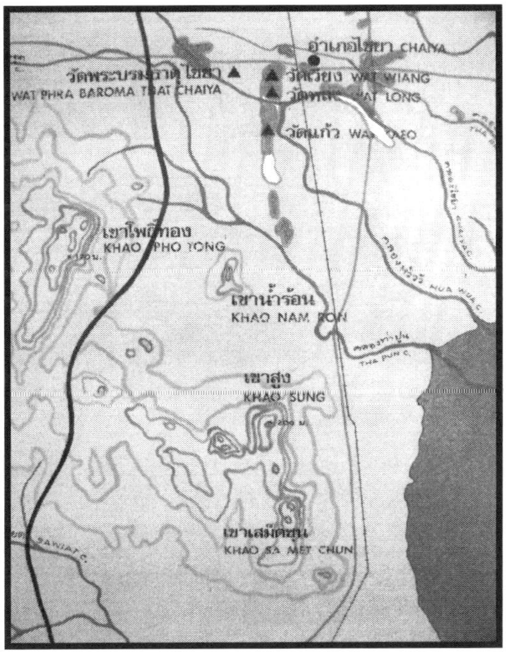

Khao Nam Ron. A hill 50 m. in height and isolated from the surrounding plain is located 1500 m. to the south of Wat Kaeo (Jacq-Hergoualc'h 2002: 307). A stone head discovered on the top of this hill displays an expression that is comparable to other depictions of Buddhist divinities. Art historians have suggested it may date from the sixth century. "Since it could not be a Buddha because it wears a diadem, it could only be a bodhisattva, probably Avalokiteśvara. The head was originally covered with a *jaṭāmukuṭa*, which would have had an image of the Buddha Amitābha in the front. The diadem is a simple band embellished with fleurons, one in front, two others above the ears, and two smaller ones in the spaces between them" (Jacq-Hergoualc'h 2002: 151-152).

According to Claeys (1931: 384-386), at the foot of this hill on the western side a hot water spring gushes from the earth at the level of the surrounding plain. For this reason, the Thais call this hill Khao Nam Ron ('Hill of hot water'). In the rocky face of the hill, Claeys discovered a cave with a depth of about 25 m. Near the entrance to this natural shelter, Claeys found a number of broken stones that still displayed the "traces of sculptures or molding". Unfortunately Claeys and his team did not have the time to excavate the floor of this cave. At the top of Khao Nam Ron, Claeys discovered the remnants of a brick shrine that had not already been "digested, as it were" by the surrounding vegetation. This structure had displayed the same type of brick-*sans*-mortar construction technique found at Wat Kaeo and elsewhere at Chaiya.[21]

The relatively close proximity of Khao Nam Ron to the heart of the ancient city led Quaritch Wales (1937: 191) to suppose that the hill "may have enjoyed peculiar sanctity" since the other hilltop sites in the area are about five miles to the west. He also believed that the royal inhabitants of Chaiya would have seen medicinal qualities in the natural pool of hot saline water situated near the base of the hill "for we know in what esteem such hot springs were held in India".

Wat Phra Borommathat Chaiya. Unlike the abandoned brick sites found elsewhere at Chaiya, it appears that the region's Buddhist monks had never forsaken Wat Phra Borommathat, which is located 600 m. to the west of Wat Hua Wieng and almost directly to the north of Khao Nam Ron (see figure 1-12). When Claeys (1931: 378-380) visited the temple in 1929, workers were replacing elements from the central sanctuary previously demolished by lightning. The ongoing restoration work gave Claeys the opportunity to verify that the original bricks of the central shrine had been placed on top of one another without the use of mortar, lime or cement as was likewise the case at Wat Long and Wat Kaeo.

Fig. 1-13. Wat Phra Borommathat (photo credit: Nicolas Revire).

Claeys agreed with the conclusion of Lajonquière that the core elements of the central sanctuary at Wat Phra Borommathat[22] must have been constructed well in advance of the Thai occupation of the Isthmus of Kra and may pertain to the period when the ancient city had been under the suzerainty of Śrīvijaya. He also observed the temple's construction similarities with Wat Phra Mahathat in Nakhon Si Thammarat (to the south of Wat Semā Müang) as well as the fact that the superstructure surmounting the temple's pedestal, which measured 12.4 m. per side, resembled some of the buildings depicted in the narrative reliefs at Barabuḍur, as Parmentier (1925) had previously observed.

Hence, Wat Phra Borommathat is comparable to the brick temple ruins at Chaiya in that it likewise integrates the same disparate architectural design elements of which the architects

[21]On his return trip from Khao Nam Ron to Wat Kaeo, Claeys noticed the stones for a foundation of 6 x 8 m.; the local inhabitants referred to this former shrine as Wat Nŏp.

[22]The GPS coordinates for Wat Phra Borommathat are 9° 23' 6.80" north latitude; 99° 11' 5.10" east longitude.

of other sites scattered throughout Southeast Asia were aware. For example, Boisselier (1969: 60) remarked that the pilasters of the four foreparts of the central sanctuary are characteristic of the Dong Duong style of Cam art dating from the second half of the ninth century.

The discovery by Prince Damrong of a majestic black bronze image of a bodhisattva just outside the enclosure walls surrounding Wat Phra Borommathat points to the site's Mahāyāna roots. Art historians believe this classic example of Pāla art may depict Avalokiteśvara, although the identity is unverifiable since the figure is missing the crown of the head, where one would anticipate seeing a small figure of Amitābha in the coiffure. The lower half of the figure below the waist is also missing. Cœdès dated this image to the ninth or tenth centuries, but other art historians have suggested dating this masterpiece to the eighth to ninth centuries (see, for example, Woodward 2003: 98).

Fig. 1-14. Bronze image found by Prince Damron outside of Wat Phra Borommathat, on display in the National Museum in Bangkok (photo credit: Nicolas Revire).

Taken as a whole, the archaeological site at Chaiya possesses a number of features comparable to those found within the environs of the Prambanan Plain to the east of Yogyakarta in Central Java, where several temples likewise arose along a north-south axis. Approximately 1.5 km to the south is a hilltop site featuring a natural spring on the western edge of the prominence, three man-made caves and a Buddhist *vihāra* on its summit dedicated to Avalokiteśvara. On the other hand, many ancient kingdoms throughout Southeast Asia had erected hilltop shrines overlooking a plain on which other temples had stood. So the most that one can say when comparing Chaiya with the Prambanan region (see the map of the Prambanan Plain and Ratu Baka prominence in Chapter VIII) is that the comparable features are perhaps greater in number than those typically found elsewhere.

Side B: Discussion, annotated transcription and revised translation

The Isthmus of Kra stele has been transcribed and/or translated in full by Cœdès (1918: 29-32 and 1961: 20-24); Chatterjee (1926: II: 40-44), Chhabra (1935, reprint 1965: 26-34), Veeraprajak (1986: 11-14), Prapandvidya (2007), and Griffiths (2011a: 22-24). In addition, Majumdar (1927), Stutterheim (1929: 14), Mus (1929: 448-449), K. Sastri (1940: 252-255), Bosch (1941, 1952), de Casparis (1950: 98-100), Poerbatjaraka (1958: 260-262), Cœdès

(1950, 1959) Damais (1968: 354), Boechari (1982, 2012: 421-424), Sarkar (1985: 324, 329), Chandra (1995: 213-214), Jordaan and Colless (2009: 55-57), and Zakharov (2012) have focused on one or the other face of the stone, either as a whole or with respect to specific Sanskrit compounds.

Given that competing interpretations of the stele's B-side have dominated the debate among scholars, the following transcription, translation and discussion segments begin with an examination of this particular face of the stone. The Sanskrit text on side B contains several defects of composition in need of restitution—including missing syllables and faults in the meter—for which Mus (1929), Chhabra (1935), and Cœdès (1950) had supplied the corrective emendations to be discussed below. For example, in the second *pāda* of the first half-verse the eighth syllable (*śa*) is light when the meter requires the syllable to be heavy; and *vapuṣman* should be read as *vapuṣmān* at the end of line two. Mus (1929: 448) proposed to repair the fault in the concluding *pāda* of the second half-verse through the emendation *prabh<ava>* in place of the emendation *prabh<u>* submitted by Cœdès (1918: 30). The emendation from Mus has been adopted by all later translators, including Cœdès (1959) himself. Chhabra (1965: 31 n. 2) also found an error in grammar. "The word like [abhāḥ] is superfluous. The text is Manmathābho vapuṣmān; it ought to be either Manmathābhāḥ or Manmatho vapuṣmān, i.e. Upamā 'similitude' or Rūpaka 'metaphor'. The author possibly intends to employ the latter."

Cœdès (1918: 30) initially read a compositum appearing in the third *pāda* as *śesasarvvāri ⌣ madavi ⌣ naś* in part because of what he perceived to be an indecipherable *akṣara* between the syllables *ri* and *ma* as well as his uncertainty concerning the identity of the *akṣara* placed between vi and naś. He subsequently offered the emended reading of *'śeṣasarvvārimadavi<ma>thanaś* (Cœdès 1950: 63). In the first case, however, Griffiths (2011a: 21, n. 8) has noted that the unidentified 'character' appears to be an extra appendage of the syllable *kṣmya* in line two having extended into line three, and with the syllable appearing between the *vi* and *naś* to be read as a *tha,* to which Cœdès affixed the syllable *ma* for which there is no indication on the stele itself. The resulting compositum *'śeṣasarvvārimadavi<ma>thanaś* is comparable to the epithet awarded to the Śailendra king who promulgated the so-called Kĕlurak (782) inscription (*vairivaravīra-vimardana,* 'Crusher of valiant enemy heroes')[23] and in a similar fashion became glorified in the Nālandā copperplate issued during the mid-ninth century (*circa* 843-850; see Jordaan and Colless 2009: 34) as *vīravairimathana,* 'Destroyer of brave foes'. It is also interesting that the final verse of the inscription found in the former *desa* Kĕlurak presents the royal appellation Śrī Saṅgrāmadhanaṃjaya, with *◦dhanaṃjaya* being the famous epithet of Arjuna glossed by *Bhagavad Gita* translators as 'Crusher of foes'. Therefore, the consecration name Saṅgrāmadhanaṃjaya, e.g. the 'Crusher of foes in battle', appears to be based on the epithet for the king found in strophe four of the same inscription.[24]

---

[23]"He had attained valor through victories over the kings in the ten directions by 'crushing (*vimarda*) the valiant (*vara*) heroes (*vīra*) of powerful enemies (*vairi*)'."

[24]In light of the similarities between all these designations for the same Śailendra monarch, it appears that the upper limit of the interval between the carving of sides A and B, as proposed by Majumdar and Cœdès, could not have exceeded 792 CE, the date of the so-called Ratu Baka inscription promulgated by his successor Samaratuṅga. If the B-side strophe were promulgated after the death of the 'Crusher of brave foes' then we would expect this text to have spoken of him using the past tense, as in the Nālandā charter.

There are two other unidentifiable marks in the text on side B. The first is located at the end of line three following *śaktyā* (). Cœdès (1950: 63) proposed reading the entire phrase as *śaktyā sau*, though the last syllable is not comparable in appearance to the *sau* appearing in the first line () of side B. Chhabra (1965: 28) read the final syllable of line three as '*so*' as did Chandra (pc 31 Aug. 2011). Additionally, a final indecipherable mark () appears at the beginning of line four and the ensuing syllable *ya* is missing the *-ḥ* or *-ṃ* for making the syllable long, which the meter requires.

Chandra thought *ya* = *yaḥ* would be a better reading grammatically than the *yaṃ* proposed by Chhabra because *yaḥ* would be in accord with *nigaditaḥ*. However, he also thought that *so 'yaṃ* provides an even better solution. "It means 'he (*so=saḥ*) is the one (*ayaṃ*) called (*nigaditaḥ*) born in the Śailendra dynasty (*śailendravaṅśaprabhava*), Śrī Mahārāja by name'; *ayaṃ:* the initial *a* was elided by *sandhi* with the *o* of *so*" (Chandra, pc 31 Oct. 2011).

The accumulation of so many mistakes within just four lines on the B-side may explain why the lapicide abruptly abandoned work on the text after the opening words of the second stanza. If the scribe had traced the original text onto the stone in charcoal, exposure to the elements would have removed any remnants of the rest of the composition. Whether the lapicide or the writer were responsible for the errors in the surviving four lines is not certain as the stonemason may have faithfully executed whatever text had been provided.

Bosch (1941) proposed that strophe B1 would actually present the names of two different kings and revised this theory in 1952 by identifying the first as the Viṣṇu(-varman) who was comparable to the sun, moon and Kāma, and the second ruler as the Śrī Mahārāja of the Śailendra family. After briefly entertaining this dual-kings hypothesis in an article published in 1950, Cœdès (1959: 45-46) ultimately concluded that the theory advanced by Bosch was untenable:

> "[I]f the compound *viṣṇvākhyo* (opposite *śrīmahārājanāmā*) refers to a different king, it should be in the first pair of *pādas*, allegedly devoted to this personage, and not at the beginning of the second pair, which is devoted to the *mahārāja.* For his part, Poerbatjaraka also thinks that the two words *eka* 'unique' and *dvitīya* 'second' refer to one and the same person, and now I, too, am prepared to admit this[. However,] instead of translating this passage as he does, 'this unique king of kings who is comparable to the sun', I should prefer to adopt Dr. de Casparis' translation: 'the supreme king of kings who is as unique as the sun'."

Following the lead of Poerbatjaraka, Cœdès revised his translation for the beginning of the third *pāda*: "the [king] named Viṣṇu who, by his prowess is like a second (Viṣṇu)". However, Chandra (pc 22 Sept. 2011) has proposed an alternative translation:

> "Viṣṇv-ākhyo means that King Śrī-Mahārāja was a veritable Viṣṇu. In the same stanza, there are two expressions: ◦*ākhyo* and ◦*nāmā*. *Nāmā* means 'name', the personal name of the King, while ◦*ākhyo* refers to him [as] being famed as Viṣṇu incarnate as he had provided security to the people by the vanquishing of enemies, [which] led to prosperity. [Furthermore, the Sanskrit word in line three] is not *dvitīyas*, but *'dvitīyas* ('= a) 'without

a second' because of his might. The words *eka* and *advitīya* are not ordinals (*prathama* 'first' and *dvitīya* 'second'). *Eka* means 'unique, the only one' like the glorious sun dispelling the darkness (*dhvānta*) of the hosts of all the enemies".

Strophe B1: Sragdharā meter

|– – –|– ⏑ –|–, ⏑ ⏑|⏑ ⏑ ⏑|⏑ –, –|⏑ – –|⏑ – –|

Fig. 1-15. Side 'B' of the stele, lines 1 through 4 (Cœdès 1918: plate IIa).

(1) svasti
yo ´sau rājādhirājas sakalaripugaṇadhvāntasūryyopa (2) maikas
svaujobhiḥ kāntalakṣmyā śaradamalaśaśī manmathābho vapu (3) ṣman=
viṣṇvākhyo ´śeṣasarvvārimadavi<ma>thanaś ca ´dvitayas svaśaktyā
so (4) ya<ṃ> śailendravaṅśaprabha<va>niga<di>taḥ śrīmahārājanāmā

Hail!
B1. He, the supreme king of kings, who alone is like the sun (having dissipated utterly) that darkness which is the assemblage of all his enemies, who is the moon without blemish in autumn by means of having natural energies and charming grace like Kāma incarnate and who is known as Viṣṇu ... (having vanquished completely) the arrogance of all (his) enemies without exception by his own prowess without a second ... (is the one called born) in the Śailendra dynasty, Śrī Mahārāja by name.

Hail (svasti)!
B1. **He** (´sau = asau, sing. third pers. pronoun), **the supreme king of kings** (rājādhirājas, read as rājādhirājaḥ),[25] **who** (yo = yaḥ) **alone** (ekas, read as ekaḥ) **is like the sun** (sūrya-upamā) [having dissipated utterly (vi<mā>tha] **that darkness** (dhvānta) **which is the assemblage** (gaṇa, 'assembly')

[25] Griffiths (2011a: 24, including n. 44) translated *rājādhirājas* as 'overlord of kings'.

of all his enemies (sakala-ripu), **who is the moon** (śaśī, sing. nom. of śaśin) **without blemish** ('mala = amala) **in autumn** (śarada, read as śārada)[26] **by means of having natural energies** (svaujobhiḥ, f. pl. instr. of svaujas)[27] **and charming** (kānta, 'pleasing') **grace** (lakṣmyā, f. sing. instr. of lakṣmī, 'beauty') **like** (ābho = ābhāḥ) **Kāma** (manmatha) **incarnate** (vapuṣman, read as vapuṣmān, sing. nom. of vapuṣmat, 'embodied'), **and** (ca) **who is known as Viṣṇu** (viṣṇvākhyo = viṣṇu-ākhyāḥ) ... [having vanquished completely (vi<ma>tha, read as vimātha, 'the act of crushing or destroying utterly')] **the arrogance** (mada) **of all** (sarva) [his] **enemies** (ari) **without exception** ('śeṣa = aśeṣa)[28] **by his own** (sva) **prowess** (śaktyā, sing. instr. of śakti) **without a second** ('dvitayas, read as advitīya)[29] ...[30] is [the one (ya<ṃ>, read as ayam, sing. third pers. pronoun) called (niga<di>taḥ) born (prabh<ava>)] **in the Śailendra dynasty** (Śailendravaṅśa),[31] **Śrī Mahārāja by name** (nāmā).[32]

Incomplete strophe B2

tasya ca sakalarā . . . . .

B2. And of him, ... of all [kings?] ... .

B2. **And** (ca) **of him** (tasya), ... [of all kings ? (sakalarā<ja>)] ....

Side A: Annotated transcription and revised translation

The transcription presented below for the most part follows the prior rendering by Chhabra released in 1935 and reprinted in 1965, except for the emendations suggested by Chandra in personal communications and by comparison with Griffiths (2011a: 18-22). However, most of the translation segments that follow the individual Sanskrit strophes diverge from the strophe translations published by Chhabra, Griffiths and other scholars with respect to the meaning of several key phrases.

---

[26]Though *śarada* is correct semantically, the meter requires an initial long syllable, e.g. *śārada*, 'autumnal'.

[27]Chhabra (1965: 31) parsed *svaujobhiḥ* as *sva-ojobhiḥ* (e.g. the pl. instr. of *ojas*), which he translated as 'through his energy'.

[28]Griffiths (2011a) interpreted *śeṣasarvvārimadavi<ma>thanaś* as meaning "being able without [the support of] Śeṣa to destroy the conceit of all enemies" or alternatively as "destroying the conceit of all enemies without exception".

[29]According to Chhabra (1965: 31), *cādvitīyas.*

[30]As indicated above, Chandra has proposed he (*so* = *saḥ*). According to Griffiths (2011a: 22), however, neither *so* or *sau* are likely readings judging from his inspection of the stone.

[31]'Lineage, race, family, stock (especially a noble race, a dynasty of kings)'.

[32]Though de Casparis (1950: 99) thought the better translation for *nāmā* would be 'entitled', Damais (1968: 354) remarked that the reports of early Arab traders state that the ruler of Zābag was 'called' the Mahārāja. "It is not a title but a name or designation, even if, as everyone knows, Śrī Mahārāja is a Sanskrit title. It seems unlikely that the use of *nāman-* in Sanskrit is not desired and it therefore appears that the word's precise meaning of 'name' must be retained". By contrast, Boechari (2012: 422) translated the final *pāda* of strophe B1 as, 'he is called Śrī Mahārāja because it is said that his origin is the Śailendrawaṃśa'.

Strophes A1 and A2: Śikhariṇī meter

| ⏑ – – | – – –, | ⏑ ⏑ ⏑ | ⏑ ⏑ –, | – ⏑ ⏑ | ⏑ – |

(1) visāriṇyā kīrttyā nayavinayaśauryyaśrutaśama-
kṣamā (2) dhairyyatyāgadyutimatidayādyakṣayabhuvā
paraṃ yasyā (3) krāntā bhuvanakubhujāṃ kīrttivisarā
mayūkhās tārāṇāṃ śaradi (4) tuhinānśor iva rucā ‖ 1 ‖

A1. By his spreading glory, the unparalleled inexhaustible arising of which is (his) prudence, modesty, valor, learning, equanimity, forbearance, constancy, generosity, brilliant understanding, compassion and the like,[33] the outpourings of the fame of the lesser kings on the earth were overwhelmed like the rays of the stars by the luster of the cool-rayed (moon) in autumn.

A1. **By his spreading** (visāriṇyā, sing. instr. of visārin) **glory** (kīrttyā = kīrtyāḥ, sing. instr. of kīrti), **the unparalleled** (adya) **inexhaustible** (kṣaya, read as akṣaya) **arising** (bhuvā, f. sing. instr. of bhū) **of which is** [his] **prudence** (naya), **modesty** (vinaya), **valor** (śauryya = śaurya), **learning** (śruta), **equanimity** (śama), **forbearance** (kṣamā), **constancy** (dhairyya = dhairya), **generosity** (tyāga, 'liberality'), **brilliant understanding** (dyutimati), **compassion** (dayā) **and the like** (param yasya, 'to be endeavored thereafter'), **the outpourings** (visarā = visarāḥ, pl. nom. of visara, 'extension, going forth or in various directions, spreading; plenty, abundance') **of the fame** (kīrtti = kīrti) **of the lesser** (ku-)[34] **kings** (bhujām, pl. genitive of bhuj) **on the earth** (bhuvana) **were overwhelmed** (ākrāntā, 'overcome, overrun')[35] **like** (iva) **the rays** (mayūkhās = mayūkhāḥ, pl. nom. of mayūkha) **of the stars** (tārāṇām, pl. genitive of tārā) **by the luster** (rucā)[36] **of the cool-rayed** (tuhinānśor, read as tuhina-aṃśoḥ, sing. genitive of aṃśu) [moon] **in autumn** (śaradi, sing. locative of śarad).

guṇānām ādhāras tuhinagiri (5) kūṭādhikarucā
guṇāḍhyānāṃ puṃsām api jagati yas tuṅga (6) yaśasām
maṇī*nāṃ* bhūrīṇāṃ duritabhidudanvān iva mahā (7) n
maṇijyotirllekhāvalayiśirasāñ cāpi phaṇinām ‖ 2 ‖

A2. (He is) a reservoir of (all)[37] virtues with more luster than (even) the (snowy) peaks of the Himalayas, who is (the support) of prominent respectable persons in the world as well as of human beings richly endowed with good qualities, a great (receptacle) of an abundance of gems like the ocean, and also the destroyer of the evil (existences) of the *nāga*-s with hoods encircled by streaks of jewel light.

[33]Or perhaps, 'the arising of which from (his) prudence, modesty, valor, learning, equanimity, forbearance, constancy, generosity, brilliant understanding, compassion and the like is preeminent (*ādi*) and inexhaustible (*akṣaya*)'.

[34]A prefix implying deficiency, depreciation, littleness, etc.

[35]Griffiths (2011a: 23): "was utterly downtrodden the diffusion of glory of the kings on the earth".

[36]In his transcription, Chhabra (1965: 29, n. 1) gave *rācā*, which he emended to *rucā*.

[37]This is implied by the contents of the previous stanza.

A2. [He is] **a reservoir** (ādhāras = ādhāraḥ sing. nom. of ādhāra) **of** [all] **virtues** (guṇānām, pl. genitive of guṇa) **with more** (adhika) **luster** (rucā) **than** [even] **the** [snowy] **peaks** (kūṭā = kūṭāḥ) **of the Himalayas** (tuhinagiri), **who** (yas = yaḥ)[38] **is** [the support (ādhāraḥ)] **of prominent** (tuṅga) **respectable persons** (yaśasām, pl. genitive of yaśas) **in the world** (jagati, sing. loc. of jagat) **as well as** (api) **of human beings** (puṃsām, pl. genitive of puṃs) **richly endowed** (āḍhyānām, pl. genitive of āḍhya) **with good qualities** (guṇa), **a great** (mahān, sing. nom. of mahat) [receptacle (ādhāraḥ)] **of an abundance** (bhūrīṇām, pl. genitive of bhūri) **of gems** (maṇīnām, pl. genitive of maṇi) **like** (iva) **the ocean** (udanvān, sing. nom. of udanvat), **and also** (cāpi = ca-api) **the destroyer** (bhid = bhit, sing. nom. of bhid) **of the evil** (durita) [existences] **of the *nāga*-s** (phaṇinām, pl. genitive of phaṇi, 'serpent') **with hoods** (śirasāñ, read as śirasām, pl. genitive of śiras, 'head, skull') **encircled by** (valayi) **streaks** (lekhā) **of jewel-light** (maṇi-jyotir = maṇi-jyotis).

Strophe A3: Hariṇī meter

|⏑ ⏑ ⏑ | ⏑ ⏑ –, | – – – | –, ⏑ – | ⏑ ⏑ – | ⏑ – ||

---

(8) dhanavikalatāvahnijvālāvalīkṣapitāśayā
yam a (9) bhipatitā ye te svā<sth>yaṃ paraṃ samupāgatāḥ
hradam i (10) va gajā nityā<śoṣyam pras>annaśubhāmbhasaṃ
savitari ta (11) paty <u>gre sevyuṃ sarojarajoruṇam || 3 ||

A3. (Whenever) those whose fortunes were decimated by waves of the flames of the fire of poverty have alighted to him, they attained perfect ease in the same manner as elephants, having resorted to a lake when the sun is burning fierce, are accustomed (to diffuse) pure, auspicious water that is perennial and ruddy with the pollen of lotus flowers.

A3. [Whenever] **those whose** (ye te) **fortunes** (āśayā = āśayāḥ, pl. nom. of āśaya, which also can mean 'hearts') **were decimated** (kṣapita) **by waves** (valī) **of the flames of the fire** (ahnijvāla, read as agnijvāla) **of poverty** (dhana-vikala, 'deprived of wealth') **have alighted to** (abhi-patita, 'fallen upon') **him** (yam, m. sing. acc. pronoun), **they attained** (samupāgatāḥ, pl. nom. of samupāgata) **perfect ease** (svāsthyam, sing. acc. of svāsthya, 'ease'; param, ind. 'at the utmost')[39] **in the same manner as** (iva) **elephants** (gajā = gajāḥ), **having resorted to** (sevyuṃ, read as sevyam, sing. acc. of sevya)[40] **a lake** (hradam, sing. acc. of hrada) **when the sun** (savitari, sing. locative of savitṛ) **is burning** (tapaty = tapati, sing. locative of tapat, 'warming') **fierce** (ugre, sing. locative of ugra), **are accustomed** (nitya) ... [to diffuse (<pras>)] **pure** (prasanna) **auspicious** (śubha) **water** (āmbhasam, sing. acc. of āmbhasa) **that is perennial** (<a>śoṣyam, sing. acc. of aśoṣya) **and ruddy** (aruṇam, sing. acc. of aruṇa) **with the pollen** (raja) **of lotus flowers** (saroja).[41]

---

[38]Griffiths (2011a: 19, n. 9): "both estampages would support reading yaṃs".
[39]Chhabra (1965: 30) read *svāsthyaṃ paraṃ*, which he translated as 'perfect ease'. Given the extent of the damage to the stone following the initial *akṣara svā* in this line, the original reading by Cœdès (1918) of *svāmyaṃ paraṃ* remains a possibility, which would mean 'ultimate dominion'. In this strophe the poet may have wished to compare the lake where elephants find relief from the scorching rays of the sun with the kingdom of the monarch, which is the 'ultimate dominion' where those felled by the scorching heat of poverty obtain relief.
[40]Chhabra (Ibid.) read *sevyaṃ* in place of *sevyuṃ* (Cœdès 1918).
[41]Chhabra (Ibid.) read *ugre* in place of *agre* (Cœdès 1918).

Strophe A4: Puṣpitāgrā meter

| ⏑ ⏑ ⏑ | ⏑ ⏑ ⏑ | ⏑ – ⏑ | – ⏑ – | – || ⏑ ⏑ ⏑ | ⏑ – ⏑ | ⏑ – ⏑ | – ⏑ – | – ||

guṇabhṛtam upa (12) gamya yaṃ guṇāḍhyā
⏑ ⏑ ⏑ ⏑ rā manunā samaṃ samantāt
(13) madhusamayam ivāmrakesarādyāś
śriyam adhikān dadhate ma (14) hīruhendrāḥ || 4 ||

A4. Having approached the bearer of virtues who is richly endowed with merit like Manu equally from all sides, (they)[42] attain abundances of bounties like the princes among trees (laden with) mango pollen, which are unparalleled (during) the spring season.

A4. **Having approached** (upagamya) **the bearer** (bhṛtam, sing. acc. of bhṛt) **of virtues** (guṇa) **who** (yam) **is richly endowed with** (āḍhya) **merit** (guṇa) **like** (nā, read as na) **Manu** (manu) **equally** (samam) **from all sides** (samantāt, sing. ablative of samanta, 'being on every side'), [they] **attain** (dadhate, third pers. pl. present, from √dhā) **abundances** (adhikān, read as adhikāni, pl. acc. of adhika) **of bounties** (śriyam, read as śriyām, pl. genitive of śrī, 'riches, wealth') **like** (iva) **the princes among trees** (mahīruhendrāḥ, pl. nom. of mahīruhendra) [laden with (āḍhyā)] **mango** (āmra) **pollen** (kesara), **which are unparalleled** (ādyāś = ādyāḥ) [during] **the spring** (madhu) **season** (samayam).

Strophe A5: Upendravajrā meter

| ⏑ – ⏑ | – – ⏑ | ⏑ – ⏑ | – – ||

jayaty ayaṃ śrīvijayendrarājā
(15) samantarājārccit<aś>āsanaśrīḥ
praśastadharmmasthiratonmukhena
vinirmmito viśvasṛjeva yatnāt || 5 ||

A5. This king (called) Śrīvijayendra,[43] the majesty of whose authority is honored by neighboring kings, who has been created by Brahmā deliberately just so by meditating upon[44] the perpetuity of the extolled Law (dharma), is victorious.

[42]Griffiths mentioned that Cœdès had proposed the emended reading of *manu<java>rā* ('the best of men') and included this in his transcription. By contrast, Chhabra (1965: 29) proposed the emendation *<jagati>narā*, which would mean 'people in the world'. However, Griffiths (2011a: 20, n. 15) remarked that Chhabra's proposed emendation "is not in conformity with the admittedly rather vague traces of akṣaras that are still visible on the estampages". The question remains open.
[43]After Griffiths (2011a: 22). Other proposed translation suggestions for *ayaṃ śrīvijayendrarājā* include, 'the Indrarāja of Śrīvijaya' (see the discussion segment for this verse).
[44]The elements of the creation become manifest as Brahmā meditates on truth (see *Viṣṇu Purāṇa* 1,6,3-5).

A5. **This** (ayam, sing. nom. pronoun) **king** (rājā, sing. nom. of rājan) [called] **Śrīvijayendra, the majesty** (śrīḥ, sing. nom. of śrī) **of whose authority** (śāsana, 'government, rule')[45] **is honored** (arccita = arcita)[46] **by neighboring kings** (samantarāja), **who has been created** (vinirmmito = vinirmitaḥ, sing. nom. of vinirmita) **by Brahmā** (viśvasṛj, i.e. 'the All-creator') **deliberately** (yatnāt, sing. ablative of yatna, lit. 'from effort'; 'very carefully') **just so** (eva) **by meditating upon** (unmukhena, sing. instr. of unmukha, 'looking at', e.g. looking thoughtfully for a long time at) **the perpetuity** (sthiratā, 'permanence') **of the extolled** (praśasta, 'praised') **Law** (dharma), **is victorious** (jayaty = jayati, third. pers. sing. present of √ji).

Strophes A6 and A7: Unidentified meters[47]

śrīvijayeśvarabhūpati (17) r eṣa guṇaughaḥ
kṣititalasarvvasamantanṛpottama ekaḥ
(18) sthāpita <ai>ṣṭikagehavaratrayam *etat*
kajakaramārani (19) sūdanavajrinivāsaṃ ‖ 6 ‖

| – ⏑ ⏑ | – ⏑ ⏑ | – ⏑ ⏑ | – ⏑ ⏑ | – – ‖
| ⏑ ⏑ ⏑ | ⏑ – ⏑ | ⏑ – ⏑ | ⏑ – ⏑ ⏑ | – – ‖
| – ⏑ ⏑ | – ⏑ ⏑ | – ⏑ ⏑ | – ⏑ ⏑ | – – ‖
| ⏑ ⏑ ⏑ | ⏑ – ⏑ | ⏑ – ⏑ | ⏑ – ⏑ ⏑ | – – ‖

A6. This king, the lord of Śrīvijaya, who is the very effusion of virtues, who is preeminent as the greatest of all the neighboring kings on the surface of the earth, has erected a triad of most excellent ... (brick) abodes, which is the seat, as it were, of Padmapāṇi, the Slayer of Māra (Buddha) and Vajrapāṇi.

A6. **This king** (bhūpatir = bhūpatiḥ, sing. nom. of bhupati), **the Lord of Śrīvijaya** (śrīvijayeśvara),[48] **who is verily** (ghaḥ) **the effusion** (eṣa) **of goodness and virtue** (guṇau),[49] **who is preeminent** (ekaḥ, sing. nom. of eka) **as the greatest** (uttama) **of all** (sarvva = sarva) **the neighboring** (samanta) **kings** (nṛpa) **on the surface** (tala) **of the earth** (kṣiti), **has erected** (sthāpita) **this** (etat) **most excellent** (vara) **triad** (trayam, sing. acc. of traya) **of dwellings** (geha) ... [made of bricks (<ai>ṣṭika, read as aiṣṭaka)[50]], **which is the seat** (āsam, sing. acc. of āsa), **as it were** (iva), **of Padmapāṇi** (kajakara, 'lotus-handed'), **the Slayer of Māra** (māra-niṣūdana, e.g. Buddha) **and Vajrapāṇi** (vajrin, 'holding a thunderbolt').

sa ⏑ tam etat trisamayacaityaniketaṃ (20) n
daśadigavasthitasarvvajinottamadattam
sarvvajagatma labhū (21) dharakuliśavaran

[45]Chhabra (1965: 30) provided this emendation to the reading of *rājārccitigmāsanaśrīḥ* by Cœdès.
[46]As proposed by Griffiths (2011a: 23, n. 34).
[47]Strophes A6 and A7 each contain 58 syllables in four quarters (*pāda*), with the first and third quarters having 14 syllables each and the second and fourth quarters having 15 syllables each.
[48]Zakharov (2012: 6) thought that °*īśvarabhūpati* would mean 'king of kings'.
[49]Chhabra (1965: 31) corrected the reading to *eṣa guṇaughaḥ* from *emaguṇo ghana* as read by Cœdès (1918), and Cœdès (1961) subsequently adopted the change. Griffiths (2011a: 20) has *eṣa guṇo ghana*.
[50]Griffiths (2011a: 20, n. 19) points out that Cœdès read *eṣṭika,* whereas Chhabra read *aiṣṭika*.

tribhavavibhūtiviśeṣadam amarapadam ‖ 7 ‖

| — ◡ ◡ | — — ◡ | ◡ ◡ ◡ | — ◡ ◡ | — — |
| ◡ ◡ ◡ | ◡ — ◡ | ◡ — ◡ | ◡— ◡ ◡ | — — ‖
| — ◡ ◡ | — ◡ ◡ | — ◡◡ | ◡ ◡ ◡ | ◡ — |
| ◡ ◡ ◡ | ◡ — ◡ | ◡ — ◡ | ◡◡ ◡ ◡ | ◡ — ‖

A7. This (contiguous) residence for the three-fold doctrine[51] in (the form of) *caitya*-s, which is presented to the best of all the Jinas situated in the ten directions,[52] is the most excellent among thunderbolts for (destroying) the mountain of impurities of the entire world, the abode of the imperishable[53] and the extraordinary endowment of prosperity[54] in the three states of cyclical existence.[55]

A7. **This** (etat) ... [contiguous (sa<ṃta>tam, n. sing. nom. of saṃtata, 'uninterrupted; linked or strung together')] **residence** (niketaṃn = niketan, read as niketam, n. sing. nom. of niketa, 'habitation')[56] **for the three-fold doctrine** (trisamaya, 'covenant; doctrine; practice') **in** [the form of] ***caitya*-s** (caitya), **which is presented** (dattam) **to the best** (uttama) **of all** (sarva) **the Jinas** (jina) **situated** (avasthita, 'having its place or abode') **in the ten directions** (daśadig = daśadik), **is the most excellent** (varan, read as varam) **among thunderbolts** (kuliśa) **for** [destroying] **the mountain** (bhūdhara) **of impurities** (mala) **of the entire** (sarvva = sarva) **world** (jagat),[57] **the abode** (padam, sing. acc. of pada) **of the imperishable** (amara),[58] **and the extraordinary** (viśeṣa) **endowment** (dam, sing. acc. of da, 'gift') **of prosperity** (vibhūti) **in the three states of cyclical existence** (tribhava).

Strophes A8 and A9: Āryā meter[59]

(22) punar api jayantanāmā rājasthaviro nṛpena suniyuktaḥ
stū (23) patrayam asi kurvv ity atas sa tad idan tathā kṛtavān ‖ 8 ‖

[51]Or: 'pledge', i.e. to "continuously maintain the view of the enlightened body, speech and mind of the buddhas" (Lingpa 2007: 205).

[52]i.e. the triad of Padmapāṇi, the Buddha and Vajrapāṇi signifying the Three Jewels (*ratnatraya*).

[53]e.g. exempt from age and death; this 'immortal abode' is *nirvāṇa* (see, for example, Burnouf 2010: 209).

[54]The thunderbolt, the immortal abode and the extraordinary endowment of prosperity pertain to Vajrapāṇi (Saṅgha - Mind), the Māra-destroyer (Buddha - Body) and Padmapāṇi (Dharma - Speech), respectively (see the discussion segment).

[55]The *kāma-loka, rūpa-loka* and *arūpa-loka*, according to Bodhiruci (Petzold & Hanayama 1995: 702).

[56]See Chhabra (1965: 29, n. 3).

[57]Griffiths (2011a: 23, including n. 37) has proposed two different possibilities for translating this part of the verse: "a perfect thunder bolt (kuliśa = vajra) against the mountains (bhūdhara) of the defilements of all worlds"; "Or: 'a perfect thunder bolt for the king (bhūdhara) against the defilements of all the people'."

[58]Cœdès (1961: 22) gave *amarapam* in place of *amarapadam.* Given the construction of strophe A6, which ends in a *pāda* containing 15 syllables, and the similar construction displayed in Strophe A7, Cœdès' transcription would fall one syllable short of the apparent model.

[59]With respect to the first and third quarters, Āryā meter should have 12 (4+4+4) measures, with — (heavy, *guru*) counting as two measures and ◡ (light, *laghu*) counting as one measure, whilst there should be 18 measures in the second quarter and 15 measures in the fourth quarter.

|⏑⏑⏑⏑|⏑ – ⏑ | – – ‖ – – | ⏑⏑– | ⏑– ⏑ |⏑⏑ – |– ‖ **first hemistich, strophe A8**
| – – |⏑⏑⏑⏑| – – ‖ ⏑– ⏑| ⏑⏑– | ⏑ | – ⏑⏑ |– ‖ **second hemistich, strophe A8**

A8. And furthermore, the senior monk, Jayanta by name, was told by the king: 'Also build a *stūpa*-triad'; hence acting as the (king's) agent he built (it) then as desired.

A8. **And furthermore** (punar-api), **the senior** (rāja, 'chief') **monk** (sthaviro = sthaviraḥ, sing. nom. of sthavira),[60] **Jayanta** ('Victorious') **by name** (nāmā), **was told** (iti) **by the king** (nṛpena, sing. instr. of nṛpa): '**Also** (asi, read as api) **build** (suniyuktaḥ) **a *stūpa*-triad**' (stūpa-trayam, sing. acc. of traya); **hence** (atas), **acting as the** [king's] **agent** (kurvv = kurva), **he** (sa =saḥ) **built** (kṛtavān, sing. nom. of kṛtavat) [it] **then** (idan) **as desired** (tathā, 'in that manner, so, thus').

svarite (24) ´smiṃs tacchiṣyo dh<ī>muktir abhūc ca nāmataḥ sthaviraḥ
iṣṭikacai (25) tyadvitayaṃ caityatritayāntike kṛtavān ‖ 9 ‖

| ⏑⏑– | – – | – – ‖ – – | ⏑⏑ –| ⏑– ⏑ | – ⏑⏑ |– ‖ **first hemistich, strophe A9**
| – ⏑⏑ | – – |⏑⏑ – ‖ – – | ⏑⏑ –| ⏑ | – ⏑⏑ |– ‖ **second hemistich, strophe A9**

A9. After he [= Jayanta] had gone to heaven, that disciple, Dhīmukti by name, became the (senior) monk and he made two of the brick *caitya*-s in proximity with the *caitya*-triad.

A9. **After he** (´smiṃs = asmin, sing. locative pronoun) **had gone** (ite, sing. locative of ita) **to heaven** (svar), **his disciple** (tacchiṣyo = tat-śiṣyaḥ, sing. nom. of śiṣya),[61] **Dhīmukti** (dhīmuktir = dhīmuktiḥ, 'Liberation through meditation, devotion or prayer')[62] **by name** (nāmataḥ = nāmatas),[63] **became** (abhūc = abhūt, third pers. sing. aortist of √bhū) **the** [senior] **monk** (sthavira) **and** (ca) **he made** (kṛtavān, sing. nom. of kṛtavat) **two** (dvitayam) **of the brick** (iṣṭika, read as iṣṭaka) ***caitya*-s in proximity** (antike, sing. locative of antika) **with the *caitya*-triad** (caitya-tritayā, sing. instr. of tritā).

Strophe A10: Sragdharā meter

|– – –|– ⏑ –|–, ⏑ ⏑|⏑ ⏑ ⏑|⏑ –, –|⏑ – –|⏑ – –|

---

vṛddhyā (26) pte śākarāje muninavarasakair mmādhavaikādaśāhe
śukle ko (27) līralagne bhṛgusutasahite cāryyamañjyotirāryye
deve (28) ndrābhena ca śrīvijayanṛpatinānyakṣitīśottamena
trai (29) lokyaikāgryacintāmaṇivapuṣa = i<va sthā>pitās s<t>ūpa<c>ai<tyāḥ> ‖10 ‖

[60]*Sthavira* is equivalent to the Pali *thera,* a monk who has spent ten years or more in the monkhood and is eligible to become a preceptor (*upajjhaya*, e.g. one who ordains other monks; see, for example, Childers 1875: 504). Xuanzang mentioned that the Siṅhalese monks of the Mahāvihāra were called the 'Hīnayāna *sthavira*' and the monks of the Abhayagirivihāra were identified as the 'Mahāyāna *sthavira*' (Baruah 2000: 53). Chhabra (1965: 33) translated *rājasthaviro* as 'royal monk'.

[61]Note that the pronoun *tat* is neut. sing. nom. whilst *śiṣyaḥ* is masc. sing. nom.

[62]Griffiths (2011a: 23) corrected Coedes' reading from *´dhimuktir* to *dhīmuktir*.

[63]Coedes (1961: 22) read *nāmatas*. Likewise, Griffiths (2011a: 21) has *nāmatas* in his transcription.

A10. When the king of the Śaka era has grown to (seven) sages, nine, and (six) savors,[64] on the eleventh day of Vaiśākha[65] in the bright fortnight, with Cancer as the ascendant[66] and with the sun as the master of the celestial world in the company of the planet Venus, the ... (*stūpa*-s and *caitya*-s), which were supreme in the three worlds owing to their wonderful appearance (as if [made out]) of wish fulfillment jewels, (were founded) by the king of Śrīvijaya with a resemblance to Indra and with preeminence over other rulers.

A10. **When the king** (rāje, sing. locative of rāja) **of the Śaka era** (śāka) **has grown** (vṛddhyāpte = vṛddhi-āpte) **to** [seven] **sages** (muni), **nine** (nava), and [six] **savors** (rasakair = rasakaiḥ), **on the eleventh** (ekādaśa) **day** (ahe, sing. loc. of aha) **of Vaiśākha** (mādhava) **in the bright fortnight** (śukle, sing. loc. of śukla), **with Cancer** (kolira = kulira) **as the ascendant** (lagne, sing. loc. of lagna) **and** (ca) **with the sun** (aryaman)[67] **as the master** (āryye = ārye, sing. loc. of ārya) **of the celestial world** (jyotir = jyotis) **in the company of** (sahite) **the planet Venus** (bhṛgusuta), ... [the *stūpa*-s and *caitya*-s (s<t>ūpa<c>ai<tyāḥ>, pl. nom. of caitya)[68]], **which were supreme** (ekāgrya = eka-agrya, eka, 'preeminent'; agrya, 'foremost') **in the three worlds** (trailokya)[69] **owing to their wonderful appearance** (vapuṣa, read as vapuṣaḥ, sing. ablative of vapus) ... [**as if** (i<va>)[70] {made out}] **of wish fulfillment jewels** (cintāmaṇi), ... [were founded (<sthā>pitās)] **by the king** (nṛpatinā, sing. instr. of nṛpati) **of Śrīvijaya with a resemblance** (ābhena, sing. instr. of ābhā) **to Indra** (devendra) **and** (ca) **with preeminence** (uttamena, sing. instr. of uttama, 'uppermost, highest') **over other** (anya) **rulers** (kṣitīśa).

Side A: Discussion of the strophes

Stanzas A1 and A2 are both composed in the Śikhariṇī ('crested'; see Morgan 2011: 148) meter, which exhibits a rhythm that audibly suggests the climbing of a mountain. "The name Śikhariṇī seems to have justification from its very rhythm, which represents the slope of the mountain in the form of the gradual transition from the heavy to the light syllables" (Mitra 1977: 110).[71] Indeed, metrical cadence is one of the important aspects of Sanskrit poetry that inevitably becomes lost in translation. "To really come alive, verses must be chanted" (Morgan 2011: 4).

Strophe A1. In my opinion, 'overwhelmed' provides a better gloss for *ākrāntā* than 'eclipses' (Chhabra 1965: 32) or 'downtrodden' (Griffiths 2011a: 22). The moon eclipses just a few stars in the sky whereas the luster of the cool-rayed (moon) in autumn, being that which is the most excellent of its kind, 'overruns' the light of all of the stars. The strophe's autumn moon simile, which has yet another parallel on the B-side of the stele, also leads me

[64] e.g. Śaka 697 = 775 CE.

[65] Mid-April to mid-May.

[66] e.g. with Cancer ascending the local horizon in the east.

[67] Aryaman is the name of the sun in the month during which the consecration occurred as well as the presiding divinity of the *nakṣatra* housing the moon on the Sunday when the king performed the rite.

[68] Other than *vapuṣa<ḥ>*, the emendations for this stanza are found in Chhabra 1965: 30-31. Due to the rules of *sandhi*, *ca-aryyaman-jyotis-āryye* became expressed in the inscription as *cāryyamañjyotirāryye*. For the identification of Aryaman with the sun, see *Yajur Veda* II.34 and *Viṣṇu Purāṇa* X.

[69] Or perhaps, 'on which the three worlds (*trailokya*) were deeply focused' (*ekāgrya*, 'closely attentive').

[70] Cœdès (1918: 30) initially proposed *i<ha>* but subsequently (1961: 22) adopted *i<va>*.

[71] For a discussion of the meter designations with respect to the contents of strophes from the Śailendra inscriptions found on Java, see the segment on compositional meters in Chapter V.

to believe that 'arising' is the preferred translation choice for *bhuvā* (sing. instr. of *bhū*) in comparison with 'sources' (Chhabra 1965: 32) or 'sprouts' (Griffiths 2011a: 22).

Strophe A2. Chhabra (1965: 32) translated *guṇānām ādhāras* as, 'he is the receptacle of virtues', though in my opinion the better choice would bc 'hc is thc rcscrvoir of virtues' and with the latter half of the strophe referring to the king as a great receptacle of an abundance of gems, with the reuse of *ādhāras* implied. Chhabra also wished to identify the king of Śrīvijaya as "[the patron] of the Nāgas with their heads haloed by the streaks of the luster of the gems, resembling [in that respect] the ocean". Chandra (pc 11 Sept. 2011) has provided a different interpretation: "Though the Nāgas are exceedingly prosperous, they are considered to be born in this inferior *yoni.* By his virtues, the monarch liberates them from their evil existences (*dur-ita*)". In either case, the term '*nāga*-s' metaphorically refers to the king's vassals and the members of his royal entourage who adorned themselves with jewels. Though both the king and the ocean are great receptacles of a multitude of jewels, the king's reservoir of virtues is so brilliant that it outshines even the snow-capped summits of the Himalayas.

This stanza can also potentially be viewed as a simple sketch in terms of traditional cosmography: with the snow-capped Himalayas to the north, with the domain of the king of Śrīvijaya in the earth's equatorial region and with the great ocean located to the south. Moreover, the *nāga*-s were associated with the netherworld below the earth's south pole. "The south, at all times, from the *Ṛg Veda* on, was known as the region of death. This was the cosmic south, below the earth. Pātāla, the netherworld, was above it. Nāgas, guilty of the crime of brahminicide, had to go to hell and leave Pātāla, the stratum of the netherworld deepest in position as well as significance" (Kramrisch 1981: 403).[72]

Strophe A3. The name for this strophe's meter, Hariṇī, designates the Indian Madder (*Rubia cordifolia*), a perennial herbaceous climber featuring a thin red bark and green leaves. The root of this plant was used to produce red textile dyes (rose madder) and paints and thus matches this stanza's poetic imagery of a lake ruddy with the pollen of lotus flowers. The Indian Madder also served as the source of an anti-inflammatory compound used in Ayurvedic medicines for the treatment of burns and other wounds (see, for instance, Sala 1996: 17 and Premila 2006: 275) and hence would have provided the traditional treatment for anyone scorched by the sun or the flames of fire (*agnijvāla*, which also can designate a 'plant with red blossoms, used by dyers') to which this strophe poetically alludes.

Strophe A4. Chhabra (1965: 32) translated this strophe as follows: "The virtuous people in the world, having from all sides turned to him, who is endowed with virtues like Manu, display a greater beauty, like mangoes, kesaras and other lordly trees on the approach of the spring season (do)". By contrast, an alternate translation for this verse proposed by Chandra (pc 11 Sept. 2011) evokes the floral splendor of the lordly trees (*mahīruhendrāḥ*)[73] 'laden with the mango pollen' (*āmrakesarādyāś* = *āmra-kesera-āḍhyāḥ*)—which is golden in color —during the spring season. The principal difficulty with his proposal is his substitution of *āḍhyāḥ* for *ādyāś*. On the other hand, his interpretation receives a modicum of support from

[72]Traditional cosmography also is embedded in strophe 15 of the Kayumwuṅan charter; see Chapter V.

[73]Though *mahīruha* literally refers to the Teak hardwood tree (*Tectona grandis*), Chandra thought it more likely that the compound *mahiruhendrāḥ* has been used here in a poetic sense.

the name for this strophe's meter. The name of this stanza's meter, Puṣpitāgrā, means 'blossoming tips' (Morgan 2011: 168). For this reason, I have attempted above to maintain Chandra's interpretation while preserving the original reading of *ādyāś*.

Strophes A5 and A6. Chhabra (1965: 33) translated *jayaty ayam śrīvijayendrarājā* as 'Victorious is this king, the lord of Śrīvijaya'. Following Stutterheim (1929), Jordaan and Colless (2009: 55-57) have argued that *śrīvijayendrarājā* should be translated as 'king over the lords of Śrīvijaya'. Griffiths (2011a: 22-23, n. 33) thought that Jordaan and Colless could have better supported their claim that Śrīvijaya had been ruled by a supreme lord through vassal kings "by citing the samantarāja/samantanṛpas of stanzas V and VI. But the evidential value of such claims is severely restricted by the fact that they are clichés in Sanskrit poetry and there is nothing specific about it in the case of Śrīvijaya."

According to Mus (1928: 520), "Indrarāja, the most frequently used appellation in Sanskrit epigraphy, can hardly be interpreted as anything other than 'the King similar [on the earth] to Indra'." In support of this interpretation, Mus cited a line from the roughly contemporary Torkhede copperplate dating from the reign of Govinda III of Gujarat (793–814 CE): "His brother Indrarāja, the equal of Indra, by his valor, a glorious king of the earth".[74]

The Upendravajrā meter selected for strophe five, which carries the meaning of a 'secondary Indravajrā' (Morgan 2011: 97), is a member of the Triṣṭubh[75] class of Sanskrit meters signifying Indra's powerful thunderbolt (Morgan 2011: 58). Given that the same monarch is compared to the lord of the gods (*devendra-ābhena*) in strophe A10, the alternate translation of *ayaṃ śrīvijayendrarājā* as 'this Indrarāja of Śrīvijaya' remains a viable secondary possibility, in my opinion.[76] As the bellicose lord of the gods, Indra is the *kṣatriya par excellence*.

In strophe A5, the designation *śrīvijayendrarājā* potentially reinforces the elevated status of the king of Śrīvijaya in comparison to all other neighboring kings on the surface of the earth, as expressly stated later on. It is also possible to view this as an allusion to Indra's palace on the summit of Mount Meru, which is elevated above the palaces of all the other *deva*-s located on the slopes of the cosmic mountain.

> "Indrarāja means 'supreme monarch'. Compare *Suvarṇa-bhās-ottama-sūtr-endrarāja*, where *Suvarṇabhāsa* (the Buddhist *sūtra*) is designated *indrarāja* to say that it is supreme among *sūtras*. Indrarāja is like the expression 'king of kings'." (Chandra, pc 30 Oct. 2011).

This interpretation of the meaning of Indrarāja resonates with two designations that appear on the reverse face of the stele: 'the supreme king of kings (*rājadhirājas*) who alone (*eka*) is like the sun' and 'by his prowess without a second' (*advitīyas*). The family name Śailendra literally means 'Lord of the mountain'. Though Śailendra is a known epithet for designating Śiva, the compound also obviously calls to mind the 'Indra of the mountain'

[74] *Brātā tu tasyendrasamānavīryaḥ śrīmāṃn* [= *ān*] *bhuvi kṣmāpatir Indrarāja.*

[75] The cadence of the Triṣṭubh meter, which is specifically identified with the *kṣatriya* caste (Morgan 2011: 93-94), is supposed to convey a powerful or warlike impression.

[76] See Sarkar (1985: 329) for examples of the designation representing the royal domain (Śrīvijayapuri) placed in advance of the king's own personal name in South India "to indicate their connection with it" (e.g. Śrīvijayaskandavarman, Śrīvijayabuddhavarman, etc).

(*śaila-indra*), e.g. the king whose royal palace on the earth is the terrestrial equivalent to the palace of Indra on the summit of the cosmic mountain.

In strophe A6, the inscription's composer refers to the Buddha as the 'slayer of Māra' (*māra-niṣūdhana*). The Sanskrit word *niṣūdana* means 'removing, destroying; killing, slaughter' and Māra is evil personified, as the references to him in Buddhist scriptures as the 'Evil One' confirm. In strophe A3, the inscription's composer designated the king of Śrīvijaya as 'the destroyer of evil [existences]'. The poet may have intended to compare the king of Śrīvijaya to the principal divinity of the inscription in the same way that elsewhere he compared the king to Indra in strophes A5 and A10. On the reverse face of the stele, as in the so-called Kĕlurak inscription and Nālandā charter, the scion of the Śailendravaṅśa likewise seems to have been identified as the 'crusher' or 'destroyer' of foes.

Though the designation *māra-niṣūdhana* applies to the historical Buddha (Śākyamuni), in theory it also can be equated with Akṣobhya—the Tathāgata of the cardinal direction east whose spiritual family (*kula*) has the *vajra* as its defining attribute. Likewise, Indra is the wielder of the *vajra* serving as the guardian of the cardinal direction east, which is associated with the rising sun. Furthermore, Indra is directly associated with the sunrise as one of the 12 Ādityas. The *Brahmā Purāṇa* contains "a passage in which the sun is alluded to under twelve names, with epithets peculiar to each, as though they were twelve distinct sun-deities: 'The first form of the sun is named Indra, the lord of the gods and the *destroyer of their enemies*'." (Wilkins 1900: 30).[77] It therefore is entirely possible that the poet had intended to represent the temple complex's royal patron as the earthly equivalent of Indra.

The appearance of the appellation *vajrin* for Vajrapāṇi in strophe A6 is also potentially significant. It may clarify Vajrapāṇi's symbolic role as the representative of the monastic community or Saṅgha in the triad presented in this verse and perhaps also provide a hint about the Buddhist viewpoint of the composer given that the following verse refers to the most excellent among thunderbolts (*vajra*) for (destroying) the mountain of impurities in the world. "Calling themselves 'possessors of mantras or scepters' (*mantrin/vajrin*), [the proponents of the system] developed rituals...for the purpose of a codified series of soteriological and non-soteriological acts and ultimately institutionalized this material in Buddhist monasteries where texts were copied, art produced, and rituals performed" (Davidson 2004: 117).

Strophe A7 This verse presents three triads: the *trisamaya* residence constructed by the king, the three states of cyclical existence (*tribhava*) and three allusions to (a) the most excellent among thunderbolts; (b) the imperishable abode; and (c) the extraordinary (*viśeṣa*) endowment (*dam*, sing. acc. case of *da*, 'granting; gift') of prosperity (*vibhūti*), which can be correlated with Vajrapāṇi (*vajra*), the Buddha (*nirvāṇa*) and Padmapāṇi (*varada-mudrā*), respectively. By contrast, Griffiths (2011a: 23) reduces the triad of potential allusions down to two: "This abode for the [Buddhas] of the three aeons, in the form of a caitya, assigned to all the Jinas residing in the ten quarters, is a perfect thunder bolt (*kuliśa* = *vajra*) against the mountains (*bhūdhara*) of the defilements of all worlds, a permanent abode for the immortals giving special power in the three existences".

In my opinion, however, the king had presented the *trisamaya* residence to the inscription's previously mentioned triad of Padmapāṇi, the Buddha and Vajrapāṇi, which

[77]Italics added to this citation by the author of the current work.

plausibly can be viewed as 'the best of all the Jinas in the ten directions' whenever they collectively signify the 'Three Jewels' (*ratnatraya*).[78] Moreover, "three eons" is a doubtful choice for the translation of *trisamaya* in the present Buddhist context given the alternatives at our disposal. This term can be equated with the three-fold doctrine of Buddha, Dharma and Saṅgha,[79] which according to Rahder (see Chhabra 1965: 33, n. 2) is applicable to the Mahāyāna Buddhist triad cited in the present inscription, as well as signify the practitioner's three-fold fundamental pledge or vow pertaining to the enlightened Body, Speech and Mind of all the Buddhas.

Strophes A8 and A9. The opening phrase 'and furthermore' (*punar api*) in strophe eight implies that the three *stūpa*-s constructed by the royal chaplain Jayanta[80]—as well as the two *caitya*-s subsequently erected by Dhīmukti—were in addition to the *trisamaya* abode erected by the king as previously mentioned in verses A6 and A7. Thus, in stanzas A6 through A9 the composer appears to be referring to three successive stages of construction prior to the consecration of the entire site by the king: (a) three (contiguous) brick abodes for Padmapāṇi, the Buddha and Vajrapāṇi, which collectively signify the three-fold doctrine of Buddha, Dharma and Saṅgha; (b) three brick *stūpa*-s; and (c) two *caitya*-s. The *trisamaya* residence mentioned in our text may refer to nothing more than three conjoined edifices. As Foucher (1900: 51) remarked, "the word *caitya*, unlike *stūpa*, has nothing to do with the shape of the building.... The *caitya* is likely to assume the most varied architectural forms".

Strophe A10. Chatterjee (1926) interpreted *mādhava* as a reference to the month of Caitra (mid-March to mid-April), presumably believing that the poet had used this Sanskrit term in the sense of 'vernal', e.g. referring to the month in which the vernal equinox took place, e.g. on 17 March 775. The composer's earlier reference to the 'spring season' (*madhu-samayam*) in strophe A5 appeared to reinforce this interpretation. Chhabra (1965: 34) disagreed and accepted *mādhava* as a direct reference to the month as Vaiśākha (mid-April to mid-May), which appears to be correct. The verse refers to the sun shining on this date as 'Aryaman'. The Āditya riding in the sun's celestial car during Vaiśākha is identified as Aryaman in the *Viṣṇu Purāṇa* (2, 10), *Brahmā Purāṇa* (31, 19-21) and *Śrīmad Bhāgavatam* (XII, 11, 34). However, Chhabra obviously erred when he wrote that the sun had been rising in the company of Venus in Cancer, which is an astronomically impossible occurrence in April. *Lagne kolira* (= *kulira*) actually refers to the celestial meridian running through the

[78]In the Old Javanese *Brahmāṇḍa Purāṇa* (Phalgunadi 2000: 16, 50-51), which dates from the tenth century, *trisamaya* is the designation used for the holy Hindu Trinity of Brahmā, Viṣṇu and Śiva.

[79]In esoteric Buddhism, the meanings of equality, fundamental vow, destruction of obstacles or re-awakening bodhi are variously attributed to *samaya*, whilst *trisamaya* "signifies the identity between all sorts of triads; e.g., our heart, the Buddha, sentient beings: Heart, Insight, and Compassion; *dharmakāya*, *saṃbhogakāya*, and *nirmāṇakāya*; Buddha, Dharma, Samgha; the actions of body, speech, and mind; and so on". The prose definition supplied by one of the chapters in the *Vairocanābhisambodhi-sūtra* (VAS) defines *trisamaya* as (1) "the gradual development of *bodhicitta* in the mind of the faithful follower"; (2) "the destruction of the obstacles"; (3) "and the identification of the faithful follower with the Buddha. Next, it is defined in verses as (1) the initial *bodhicitta*, that is to say, the Buddha who resides in the innermost depth of ourselves; (2) the Dharma; (3) the Samgha, that is to say, the totality of the faithful followers who gradually realize the Dharma" (Wayman & Tajima 1993: 329-330; see also Abe 1999: 217, 503).

[80]"The three temples had been constructed and the king commanded the royal preceptor named Jayanta to further construct three *stūpas* related to them" (Chandra, pc 11 Sept. 2011).

constellation Cancer, which must have been ascending the local horizon when the king consecrated the temple complex. Similarly, the Canggal inscription of king Sañjaya refers to *kumbha-lagne* (e.g. with Aquarius as the ascendant) as is likewise the case with the aforementioned Kañjuruhan inscription (760 CE) from East Java (de Casparis 1978: 22).

Strophe A10 specifies the auspicious elements of the consecration date as follows:

- Auspicious month: spring;
- Auspicious bright fortnight when propitious rituals are typically performed;
- Auspicious eleventh *tithi* dedicated to fasting, devotional activities, and remembrance of the Supreme Lord among Hindus;
- Auspicious *lagna* as the ascendant: Cancer (*kulīra*) incorporates the highly auspicious *nakṣatra* Pusya, the asterism associated with the Buddha's immaculate conception;
- Auspicious planet: Venus (Śukra, associated with Kubera, the god of prosperity);
- Auspicious time of day: when the sun (Aryaman) was in the vicinity of the zenith;
- Auspicious Śrīvijayan anniversary: the same date as the Kedukan Bukit inscription.[81]

As Griffiths (2011a: 23-24, n. 39) has observed, *cāryyamañjyotirāryye* (*ca-aryyaman-jyotis-āryye*) is difficult to translate given that the compound *jyotirārya* does not appear to be attested elsewhere though the two-word sequence of *jyotir āryam* does appear in the *Ṛgveda* (10, 43, 4d) as a possible reference to the sun. Having examined the celestial state of affairs on the consecration date, in my opinion the most plausible translation would be, 'and (*ca*) with the sun (*aryaman*) as the master (*āryye*) of the celestial world (*jyotis*)'. From the astrological viewpoint, Aryaman was the master of the celestial world when the inscription was issued for the following reasons:

- The sun is called Aryaman in the month Vaisākha;
- The eleventh day of the bright half of Vaisākha was a Sunday;
- The moon was in the *nakṣatra* Uttara Phalguni, which has Aryaman as its presiding divinity and the sun as its ruling planet, respectively;[82]

[81]According to the Kedukan Bukit inscription (Cœdès 1930: 34), the king of Śrīvijaya embarked on a *siddhayātra* on *ekādaśī-śuklapakṣa* in Vaiśākha during Śaka 605 (e.g. Sunday, 16 April 683 CE). Hence, it is possible that the composer of the Isthmus of Kra stele had specifically intended to commemorate an anniversary of importance to Śrīvijaya, though the precise meaning of the word *siddhayātra* has been hotly debated. Boechari (2012: 370-371) speculated that the Kedukan Bukit inscription was intended to commemorate the establishment of a new capital in Palembang for the Śrīvijayan empire. He also suggested that the king of Śrīvijaya had embarked on the eleventh day in the bright half of Vaiśākha in order to reach a distant Buddhist shrine in time for celebrating the anniversary of the Buddha's birthday and *parinirvāṇa* on the full moon of this particular month (Boechari 2012: 378, 390-391). However, the selection of the eleventh day in the bright half of Vaiśākha for the Isthmus of Kra stele suggests to me that the identical date appearing in the Kedulan Bukit inscription had been significant on its own.

[82]According to the sixth century astronomer Varāhamihira, the activities suitable for performing when the Moon passes through Uttara Phalgunī, as well as other *nakṣatra*-s belonging to the same class of stable (*dhruva*) asterisms, include the coronation of kings, expiatory ceremonies, planting of trees, the building of towns, acts of public utility, the sowing of seeds and acts of permanent effects (Varaha Mihira & Iyer, vol. II, 1884: 229-230. Varāhamihira also remarked that Pūrva and Uttara Phalgunī form the genitals of the stellar body known as the *nakṣatra puruṣa* (Ibid., p. 255).

- the sun was in the vicinity of the apex of its daily path across the sky;
- Aryaman was in Aries—the sun's constellation of exaltation,[83] according to Varāhamihira (*Bṛhat Jātaka* I, 13).

Besides, with Cancer on the local horizon during mid-April, the sun would have been in close proximity to the zenith, i.e. when the sun transits the local meridian at the time of local noon. The Hindu-Buddhist equivalent of an hour, the *muhūrta*, is roughly 48 minutes in duration. The eighth *muhūrta* of the daylight hours, which straddles the time of local noon (24 minutes to either side), is known as Abhijit, which means 'victorious'. On the inscription's date, the sun would have been in the vicinity of the zenith—the high point of the arc at which the sun transits the local meridian—when the constellation Cancer was on the local horizon (approximately 10:47 am to 1:00 pm local time).

In ancient India, Puṣya (=Tiṣya) was regarded to be a particularly auspicious asterism in general, and the composers of early Mahāyāna Buddhist texts associated this particular asterism with either the conception or birth of the historical Buddha. "Then as soon as Pushya became propitious, from the side of the queen, who was hallowed by her vows, a son was born for the weal of the world, without her suffering either pain or illness" (*Buddhacarita* I, 9, 10).

The usual astrological meaning one would be inclined to infer from *bhṛgusutasahite* is 'in conjunction with the planet Venus'. However, the Sun and Venus did not occupy the same constellation during April of 775 CE. Perhaps the poet had intended to use *bhṛgusutasahite* as a way to stress the fact that Venus was likewise occupying its own constellation of exaltation, Pisces, at the time of consecration. "When planets are inclined to give good they give full when they are in exaltation...." (Varāhamihira et al 1986: 454).[84] Furthermore, on the consecration date the sun was in the *nakṣatra* Bharaṇī, which has Venus as its planetary ruler. In any case, the planet Venus was in Pisces while the sun was in the next zodiac sign Aries when the inscription was promulgated. So both were shining in the sky overhead but were not located in conjunction or close proximity to one another.

Chhabra (1965: 28) gave the inscription's date as Thursday, 14 April 775 based on calculations provided by a member of the Oriental College at Lahore. According to the South-East Asian Calendars (SEAC) software application developed by J.C. Eade at the Australian National University and Lars Gislén at Lund University, however, the equivalent Gregorian calendar date is Sunday 20 April 775. Comparable results are delivered by the Jagannatha Hora software program developed by P. V. R. Narasimha Rao.

Griffiths (2011a: 23-24) translated strophe A10 as follows: "And the stūpas and caityas were founded here for [the Buddha] whose appearance is that of a wish-jewel for single-mindedness in the three worlds, by the king of Śrīvijaya, who resembled Indra among the gods in that he was the foremost among other kings, when the king of the Śākas has grown to (7) sages, nine, (6) aromas (i.e. in 697 Śaka), on the eleventh day of Mādhava (i.e. Vaiśākha), in the waxing (fortnight), with Cancer as the ascendant, and with the Sun (?,

[83]A planet in its own exaltation sign is considered to be exceedingly powerful whilst a planet occupying its debilitation sign is considered to be exceedingly weak.

[84]Additionally, Saturn was exalted on the same date in the constellation Libra. The sun's exaltation = +95 percent, whereas the exaltation of Venus and Saturn were +89 percent. By contrast, a planet's strength at debilitation (-180 degrees from exaltation) only ranges from 0 to 12.5 percent.

āryamañjyotirārya), in the company of Venus". In my opinion, however, the translation for v.A10 presented earlier in this chapter is preferable in that it adopts an astrological top-down point of view: with the macrocosmic state of affairs in heaven preceding the terrestrial details, which are ideally presented as heaven's mirror image. The two half-verses are mutually intertwined on the macrocosmic and microcosmic levels because of the highly auspicious nature of the astrological components of the consecration date.[85] Moreover, Griffiths' assumption that the *stūpa*-s and *caitya*-s solely pertain to the Buddha is in my opinion incorrect given their identification with the *trisamaya* and its correlation with Padmapāṇi, the Buddha and Vajrapāṇi as a triad signifying the Three Jewels.

Body	Longitude	Nakṣatra	Pāda	Rasi	Navāṃśa
Lagna	14 Cancer 23' 06.49"	Puṣya[86]	4	Cn	Sc
Sun	22 Aries 10' 20.29"	Bharaṇi	3	Ar	Li
Moon	29 Leo 42' 23.53"	Uttara Phalguni	1	Le	Sg
Mars	20 Aquarius 04' 50.98"	Purva Bhādrapadā	1	Aq	Ar
Mercury	25 Pisces 50' 44.86"	Revatī	3	Pi	Aq
Jupiter	19 Capricorn 17' 28.22	Sravaṇa	3	Cp	Ge
Venus	8 Pisces 17' 43.86"	Uttara Bhādrapadā	2	Pi	Vi
Saturn	2 Libra 42' 27.06"	Citra	3	Li	Li
Rahu	15 Taurus 28' 39.43"	Rohiṇī	2	Ta	Ta
Ketu	15 Scorpio 28' 39.43"	Anurādhā	4	Sc	Sc

Date: 20 April 775 (Gregorian calendar)
Time: 11:50:19 (Cancer was on local horizon between 10:47 am and 1:00 pm)
Time Zone: 7:00:00 (East of GMT)
Place: 99 E 11' 25", 9 N 22' 41"
Chaiya, Surat Thani, Thailand
Lunar Yr-Mo: Rākṣasa - Vaiśākha
Tithi: Śukla Ekādaśī (Ma) (37.21 percent left)
Vedic Weekday: Sunday (Su)
Nakṣatra: Uttara Phalgunī (Su) (77.20 percent left)

Fig. 1-16. Astrological details pertaining to the A-side of the Isthmus of Kra stele.

[85]There is another astrological aspect that perhaps can be associated with the position of the sun in Aries and thus conceivably lend support to the view that the *stūpa*-s and *caitya*-s were shining as if [made out] of wish fulfillment jewels. According to the *Bṛhat Jātaka*, the constellation Aries can signify, among other things, mines where precious stones are found.

[86]The other *nakṣatra*-s that span the remaining parts of the constellation Cancer are Punarvasu (20° 00' Gemini — 03° 20' Cancer) and Aśleṣā (16° 40' Cancer — 00° 00' Leo).

A critical review of the Dharmasetu hypothesis

In his 1959 article devoted to the 'stele of Ligor', Cœdès examined the various contradictory arguments previously presented by himself, Bosch, Poerbatjaraka, and de Casparis and proposed the following synthesis. The Śailendra Mahārāja Śrī Bālaputradeva cited in the Nālandā charter must have ascended the throne of Suvarṇadvīpa (presumed by Cœdès and others to be a reference to Śrīvijaya) as the result of an inheritance brought to him by his mother Tārā, the daughter of Śrī Dharmasetu.

> "The king in Śrīvijaya mentioned on side A and the founder of a Buddhist monastery in 775 is almost certainly the king Dharmasetu named in the Nālandā charter.... [T]his name is not actually mentioned on the Ligor stone, [though] it is at least alluded to" (Cœdès 1959: 47).

As this interpretation subsequently became the consensus opinion among historians, we shall critically review Cœdès' source materials as well as the merits of the individual elements of his synthesis. First, an abridged translation of the Nālandā charter segment on which Cœdès based his Dharmasetu hypothesis:

> "There *was* a king of Yavabhūmi (or Java) who *was* the ornament of the Śailēndra dynasty.... He had a son, who possessed prudence, prowess, and good conduct, whose two feet fondled much with the diadems of hundreds of mighty kings (bowing down). He *was* the foremost warrior in battlefields and his fame *was* equal to that earned by Yudhiṣṭhira, Parāśara, Bhīmasēna, Karṇa and Arjuna... Tārā *was* the consort of that king, and *was* the daughter of the great ruler Dharmasētu [correctly Varmasētu—Ed.] of the lunar race and resembled Tārā (the Buddhist goddess of the same name) herself" (K. Sastri 1942: 101-102).[87]

In potential support of his identification of Śrī Dharmasetu with the king of Śrīvijaya, Cœdès (1959: 44) cited strophe five from the A-side of the stele. "[T]he King of Śrīvijaya 'was deliberately created by Brahmā as if this god's only aim was the stability of the praiseworthy Dharma' (*praçastadharmasthiratonmukhena*); it appears that this *dharmasthiratā* must be the main aim of a *Dharmasetu* who is a 'buttress of the law'." Still, his proposed allusion is a rather weak linkage without something more to support it.[88] Cœdès also never directly addressed the contrary observations made by K. Sastri (1942) and Majumdar (1933)—with the latter having considered it "beyond doubt"—that the Sanskrit appellation (or epithet for this king) given in the charter is Śrī Varmasetu and not Śrī Dharmasetu.

Cœdès' Dharmasetu hypothesis has proven so seductive because it provides plausible, easily understood explanations for several issues that previously had remained unaddressed,

---

[87]Italics added by the author of the current text. All of these ancestors of Bālaputradeva apparently were deceased when Devapāla issued the Nālandā charter.

[88]Cœdès could have made a stronger case for his hypothesis by citing an entirely different phrase found in strophe A2: "[He (e.g. the king of Śrīvijaya) is] a reservoir of virtues (*guṇānām ādhāras*)...." Among other things, *ādhāra* means 'a dike, a dam' as is likewise the case with *setu*.

such as why the Nālandā charter identifies the Śailendra Mahārāja Śrī Bālaputra as the king of Suvarṇadvīpa instead of Java. It also potentially explains why an inscription presumably naming his Śailendra grandfather would have appeared on the other side of a stele promulgated by the king of Śrīvijaya. Still, there is no evidence that the kings of Śrīvijaya had ever considered themselves to belong to the *somakula* whereas a comparable lunar family designation appears in an inscription from Central Java dating from the mid-ninth century.[89]

One major flaw in the Dharmasetu hypothesis is the ill-founded belief that Bālaputra did not begin to reign in Śrīvijaya until after 856 CE. In this respect, the translation and highly speculative interpretation of the Śivagṛha inscription (856 CE) published by de Casparis in 1956 appears to have led many historians astray:

> "Bālaputra, presumably after a defeat in the open country, retired to a place [in Central Java] ... which could be transformed into a stronghold by means of defense works built up with hundreds of stones. However, before having succeeded in establishing an almost unconquerable position, he was attacked and defeated by Kumbhayoni, who was as swift as the wind, and wiped off from there. Presumably Bālaputra was not killed in battle..." (de Casparis 1956: 293). "Unless one should assume that Bālaputra interfered with Central Javanese affairs in a time when he was already a king of Śrīvijaya—*which is extremely unlikely*—it is necessary to conclude that he became a king in Sumatra after 856 A.D." (de Casparis 1956: 295).[90]

As we have previously seen, Jordaan and Colless now believe that King Devapāla had promulgated the Nālandā copperplate *circa* 843-850 CE, or perhaps even earlier. We may also safely presume that Bālaputra had been ruling in Suvarṇadvīpa for a period in advance of the arrival of his messenger at the royal court of Devapāla in Bengal. Consequently, the description of events offered by de Casparis concerning an insurrection in Central Java presumably led by Bālaputradeva[91] in 855-856 is debatable. Acri (2010) has argued that Bālaputradeva may have aimed at overthrowing the local Javanese ruler, perhaps through covert means at the time of the succession. This interpretation based in major part on his reading of the Old Javanese *Rāmāyaṇa* as a metaphorical document pertaining to the event.

Damais (1968) devoted several pages to highlighting the series of conjectures that de Casparis' had to adopt to arrive at his dubious historical 'reconstruction'. Among other things, de Casparis mistakenly equated Rakai Pikatan (847–855) with Rakai Walaiṅ pu Kumbhayoni—the promulgator of the Wukiran inscription found at Pereng near the foot of the Ratu Baka Plateau to the southeast of Prambanan as well as several *liṅga* inscriptions unearthed in the vicinity of Dawangsari and other locations atop the eastern prominence of Ratu Baka. His restoration of a missing syllable is questionable and the remainder of his

[89]Chandra (1995: 234, 236) remarked that a lunar family designation is applied to the Javanese aristocrat Rakai Walaiṅ pu Kumbhayoni in the Ratu Baka Xc inscription from the mid-ninth century.

[90]Italics added by the current text's author.

[91]Chandra (1995: 232) has glossed the name Bālaputra as 'young prince', which strikes me as a highly unusual name for a Śailendra Mahārāja. Citing the *Mahābhārata,* the online *Cologne Digital Sanskrit Lexicon* defines Bālaputra as 'having children' or 'young'.

interpretation of events relies on his speculative reading of a key Old Javanese word that does not conform to any of the known definitions.

> "I have gathered these scattered remarks to show how everything is conjectural. He has not only added a syllable conjecturally but he is also obliged to give a word, introduced by him, an unattested sense... For my part, I consider that the deductions made about such an incomplete text can only be speculative. Additionally, the uncertainty of the date of the Nālandā charter makes it particularly difficult to interpret the role of Bālaputra here. De Casparis, who wishes that the latter had waged war with Java (pp. 295 and 297, including n. 69) before he became king of Śrīvijaya, is obliged to consider that he was 'presumably' not killed. If one engages in speculation, however, it is just as easy to conceive theoretically that he came from Sumatra 'to wage war' on Java; though to do that, it is obvious that the charter of Nālandā predated 856 CE. The question remains open" (Damais 1968: 483).

The Nālandā charter identifies the paternal grandfather of Śrī Mahārāja Bālaputra as the king of Java (*yavabhūmipāla*) and scholars have generally presumed that his son, who is described as the 'foremost warrior in battlefields' (*samarāgravīra*), must have likewise held the same title. However, if Bālaputra had been planning to invade Java then it would have been in his best interests to ensure that the Nālandā charter clearly enunciated his own father's ascendance to the Javanese throne. Additionally, why would Śrīvijaya—which did not resume sending trade missions to China until 905 CE—have found it desirable or even practical to adopt an expansionist policy so ambitious that it included plans for an outright invasion of its far larger and more populous neighbor?

Stutterheim (1929: 9) surmised that the Nālandā charter's Sanskrit compound *samarāgravīra* would be an epithet for the Śailendra king Samaratuṅga, whose own consecration name one may gloss as 'exalted in war' or 'preeminent in battle'. Though Bosch eventually adopted Stutterheim's supposition, his initial reaction was to think it unnecessary to deem *samarāgravīra* as having any special significance. He noted that Śrī precedes all the other royal appellations from the Nālandā charter, including the epithet *vīravairimathana* for the grandfather of Bālaputra from strophe 24. However, the same royal honorific does not precede the phrase 'foremost warrior in battlefields' (Bosch 1930: 135, n. 2).

It is entirely possible that Śrī Saṅgrāmadhanaṃjaya had multiple male offspring who were destined to become warriors. Therefore, the similarity in meaning between the descriptive compound *samarāgravīra* and the royal consecration name Samaratuṅga may signify nothing more than the existence of at least two sons of the 'Crusher of foes in battle' who had been, so to say, chips off the same block. If we are to regard Stutterheim's surmise as historical fact then something more is required, such as the appearance of a similarly worded epithet for Samaratuṅga in one of his own inscriptions, just as has proven to be the case with respect to the so-called Kĕlurak inscription of Samaratuṅga's presumed father. However, neither the Abhayagirivihāra (792/3) or Kayumwuṅan (824) charters mentioning

Samaratuṅga exhibit any traces of such an epithet, nor do they name his queen,[92] or contain even the slightest hint about whether Samaratuṅga even had a male heir. One might argue that the extensive lacunas in these two charters may have conceivably provided the requisite space for one or more of these missing elements. Still, the equal attention that the poet devotes to both Samaratuṅga and his daughter in the Kayumwuṅan charter suggests the possibility that Śrīmat Prāmodavarddhanī had been the monarch's principal heir in 824 CE.

Trade missions to China from Southeast Asia

Beyond the speculative underpinnings already cited above, there are two other major problems with Cœdès' Dharmasetu hypothesis, the first of which is the relatively late date it advances for the inception of an alliance, achieved through marriage or other means, between Śrīvijaya and the Śailendravaṅśa. From 768 through the end of 852, the embassies arriving from the Malay-Indonesian Archipelago had come from Java exclusively. The abrupt end of lucrative trade missions from Śrīvijaya to China in 742 and the three consecutive annual embassies from Ho-ling to China in 768, 769 and 770 also suggest that the triggering event or series of events responsible for Java's ascendancy are more likely to have occurred prior to 775 CE. Additionally, Cœdès' Dharmasetu hypothesis does not account for why the king of Śrīvijaya would have promulgated his own inscription on the A-side of the stele using a variety of Palaeojavanese script instead of the Pallava type favored by Śrīvijaya during the late seventh century.

As Cœdès pointed out, there are no direct references to the Śailendravaṅśa in the earlier epigraphical records of Śrīvijaya, of which all the dated inscriptions pertain to the period 683–686 CE. The little else we know about the activities of Śrīvijaya between 686 CE and 775 CE comes from the remarks recorded by the Chinese monk Yijing for the period 672–692 as well as the royal court records of the Chinese emperor covering the decades between 695 and 742 CE. Despite the assertion by Cœdès (1948: 185) that Bālaputra was without doubt the first Śailendra sovereign of Śrīvijaya, it certainly remains possible—and perhaps even likely as we shall see below—that the Śailendravaṅśa had established itself in the Malay-Indonesian Archipelago at some point in time during the three decades (743–774) for which we possess no historical reports.

Chinese court officials employed the designation Shih-li-fo-shih, or simply Fo-shih, for the embassies from Śrīvijaya, with the kingdom's initial trade mission having arrived in China *circa* 670–673 (Jordaan and Colless 2009: 67). The Śrīvijayan trade missions overview presented by K. Sastri (1940: 252) provides us with a modicum of insight into what these embassies had entailed. In 695, Chinese court officials decided to regulate "the provisions to be supplied to the embassies from different foreign countries", with the trade missions from Śrīvijaya receiving the same five months of provisions as the embassies

[92]Though a fragmentary line from the Plaosan inscription (see de Casparis 1956: 193) includes the phrase, "... a wife (*bhāryyā*) dignified (*virājati*) like Tārā (*tāreva*)", nothing else appears in this Sanskrit text that would lead us to believe that this phrase must specifically refer to the wife of Samaratuṅga. Since Caṇḍi Kalasan was dedicated to the worship of this goddess the Plaosan text fragment may simply be a general reference to a quality of the goddess that the wife of an unnamed royal personage had likewise possessed.

from Chen-la and Ho-ling. Subsequent reports indicate that Śrīvijaya (Fo-shih) did send embassies to China in 702 and 717 CE.

In 724, the Chinese emperor's court received an ambassador bearing the designation Kumāra; it is possible he had been the crown prince of Śrīvijaya. Kumāra "presented to the emperor two dwarfs, a Zengi (Negro) girl, a troupe of musicians and five-colored parrots" and the emperor in turn conferred a title on the Kumāra and gave him one "hundred pieces of silk before sending him back to his country". Additionally, the Chinese emperor conferred a title on the king of Śrīvijaya named Che-li-to-lo-pa-mo, which Krom (1930: 120) considered to be the Chinese transliteration of Śrīndravarman.

> "The present of multi-coloured parrots by yet another embassy is recorded in 728. The last of the embassies of this period falls in the beginning of 742 A.D. when another prince of Śrī Vijaya visited the Chinese court and the emperor conferred another title on the king who had sent the embassy" (Sastri 1940: 252).[93]

Given the potential political and trade benefits of these exchanges, it is an utter surprise that no other Śrīvijayan embassies came to China after 742, especially in light of the statement by Yijing that the capital of Śrīvijaya had been the chief trading port with China during the late seventh century (1896: xl).[94] Furthermore, from the beginning of the eighth century through the end of the ninth century, the trade missions from Śrīvijaya and Java had never overlapped, which is extraordinary and in all probability highly important for our understanding of political developments within the Malay-Indonesian Archipelago.

> "The [Chinese] emperor graciously accepted the 'tribute' offered, but gave more expensive presents in return. Of course, foreign embassies also brought goods for trade, and the Chinese well appreciated their commercial value.... Some [embassies went to China] in response to the invitation of Chinese emperors who sought exotic products or the gratification of barbarian submission. Some Southeast Asian rulers dispatched embassies in order to reinforce or legitimize their own power. Presentation of fine clothing, titles and regalia [by the Chinese emperor] raised the status of rulers of small kingdoms like Funan, giving them the edge over their rivals in the cutthroat politics of Southeast Asian mandalas. Most embassies, however, were sent to promote trade, particularly in Chinese luxury products, such as silk and later fine porcelain, desired as status symbols by Southeast Asian elites" (Stuart-Fox 2003: 30-31).

It is notable that Kedah (Ko-lo) sent embassies to China on a regular basis between 742 and 759 CE, e.g. immediately following the final trade mission from Śrīvijaya, which suggested to Jordaan and Colless (2009: 67, n. 1, see also 216-217) "that a change in its political relationship towards Śrīvijaya" had occurred. Located on the west coast of the Malay Peninsula near Malacca, Kedah had been one of the major stopover points for journeys between Śrīvijaya and India during the closing decades of the seventh century,

---

[93]Bielenstein (2005: 59) gives the year of the next-to-last trade mission from Śrīvijaya as 727 CE.

[94]Trade missions from Ho-ling arrived in China in 640, 649 and 666 but did not return to China until the consecutive annual missions of 768, 769 and 770 CE.

according to Yijing (1896). Here it is worth repeating an observation made by Quaritch Wales (1937: 172): "Kedah, situated at the western entrance to the Straits, and in a position to patrol them throughout their length, certainly seems better placed to exercise this control than does Palembang, which lies fifty miles up a river, the mouth of which is 250 miles distant from Singapore".

Campā (coastal region of south-central Vietnam)	Lin Yi							Huan Wang			Chang Ch'eng		
		623 625 627- 631 639	642 645 653 654 657	668 669	686 695 699	703 706 707 710 712 714 715	731 734- 736 748 749		793 797	809		877	958/59 961/62 966/67 974 976
Khmer Cambodia	Wen Tan (Chenla)									Angkor			
	607 616 617	623 625 628 635	651	682	698	707 710 717	750 753	771	799	813 814			
Java	Ho-ling												
			640 649	666 676				768- 770	813 815 818				
	She-po												
										820 831	839	860~ 874	992 993
Malay Peninsula or Bali	Po-li												
	616	630											
Malay Peninsula	P'an-P'an												
	616	633 635	641 648										
Kedah, Malay Peninsula	Ko-lo												
	608		650~ 656				742~ 759						
Jambi, Sumatra	Mo-lo-yu (*Malāyu*)							Chan-pei (*Jambi*)					
			644- 645								853	871	
(Shi-li-)Fo-shih: Sumatra; (San-)Fo-shih: Sumatra or the Malay Peninsula	(Shi-li-) Fo-shih or (San-) Fo-shih (*Śrīvijaya*)												
				670~ 673		702 716 724 727 742						904	960- 962 971 974 976 980 984 988 990 992

Fig. 1-17. Embassies from Southeast Asia to China: 607 - 992 CE.

One might suppose that trade missions from Śrīvijaya had ceased during the two decades following 742 because of the An Lu-shan rebellion (755–763) underway in China, which nearly succeeded in overthrowing the T'ang dynasty. Still, China's internal turmoil had not prevented Kedah from sending its own embassies during this period. Once the An Lu-shan rebellion had run its course, Ho-ling (Central Java) was the only polity from maritime

Southeast Asia to appear at the emperor's court and this continued to be the case until 853 CE. The question is, what role did the Śailendravaṅśa play in this major turn of events?

It is tempting to suggest that a rivalry had sprung up between Śrīvijaya and Java over controlling the region's lucrative maritime trade routes, which had inevitably led to armed conflict. Having won the war, Java prohibited Śrīvijaya from sending embassies to China thereafter. However, the face of the stele promulgated by the king of Śrīvijaya presents him as he wished to be considered: as the supreme monarch over all *neighboring* kings on the surface of the earth. The posting of such a proclamation at a major crossroads of maritime trade does not at all suggest that Java had managed to transform Śrīvijaya into a subject state by 775 CE. Another obvious suggestion to propose is that Śrīvijaya and Central Java had reached an amicable accord under which all subsequent embassies to China came solely from Ho-ling[95] but had represented the interests of Śrīvijaya as well as Java. A major goal of such an alliance would have doubtlessly been to establish a monopoly with respect to all maritime trade with China. Under this hypothetical scenario, the launch of coordinated attacks on potential regional rivals—either directly or through 'pirate' surrogates—would have been an excellent strategic move. The extensive trade mission activities of Cam and Khmer polities prior to 768 suggest that these kingdoms on the mainland naturally would have been prime targets.

Figure 1-17 presents the dates for the embassies that arrived in China from various kingdoms in maritime Southeast Asia between 616 and 992 CE. Though generally based on the research of Bielenstein (2005), the table's expanded time-line also includes additional data gathered from Bowman (2000: 418), Briggs (1950: 272-274), Damais (1964: 128-130), K. Sastri (1940: 246), Southworth (2004: 324-326) as well as Jordaan and Colless (2009: 67, n. 1; 69, n. 1). These additional sources supply the embassy dates for Jambi, Java, Kedah, Malayū and other polities in Southeast Asia not covered by Bielenstein.[96]

During the ninth century, the first polity other than Java to arrive in China from maritime Southeast Asia was Jambi, which was strategically located at the other end of the Straits. Jambi's first embassy to China in 853 CE likely postdated the Nālandā charter (*circa* 843-850) by a few years and a second trade mission followed in 871 (Jordaan and Colless 2009:

---

[95]Jordaan and Colless (2009: 67, n. 1) have referred to Ho-ling as 'Buddhist Java' and Shê-pò as 'Hindu Java' but without providing any further clarification about why we should believe the trade missions of Ho-ling should be considered as having come from 'Buddhist Java' during the seventh century.

[96]The encyclopedic trade mission history prepared by Bielenstein proves to be a useful reference as the author typically provides specific Chinese text references for the individual embassy dates from across Asia and presents them all in a single work, whereas the other source materials cover the missions from specific Southeast Asian polities. However, the special focus on Java by Damais (1964) is the source of data not sufficiently evaluated by Bielenstein (2005: 74). Bielenstein provides a Chinese court notice about a queen ruling in Java between 766 and 779 CE, which might be an error. A Chinese record dated about a century earlier refers to queen Ximo (Sima) who is said to have been ruling in 674 CE (*New History of the T'ang* 222.2). Missions from Ho-ling arrived in China during 666–676 CE so it is possible that Bielenstein has erred on the date; a Chinese-language specialist will need to investigate this apparent discrepancy. Bielenstein also employs the designation K'o-ling in place of Ho-ling without any explanation for the change, perhaps because of the old hypothesis that the transliteration had been derived from the toponym Kaliṅga (see, for example, Damais 1964: 94-97). Additionally, he states that the dates of the trade missions from Shê-pò and 'K'o-ling' had overlapped after 820 CE. This contradicts the conclusion reached by Damais (1964: 130), a scholar who was characteristically cautious when publishing materials of major importance to Javanese history.

69). Jambi was the superior site for guarding the Straits and therefore a more logical location than Chaiya to propose for the capital of Suvarṇadvīpa during the reign of the Mahārāja Bālaputra and his immediate successors. It was not until 904 that the Chinese recorded the arrival of an embassy from Fo-chi, the designation formerly employed by Chinese court officials for Śrīvijaya between 670 and 742 CE. This suggests the possibility that it had taken some time for Bālaputra and his Śailendra descendants to consolidate their control over the *entrepôts* of the Malay-Indonesian Archipelago.

The raids on mainland Southeast Asia

The hypothesis that Śrīvijaya and Central Java had reached an accord under which they could dominate all maritime trade through Southeast Asia to and from China appears to dovetail nicely with several known historical events that occurred during the latter half of the eighth century. These include the naval raids on the coastal cities of Campā and Annam. As reported in one of the Annamese Annals (*Dai Viet su ky toan thu*), maritime invasions of the Protectorate of Annam and the Cam kingdom of Huan-wang to the south occurred in 767 CE. According to Taylor (1983: 198-199, 250), the new protector general of Annam Chang Po-I was immediately challenged by the K'un-lun and Shê-p'o forces arriving by sea, which seized the citadel Tu-thanh (Chinese = Tzu-Chěng) and raided the lowlands at will. Chang Po-I requested help from Kao Cheng-p'ing, a military official from further north, who sent the soldiers who ultimately defeated the sea-borne invaders in Annam. Subsequently, Chang Po-I constructed a new citadel for the government seat at La-thanh (Chinese = Lo-Chěng) after Tu-thanh was destroyed.

It is significant that the Annamese report refers to the forces of Shê-p'o (Java) as well as the Kunlun, a term the Chinese often used as a generic reference to people from the islands of Southeast Asia as well as Siam and the coastal polities of the Malay Peninsula. According to Chavannes, however, the *History of the T'ang* (chapter CCXXII c) mentions the same designation as a title of the sovereign of P'an-P'an (Chaiya): 'emperor Koen-loen or Kou-long' (see the citation in Yijing 1896: 11, n. 1). Yijing (1896: xli) also used the term Kun-lun to refer specifically to the Old Malay language.

Given that the Annamese report clearly differentiates between the forces of Shê-p'o (Java) and the Kun-lun (Malay), the author must have used the latter designation in a restricted sense rather than as general term for referring to all foreigners from Southeast Asia. It offers support for the hypothesis that the Javanese had forged an alliance with one or more polities on the Malay Peninsula by no later than 767, and in all probability at a somewhat earlier date given the additional time required for planning, organizing and launching multiple attacks. As this particular report clearly indicates that the protector governor of Annam had to request aid from a military official in the north, it must have taken some time for this military official to receive the request for assistance, to marshal his troops and finally arrive on the scene and repel the invaders. In other words, he had to conduct a coordinated military campaign to thwart these 'raids'.

According to Cam inscription C.38, ferocious, pitiless, dark-colored people of other countries, whose food was more horrible than that of vampires, came in ships and sacked the Cam temple of Po Nagar at Na Tran in 774 CE (Golzio 2004: 34-35).[97] What's more,

[97]See Schweyer 2005: 110-111 and Majumdar 1927: III: 50.

Cam inscription C.25 states that due to the innumerable faults of the Kali Yuga, the armies of Java, coming by means of ships, burnt the temple of the Cam state divinity Bhadrādhipatīśvara in Phan Rang during 709 Śaka,[98] e.g. 787 CE (Jacques 2005: 22). In addition, according to a romanticized account recorded by the Arab trader Abū Zaid (Briggs 1951: 68; Cœdès 1968: 93), the naval raids that took place during this period may have included a surprise attack on the capital of a Khmer kingdom (see figure 1-18), though Vickery (2003: 134) has rejected the tale as a mythic fantasy. "[T]he entire conception of an Indonesian fleet conquering far up the Mekong to Kratie in the 8th century is fantastic, and the quickly repelled coastal attacks on Vietnam and Champa...do not at all constitute support, rather the contrary".

However, this blanket statement is debatable insofar as the coastal attacks of 767 are concerned, and the reference to the 'army of Java' in the Cam inscription dating from 787 CE suggests that this particular attack also had a military purpose. Consequently, it is entirely possible that the report of Abū Zaid contains a kernel of truth amidst the more fantastic elements of the story. Several Khmer inscriptions lend the account threads of support, beginning with the Sdok Kăk Thom inscription (K.235, 1053 CE) dating from the reign of the Khmer monarch Udayādityavarman II.

One segment from the Sdok Kăk Thom inscription refers to the consecration of the Khmer ruler Jayavarman II as a *cakravartin* on the Mahendraparvata (Phnom Kulen to the north of the ancient city of Angkor) in 802 CE. Moreover, the text refers to a Śivaite rite performed by the Brahmin Hiraṇyadāma to ensure that the kingdom of Jayavarman II would no longer be subject to the suzerainty of 'Javā'. "The Venerable Parameśvara [the late Jayavarman II] requested him to perform a ritual in order that this land of Kambuja (Kambujadeśa) should not continue to be a dependency of Javā and so that only one king should be universal ruler [in this region]" (Sanderson 2003-2004: 357). The Sdok Kăk Thom stele also states that Jayavarman II had returned to Khmer territory from Javā but does not say when or whether he had left Kambujadeśa voluntarily or even had been seized as a hostage, as speculated by Cœdès (1966: 96-97; 1968: 97-98) .

Secondly, the tenth century inscription of Vat Samrong (K.956, Ba Phnom) states that Jayavarman II also commanded that Mratāñ Śrī Prathivinarendra perform a ritual in the south to ensure that Kambujadeśa would remain free from the suzerainty of Javā (see Chouléan 1997: 336). Additionally, two other Khmer inscriptions refer to 'Javā', including the inscription of Sab Bāk (K.1158, 1066 CE) referring to Vajrayāna Buddhist divinities.[99]

> "Indeed, the images of Vraḥ [the adorable] Buddhalokeśvara were installed by the Venerable Śrisatyavarman, who had supernatural power, in the past, on Abhayagiri, with the intention that Javā may not attack Kambuja. Later on, the nine images deteriorated. The venerable teacher by the name of Dharaṇīndrapura has renovated the deteriorated images and reinstalled them once again. Indeed, his pupil, Vraḥ Ācāryya Dhanu, has installed these images in the year 988 [Śaka], which is in the reign of His Majesty King

---

[98]Stele of Datrang C.25, face B, lines 6-7*: tataś ca kaliyugadoṣātiśayabhāvena nāvāgatair jjavavalasaṃghair nnirddahyate þi navāmvarādri*(7)*yamite śakakāle sa eva śūnyo 'bhavat* //

[99]Discovered in Bān (village) Sab Bāk, Ampher (district) Pak thong Chai, which is approximately 40 km southwest of Nakhorn Ratchasima (Prapandvidya 2007).

Udayādityavarmadeva. May he live long and remain powerful for the rest of his reign" (Prapandvidya 1990: 13; see also Prapandvidya 2007).[100]

Griffiths (2013a: 74-75) has speculated that the inscription K.1158 refers back to the time of the eighth century Cam King Satyavarman and that the reference to the Abhayagiri intentionally echoes the designation of the Śailendra religious foundation on Central Java's Ratu Baka Plateau in Central Java. The fourth inscription is the Praḥ Khan stele (K.908, 1191 CE), which identifies the lord of Yavana (*yavaneśvara;* a Thai ruler according to Jacques 2005), two Cam monarchs (*cāmpendrau*) and the king of Javā (*javendro*) as vassals of King Jayavarman VII (reigned *circa* 1181—1200 CE).[101]

Jacques (2005) doubted that the designation 'Javā' in all of the examples cited above could be a reference to any kingdom on the isle of Java or to the entire island itself. Among other things, he noted that the *Rāmāyaṇa* and other ancient texts from India designate Java Island as Yavadvīpa as does the charter of the Javanese king Sañjaya (732 CE). The designation Yavadvīpa also appears in verse 20 of the Prasat Kandal Do'm North inscription from Cambodia (K.809): "On the haughty heads of the kings of China, Campā and the isle of Yava his edicts [e.g. those of King Indravarman I]—immaculate garlands of jasmine—form a crown" (Jacques 2005: 20). Plus, Yavadvīpapura appears twice in Cam inscription C.149 (from Nhan-Bieu *circa* 908—911) and Yavadvīpa appears once in C.22.

With respect to the geographic identity of Javā, Jacques observed that the Siṅhalese *Cūḷavamśa* refers to the forces of King Candrabhānu, the previously mentioned Lord of Tāmbraliṅga from the Isthmus of Kra, as 'Jāvaka'.[102] He also mentioned that the term 'country of Java' (*bhūmi-java*) appears in the Kota Kapur (Bangka Island) inscription in reference to the launch of a military expedition by Śrīvijaya in 686 CE against a foreign state that had refused to submit to its suzerainty. The last trade mission sailing from P'an P'an (Chaiya) to China arrived in 648 CE. "It appear that there is no objection to this 'land of Java' being situated on the Malay Peninsula itself, since the island of Java was not called Java 'from time immemorial'..." (Jacques 2005: 22).[103] Given that the Nālandā charter refers to the king of Java as the *yavabhūmipālaḥ*. Jacques concluded that in ancient Cambodia the designation Javā most likely had been such a well-known term for a vassal kingdom with a Malay population that the inscriptions' composers had no need to characterize it any further. However, Arlo Griffiths disputes this conclusion.

---

[100]The so-called Ratu Baka charter (792 CE) promulgated by the Śailendra monarch Samaratuṅga refers to the consecration of an Abhayagirivihāra on Central Java's Ratu Baka Plateau. The same inscription refers to an image of Padmapāṇi the Compassionate, the spiritual son of Amitābha.

[101]A brief Khmer inscription, found at Chaiya, refers to "the casting of a statue on the orders (or during the reign) of a personage named Kamrateṅ Añ Mahārāja Śrīmat Trailokyarāja Maulibhūṣaṇavarmadeva" in 1183 CE (Jacq-Hergoualc'h 2004: 421).

[102]This latter designation also suggests an affinity with the Arab designation Zābag, the kingdom of the Mahārāja who supposedly led the legendary raid on the Khmer kingdom. "The etymology of the word Jāvaka suggests the expansion of the Śailendras' rule from Java to the area around the Straits of Malacca in the second half of the eighth century..." (Nguyên and Ishizawa 1999: 43). "Arab authors and navigators applied the name Jawa to both Sumatra and Java, and the adjective Jawi to products of the Malayan world as well as to Muslim Indonesians, especially to the natives of Malaysia proper" (Gonda 1973: 349).

[103]For other interpretations/localizations of Java in NE Thailand (Wendan), see Woodward 2010: 93 and Ferlus 2010.

> "This argument amounts to a willful denial of the nature of royal inscriptions as instruments of propaganda, that we see throughout the Indianized world, and the corollary attempts of 19th and 20th century Western historians to build *histoire événementielle* by treating epigraphical data as factual descriptions of historical events need to be treated with utmost care. That is, Claude Jacques chooses to deny just about the most important advance in historiographical understanding in the study of pre-modern South and Southeast Asian history of the past few decades (cf. Pollock 2006: §3.3). And this methodological atavism becomes the starting point for a wild goose chase in search of alternative identifications of Java/ā and Yavana, which Jacques finds respectively in "un royaume vassal de population malaise" and "les Thaï". But as soon as we accept that the Khmer king was just as liable to make counterfactual claims to suzerainty over his neighboring kings, as were his peers throughout the epigraphically recorded history of the entire Indianized world—including the kings of Java—the very basis of Jacques' reasoning falls away, and we no longer have any ground to refuse to acknowledge what the epigraphical evidence clearly reveals, namely that in the inscriptions of Campā and Cambodia the terms Java and Yavana referred to Java and Đại Việt" (Griffiths 2013a: 62-63).

The activities of Jayavarman II prior to 802 CE continue to be the subject of debate among historians today. The Práḥ Thãt Práḥ Srĕi inscription (K.103, 770 CE) found south of Kompoṅ Čaṃ refers to a royal personage bearing the name Jayavarman I *bis*. The same appellation likewise appears in the Lobŏ'k Srót inscription (K.134, 782 CE) discovered at Kračèḥ near Śambhupura as well as two other undated inscriptions from Kračèḥ (Dupont 1943: 19). Whether this personage and Jayavarman II had been one-and-the-same remains an intriguing working hypothesis (see Vickery 1986: 102-104, Golzio 2000 and Vickery 2001). If future research provides additional support for the equation of Jayavarman I *bis* with Jayavarman II then the attacks launched in 767 CE by Shê-p'o and the K'un-lun against two or more polities in mainland Southeast Asia suggest a plausible time for his reported departure from Kambujadeśa as well as his return home in 770 CE.

Vickery points out that according to inscription K.583 Jayavarman II was already ruling in 790. This badly damaged stele, however, is the document of a tenth-century official who had lived during the reign of Rajendravarman and who had claimed that Jayavarman II and one of his sons were his ancestors. "The date '790' is as suspect, or as reliable, as '802', but it is important as showing that in 10th-century Angkor there was another tradition about the reign of Jayavarman II" (Vickery 2001). In the absence of further details, however, it is difficult to ascertain the significance of inscription K.583.

More than one stele refers to the consecration of Jayavarman II as a 'universal sovereign' (*cakravartin*) in 802 CE. "There was a king (named) Śrī Jayavarman, who ruled the earth to the ocean in 724 [Śaka = 802 CE] and established his residence on Mount Mahendra" (Trapãṅ Run, K.598; see Jacques 1972: 206). Consequently, the reference to Jayavarman II already ruling in 790 probably had nothing to do with an alternate tradition. As the Vat Samrong inscription reports a second ritual in the south it is equally possible that Jayavarman II had ruled as a king in the south first. As Jacques (1972: 207-208) noted, his subsequent consecration as a *cakravartin,* e.g. as the supreme monarch ruling all the lands lying between Mount Mahendra and the ocean, may simply have been a supplemental rite performed for the benefit of his successors: "It is not implausible to assume that Jayavarman II, coming from Javā—regardless of the place that this name represents—had conquered or at least had been recognized as the king of a number of Khmer principalities prior to being proclaimed and recognized as a 'universal monarch' in 802 A. D." This would explain why inscriptions from the reigns of later monarchs preferred to refer to it.

Archaeologists have not unearthed any inscriptions known to have been promulgated by Jayavarman II himself or his son and successor Jayavarman III. Moreover, the significant interval between the dates of the Sdok Kăk Thom and the Vat Samrong inscriptions (1053 and 1066 CE) and the coronation date of Jayavarman (802 CE) raises the question of whether we should perhaps view the tale of Jayavarman II's return from the mysterious land of Javā and his unification of Kambujadeśa as mythical (Vickery (2001). On the other hand, a significant number of inscriptions from the Angkor period identify Jayavarman II with the beginning of a great political movement of historic proportions. Chouléan has suggested that the Khmer people had retained a 'collective memory' of Jayavarman II as their liberator.[104] This would help to explain why all the lists of kings dating from the ninth century onward begin with Jayavarman II rather than a monarch from the pre-Angkor period. The ancient name of the Preah Kô temple founded in the ancient city of Hariharalaya (near modern-day Rolous, Cambodia) by Indravarman in 879 CE is Parameśvara, the posthumous name awarded to Jayavarman II. "The statue of the latter, 'deified' in the guise of Śiva, occupies the central position. This is highly significant: Preah Kô is not dedicated primarily to the direct ancestors of the royal constructor, but to Jayavarman II" (Chouléan 1997: 334-335).

Conclusion

Jordaan and Colless (2009) contend that the influence of the Śailendra monarchs had extended over Sumatra and the Malay Peninsula at a much earlier date than has generally been accepted in the past. Among other things, their hypothesis potentially accounts for the general confusion among the early Arab trader-chroniclers, who described the Śailendra Empire in ways that conflate geographic elements from Java with those of Sumatra. It also explains why no convincing archaeological evidence has been uncovered to date in Palembang that would establish the location for the early capital of the so-called Śrīvijayan Empire. According to Jordaan and Colless, the Śailendra had ruled over a symbiotic state consisting of a 'rice basket' located in Central Java that in turn supported the rest of the empire's array of trading ports in Sumatra and on the Malay Peninsula. Through this arrangement, the Javanese side of the empire would have gained access to gold and silver not found on Java itself, and benefited from a constant flow of the trading goods and even luxury items from abroad that permeated the empire's array of trading ports in Sumatra and on the Malay Peninsula. For their part, the vassal kings of these ports gained access to an

[104]As the remarks of Stutterheim (1935: 29) concerning the charter of Tīrtha Empul (962 CE) effectively demonstrate, collective memory does play a role in the preservation of historical data. The Balinese residents of the village Manukaya nearby the *tīrtha* were able to recall the site's precise foundation date though they were no longer capable of deciphering the charter itself.

abundant supply of rice and liberated from the constant fear that Java's far more sizable Javanese ethnic group would decide to overrun their territories.

In my opinion, the Śailendra Empire as envisioned by Jordaan and Colless is far more plausible if we suppose that it had operated as a 'family business', e.g. with each of the two major divisions having been administered by different members of the Śailendravaṅśa. Otherwise, the vast distances involved in maintaining communications and control over multiple island polities would have presented formidable obstacles.

The appearance of the Palaeojavanese script on both faces of the stele from the Isthmus of Kra suggests the application of a hypothetical 'double-kingdom' scenario about which Jordaan and Colless (2009: 136-138) have already made some preliminary remarks.[105] The Kañjuruhan charter provides us with a classic model that enables us to posit what the missing text segment from the B-side of the stele may have included. The first stanza of the Kañjuruhan inscription refers to Devasiṁha, the father of the reigning king who had already gone to heaven. The second stanza is devoted to Devasiṁha's son Gajayāna—the actual promulgator of the Kañjuruhan inscription—and the third stanza refers to Gajayāna's daughter Uttajanā and her spouse Jananīya (see Griffiths 2011a: 37-38). The presentation of genealogical records for the promulgators of charters is likewise a part of many epigraphical records from ancient India (Bosch 1924: 230). Though Devapāla actually issued the Nālandā charter, this copperplate likewise presents a genealogical record for Bālaputra that spans three generations.

The incomplete B-side of the Isthmus of Kra stele presents an opening stanza that lauds the Śrī Mahārāja of the Śailendravaṅśa. There is one essential difference from the first stanza from the Kañjuruhan charter: the Śailendra monarch known as Śrī Mahārāja by name appears to have been alive at the time the stele first appeared. Chhabra (1965: 31) translated the opening words of the following incomplete Prākṛti verse, which abruptly breaks off in the middle of a word: "And of him, ...of all kings (?) ..." (*tasya ca sakalarā<ja>*). Therefore, it is theoretically possible this opening phrase had been part of a strophe referring to the actual promulgator of the A-side text.

Boechari (1982) proposed that the B-side of the stele would have presented a family tree covering several generations, with *tasya*—the first word of the unfinished strophe B2—being translated as 'of him' or 'his'. However, Boechari also theorized that Bālaputradeva had been the promulgator of the B-side text in or around 850 CE. "Being the first Śailendra on this throne, Bālaputradeva supposedly deemed it necessary to enlarge the foundation of his grandfather, a meritorious act he would have wanted to record on the reverse side of Ligor A 'to show his rights to the people of the Isthmus'" (as cited in Jordaan 1999a: 9).

Though Jordaan agreed it was entirely possible that the composer of the B-side of the stele had intended to present a Śailendra genealogy, he objected to an attribution of the event to the mid-ninth century.

[105]As Jordaan and Colless have already suggested, beginning with Ho-ling's first trade mission to China in one hundred years, this double kingdom would have appeared to the Chinese court and other foreign observers as if it were a unitary state. "The notion of double kingdom calls to mind the Chinese account of Śrīvijaya (Shih-li-fo-shih), from the Tàng era. 'This country counts fourteen cities and is divided into two kingdoms; they have separate administrations; the western is called Lang-pò-lu-ssŭ' (*Hsin Tàng shu* 222B, 5a). However, this statement has always been interpreted as pertaining to a regional division in Sumatra". (Jordaan & Colless 2009: 137).

> "Boechari's suggestion that Ligor B was at least one generation younger than Ligor A and was issued by Bālaputradeva raises more questions than it solves. Paleographically, because the differences between face A and B are small, as Boechari himself admits: 'they are very slight as to warrant a difference of time of one generation at the most' (1982b: appendix 4A, page 2). Significantly, the script of Ligor B is said to look even more archaic than contemporaneous Old-Javanese inscriptions" (Jordaan 1999a: 9).

Jordaan also characterized as 'far-fetched' the attempts made by Boechari to explain away the archaic appearance of the script on side B as "the result of certain local circumstances and developments as well as his theory that Bālaputra had deliberately ordered his scribe to 'imitate as close[ly] as possible the script of Ligor A' (1982b: appendix 4A, page 3). Besides if Bālaputradeva indeed attached so much importance to the inscription why was the text left unfinished?"

Jacq-Hergoualc'h (2002: 304) and Woodward (2003: 83) have likewise supported the notion that Bālaputra had subsequently promulgated the B-side of the stele during the ninth century. But nobody has tendered a plausible explanation for why Bālaputra would have refrained from referring to his grandfather in the past tense, just as the opening strophe of the Kañjuruhan charter does for Gajayāna's father Devasiṁha and is likewise the case in the Nālandā charter (H. Sastri 1942: 101).[106] Beginning in 778 CE, the Śailendra monarchs on Java began using the Siddham script for all their charters. Therefore, it is difficult to envision why the presumed son of Samaratuṅga would have promulgated his own inscription by reverting to a type of script used earlier—unless, of course, we consider the previously tendered hypothesis that Bālaputra had not been the son of Samaratuṅga and had never even resided on the island of Java.

For a number of other reasons, I am unable to accept an alternate hypothesis expressed by Jordaan (1999a: 10): "that Ligor B must have been made between 775 and 778, that is to say, just before the migration of the Śailendras from the Malay Peninsula to Central Java". Among other things, Jordaan has proposed that the Śailendravaṅśa was of foreign origin, e.g. from beyond Java's shores. Three years is entirely too short a period for a foreign dynasty to have established itself on Java as well as stimulated the construction and consecration of a Buddhist temple and monastery dedicated to Tārā, which must have had a supporting monastic community already in place at the time of the temple's consecration. If the Śailendra kings had indeed been foreigners, as Jordaan and Colless have argued, it would be far more plausible to propose that they had established themselves in Central Java considerably earlier than 775. This would account for their familiarity with Palaeojavanese, help explain how this particular script had subsequently appeared on the Isthmus of Kra, and also clarify why Ho-ling—the Chinese term for Java—had first appeared in T'ang dynasty court documents dating from the mid seventh century.

In my opinion, the best hypothesis for explaining the inception of the double kingdom proposed by Jordaan and Colless remains the marriage of a princess or queen from Śrīvijaya with a Śailendra prince or king and with the ascent to the throne of Suvarṇadvīpa by Bālaputradeva having ultimately stemmed from it. However, I believe the requisite

[106]Italics added by the author of the current text.

marital union that historians have come to take for granted is far more likely to have occurred at a date considerably earlier than 775 CE, when the king of Śrīvijaya promulgated the A-side of the stele using the Palaeojavanese script. With respect to the groom, it is doubtful that this personage had been Samaratuṅga given that his reign on Java had extended for a minimum of 32 years (792–824), and probably had endured for even longer.

It presumably would have taken several years for the 'Indrarāja' of Śrīvijaya to erect the *trisamayacaitya* cited on the A-side of the stele, and for two of his royal chaplains to have contributed additional *stūpa*-s and *caitya*-s to the original religious foundation thereafter. Consequently, the actual construction work may have begun *circa* 767–768, e.g. the period during which the initial raids along the coast of mainland Southeast Asia occurred and when the first Ho-ling embassy in one hundred years had arrived in China. Though any further remarks can only be highly speculative in nature, it may prove useful to sketch the bare outlines for a few plausible scenarios. One of the top candidates for the groom would be the 'Crusher of enemy foes', with his bride having been a queen or princess of Śrīvijaya, and with one of his sons having been the promulgator of the A-side of the stele from the Isthmus of Kra.[107] Under this scenario, we may even retain the long cherished Dharmasetu hypothesis so long as we view another son of the 'Crusher of enemy foes' as having occupied the throne of Śrīvijaya prior to 775 CE. Under any of these scenarios, the presumption of an 'inheritance' that had enabled Bālaputradeva to ascend the throne of Suvarṇadvīpa would remain a plausible scenario and with the double-kingdom envisioned by Jordaan and Colless presumed to initially have been under the coordinated supervision of the Śrī Mahārāja of the Śailendravaṅśa (stele, side B) and one of his sons (stele, side A). Following the death of the 'Crusher of foes in battle' between 782 and 792, the elder and younger sons hypothetically could have administered the two major divisions of the Śailendra Empire from their respective capitals. Ultimately, Samaratuṅga and his nephew Bālaputra might even have ruled these same two divisions until the old double-kingdom model dissolved during the first half of the ninth century.

In the absence of additional corroborating historical evidence, of course, all of the above scenarios are conjectural as is likewise the case with the old Dharmasetu model as enunciated by Cœdès. The most important conclusion that one may draw presently is that historians have needlessly limited their evaluation of the stele from the Isthmus of Kra to a single hypothesis that is no more plausible than other theories. In fact, the original Dharmasetu hypothesis appears to provide a worse fit than the alternate scenarios sketched above when we attempt to account for all of the historical facts and epigraphy details available to us.

---

[107]The Nālandā charter (Sastri 1942: 99, 102) identifies the father of Bālaputra as someone 'who possessed prudence (*naya*), prowess (*parākrama*), and good conduct (*śīla-śālī*)'. Likewise, the opening verse on the A-side of the Isthmus of Kra stele similarly cites prudence (*vaya*), propriety of conduct (*vinaya*) and prowess (*śaurya*) as three among the many inexhaustible sources of the widespread glory possessed by the king of Śrīvijaya. Should we think it purely coincidental or extraordinary to encounter two Sanskrit inscriptions—each hailing from a different geographic area and period—in which their respective composers had described royal personages using phrases with meanings that were similar or even identical? Acri (pc 22 May 2014) argues that such similarities are striking and invite further scrutiny. "These documents are full of metaphors, and often speak via such subtle linguistic plays".

II: The Kalasan charter and the Śailendra 'Lion among kings'

The Kalasan charter (D.147; figure 2-1), which measures 67 cm. in length and 46 cm. in width, was discovered near the railway line running between the villages of Kalasan and Prambanan on the outskirts of the eastern part of the city of Yogyakarta (Brandes 1886: 240). The Sanskrit composition consists of fourteen lines that collectively present a dozen strophes: seven composed in the Āryā meter (vs.3-8 and v.12), and with the remaining five stanzas composed in the Vasantatilakā (v.1), Udgīti (v.2), Sumānikā (v.9), Śālinī (v.10) and Upendravajrā (v.11) meters, respectively.

Fig. 2-1. The Kalasan charter (photo credit: OD-6366).

The initial production of a transcription and translation of this charter by J. L. A. Brandes (1886) was a pivotal event in the development of archeological research in maritime Southeast Asia.

"Significant in more than one sense, this nearly undamaged remnant of a lost civilization from the year 700 Śaka (778 A.D.) contains a reference to a sanctuary for Tārā inaugurated by an indigenous ruler. Considering that Tārā is the well-known name of a female being, who like her male counterpart, the Bodhisattva Avalokiteśvara, is held in special veneration in the Mahāyāna branch of the Buddhist Church, we can be sure that Mahāyānism had penetrated into Java as early as the eighth century. Additionally, the fact that the inscription was written in Nāgarī, the script commonly used in the northern part of India, furnishes evidence that Buddhists from northern India were involved in the construction of the sanctuary. Although in his translation Brandes erred in a few points, he gave an essentially correct explanation of the Sanskrit poem, which we can regard as the foundation charter of the sanctuary dedicated to Tārā" (Kern 1906: 35).

Fig. 2-2. Caṇḍi Kalasan after the partial restoration of the temple in 1928 and 1929 (photo credit: Collectie Tropen Museum).

According to the Kalasan inscription, the king had donated the village Kālasa[1] for the purpose of supporting the Tārā temple and its associated cloister. Given that the name of the *desa* in which the stone was recovered is Kalasan, Brandes thought it probable that the two religious foundations mentioned in the inscription could be linked with "two of the many masterpieces of construction out of ancient times, now in such a dilapidated state, that are found in the eastern part of the Yogyakarta area...." (Brandes 1886: 255). For the Tārā foundation he proposed the temple site that the region's indigenous residents knew as Caṇḍi Kali Bening after the riverlet nearby, which was also called Caṇḍi Kalasan (figure 2-2) after the name of the *desa* in which it is located.[2]

[1]According to Damais (1968: 392-393), Kālasa is a Sanskritization of the Old Javanese toponym Kalasan, which literally means 'forest', and it would seem, all uncultivated land. According to Jordaan (pc 23 Sept. 2013), "This toponym can be linked with the noun ke-alas-an, based on the stem alas. It is this root word, alas, that means uncultivated land (forest, jungle, etc.)".

[2]A chapter of the *Mañjuśrīmūla-kalpa* (MMK) called the prophecy of the kings (*rāja-vyākaraṇa*) "recounts the dynastic history of several kingdoms up to about 770 A.D., presenting it as a prophecy by the Buddha ... Hidden away toward the end of this lengthy and tedious chronicle are some verses on Tārā ... [that cite] some of the places where Her cult flourished" in the world. MMK 53, 832: "[Then the wrathful mantras are practiced in the southern region, In the lands of thieves and *mlecchas*, and likewise in the oceans]". MMK 53,

For the monks' abode or *vihāra* Brandes suggested Caṇḍi Sari, which is located about 200 m. to the north. Several architectural characteristics of Caṇḍi Sari—the rectangular ground plan; multiple storeys with a minimum of at least one upper interior level, presumably reached via a wooden staircase; windows; and barrel-shaped roof—are comparable to the monastic residences called *pāsāda* (*uposathaghara*) constructed in the ancient city of Anurādhapura on Sri Lanka, including at the famous Abhayagirivihāra (see, for example, Bandaranayake 1974: 253-259). Perhaps the Siṅhalese monks who had founded a branch of the Abhayagirivihāra in Central Java during the late eighth century, as attested by the Abhayagirivihāra (Ratu Baka) charter from 792/3 CE, had brought a design prototype to Java that Javanese architects subsequently modified to suit their own needs.

The architectural features of Caṇḍi Sari as well as the two younger structures at the center of Caṇḍi Plaosan Lor led early Dutch archaeologists to suggest that these buildings had either served as cloisters or repositories for Buddhist scriptures. However, Caṇḍi Sari and the twin Plaosan *vihāra*-s depart from the typical Siṅhalese design, which features a central *cella* or chapel surrounded by open interior space punctuated by pillars for supporting the upper storeys (Bandaranayake 1974: 254, 258). By contrast, the interior spaces within the Caṇḍi Sari and Caṇḍi Plaosan *vihāra*-s are each divided into three chambers of almost identical dimensions, separated by solid walls.

Though the design of Caṇḍi Sari must be considered the early prototype for the Plaosan *vihāra*-s, it is unclear whether its first phase of construction could have occurred as early as 778/9 CE or even have actively supported the early religious services held at Caṇḍi Kalasan.

> "[I]t is hard for us to see in Caṇḍi Sari the monastery of Kalasan; the latter must have been a *saṅghārāma*, the place where monks who took charge of the service in the Kalasan temple were living [literally, found shelter], and not a sanctuary as such where the statues to be venerated occupied the foremost space [literally, the most important place] and the monks living on the upper storey obviously were primarily responsible for the service of the statues below, not for another sanctuary several hundred metres away" (Krom 1923: I: 269).

However, another structure formerly stood to the south of Caṇḍi Kalasan that is no longer in evidence today. This building nearby, which featured an interior space punctuated by pillars, may have served as a monastic audience hall in which monks had engaged in group recitations from the Mahāyāna scriptures, periodically presented their confession of sins and in which new monks were ordained.

Klokke (2006: 50) has suggested that the Kalasan inscription might be connected with a series of non-narrative relief sculptures depicting female deities that were found in the hamlet of Tirtomartani located midway between Caṇḍi Kalasan and Caṇḍi Prambanan

---

833: "And then a mighty *yakṣa*-king also practices Tārā. In Harikela, Karmaraṇga, Kāmarūpa and Kalaśa" MMK 53, 833: "[Many female envoys and *yakṣas* achieve great miracles]" (Willson 1986: 42-43). Ghosh 1980: 13) believed that this reference to Kalaśa could be equated with Caṇḍi Kalasan in Java. However, this inexact name association may very well be nothing more that sheer coincidence, given that *kalaśa* means 'a round pinnacle on the top of a temple—especially the pinnacle crowning a Buddhist *caitya* or *stūpa*'—as well as 'a waterpot, pitcher, jar, dish' (with the breasts of a woman frequently compared to jars in Sanskrit texts).

(Fontein 1990: 140-141) and thus could have come from a temple no longer in evidence that was dedicated to a Tārā image. In absence of the discovery of any other temple remains in their vicinity, however, there is no way to ascertain whether these reliefs belonged to the place of their discovery or had been later moved to this location from another site such as Caṇḍi Sanan (see figure 8-1 in Chapter VIII), a temple that formerly stood near the bank of the Progo River further to the south of. Caṇḍi Kalasan. Several Buddha images and a sculpture of Tārā were found at this location (Krom, 1923: I: 255).

Fig. 2-3. *Kīrtimukha* with goddess seated above.

There are several reasons why Caṇḍi Kalasan is far more likely to have been the Tārā abode mentioned in the inscription (Long 2011). The temple's architectural design includes 16 exterior niches as well as 21 interior locations for the placement of images, or 37 free-standing images in total when not including the main image seated in *bhadrāsana* that was enthroned within the temple's main *cella*. Both the numbers 21 and 37 are associated with the goddess Tārā: there are 21 forms of the goddess to which devotees paid homage and 37 wings to enlightenment (*bodhipākṣika-dharma*) with which the goddess is associated. "Endowed with the thirty-seven Aids to Bodhi, Dhyānas, and many *samādhis* and Liberations", Tārā has realized inseparably the space-like Dharmakāya, but shows "Form-bodies, like rainbows, to migrators. Always, supreme chief of all the *maṇḍalas*, Tārā, You save migrators from *sāmsara's* straits" (Willson 1986: 212-221).

Figs. 2-4 & 2-5. The goddesses above the entrances.

In addition to the female divinities above each of the temple's doorways, a second goddess was carved in relief just above the so-called 'face of glory' (*kīrtimukha*) on each of the four exterior facades. Besides, each of the female figures on the temple's doorway lintels is seated with both legs crossed and holds the stem of a lotus in either hand, an iconographic trait more typically associated with the mother goddess Lakṣmī-Śrī than Tārā herself. Additionally, a number of the 52 *stūpa* structures that had originally lined the monument's base at ground level, which appear to have contained items belonging to monks, were originally adorned with the images of goddesses (Bernet Kempers 1982: 45-46; Bernet Kempers & Soekmono 1954: fig. 21; OD-10076). What the prevalence of goddesses on the exterior of the temple does seem to demonstrate is that the designers of Caṇḍi Kalasan had elected to accentuate the female principle to a greater extent here than is found elsewhere on the exteriors of other Javanese Buddhist temples dating from the same period.

Baker and Mackenzie each observed the vestiges of a raised platform or *pĕṇḍapa* on a small height located approximately 130 m. to the south of Caṇḍi Kalasan. Mackenzie called this structure a "temple" while for Baker it was a "hall of audience or state". The first thing Baker encountered on his visit to the site were two pairs of *dvārapāla* statues guarding the eastern approach. One pair was later moved to the garden of the Residency House at Yogyakarta (see figure 2-6). The other pair, which was initially sent to the Dutch Residency House in Yogyakarta after being rediscovered and unearthed in 1925, was subsequently transferred to the seat of the Governor General[3] in Batavia (Jakarta).

> "[Each figure] knelt on one knee, leaning the right arm on a short thick mall or club, round the left a Serpent winded or clung—its position rather leaning forward and inclining to the left; while its companion, which we immediately after found, leaned forward inclining to the right—both these figures seemed by their countenance, position and half inclined half forward expression and gesture, leaning on their clubs, to be watching with assiduity the approach of any profane foot to the temple.... [T]he curled hair was loose, neatly parted on the forehead; behind it flowed down over the neck into three rows of curls carefully arranged...."
>
> "Of the Temple behind nothing remained but several great round pedestals (and capitals) of several large pillars, forming the enceinte of an oblong structure, and several blocks and fragments of stones of a large size—no vestiges of a wall; I am uncertain which part of these were capitals or pedestals—if all the latter, a considerable difference existed in the formation of each—a mound formed by a kind of ditch inclosed these, and had such effect in preventing their being seen from the road, and is so completely ruined, that it cannot be observed without approaching immediately to it" (Mackenzie 1814: 30-32).

According to Baker (see Raffles 1817: II: 30), the roof of this so-called "hall of audience or state" had originally stood:

> "on fourteen pillars, with a verandah all round it standing on twenty-two pillars. The porters guarded this building exactly in the centre of its eastern front: the nearest pair scarcely thirty feet distant from it. The greatest length of the building was east and west. The inner apartment over all gave forty-seven feet in length, including the pillars: the width of the hall was twenty-eight feet and a half in the same way. A verandah, of twelve feet and a half wide all round over the pillars, surrounded the hall".

IJzerman (1891: 15) thought that the structure's roof had probably rested on wooden posts, supported by colossal pedestals with a band of lotus leaves on top and in which the shaft of the lost columns would have fitted. He also noted that these artifacts laid partly

[3]Following Indonesia's war of independence, the former seat of the Dutch Governor General was renamed the Presidential Palace.

buried in the ground and partly loose on the surface. Additionally, the rubble found at this site only consisted of bricks, which led IJzerman to surmise "that except for the base of the posts little or no natural stones were used for this building and that the roof therefore also consisted of impermanent materials".

Fig. 2-6. A Kalasan *dvārapāla*.

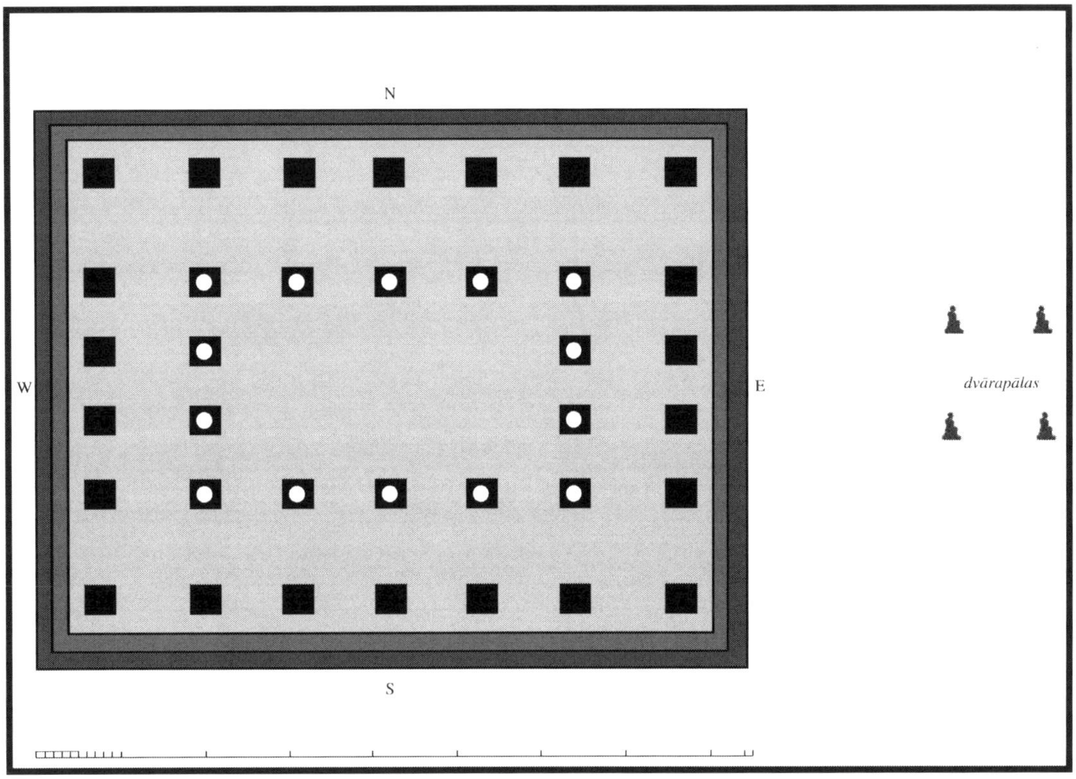

Fig. 2-7. Kalasan *pĕṇḍapa* architectural plan, after Baker (in Raffles 1844).

During the partial restoration of Caṇḍi Kalasan, workers discovered that the present building had been built on top of an earlier structure (Oudheidkundig Verslag 1929: 12-13), which Bernet Kempers and Van Romondt (Bernet Kempers & Soekmono 1954) associated with the Kalasan charter. The residual remains of the site's first building phase consisted of a simple square plan that was subsequently cleared from the foundation to make way for the more elaborate construction visible today. Though this would seem to also raise questions concerning the date when the Kalasan *pĕṇḍapa*[4] had been constructed, van Lohuizen-de Leeuw (1981) noted that in comparison to the *dvārapāla* statues installed at the entrances to Sewu, Plaosan and Sojiwan, the Kalasan *dvārapāla* images display archaic features which suggest that the structure they originally guarded had been built during an earlier stage in the development of Buddhist architecture in Central Java. At Caṇḍi Sewu, for example, the *dvārapāla* pairs display additional attributes that are symbolic of a slight increase in aggressive tendencies, such as snake-formed arm-bands, *upavīta* and diadem as well as wilder hair curls. Though similar, the statues belonging to the even younger Plaosan Lor and Caṇḍi Sojiwan temple complexes also display evolutionary developments, such as profuse heavy jewelry as well as large diadems that resemble a crown.

[4]According to Bernet Kempers (1959: 17-18), the Old Javanese term *pĕṇḍapa* was derived from the Sanskrit *maṇḍapa*, 'open hall, pavilion; temple'.

"There is no reason whatsoever to assume that the [Kalasan] *vihāra* was only built when the temple underwent its third and final reconstruction.... On the contrary, it is much more likely that the monastery was erected roughly about the time when the first phase of Caṇḍi Kalasan was built. In fact, it was almost certainly constructed even a little before A. D. 778, for the monks had to settle down first in order to be able to perform the initial ceremonies, such as the dedication of the *sīmā*, after which they had to supervise the building activities as these gradually developed. That this was the normal sequence of events is known from other instances" (van Lohuizen-de Leeuw 1981: 18-19).

Other evidence suggests that a Buddhist monastery had formerly existed on the south side of Caṇḍi Kalasan. In November of 1927, a Javanese laborer unearthed an ornate bronze bell with a silver patina at a depth of about two feet below the surface of a sugarcane field located about 400 m. to the southwest of the temple and 270 m. south of the platform discovered by Baker. Cast in the shape of a *stūpa*, the bell measures 57.5 cm. in height and at its greatest width measures 42 cm. in diameter. It is crowned with a prancing lion seated on a lotus cushion (see figures A-12 and A-13 in Appendix E).

"Right next to the bell was a large Chinese vase, the inside and outside of which was covered up to [a level of] 14 cm. from the bottom with a coating of greenish glaze. Around the neck are six small ears. The height of the vase measures 0.645 m. The find spot of the two objects also yields an indication of their original purpose. The immediate vicinity of the monastery suggests that the remains belonged [to it]. With the bell we have presumably recovered the monastery bell, whereas the big vase may have served as a water vessel" (Oudheidkundig Verslag 1927: 106).

An iron chain from which the bell may have once hung was also unearthed at the same spot in 1928 (Oudheidkundig Verslag 1928: 88). Still, the discovery of these artifacts does not necessarily indicate that a monastery had been located at this precise spot, as demonstrated by the discovery of one of the *Rāmāyaṇa* narrative reliefs from Prambanan in the perimeter wall of a Javanese household located 400 m. west of Kalasan. "Furthermore, two large *makaras* were removed from the village Glongang, located about 200 m. northwest of Kalasan, and transferred later to the temple grounds. Significantly, the top piece of one of these *makaras* was unearthed in the *desa* Kali Bening just behind the temple" (Oudheidkundig Verslag 1927: 107-108).

The script of the Kalasan charter

Bhandarkar (1887-1889: II: 2-10) was the first to observe that the Siddhamātṛkā script—the so-called *prae-nāgarī* of the early studies by Dutch scholars beginning with the Kalasan charter—bears a striking resemblance to the script employed in an inscription from King Devapāla of Benares, which was discovered at Magadha in Ghosrāwa. To this Bosch (1929a: 13-15) added that only slight deviations are observable between the Kalasan Sanskrit characters and the script type used in the Khālimpur (in Gaur) and Mungir charters of Devapāla's predecessor Dharmapāla. Furthermore, several Nepalese inscriptions representing the edicts of King Aṃśuvarman and his successors into the ninth and tenth centuries were written in a script that is very closely related to the one featured in the Kalasan and Abhayagirivihāra (Ratu Baka) charters. In the absence of any evidence of direct contact between Java and Nepal during this period, Bosch characterized the striking resemblance between the Nepalese and Javanese Sanskrit scripts as likely borrowings from a common source, with Nālandā being his prime candidate. Moreover, he credited Buddhist institutes of learning for the transmission of the script innovations found in Javanese charters prior to their subsequent appearance in the inscriptions of ancient India.

> "There is no doubt that we here have a consequence of the lively and continuous spiritual exchange that took place between the home land of Buddhism and the countries of the southern ocean during the heyday of Śrīvijaya. Through the stream of manuscripts that flowed out from the great monasteries in northern India to centers of learning in the Archipelago, the latest developments in the script were also diffused immediately after they were created. Thus it is easy to see that in the development of *prae-nāgarī* Sumatra and Java were ahead of the territories in India whose relations with learned Buddhist circles were looser" (Bosch 1929a: 13).

Bosch also detected major script differences between the Kalasan and Abhayagirivihāra (Ratu Baka) charters on one hand and the Śrī Saṅgrāmadhanaṃjaya (Kĕlurak) and Plaosan inscriptions on the other, with the two latter inscriptions displaying more developed script-characteristics and fewer errors than the former. One possible explanation is that the script's initial introduction and subsequent changes had come about as the direct result of the arrival of venerable Buddhist visitors from abroad such as the Śailendra *guru* Kumāraghoṣa mentioned in the so-called Kĕlurak inscription as well as the unnamed pilgrims from Gujarat to which the Plaosan inscription refers. The reversion to the older form in the Abhayagirivihāra charter might be an indication that Kumāraghoṣa was no longer residing on Java in 792/3 and that for the so-called Ratu Baka charter King Samaratuṅga had turned to the same person who had formerly traced the characters for the lapicide to follow onto the Kalasan stone.

> "The numerous peculiarities in the Kalasan script reappear in the Ratu Baka inscription, whilst noticeable differences do not occur. It is beyond doubt that the two inscriptions date from the same period, indeed were probably executed by one and the same hand.... It is remarkable that the script of the Kĕlurak charter deviates quite strongly from [that of] Kraton Ratu Baka considering that the date of promulgation of the first is only four years removed from that of Kalasan" (Bosch 1929a: 6-7).

The introduction of the Siddhamātṛkā Sanskrit script on Java is often cited as an indication that the Śailendra dynasty had originated from beyond Java's shores (see Jordaan 2006: 6, for example). Based on the brief summary presented above, one might think that Java's introduction to Siddhamātṛkā—as well as silver coinage featuring the same script—had simply occurred as the direct result of the Śailendra family's religious affiliation with Mahāyāna Buddhism, irrespective of the dynasty's geographic origin. The disappearance of Siddhamātṛkā from the kingdom's charters does appear to have coincided with the presumed disappearance of the Śailendra dynasty from Java, though it is also found on a silver plate embedded in the base of the famous silver Mañjuśrī image found near Semarang, which Bosch dated to the first quarter of the tenth century (Bosch 1929b: 45).

Annotated transcription and revised translation

Having rendered it plausible that the inscription belongs to the temple in the village Kalasan, we shall now turn our attention to the contents of the Kalasan charter. The following transcription, translation and discussion segments covering this inscription includes major contributions as well as some minor remarks made by Brandes (1886), Bhandarkar (1887), Bosch (1929a), Chatterjee (1933), Majumdar (1933), de Casparis (1950), Damais (1952), Boechari (1966; 2012: 358, inc. n. 8), Sarkar (1971/2: I), Chandra (1995), Santiko (2010) and Zakharov (2012). The transcription segments that appear in front of their corresponding verse translations are almost entirely based on the treatment published by Bosch (1929a: 57-62) plus the emendations proposed by de Casparis (1950), Damais (1952) and Sarkar (1971/2: I), which are placed between angle brackets. Bosch worked directly from the stone itself, whilst Bhandarkar had to rely on a single photograph and Brandes worked from a photo and a *papier-mâché abklatsch* because the original had gone missing. The stone was later recovered from a private collection and cataloged in the Batavia Museum as number D.147, allowing Bosch to study the original and compare it with the prior transcriptions of Brandes and Bhandarkar. "In the event of differences between the two, the correct reading could be established in most cases" (Bosch 1929a: 57).

Salutation and strophe one in Vasantatilakā[5] meter

| – – ⏑ ¦ – ⏑ ⏑ ¦ ⏑ – ⏑ ¦ ⏑ – ⏑ ¦ – ⏓ ||

Namo bhagavatyai āryatārāyai //

Homage to the divine Ārya Tārā!

yā tārayaty amitaduḥkhabhavābdhimagna<ṃ> [6]
lokaṃ vilokya vidhivattrividhair u- [2] payaiḥ / [7]
sā vaḥ surendranaralokavibhūtisāraṃ
tārā diśatvabhimataṃ jagadekatārā // (1)

1. The one who, having duly seen the world of human beings immersed in the endless suffering of the ocean of existence, delivers (it) by three-fold skill-in-means, may she, (Tārā), the sole savioress of the world, grant unto you the desired quintessence of prosperity in the celestial and human worlds.

---

[5]'Spring ornament' (Morgan 2011: 133).
[6]Bosch (1929a: 58) has *magnam*, which was corrected to *magnaṃ* by Sarkar (1971/2: I: 35).
[7]The meter requires *upāyaiḥ* in place of *upayaiḥ*.

Chapter II: The Kalasan charter and the Śailendra 'Lion among kings'

1. **The one who** (yā), **having duly** (vidhivat) **seen** (vilokya) **the world of human beings** (lokam, sing. acc. of loka) **immersed in** (magnam, sing. acc. of magna) **the endless** (amita) **suffering** (duḥkha) **of the ocean** (abdhi) **of existence** (bhava), **delivers** (tārayati, supposedly from √tṝ)[8] [it] **by threefold** (trividhair = trividhaiḥ, pl. instr. of trividha) **skill-in-means** (upayaiḥ, read as upāyaiḥ, pl. instrumental of upāya),[9] **may she** (sā), [Tārā], **the sole** (eka) **savioress** (tārā) **of the world** (jagad), **grant** (diśatv = diśatu the third pers. sing. imperative of √diś) **unto you** (vaḥ) **the desired** (abhimatam, sing. acc. of abhimata) **quintessence** (sāram, sing. acc. of sāra) **of prosperity** (vibhūti)[10] **in the celestial** (surendra) **and human** (nara) **worlds** (loka).[11]

Strophe two in Udgīti[12] meter

ā<varjy>a[13] mahārājaṃ *dyāḥ* pañca- [3] paṇaṃ panaṃkaraṇam /
śailendrarājagurubhis tārābhavanaṃ hi kāritaṃ śrīmat // (2)

| — — | ⏑⏑— | — — ‖ — — | ⏑⏑— | ⏑ | —⏑⏑ | — ‖ **first hemistich**
| — — | ⏑—⏑ | ⏑⏑— ‖ — — | ⏑⏑— | ⏑—⏑ | — — | — ‖ **second hemistich**

---

[8]See Jamison 1983: 101. Here the poet employed *tārayati* as a pun on the name of the Buddhist goddess.

[9]In Mahāyāna Buddhism *upāya* signifies the 'skill-in-means' that bodhisattvas exercise when teaching the Dharma to others. In his commentary on the *Nāmasaṃgīti*, the eighth century *ācārya* Vilāsavajra defined skill-in-means (upāya) as, "acting for the [ultimate] purpose of all beings by explaining all mundane and supramundane samādhis according to [the individual's] suitability" (Tribe 1994: 77). Furthermore, Bhandarkar (1887-1889: II: 2) noted that three *upāya*-s are mentioned in the *Dharmasaṃgraha* (111): *upāyastrividhaḥ / tadyathā - sarvasattvāvabodhakaḥ, sattvārthābhāvakaḥ, kṣiprasukhābhisaṃbodhiśceti //* .

[10]Sarkar (1971/2: I: 37, 39) translated *vibhūti* as 'wealth' while noting the difficulty of arriving at a precise English equivalent. "English phraseology does not convey the exact significance of the word *vibhūti* and we use the above word for want of a better one".

[11]Lit. 'in the worlds (*loka*) of Indra (*surendra*) and of men (*nara*)'.

[12]'Singing, singing loud; chanting'. With respect to the first and the third quarters of a strophe composed in the Udgīti meter there should be a total of 12 measures in each, with — (heavy, *guru*) counting as two measures and ⏑ (light, *laghu*) counting as one measure, whilst there are 15 measures in the second quarter and 18 measures in the fourth quarter.

[13]In the initial transcription for this charter published by Brandes (1886: 247), the first hemistich of this strophe reads ā — — mahārā — — — — pañcapanampanamkaranam. Next, Bhandharkar (1887-1889: II: 1) submitted the following reading: āvarjya mahārājaṃ — — — — paṇaṃ panaṃkaraṇaṃ. For his part, Bosch did not indicate he had any doubts about his own reading of *āvarja* in his transcription: āvarja mahārājaṃ dyāḥ pañcapaṇaṃ panaṃkaraṇaṃ. By contrast, de Casparis proposed *ā<vāh>ya*, 'to be invoked, invited' whilst Sarkar (1971/2: I: 36, 38, n. 18) followed the reading of *āvarjya* proposed by Bhandarkar. Damais (1952: 23-24, n. 4) excluded both *āvarjya* and *āvarja* from consideration, although he had no recourse to the stone itself or an estampage. He thought that the second *akṣara* was a *-va*, though he admitted that it was very difficult to read from the photograph published by Bosch, and with the final *akṣara* being a *-ya* with certainty and which can "hardly be read otherwise than *-tya*", e.g. *ā<va>tya*.
Upon examining the stone, however, Sundberg made the following observations: "The word occurs in a portion of the stone which is difficult to read, and which would greatly benefit from a better viewing with variable-angle lighting, which Bosch must have had when he was reading the stone, whereas I had to take whatever the sky would offer. Regarding the characters on the stone: A long 'a' was very clear to me. I couldn't see the 'va', but then again I couldn't really see any other letter.... In short, I am certain that the word must fit the pattern 'ĀX?j?a', where the 'X' denotes an unknown which is demonstrably present and the ? means the possible presence of a character" (Sundberg, pc 28 Jan. 2011).

2. [After persuading (e.g. to make the gift)] the Mahārāja Paṇaṃkaraṇa dyaḥ Pañcapaṇa, the residence of Tārā was assuredly caused to be made glorious by the preceptor(s) of the Śailendra king.

2. [After persuading (ā<varjy>a,[14] 'bending, inclining')] **the Mahārāja** (mahārājam) **Paṇaṃkaraṇa** (panaṃkaraṇam) **dyaḥ** (dyāḥ) **Pañcapaṇa** (pañcapaṇam),[15] **the residence** (bhavanam, n. sing. nom. of bhavana) **of Tārā** (tārā) **was assuredly** (hi, adverb) **caused to be made** (kāritam, n. sing. acc. of kārita) **glorious** (śrīmat, n. sing. acc. of śrīmat) **by the preceptor**(s)[16] (gurubhis = gurubhiḥ, the pl. instr. of guru) **of the Śailendra-king** (śailendrarāja).

Strophes three through eight in Āryā[17] meter

---

gurvājñayā kṛtajñais tārādevī [4] kṛtāpi tadbhavanam /
vinayamahāyānavidāṃ bhavanaṃ cāpyāryabhikṣūṇām // (3)

| – – | ⏑–⏑ | – – ‖ – – | – – | ⏑–⏑ | –⏑⏑ |–‖ **first hemistich**
|⏑⏑⏑⏑| – – |⏑⏑ – ‖⏑⏑ – | – – | ⏑ | – – |–‖ **second hemistich**

3. With awareness of the matters done by the order of the preceptor(s) was assuredly made ready the dwelling of the goddess Tārā, and also the place of abode for highly esteemed monks who have (full) knowledge of the monastic rules of the Mahāyāna.

3. **With awareness of the matters done** (kṛtajñais = kṛtajñaiḥ, pl. instr. of kṛtajña) **by the order** (ājñayā, sing. instr. of ājñā) **of the preceptor**(s) (gurv = guru) **was assuredly** (api, as a separate adverb) **made ready** (kṛta) **that** (tad, n. sing. acc. pronoun) **dwelling** (bhavanam, n. sing. acc. of bhavana) **of the goddess Tārā** (tārādevī) **and also** (cāpy = ca-api) **the place of abode** (bhavanam, n. sing acc. of bhavana) **for highly esteemed** (ārya) **monks** (bhikṣūṇām, pl. genitive of bhikṣu) **who have** [full] **knowledge** (vidām, pl. acc. of vida) **of the monastic rules** (vinaya) **of the Mahāyāna.**

paṅkuratavānatīripa- [5] nāmabhir ādeśaśastribhīrājñaḥ /
tārābhavanaṃ kāritam idamapi[18] cāpyāryabhikṣūṇām // (4)

| –⏑⏑ | ⏑–⏑ | –⏑⏑ ‖ –⏑⏑ | – – | ⏑–⏑ | – – |–‖ **first hemistich**

---

[14]*Epigraphia Indica* 22 (1935: 67) discusses the use of *āvarjjya* (derived from *ā-* √*vṛj*, 'to turn over, incline, bend') in another *praśasti*, perhaps as an absolutive clause for indicating 'being inclined, i.e. induced (to make the gift)', though the journal's editor thought that 'being accepted' was the preferable meaning in this other instance given that *āvṛj* can also mean 'to choose' or 'to bring into possession'.
[15]It appears that the second verse of the Kalasan charter includes the Sanskritization of the Old Javanese honorific (*dyaḥ*), the king's personal name (*pañcapaṇa*) and the toponym with which the monarch was specifically associated (*paṇaṃkaraṇa*). See also footnote 41 for a discussion of *kariyāna* (title) *paṇaṃkaraṇaḥ* (toponym), which appears in v.12 of this inscription.
[16]It is entirely possible that the pl. instr. for *guru* had been granted to a single Śailendra preceptor out of respect (*pluralis majestatis*). Otherwise this would suggest the participation of three or more preceptors.
[17]Āryā means 'The Lady' (Morgan 2011: 172).
[18]Sarkar (1971/2: I: 38, n. 22) proposed *kāritam idaṃ mapi* but this would break the meter.

| — — | ⏑⏑ — | — ⏑⏑ || ⏑⏑⏑⏑ | — — | ⏑ | — — | — || **second hemistich**

4. By the executors of the king with the appellations of Paṅkur, Tavāna and Tīripa was caused to be made the residence of Tārā, and also (the dwelling) of the highly esteemed monks.

4. **By the executors** (ādeśaśastribhī, read as ādeśa-śastribhiḥ, pl. instr. of śastrin)[19] **of the king** (rājñaḥ, sing. genitive of rājan) **with the appellations** (nāmabhir = nāmabhiḥ, pl. instr. of nāman) **of Paṅkur, Tavāna and Tīripa was caused to be made** (kāritam, n. sing. acc. of kārita) **the residence** (bhavanam, n. sing. acc. of bhavana) **of Tārā, and also** (cāpy = ca-api) [the dwelling] **of the highly esteemed** (ārya) **monks** (bhikṣūṇām, pl. genitive of bhikṣu).

rājye pravarddhamā- [6] ne rājñaḥ śailendravaṅśatilakasya /
śailendrarājagurubhis tārābhavanaṃ kṛtaṃ kṛtibhiḥ // (5)

| — — | ⏑ — ⏑ | — — || — — | — — | ⏑ — ⏑ | ⏑⏑ — | — || **first hemistich**[20]
| — — | ⏑ — ⏑ | ⏑⏑ — || — — | ⏑⏑ — | ⏑ | — ⏑⏑ | — || **second hemistich**

5. Since the sovereign was in the empire excessively flourishing for the ornament of the Śailendra dynasty,[21] the residence of Tārā was constructed by the pious preceptor(s) of the Śailendra-king.

5. **Since the sovereign** (rājñaḥ, sing. ablative of rājan) **was in the empire** (rājye, sing. locative of rājya) **excessively** (pra) **flourishing** (varddhamāne, read as vardhamāne, sing. locative of vardhamāna, 'thriving') **for the ornament** (tilakasya, sing. genitive of tilaka)[22] **of the Śailendra dynasty** (śailendravaṅśa), **the residence** (bhavanam, n. sing. nom. of bhavana) **of Tārā was constructed** (kṛtam, n. sing. acc. of kṛta) **by the pious** (kṛtibhiḥ, pl. instr. of kṛtin) **preceptor**(s) (gurubhis = gurubhiḥ, pl. instr. of guru) **of the Śailendra-king** (śailendra-rāja).

śak<a>nṛpakālātītai- [7] r varṣaśataiḥ saptabhir mmahārājaḥ /
akarod gurupūjārthaṃ tārābhavanaṃ paṇaṃkaraṇaḥ // (6)
grāmaḥ kālasanāmā [8] dattaḥ saṃghāya sākṣiṇaḥ kṛtvā /
paṅkuratavānatīripadeśādhyakṣān mahāpuruṣān // (7)

| ⏑⏑⏑⏑ | — — | — — || — ⏑⏑ | — — | ⏑ — ⏑ | — — | — || **first hemistich**
| ⏑⏑ — | ⏑⏑ — | — — || — — | ⏑⏑ — | ⏑ | — ⏑⏑ | — || **second hemistich**

| — — | — ⏑⏑ | — — || — — | — — | ⏑ — ⏑ | — — | — || **first hemistich**
| — ⏑⏑ | ⏑ — ⏑ | — ⏑⏑ || — — | — — | ⏑ | — ⏑⏑ | — || **second hemistich**

[19]Sarkar (1971/2: I: 39, n. 38) thought this term referred to persons connected with weapons. He overlooked the earlier observation by Bosch (1952a: 114) that *ādeśaśastrin* literally means 'armed with warrants'.
[20]The last syllable of a half-verse or verse is considered long because of the breath pause or caesura indicated by the single or double *daṇḍa* marks.
[21]Or, following Sarkar (1971/2: I: 37): 'As the kingdom (*rājye*) of the king (*rajñaḥ*) who is an ornament (*tilakasya*) of the Śailendra dynasy (*śailendravaṅśa*) was flourishing (*pravarddhamāne*) ...'.
[22]This appears to be another of those instances in which a genitive is used in the sense of the dative.

6-7. When seven hundred years of the era of the Śaka king had elapsed [e.g. 778/9 CE], the Mahārāja Paṇaṃkaraṇa enacted the residence of Tārā for the sake of the [daily] worship activities of the preceptor(s), after having made the high officials Paṅkura, Tavāna and Tīripa and the supervisors of the region witnesses to the donation of the hamlet named Kālasa for the sake of the Saṅgha.

6-7. **When seven hundred** (śataiḥ saptabhir = saptabhiḥ, the pl. instrumentals of varṣaśata and saptan, respectively) **of the years** (varṣa) **of the era** (kāla) **of the Śaka-king** (śaka-nṛpa)[23] **had elapsed** (atita), **the Mahārāja Paṇaṃkaraṇaḥ** (sing. nom.) **enacted** (akarod = akarot, third pers. sing. imperfect of √kṛ) **the residence** (bhavanam, n. sing. acc. of bhavana) **of Tārā for the sake of** (artham) **the** [daily] **worship activities** (pūjā) **of the preceptor**(s) (guru),[24] **after having made** (kṛtvā, the absolutive of √kṛ) **the high officials** (mahāpuruṣān, pl. acc. of mahāpuruṣa, 'eminent man') **Paṅkur, Tavāna and Tīripa and the supervisors** (adhyakṣān, pl. acc. of adhyakṣa, 'overseer') **of the commands** (deśa = ādeśa *metri causa*)[25] **witnesses** (sākṣiṇaḥ, pl. acc. of sākṣin) **to the donation** (dattaḥ) **of the hamlet** (grāmaḥ) **named** (nāmā) **Kalasan** (kālasa) **for the sake of the Saṅgha** (saṃghāya, sing. dative of saṃgha = saṅgha).

bhurada- [9] kṣineyam atulā dattā saṃghāya rājasiṅhena /
śailendravaṅśabhūpair anuparipālyāryasantatyā // (8)

|⏑⏑ – |⏑ – ⏑ |⏑⏑ – ‖ – – | – – | ⏑ – ⏑ | – – | – ‖ **first hemistich**
| – – |⏑ – ⏑ | – – ‖⏑⏑⏑⏑| – – | ⏑ | – – | – ‖ **second hemistich**

8. Given to the Saṅgha by the Lion among Kings, this gift in ample (measure), which is incomparable, is to be cared for thereafter by the princes of the Śailendra dynasty together with an uninterrupted succession of Buddhist priests.

8. **Given** (dattā) **to the Saṅgha** (saṃghāya, sing. dative of saṃgha = saṅgha) **by the Lion** (siṅhena, sing. instr. of siṅha = siṃha) **among Kings** (rāja),[26] **this** (iyam, f. sing. nom. pronoun) **gift** (dakṣinā, f. sing. nom.)[27] **in ample** [measure] (bhura, read as bhūri, 'abundant, extensive'),[28] **which is incomparable** (atulā, f. sing. nom.), **is to be cared for** (paripālya, in comp. for paripālanīya) **thereafter** (anu, 'afterward') **by the princes** (bhūpair = bhūpaiḥ, pl. instr. of bhūpa) **of the Śailendra dynasty** (śailendravaṅśa) **together with an uninterrupted succession** (santatyā, sing. instr. of santati in comp. for saṃtati) **of Buddhist priests** (ārya).[29]

[23]704 Śaka = 778/9 CE.
[24]Sarkar (1971/2: I: 37 and 40, n. 40) corrected Bosch's published reading from *saknṛpa* to *sak<a>nṛpa* and translated *gurupūjārtham* as 'for the worship of (his) preceptors (to the deity)' whilst Chandra (1995: 215) rendered the compositum as 'out of respect to the guru'. In the *Śrīmad Bhāgavatam* (11,27,50), *pūjā* is used in the sense of 'for regular daily worship'.
[25]See Bosch 1952a: 114.
[26]See the discussion segment for this verse.
[27]Bhandarkar (1887, II: 3) translated *dakṣina* as 'gratuity'.
[28]Sarkar (1971/2: I: 40, n. 41) viewed *bhura* as "an unfortunate mistake of the scribe for *bhuri*", e.g. *bhūri*. He also thought that *bhūridakṣiṇa* would be equivalent to the Old Javanese *pasĕk-pasĕk*, which conveys the meaning of gifts in ample measure. See also Gonda (1954: 191) in relation to the use of *bhūridakṣiṇa* in the *Mahābhārata* (15, 5, 32; 12,66,10; etc.).

Strophe nine (Sumānikā meter)[30]

[10] sa<ṇḍa>paṅkurādibhiḥ san tavānakādibhiḥ /[31]
saṅ tīripādibhiḥ pat<n>ibhiśca sādhubhiḥ // api ca //[32] (9)

– ⏑ – ⏑ – ⏑ –
– ⏑ – ⏑ – ⏑ – /
– ⏑ – ⏑ – ⏑ –
– ⏑ – ⏑ – ⏑ – // ⏑ ⏑ – //

9. And moreover, (to be maintained) by ... [Saṅ ḍa] Paṅkur and his staff, Saṅ [ḍa] Tavāna and his staff, Saṅ [ḍa] Tīripa and his staff, as well as by their wives of honorable descent.

9. And moreover (api ca) [to be maintained (paripālya)] **by** ... [Saṅ ḍa (sa<ṇḍa>)] **Paṅkur and his staff** (ādibhiḥ, lit. 'and so on,'), **Saṅ** [ḍa] **Tavāna** (san tavāna, read as saṅ tavāna) **and his staff** (ādibhiḥ), **Saṅ** [ḍa] **Tīripa and his staff** (ādibhiḥ), **as well as** (ca) **by their wives** (patnibhiś = patnibhiḥ, pl. instr. of patni) **of honorable descent** (sādhubhiḥ, pl. instr. of sādhu).

Strophe ten in Śālinī[33] meter

|– – – ¦ –, – ⏑ ¦ – – ⏑ ¦ – –||

[11] sarvān evāgāminaḥ pārthivendrān
bhūyo bhūyo yācate rājasiṅhaḥ /
sāmānyo ya<ṃ> dharmmasetur na- [12] rāṇāṃ[34]
kāle kāle pālanīyo bhavadbhiḥ // (10)

[29]De Casparis (1950: 186, n. 1) also saw the possibility of connecting *āryasantati* with the Sanskrit term *gotra:* 'family, race, lineage, kin'. So *śailendravaṅśabhūpair anuparipālyāryasantatyā* can also perhaps be read as *śailendravaṅśabhūpaiḥ anu-paripālyā-arya-santatyā*, which can mean 'to be cared for thereafter by the princes of the Śailendra dynasty together with their devoted (*arya*, f.) offspring (*santatyā*, f.)'.

[30]"Four lines of seven syllables, alternately long and short, starting with long" (de Casparis 1950: 136, n. 4; see also Damais 1952: 25, continuation of n. 4). *Su-mānikā* literally means 'excellent weight or measure'. In theory, this potential reference to standard units of measure might be applicable to the Javanese public works officials mentioned in this stanza, who appear to have been in charge of implementing and maintaining the orders of the king, presumably with respect to the size, amount, or degree of compliance.

[31]De Casparis' (Ibid.) emendation *sa<ṇḍa>paṅkur* is equivalent to the Old Javanese *saṅ ḍa paṅkur*.

[32]Damais (1952: 25, continuation of n. 4) remarked that Brandes (1886: 247) had read this as *patnibhiśca* as opposed to the reading of *pattibhiśca* by Bosch and with *patnibhiḥ* (the pl. instrumental of *patni*) meaning 'by their wives'. Many other inscriptions found on Java refer to the participation of the wives of officials. Damais also wrote that a comparison to the form of the word *dattā* in line nine makes it evident that *pattibhiśca* is an incorrect reading for line 10, and that *sādhubhiḥ* could be interpreted as either a reference to the Paṅkura, Tavāna and Tīripa or their wives.

[33]'Possessing a house; amply furnished with; praiseworthy'.

[34]Bosch (1929a: 59) has *sāmānyo yan*, which was emended by Sarkar (1971/2: I: 59) to *sāmānyoyaṃ*.

10. The Lion among Kings solicits again and again all of those greatest of princes from the future just so: "This bridge to the Dharma, which is common property among men, should be maintained by you always at the right time".

10. **The Lion** (siṅhaḥ, sing. nom. of siṅha = siṃha) **among Kings** (rāja) **solicits** (yācate, third pers. sing. middle present from √yāc) **again and again** (bhūyo bhūyo = in comp. for bhūyas, adverb) **all of those** (sarvān, pl. acc. of sarva) **greatest** (indrān, pl. acc. of indra, 'best') **of princes** (pārthiva) **from the future** (āgāminaḥ, sing. ablative of āgāmin) **just so** (eva): "**This** (yaṃ = ayam, m. sing. nom. pronoun) **bridge** (setur = setuḥ, m. sing. nom. of setu) **to the Dharma** (dharmma = dharma), **which is the common property** (sāmānyo = sāmānyaḥ, sing. nom. of sāmānya, 'shared by others') **of men** (narānām, pl. genitive of nara), **should be maintained** (pālanīyo = pālanīyaḥ) **by you** (bhavadbhiḥ, pl. instr. of bhavat) **always at the right time** (kāle kāle, sing. locative of kāla)".[35]

Strophe eleven in Upendravajrā[36] meter

|⏑–⏑¦––⏑¦⏑–⏑¦––||

---

anena puṇyena v<i>hārajena[37]
   pratītya jātārthavibhāgavi- [13] jñāḥ /
bhavantu sarve tribhavopapannā
   janā jinānām anuśāsanajñāḥ // (11)

11. By means of this spiritual merit accruing from (the construction of) this monastery may there be experts in the exposition of the (philosophical) meaning of the chain of causation (and may) all living beings produced in the three states of existence (become) conversant in this instruction of the Jinas.

11. **By means of this** (anena, third pers. sing. instr. pronoun) **spiritual merit** (puṇyena, sing. instr. of puṇya) **accruing from** (jena, sing. instr. of ja, 'produced or caused by; descended from') [the construction] **of this monastery** (vihāra) **may there be** (bhavantu, third pers. pl. imperative from √bhū) **experts** (vijñāḥ, pl. acc. of vijñā, 'wise, clever'; 'wise man') **in the exposition** (vibhāga)[38] **of the** (philosophical) **meaning** (artha) **of the chain of causation** (pratītya-jāta, e.g. pratītya-samutpāda) [and may] **all** (sarve, pl. nom. of sarva) **living beings** (janā = janāḥ, pl. nom. of jana) **produced** (upapannā = upapannāḥ, pl. nom. of upapanna) **in the three states of existence** (tribhava)[39] [become] **conversant in** (jñāḥ, pl. accusative of jñā, 'familiar with') **this instruction** (anuśāsana) **of the Jinas** (jinānām, pl. genitive of jina).

---

[35] Or 'always in time'. See Mcdonnell 1893: 67 and Monier-Williams 1899: 278.
[36] 'Secondary Indravajrā' (Morgan 2011: 97).
[37] Bosch (1929a: 59) has *vīhārajena*, corrected to *vihārajena* by Sarkar (1971/2: I: 36).
[38] Rahder remarked about *vibhāga* being equivalent to the Pali Buddhist term *vibhanga* in Bosch 1931: 379.
[39] The same expression appears in verse A7 of the Isthmus of Kra stele.

Strophe 12 (Āryā meter)

---

kariyānapaṇaṃkaraṇaḥ śrī- [14] mān abhiyācate tra bhāvi<n>ṛpān /[40]
bhūyobhūyo vidhivad v<i>hāra paripālanārtham iti // [41] (12)

|⏑ ⏑ – | ⏑⏑ – |⏑⏑ – ‖ – – | ⏑⏑ – |⏑ – ⏑ | – ⏑⏑ | – ‖ **first hemistich**
|– – | – – |⏑⏑ – ‖⏑ – ⏑ | ⏑⏑ – | ⏑ | – ⏑⏑ | – ‖ **second hemistich**

12. The illustrious Kariyāna Paṇaṃkaraṇa entreats the kings among the protectors in the future over and over again for the sake of the (proper) care of this monastery and so forth in accordance with the prescribed regulations.

12. **The illustrious** (śrīmān, sing. nom. of śrīmat) **Kariyāna**[42] **Paṇaṃkaraṇaḥ** (sing. nom.) **entreats** (abhiyācate, third pers. sing. middle present from abhi- √yāc, 'to ask for, solicit, request') **the kings** (nṛpān, pl. acc. of nṛpa)] **among the protectors** (tra) **in the future** (bhāvi, in comp for bhāvin) **over and over again** (bhūyo bhūyo = in comp. for bhūyas, adverb) **for the sake of** (artham) **the** [proper] **care** (paripālana) **of this monastery** (vihāra) **and so forth** (iti) **in accordance with the prescribed regulations** (vidhivad = vidhivat, 'according to rule').

Strophe discussion segment

Two different theories have been adopted by the various scholars who have commented upon individual strophes from the Kalasan charter. Proponents of the single-dynasty theory believe that the Javanese *mahārāja* Paṇaṃkaraṇa prominently featured in the Kalasan charter had been a descendant of the Śailendravaṅśa. By contrast, proponents of the two-dynasties theory believe that this inscription delineates the participation of two different monarchs in the construction of the Tārā abode and its associated cloister. The individual points that pertain to specific stanzas of the inscription raised by proponents of both camps will be discussed in accordance with the order of the strophes. Critical comments pertaining to the overall merits of the single-dynasty and two-dynasties theories will be reserved for presentation in this chapter's concluding segment.

Salutation and verse one. Brandes (1886: 252) thought the opening salutation *bhagavatyai āryatārāyai* probably referred to "the *śakti*, or as the Buddhists used to say, the

---

[40]Bosch (1929a: 59) has *trabhāviṇṛpān*, which Sarkar (1971/2: I: 36, 39 n. 32) corrected to *bhāvi<n>ṛpān*. However, Sarkar appears to have accidentally omitted *tra*, which is required to complete the meter.

[41]The transcription published by Bosch (1929a: 59) has *vīhāra* instead of *vihāra*. Sarkar (1972: I: 39, n. 33) also observed that "*hāraparapari* is evidently a printer mistake" as the addition of *-para-* would present too many syllables for the meter to accommodate.

[42]According to de Casparis (1950: 53-54), this is a Sanskritization of the Old Javanese title *rakarayān* (as in Ra karayān Patapān of the Kayumwuṅan charter) and what appears to be its Old Malay equivalent, *ḍang karayān*, which he translated as "His Highness". From this, de Casparis concluded that the respective meanings of *mahārāja* and *kariyāna* must have overlapped to a considerable degree. Damais (1968: 357, 370) disagreed. The later use of the Old Javanese titles Raka, Ra kriyān or Ra karayān is attached to a function that appears to encompass a territory, which for the sake of convenience Damais dubbed a "prerogative". In Damais' view, Kariyāna Paṇaṃkaraṇa is the name for a prerogative specific to the Javanese sovereign, with Paṇaṃkaraṇa specifying the toponym, whilst *mahārāja* was his title.

Tārā of the Dhyānibuddha Amoghasiddhi". By contrast, Jordaan (1998) viewed this salutation[43] as potentially a reference to a specific form of the Buddhist goddess when Āryatārā is understood as an alternative name for Vyaśatārā, whose prescribed sitting position in iconographic texts is compatible with the *bhadrāsana* posture appropriate for the now empty throne within the main *cella* at Caṇḍi Kalasan.[44]

> "The symbolic meanings assigned to the sitting posture and the throne seem to support the identification proposed here. According to Ghosh (1980: 35), the *bhadrāsana* stands for 'sovereignty', which would accord well with the designation Vaśyadhikara-Tārā, which ... means 'Tārā having authority over the subjected ones' .... [this] is precisely the symbolic meaning ascribed to the ornamentation of the throne, comprising of a *makara*, a rampant lion, and an elephant on either side of the throne (Auboyer 1937; Saunders 1960: 129). Obviously, Vaśya-Tārā's independent status underscored her status as supreme goddess in the pantheon of Kalasan" (Jordaan 1998: 173).

In the Nālandā charter, the Sanskrit term Tāreva ('like the goddess Tārā') appears in reference to the mother of the Śailendra king Bālaputradeva, who is also identified as the spouse of a royal personage described as 'the foremost warrior in battlefields' (*samarāgravīraḥ*), whose father was the king of Java known by the epithet *śrī vīra-vairi-mathana* ('illustrious destroyer of brave foes'). Therein the mother of Bālaputra is also identified as the daughter of Śrī Dharmasetu (or Varmasetu) of the lunar race (Sastri 1942: 101-102). Cœdès (1968: 84, 109) associated her father with the king of Śrīvijaya, who is prominently featured on side 'A' of the Isthmus of Kra stele but not specifically designated by name. The designation Tāreva also appears in the Plaosan inscription, but the context is unclear since the expression is found in one of the early fragmentary lines.

The compositum *jagadekatārā* from the benedictory verse of the Kalasan charter can convey the secondary meaning of 'the sole (guiding) star of the world' because the Sanskrit word Tārā conveys the double meaning of 'She who carries across' as well as 'Star Lady'. Buddhists considered Tārā to be their guiding light with respect to crossing the 'ocean' of existence and arriving safely on the other shore of *nirvāṇa*. As her name suggests, however, the savioress from the eight perils was also the patron divinity of sailors and merchants who crossed the ocean in pursuit of their respective trades.[45]

---

[43]Jordaan argued that the composer's presumed use of *ārya* as a generic honorific seemed superfluous given that the Sanskrit words *bhagavatī* and *ārya* both can convey similar meanings, but that the redundancy could be satisfactorily explained by taking Ārya as a specified form of address for the particular Tārā residing at Kalasan. *Bhagavatī*, is the feminine form of *bhagavat*, which means 'glorious, illustrious, divine, adorable, venerable' or 'possessing fortune'. However, Jordaan (pc 20 Oct. 2012) does not agree that these meanings for *bhagavatī* would have provided sufficient differentiation from Ārya. "Wouldn't the Javanese stress the great overlap between noble, glorious, divine, and venerable?" *Bhagavatī* is also a name of Lakṣmī, which is of interest since the many goddesses displayed on the exterior facades at Caṇḍi Kalasan present attributes that are consistent with her iconography.

[44]This throne is comparable to the one on which the Buddha is seated in *bhadrāsana* at Caṇḍi Mendut.

[45]Jordaan and Colless (2009: 76) speculated that the later Śailendra kings had funded temples at Nālandā and Nagapattinam (Nākappaṭṭinam) in South India to ensure the safe passage of their ships after losing their ritual access to her temple in Central Java.

Buddhist monks, pilgrims, merchants and sailors braving the perils of the sea prayed to the goddess for a safe journey to the other shore. She is said to have answered their prayers by appearing with her attendants to frighten sea monsters away (Willson 1986: 223) and just to think of her calmed the waters: "One's ship is broken amidst an ocean whose commotion towers up high as the Brahmā heavens, (by) fish and sea monsters of terrifying forms: but thinking of Tārā, one finds security" (Willson 1986: 237). What's more, "One who stands paralyzed with fear on the deck of a sinking ship may suddenly be standing on the shore" (Shaw 2006: 310).

The popularity of the goddess among the Pāla rulers of northern India is attested by the Nesari plates (805) of the Rāṣṭrakūṭa king Govinda III, which indicate that his rival Dharmapāla had venerated the Buddhist goddess Tārā to such an extent that his banner or standard had borne the image of the goddess (Sircar 1971: 100). Having voluntarily submitted to Govinda III, Dharmapāla also gifted an image of Tārā. Hence, the adoption of a Tārā abode on Java during roughly the same period suggests the existence of strong ties between the Śailendra dynasty and the region of ancient India over which the Pāla kings had ruled, which included the famous Buddhist religious institution of Nālandā.

Verse two. Strophe two appears to have been composed in the Udgīti meter, in which the number of measures in the second and fourth quarters of a verse are reversed in comparison to the Āryā meter, hence incorporating 15 and 18 measures, respectively. The interpretation of this stanza, together with the strophes thereafter, is important for the reconstruction of the history of Central Java. According to the two-dynasties theory proposed by van Naerssen, which in turn had been inspired by an earlier observation made by Vogel, the Kalasan charter would refer to two rulers: a Śailendra overlord who hailed from beyond Java's shores and the representative of the indigenous royal Javanese lineage founded by Sañjaya, which had continued to exercise limited authority during the period of the so-called Śailendra interregnum (van Naerssen 1947: 249-253).

> "In the protocol the two parties, who most come to the fore in effecting the donation, are purposely mentioned separately.... After an introductory stanza, there follows a general communication in which the two principal co-operators of, and the manner in which the institution has been found are named, viz.: 'After the *gurus* of the Çailendra prince having prevailed upon the Mahārāja dyāḥ Pañcapaṇa Panangkaraṇa, they caused a magnificent Tārā temple to be built.' (stanza 2). After this preliminary discussion there follows a further elaboration of it, namely in stanza 3, of the share the Çailendra-clerics (*gurus*) had in it, and in stanza 4 of the share of the principal functionaries in the reign of the Javanese princes. In stanzas 5 and 6 homage is again paid to the illustrious takers of the initiative: 1. to the prince who is the ornament of the Çailendra dynasty, and 2. to the great-king Panangkaraṇa. So far mention has been made of the building of a temple. In the 7th stanza the Javanese *pankur*, *tawan* and *tirip* and the 'notable *desa*-heads' are brought on the scene, the *rāmas* of the Old-Javanese deeds. These were namely the representatives of the desas on whose grounds the institution was founded. In olden times even a prince could not dispose at will ground belonging to a desa community. Further the 'protection' and the 'maintenance' of the institution are guaranteed in stanzas 8 and 10 by the Çailendra dynasty, and the 'series of nobles succeeding each other', and finally

in stanzas 9 and 12 by the 'illustrious *rakryan* Panangkaraṇa' and the 'princes reigning here later'." (Naerssen 1947: 250-251).

Given that *mahārāja* is not an indigenous Javanese title for a king, van Naerssen proposed that the Śailendra *guru(s)*[46] had awarded it to Paṇaṃkaraṇa, perhaps in recognition of his cooperation in the founding of the Tārā temple. "They were the most suitable officials to perform the act of bestowing the honourable title. This title, however, was apparently not yet of such great importance to a *raka* as it was to be about a century later" (Naerssen & de Iongh 1977: 39).

Verse three. *Kṛtajña* can mean 'knowing what is right, correct in conduct' (see, for example, *Mahābhārata* 12,104,6), which led Sarkar (1971/2: I: 37, 39, n. 37) to gloss *kṛtajñaiḥ* as 'by the experts'. On the other hand, Chandra (1995: 215) has proposed 'mindful of right conduct' with the pl. instrumental *kṛtajñaiḥ* having been granted out of respect, *pluralis majestatis*. Still, this translation does not account for the poet's use of the instrumental case in this instance.

Though typically glossed as grateful (e.g. 'knowing the matter done, one who has the sense of gratitude'; see Higashimoto 1965: 89), *kṛtajña* also can mean 'knowing what was done' (Bilimoria *et al* 2007: 194) as well as 'the act of being aware of what has been done (*kṛta*) for one or the agent thereof' (Carman & Streng 1989: 78). Given the context, I have translated *gurvājñayā kṛtajñais* as 'With awareness of the matters done by the order of the (Śailendra) preceptor(s)'.

Sarkar (1971/2: I: 37) translated the entire verse to accommodate his own interpretation of the meaning of *kṛtajñaiḥ*. "By experts, at the command of the preceptors, were made (the image of) the goddess Tārā and a temple for her; so also was made an abode for the venerable monks who knew the Great Vehicle of Discipline".

The translation for *vinayamahāyānavidāṃ* has been revised herein as 'who have knowledge of the monastic rules of the Great Vehicle (Mahāyāna)'. It is also worth noting that *ārya* does not actually automatically mean 'venerable', as Sarkar and Chandra have consistently translated this Sanskrit word, but rather 'honorable, noble, highly esteemed'. When applied to an entire monastic community as opposed to the most senior monks in the Saṅgha, it would seem more prudent to apply one of the latter meanings. Moreover, both Sarkar and Chandra have typically glossed *bhavana* as 'temple', though the word actually means 'dwelling, residence, place of abode'.

Verse four. Bhandarkar (1887: 6) observed that the kings of ancient India had addressed their royal mandates to various personages invested with authority over village communities and entire districts, called Separatists, Gramapatis, Ayuktaka, Niyuktaka, and so forth, and surmised that the Kalasan inscription's references to *paṅkura*, *tavāna*, and *tīripa* were similarly intended. De Casparis noted that this triad was collectively known as the 'three honored ones' (*sang māna katrīṇi*) and usually preceded the Javanese tax farmers (*maṅulala*) in the lists of royal officers presented in Javanese charters. Though their precise role in Javanese medieval society is unclear, they do not seem to have merely represented

[46]Chandra (1995: 214-217) has adopted the view that only a single Śailendra preceptor is ever mentioned in the Kalasan charter, with the plural *rājagurubhiḥ* then presumably having been awarded as an indication of respect.

the interests of a single community, as van Naerssen thought, but rather served the Javanese king in a broader capacity related to the collection of taxes.

> "In the later Old Javanese inscriptions the stereotyped formula is that the area which is to become a *sīma* is not to be entered by (*tan katamāna de*) the *māna katrīṇi: pangkur, tawān* and *tirip*, nor by all those 'claiming the king's property'. Some inscriptions of the time of Pu Siṇḍok have, however, a slightly different formulation, when it is stated that the *sīma* is not to be entered by all those acting by order of (literally: borne by, *winawa*) the *māna katrīṇi*.... The latter formulation suggests that this trio controlled to some extent the activities of the tax farmers" (de Casparis 1962: 59).

Writing about the younger East Javanese kingdom of Majapahit, Hall (2000: 69) noted that the trio was "distinguished as having income rights as a consequence of their having local spiritual authority and special titles of distinction: Pangkur, Tawān and Tirip. *Mangilala dĕrwaya haji*, the collectors of the king's due, are in contrast collectively termed *wulu-wulu* 'persons of low standing' who are forbidden to 'trouble' or 'visit' the community, as are a list of other royal officials who might 'claim the Lord's due'." So the participation of the *pangkur, tawān* and *tirip* in the founding of the temple and monastery appears to have had religious overtones. Their witnessing of the king's donation was also an affirmation that the tax exempt status of the religious foundation would be observed.

Verse five. Santiko (2010: 629) has expressed the opinion that the Śailendra king mentioned in strophe five had actually occupied a position subordinate to the Mahārāja Paṇaṃkaraṇa, who Santiko viewed as the emperor at the time, rather than the other way around. This unique two-dynasties interpretation is based in part on her translation of *rājye pravarddhamāne* as "in the kingdom (which) is growing", e.g. which is still in the formative stages of its development. In my opinion, however, it was the thriving and prosperous status of the Śailendra kingdom that enabled the monarch's preceptors to proceed with the construction of the Tārā abode. There is also reason to believe that Santiko has misrepresented the meaning of *āvarjya* from strophe two by interpreting the Sanskrit term as an indication that the Śailendra king, through his preceptors, had to request the approval of Paṇaṃkaraṇa.

Verses six and seven. The next two strophes in the Āryā meter appear to form a conjoined pair due to the presence of the gerund *kṛtvā*. With respect to verse six, Sarkar (1971/2: I: 36) surmised that Paṇaṃkaraṇa had built the residence of Tārā for the worship of (his) preceptors. Given the repeated references to the Śailendra *guru*(-s) in this charter, the proponents of the two-dynasties theory believe it is more probable that the Javanese king had built the Tārā abode for the worship activities of the (Śailendra) preceptors.

Strophes very similar to verse six of the Kalasan charter appear in the Abhayagirivihāra (792/3) and Kĕlurak (782) charters, with the former giving the Śaka year during which the Javanese branch of the Abhayagirivihāra had been constructed (de Casparis 1961: 242) and the latter providing the Śaka year during which the Śailendra *guru* Kumāraghoṣa established a Mañjughoṣa image and/or temple. In the Kalasan inscription, however, it is the Mahārāja Paṇaṃkaraṇa who fills the principal role in 700 Śaka (=778/9 CE), albeit one that is not easy to define since the inscription's composer elsewhere credits the Śailendra preceptor(s) and a trio of officials representing the rural gentry for the various construction activities mentioned in the text. Van Naerssen examined this issue from the viewpoint of his two-dynasties theory.

> "What actual part the Śailendra kings played in the erection of the sanctuaries, in other words: what is involved in this 'building of a temple', is not clear to us. But we may expect that at this early stage of Hindu-Javanese history only the Śailendra kings were able to have a buddhist temple (or other religious building) consecrated according to buddhistic rituals and ceremonies, because only they had at their disposal Buddhist priests who could properly accomplish the consecrations. However, as these Śailendra kings belonged to a dynasty which apparently was of foreign origin, they were not entitled to dispose of local land and labor, the necessary assets for the completion of great works. The inscription of Kalasan leaves no doubt whatever as to who had the rights of disposal of the revenue and labour of the subjects: the Javanese Raka (or Rakarayan) Panangkaran" (Naerssen & de Iongh 1977: 38).

Strophe seven refers first and foremost to the triad of officials collectively known on Java as the 'three honored ones' (*sang māna katrīṇi*). According to Bosch, the *ādeśaśastribhīr paṅkuratavānatīripanāmabhir* mentioned in strophe four are obviously the same people subsequently identified as the *paṅkuratavānatīripadeśādhyakṣān* in strophe seven.

> "The first part in the latter compositum implies a specification of *deśādhyakṣān*, not therewith forming a *dvandva*, as was wrongfully assumed in the translation [by van Naerssen]. Deśa in this [compositum] stands *metri causa* for the usual *ādeśa* (both having the meaning 'instruction', 'order'). By means of both the *deśādhyakṣa* of strophe seven and the *ādeśaśastrin* (literally 'armed with warrants') of strophe four are the *pangkur*, *tawan* and *tirip* denoted as [belonging to] a category of officials who were charged with monitoring the implementation of the orders of the king, presumably a sort of inspectors of public works, including works of a religious nature. Needless to say that the changed division of tasks between the Śailendra monarch and Paṇaṃkaraṇa proposed here, the importance of the first versus the last is further accentuated rather than weakened, so that van Naerssen's idea—namely that the second holds a subordinate position towards the first—can be maintained unabated" (Bosch 1952a: 114).

Verses eight and nine. Though Sarkar (1971/2: I: 37) initially translated *āryasantatyā* as 'by the nobility', he subsequently suggested 'by the scion of Ārya(-land)' to fit his conjectural theory about the Śailendra dynasty having originated in South India. "The incomparable presents given in profusion to the congregation by the king, who is a lion among monarchs and scion of Ārya-land, must be protected by the rulers of the Śailendra dynasty" (Sarkar 1985: 326-327). By contrast, Chandra (1995: 215) surmised that °*ārya-santatyā* would mean 'by the noble traditions to be observed'. However, *santatyā* (e.g. the sing. instrumental of *santati*, read as *saṃtati*) actually means 'continuation', 'succession' or 'lineage', or even 'progeny' and 'offspring'.

Though *bhupaiḥ* does potentially mean 'by the kings', the contents of the following stanza, which begins with 'and moreover', suggests that *bhupaiḥ* was intended to refer to the Śailendra princes living during the same period as the officials subsequently mentioned in v.9. By contrast, the *mahārāja* entreats the greatest of princes from the more distant future to care for the monastery in the charter's final strophe.

Chandra (1995: 215) translated *rājasiṃhena* in v.8 as 'by the mighty king' and *rājasiṃha* in v.10 as 'mighty king'. As we shall see in the discussion of v.10, however, the inscription's reference to the Lion among Kings (*rājasiṃha*) may rather be understood as an epithet applicable to the Buddha, at least within the specific context of the following strophe.

Verse 10. Though Chandra (1995: 216) translated *dharmasetu* as 'religious foundation' he also noted that the additional meaning of 'bridge of religion' would be highly appropriate for a temple dedicated to the Buddhist goddess Tārā: "In this context *dharmasetu* also signifies the bridge of Dharma to cross over the ocean of existence (*bhava-sagara*), as Goddess Tārā takes beings across. Tārā is from the root *tar* 'carry through or save, pass across or over, cross over, sail across'. Tārā is so-called as she carries across the ocean of mundane existence". However, Sundberg believes that the Buddhist temple dedicated to the worship of the goddess had served a parallel purpose in commemorating the presumed marriage of Samaratuṅga to the historical Tārā, based on the widely adopted interpretation of the Nālandā inscription as having referred to Samaratuṅga through the use of the epithet *samarāgravīra* and also having referred to Tārā's father as 'Dharmasetu' instead of Varmasetu.

> "As nearly as can be told, the Kālasan inscription seems to be a *praśasti* which flattered the Somavaṃśa by artfully incorporating the names of the father, Dharmasetu and the daughter Tārā into the text. Of the tens of thousands of terms which might be selected out of an extensive Sanskrit vocabulary to include in the short dedication of a temple to the Buddhist goddess Tārā, for whom his daughter-in-law and a future queen of the family was named, the Śailendra king managed in prophetic anticipation to select the term '*dharmasetu*' ('Bridge of Religion'), the exact name of the Somavaṃśa king who was the maternal grandfather of the Killer's grandson Bālaputradeva. I consider it beyond happenstance that an inscription of 778 would anticipate the marriage into the Śailendra fold of two individuals whose names are repeatedly employed in that very inscription. If the Nālandā inscription told us other names of the family, we should not be surprised to find that name woven into the Kālasan inscription too. We must therefore put a limit of the year 778 on the date of the marriage, with great consequences for our understanding of the dynastic history of ancient Central Java as well as the location of the heart of the Śailendra kingdom" (Sundberg 2011: 145, n. 4).

In covering much the same territory, however, Bosch (1929a:141-142) noted that the composers of both the Kalasan and Kĕlurak inscriptions had employed *dharmasetu* as a term, whereas it appears as a proper name in the Nālandā inscription. Bosch also cited the statement by Majumdar (1926: 13) that this proper name more probably reads Varmasetu, not Dharmasetu, and if thought correct this would render moot any further arguments concerning the possible use of this Sanskrit word in these two inscriptions to refer to the father of Tārā, though he did note that Varmasetu sounded considerably stranger to the ears than Dharmasetu.[47]

During medieval times in India and elsewhere in southern Asia, *dharmasetu* was the term often used specifically to refer to royal land grants (*rājaśāsana*, lit. 'the decree [*śāsana*] of a ruler [*rājā*]'). "For the guidance of future kings and vassals the king should write that the violation of the grant will lead to condemnation in hell lasting for sixty thousand years, and its observance to the attainment of heaven for the same period. The grant is called *dharmasetu*, which should be observed by all future kings in all ages" (Sharma 2002: 167).

The composers of several early ninth century inscriptions used the term *dharmasetu* in precisely the same sense as in the Kalasan inscription. For example, an almost identical stanza was appended to the traditional minatory[48] verses of Vyāsa "from about the beginning of the ninth century, and first in Rāṣṭrakūṭa domains. Among the earliest instances I have located are the Sīsavai Grant of Govinda III (AD 807) [Rāṣṭrakūtas of Guajart] *EI*, 23.212 (Rāmacandra), and the Nilgund Inscription of Amoghavarṣa I (AD 815-75), *EI*, 6.105 (Rāmabhadra)" (Vyas and Shah 1995: 155, n. 33).

Brandes (1886: 259-260) also noted the similarities between strophe ten of the Kalasan inscription and a strophe from a substantially younger Indian charter: the Amgachi Grant of Vigrahapāla III that presents the lineage of the Pāla-kings of Bengal (Asiatic Society of Bengal 1885: II: 213). The Amgachi Grant is comparable to the Kalasan inscription with respect to the original order of the half-verses as they actually appear in the Śailendra charter. Except for the simplification of the royal appellation, which in this instance is given as Rāma, once again the message is essentially the same as in earlier examples.

For comparative purposes, the relevant stanzas from the Sisavai and Amgachi grants are presented below, together with the equivalent passage from the Kalasan charter. Given that *bhāvinaḥ* (from *bhāvin*, 'future') in the Sīsavai Grant conveys the same meaning as *āgāminaḥ*, the two statements are quite similar, except for the exchanges of *nṛpānāṃ* ('kings' e.g. 'common to all kings') for *narāṇāṃ* ('men', e.g. 'common property among men') and either *rāmacandraḥ or rāmaḥ* in place of *rājasiṃhaḥ*. What's more, the order of the half-verses alternates between the Sīsavai Grant and the Kalasan charter.

By contrast, in the Amgachi Grant promulgated by the twelfth ruler of the Pāla royal line, the half-verses appear in the same order as they do in the Kalasan charter. *Bhāvina* once again conveys the same meaning of 'future' as *āgāmina*, while *prārthayati* ('desire, wish, ask for') is comparable to *yācate* ('solicit, ask for') and *krameṇa* ('in order' e.g. each succeeding future king) replaces *bhavadbhiḥ* ('by you').

---

[47]Sundberg believes that a 'dh' is there to be read in the name of the king, having already examined the *abklatsch* that Shastri (1924) published with his edition of the Nālandā inscription. In explaining why the composer of the so-called Kĕlurak inscription would have also employed the word *dharmasetu* after its earlier appearance in the Kalasan inscription, Sundberg notes that the Kĕlurak inscription is quite difficult to read. "Bosch spent three years working on it, and encouraged others to try their hand at it, as he was not entirely certain of his readings and I would concur; it begs for rigorous documentation, done with modern understandings of the fluorescence signatures" (Sundberg, pc 17 April 2010).

[48]'Expressing or conveying a threat'.

Sīsavai Grant:

Sāmānyo 'ya dharmasetur nṛpānāṃ kāle kāle pālaniyo bhavadbhiḥ /
sarvān etān bhāvinaḫ pārthivendrān bhūyo bhūyo yācate rāmacandraḥ //

Kalasan Charter:

Sarvān evāgāminaḥ pārthivendrān bhūyo bhūyo yācate rājasiṃhaḥ /
Sāmānyo 'ya dharmmasetur narāṇāṃ kāle kāle pālanīyo bhavadbhiḥ //

Amgachi Grant:

Sarvān etān bhāvinaḥ pārthivendra[n] bhūyo bhūyaḥ prā[r]thayaty esha rāmaḥ /
Sāmānyo 'y[an dh]armasetur nṛipāṇā[ṃ] kāle kāle pālanīyaḥ krameṇa //

In the Baroda copperplate of Rāṣṭrakūṭa Karkkarāja II (812 CE), which "records the grant of the village of Vaḍapadraka to Bhānu, son of Bhaṭṭasomāditya, by Karkkarāja [II] Suvarṇavarṣa, the Rāṣṭrakūṭa king of Gujarat" (Solomon 1998: 284), the proper name Rāmabhadra is given in place of Rāmacandra. "And also the Lord Rāmabhadra said: 'Over and over Rāmabhadra begs all the future kings: this bridge to the Dharma, which is common to all kings...'." (Solomon 1998: 294).[49]

The similarities between the examples presented above, as well as a number of other comparable verses found in additional inscriptions from ancient India, Campā and Nepal, strongly suggest the existence of an even earlier source of this statement from which the composers of all these charters had drawn.[50] It is interesting that the Kalasan inscription

---

[49]Uktāñ=cha bhagavatā rāmabhadreṇa / Sarvvān=etān=bhāvinaḥ pārtthivendrān bhūyo bhūyo yāchate rāmabhadraḥ / sāmānyo=yaṃ dharmma-setur=nṛipāṇāṃ kāle kāle pālanīyo bhavadbhiḥ // (Fleet 1883: 161).

[50]Among the numerous other examples of this traditional formula pertaining to land grants are three inscriptions of the minor Chalukya dynasties of Andhra Pradesh: The Arikēsari (III) inscription of 968, which records the donation of lands by a chief Vujaya to a Jain Jinālaya constructed by king Arikēsari; the Guṇagarasa inscription of 1004 concerning the bestowal of a gift to the god Mallikārjuna; and the eleventh century Kusumāyudha (IV) grant of Mogaluchurvula to a Brāhmaṇa (Suryanarayana 1993: 22, 34, 36). Other examples were noted by Sarkar (1971/2: I: 40, n. 45) as well as Sircar (1965: 193), who also cited the following example from the *Skanda Purāṇa* (v.40):

Dattvā bhūmiṃ bhāvinaḥ pārthiveśan=bhūyo bhūyo yācate rāmacandraḥ / sāmānyo='yaṃ dharma-set r==nṛpāṇāṃ sve sve kāle pālanīyo bhavadbhiḥ //

A section of an old palm-leaf manuscript entitled the *Skanda Purāṇa* written in the Gupta script was discovered in the royal library of Nepal by M. Haraprasad Sastri, who dated this material to the seventh century on paleographic grounds. "Professor Bendell and myself carefully examined the palaeography of the MS. at the Durbar Library, and we came to the conclusion that the work must have been copied at least two hundred years before the *Parameśvaratantra* in transitional Gupta character, described by Prof. Bendell in his Cam. Cat. So the MS. must have been copied before 659 A.D., as the *Parameśvaratantra* was copied in Harṣa era 252=859 A. D." (Sastri 1905: lii). However, the vast contents of the *Skanda Purāṇa* doubtlessly must have grown over the course of centuries, which means there is no way of knowing whether this particular text had served as the original source for the composer of the Kalasan inscription, short of finding it in the represents the earliest dated example of this type of traditional verse known to us; it may also be significant that the other earliest examples had originated from Gujarat. Strophe 14 of the Plaosan inscription refers to the pilgrims "who continually arrived from Gujara country (*gurjaradeśa*), bowed by the burden of devotion to the Buddhas ..." (de Casparis: 1956: 202).

All of these comparable verses from beyond Java's shores contain statements represented as ostensibly having been made by the epic hero Rāma (*rāmacandra, rāmabhadra* or *rāma*) in his role as the classic example of a "superordinate king" (Vyas and Shah 1995: 146). However, K. Bhattacharya (1972: 48) also observed that these references to Rāma, Rāmabhadra and Rāmacandra may actually properly pertain to the royal donor himself, who symbolically speaks in his role as the superordinate 'Rāma' of the era in which each charter was issued. Given that the Buddha's identification as a 'universal sovereign' (*cakravartin*) is a such a common theme in Buddhist art and literature, it is not difficult to view Rājasiṃha and Rājasiṃhena as having been intended to signify the Buddhist counterpart for Rāma, with the Śailendra donor speaking on behalf of the historical Buddha known by the epithet Śākyasiṃha.

Verse 11. *Pratītya-jāta* (e.g. *pratītya-samutpāda*) refers to the chain of consecutive links of Dependent Co-origination that comprise the stream of death and rebirth comprising *saṃsāra*, which includes ignorance; predisposition; consciousness; mind and body; six organs of sense; contact; feeling; craving; attachment; action; rebirth; old age and death. Moreover, the existence (and cessation) of each link in the chain is entirely dependent on the origination (and cessation) of the preceding link. A Buddhist Sanskrit treatise on *pratītya-samutpāda* incised on gold plates was discovered in Indonesia at some point during (or shortly after) World War II, at which point it was placed in the Batavia Museum in Jakarta. However, the original finding place and discoverer of this treatise remain unknown. Having examined these gold plates, de Casparis was of the opinion that the script represents:

> "a transitional phase between the Pallava script and the Old Javanese script of the oldest period. Very archaic forms frequently occur side by side with relatively modern forms" (1956: 49). "Allowing a wide margin, we might conclude that the most probable time of engraving would be between about 650 and 800 A. D." (1956: 52). "[T]here is hardly any doubt that the plates once belonged to an important religious foundation" [and] "there are only two centers which seriously come into consideration: the empire of Çrīvijaya and the Çailendra empire in Central Java" (de Casparis 1956: 56, including n. 23).

Given that it was reproduced in gold, this treatise was undoubtedly held in extremely high regard by the Buddhists who had produced it. It is also noteworthy that a text was chosen that contains a segment in which the chain of Dependent Co-origination is compared to the evolution of a ruler and his kingdom (see de Casparis 1956: 147), which suggests that this scripture may have been used in the instruction of kings and princes.

Nepalese version. "Some of the mythology of the *Skanda Purāṇa* is undoubtedly post-Gupta and consistent in spirit with the medieval South" (Clothey & Ramanujan 1978: 224).

Strophe 11 expresses the wish that all of those living beings produced in the three worlds become conversant in the instruction of the Jinas known as the chain of causation by means of the merit accruing from this *vihāra*. The expression *pratītya-jāta* is actually a synonym for the Buddhist philosophical term *pratītya samutpāda*, or chain of Dependent Co-Origination, and is comparable to the phrase *pratītya jātā dharme imi* that appears in *Lalitavistara* v.340.3 (see Chandra 1995: 216 and Karuṇāratne 1988: 35-37). Given the presumed importance of the aforementioned treatise on gold plates, we might speculate that Paṇaṃkaraṇa had received a personal instruction in Dependent Co-Origination from a Śailendra *guru* concerning "the prince who, with the help of his army commanders and ministers, attacks his neighbors and succeeds in building up an empire, — which, however, he loses afterward.... [J]ust as the foundation of an empire is necessarily followed by its dissolution, in the same way rebirth is always followed by redeath" (de Casparis 1956: 148, continuation of n. 126).

Verse 12. In the final strophe of the Kalasan charter, Paṇaṃkaraṇa delivers a message that is almost identical to the one given by the 'Lion among Kings' in strophe ten: for future kings to maintain this 'bridge to the Dharma' (*dharmasetu*). I can recall of no other example of such a redundancy occurring within a single Sanskrit inscription from Central Java, and as far as I am aware no scholar other than Bosch has offered a cogent explanation for why this would be the case. Moreover, none of the other inscriptions from southern Asia that refer to the maintenance of a *dharmasetu* possess more than one verse dedicated to this purpose.

Our discussion of the individual stanzas comprising the Kalasan charter would not be complete without commenting upon the instances in which specific key phrases were subsequently duplicated in the Abhayagirivihāra (Ratu Baka) charter of 792/3 CE. The initial half-verse of v.4 from the Kalasan charter is comparable to the expression *<r>ājye pravarddhamāne...samaratuṅgasya śailendra*...that appears in v.14 of the Abhayagirivihāra charter (de Casparis 1961). The compositum *vihāraparipālanārtham* from v.12 of the Kalasan charter also is found in line 15 of the Abhayagirivihāra charter, whilst the compound *jātārthavibhāgavijñāḥ* found in the same strophe from the Kalasan charter, which pertains to the Buddhist doctrine of Co-Dependent Origination (*pratītya-samutpāda*), likewise appears in the final strophe of the Abhayagirivihāra charter, as we shall see in Chapter IV. Additionally, in line 16 of the Abhayagirivihāra charter of 792/3 we encounter the phrase *san tavānakādibhiḥ saṇ* = *ḍa*..., the first part of which closely resembles the phrase *saṅ tavānakādibhiḥ* in v.9 of the Kalasan charter. It is also possible that the ensuing *saṇ* = *ḍa*... from the Abhayagirivihāra inscription had been the start of the title for another Javanese official, such as *saṅ ḍaputa ramyah* or *saṅ ḍapu hyang* (de Casparis 1956: 9-10, n. 52).

Yet when it comes to the discussion of spiritual matters, there are considerable differences between the two inscriptions. The Abhayagirivihāra charter expounds at considerable length on Buddhist religious themes throughout multiple stanzas. By contrast, we have already seen that the spiritual content in the Kalasan inscription is limited to the benedictory verse dedicated to Tārā and the next to last strophe dedicating the merit accruing from the establishment of the *vihāra*. The remainder of the composition refers to the donation of land in support of the temple and associated monastery as well as their presumed receipt of a tax except status, if our understanding of the official role of the 'Three honored ones' (*sang māna katrīṇi*) is correct.

What is also worth mentioning in our discussion of the Kalasan inscription is the composer's selective use of metrics. One way for a poet to display his prowess is through the extensive use of meter variations. With respect to the Kalasan charter, however, the poet employs a standard workhorse for Sanskrit poets—the Āryā meter or its Udgīti variant—in all but four of the composition's twelve strophes. The alternate use of Vasantatilakā ('spring ornament') for the opening strophe is perfectly understandable given that it is obviously intended to stand apart from the remainder of the text as an invocatory verse (*maṅgalācaraṇa*) honoring the composition's principal divinity Tārā. However, we naturally wonder whether the composition's transition from Āryā meter to the Sumanika (v.9), Śālinī (v.10) and Upendravajrā (v.11) meters was expressly intended to differentiate each of these three verses before reverting to the Āryā meter in the final strophe of the inscription. Here, the meaning of 'The Lady' for Āryā may be relevant.

A critical review of the single-dynasty and two-dynasties theories

Zakharov (2012: 4) has argued against the aforementioned two-dynasties theory for interpreting the Kalasan charter by posing and answering the following two questions: "why is the suzerain called simply 'king' (*rājan*) while his vassal claims to be [a] 'great king' (*mahārāja*); second, why does the name of the suzerain not occur as well as the lineage of his vassal? Using Ockham's principle, the simplest answer is that there was only one king who was called *dyāḥ* Pañcapaṇa Paṇaṃkaraṇa, 'ornament of the Śailendra dynasty' (*śailendravaṅśatilaka*), great king (*mahārāja*), 'lion of kings' (*rājasiṅha*), and *kariyāna*..."

In some respects the above argument echoes the views of Boechari (1966: 246-248; 2011: 358) and Damais (1968: 356), and in all three cases the proponents have clearly weighted the evidence in favor of their respective arguments.[51] In my opinion, the issue of whether or not Paṇaṃkaraṇa (746-784) had been a member of the Śailendra dynasty is in need of a more balanced evaluation.

Damais wrote that it would be inconceivable from the perspective of protocol for a royal charter to assign the title Śrī Mahārāja to a king who was dependent on another sovereign during a period in which this designation was allegedly the highest title in use, while his lord or supreme king would be indicated by an dynastic epithet, without any name or title. It should be noted, however, that the Kalasan charter never actually refers to Paṇaṃkaraṇa as Śrī Mahārāja. Furthermore, we do not necessarily need to presume that Paṇaṃkaraṇa had

[51]Boechari's viewpoint also was influenced by de Casparis' (1950: 21, n.4) reading of the first quarter of the second strophe of the Kalasan charter as *āvahya mahārājaṃ tejaḥpūrṇnāpaṇaṃ paṇaṃkaraṇam,* which was not adopted in this chapter's preceding transcription and translation segment. "Moreover, it is not very likely that a vassal king should use such lofty *epitheta ornantia* as *mahārāja tejaḥpūrṇāpaṇa paṇaṃkaraṇa*" (Boechari 1966: 246; 2011: 358). It also should be noted that de Casparis' initial reading of v.2 from the Kalasan charter originally was presented in tandem with his speculative reconstruction of the following verse fragment from the Abhayagirivihāra charter: *rājyaṃ alaṃkurvāṇaṃ tejaḥpūrṇnāpa<ṇaṃ paṇaṃkaraṇam>,* which he regarded as a reference to Paṇaṃkaraṇa following his presumed abdication (de Casparis 1950: 21). As we shall see in Chapter IV, however, a more plausible interpretation of v.10 from the Abhayagirivihāra charter can be proposed that does not involve any reference to the preceding Śailendra monarch.

been the vassal of a Śailendra king in 778 CE.[52] It would not be surprising for an independent monarch to have been declared a 'great king' within his own dominions.

Zakharov, Damais and Boechari never addressed an even bigger question: why would the Śailendra monarch have identified himself as "Śrī Mahārāja by name" on the B-side of the Isthmus of Kra stele—a point which Damais himself had emphasized elsewhere in the same article—and also have promulgated a roughly contemporary inscription on Java that presents his proper name together with his Sanskritized Javanese title (*kariyāna*) as well as the royal Sanskrit appellations *mahārāja* (vs.2,6) and *śrīmān* (v.12)? It was not until the promulgation of the so-called Kĕlurak inscription of 782 CE that a variant of the Śailendra king's destroyer-of-foes epithet became transformed into a Sanskritized coronation name, as we shall see in the following chapter. Within the context of the Kalasan charter, especially v.10, the inscription's composer may even have considered Rājasiṃha to have been a regal appellation superior to that of *mahārāja*, or at a minimum one that would avoid the potential for confusion with respect to references to the Mahārāja Paṇaṃkaraṇa.

If Paṇaṃkaraṇa had indeed been the Śailendra king designated as the 'ornament of the Śailendra dynasty' in the Isthmus of Kra, Kĕlurak and Nālandā inscriptions, then why did the Javanese refrain from perpetuating the dynastic designation *śailendravaṅśatilaka* on Java following the death of Samaratuṅga? Jordaan (2006: 11-12) argues that one would logically expect that at least some of the kings ruling in Central Java from the mid-ninth century onward would have claimed descent from the famous Śailendravaṅśa in order to legitimize their claims to the throne. And even if one were to presume that this illustrious family had been a dynasty of Javanese origin,[53] then Jordaan believes it stands to reason that the Javanese people would have called upon a member of the Śailendravaṅśa to ascend the throne during the 'leaderless' (*ana-yaka-*) period (February 887 – November 894) during which there was no supreme sovereign ruling the kingdom, according to the Wanua Tĕngah III inscription. "It is well known that for the Javanese a situation of 'leaderlessness' is generally put on a par with social and political unrest and lawlessness, often leading them to look for 'strong' persons whom they hope will restore public order. The passing over of the Śailendras is the more remarkable given the fact that they had left Java only recently, that is to say within living memory".

The disappearance from Java of all references to the Śailendra dynasty after 824 CE suggests that this regal designation had been associated with a rival royal family that had been ousted out of power and expelled from the country. As Jordaan points out, all we

[52]The vassal theory rests upon the contents of the Nālandā copperplate (Sastri 1942: 102), which refers to an unnamed Śailendra monarch as the king of Yavabhūmi (Java). However, the Nālandā charter was promulgated in Bengal, India more than 60 years after the Kalasan inscription. As Pollock (2006: 149) has argued, "distinguishing the reality of lineage affiliation from its mere representation poses serious problems".

[53]De Casparis (1956: 318, n. 20) thought that the ascension to the throne of Rakai Kayuwaṅi dyaḥ Lokapāla (855–885 CE) mentioned in v.9 of the Śivagṛha inscription (856 CE) had been "represented as a national liberation (cf. the use of *swastha*). The result of the restauration was that also the Brāhmaṇic structure of the society was introduced (or re-introduced), at least in theory." This would seem to provide a modicum of support for the hypothesis that a dynasty of foreign origin had been expelled from Central Java in 855 CE. On the other hand, Acri (2010: 490, including n. 27) subsequently translated the Old Javanese word *swastha* in the more general sense of 'happy, satisfied, safe', etc. "The kingdom and the palace were taken by other hands. Prince Lokapāla, who was regarded (by Rakai Pikatan) as a younger brother, was King. The subjects were safe, divided into the four classes with the Brahmans ahead".

know for certain is that the scions of the Śailendravaṅśa had resettled on the Malay Peninsula from whence they gradually rebuilt their empire.[54]

The critics of the two-dynasties theory are rightfully skeptical of van Naerssen's presumption that Paṇaṃkaraṇa must have been a vassal of the Śailendra monarch. Referring to the relationship existing between the Śailendra dynasty and Rakaryān Patapān pu Palar in the founding of the Veṇuvanavihāra, as reflected by the contents of the Kayumwuṅan charter, van der Meulen (1979: 36, n. 52) stressed the lack of any evidence for suggesting that land or rent grants were ever made by a lower-status royal personage to another ruler enjoying a higher status, which would be "contrary to the spirit of a feudal hierarchy".

On the other hand, both the Nālandā charter and Larger Leiden grant provide us with examples of two different monarchs cooperating in the endowment of a Buddhist monastery without any indication that either king had been considered the vassal of the other. Indeed, the Larger Leiden grant records that in the twenty-first year of the reign of Rājarāja (1006 CE) the Cōḷa king donated a village to the Buddha residing in the Cūḷāmaṇivarmavihāra founded and constructed in the vicinity of Nagapattinam, South India by the Śailendra monarch Cūḷāmaṇivarman and his son Śrī Māravijayottuṅgavarman (Sastri 1940: 281-282).

Finally, the Nālandā charter states that Bālaputra had not only constructed a Buddhist *vihāra* within the territory of Devapāla, but also had granted the income from five villages as this monastery's endowment after having requested a royal edict for this purpose from the king of Bengal, according to the translation of v.33 submitted by Bosch.[55]

> "After all, by placing a comma after ['Having requested'] and inserting ['King Devapāladeva'] between commas, [Shastri (1924: 327)] suggests to the reader that Devapāladeva was the donor of the five villages and that this end of the document corresponds to what is communicated in the first part of the inscription. Now this is very definitely not the case. The name of the monarch Devapāladeva is in the accusative and can therefore never be the subject of *dadau*, 'donated'. The subject of the sentence is *asau* (second *pāda*), which refers to the Bālaputra designated in the preceding strophes. The purpose of v.33, what the poet also expresses on grammatical [grounds], cannot be anything other than this: 'He (Bālaputra), having solicited Devapāladeva by messengers for authorization and having an edict issued, donated the five villages whose use is designated above'.... Thus, we face the fact that Devapāla acts as the donor in the first part of the document whereas Bālaputra [acts as the donor] of the same five villages in the last part. To explain this contradiction we suggest the supposition that Devapāla's donation had not been made directly to the monastery founded at Nālandā, but to the

[54]That is, if de Casparis' emendation of *śailendravaṅśatilaka* to strophe five of the Kayumwuṅan charter is correct as Bosch (1952b) believed. De Casparis (1950: 39, 45) thought that this expression had also originally appeared in the Kayumwuṅan inscription, but only the syllable *śai-* could be read from the stone itself, though the outstanding syllables falling within the ensuing lacuna are indeed metrically compatible with this designation.

[55](Bosch 1925: 525): bhaktyā tatra samastaśatruvanitāvaidhavyadīksā guruṃ krtvā śāsanam āhitādharatayā yam prārthya dūtair asau | grāmān pañca vipañcitopariyathoddeśān imān ātmanaḥ pitrorllokahitodayā ca dadau śrī Devapālaṃ nṛpaṃ || 33

patron, Bālaputra, and that he in turn handed over the five villages, which he had acquired under this grant of disposal for covering the maintenance of the building and the necessities of monks, to the monastery foundation" (Bosch 1925: 526-527).

The absence from the Kalasan charter of any laudatory phrases or outright expressions of Buddhist sentiments that we might directly attribute to the king might plausibly be explained as due to the Śailendra monarch's absence from Java at the time that this charter had been composed, which is implied by the translation of strophe five as it is presented above. This could help to explain why the temple was said to have been constructed by the Śailendra preceptor(s) in this instance. Several Cam inscriptions, the Chinese annals and a tale preserved by the Arab trader Suleiman strongly suggest that military expeditions from the Indonesian Archipelago had been actively engaged in campaigns against the rulers of Cam and Khmer kingdoms on mainland Southeast Asia during this period (Sundberg 2011: 140-141; Jordaan and Colless 2009: 61; and Griffiths 2013: 43-81).

Moreover, the following hypothesis advanced by Bosch as an evolved interpretation of van Naerssen's two-dynasties theory offers a coherent explanation for why two different verses in the same charter present declarations calling upon future rulers to support the religious foundation.

"Although I do agree with his theory, I can not quite reconcile it with the roles accorded to the Śailendra king and Paṇaṃkaraṇa as proposed by van Naerssen. In his view there are two parties—on the one side the Śailendra with his gurus, on the other the Javanese king with the Javanese *desa*-heads–who teamed up in unison in the establishment of the foundation and are named in turn in the text, each time under the mention of a new particularity. However, if we continuously distinguish between the *mahārāja* (or *kariyāna*) named Paṇaṃkaraṇa and the Śailendra king referred to as *rāja* or *rājasiṃha*, the distribution [of tasks] becomes completely different. Then the strophes 2, 3, 4, 5, 7, 8, 9 and 10 are all related to the Śailendra whilst Paṇaṃkaraṇa only figures in strophes 2, 6 and 12" (Bosch 1952a: 113).

Bosch's interpretation offers a simple explanation for what otherwise amounts to an excessive duplication of statements throughout the Kalasan charter. For example, the almost identical declarations made in strophes 10 and 12 make better sense when we view them as expressing the entreaties of two different monarchs. In my opinion, however, strophes two through four seem more likely to pertain to Paṇaṃkaraṇa considering the context. In other words, the previously mentioned temple construction activities of Paṇaṃkaraṇa can be viewed as having been performed at the behest of the royal preceptor(s) of the Śailendra monarch and thus with the Śailendra 'Lion among Kings' having subsequently endowed the Saṅgha, according to strophe eight.

The appellation *rājasiṅha* appears to place the Śailendra monarch in the same role of superordinate king that Rāma fulfills in the inscriptions from Rāṣṭrakūṭa domains, whilst the second similar declaration by Paṇaṃkaraṇa in v.12 seems to be the mere echo of the prior entreaty. This suggests the possibility that Paṇaṃkaraṇa and his court officials had carried out the orders of the Śailendra preceptor(s) whilst the Śailendra monarch was engaged elsewhere. For his part, Paṇaṃkaraṇa (or the *sang māna katrīṇi* acting on his behalf) had installed the principal image, prepared the temple and monastic residence, and also had granted the hamlet of Kalasan for the support of the monastic community, presumably together with the granting of freehold rights.

As witnesses to the agreement, the *sang māna katrīṇi* as well as the *adhyakṣān* also undoubtedly helped with the provision of local labor, e.g. "caused to be made" (*kārita*). One potential argument for the two-dynasties theory would be that it was for this very reason that the declaration of Paṇaṃkaraṇa in strophe 12 pertains to the *vihāra*, whilst the comparable declaration in strophe 10 to be observed by the kings of the Śailendra dynasty pertains to the Tārā temple, therein identified as the 'bridge to the Dharma' (*dharmasetu*), as would also be thought to have been the case with the Mañjughoṣa *dharmasetu* subsequently mentioned in the so-called Kĕlurak inscription.

One point potentially in favor of the single-dynasty theory is the fact that the Mahārāja Paṇaṃkaraṇa (746—784) had also donated irrigated rice fields to another Buddhist religious foundation[56] soon after ascending the throne in 746 CE, according to the Wanua Tĕngah III charter. This was the Buddhist monastery at Pikatan founded by rahyangta i Hāra, who is presumed by Wisseman Christie (2001: 33-34) to have either been the younger brother of Sañjaya—the founder of Central Java's most celebrated lineage of kings—or the subordinate ruler ('younger brother') of another kingdom subsumed by Sañjaya.[57]

Though Paṇaṃkaraṇa appears to have developed a strong relationship with the Buddhist community in Central Java, his donations do not prove that the Javanese *mahārāja* had been a Buddhist. For example, if Paṇaṃkaraṇa had been the son of King Sañjaya, as historians generally presume, then his grant to a Buddhist monastery founded by his uncle may have been solely for the purpose of supporting the efforts or memory of his father's brother. Besides, other local Javanese aristocrats such as Ra karayān Patapān pu Palar likewise had donated irrigated rice-fields in support of another Buddhist temple and *vihāra* built by a member of the Śailendra family, as the Kayumwuṅan charter (824) demonstrates.

None of the proponents of the single-dynasty theory have been able to establish a convincing link between any of the Javanese rulers listed in the Mantyāsiḥ I and Wanua Tĕngah III charters and any of the Śailendra kings named in other inscriptions. Sundberg (2011), for example, has argued in an unconvincing manner that Samaratuṅga—who he attempted to equate with Rakai Panaraban (784-803), the successor of Panaṅkaran—had been deposed and imprisoned by his own son (e.g. by Rakai Warak dyaḥ Manara, 803-827). Among other things, his hypothesis is based on the contents of the Old Sundanese *Carita Parahyangan*, which is significantly younger than the relevant Javanese *praśasti*-s dating from the eighth and ninth centuries. Moreover, Sundberg does not explain why a charter promulgated in 824 CE, e.g. during the reign of the presumed usurper Rakai Warak, would have continued to laud Samaratuṅga if he had been deposed. In light of the emphasis given to Prāmodavarddhanī in the Kayumwuṅan charter as well as the fragmentary state of this

[56]His successor Rakai Panaraban (784—803) took no action affecting this grant, but the Pikatan monastery's so-called *sīma* rights were subsequently withdrawn by Rakai Warak (803—827), only to be later reinstated in 829 by Rakai Garung (Wisseman Christie 2001: 29-30).

[57]"It was he, known as the holy ancestor of Hāra, younger brother of the holy ancestor of Mḍang [e.g. Sañjaya], who founded the Buddhist monastery at Pikatan, as a permanent sign [of his piety]" (Ibid.).

inscription, the only plausible explanation which occurs to me, and was also the suspicion of Damais (1968: 361), is that Samaratuṅga had died prior to 824 CE (see Chapter V).

Sundberg (2011: 142, n. 10) also points out that the Wanua Tĕngah III charter refers to the posthumous remains of Rakai Warak dyaḥ Manāra having been 'interred' (*lumaḫ*) at Kelāsa, which Wisseman Christie had earlier sought to link with the village Kalasan donated by Paṇaṃkaraṇa to the residence of Tārā. Under Sundberg's theory, Paṇaṃkaraṇa would be the grandfather of Warak, hence potentially explaining why Rakai Warak might have selected this hamlet as the locale for a final resting place. On the other hand, it was Warak who had first vacated the *sīma* rights that Paṇaṃkaraṇa had granted to the Buddhist monastery at Pikatan.

The proposition that Warak had actually been 'interred' at Kalasan, e.g. with his relics, not his ashes, having been placed in a separate structure located nearby, seems an odd choice for a king who had vacated the *sīma* provisions of the Buddhist monastery at Pikatan founded by Sañjaya's 'younger brother' and supported by Rakai Warak's presumed grandfather Paṇaṃkaraṇa under Sundberg's theory. And given that Damais (1968: 392-393) has characterized Kālasa as a Sanskritization of the Old Javanese toponym Kalasan, one naturally wonders why it would have been rendered as Kelāsa in a later Old Javanese inscription.

Several ninth and tenth century Javanese inscriptions warn against taking any actions that are detrimental to the well-being of religious foundations, notifying potential transgressors that they risk being "thrown off the firmament" as a result. And it is not any stretch of the imagination to suppose that one's risk of being denied a posthumous ascent to heaven would only be compounded by the commission of an act that transgressed the express wishes of a highly esteemed ancestor. Sundburg's explanation that Rakai Warak may have vacated the Pikatan *sīma* rights because he was in need of additional tax revenue would hold greater weight if the overall theory did not also attempt to represent this Javanese king as a direct descendant of Sañjaya.

III: The Śrī Saṅgrāmadhanaṃjaya inscription from the *desa* Kĕlurak

In 1868, a Sanskrit inscription was reported as having come into the possession of the Batavian Society through the efforts of Raden Saleh (NBG 1868: 60). Cataloged as D.44, the stone measures 45 cm. in height by 73 cm. in breadth and displays 16 lines of small inscribed characters of the Siddhamātṛkā script. The inscription was discovered in the *desa* Kĕlurak formerly located to the north of the latitude of Caṇḍi Prambanan, which is approximately 15 kilometers to the east of Yogyakarta in Central Java. However, the precise location of the stone's place of discovery within the former *desa* was never specified. The southern perimeters of the Buddhist temples of Caṇḍi Bubrah and Caṇḍi Sewu are located approximately 520 m. and 725 m., respectively, to the north of the Prambanan complex's second enclosure gate in the north; and the distance separating Prambanan's second enclosure gate in the north and the southern perimeter of Caṇḍi Lumbung to the northeast is approximately 350 m.[1]

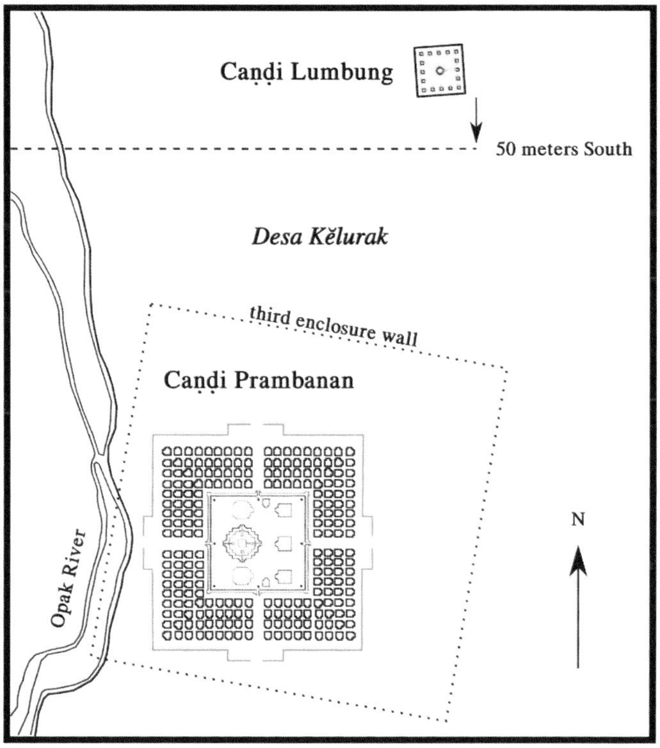

Fig. 3-1. The former *desa* Kĕlurak.

"The *desa* Kĕlurak covers a fairly large area: the southern border runs approximately five m. to the south of the third northern enclosure-wall of the Prambanan complex: the northern border about 50 m. south of Caṇḍi Lumbung; the western border is in line with the present-day western line of demarcation of the Prambanan terrain, whilst the eastern border continues the eastern border of the Lumbung temple complex. Although there is therefore a chance in theory that the stone originated from the border of Prambanan, it is nevertheless much more likely that it was found close to the Buddhist sanctuary than near the Śaivaite complex" (Bosch 1929a: 50).

[1]These distance calculations were performed using satellite view within Google Maps in tandem with an online software program hosted at http://movable-type.co.uk/scripts/latlong.html (active as of 14 July 2014).

The first western Sanskrit epigraphy expert to examine the stone was A. C. Burnell, who declared it to be "very illegible" (1878: 53, n. 5). In 1886, however, Brandes succeeded in reading the opening words *namo ratnatrayāya*, wherewith it became apparent to him that just like the previously known inscription found in the vicinity of the *desa* Kalasan, the *praśati* found in the *desa* Kĕlurak was a Buddhistic inscription composed in Sanskrit. Having assigned the stone a tentative date of Śaka 704, Brandes also concluded that the so-called Kĕlurak inscription had been sponsored by the same king of the Śailendra dynasty who promulgated the Kalasan charter of Śaka 700 (778 CE). Given that the inscription speaks of the Buddha, Dharma and Saṅgha having been established in a religious foundation, it seemed to Brandes (Groeneveldt & Brandes 1887: 389) that the inscribed stone would have belonged to Caṇḍi Lumbung, a Buddhist temple which in Brandes' opinion was also dedicated to the *ratnatraya*, based on the presence of the three niches in the back wall of the central shrine.

Fig. 3-2. The inscription from Kĕlurak (photo credit: Gunkarta Gunawan Kartapranata).

On the other hand, the interior chamber of Caṇḍi Lumbung's central temple also contains three more niches in either sidewall plus one each on either front wall flanking the doorway, thus eleven niches in total. In discussing the possibility that the Sanskrit inscription found in the *desa* Kĕlurak might originally have come from Caṇḍi Sewu, as Rouffaer (1909: 150) had previously suggested, Krom (1923: I: 270-271) remarked that four short inscriptions discovered at Sewu feature a variant of the so-called Early Kawi (dubbed Palaeojavanese by Damais) script that in his opinion did not gain currency until some time after the attested date of the so-called Kĕlurak inscription. Furthermore, Krom observed that a Sewu find place would put the original location of the stone considerably further to the north than Caṇḍi Lumbung. With respect to the inscription's possible relationship with either Caṇḍi Sewu or Caṇḍi Lumbung, more will be said later in this chapter.

Annotated transcription and revised translation

The annotated transcription that appears below is based on the one from Bosch (1929a: 1-56), who also provided an extensive translation. Chatterjee (1926: 60), Majumdar (1933: 122-123), de Casparis (1950: 102-103, 144-146), Damais (1955: 205), Sarkar (1971/2: I: 41-47; 1977/8: 929), Chandra (1995: 218-224) and Zakharov (2012: 4-5) also have contributed emendations and/or partial translations as well as short comments. Moreover, the present author has inserted a metric correction in one of the strophes and also has extensively revised the stanza translations.

Opening Salutation; strophes one and two (Āryāgīti[2] meter)

// namo ratnatrayāya //

Homage to the Three Jewels!

jayalokeśvarasugatapadākṣara jayabhadreśvarasugatapadākṣara /
jayaviśveśvarasugatapadākṣara jaya — — śvarasugatapadākṣara // (1)

| ⏑⏑— | —⏑⏑ | ⏑⏑⏑⏑ ‖ —⏑⏑ | ⏑⏑— | —⏑⏑ | ⏑⏑⏑⏑ | —⏑⏑ ‖ first hemistich
| ⏑⏑— | —⏑⏑ | ⏑⏑⏑⏑ ‖ —⏑⏑ | ⏑⏑— | —⏑⏑ | ⏑⏑⏑⏑ | —⏑⏑ ‖ second hemistich

1. O, the unchanging intrinsic nature of the Buddhahood of the Lord of the World, hail to thee! O, the unchanging intrinsic nature of the Buddhahood of the Lord of Well-being, hail to thee! O, the unchanging intrinsic nature of the Buddhahood of the Lord of the Universe, hail to thee! O, the unchanging intrinsic nature of the Buddhahood of the Lord of ..., hail to thee!

1. O, the unchanging intrinsic nature (akṣara, sing. vocative)[3] **of the Buddhahood** (sugatapada)[4] **of the Lord of the World** (lokeśvara),[5] **hail to thee** (jaya)![6] **O, the unchanging intrinsic nature** (akṣara) **of the Buddhahood** (sugatapada) **of the Lord of Well-being** (bhadreśvara), **hail to thee! O, the unchanging intrinsic nature** (akṣara) **of the Buddhahood** (sugatapada) **of the Lord of the**

---

[2] The first two strophes of the Śrī Saṅgrāmadhanaṃjaya inscription were composed in Āryāgīti meter, which is also known as *skandhaka*—a form of musical bar meter (*gaṇachandas*). Bosch thought v.3 might also have been composed in the Āryāgīti meter.

[3] See the discussion segment for this verse.

[4] *Sugatapada* also can potentially mean Bodhisattvahood; see the discussion segment for this verse.

[5] A designation associated with Amitābha as well as his spiritual family, otherwise known as the *padmakula*.

[6] Chandra (1995: 218; pc 2 Nov. 2010) noted that *jaya* can be interpreted as the verbal imperative 'hail to thee', which is found in Bengalese oral folk-tales (Kundu 2008: 301) and the literary traditions of India (Shanbhag 2007: 171). Perhaps another plausible translation for *jaya* would be, 'who is victorious'.

Universe (viśveśvara), **hail to thee! O, the unchanging intrinsic nature** (akṣara) **of the buddhahood** (sugatapada) **of the Lord of** ...,[7] **hail to thee!**

dharṣati yo [2] lokeśa<ṃ> dhartu<ṃ> mūrdhnāmitābham api lokeśvaraṃ /
praṇamata taṃ lokeśaṃ sakaladigantāvabhāsanālokeśaṃ // (2)

| — ⏑ ⏑ | — — | — — ‖ — — | — — | ⏑ — ⏑ | ⏑ ⏑ — | — ⏑ ⏑ ‖ first hemistich
| ⏑ ⏑ ⏑ ⏑ | — — | — — ‖ ⏑ ⏑ ⏑ ⏑ | — — | ⏑ — ⏑ | — — | — — ‖ second hemistich

2. Pay homage unto Him, the Lord who dares to bear on his head even the Lord of the Worlds Amitābha, the Lord illuminating all the directions, the Lord of Light.

2. **Pay homage** (praṇamata, read as praṇamatha, sec. pers. sing. present active of pra- √nam, 'make homage to') **unto Him** (tam), **the Lord** (lokeśam, sing. acc. of lokeśa) **who** (yo = yas) **dares** (dharṣati, third person sing. present from √dhṛṣ) **to bear** (dhartum, the indeclinable infinitive of √dhṛ)[8] **even** (api) **the Lord of the worlds** (lokeśvaram, sing. acc. of lokeśvara) **Amitābha** (amitābham, sing. acc. of amitābha) **on his head** (mūrdhna, read as mūrdhan), **the Lord** (lokeśam, sing. acc. of lokeśa) **shining** (avabhāsana) **in all the directions** (sakala-diganta), **the Lord** (īśam, sing. acc. of īśa) **of light** (āloka).[9]

Strophe Three (Āryā or Āryāgīti meter ?)

---

yātasthā*mavacaratayaḥ* śarumān — — — — — — — — /
saṅgata — navaratnaṃ mām api [3] bhayabhītam avacara<n>taṃ // (3)

Given the lengthy lacuna and the uncertainty about the identity of the meter, further discussion of this verse shall be reserved for a later chapter segment.

Strophes four, five and six (Vasantatilakā meter)

— — ⏑ | — ⏑ ⏑ | ⏑ — ⏑ | ⏑ — ⏑ | — ⏓ ‖

---

sāmantamantripati*saṃskṛ*tasatkrameṇa
dikcakrarājavijayārjitavikrameṇa /
— — *ravairi*varavīravimardanena
nityaṃ parā*rtha*karu<ṇā> ⏑ ⏑ — <⏑>[10] mena // (4)

---

[7]Perhaps, 'Lord of speech' (*<vāgī>śvara*), 'Lord of wealth' (*<ratne>śvara*) or 'Lord of the thunderbolt' (*<vajre>śvara*).
[8]See Whitney 1885: 84.
[9]Vilāsavajra, the eighth-century *Namasaṃgīti* (NS) commentator and student of the celebrated *ācārya* Mañjuśrīmitra, linked *āloka* to *ādarśa* and thus to the Mirror-like Awareness of Akṣobhya (*ādarśanajñāna*). So *ālokeśa* might alternately mean 'the lord of sight' (see Tribe 1994: 96, n. 84).
[10]Though not marked on the original transcript, this additional short syllable is required to complete the meter based on the entire reading by Bosch. Sarkar (1971/2: I: 42) likewise failed to detect this.

4. Prepared by a venerable succession of feudatory princes, ministers and lords, with valor being attained through victories over kings in all the directions by crushing the valiant heroes of (powerful) enemies, ... he always (is compassionate) for the sake of others.

4. **Prepared** (saṃskṛta) **by a venerable** (sat) **succession** (kramena, the sing. instr. of krama) **of feudatory princes** (sāmanta), **ministers** (mantri, read as mantrī) **and lords** (pati), **with valor** (vikramena, the sing. instr. of vikrama) **being attained** (arjita, past passive participle, from √ṛj) **through victories** (vijaya) **over kings** (rāja) **in all the directions** (dikcakra) **by crushing** (vimardanena, the sing. instr. of vimardana) **the valiant heroes** (varavīra) **of** ... [powerful][11] **enemies** (vairi)[12] ... **he always** (nityam, an adverb) [is compassionate (karu<ṇāyati>, third pers. sing. present of √karuṇ)] **for the sake of others** (parārtha).[13]

śailendravaṅśatilakena maho [4] dayena
yasya kramāmbujarajaḥ *śiras*ā praṇamya /
sampūjya*te pravararatna*saroruhādyai
rājñā dhṛtā dhṛtimatā dharaṇīndra<nāmnā>[14] // (5)

5. By the ornament of the Śailendra dynasty who is conferring prosperity as the dust of his lotus feet is worshiped with excellent jewels, lotus flowers and so forth (by persons) after having bowed down with the head (in homage), by (that) king of steadfast (disposition) ..., the earth is sustained.

5. **By the ornament** (tilakena, sing. instr. of tilaka) **of the Śailendra dynasty** (śailendravaṅśa) **who is conferring prosperity** (mahodayena, sing. instr. of mahodaya) **as the dust** (rajaḥ) **of his** (yasya, sing. genitive pronoun) **lotus feet** (kramāmbujaḥ)[15] **is worshiped** (sampūjyate, third pers. sing. passive of sam + √pūj) **with excellent** (pravara) **jewels** (ratna), **lotus flowers** (saroruh) **and so forth** (ādyai = ādyaiḥ, pl. instr. of ādya) [by persons] **after having bowed down** (praṇamya, absolutive of √praṇam) **with the head** (śirasā, sing. instr. of śiras) [in homage], **by** [that] **king** (rājñā, sing. instr. of rājan) **of steadfast** [disposition] (dhṛtimatā) ...,[16] **the earth** (dharaṇī, sing. nom. of dharaṇī) **is sustained** (dhṛtā, 'borne, held, maintained, supported').

tenendra — ⏑ ⏑ ⏑ — ⏑ ⏑ — vilokya
lokaṃ kṛpaparigatena jaga*ddhit*āya /
vai [5] *pulyavipra*tilakena tathāgato*ktam*

[11]Based on the other known epithets for this particular Śailendra monarch, it is plausible to suggest that 'enemies' (*vairi*) had been qualified by a Sanskrit adjective ending in *-ra* meaning 'powerful'.
[12]Sarkar (1971/2: I: 45, n. 27) expressed doubt about Bosch's readings of *vīra* and *vairi.*
[13]The fragment *-mena*, is probably the sing. instr. ending of a Sanskrit word lost in the preceding lacuna.
[14]The alternate reading of *dharaṇīndra<rena>* was proposed by de Casparis, who thought that this would simply mean 'by the (Śailendra) king' (see Cœdès 1959: 48). However, the facsimile of the inscription is not clear. "The letters *<rena>* have been read by [F.D.K. Bosch and] H.B. Sarkar as *nāmnā*. The reading *-ndra<rena>* cannot be accommodated. It will have to be read on the original stone where the chisel marks may contribute to a meaningful reading" (Chandra, pc 7 June 2014).
[15]This expression is comparable to *padāmbuja*, which conveys the same meaning, though the singular *kramāmbujaḥ* might have been intended to convey an additional nuance pertaining to the sitting posture known as royal ease (*rājalīlāsana*), in which only one leg is pendant.
[16]Sarkar (1971/2: I: 45) translated *indranāmnā* as, 'of the name of Indra'.

— — ⏑ — ⏑ balinā bala — utena // (6)

6. By him ... who, after having seen the world of human beings..., was overpowered by compassion for the sake of the welfare of the people, by the ornament of theologians (learned in) the *sūtra*-s of great expansion (was uttered) a saying of the Tathāgata ... .

6. **By him ...** (tenendra = tena-indra: tena, third pers. sing. instr. pronoun; indra, the initial part of a compound lost in the ensuing lacuna)[17]... **who, after having seen** (vilokya, the absolutive of vi-lok) **the world of human beings** (lokam, sing. acc. of loka) ...[18] **was overwhelmed** (parigatena, sing. instr. of parigata) **by compassion** (kṛpa, read as kṛpā) **for the sake of the welfare** (hitāya, sing. dative of hita) **of the people** (jagadd = jagat), **by the ornament** (tilakena, sing. instr. of tilaka) **of theologians** (vipra, 'learned theologian') [learned in] **the *sūtra*-s of great expansion** (vaipulya) [was uttered] **a saying** (uktam) **of the Tathāgata** ... .[19]

Strophes seven and eight (Śārdūlavikrīḍita meter)

— — — | ⏑ ⏑ — | ⏑ — ⏑ | ⏑ ⏑ —, | — — ⏑ | — — ⏑ | ⏓ ||

---

gauḍīdvīpagurukramāmbujarajaḥpūtottamāṅgātmanā
<saṃgūḍh>*ārthavi*<bhāma>*hārddhisahadā* *saṃveda* — — ⏑ ⏓ /[20]
— — — ⏑ ⏑ — ⏑ — ⏑ ⏑ ⏑ — [6] prāptābhiṣekaṃ śriyā
śreyaḥ kāra ⏑ — ⏑ — ⏑ ⏑ ⏑ — — — ⏑ *vidvadriyā* // (7)

7. By him, whose head was purified by the dust of the lotus-feet of the preceptor from Gauḍīdvipa, (who) was illuminated by the esoteric significance, (who attained) great supernatural power equally with the ... of consciousness ... who obtained consecration with the enrichment of well-being ... .

7. **By him** (ātmanā, sing. instr. of ātman) **whose head** (uttamaṅga) **was purified** (pūta) **by the dust** (rajaḥ) **of the lotus-feet** (kramāmbuja = krama-ambuja) **of the preceptor** (guru) **from Gauḍīdvipa, who was illuminated** (vibhā) **by the esoteric** (saṃgūḍha, 'completely concealed or hidden from view') **significance** (artha, 'meaning, true sense'), [who attained (prāpta)] **great supernatural power** (mahārddhi = mahāṛddhi) ...[21] ... **of consciousness** (saṃveda), ... **who obtained** (prāpta) **consecration** (abhiṣekam, sing. acc. of abhiṣeka) **by means of the enrichment** (śriyā, sing. instr. of śrī, 'wealth, treasure, riches') **of well-being** (śreyaḥ = śreyas 'welfare, prosperity, bliss') ...[22] ... .[23]

---

[17]Given that so many Sanskrit compounds begin with *indra*° it is not possible to know exactly what the inscription's composer had intended to convey. Though *dharaṇīndrarena* from the prior verse can literally mean 'the Indra on the earth', we would expect *tenendra* in verse six to be reference to the Śailendra *guru* (i.e. the *vaipulyavipratilaka*).

[18]Sarkar (1971/2: I: 45) thought that 'steeped in miseries' would fit the context of the initial half verse.

[19]For the text fragment in the fourth quarter, Chandra (pc 20 Nov. 2010) suggested 'with mighty (*balinā*, sing. instr. of *balin*) [ritual] power (*bala*)'.

[20]Sarkar (1971/2: I: 43) failed to note the emended readings previously provided by de Casparis (1950: 144).

[21]In place of the uncertain reading of *sahadā*, can be proposed samadhā, 'equally with'.

[22]The fragment *kāra-* has been left untranslated.

[23]Bosch's uncertain reading of *vidvadriyā* has been left untranslated.

sarvajño ⏑ ⏑ – ⏑ – ⏑ ⏑ ⏑ – – – *prad*ā*v*ojvalaḥ
sarvasthākhilaloka – ⏑ ⏑ ⏑ – – – ⏑ nīlotpalaḥ /
maṃjuśrīr ayam aprameya*su* [7] *gataprakhy*ā*ta*kīrttimahā
– – – ⏑ ⏑ – ⏑ rājaguruṇā lok*ā*r*thasa*ṃ*sth*āpitaḥ // (8)

8. Radiant in majesty ... omniscient ... of the blue lotus ... who is omnipresent throughout the entire world, this (image of) Mañjuśrī, whose abundance of glory has been enunciated by innumerable Sugatas ... was established by the preceptor of the king for the benefit of the world.

8. **Radiant** (ujvalaḥ, read as ujjvalaḥ, sing. nom. of ujjvala) **in majesty** (*prad*āva, read as prabhāva)[24] ... **omniscient** (sarvajño = sarvajñaḥ, sing. nom. of sarvajña) ..., ... **of the blue lotus** (nīlotpalaḥ) ... **who is omnipresent** (sarva-stha, 'everywhere abiding') **throughout the entire** (akhila) **world** (loka),[25] **this** (ayam) [image of] **Mañjuśrī** (maṃjuśrīr = mañjuśrīḥ, sing. nom. of mañjuśrī) **whose abundance** (mahā, sing. nom. of mahan) **of glory** (kīrtti = kīrti) **has been enunciated** (prakhyāta, 'told') **by innumerable** (aprameya, 'immeasurable') **Sugatas** ..., **was established** (saṃsthāpitaḥ, 'fixed, placed') **by the preceptor** (guruṇā, sing. instr. of guru) **of the king** (rāja) **for the benefit** (artha) **of the world** (loka).

Strophe nine (unidentified meter)[26]

d<ṛ>ṣṭ*a*ḥ[27] spṛṣṭaḥ smṛti*mi* .... itaḥ .... *tit*āpa . *iti*ḥ *sasu*khasya ....
setur mmaṃjughoṣaḥ saṃtoṣaḥ [8] .smāttasmādbhavadbhir ......
satkṛtta .... jjapadadṛṣtarataḥ kīrttist*ambha* .. smṛttiḥ // (9)

Strophe 10 (Śārdūlavikrīḍita meter)

|– – –| ⏑ ⏑ –| ⏑ – ⏑| ⏑ ⏑ –,|– – ⏑|– – ⏑| ⏓ ‖

prīyaṃ buddha ⏑ – ⏑ – ⏑ ⏑ ⏑ – – – ⏑ – – ⏑ ⏓
trailoky*ā*r*cita*saṃkramasya jagataḥ [9] trātur vidhātuḥ śriyaḥ /
kṛtvemāṃ pratimāṃ mayā *yadamita*ṃ prā*pta*ṃ *guru*ṃ *bhaktita*ṃ
sevā – ⏑ ⏑ locanaḥ smarajitaḥ – – ⏑ maṃjuśriyaṃ // (10)

10. ... the treasures of the three worlds were offered with reverence for the transition of the protector of the universe from the Creator; [speculative translation options for the problematic second half verse are presented in the discussion segment].

---

[24]Reading proposed by Chandra (1995: 220).
[25]Chandra (pc 20 Nov. 2010) conjectured that the preceding segment had referred to ['the benefactor'] of the entire world by all (*sarva*) his (*sva* in place of *sthā*) ['power'].
[26]A speculative translation for the following fragmentary strophe will be discussed later.
[27]See Sarkar 1971/2: I: 46, n. 14.

10. ...[28] **the treasures** (śriyaḥ, pl. nom. of śrī) **of the three worlds** (trailokya) **were offered with reverence** (arcita) **for the transition** (saṃkramasya, sing. genitive of saṃkrama) **of the protector** (trātur = trātuḥ, sing. genitive of tratṛ) **of the universe** (jagataḥ, sing. genitive of jagat) **from the Creator** (vidhātuḥ, sing. ablative of vidhātṛ);[29] ....

Strophes 11 and 12 (Āryā meter)

śakanṛpakālātītair varṣaśataiḥ saptabhiścaturbhirapi /
varṣaiḥ ku [10] māraghoṣaḥ sthāpitavān maṃjughoṣam imaṃ // (11)

|⏑⏑⏑⏑| — — | — — ‖— ⏑⏑ | — — | ⏑—⏑ | — ⏑⏑ | — ‖ first hemistich
| — — | ⏑—⏑ | — — ‖— ⏑⏑ | — — | ⏑ | — ⏑⏑ | — ‖ second hemistich

11. When four and seven hundred of the years of the era of the Śaka king had elapsed, Kumāraghoṣa established this Mañjughoṣa during the rainy season.

11. **When four** (caturbhir = caturbhiḥ, pl. instr. of catur) **and** (api) **seven** (saptabhiḥ, pl. instr. of sapta) **hundred** (śataiḥ, pl. instr. of śata) **of the years** (varṣa) **of the era** (kāla) **of the Śaka king** (śaka-nṛpa) **had elapsed** (atītair = atītaiḥ, pl. instr. of atīta, 'gone by'),[30] **Kumāraghoṣaḥ** (sing. nom.) **established** (sthāpitavān, sing. nom. of sthāpitavat, 'one who has fixed or placed') **this** (imam, third pers. sing. acc. pronoun) **Mañjughoṣa** (mañjughoṣam, sing. acc. of mañjughoṣa) **during the rainy season** (varṣaiḥ, pl. instr. of varṣa, lit. 'together with the rains').

*Vyatiṣyamvicinā̆manisara*guru. . . . . . .
kala . . *saptame* māse sthapitavāñca yathāham — // (12)

12. Given the uncertainty of Bosch's original transcription for strophe 12—indicated by the *akṣaras* presented in italics below—any further comments concerning a possible translation for v.12 shall be reserved for a later discussion of the segment.

Strophes 13, 14, 15 and 16 (ślokas)

---

kīrttistambho 'yam atulo [11] dharmmasetur anuttaraḥ /
rakṣārthaṃ sarvasatvānāṃ maṃjuśrīpratimākṛtiḥ // (13)

13. This peerless pillar of glory, this excellent bridge to the Dharma, this relics-house for the image of Mañjuśrī[31] is for the sake of the protection of all living beings.

---

[28]The first *pāda,* of which only *prīyaṃ buddha-* has survived, has been left untranslated.
[29]'A name for Brahmā as the creator of the world and the disposer of human fate.
[30]Śaka 704 is equivalent to 782 CE.
[31]Or, 'this creation (*kṛtiḥ*) for the likeness (*pratimā*) of Mañjuśrī'. Strophe 19 later identifies the *dharmasetu* as having been an edifice constructed for the image of the Kumāra, e.g. Mañjuśrī. Furthermore, Chandra (1995: 222) noted that *mañjuśrīpratimākṛtiḥ* can be an example of a *śleṣa* that also describes the exterior of the *kīrtistambha,* "which is resplendent (*śrī*) with the grace (*mañju*) of the forms (*ākṛtiḥ*) of the images

13. **This** ('yam = ayam, third pers. sing. nom. pronoun) **peerless** (atulo = atulaḥ, sing. nom. of atula 'unequaled') **pillar of glory** (kīrtistambho = kīrtistambhaḥ, sing. nom. of kīrtistambha), **this excellent** (anuttaraḥ, the sing. nom. of anuttara) **Bridge to the Dharma** (dharmmasetur = dharmasetuḥ, sing. nom. of dharmasetu), **this relics-house** (kṛtiḥ, sing. nom. of kṛti) **for the image** (pratimā) **of Mañjuśrī is for the sake of** (artham) **the protection** (rakṣā) **of all** (sarva) **living beings** (satvānāṃ = sattvānāṃ, pl. genitive of sattva).

atrabuddhaścadharmmaścasanghaścāntargataḥ sthit<ā>ḥ /[32]
dṛstavyo dṛśyaratne 'smin smarārāti [12] nisūdane //(14)

14. The Buddha, the Dharma and the Saṅgha which are present here, existing within (this pillar of glory), should be seen in this jewel of visible objects[33] as the destroyer of Desire's malevolence.

14. **The Buddha** (buddhaś = buddhaḥ, sing. nom. of buddha), **the Dharma** (dharmmaś = dharmmaḥ, sing. nom. of dharma) **and** (ca) **the Saṅgha** (sanghaś = saṅghaḥ, sing. nom. of saṅgha) **present** (sthit<ā>ḥ, pl. nom. of sthita) **here** (atas), **existing within** (antargataḥ) [this pillar of glory], **should be seen** (dṛstavyo, read as dṛstavyā)[34] **in this** (asmin, sing. locative third pers. pronoun) **jewel of visible objects** (dṛśyaratne) **as the destroyer** (nisūdane, sing. locative of nisūdana) **of Desire's malevolence** (smara-arāti).

ayaṃ sa vajradhṛk śrīmān brahmā viṣṇurmmaheśvaraḥ /
sarvadevamayaḥ svāmī maṃjuvāg iti gīyate // (15)

15. He the wielder of the thunderbolt (Indra), this one possessed of glory (Kubera), the Brahmā-Viṣṇu-Maheśvara, the Lord containing all the gods is thus hymned as 'Sweet-voiced' (Mañjuvāk).

15. **He** (sa = sas) **the wielder of the thunderbolt** (vajradhṛk, sing. nom. of vajradhṛk; i.e. Indra), **this** (ayam) **one possessed of glory** (śrīmān, the sing. nom. of śrīmat, a name for Kubera),[35] **the Brahmā-Viṣṇu-Maheśvara** (sing. nom.),[36] **the Lord** (svāmī, sing. nom. of svāmin) **containing all the gods** (sarvadevamayaḥ, sing. nom. of sarvadevamaya), **is thus** (iti) **hymned** (gīyate, third pers. sing. passive present of √gā 'praised', 'addressing with praise, verse, song') **as 'Sweet-voiced'** (maṃjuvāg = mañjuvāk).[37]

(*pratimā*)".
[32]Sarkar 1971/2: I: 44 & 46, n. 17.
[33]Or, 'jewel of the visible world'.
[34]Sarkar (1971/2: I: 46, n. 18) proposed reading *dṛṣtavyo* as *dṛṣtavyā,* which appears to be a variant spelling for *draṣṭavyā,* from √*dṛś*.
[35]See, for example, the entry for *śrīmat* in the *Monier-Williams Dictionary* and Gonda 1954: 195.
[36]e.g. the Hindu Trimūrti.
[37]A Sanskrit inscription carved on a rock at Tiriyay in Sri Lanka refers to Avalokiteśvara, Mañjuvāk (=Mañjuśrī) and the sanctity of the Girikaṇḍika-caitya (see Malalasekera 1961: 617). According to Vilāsavajra, "[In the expression] the Knowledge-Being Mañjuśrī {mañjuśrī:jñānasattva}, 'Mañjuśrī' means 'one possessing splendour (śrī) which is sweet (mañjuḥ > komala)' {mañju;śrīḥ}. He is a 'Knowledge-Being' since he dwells in the heart, [that is, the consciousness] of all the Tathāgatas. The Knowledge-Being Mañjuśrī

deśasya*ta*sya parārakṣāṃ parasvasya yatanaṃ sthiraṃ / [13]
maṃjuśrīr ayam atrāste kurvan *tavýohi*taśriyā // (16)

16. Situated in this place for welfare and prosperity, this Mañjuśrī who is active and strong shall be the paramount protection of another's property making a steadfast effort for his region.

16. **Situated** (aste, sing. locative of asta, lit. 'at home') **in this place** (atra) **for welfare** (*hi*ta, *metri causa* for hitā) **and prosperity** (śriyā), **this** (ayam) **Mañjuśrī** (maṃjuśrīr = mañjuśrīḥ, sing. nom. of mañjuśrī) **who is active** (kurvan, sing. nom. of kurvat) **and strong** (*tavyo*, = tavyaḥ, sing. nom. of tavya) **shall be the paramount** (parā) **protection** (rakṣām, sing. acc. of rakṣā) **of another's property** (parasvasya, sing. genitive of parasva) **making a steadfast effort** (yatanam, sing. acc. of yatana, 'making effort'; sthiram, sing. acc. of sthira, lit. 'firm, steady, not wavering or tottering') **for his region** (deśasya, sing. genitive of deśa; tasya, masc. sing. genitive pronoun).

Strophes 17 and 18 (Āryā meter)

---

da ⏑ <bo>*dhicitta*mūlaḥ karuṇāskandho mahākṣamāśākhaḥ /
abhivā<ñ>chitāśrayalavaḥ kalinavakalpadrumo ja [14] yati // (17)

| ⏑ ⏑ – | ⏑ – ⏑ | – – ‖ ⏑ ⏑ – | – – | ⏑ – ⏑ | – – | – ‖ first hemistich
| ⏑ ⏑ – | ⏑ – ⏑ | ⏑ ⏑ – ‖ ⏑ ⏑ ⏑ ⏑ | – – | ⏑ | – ⏑ ⏑ | – ‖ second hemistich

17. (This) new Wishing Tree of the Kali [Yuga],[38] whose root ... (is the Mind of Enlightenment), whose trunk is compassion, whose branches are the great forbearance, whose leaves are the highly desired shelter, is victorious (in the ceasing of rebirth).

17. [This] **new** (nava) **Wishing Tree** (kalpadrumo = kalpadrumaḥ, sing. nom. of kalpadruma) **of the Kali** [Yuga], **whose root** (mūlaḥ, sing. nom. of mūla) ...[39] [is the Mind of Enlightenment (<*bo*>*dhicitta*)],[40] **whose trunk** (skando = skandhaḥ, sing. nom. of skandha) **is compassion** (karuṇā), **whose branches** (śākhaḥ, read as śakhāḥ, the pl. nom. of śakhā) **are the great forbearance** (mahākṣamā), **whose leaves** (lavaḥ, read as lavāḥ, the pl. nom. of lava, lit. 'a fragment, piece, particle, bit, little piece')[41] **are the highly desired** (abhivāñchita)[42] **shelter** (āśraya), **is victorious** (jayati, third person sing. present of √ji) [in the ceasing of rebirth (ja-yati); see the discussion segment].

---

is not the Bodhisattva who is the master of the ten stages (bhūmi). Rather, he is Non-dual Awareness (advayajñānam), the Perfection of Wisdom itself" (Tribe 1994: 84).

[38]*Kali* can also mean 'hero'. So this also can be a pun pertaining to the Śailendra monarch, who is called 'the best of heroes' in v.20 of this inscription.

[39]... of 'unfolding growth' (*da<la>*, 'a small shoot, blade, petal, leaf').

[40]With respect to the two syllables following the initial *da*, Sarkar (1971/2: I: 47, n. 20) remarked that the "following two letters appear to me like jatra". However, *tra* would make the preceding *ja* heavy and thus break the meter. Besides, Sarker retained *bodhicitta* in his own translation of this verse.

[41]The sing. nom. *śakhaḥ* and *lavaḥ* were used here in place of the pl. nominatives *śakhāḥ* and *lavāḥ*.

[42]As emended by Sarkar (1971/2: I: 44) from *abhivānchita* (Bosch 1929a: 20).

. . . smabhūta . . . sukha . . . . . rājā /
tārkṣyo rakṣasi rakṣāṃ maṃjuravaḥ sarvabhītiharaḥ // (18)

| - - - - - | - - - - - | - - - - ‖ - - - - - | - - - - | - - - - - | - - - — | — ‖ first hemistich
| — — | — ⏑ ⏑ | — — ‖ — ⏑ ⏑ | — — | ⏑ | — ⏑ ⏑ | — ‖ second hemistich

18. ... ... / Ye the Tārkṣya (please) guard the defense (of the region) by destroying all dangers with (your) charming roar.

18. ... ... /[43] **Ye the Tārkṣya** (tārkṣyo = tārkṣyaḥ, the sing. nom. of tārkṣya)[44] [please] **guard** (rakṣasi, sec. pers. sing. present of √rakṣ) **the defense** (rakṣām, sing. accusative of rakṣā) [of the region][45] **by destroying** (haraḥ) **all** (sarva) **dangers** (bhīti) **with** [your] **charming roar** (maṃjuravaḥ = mañjuravaḥ, an epithet of Mañjuśrī).

Strophe 19 (Vasantatilakā meter)
| — — ⏑ | — ⏑ ⏑ | ⏑ — ⏑ | ⏑ — ⏑ | — ⏓ ‖

---

yāce tri —⏑ caritocitacāruvṛ [15] ttān
āgāminaḥ kṣitipatīn ava —⏑ sarvān /
yuṣmābhir aprati ⏑ *maḥ pratip*ālanīyaḥ
śrīdhammasetur ayaṃ —⏑ ⏑ bhṛtkumāraḥ // (19)

19. I implore all of those future kings ... whose virtuous activities of ... conduct are heaped with splendor, that by you be guarded this Śrī Dharmasetu,[46] which is highly esteemed (as without a parallel), for the Prince who is the bearer of the (blue lotus).

19. **I implore** (yāce, first pers. sing. present middle of √yāc) **all of those** (sarvān, pl. acc. of sarva) **future** (āgāminaḥ = pl. acc. of āgāmin) **kings** (kṣitipatīn, pl. acc. of kṣitipati) ... , **whose virtuous activities** (vṛttān, pl. accusative of vṛtta) **of** ...[47] **conduct** (caritaḥ) **are heaped** (cita) **with splendor** (cāru), **that by you** (yuṣmābhis, sec. pers. pl. instr. pronoun) **be guarded** (pratipalānīyaḥ) **this** (ayam, sing. nom. pronoun) **Śrī Dharmasetu** (dharmasetuḥ, sing. nom.), **which is highly esteemed** (mah) ... [as without a parallel (aprati<ma>)], **for the Prince** (kumāraḥ)[48] **who is the bearer** (bhṛt, sing. nom. of bhṛt) **of the** ...[49] .

[43]The first hemistich is too fragmented to translate.
[44]Though best known as an epithet of the Garuḍa, the designation Tārkṣya also potentially pertains to legends concerning the birth of Mañjuśrī; see the later discussion segment for this verse.
[45]This conjectural addition is based on the content of v.16.
[46]Though *śrī* is fem. in gender, it serves here as a respectful title for the name of a sacred religious foundation having a masc. gender.
[47]The syllable *tri-* implies a grouping of three such as thought, word and deed, though an obvious choice that also would comply with the meter (*tri<satya*>, 'trebly truthful'>) is not an epigraphical possibility.
[48]The 'heir-apparent associated in the kingdom with the reigning monarch'; an epithet of Mañjuśrī.
[49]blue lotus (<*utpala*>).

Strophe 20 (Āryā meter)

śrīsanggrāmadhanaṃja [16] yanaravarasa<ṃskā>ralab*dha*guru-<nāmnaḥ> / [50]
kṛtir iyam .... // (20)

| — — | — ᴗ ᴗ | — ᴗ ᴗ ‖ ᴗ ᴗ ᴗ ᴗ | — — | ᴗ — ᴗ | ᴗ ᴗ — | — ‖ first hemistich
| ᴗ ᴗ ᴗ ᴗ | - - - - | - - - - ‖ - - - - | - - - - | | - - - - | — ‖ second hemistich

20. Of the most excellent of heroes going by the name of Śrī Saṅgrāmadhanaṃjaya ('Illustrious Crusher of Foes in Battle'), who has found the preceptor through (noble) impressions on the mind of acts performed in previous states of existence, this relics-house ... (is his).

20. **Of the most excellent of heroes** (naravara) **going by the name** (nāmnaḥ, sing. nominative of nāmna) **of Śrī Saṅgrāmadhanaṃjaya** ('Illustrious Crusher of Foes in Battle'), **who has found** (labdha) **the preceptor** (guru) **through** [noble] **impressions on the mind of acts performed in previous states of existence** (saṃskāra), ... **this** (iyam, f. sing. nom. pronoun) **relics-house** (kṛtir = kṛtiḥ, f. sing. nom. of kṛti)[51] ... [is his] .

Discussion of the strophes

Verse one. Bosch (1929a: 44-46) surmised that the *sugatapadākṣara* cited four times in v.1 —each time in tandem with a different designation that ends in ◦*iśvara*—was intended to designate a Tathāgata: Lokeśvara for Amitābha (west, whose spiritual son is Padmapāṇi, also called Avalokiteśvara); Bhadreśvara for either Vairocana or Akṣobhya (east, Samantabhadra);[52] Viśveśvara for Amoghasiddhi (north, whose emblem is the *viśvavajra* and whose spiritual son is called Viśvapāṇi); and with the incomplete fourth ◦*iśvara* hypothetically having been either Vajreśvara for Akṣobhya (east, Vajrapāṇi), or Ratneśvara for Ratnasambhava (south, Ratnapāṇi).

> "The first strophe, composed in a rare variety of the Āryā meter, consists of four composites, all of which have a name of a deity ending in *īśvara* and besides are homophonic. Given that all four end in the undeclined form of the stem, it must be assumed that it concerns vocatives. The difficulty lies mainly herein: that it is not the *īśvaras* themselves who are called upon [in prayers] but the *sugatapadākṣaras* of these deities. We did not succeed in finding a satisfactory explanation for this expression. Does ◦*īśvarasugatapada* mean 'the footstep (or footprint) of the ◦*īśvarasugata*' or 'the *sugata* residence (or Sugataship) of the ◦*iśvara*'? And should the last word *akṣara* also be

[50] De Casparis proposed two important emendations to line 16 that Sarkar (1971/2: I) failed to note. "The deviations from Bosch's reading are (a) *saṃskāra* instead of *satkara*; in the upper part of the ligature a [letter] *sa* can be recognized, whilst behind it a length sign is visible that is not extended as far as the bottom of the line, and (b) the addition *nāmnah*, of which only the *na* sign beneath the [letter] *ma* is not entirely clear" (de Casparis 1950: 102, n. 5).

[51] Or ... 'this construction is his', according to Sarkar 1971/2: I: 46.

[52] In some Vajrayāna texts, Vairocana is located in the east and Akṣobhya occupies the center or zenith.

interpreted as the (mystic) syllable (meaning *bījākṣāra* inscribed in this footprint or perceived as the symbol of the Sugata faith or the Sugataship) or likewise be there to denote the 'imperishable principle' of the Sugataship of the ◦*iśvara*? For the elucidation of this strophe the one element that provided a clue is the names of the three *iśvaras:* Lokeśvara, Bhadreśvara and Viśveśvara (the fourth is unreadable). Although recognizable as the not unusual aliases of Śiva in his *liṅga* manifestation, it is not very likely in this context—namely, preceded by the purely Buddhistic Tritratna and followed by the no less Buddhistic Avalokiteśvara [e.g., who Bosch surmised would be the Lord who dares to bear Amitābha on his head in v.2]—that the supreme deity of the Śaiva pantheon would here appear onto the stage. The word *sugata*, which forms an integral component of the four composites concerned, makes it more plausible that the four *sugatas par excellence* are intended, i.e. the four Tathāgatas" (Bosch 1929a: 43-44).

De Casparis (1950: 144, n. 1) was skeptical of Bosch's hypothesis. "It seems improbable that we can identify *sugata* with Buddha or Tathāgata without further investigation". Indeed, we can find no example of a Buddhist text in which an entire Tathāgata grouping has been awarded °*iśvara* epithets, though Lokeśvara can certainly be taken as an alternate designation for Amitābha, as the *Guhyasamājatantra* demonstrates.

Chandra (1995: 218) interpreted the opening strophe as an invocation of the inscription's principal divinity Mañjuśrī by means of four epithets. However, he also wrote that "the possibility of their being his four manifestations cannot be ruled out". More recently, he has expressed the hypothesis that these four epithets may refer to Mañjuśrī in his four aspects: (1) 'Lord of the world' (*lokeśvara*); (2) 'Lord of well-being' (*bhadreśvara*); (3) 'Lord of the universe' (*viśveśvara*, *viśva* 'universe'); and (4) 'Lord of the logos' (*<vāgī>śvara*). As the interlocutor of several Buddhist *sūtra*-s, Mañjughoṣa is the lord of the sacred word. "Mañjughoṣa is a Bodhisattva, a Mahābodhisattva, but one who is accorded the rank of a *sugata*. Akṣara ('immutable') refers to the connection of Mañjughoṣa with the Word, the Sūtras, to his evocative epithet *vāg-īśvara*, *akṣara* 'word'." (Chandra, pc 20 Nov. 2010).

In the *Nāmamantrārthāvalokinī,* the *ācārya* Vilāsavajra has explained the esoteric meaning of *akṣara* as follows:

> "By etymological analysis, *syllable* (akṣaraḥ) [is seen to] mean 'that which does not (na < a-) perish (kṣarati < -kṣaraḥ)'. This is because it is without change, due to having the Limit of Reality as its nature. [Hence the word] paramākṣaraḥ' means the *supreme syllable*, [that is to say, 'the supreme unchangeable reality'] .... And that same [nature], since it is completely free from all obstacles, should be understood to be the nature, one by one, of each of the maṇḍala-deities arising in the consciousness of yogins" (Tribe 1994: 118; see also 33, n. 91).[53]

Furthermore, Buddhaguhya provided two explanations for *akṣara* ('letter', 'immutable') in his commentary on the *Vairocanābhisambodhi-sūtra* (VAS):

[53]The supreme syllable is A in the *Nāmasaṃgīti* and its various commentaries.

"'Letter' (*yi ge*) is a word [meaning] 'immutable' (*mi 'gyur ba*). Furthermore, what are they? Concerning that, letters are said to be of two types—'sounds and minds of enlightenment'. Concerning that, sounds are the forms of mantra letters. They are called 'immutable' (*mi 'gyur ba*) because they do not change (*mi 'gyur ba*) from the nature of indicating the release of conventional and ultimate deities.... The mind of enlightenment [*bodhicitta*] is to be taken as a moon disc; the mind of enlightenment which has the nature of thusness is blessed [to appear] as a moon disc because it is implanted with the seal (*phyag rgya, mudrā*) of the mind of enlightenment as a moon disc. The mind of enlightenment is called 'immutable' (*mi 'gyur ba*) because it does not change ('immutable') from having consideration of the nature of emptiness as without the aspects of apprehended object and apprehending subject, etc., since it is thoroughly established as non-erroneous" (Hopkins 1985: 76).

The complete title of the VAS (Hodge 2003: 25) includes 'the King Indra of expanded scriptures' (*vaipulyasūtrendrarāja*) and the NS is likewise described as 'having a profound and extensive broad scope' (*gambhīrodāravaipulyo*). So both texts would have fallen under the purview of the Śailendra *guru* characterized in v.6 as an ornament (*tilaka*) of sages [learned in] (*vipra*) the *sūtra*-s of great extension (*vaipulya*). Hence, based on the comments of Buddhaguhya cited above, *akṣara* may be glossed as 'immutable intrinsic nature' (e.g., *bodhicitta*). Besides, the identification of Mañjuśrī as the awakener of *bodhicitta* in scriptures such as the *Gaṇḍavyuha-sūtra* potentially answers the question posed by Bosch concerning why the first stanza invokes *sugatapadākṣara*-s instead of the ◦*īśvara* deities themselves.

Sarkar (1971/2: I: 44) translated *sugatapada* as 'buddhahood' without further discussion. He may had simply taken this compound as a Sanskrit synonym for *buddhapadam* or *buddhatvam*, or had been influenced by Sastri's translation of the *Bāhyārthasiddhikārikā* (*circa* 650–750; see Śubhagupta & Sastri 1967: 29) in which *saugatapadam* became glossed as Buddhahood (lit. 'the state of well-faring'). Moreover, *sugatapadam* appears in the final stanza of the *Śikṣāsamuccaya* by Śāntideva (*circa* 650–750),[54] which is immediately preceded by a lengthy homage to Mañjuśrī (see Harrison 2007: 247-248). By contrast, *sugatapada* also suggests the meaning of 'bodhisattvahood' given that *pada* can mean the 'object or cause of' the *sugata,* and with the four ensuing designations ending in ◦*īśvara* signifying aspects, characteristics or functions thereof. In his commentary (*pañjikā*)

[54]iti jinatanayānāṃ sarvathātyadbhutānāṃ caritam
upanibandhyopārjitaṃ yac chubhaṃ me /
bhavatu sukham anantaṃ dehināṃ tena yāvat
sugatapadam anantavyomasīmādhipatyaṃ // XIX.73

Thus (*iti*), after having written (*upanibandhya*) of the sons (*tanayānām*, pl. genitive of *tanaya*) of the Conquerors (*jina*), and of their extraordinary (*ati*) marvels (*adbhutānām*, pl. genitive of *adbhuta*) in every respect (*sarvatha*), by whatever (*yad*) has been acquired (*upārjitam*, sing. acc. of *upārjita*), practiced (*caritam*, sing. accusative of *carita*), and a benefit (*śubham*, sing. acc. of śubha) to me (*me*, sing. dative pronoun), let there be (*bhavatu*) happiness without end (*sukham anantam*, sing. acc. of *sukha* and *ananta*, resp.) for living beings (*dehinām*, pl. genitive of dehin) thereby (*tena*) until (*yāvat*) the state of the one gone to bliss (*sugatapadam*) is the governing influence (*ādhipatyam*, sing. acc. of *ādhipatya*, 'sovereignty, supremacy') to the furthest extent (*sīma*, in comp. for *sīman*) of the boundless (*ananta*) sky (*vyoma*).

on Śāntideva's *Bodhicaryāvatāra*, the eleventh century monk Prajñākaramati apparently used the term *sugatapada* to indicate 'bodhisattvahood' (see Śāntideva *et al.* 1990: 362). So *sugatapadākṣara* might alternately signify the unchanging intrinsic nature of four bodhisattvas.

De Casparis claimed that the Sanskrit word bodhisattva never appears in the *praśasti* hailing from Central Java.

> "Now it is very striking that it is precisely this word, which must be one of the central terms of Śailendra Buddhism, is not found in any of their inscriptions. Nevertheless, hardly any value can be attached to the absence of this term if it were not that a different word is used at the places where the word [bodhisattva] is expected, namely *sugata* ... [which] either must mean bodhisattva or a specific type of bodhisattva. Regarding the latter [possibility], we should bear in mind that different systems distinguish between a kind of 'independent' bodhisattva and the bodhisattvas who have reached a certain stage of the Path [e.g. the tenth stage known as *dharmamegha*] who are designated as Bodhisattva Mahāsattva" (de Casparis 1950: 145).

According to the *Dharma-kośa-saṅgraha* (folio 9a), however, Vairocana emanates Samantabhadra, Akṣobhya emanates Vajrapāṇi, Ratnasambhava emanates Ratnapāṇi, Amitābha emanates Padmapāṇi, and Amoghasiddhi emanates Viśvapāṇi. Hence, there is no mention of a Lokeśvara or Avalokiteśvara emanation of Amitābha under the *pañca-bodhisattva* system.

The next point to consider is how we should interpret the preceding salutation dedicated to the *ratnatraya*. Bosch compared the so-called Kĕlurak inscription with the Kalasan charter of 778/9 CE, which features both an opening salutation and initial benedictory verse devoted to the Buddhist goddess Tārā.

> "The affinity between the inscription of Kalasan and that of Kĕlurak has prepared us for [seeing] the divinity to which the [latter] inscription is devoted; thus Mañjuśrī should have been honored in the salutation, just like the Tārā of the Kalasan text. The fact that [the Kĕlurak inscription] should invoke the Triratna in [his] place does not now seem in conflict but rather in accordance with this expectation. Indeed, if the meaning of the fourteenth strophe is correctly interpreted above, then according to the dogma developed in that strophe the Triratna was equal to the divinity Mañjuśrī venerated in the inscription itself. Thus, in the opening words of the inscription the faithful not only presented homage to the Three Jewels; the salutation also named the divinity in which the Three Jewels are contained, the Mañjuśrī, to whose image emplacement the inscription was devoted" (Bosch 1929a: 43).[55]

[55]Amitābha, Avalokiteśvara, Śākyamuni, Tārā and other Buddhist divinities are each in turn declared the 'embodiment of the Three Jewels' in various texts. Besides, devotees also regarded their Buddhist spiritual teachers in precisely the same way. "Visualize that your maṇḍala deity, who is an embodiment of the Three Jewels and is inseparable in nature from your spiritual master, appears in the space in front of you, or above the crown of your head" (Mullin 2006: 152). For Mahāyāna Buddhists, Mañjuśrī is the *guru par excellence*.

Verse Two. Sarkar (1971/2: I: 44) translated the second stanza as follows: "Pay homage to that Lokeśa, the lord of thc worlds, who illuminates all regions, who is Lokeśvara, daring to bear on (his) forehead Amitābha, the ruler of the worlds!" Among other things, however, Sarkar overlooked a valuable observation made by de Casparis (1950: 144), who noticed that the second hemistich also can be read as *lokeśaṃ sakala-diganta-avabhāsana-āloka-iśaṃ:* 'the Lord (*lokeśa*) illuminating (*avabhāsana*) all the directions (*sakala-diganta*), the Lord of light (*āloka-īśa*)'.

Bosch (1929a) and Sarkar (1971/2: I) believed that the reference to the Lord who dares to bear Amitābha on his head must indicate the bodhisattva Avalokiteśvara, whose images typically display a small figure of his spiritual progenitor Amitābha in the coiffure. Within the overall context of the present inscription, however, Mañjuśrī clearly plays the principal role. So we cannot rule out the possibility that v.2 might actually be referring to a manifestation of Mañjuśrī. Indeed, given that the Buddha calls Mañjuśrī 'the father and mother of the bodhisattvas' (for example, in the *Ajātaśatrurāja-sūtra;* see Wayman 1985: 4), the initial two strophes may be envisioned as pertaining to Mañjuśrī in his role as the 'spiritual progenitor' of Buddhahood through the awakening of *bodhicitta*.

Family (*kula*):	Tathāgata (Cakra)	Vajra	Ratna	Padma	Karma
Tathāgata:	Vairocana	Akṣobhya	Ratnasambhava	Amitābha	Amoghasiddhi
Awareness (*jñāna*):	Awareness of the Perfectly Pure Dharma-Sphere	Mirror-like Awareness	Awareness of Equality	Discriminating Awareness	Awareness of the Performance of Action
	suviśuddha-dharmadhātu-jñāna	*ādarśajñāna*	*samatājñāna*	*pratyavekṣaṇā-jñāna*	*kṛtyānuṣṭhāna-jñāna*
Poison (*kleśa*):	Ignorance (*moha*)	Anger (*dveṣa*)	Pride (*manas*)	Desire (*rāga*)	Jealousy (*īrṣyā*)
Aggregate (*skandha*):	Consciousness	Form	Feeling	Perception	Volition
Color:	White	Blue	Yellow	Red	Green
Direction:	Center[56]	East	South	West	North

Fig. 3-3. Five-fold Awareness (*jñāna*) of the Buddhistic spiritual families.[57]

[56]Vairocana and Akṣobhya exchange positions in certain *tantras*.

[57]The two rows associated with the main header dedicated to Awareness are given in Tribe 1994: 91.

A crowned Mañjuśrī image is the five-fold Awareness (see figure 3-3) personified: the mind of enlightenment which has fully realized the transcendental Gnosis (*jñāna*) exemplified by each member of the Tathāgata pentad and their respective spiritual families. It is possible that four of these aspects are put forward in strophe one (e.g. those of the *padma*, *vajra*, *karma* and *ratna* families, respectively) and with the fifth and foremost (e.g. the Tathāgata family signifying the Awareness of the essential nature of the *dharmadhātu*) brought forward in strophe two. We shall examine this issue in more detail later.

Verse Three. Bosch and Sarkar mentioned that the first hemistich of v.3 is difficult to interpret due to the uncertainty over the reading of several *akṣara*-s as well as an extensive lacuna at the end. Both translators thought that the stanza would refer to terror-stricken (*bhayabhītam*) worshipers invoking the protection of the divinity mentioned in the prior strophe as bearing Amitābha on his head. "From the reference to *māmapi bhayabhītam*, it appears that Lokeśvara is invoked here for protection" (Sarkar 1971/2: I: 45). However, there is nothing else in what remains to be read in this stanza that would offer support for this hypothesis. Mañjuśrī is the deity invoked repeatedly for protection in the remainder of this inscription.

Chandra (1995: 221) initially envisioned the unnamed principal figure in strophe three as the Śailendra king's preceptor. Noting that this stanza features the phrase *navaratna*—a possible reference to the 'nine gems' offering protection from the astrological influences of the nine planets or else the nine literati of a king's court—Chandra envisioned the verse to be a description of how the Śailendra king's preceptor had won a debate with a group of nine scholars (*navaratna*) from the Javanese branch of the Abhayagiri monastery on the Ratu Boko Plateau, who supposedly panicked away in fright (1995: 219). However, it was not until a full decade later that the next Śailendra monarch sponsored the construction of a *vihāra* for Siṅhalese monks, according to the Abhayagirivihāra charter of Samaratuṅga dating from 792/3 CE. Anyway, Chandra's interpretation is based on his doubtful alternate reading of *saṅgata* as *saugata*, which he subsequently has abandoned (Chandra, pc 21 Nov. 2011).

The construction of this verse's second hemistich, according to Bosch's transcription, suggests that v.3 had been composed in the Āryā meter, at least if one refrains from accounting for his <*n*> emendation *avacara*<*n*>*taṃ* in the diagram presented below. To bring the first hemistich into conformance with this meter, the following hypothetical diagram has been provisionally tagged at the end of the first *pāda* (◊) to suggest one potential way that a transformation from a light to a heavy measure (*mātrā*) could have made the text conform to the Āryā meter's specific requirements.

yātasthā*mavacarata ya*ḥ śarumān ——————— /
saṅgata — navaratnaṃ mām api [3] bhayabhītam avacarataṃ // (3)

Hypothetical verse in Āryā meter:

```
| — — | — ⏑ ⏑ | ⏑ ⏑ ◊ ‖ — ⏑ ⏑ | — - - | - - - - | - - - - | - ‖   emended first hemistich
| — ⏑ ⏑ | - ⏑ ⏑ | — — ‖ — ⏑ ⏑ | ⏑ ⏑ — | ⏑ | ⏑ ⏑ ⏑ ⏑ | — ‖   emended second hemistich
```

Strophe four refers to the Śailendra king's triumphs on the field of battle in all directions, so we naturally wonder what had transpired here in the second hemistich of v.3 that would have justified the use of *bhayabhītam* (lit. 'fearful and afraid'). Moreover, Bosch's tentative reading of *avacarata* in the first hemistich suggests the possibility of a pun on *avacara<n>tam* ('moving about, roaming around'). But there are a number of uncertainties concerning the contents of this strophe. For example, *śarumān* can be interpreted as the singular nominative of *śarumat,* 'armed with missiles'. On the other hand, *śarumān* merely may have been the initial part of a Sanskrit compositum: *śarum*° (sing. acc. of *śaru,* 'passion, anger'; 'arrow, dart, spear; or a missile weapon, especially Indra's thunderbolt and weapon of the Maruts'), and with °*ān-* being the initial syllable of another compound lost in the ensuing lacuna.[58]

Through the inclusion of a question mark following Āryāgīti in advance of his transcription, Bosch (1929a: 18) tentatively suggested that the text's composer may have intended to once again employ this particular meter in verse three. On the other hand, his presentation of a single *daṇḍa* at the end of what he surmised to be the first hemistich in his transcription for this verse would mean that the presumed second hemistich would not then contain a sufficient number of measures (*mātrā*) for reconstructing a strophe in the Āryāgīti meter. Besides, one of the light measures in the italicized portion of first hemistich would actually need to be heavy (◊) plus we would need to account for his <n> emendation for the second hemistich as potentially being a scribal error.

Hypothetical reconstruction in the Āryāgīti meter:

yātasthā*mavacarata ya*ḥ śarumān −−−−−−−− /
saṅgata − navaratnaṃ mām api [3] bhayabhītam avacara<n>taṃ // (3)

| − − | − ⏑ ⏑ | ⏑ ⏑ ◊ ‖ − ⏑ ⏑ | − - - | - - - - - | - - - - - | - - - - - ‖ first hemistich
| - - - - - | − ⏑ ⏑ | − ⏑ ⏑ ‖ − − | − ⏑ ⏑ | ⏑ ⏑ − | ⏑ ⏑ ⏑ ⏑ | − − ‖ second hemistich

The appearance of the Āryāgīti meter in the inscription's first three stanzas would suggest the possibility that the poet had intended to form a discrete segment of the text dedicated to the Buddha, the Dharma and the Saṅgha, respectively:

- (v.1) with the four °*īśvara* designations expressing the qualities or characteristics of the Buddha by means of four epithets;

[58]With respect to the second hemistich, the only potentially coherent translation possibility that occurs to me would require *saṅgata–* to be interpreted as incorporating the Old Javanese honorific *saṅ*, which previously appeared in the Kalasan inscription, followed by *gata<bhīḥ>* (the masc. sing. nom. of *gatabhī*). Then the second hemistich would mean, 'the honorable one (*saṅ*) free from fear (*gata<bhīḥ>*) [e.g. Kumāraghoṣa] was roaming around (*avacara<n>tam*) me (*mām*, masc. sing. acc. pronoun) as well as (*api*) the group of nine court literati (*navaratnam*, sing. acc. of *navaratna*), which was terror-stricken (*bhayabhītam*, sing. acc. of bhayabhīta)'. But this is a highly speculative translation as is likewise the case with the rest of the translations of verse fragments presented hereafter, and especially so given that *saṅ* only appears as the title for indigenous Javanese officials in the Kalasan charter.

- (v.2) with the Lord who dares to bear Amitābha on his head symbolizing the Dharma; and
- (v.3) with a divinity or spiritual personage potentially representing the Saṅgha in this fragmentary verse.[59]

By way of comparison, the Abhayagirivihāra charter (792/3) opens with three stanzas composed in the Śārdulavikrīḍita meter that allude to each of the Three Jewels in turn (v.1: Sambuddha, v.2: fire of the Dharma, and v.3 the monastic community). Likewise, the initial three verses in Sragdharā meter from the fragmentary Kayumwuṅan charter (824) are open to the same interpretation, as we shall see in Chapter V. Besides, we have already seen in Chapter I that the A-side of the Isthmus of Kra stele mentions a tripartite construction (*traisamayacaitya*) that provided the seats, as it were, for the Buddha, Padmapāṇi and Vajrapāṇi, a well-known triad for designating the Three Jewels. All things considered, however, Āryā appears to be the least problematic candidate for this verse's meter.

Verses four, five and six. The Śailendra king's epithet 'Crusher of valiant enemy heroes' (*vairivaravīravimardana*, v.4) is subsequently echoed by the Sanskritized name awarded to the monarch in v.20: the illustrious 'Crusher of foes in battle' (*saṅgrāmadhanaṃjaya*). Both are comparable to the epithet 'Illustrious Tormentor of brave foes' (*śrīvīravairimathana*) from the Nālandā copperplate promulgated by the king of Bengal Devapāladeva as well as the epithet *sarvvārimadavi<ma>thana* from the B-side of the Isthmus of Kra stele, which also identifies him as an 'ornament of the Śailendra dynasty' (*śailendravaṅśatilaka*). Following the methods adopted by Damais (see, for example, 1952: 28, n. 1 and 1968: 353) for naming an inscription, then first preference should be given to the name of a toponym mentioned in the text, or if one is unavailable then either the name of the religious foundation or that of the donor. For this reason, the *praśasti* originally named after the old *desa* Kĕlurak is designated as the Śrī Saṅgrāmadhanaṃjaya inscription herein, as did Damais (1964).

In a letter to Cœdès (1959: 48), de Casparis had proposed the revised reading of *dharaṇīndrarena*—which would simply mean 'by the king'—in place of *dharaṇīndranāmnā* in v.5. However, *dharaṇīndrarena* would then be entirely superfluous given the presence of *rājñā* in the same quarter of the verse. Excluding *-ndranāmnā* or *-ndrarena,* the prose order would be: *yasya kramāmbuja-rajaḥ śirasā pranamya, pravara-ratna-saroruhādyaiḥ sampūjyate, śailendra-vaṅśa-tilakena mahodayena dhrtimatā rājñā dharanī dhrtā,* according to Chandra (pc 7 June 2014).

It is also of interest that vs. 4-6 and v.19 are all composed in the meter known as Vasantatilakā, which means 'spring ornament'. In addition to the compositum *śailendravaṅśatilaka* encountered in v.4, the Śailendra preceptor is identified in v.6 as a *vaipulavipratilaka.* Hence, the poet's selection of the Vasantatilakā meter for these four verses may have been intended to emphasize the parallels existing between the king and his preceptor, with the latter apparently being the principal personage mentioned in v.6.

[59]The Śailendra king's preceptor "was a *vaipula-vipra-tilaka*, namely a brāhmaṇa (vipra) by caste.... The name of the Guru [Kumāraghoṣa] indicates his initiation (*abhiṣeka*, st. 7) into Vāgīśvara Mañjughoṣa. Thus the consecration of the image got special sanctity as it was done by a *brāhmaṇa* who was so to say the veritable Divinity Himself" (Chandra 1995: 221).

"It speaks of the Guru who is an ornament of vipras versed in the Vaipulya traditions: *Vaipulya-vipra-tilakena* corresponds to *Śailendra-vaṁśa-tilakena.* Sarkar (n. 28) feels that the word *vipra* is "perhaps used here in the sense of a learned priest", to pun with vaipulya. The teacher was a brāhmaṇa (*vipra*) by caste and hence its specific mention. Just as the king was of noble descent by virtue of his dynasty (*vaṁśa*), likewise was the Guru born high as a brāhmaṇa (*vipra*). This becomes clear in the seventh stanza which point out that the head of the King was purified by the dust of the lotus feet of the Guru from Gauḍī-dvīpa. It is in apposition to the statement in the fifth stanza that the dust of the feet of the ornament of the Śailendra dynasty was saluted by feudatories, ministers and others with their heads" (Chandra 1995: 220).

Verse seven. This strophe's revised transcription and translation segments are based on a reading of the Sanskrit verse submitted by de Casparis (1950: 144) following his examination of the stone: "Also the curious term *saṃgūḍhārtha*, 'hidden meaning', is found in strophe seven, wherein the second line starts with the words *saṃgūḍhārtha-vibhāga*, synonymous with *saṃgūḍhārtha-vicāraṇā* of the Ratubaka inscription, [which] Bosch transcribed as: — — *ārthavidāma*". Unfortunately, Sarkar (1971/2: I: 45) failed to discuss this observation when preparing his own transcription.

Stanza seven begins with a proverbial expression well known in both the Hindu and esoteric Buddhist traditions concerning the placement of the disciple's head at the feet of the *guru.*[60] Hindu disciples, for example, obtain sanctity through the application of the dust from the guru's lotus-feet upon their heads or by placing the dust on their forehead at the spot above the eyebrows as a token (*tilaka*) of their spiritual affiliation. In the *Bodhicittabhāvana* ('Cultivation of Enlightened Mind'),[61] vs. 132-141 identify reverence for the *guru* alone as a valid path to Great Enlightenment. "Simply through the generation of veneration for one's Guru, who is the Supreme Lord of the threefold Universe and by making Offerings (*pūjā*) according to the practice of proper disciples (*śrāvaka*), one may overcome with splendour all the devil's hosts. This Great Method is the particular mystical practice of the Bodhisattvas".

The person whose head is purified by the dust of the preceptor's lotus feet is not specified in the readable portion of v.7, though it is obvious that this must have been the head of a living being rather than part of the consecration ceremony for the Mañjuśrī image. Given

[60]See, for example, v.3 of the *Gurupañcāśikā* ('Fifty stanzas of guru-devotion') by the 'tantric' Aśvaghoṣa: "At the three times, supremely faithful, with flower, mandala and palms pressed together, devote yourself to the teacher *guru* and pay homage to his feet [by touching them] with your head" (*trikālaṃ parayā bhaktyā sapuṣpāñjalimaṇḍalaiḥ / paryupāsyo guruḥ śāstā śirasā pādavandanāt // 3 //*). The central premise of the "Fifty stanzas", which cites several early Mantrayāna texts, is that the *sādhaka* reaches the divinity by way of the *guru* who is identified with the deity and invested with the power to bestow the requisites that the *sādhaka* requires to likewise serve and identify with that divinity (Wayman 1997: 217).

[61]The colophons in the surviving Tibetan translation (*rDo la gser zhun*) of this lost Sanskrit text attribute the authorship to the celebrated eighth-century *ācārya* Mañjuśrīmitra and the Tibetan translation to Mañjuśrīmitra's disciple Śrī Siṃha and the Tibetan translator Bhikṣu Vairocanarakṣita (Mañjuśrīmitra; Kunpal Tulku 1995).

that the Śailendra monarch is the only other human being mentioned in the inscription it is reasonable for us to presume that the purified head had been that of the king.[62]

Responding to a request for his response to de Casparis' emendations for v.7, Chandra observed that the revised transcription for this strophe can be envisioned as encompassing five steps:

> "(i) Even though he was a mighty monarch whose feet were graced by feudatory princes, he himself felt purified by touching the feet of the Guru who hailed from the hallowed land of Gauḍīdvīpa. This is *śraddhā*.
> (ii) The monarch came to understand the esoteric doctrines in depth from the Guru who was well versed in the *vaipulya* traditions (st. 6). The Guru was the crowning scholar as well as endowed with the *saṃskāra* of being a *brāhmaṇa* (*vipra*). This is the dawning of *jñāna*.
> (iii) By faith (*śraddhā*) and knowledge (*jñāna*) the monarch attained great supernatural power (*mahārddhi*). *Mahārddhi* is of Ṛṣis, of Buddhas, of deities, and of others. This is the culmination of *siddhi*.
> (iv) After them the monarch was given initiation (*abhiṣeka*) by the Guru.
> (v) By this auspiciousness (*śrī*) the monarch dedicated himself to the welfare and prosperity of sentient beings.
> *Preyas* and *śreyas* are two technical terms in *yoga*. To me the sequence is clear: *śraddhā* → *jñāna* → *siddhi* or *ṛddhi* → *abhiṣeka* (these four are *preyas*) → *śreyas*. The statement of the inscription is in general terms. Though logical in sequence, it is not a liturgical sequence" (Chandra, pc 20 Nov. 2011).

So it would seem that the *guru* had bestowed a Mañjuśrī empowerment upon the king, especially because of the presence of the word *abhiṣeka*, which is indicative of a ritualized 'consecration'. Such empowerments are by nature esoteric transmissions that are only available to initiates.

In Hinduism, the designation *darśana* (Pali = *dassana*) means 'sight' (from √*dṛś* 'to see') in the sense of 'seeing or beholding', or a 'vision, apparition, or glimpse'. "Darsana is the act of seeing (and simultaneously being seen by) a god or an auspicious person. Darsana is 'given' by the god and 'taken' by the person. It is often explained as a discharge of power [that is] mediated by sight or touch" (Morinis 1992: 85). For example, the exchange that takes place between deity and devotee within the inner sanctum of a temple is typically one of glances, with the worshiper not only seeing the deity residing within the image, but the deity also seeing the worshiper. Additionally, *darśana* is the 'reception of a vision' granted by a deity in the temple or by a *mahāguru*, with the end result being a heightening of consciousness or spirituality.

Another integral aspect of *darśana* is the touching of the feet (*pranāma*) of the *guru*, *mūrti* or icon of a divinity.[63] During *pūjā*, for example, devotees may either touch the feet

---

[62]By way of a divine comparison, the *Śrīmad Bhāgavatam* (6,7,21) relates how the lord of the gods Indra had touched with his head the lotus feet of his spiritual preceptor Bṛhaspati.

[63]A well-known example of a Hindu *darśana* appears in the *Bhagavad Gītā* (XI.17): "At that time the son of Pāṇḍu [Arjuna] saw the entire universe with its diversity and variety united in the body of the God of gods.

of a *guru* or remove the dust from his feet to place on the forehead or on top of the head. "The idea is that when a man prostrates himself at the foot of a saint the dust of the saint's feet purifies him. The climax of beatitude is attained when the dust of the soles of the saint's feet falls on the worshiper's head" (Macauliffe 1909: 34).

Mahāyāna Buddhism similarly associates the dust of the Bodhisattva's lotus-feet with occult or mystic power. The *Jātakamālā*, for example, presents the Bodhisattva's birth story as the navigator *par excellence* Supāraga. Despite the Bodhisattva's advanced age and diminished physical capabilities, sea-faring merchants nevertheless sought his mystic aid: "'The dust touched and hallowed by your lotus-like feet will be auspicious to our ship and procure her a happy course over yonder sea, even if assailed by great danger. With this in mind we have applied to you'." (Āryāśūra & Speyer 1895: 175; see also Sastri 1937: 134-135).

Verses eight and nine. The principal theme of strophe eight is the Śailendra preceptor's installation of an image of Mañjuśrī, presumably holding a blue lotus. Moreover, the initial half of the following fragmentary stanza appears to refer to a *setu* ('dam, bulwark, bridge') that is either of Mañjughoṣa or which is (verily) Mañjughoṣa,whereas the second half-verse seems to equate this *setu* with a 'pillar of glory' (*kīrtistambha*). Because of the extensive lacunas, however, the following speculative translation should be regarded with caution.

> *d*<ṛ>ṣ*ṭaḥ* spṛṣṭaḥ smṛt*imi* .... itaḥ .... *titā*pa . *itiḥ sasu*khasya .... *setur*
> mmaṃjughoṣaḥ saṃtoṣaḥ [8] <ya>smāttasmādbhavadbhir ...... satkṛtta ....
> jjapadadṛṣtarataḥ kīrttist*ambha* .. smṛttiḥ // (9)

Visualized, touched, ... with mindfulness, ... blissful, because this ... bridge ... which is [verily] Mañjughoṣa ... has been [our] rejoicing / hence ... the memory of this pillar of glory should be honored by you ... who are always engaged in prayer for that which is beyond the reach of observation or consciousness ... //.

Visualized (dṛṣṭaḥ, sing. nom. of dṛṣṭa), **touched** (spṛṣṭaḥ, sing. nom. of spṛṣṭa), ... **with mindfulness** (smṛti), ...,[64] **blissful** (sa-sukhasya), **because** (<ya>smāt) **this** ... **bridge** (setur = setuḥ, sing nom. of setu) **of Mañjughoṣa** (mmaṃjughoṣaḥ) ... **has been** [our] **satisfaction** (saṃtoṣaḥ) / **hence** (tasmād = tasmāt) ... **the memory** (smṛttiḥ = smṛtiḥ, sing. nom. of smṛti)[65] **of this pillar of glory** (kīrtistambha) **should be honored** (satkṛta) **by you** (bhavadbhir = bhavadbhiḥ, pl. instr. of bhavat) ... **who are engaged** (rataḥ) **in prayer** (japad) **for that which is beyond the reach of observation or consciousness** (adṛṣṭa) ... //.[66]

Then overwhelmed with astonishment and his hair standing on end, Dhanaṃjaya ['Crusher of foes', Arjuna's famous epithet] bowed his head over folded hands to the Supreme Person and spoke: Arjuna said: O Lord, I see all the gods in your body, and a variety of creatures assembled, the sovereign god Brahmā seated on his lotus seat, all the seers as well as the divine serpents. I see you everywhere in an infinite form, having unlimited arms, bellies, mouths and eyes; I behold in you no end, no middle and no beginning, O Lord of all, whose form is the entire world" (Theodor 2010: 94).

[64]Perhaps, honoring through reflection (<*cin*>*titāpa*<*c*>*itiḥ*).

[65]"The practices of devotion to, and visualization of, the Buddha involve a variety of memory akin to commemoration" (Gyatso 1992: 1).

[66]My thanks to Chandra (pc 20 Nov. 2010) for his provisional interpretation of this fragmentary stanza.

The expression *dharmasetu* ('bridge to the Dharma') appears in several later strophes and we have previously encountered this last Sanskrit compound twice in the Kalasan charter in relation to the founding of a residence for an image of the Buddhist goddess Tārā as well as a *vihāra* for Buddhist monks. For the moment, however, we shall confine our discussion to *setu*.

> "[It] originally meant an earthwork across a flooded area, and so can mean 'dam' or 'barrier' as well as 'bridge'. The [*Śvetāśvatara Upaniṣad*] emphasizes the former meaning, but the Self or God [Ātman] as a bridge from our present state to infinite consciousness is also a common image" (Easwaran & Nagler 1987: 359).

> "As such a sustainer of the imperishable and the perishable, the Ātman implies both the dam (*setur vidhṛtiḥ*) extending between the different worlds and at the same time the connecting bridge (*setu* implies both) between this worldly existence and the yonder world (the world of Brahman). No wickedness, no evil, no incompleteness can cross the bridge. The way to attain the Brahman world, is *Brahmacaryam* ... the life of a Brahmacārin, a student studying Brahman, devoted to study and renunciation" (Deussen 1990: 190).

Though the meaning of v.9 as a whole remains uncertain, the stanza contains several key elements which likewise suggest that the entire religious foundation was verily Mañjughoṣa (e.g. the divinity's monumental body, perhaps even one designed to function as a three-dimensional architectonic *maṇḍala*). The fragmentary verse also appears to forge an inextricable link between the terms *setu* and *kīrtistambha*.

Verse 10. Chandra (1995: 221) initially suggested that the uncertain reading of *gurum̐* presented by Bosch in his original transcription should be changed to *puṇyam̐* based on the content. He also noted that *bhaktitam̐* is grammatically incorrect and thought this should be read as *bhaktitaḥ*, the sing. ablative of *bhakti*. In addition, *mañjuśriyam̐* is in the accusative case when in his opinion it should be in the genitive case.[67] However, his reading of *puṇyam̐* in place of *gurum̐* would break the meter and the three case ending changes proposed by Chandra need to be viewed with caution given the characteristically careful way that Bosch declared his degree of certainty for the readings presented in his transcriptions.

With respect to the tentative nature of Bosch's readings for multiple words in the third quarter of this stanza, together with the lacuna in the first half verse, all translations for this strophe can only be regarded as speculative. Here is what seems most plausible to me as an partial translation for the second half-verse.

[67]Chandra (pc 20 Nov. 2010) subsequently revised his translation: "Having constructed (*kṛtva*) with devotion (*bhaktitam̐* = *bhaktitaḥ*), this (*imām̐*) image (*pratimām̐*) of Mañjuśrī (*mañjuśriyam̐* = *mañjuśriyaḥ*), who has vanquished Desire (*smarajitaḥ*), whose feet (*saṁkramasya*) are worshiped (*arcita*) by the three worlds (*trailokya*), who is the protector (*trātur*) of the universe (*jagataḥ*), who ordains (*vidhātuḥ*) affluence (*śriaḥ*), and thereby (*yad*) the immense (*amitam̐*) merit (*gurum̐* = *puṇyam*) I (*mayā*) have attained (*prāptam̐*) ... [has led to bounties indicated in the following stanzas]." In my opinion, however, it is preferable to refrain from mixing and matching compositional elements found in different halves of the same stanza whenever their true significance remains debatable due to extensive lacunas.

kṛtvemāṃ pratimāṃ mayā *yadamitaṃ* prā*ptaṃ guruṃ bhaktitaṃ*
sevā — ⏑ ⏑ locanaḥ smarajitaḥ — — ⏑ maṃjuśriyaṃ // (10)

On account of (great) devotion having established this image, which is immeasurable,[68] by me was found the *guru* in the service ... of the illuminating (one) who has conquered Desire ....

On account of [great] **devotion** (bhaktitaṃ, read as bhaktitaḥ, sing. ablative of bhakti)[69] **having established** (kṛtvā, absolutive of √kṛ) **this** (imām, sing. acc. pronoun) **image** (pratimām, sing. acc. of pratimā) ...,[70] **which** (*yad*) **is immeasurable** (*amita*m, sing. acc. of amita, 'without a certain measure'), **by me** (mayā, first pers. sing. instr. pronoun)[71] **was found** (*prāpta*m, sing. acc. of prāpta)[72] **the *guru*** (*guru*m, sing. acc. of guru)[73] **in the service** (sevā-) ... **of the illuminating** [one] (locanaḥ) **who has conquered Desire** (smarajitaḥ, sing. genitive of smarajit)[74]....

Verses 11 and 12. We are informed in stanza 11 that the royal preceptor had installed (*sthāpitavān*) the 'Mañjughoṣa' in the Śaka year 704, which is equivalent to 782 CE.[75] Bosch, Sarkar and Chandra have all assumed that this 'Mañjughoṣa' was none other than the same Mañjuśrī image previously lauded in v.8. In my opinion, however, it is equally plausible to suggest that here Mañjughoṣa actually refers to the religious foundation in its entirety as also may have been the case in v.9. The reasons for adopting this different point of view shall be explained in a later segment of this discussion.

The Śailendra preceptor's name combines Mañjuśrī's famous Kumāra epithet with the latter half of yet another celebrated designation for the same divinity, e.g. *-ghoṣa*. Based on the inscription's repeated references to Mañjuśrī, Mañjughoṣa and Kumāra, as well as other epithets such as Mañjurava and Mañjuvāk, Kumāraghoṣa can be glossed as the 'Voice of the Kumāra' or perhaps even interpreted as meaning the 'Sound of the prayer-recital of the Kumāra'.

Damais (1955: 205) provided a revised reading for v.12 which suggests that its purpose was to supply the month and day on which the Śailendra preceptor had consecrated the image of Mañjuśrī cited in v.8 or the entire religious foundation, which is subsequently identified as a *dharmasetu* in v.19.

"Following stanza 11 (line 9) where the year is given in words [e.g. seven hundred (varṣa-śata-saptabhiś) and four (caturbhir api)], the date is specified in the following

[68]According to Vilāsavajra, Mañjuśrī is "immeasurable, since, for the whole [immeasurable] mass of living beings, he possesses the love [one feels] for an only son" (Tribe 1994: 138).
[69]Presuming with Chandra (see above) that this is a grammatical error.
[70]Chandra (1995: 221) proposed adding 'of Mañjuśrī' (i.e. with *maṃjuśriyam* being read as *mañjuśriyaḥ*).
[71]e.g. the Śailendra monarch.
[72]Strophe 20 explains that the Śailendra king had found the *guru* by means of his (noble) *saṃskāra*.
[73]Chandra (1995: 221) proposed reading *guruṃ* as *puṇyam*, the sing. acc. of *puṇya* ('religious merit'), based on the context. However, *puṇyam* would not comply with the meter.
[74]Compare with *kāmajit*, 'conquering Desire', a name of Skanda.
[75]The presentation in v.11 is comparable to how the composers of the Kalasan and Abhayagirivih āra charters had likewise expressed their year dates.

stanza (line 10) in contrast to the stele of Kalasan, where only the year is given. The meter is a variety of Āryā. The inscription is very faded and difficult to read at this place (Bosch only transcribed a few syllables) and my own reading is very fragmentary. Here, however, is what I believe that I can decipher ....

wyā*ti* -rā-*sita*-*nā*mani suraguruwāre ca . . . . ṇaśya-tithau /
kala-wi*ra* -*aś*<->*ina* māse sthā*pitava*<-> . . . . . ya . . . . ha . . . . // (12)

"To me, *suraguru* (=Bṛhaspati) seems secure, *sita* (=*śukla*) is possible palaeographically [and] Āświna (=Aśuji) seems probable but with no certainty.... If the month starts the day after the astronomical new moon, the Thursdays are 7 and 14 Śukla and 6 and 13 Kṛṣṇa. Between *wāre* and *tithau*, within which the date indication must be, there is nothing we can decipher satisfactorily. The words *pratipada* [and] *aṣṭama* seem unlikely palaeographically. Since there appears to be subscribed letters, one of the expressions designating the full moon seems to me that which is more probable and [which] is why I propose Thursday, 26 September 782 CE [Julian calendar] but with reservations" (Damais 1955: 205).

Following Damais, the most obvious metrically compatible term to consider for designating the full moon is derived from *pārvaṇa:* 'increasing, waxing; belonging or relating to a division of time or to the changes of the moon; full'; the singular genitive *pārvaṇasya* would signify the full-moon *tithi*. A well-known Hindu rite is performed on the days of the new moon and full moon. It consists of fasting as well as offering cooked oblations to the deities of those days, together with appropriate *mantra*-s. Hence, it is also potentially significant that the inscription refers to a consecration which occurred on a Thursday, the day of the week for offering oblations to the *guru par excellence:* Bṛhaspati. Moreover, the full moon night in Āśvina known as Śārad Pūrṇimā is the brightest of the year. This is when devout Hindus believe that the moon showers the earth with *amṛta*. To absorb the ambrosia, milk thickened with rice and mixed with sugar is left outside to be bathed in the moonbeams all evening long (see Sehgal 1999: 509). Based on the above, the following—which builds upon elements from the respective readings by Bosch and Damais —is presented below as a tentative transcription and translation:

vyā*ti* -rā-sita-nāmani suraguruvāre ca — ⏑ ṇaśya-tithau /
kalavira<-ā>ś<v>ina māse sthāpitavañ ca yathaham . . . . // [12]

| — — | — ⏑ ⏑ | — ⏑ ⏑ ‖ ⏑ ⏑ ⏑ ⏑ | — — | ⏑ — ⏑ | — ⏑ ⏑ | — ‖ first hemistich
| ⏑ ⏑ ⏑ ⏑ | — ⏑ ⏑ | — — ‖ — ⏑ ⏑ | — ⏑ ⏑ | ⏑ | — ⏑ ⏑ | — ‖ second hemistich

12. ... in the bright half (of the month) on the lunar day ... [of the full moon] and on the day of the week called Suraguru, in the month ... (of Āśvina) was established ... [the image and/or temple] by that melodious eminent man as well as myself.

12. ... **in the bright half** [of the month] (sita) **on the lunar day** (tithau, sing. locative of tithi) ... [of the full moon (<pārva>ṇaśya, read as pārvaṇasya, sing. genitive of pārvaṇa)] **and** (ca) **on the day of the week** (vāre, sing. locative of vāra) **called** (nāmani, sing. locative case of nāman) **Suraguru, in the month** (māse, sing. locative of māsa) ... [of Āśvina (<ā>ś<v>ina)] **was established** (sthāpitavāñ = sthāpitavān, sing. nom of sthāpitavat) ... [the image and/or temple] **by that melodious** (kala) **eminent man** (vira)[76] **as well as** (ca) **myself** (yathaham, read as yathāham).

Body	Longitude	Nakṣatra	Pāda	Rāśi	Navāṃśa
Lagna	29 Virgo 18' 17.74"	Citra	2	Vi	Vi
Sun	29 Virgo 16' 09.94"	Citra	2	Vi	Vi
Moon	24 Pisces 48' 54.48"	Revatī	3	Pi	Aq
Mars	19 Scorpio 59' 53.40"	Jyeṣtha	1	Sc	Sg
Mercury	17 Libra 01' 36.50"	Svāti	4	Li	Pi
Jupiter	4 Virgo 59' 41.41"	Uttara Phālgunī	3	Vi	Aq
Venus	14 Scorpio 33' 09.58"	Anurādha	4	Sc	Sc
Saturn	21 Sagittarius 14' 25.35	Pūrva Aṣāḍha	3	Sg	Li
Rahu	21 Sagittarius 21' 01.26"	Pūrva Aṣāḍha	3	Sg	Li
Ketu	21 Gemini 21' 01.26"	Punarvasu	1	Ge	Ar

Date:	30 September 782 (Gregorian calendar)
Time:	5:27:12 (arbitrarily set at dawn; however, no lagna was given)
Time Zone:	7:00:00 (East of GMT)
Place:	Prambanan, Central Java, Indonesia (110 E 30' 17", 7 S 44' 26")
Lunar Yr-Mo:	Dundubhi - Āsvayuja
Tithi:	Purṇimasya (full moon) (37.12 percent left)
Vedic Weekday:	Thursday (Bṛhaspati/Guru)
Nakṣatra:	Revatī (38.89 percent left)
Yoga:	Harṣaṇa (94.37 percent left)

Fig. 3-4. Astronomical details hypothetically presented in the inscription.

Both v.11 and v.12 apparently refer to the dating of a consecration event but whether one pertains to the temple and the other to the image remains unclear. The initial verse from this pair of stanzas refers to Kumāraghoṣa as the sole performer of the consecration rite for the 'Mañjughoṣa' in the Śaka year 704. Based on the above interpretation of Bosch's transcription for the final part of the second hemistich, it would seem that both the king and his preceptor had been joint participants, which leaves open the possibility that v.11

[76]Just like Mañjuśrī, Kumāraghoṣa may have been thought to possess a remarkably melodious voice.

provides the year in which the edifice was consecrated and v.12 reveals the specific date on which they installed the principal image.

Strophe 12 refers to the event as having occurred on a Thursday and hence ritualistically associated with Bṛhaspati as the divine incarnation of the Hindu priesthood.[77] As Bosch (1968: 258) observed, the *Ṛgveda* calls Bṛhaspati the 'Lord of the powerful magic word' (Brahmaṇaspati). In Mantrayāna texts the same role is assigned to Mañjuśrī, to whom, among other things, is attributed the invention of the famous *Aracapana* mystic alphabet. Bosch also cited several other striking features shared by Bṛhaspati and Mañjuśrī as deities of wisdom. Among other things, their equivalence is reflected by the fact that both are known as the 'Lord of Speech' (Vāgīśvara, Mañjuśrī; Vācaspati, Bṛhaspati) and bear a sword as one of their defining attributes. Though Mañjuśrī is identified in v.15 as the 'Lord' (*svāmī*) containing all the gods, it is also worth noting that *svāmī* can equally mean 'spiritual preceptor'.

Verses 13, 14, 15 and 16. In v.9 the composer appears to have equated the 'bridge' (*setu*) of Mañjughoṣa with the *kīrtistambha,* though the lacunas leave room for doubt. In vs.13-16 we gradually realize that this so-called 'pillar of glory' is identifiable with the religious foundation in its entirety rather than with the image of Mañjuśrī alone, as Bosch originally had proposed. Bosch also noticed that the composer seems to symbolically link the *kīrtistambha* with its classical predecessor: the Vedic 'world pillar' or *skambha*: "The mighty adorable spirit at the centre of the world, engrossed in penance on the surface of water, on Him rests all the gods that are, even as branches round the trunk of a tree" (AV.10). As Bosch (1929a: 34, n. 1) observed, "It is quite remarkable, then, that it is said of the *skambha* as well as of the *kīrtistambha* of the present inscription (see v.15) that he contains (three and 30) gods", and that both are compared with a tree (v.17 and AV.38). He also observed that the parallel meanings shared by *stambh* ('to make firm [create], to stop, make immovable') and *skambh* ('to make firm [create], to support, to stop, obstruct, impede').

The underlying linkage between the *stambha* ('a post, a pillar, a stem, obstruction') and the Vedic *skambha* ('the fixed, the immovable, that on which a superstructure rests') persists throughout the remainder of the composition. It metaphorically implies that the *kīrtistambha* is a 'bridge' (*setu*) between two places: heaven and earth which are symbolically salvation and *saṃsāra,* respectively. For Buddhists this 'bridge' naturally connects to the Dharma: the Doctrine of the Buddha that enables devotees to cross the divide. Both of these terms correlate very well with the Vedic *skambha*, about which the *brāhmaṇa* Kumāraghoṣa was doubtlessly aware. The Śailendra preceptor seems to have been a learned theologian (*vipra*)[78] who found joy in reintroducing ancient Brahmanic concepts within a Buddhist context, as likewise appears to have been the case with the composer of the *Vairocanābhisambodhi-sūtra* (see Wayman & Tajima 1992: 8).

---

[77]The Kayumwuṅan charter of 824 CE likewise states that the installation of the image of Śrī Ghananātha had taken place on a Thursday.

[78]From √vip, 'trembling, shaking, vibrating; those who vibrate like a power house of energy; mystical heat'. A *vipra* is he whose powers are amassed "through the building up of inner heat, which ultimately enables him to take the place of both fire and the sun—transforming his whole being, as it were into pure energy—and to attain heaven and conquer the realms of the gods" (Mitchiner 1982: 188).

Chapter III: The Śrī Saṅgrāmadhanaṃjaya inscription from the desa Kĕlurak

The way to salvation is represented in a variety of different ways in Buddhist art and scripture, with the most frequently encountered motif being the horizontally-oriented path for bridging a 'chasm' or the boat for sailing across the 'ocean' and with the ocean and chasm equally symbolizing existence in *saṃsāra*. However, Buddhist art also knows of a vertically-oriented path for bridging heaven and earth: the so-called Jacob's Ladder. In the *Vimalakīrtinirdeśa-sūtra* this is the ladder connecting the paradise of Abhirati[79] in Jambudvīpa (hence apparently a terrestrial location rather than a heavenly abode) with the Trayastriṁśa heaven "and on that noble ladder the Trayastriṁśa's gods descend into the Jambudvīpa to see the Tathāgata Akṣobhya and do him homage, worship him and to hear the Law" (Richardson & Pal 1983: 139-140).[80]

The concluding segment of the *Mañjuśrīkumārabhūta-aṣṭottaraśatakanāma* (see Giebel 2011), a Siddham text that Kūkai brought to Japan in 806 CE, refers to the text's preceding presentation of the 108 Names of Mañjuśrī with a Thousand Bowls (T. 1177B), as 'this ladder of unequaled power' (*īmaṃ jiner [=jinair] atulabalādhirohiṇī*). In the Tibetan translation of this work, however, *dhāraṇī* appears to have been substituted for 'ladder'.

> "This ladder (*Tib. dhāraṇī*) of unequaled power, standing in the preeminent path, radiant, honoured by those who have a pledge with the gods, captivating, and earnestly beheld (*Tib.* desired) by gods and demigods, was well chanted by the Victors (i.e., Buddhas). Here ends the One Hundred and Eight Names" (Giebel 2011: 335).

Verse 19 of the Śrī Saṅgrāmadhanaṃjaya inscription suggests that the term *dharmasetu* applies to the structure for housing the image of Mañjuśrī (=Kumāra). Given the equivalence established between the *kīrtistambha* and the *dharmasetu* in v.13, and perhaps in v.9 as well, it is entirely possible that the Three Jewels had been represented—either inside the principal structure or within external niches—as an image triad, which seems to be the case within the inner sanctum at Caṇḍi Mendut. In fact, we shall subsequently see that Mañjuśrī plays the principal role with respect to the creation of an entire *maṇḍala* filled with both Buddhist and Hindu divinities, according to the early NS commentators. Strophe 15 suggests the possibility of such a connection by referring to Mañjuśrī as the Lord (*svāmī*) containing all divinities.[81]

---

[79]Abhirati is also the heaven that potentially can be associated with Mañjuśrī given that he is the spiritual son of Akṣobhya.

[80]In a hymn dedicated to Bṛhaspati from the *Ṛgveda* (2,28,6), Indra's close companion is the personification of *mantra* and sacred songs whose heavenly manifestation is the 'voice of the thunder'. Therein, Bṛhaspati is also called the *pathikṛt:* 'preparer of the path' or 'path-maker': "Thou art our keeper, wise, preparer of our paths: we, for thy service, sing to thee with hymns of praise. Bṛhaspati, whoever lays a snare for us, him may his evil fate, precipitate, destroy".

[81]Chandra (1995: 223) noted that *vajradhṛk* can also be interpreted as a reference to Vajradhara, which is of interest in light of Vilāsavajra's remark that when the opening verse of the NS refers to Vajradhara as 'glorious' (*śrīmān*)—as is perhaps likewise the case in v.15 of the inscription—this can mean "one who possesses (-mān) 'śrī', that is to say, [one who possesses] 'goddesses'. And this alludes to his extensiveness (audārya)". The text's translator adds: "Śri is identified as devatī, a word used in Buddhist contexts as equivalent to devata. This is seen, for instance, in sādhanas devoted to Tārā where the term denotes the offering goddesses (pūjādevī).... Thus to say that Vajradhara is glorious is to say that he is surrounded by a maṇḍala of deities. The maṇḍala deities represent the active, compassionate, all-pervading aspect of the deity

The verse's compositum *sarvadevamayaḥ* echoes the Vaiṣṇava expression *sarvadevamaya hari,* which means 'Hari represents in himself all the gods'; it also reminds of another expression well known in India: *sarvadevamayaḥ guruḥ*, 'the *guru* is made up of all divinity'. From a doctrinal point of view, saying that Mañjuśrī includes all the gods is not substantially different from what the *Kāraṇḍavyūha-sūtra* suggests about Ārya Avalokiteśvara by stating that the sun (Āditya) and moon (Candra) are born from the bodhisattva's eyes, Maheśvara [Śiva] from his brow, Brahmā from his shoulders, Narayāna [Viṣṇu] from his heart, Sarasvatī from his teeth, Vāyu from his mouth, the Dharaṇī from his feet and Varuṇa from his stomach.

"Avalokiteśvara, thereby, is associated with one of the central tenets of the *īśvara* doctrine—the idea of the cosmic *puruṣa*—without offending Buddhist norms. The sūtra version of the *puruṣasūkta* myth, in the end, reads like a variation on the classic Mahāyāna belief that Avalokiteśvara is able to manifest in different forms according to the needs of different individuals" (Studholme 2002: 44).

The Vedic *skambha* was similarly envisioned as the embodiment of the cosmic *puruṣa* within whose one limb all the Gods, three and thirty in number, are affixed. Hence, the present inscription's potential representation of the *kīrtistambha* as the monumental embodiment of Mañjuśrī would be comparable to the Vedic tradition after which it may have been modeled. What's more, Mañjuśrī is capable of manifesting himself in a multiplicity of divine forms, as early Mantrayāna texts such as the *Mañjuśrīmūlakalpa* (MMK) attest.

Verse 17. This stanza evokes the mental image of a *kalpadruma* "whereof the roots are the bodhicitta, the trunk is the compassion, the branches are the great forbearance, [and] the leaves are the desired shelter" (Sarkar 1971/2: I: 46). In the previously cited homage to Mañjuśrī written by Śāntideva, which appears near the end of the *Śikṣāsamuccaya* (XIX.70a), the bodhisattva is lauded as "the wishing-tree (*kalpapādapaṃ*) with the fruits (*phala*) abounding in (*sphīta*) the ten regions (*daśadik*) that are desired (*iṣṭa*) by the world (*jagad*), that is venerated (*arcitam*, sing. acc. of *arcita*, 'honored, worshiped, respected, saluted') by the lotus-eyes (*netra-utpala*) of people (*jagan* in comp. for *jagat*) delighted (*saṃhṛṣṭa*) by the attainment (*prāpti*) of their desires (*prārthita*)".

This quintessential Wishing Tree is the Bodhi Tree—Mahāyāna Buddhism's symbol *par excellence* for signifying the attainment of enlightenment—and therefore a popular metaphor encountered in texts devoted to discussing the spiritual growth that arises from the root of compassion, such as the *Prajñāpāramitā-sūtra* (Conze 1961: 524-525), the *Avataṁsaka-sūtra* (Cleary 1993: 1001) and the *Mahāyānasūtralaṁkāra* (Nagao and Silk 2000: 13-15). In the Śrī Saṅgrāmadhanamjaya inscription, however, the tree's root is *bodhicitta* whereas the trunk is compassion and the ensuing analogies pertaining to the branches, and leaves proceed without any mention of the flowers or fruits. These significant points of difference strongly suggest the application of a different philosophical viewpoint in which *bodhicitta* was considered the essential primordial component. From the tenor of

at the centre of the maṇḍala and so the term śrīmān can also be associated with Vajradhara's skill in means (upāya)" (Tribe 1994: 73, including n. 28).

the inscription as a whole, which repeatedly refers to Mañjuśrī by name or epithets (Mañjughoṣa, Mañjurava, Mañjuvāk, etc.), one suspects that the underlying philosophical system must be one in which Mañjuśrī plays a major role.

Stanzas 5-10 of the *Bodhicittabhāvana* characterize *bodhicitta* "as the very essence of the Dharma and the essence itself of the 'Eternal Mañjuśrī'; as the mother of all the Blissful Ones (*sugata*), the sole path of all the Victors (*jina*); as the basis of the path of the vast collection of spiritual practices, beginning with Virtue (*sīla*), and so forth. This is the immaculate Enlightened-mind (*bodhicitta*), inherently ripe with the most excellent attributes (*guṇa*)". And as an anonymous Tibetan-language commentary further explains: "If one has not taken hold of the ten ways of overcoming (limitations), such as ethical conduct, etc., as well as other wholesome activities, which is this primordial state [of *bodhicitta*], then the accumulation (of merit) that leads to the state of an Awakened One has not been accomplished. Thus, it is also shown that [*bodhicitta*] is the basis of all the merits accumulated for the sake of reaching the state of an Awakened One" (Mañjuśrīmitra *et al.* 1986: 72).[82] It is in this particular sense of *bodhicitta* that the Wishing Tree of the present inscription can be viewed as the 'Tree of Practice' (*kalpa,* 'manner of acting, proceeding, practice'; *druma*, 'tree') by means of which bodhisattvas engage in the cultivation of the Enlightened Mind on behalf of all sentient beings.

The Wishing Tree's 'trunk' (*skandha*) is equated with compassion in v.17. However, the Sanskrit word *skandha* also carries the meaning of 'aggregate'. And the 'branches' of the *kalpadruma* signify the 'great forbearance' (*mahākṣamā*), whereas the 'leaves' are the 'highly desired shelter' or 'highly desired place of refuge' (*abhivāñchita-āśraya*).[83] On the other hand, *āśraya* also may have been intended to evoke the Buddhistic doctrine of *āśraya-parāvṛtti:* the fundamental transformation or 'revolution of the basis' that enables advanced bodhisattvas to perform their salvation activities in the midst of mundane existence while remaining high above it, free from delusions like a lotus unstained by the mud from which it has arisen. By means of *āśraya-parāvṛtti*, "'Cognition is revolved and Wisdom is acquired' ... , it is said, and this wisdom is none other than the essence of the threefold body of Buddha. Thus, the doctrine of *āśraya-parāvṛtti* is an attempt to clarify that the human way of being, along with its basis, revolves itself and becomes the Buddha's way of being, or realizes the Buddha's body, his basis" (Nagao and Kawamura 1991: 116-117). According to Asaṅga (*Mahāyānasaṃgraha* 9.1), the end result is the 'non-abiding *nirvāṇa*' (*apratiṣṭhita-nirvāṇa*),[84] which then serves as the foundation (*āśraya*) that enables

---

[82]*Primordial experience: An introduction to rDzogs-chen meditation* is the only translation of the *Bodhicittabhāvana* and its anonymous Tibetan commentary (*Byaṅ chub sems bsgom pa don bcu gnyis bstan pa*) published to date in print form. Unfortunately, the translators have distorted the meaning of several key phrases (see Nordstrom 1989: 355-357) by avoiding traditional Buddhist technical terminology, which the translators dismiss as 'tribal jargon'. For this reason, a 1995 translation by the Kunpal Tulku for the Dharma Fellowship of His Holiness the Gyalwa Karmapa posted online is cited in the vast majority of cases herein. See http://www.dharmafellowship.org/library/texts/cultivation-of-enlightened-mind.htm, accessed 24 Feb. 2014.

[83]Abhi is a prefix for expressing superiority or intensity; *vāñchita* means 'to desire, wish, ask for, strive after, pursue'.

[84]According to Mus (1934: 272), this *apratiṣṭhita-nirvāṇa* of Buddhahood is comparable to viewing the world as if from the summit of a mountain. For the Mahāsattva elevated to these heights, the old 'background' was not destroyed, but was rather purified. The activities of the senses, the apprehensions of the mind, and other

advanced bodhisattvas to eliminate afflictions (*kleśa*) without rejecting the world of cyclic existence (Makransky 1997: 81).

Strophe 17 ends with the normally short syllable 'ti', but this automatically becomes long because of the pause that naturally occurs at the end of a stanza. This caesura is also called a '*yati*', which means 'stopping' or 'ceasing' (Egenes 2000: 88). So the composer's choice of *yati* for the final two syllables of this verse might be more than a coincidence. Besides, *ja* is the last syllable that appears at the end of line 13, whilst *yati* is found at the beginning of the following line, just before the double *daṇḍa* indicating the end of the strophe. Within the context of the reading experience, the hiatus between *ja* and *yati* may very well have had the purpose of emphasizing the cessation of rebirth as the concluding theme of this verse. Sarkar (1971/2: I: 46) glossed *jayati* as 'be victorious' and placed the contents of the second hemistich at the beginning of his translation of strophe 17. However, the translation of *jayati*[85] as 'victorious [in the ceasing of rebirth]' not only would complete the meaning of the verse but also be entirely appropriate and felicitous in the present context.

Another issue that needs to be addressed is the parsing of this verse's initial Sanskrit word, for which only the first syllable *da* remains. The available choices for *da* ˘ that would seem to fit the strophe's overall context are *dadha* ('bestowing'), *dala* ('a small shoot' in reference to plantlike growth) and *dama* ('residence, house'). Given that the inscription's 'Tree of Practice' serves as a metaphor for spiritual growth, the emendation *da<la>* has been proposed here-above in a translation segment footnote.

Āśraya means 'place of refuge' and thus is potentially applicable to the religious foundation as a whole. In BB vs.1-4, the text's composer presents his analysis of the Three Jewels[86] and then concludes with the following statement: "to this triad that is one throughout, with a characterless mind of supreme faith, we make salutation". As the anonymous Tibetan commentary further explains, "The place of refuge is the three jewels. The ultimate content of what is, is the unerring path. This is what is to be known; the Awakened Ones and those heroically committed to Awakening are those who know this" (Mañjuśrīmitra *et al.* 2001: 71). This provides us with a potential framework for viewing v.17 of the present inscription as encompassing the entire Buddhahood continuum: as the 'ground' (the root); as the 'path' whereby the 'unfolding growth' of one's ordinary body, speech and mind is transformed into the divine Body, Speech and Mind (trunk, branches and leaves); and as the 'perfected fruition state' (e.g. the ceasing of rebirth).[87]

---

factors with which this basis (*āśraya*) had previously been impregnated, also are eliminated through the intervention of Bodhi, which is to say the absolute and sublime wisdom pervading the depths of human consciousness. So these internal conditions of differentiation and error disappear within the advanced bodhisattvas and with external conditions materializing around them that serve as the stage for the operations of their enlightening minds.

[85]With respect to *mantra*, the syllable JA is identified in the *Prajñāpāramitā-sūtra* (Conze 1961: 160) as a door to all *dharma*-s "because of the non-apprehension of birth (*jāti*)"; likewise, in chapter two of the VAS (Wayman & Tajima 1992: 133), JA is a gate of all dharmas "because there is no apprehension of birth (*jāti*)".

[86]As (a) "the Blissful One (*sugata*), the Embodiment of the inconceivable Gnosis of the Source of Reality (*dharmadhātu jñāna*), who is without either (personal or phenomenal) identity"; (b) "the Quiescent Nature (*santi-svabhāva*) of all (phenomena), arrived at through the supreme path of neither acceptance nor rejection"; and (c) "all the Followers of the Lord (*bhagavat*), possessing the ten powers of not falling-back, etc.".

[87]As the eleventh century NS commentator Smṛtijñānakīrti explained, "There are three kinds of Mañjuśrī: (1) Mañjuśrī of the self-existence cause, attended with all bonds; (2) Mañjuśrī of the cultivation-path not free

Comparable to the sap that arises from the roots to nourish the entire tree, *bodhicitta* is the very essence that sustains every single unfolding stage of growth, from the initial Thought of Enlightenment that is the 'cause'—and the path unfolding therefrom—to the Mind of Enlightenment as the 'perfected fruition state'. Along the entire Buddhahood continuum, *bodhicitta* serves as both the cause and the fruit of each successive stage of growth. "Every Enlightened-being (bodhisattva), belonging to the immortal great lineage of the saints, could not have come into being except for this [Enlightened-mind (*bodhicitta*)], and this is the Path itself of supreme Liberation" (BB vs.16-17).

Strophe 17 is a natural extension of the symbolic linkage between the *kīrtistambha* and the Vedic cosmic pillar (*skambha*) mentioned earlier.

> "The pillar symbolizes the link between heaven and earth, and is also the embodiment of the universe; it both contains and also indicates the path leading from earth to heaven—just as it was in the pillar (in the form of the sacrificial *yūpa*) that the gods hid the sacrifice.... The *skambha* is in a sense a further embodiment of *brahman* and Prajāpati, and the appearance of both the Ṛṣis and eka-Ṛṣi within it underlines the role of both as manifestations of *brahman* and as the links which bind together the divine and human realms" (Mitchiner 1982: 306-307).

Though v.17 of the inscription characterizes the *kalpadruma* as the new Wishing-tree of the Kali Yuga—the current World Age which is the least auspicious of the four periods that comprise a *kalpa*—Mañjuśrī's powers to transform the inauspicious into the auspicious is signaled by his close identification with the Great Being standing in the midst of the world in the form of the cosmic pillar to whom all the *devas* are joined as if they were the branches surrounding the trunk of a tree.

> "This world tree is the tree of life. Its stem passes through the centre of all life, of every state of being; from it they ramify; at the top of this tree is the sun, its fruit. In this tree all the birds make their nest as man did when he still lived near the age of Truth, the Perfect age, the Satya or Kṛta Yuga, when the tree witnesses his gradual engagement and still supports him as tree of knowledge" (Kramrisch 1946: 118).

Verse 18. The evocation of the protective powers of the Mañjuśrī image, together with his monumental embodiment, is a theme to which the composer of the present inscription repeatedly returns. The classical Mahāyāna Buddhist texts do not provide us with any strong evidence that their authors had regarded Mañjuśrī as the possessor of strong protective powers. It is only when we turn to the early Mantrayāna texts, as well as the later Vajrayāna scriptures, that Mañjuśrī's protective capabilities step to the foreground.

> "In company with Avalokiteśvara and Vajrapāṇi, Mañjuśrī forms a well-known triad of protectors, one of the earliest examples of which is found in the *Mañjuśrīmūlakalpa* [MMK]. In the same text, Yamāntaka, later identified as a wrathful manifestation of Mañjuśrī, is portrayed as being at Mañjuśrī's service" (Tribe 1997a).

---

from some side (*pakṣa*); (3) Mañjuśrī of the final result, free from extremes" (Wayman 1985: 60).

The role of Mañjuśrī as a protector divinity rose to prominence in Japan during the early ninth century. For example, Mañjuśrī is the chief deity in the fire ritual (*homa*) of protection (*śāntika*) that Kukai imported from China (White 2000: 489-490). And Mañjuśrī became closely associated with protective spells, amulets and charms in Tibet through his close association with a wrathful 'Destroyer of Death' (Yamāntaka).

As we have previously seen, the Śrī Saṅgrāmadhanaṃjaya inscription incorporates several names and epithets for the composition's principal divinity: Mañjuśrī (from *śrī*, 'glory'; vs. 8, 10, 16) and Sarvajña (v.8); Mañjughoṣa (from *ghoṣ*, 'voice'; vs. 9, 11); Mañjuvāk (from *vāg*, 'speech'; v.15); Mañjurava (v.18) and Kumāra (v.19).[88] What is atypical about v.18 is the identification of the text's principal divinity as "Ye the Tārkṣya" (Garuḍa).[89] To my knowledge, the Garuḍa manifestation of Mañjuśrī is only attested in the MMK, which integrates colophons that identify this text as a *vaipulya-sūtra* and hence yet another text that presumably fell within the purview of the Śailendra preceptor (see v.6).

> "In chapter 2 we are given a number of *mantras* associated with different deities, including the major Hindu deities Śiva and Viṣṇu. When we come to the *mantra* of Viṣṇu we are told that in fact such *mantras* in the Vaiṣṇava *tantras* were actually proclaimed by Mañjuśrī, disguised as Viṣṇu as a skillful means to help living beings (31). Similarly it is Mañjuśrī who has proclaimed the *mantras* in the Śiva *tantras* (33) and the Garuḍa *mantra* to cure snake bite (34-35). In order to help living beings and destroy snakes, Mañjuśrī appeared as Garuḍa. We are then told: *yāvanto laukikā mantrah te 'smi kalpa udāhṛtāḥ / vaineyārthaṃ hi sattvānāṃ vicarāmi tathā tathā //* [MMK 2.39]. A free translation of this, that I feel captures its meaning, would be as follows: 'All of the *laukika* (Hindu) *mantras* that are proclaimed in this ritual text are proclaimed by me taking this or that form for the sake of teaching living beings'." (Laughlin 2000: 409).

In his search for a plausible explanation for the identification of Mañjuśrī with the appellation Tārkṣya, as indicated in v.18, Bosch (1968: 241-261) examined a number of legends pertaining to Mañjuśrī and noted that a Tibetan tale describes his birth atop a lotus blossom which had sprouted from the Trkṣa (a *jambu* tree, *Eugenia jambolana*) located on the southern spur of the five-peaked Gandhamadana mountain chain, which is comparable to Mount Meru in several respects.[90] According to Bosch, Tārkṣya would mean the 'son of

---

[88]This wide range of names for the same divinity is most unusual for a Central Javanese charter but is one of the defining characteristics of the NS.

[89]Though the designation Garuḍa is more widely attested in Mahāyāna Buddhist scriptures, the divinity's alternate name of Tārkṣya appears in the *Buddhacarita*.

[90]The fame of Mañjuśrī as the eternally youthful crown prince (Kumārabhūta) may stem in part from the fact that the fruit of the *jambu* tree, at least with respect to the Meru cosmological model, is said to possess a juice that enables the inhabitants of Jambudvīpa to "pass their days in content and health, being subject neither to perspiration, to foul odors, to decrepitude, nor organic decay", according to the *Viṣṇu Purāṇa*. His ability to assume different bodily forms also may be attributed to his Ṛṣi lineage. By means of the fire of *tapas* amassed from ascetic austerities, the Ṛṣis are able to transmute their entire beings into fiery heat and energy, which underlies their "ability to attain rejuvenation and renewal of bodily forms" (Mitchiner 1982: 211).

the *jambu* tree named the Trkṣa'. He also mentioned that many other story elements from this Tibetan legend equally apply to the sire of the Garuḍa: the *ṛṣi* Kaśyapa.[91]

Among other things, this Vedic sage and member of the Seven Ṛṣis likewise was born from a *jambu* tree on the southern mountain of the five-peaked Gandhamadana, and with both Mañjuśrī and Kaśyapa playing similar key roles in legends pertaining to the birth of the kingdoms of Nepal and Kashmir. These parallel developments led Bosch to conclude that the allocation of the name Tārkṣya to Mañjuśrī as well as Garuḍa—the most famous of the many descendants of Kaśyapa—demonstrates that, at the very least, these two divinities were thought to share the same Ṛṣi bloodline.[92]

Earlier in his professional career, Bosch (1929b: 39-43) demonstrated that Buddhist artisans were well aware of Mañjuśrī's *ṛṣi* lineage. This knowledge is exemplified by the unusual hair-style borne by the famous statue of Mañjuśrī (8.25 kg, 92% silver) that a rice farmer discovered while cutting grass on his land in Ngĕmplak Sĕmongan, Semarang, Central Java. In his discussion of this unique find, Bosch succeeded in identifying the 28-cm-high figure as the depiction of a specific form of Mañjuśrī known as Śikhādhara ('Lock-bearer'), which is mentioned in a Nepalese text entitled the *Trikaṇḍaśeṣa*.

According to Bosch (1929b: 42), families in ancient India performed a special ceremony (*cūḍākaraṇa,* lit. 'tonsure') for Hindu male youths during which the head was shaved, and with the prescribed number of hair locks retained on the crown being based on the youth's family lineage. Several locks (*cūḍā*) were retained whenever Ṛṣis were named in a boy's pedigree. The silver statue displays three hair-locks, which are located at the middle, right and left of the crown.

The Sanskrit term *śikhara* ('mountain summit'), which can refer to the crowning cupola of a Hindu temple, is derived from *śikha*,

> "and more specifically refers to the hair-tuft worn by Hindus at the scapular foramen [e.g. the crown of the skull] to mark the location of the 'aperture of Brahman' (*brahmarandhra*), the point where the axis of the body (*merudaṇḍa*, *brahmadaṇḍa*) emerges from the top of the head. The same associations are connected with the word *stūpa*, which in its literal sense also means 'topknot' or 'crest'; whence its derivative,

---

[91]"The word *kaśyapa* means a tortoise, and in the *Brāhmaṇas* he is identified in this role both with Prajāpati and also with the sun" (Mitchiner 1982: 259-260). It is also doubtlessly by way of his Ṛṣi lineage that Mañjuśrī is known as the 'Lord of speech' (Vāgīśvara). "[T]he role of the Ṛṣis as seers and composers of both hymns and other works ... arises in part from the very nature of sacred speech or *vāc*, which is seen as a form of breath (*prāṇa*) and also as a form of both fire and the sun: whence the use of *vāc*—particularly in chanting hymns—enables the chanter both to attain heaven and also defeat his enemies" (Mitchiner 1982: 176-177). "Ṛṣis were viewed as a king of oracle, an infallible speaker whose speech alone literally carries power and authority—a fiery utterance from a receptacle of fire and tapas" (Mitchiner 1982: 210).

[92]"Another word which is frequently used—from the *Ṛgveda* onwards—as a synonym of the term Ṛṣi is *vipra*, and the Seven Ṛṣis are frequently referred to as the seven *vipras* or *vipra*-Ṛṣi, especially in connection with the singing of hymns and the performance of the soma-sacrifice" (Mitchiner 1982: 187). As the hereditary family priests of monarchs (*purohita*), Ṛṣis played a powerful role in the ruling of the kingdom as the ruler's *guru*. They "frequently accompany a king on his military expeditions, often taking an active part in any conflicts" (Mitchiner 1982: 220). "The very presence of a Ṛṣi was like that of a smoldering and threatening fire ready to blaze forth and consume the worlds; and when a king of people obtained the favor of a Ṛṣi, well might their enemies tremble" (Mitchiner 1982: 222).

stūpikā, which is the topmost finial of a building, the portion of its axis that emerges above the capstone. As does *śikha*, the term *stūpa* signifies the hair-tuft at the topmost point of the human body; by way of analogy it comes to indicate the topmost point of the building; and finally it is applied to the edifice as a whole: the building is named for its crowning and focal element" (Snodgrass 1985: 263).

By analogy, the statue's distinctive three hair-lock (*śikhaṇḍaka*) coiffure may signal the divinity's special affinity with the *ratnatraya*, just as other representations of Mañjuśrī with five locks (*pañcaciraka*), five top knots (*pañcaśikha*) or a crown adorned with a Tathāgata pentad symbolically evoke his place of birth on the summit of the aforementioned five-peaked mountain as well as his mastery of the five-fold transcendental Awareness. The two curved protrusions of the middle part of the silver Mañjuśrī statue's neck chain represent tiger's claws, an iconographic attribute that was exclusively given to Mañjuśrī sculptures in India (Mallmann 1964: 34-35). Within cave 10 at Ellora (Malandra 1993: 101), for example, there is a Mañjuśrī sculpture that displays three hair-locks, a book atop a lotus and a tiger claw necklace or *vyāghraṇakha.* Mañjuśrī is also depicted as seated on the back of a tiger (or a lion) in some cases.[93]

Fig. 3-5. Silver statue of Mañjuśrī Śikhādhara (photo credit: Collectie Tropen Museum).

The Sanskrit meter known as 'Tiger's play' (Śārdūlavikrīḍita) is featured in vs. 7, 8 and 10 of the present inscription. Stanzas eight and 10 refer directly to the Mañjuśrī image, while v.7 pertains to the Śailendra preceptor. This potentially reinforces Chandra's surmise that the king had regarded his *guru* to be an incarnation of this Buddhist divinity, a deduction that also potentially receives a modicum of support from the expression *kalavira* ('melodious eminent man') in v.12.

Verses 19 and 20. Here it is helpful to compare the use of *dharmasetu* in strophe 19 of the present inscription to how the same designation was employed in v.10 of the Kalasan

[93]Based on his epigraphical analysis of an inscribed silver plate found embedded in the base of the figure, Bosch suggested an early tenth-century date for the statue's creation. He also concluded that a local Javanese artisan must have created this silver statue of Śikhādhara, due to the similarities between the ornamental motives adorning the figure's garments and those displayed at several Central Javanese temples. However, Bernet Kempers (1959: 52) was inclined to regard this image as an import from India.

charter. In either example, the composer used the Sanskrit term to refer to a Buddhist religious foundation. Moreover, v.13 of the present inscription suggests that the terms *dharmasetu* and *kīrtistambha* are mutually exchangeable.

The final verse of the Śrī Saṅgrāmadhanaṃjaya inscription provides us with the consecration name of the Śailendra king responsible for the construction activities previously mentioned in the Sanskrit text. The appellation's predicate is the famous epithet of the epic hero Arjuna, which the ever vigilant reader no doubt had already noticed: "They call me Dhanaṃjaya because I stand in the midst of booty after conquering all the country-sides and plundering their entire wealth" (*Mahābhārata* 4,[47],39,10-15). *Saṅgrāma* means 'an assembly of people, host, troop, army' and 'battle, war, fight, combat, conflict', whereas Arjuna's epithet *dhanaṃjaya* can either be translated as 'conqueror of wealth' or 'crusher of foes'. Hence, Śrī Saṅgrāmadhanaṃjaya can be glossed as the 'Illustrious Crusher of foes in battle'—especially if we presume that the composer's intent was to build upon the epithet previously awarded to the Śailendra monarch in v.4: 'Crusher of valiant foes of [powerful] enemies' (*vairivaravīravimardana*).

Only the initial 18 *akṣara*-s contained in line 16 have been transcribed, even though the concluding line of this inscription extends all the way to the far side of the stone. The size of the *akṣara*-s are significantly larger at the bottom of the stone than at the top, with line 15 having originally contained 50 *akṣara*-s. This last figure provides us with a rough guideline for determining that ample space remained in line 16 for accommodating the remainder of what is presumed to have been v.20's second hemistich, together with an addendum.[94] Hence, line 16 easily could have encompassed a reference to a donation made by the king to the monastic community for the upkeep of the Mañjughoṣa foundation. The equivalent declaration in the Kalasan charter only spans a portion of the first hemistich of the stanza seven in Āryā meter.

The Śrī Saṅgrāmadhanaṃjaya inscription's 'pillar of glory'

Chandra (1995: 221-222) has expressed the opinion that the *kīrtistambha* mentioned repeatedly in the present inscription must have been an immense tower or gate featuring niches filled with images and narrative reliefs illustrating scenes pertaining to the Mañjuśrī cycle of tales from the Mahāyāna Buddhist scriptures. One of the more striking Hindu parallels would be India's famous 'Tower of Fame' constructed from 1439 to 1459 at Chittor in commemoration of a victory by the ruler Mahārāṇā Kumbhā. This gracefully exuberant building is adorned with the images of Hindu divinities, is 37.2 m. high; one of the inscriptions attached to the structure identifies it as the *mahāmeru-śrī-kīrtistambha* (Sircar 1966: 181).

It was a common practice in India and elsewhere in South Asia for kings to erect a pillar or tower to commemorate their victories. These monolithic structures, which temple donors also erected to celebrate the generous gift-giving, often bore inscriptions that detailed the celebrated events that led to their establishment. Moreover, these monolithic structures invariably stood in relation to a temple in its immediate vicinity, with the pillar or tower most often located on the entrance side of its associated temple.

---

[94]We have already encountered a comparable example at the end of v.9 in the Kalasan charter.

According to Lévi (1905: 14), one of the most popular auxiliary religious structures in ancient Nepal was the independent pillar established in front of Buddhist and Śivaite temples. Whether planted directly in the ground or installed on top of a tortoise base, these pillars were almost always crowned with a capital in the form of an open lotus, which also served as the base for an image in some cases. For example, an engraved pillar was erected during 464 CE presumably in celebration of the victories of Licchavi Mānadeva (464-506) over the Mallas, which enabled the Nepalese king to return to his capital with a wealth of booty (Riccardi 1989). The pillar originally was located directly in front of the west-facing entrance to the Caṅgu Nārāyaṇa temple in Nepal's Kathmandu Valley (see Juramie 2003: 37, fig. 2) and originally may have had an image of a Garuḍa on its capital prior to its collapse.

The question is whether an actual *kīrtistambha* had once stood beside a religious foundation where an image of Mañjuśrī had been honored as an important, if not the principal, divinity. Bosch rejected this hypothesis on several grounds. Among other things, no ancient remains have ever been uncovered on Java that would suggest they had originated from either a tall pillar, tower or *toraṇa.* This led Bosch to conclude that the composer of the inscription had used the Sanskrit term *kīrtistambha* in a metaphorical sense. To support this interpretation, he cited the Khmer inscription of Kdĕi Aṅ, which states that a physician of King Jayavarman had erected a *liṅga* and founded a sanctuary devoted to Śiva-Vijayeśvara in 589 Śaka. The text mentions that an ancestor of this physician had established statues of Hara and Hari, which were 'erected high like two pillars of glory, destined to remain standing for as long as the earth will be standing'.

> "Although a word such as *iva* to express a comparison is lacking in the Kĕlurak inscription, the above has nevertheless made it very probable that in verses nine and 13 the word *kīrtistambha* has no bearing on the outward appearance or positioning of the Mañjuśrī statue but that the said image, just as in the Cambodian inscription, is metaphorically compared with 'a pillar of glorious piety', which in Indian figurative language usually means identified with. If we accept the above explanation of *kīrtistambha* as correct, we are not forced to resort to a strange and inappropriate representation within the framework of Hindu Javanese art, but are allowed to assume that the Mañjuśrī statue had been placed on a lotus cushion in the usual bodhisattva posture and that this [cushion] rested on a pedestal (wherein the stone [inscription] was bricked in?)" (Bosch 1929a: 33-34).

As previously stated, however, v.19 suggests that a statue of the Kumāra had resided within a religious foundation (*dharmasetu*). Moreover, the identification of this religious institution (*setu*) with the *kīrtistambha* is implied in v.9 and v.14, and by extension also identified with the Wish-fulfillment Tree presented in v.17.[95] Therefore, one alternate explanation is that the inscription's composer had intended to metaphorically compare the entire construction—presumably a temple with a vertically-oriented superstructure seated on a plinth—with 'a pillar of glorious piety'.

[95]By contrast, *iva* clarifies the metaphorical nature of the comparison being made between the *stūpa*-s and *caitya*-s and wish-fulfillment jewels in v.A10 of the Isthmus of Kra stele.

The location where this religious foundation had formerly stood remains an open question that demands a closer examination of the general area in which the inscribed stone was found. Our investigation of the area in which the old *desa* Kĕlurak had formerly stood is complicated by two factors: (a) a number of other temple constructions had formerly stood in the general vicinity of Prambanan that are no longer in evidence today because the Javanese had removed their stones for use in more recent construction projects;[96] and (b) the evidence suggests that a sizable number of temple stones from the general vicinity of Caṇḍi Sewu had been moved to the east. With respect to the latter point, it does not seem likely that a relatively large inscription formerly placed in the immediate vicinity of Caṇḍi Sewu would had been moved a half-kilometer to the south instead of the east.

Brumund's examination of the last remnants of Caṇḍi Asu, which were located several hundred meters to the east of Caṇḍi Sewu, sheds additional light on the removal and use of stones from the entire Sewu temple complex during the middle of the nineteenth century.

> "Caṇḍi Asu is situated just right behind an abandoned *dalem* [an enclosed royal residence] of considerable size, surrounded by a 12-foot-high wall built up from caṇḍi-stones. This *dalem*, for which Caṇḍi Asu and Caṇḍi Sewu had supplied the stones, was 20 years ago built and occupied by the Toemengoeng [a title of nobility] Wirio-Negoro. He and his son were later deprived of their posts. The Javanese say that this was the punishment that most assuredly had struck them because of their destructive offense against the *caṇḍis*. But they themselves [the common people] commit no less offenses by putting the stones [from the temples] to use as the thresholds or foundations for their huts, also for water conduits and for other purposes" (Brumund 1854: 25).

Brumund also mentioned the possibility that another man-made structure had perhaps existed in the general vicinity of Lumbung and Prambanan during ancient times.

> "Behind Caṇḍi Lumbung is a hill from which some hewed stones protrude. There too a *caṇḍi* was located in the past; we gave [the site] the name of Telogo ('lake, pond'), after the nearby pond. This so-called lake, nowadays dry and elevated, is still recognizable in its perimeter as a great oblong quadrangle. We suspect this also dates from the time of the *caṇḍis* and contained water for purification or holy water" (*Ibid*).

However, when IJzerman (1886: 77) visited the Telogo site, located 735 m. due east of Prambanan's north gate and 610 m. southeast of Caṇḍi Lumbung's eastern perimeter, he found a pond full of water but encountered no surface traces of a former temple. This may be the very same body of water that Crawfurd encountered in 1816 while traveling between the villages of Plaosan and Prambanan. Crawfurd thought the pool was a man-made tank.

[96]See, for example, the remarks made by Stutterheim (1926a and 1926b) about the remnants of the temple foundations that formerly lined the road to the south that had presumably led to the building complex situated on top of the Ratu Baka prominence as well as the observation made by the Dutch architect C. F. Reimer in the late eighteenth century concerning two temples he described as being located on either side of the road "a few hundred strides" from Prambanan (see Bosboom 1902).

> "The site of the temples of *Prambanan* is abundantly supplied with fine water, so much desired by the *Hindus*, and so necessary to the performance of their rituals. Besides two rivers of the purest water, there is between the villages of *Prambanan* and *Plaosan* a small tank, evidently an appendage of the temples. This little piece of water is a square of about 200 feet to a side. The ground around it is elevated and there is every appearance of it being an artificial excavation. The whole tank is covered with the blue *Lotus*, the flower of which is so conspicuous an ornament of the sculptures on the temples.
> The *Lotus* though a native of *Java*, is generally propagated in the first instances by art, after which it perpetuates itself, so that we may hazard a conjecture, that the plants which now cover this little sheet of water, are from the original stock planted by the first founders of the temples" (Crawfurd 1820: 346).

Crawfurd's observations are of particular interest because the indigo-blue lotus or *utpala* was closely associated with Mañjuśrī. Moreover, the Sanskrit word *setu,* which among other things, means 'bridge, dike, dam', appears in v.9 of the Śrī Saṅgrāmadhanaṃjaya inscription. Still, according to IJzerman the site itself yielded no evidence that a temple structure had formerly stood at this location. The only other possibility that occurs to me is that the religious foundation commemorated in the Śrī Saṅgrāmadhanaṃjaya inscription had formerly occupied the site on which Caṇḍi Prambanan now stands but had been leveled during the first half of the ninth century to make way for a grander construction believed to more appropriately represent the new spirit of the kingdom, in which case the so-called Kĕlurak inscription might represent the only remaining trace of any leveled structure.

Envisioning a Mañjughoṣa foundation on the Prambanan Plain

The inscription's second stanza is remarkable in that a variant of the Sanskrit word for 'Lord' appears in four different parts of the strophe (*lokeśa*, *lokeśvara*, *lokeśa* once again and *ālokeśa*) plus the name Amitābha. Bosch and Sarkar viewed this stanza as being devoted entirely to Avalokiteśvara, the bodhisattva of Great Compassion. Ronald Davidson (pc 22 June 2011) also thought this verse would be "a straight-forward homage to Lokeśvara, a common name for Avalokiteśvara, and that would explain the Amitābha on his head"—unless there were other indications to the contrary. Some art historians (see, for example, Fontein 2013: 9) believe it likely that forms of esoteric Buddhism did not spread to Java prior to the tenth century. Still, the meaning of the compositum *sugatapadākṣara* in v.1, which was discussed above, does suggest the possibility of an esoteric influence. So we shall now turn our attention to the alternate proposal that strophe two might actually pay homage to a single esoteric Buddhistic deity believed to encompass the attributes of multiple divinities.

Forms of Mañjuśrī known as Dharmadhātuvāgīśvara Mañjughoṣa, Vāgīśvara and Mañjuvara were either depicted with a small figure of Amitābha in his coiffure or with Amitābha as one among the five Buddhas gracing his crown (see, for example, Bhattacharyya 1958: 104, 116-117; Wayman 1985: 27; and Śākya 1994: 90). This leads us to consider whether the religious foundation to which the inscription refers might have been an architectonic depiction of the Dharmadhātuvāgīśvara Mañjughoṣa *maṇḍala,* the principal Buddhist divinity of which is described as follows in the *Sādhanamālā* (46):

> "The worshiper should think himself as the god Dharmadhātu-Vāgīśvara who is eight-armed, four-faced and of reddish-white colour. His right face is red, the face behind is of lotus-red colour, and the left is of yellowish-red colour. He holds the bow and the arrow in one pair of hands, the noose and the goad in another pair, the Prajñāpāramitā manuscript and the sword in the third and the Ghaṇṭa and the Vajra in the fourth. He displays the sentiment of Śṛṅgāra (amour), and sits on the moon on a double lotus in the Lalita attitude. He is decked in celestial garments and ornaments and bears on his *jaṭamukuṭa* (crown of matted hair) the effigy of Amitābha" (Bhattacharyya 1958: 104).[97]

The four faces and eight arms of this particular divinity suggest the possibility of a relationship with the four *◦īśvara* designations previously designated in strophe one and the four variants for 'Lord' that appear in strophe two. According to *sādhana* 46, Dharmadhātuvāgīśvara is stationed at the center of a group flanked by Candraprabha and Sudhana (right) and Yamarī and Sūryaprabha (left). Surrounding them are Vairocana (E), Ratnasambhava (S), Amitābha (W) and Amoghasiddhi (N) and with the four Tathāgata consorts Locanā (SE), Māmakī (SW), Pāṇḍarā (NW) and Tārā (NE) occupying the intermediate directions. These twelve divinities presumably signify the twelve syllables at the beginning of NS v.26 explained in the *Nāmasaṃgīti-upadeśa* (see below). The *mantra* of the ensemble's principal divinity is given as '*Oṃ Dharmadhātuvāgīśvara muḥ svāhā*'.[98]

A unique sequence of seed syllables associated specifically with Dharmadhātuvāgīśvara Mañjughoṣa appears in several ancient texts of Javanese origin preserved on Bali. According to Nihom (1994: 104-106), one of these texts is a hymn that "is also widely known in Nepal".[99] Moreover, Nihom cited the following passage from the Old Javanese *Sutasoma:* "in pleasure and in pain let the sounds *aḥ hūṃ traṃ hrīḥ* and *aḥ* be the foundation of your heart". Additionally, he determined that *sādhana* 61, which describes the white Dharmadhātuvāgīśvara with four faces and eight arms who wears the crown of five Tathāgatas, is the only one out of the 312 *sādhana*-s presented in the *Sādhanamālā* which incorporates the sequence of *āḥ hūṃ traṃ hrīḥ āḥ.*

> "[He is] endowed with the sentiments beginning with the erotic sentiment and with raiment and heavenly jewels, two of whose hands are marked by the *dharmacakra* hand-gesture, the three of whose [remaining] right hands [bear] a sword, a bow and a *vajra*, the three of whose [remaining] left hands [bear] a volume of the Prajñāpāramitā-sūtra(s), a bow and a *vajra*-bell, and in the *vajraparyaṅka* posture. One [then] meditatively produces

---

[97](Diacritics added by the present writer.) This description emphasizes the association of Amitābha, as well as the *padma-kula* over which he presides, with the god of Desire by way of the divinity's hand-held attributes, according to Donaldson (2001: 174): "The goad and noose are the conventional second pair of weapons for Kāma, the Brahmanical god of love, so that the iconography, combining the attributes of Kāma (bow, arrow, goad, noose) with those of Mañjuśrī (sword, *vajra*, *ghaṇṭā*), parallels developments in Hinduism where Kāma is similarly absorbed into Viṣṇu in his Puruṣottama-Trailokyamohana form".

[98]My thanks to Chandra for providing the additional details from *sādhana* 46. The respective identities of the divinities as well as their arrangement surrounding Mañjughoṣa is duplicated in another *sādhana* (Foucher 1918: 40-41), with the principal differences being that Śrī Vādirāṇ Mañjughoṣāya only displays two hands and a small figure of Akṣobhya in his coiffure.

[99]The *Pañcabuddhastava* is one of the three titles by which this particular work was known, the other two being the *Nāgavāyusūtra* and the *Anaṅgavāyusūtra* (Nihom 1994: 104) .

oneself as endowed with four *mudrās* [see figure 3-6]. One should then ground oneself with the *mantra*[100] ...." (Nihom 1994: 105-106).

In *yoga-tantra* texts, each *mudrā* signifies one of the four ascending planes of meditation that a *yogin* employs during the intense contemplation of a divinity, with the sequence differing depending on the school. The symbols and colors associated with the four ascending planes can be associated with the same four Buddhistic families previously proposed for linking with the four *īśvara* appellations from verse one.

Syllable	Color	Mudrā	Location	Symbol
āḥ	white	Dharmadhātuvāgīśvara		
hūṃ	blue-black	*mahāmudrā*	heart	*vajra*
trāṃ	yellow	*dharmamudrā*	*ūrṇā*	*ratna*
hriḥ	red	*samayamudrā*	throat	*padma*
āḥ	green	*karmamudrā*	head	*viśvavajra*

Fig. 3-6. Details concerning the four meditative planes presented *Sādhanamālā* 61.

Yet another potential alternative to Avalokiteśvara is the divinity Vāgīśvara, who is still highly revered in Nepal (Śākya 1994: 90). The *Sādhanamālā* states that the single-faced two-armed Vāgīśvara is red in color: He holds the stem of a blue lotus in the left hand and his "head is beautified by the images of the five buddhas". His *mantra* is '*Oṁ Vāgīśvara mūḥ*' (Bhattacharyya 1958: 116-117).

Strophe two of the Śrī Saṅgrāmadhanaṃjaya inscription may now be reexamined in light of the data presented above: Pay homage unto Him (*praṇamatha tam*) the Lord (*lokeśam*) who (*yo*) dares (*dharṣati*) to bear (*dhartum*) even (*api*) the Lord of the Worlds (*lokeśvaram*) Amitābha on his head (*mūrdhna*), the Lord (*lokeśam*) illuminating (*avabhāsana*) all the directions (*sakala-diganta*), the 'Lord of light' (*ālokeśam*).[101]

Rays of light play the quintessential role in the *Nāmasaṃgīti-upadeśa* commentary, wherein the famous eighth-century *ācārya* Mañjuśrīmitra elaborated upon the essential elements for the ritual recitation of the *Nāmasaṃgīti* ('perfect chanting of names') for producing the numerous *maṇḍala* deities surrounding Dharmadhātuvāgīśvara. During the

[100]The *mantra* presented in *sādhana* 61, "*Oṃ hūṃ hriḥ bhagavan jñānamūrti vāgīśvara mahāvāca sarvadharma gaganāmalasupariśuddha dharmadhātu-jñānagarbha āḥ,* was directly lifted from the NS text segment (Davidson 1981: 68) known as the 'Arrangement of the *mantra*'. "O blessed one, O Lord of Speech who is embodied gnosis, with great speech, O embryo of the gnosis, of the dharmadhātu being perfectly pure, immaculate like the spatial field of all phenomena—āḥ" (Davidson 1995: 124).

[101]It is also possible that v.2 refers to a Buddhistic triad composed of Avalokiteśvara, Vairocana (e.g. illuminating all the directions) and a third divinity from the Akṣobhya family, based on the implied identification of *āloka* with Mirror-like Awareness in Vilāsavajra's NS commentary (see footnote 9). The resulting triad in turn would be theoretically identifiable with the 'triple family' (*kulatraya*) led by Vairocana in the NS, so-called "because it has [the triad of] body, speech and mind as its nature" (Tribe 1994: 96).

mid-eighth century, the famed *ācārya* Mañjuśrīmitra[102] and his student Vilāsavajra were living in the same general area of northern India as the Śailendra preceptor from Gauḍīdvīpa. So Kumāraghoṣa would have had ample opportunity to encounter their influential NS commentaries and other works or might even have been personally acquainted with either *yogin*.

We shall begin our review of Mañjuśrīmitra's *Nāmasaṃgīti-upadeśa* commentary by recapitulating v.25 from the *Nāmasaṃgīti*: "[Śākyamuni] pronounced this mystic verse, having six kinds of mantra and possessing unarisen characteristics, being nondual in arising and joined with the vocal lord [Mañjuśrī]" (Davidson 1995: 108). Next is the segment from the *Upadeśa* concerning NS vs.26-27:

> "First thinking, 'I will obtain Buddhahood for the sake of all beings', then through saying, '*a ā i ī u ū e ai o au aṃ aḥ*', rays of light, being the light of one's own mind from the proper nature of emptiness and considered as the vowels (*āli*) and consonants (*kāli*), construct the basic *maṇḍala*. At the center of that *maṇḍala* [the *mantrin*] visualizes a lion throne on a *maṇḍala* of the sun. Then with the remainder of the words" [e.g. 'Situated in the heart, I'm deep awareness embodied, the Buddha of the Buddhas occurring in the three times', (NS v.26)] "he visualizes [on the throne] Mahāvairocana Samantamukha.[103] Visualizing in Mahāvairocana's heart the Ādibuddha [Mañjuśrī], in the heart of the Ādibuddha [the *mantrin*] contemplates the Wheel of Insight (*prajñācakra*). While saying the *mantras*" [e.g. 'Oṃ Sharp as a Vajra, homage to you; Oṃ Cutter of Suffering, homage to you; Oṃ Embodied Knowledge of Insight, homage to you; Oṃ Gnostic Body, homage to you; Oṃ Lord of Speech, homage to you; Oṃ Arapacana, homage to you',[104] (NS v.27)], "he visualizes the six spokes on the Wheel of Insight. Above the Wheel [the *mantrin*] contemplates the gnostic entity (*jñānasattva*) [as the syllable] *a* on a moon. He imagines the light rays of the [syllable] *a* entering himself [in the form of] the six gnostic (*jñāna*) *maṇḍalas*" (Davidson 1981: 45-46)[105].

The *mantrin* then recites NS vs.28-157. The visual words corresponding to the 'Names' being recited then arise from the gnostic entity (*jñānasattva*), the syllable A on a moon. They turn into the groups of deities belonging to the six *maṇḍala*-s: (a) of the "blessed Bodhicittavajra" (vs.28-41), and "having gone forth they work for the sake of beings; returning they assemble again in the *maṇḍala* ... taking their place surrounding Mahāvairocana"; (b) of Vairocana (vs.42-66c), and "having worked for the sake of beings they return to become the immediate retinue of Mahāvairocana"; (c) of Akṣobhya (vs.66d-76), and having tamed the noxious beings of the world they "occupy their position in the eastern portion of the *maṇḍala*"; (d) of Amitābha (vs.77-118), and "having worked for the

---

[102]Mañjuśrīmitra was originally a native of Sri Lanka, according to Davidson (1981: 5).

[103]'Facing in all directions', a designation applied to Avalokiteśvara in Chapter 25 of the *Lotus Sūtra*. The 72 images displaying the *dharmacakra-mudrā* on the summit of Barabuḍur face in all directions.

[104]The Arapacana *mantra* was associated with the Bodhicittavajra family in the earliest NS commentaries (Davidson 1981: 22, n. 63).

[105]The Buddhistic term *jñānasattva* ('gnostic entity') may be applied to any divinity invited "from the realm of the sky" after the *mantrin* has visualizing himself as the *samayasattva* ('pledge being'), "Mañjuśrī, however, comes by this title through being the *jñānasattva* par excellence" (Davidson 1981: 19, n. 56).

benefit of beings" they return to the western portion of the *maṇḍala*; (e) of Ratnasambhava (vs.119-142), and having worked for the benefit of beings they return to the southern portion of the *maṇḍala*; and (f) of Amoghasiddhi (vs.143-157), and "having accomplished the thought of beings", they return to assemble in the northern portion of the *maṇḍala* (Davidson 1981: 46-47).

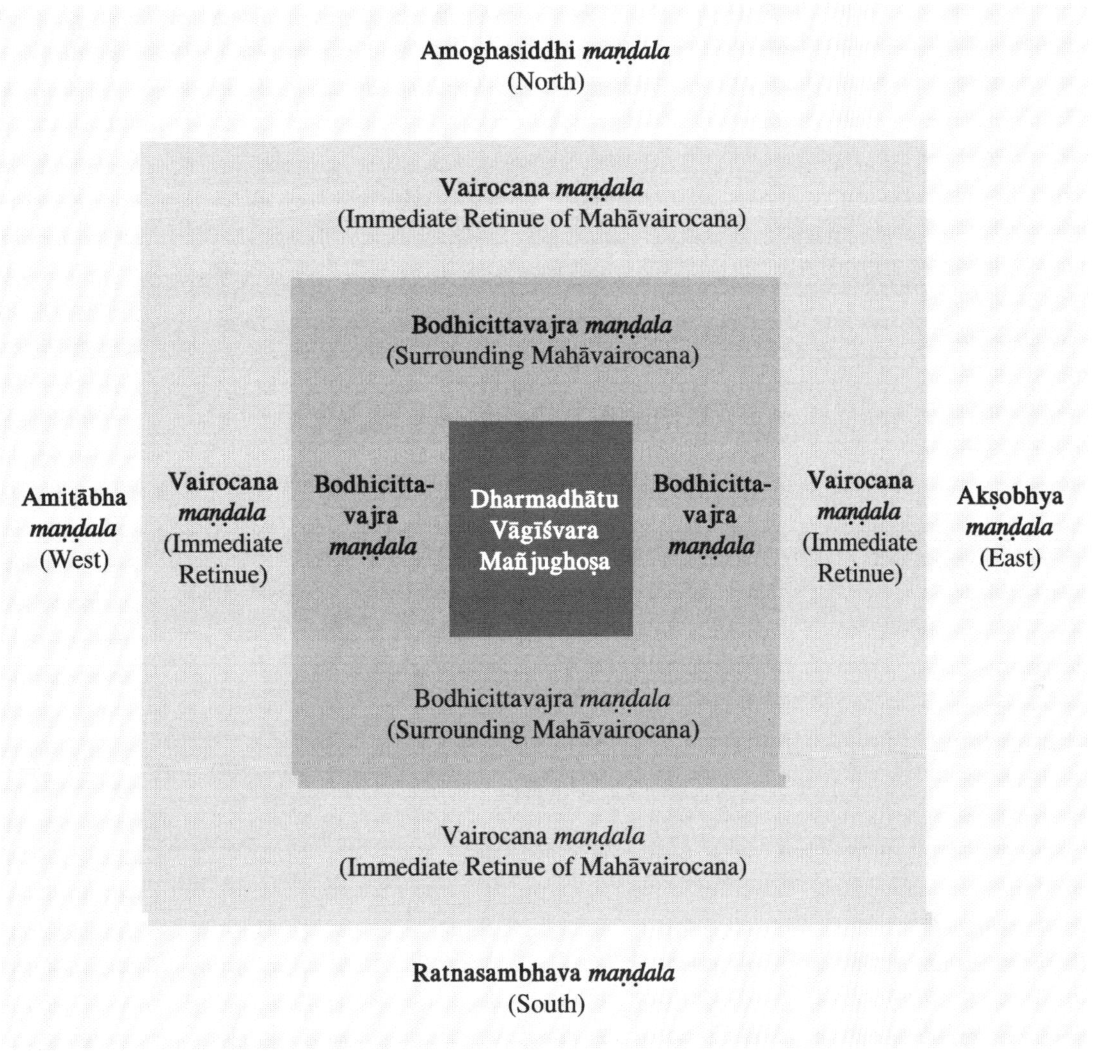

Fig. 3-7. Placement of the six *maṇḍala* groups, according to the *Upadeśa*.[106]

Mañjuśrīmitra's brief description of the NS *maṇḍala* in all its glory is potentially significant with respect to two of the Buddhist temples located in the general area (within

[106]Mañjuśrīmitra's description of the generation of the deities belonging to the six Buddha families from the *Nāmasaṃgīti* parallels the layout of the Buddha images at Barabuḍur in general. Moreover, the perforated walls of the 72 *stūpa*-s on the highest levels of the monument potentially provide the means for the emanation and return of the lower deity groups to the Bodhicittavajra, which is "a hypostasisation of bodhicitta [that] subsumes the other five families. Mañjuśrījñānasattva is the source or nature of all six" (Tribe 1994: 48).

one kilometer) in which the Śrī Saṅgrāmadhanaṃjaya inscription was found. Due to space limitations only a brief review can be provided herein concerning the two largest complexes located to the north of the old *desa* Kĕlurak: Caṇḍi Sewu and Caṇḍi Lumbung.

Caṇḍi Sewu. Though either site hypothetically might have served as an architectonic *maṇḍala*, only Caṇḍi Sewu conforms to the classic design featuring the four entrances that face the cardinal directions, and with each of the four gates guarded by a pair of huge gatekeepers. J. E. van Lohuizen-de Leeuw (1981: 19) and other scholars have argued that the Śrī Saṅgrāmadhanaṃjaya inscription would best fit Caṇḍi Sewu because of the later discovery of the Mañjuśrīgṛha inscription (Boechari 2011: 476-477) of 792 CE near a subsidiary shrine at the west end of the Sewu temple yard (Miksic 2001). Dumarçay (2007: 203-205) has published a complete inventory of all the statue pedestals located at Sewu, which suggests that the entire temple complex in its final form had accommodated more than 500 images.

Dumarçay (2007: 179) rejected the Vajradhātu *maṇḍala* theory proposed by Bosch (1961) for Caṇḍi Sewu because of the later modifications that occurred to the site's core structure through the emplacement of 16 new statues, with four having been added at the interior corners of each of the four chapels attached to the main shrine (see the drawing in Dumarçay 2007: 163). However, the extent to which the original temple pentad had been surrounded by auxiliary shrines during the late eighth century is unclear. The subsidiary shrine (*perwara*) next to the find spot of the Mañjuśrīgṛha inscription presumably had been constructed prior to 792 CE. Dumarçay (2007: 199) also noted distinct stylistic differences between the *perwara* structures of the first and fourth rows and those of the second and third, which suggest that the two groups may have been added during different periods. Additionally, the interior of the *cella* at the center of the temple yard, together with the entire religious foundation's principal image, had undergone significant modifications at a date subsequent to the founding of the original temple (see Dumarçay 2007: 163, Pl. 49).

What is intriguing about the initial state of the main shrine is that prior to the emplacement of 16 new sculptures, the singular statue within the main *cella* had been surrounded by a total of 33 images: three triads in the exterior *cella* walls facing the south, west and east, together with six more sculptures in each of the four surrounding structures in the cardinal directions. The number 33 symbolically represents the total number of deities residing on Mount Meru, and hence the symbolic numerical equivalent to the phrase "all the gods" identified with Mañjuśrī (e.g. Mañjuvāk) in v.15 of the Śrī Saṅgrāmadhanaṃjaya inscription. Unfortunately, none of the original 33 images have survived and no other contemporary iconographic texts have been discovered to date that would enable us to flesh out the names of the specific divinities comprising the elaborate *maṇḍala* sketched above by Mañjuśrīmitra.

On the other hand, Wayman (1985: 68-73) noted that there are only 33 verses in the NS available for assignment to the core *maṇḍala* divinities subsequently identified by the later NS commentaries of Candrabhadrakīrti and Smṛtijñānakīrti, with none remaining for the four gatekeepers. Wayman (1985: 29) also observed that the *Niṣpannayogāvalī*—a Vajrayāna Buddhist iconographic text written by Abhayākaragupta, a contemporary of king Rāmapāla (1072—1126 CE) of Bengal—lists the addition of 16 bodhisattvas to the core area of the Dharmadhātuvāgīśvara *maṇḍala*. So these later modifications might help to explain the subsequent addition of emplacements for 16 new images to the original core structure at Caṇḍi Sewu mentioned above by Dumarçay.

Bosch (1961; 125-130) proposed that the cluster of temple complexes on the Prambanan Plain, of which Caṇḍi Sewu is merely one component, may have been based on an integrated plan that was to be completed over time. He attempted to demonstrate that Caṇḍi Lumbung had been dedicated to the *ratnatraya*, whereas the deities of the Vajradhātu had resided at Caṇḍi Sewu. He also believed that it was entirely possible that Prambanan's Hindu pantheon had been part of the overall plan.

> "Indeed, we may take the view that once the great design embodied in the doctrine of the multiple unfolding of Mañjuśrī—the Supreme Deity—had been accepted in outline, there would be no dogmatic objections to allocating the execution of the construction of the [constituent] parts over a long period of time. 'Those who believe hasten not'. Here not only to one, but to a series of monarchs was offered the opportunity for acquiring imperishable *puṇya* through the creation of statues, the founding of sanctuaries, [their] donation of land and other pious work for themselves and for their offspring. Their merit would not be affected when unity was lost in the style of buildings and other foundations, which in religious terms once and for all had been established" (Bosch 1929a: 54).

Caṇḍi Lumbung. The architectural layout of Caṇḍi Lumbung consists of a central temple facing the east that is surrounded by 16 *perwara*-s, with groups of five facing the east, south and north and with only a singular shrine facing the west (approximately 4° S of due west). Moreover, the entire complex originally had been surrounded by an enclosure wall, the traces of which were found in 1920, with an entrance on the eastern side guarded by a pair of *dvarapāla* statues.[107]

Only the *perwara* structures on the west and north sides of the temple complex have yielded sufficient remains to enable archaeologists to restore them. Though the temple complex displays few overt signs of having been a Buddhist sanctuary and is located close enough to Prambanan to have raised the issue of religious affiliation in some minds in the past, the following observation made by Crawfurd in the early nineteenth century suggests that it had been a Buddhist religious foundation.

> "[P]roceeding still further in the same direction, but not in all above 300 yards from the 'thousand temples' [Caṇḍi Sewu], we come to a small group, which contains about 15 temples including one large central one. These are of the same pyramidal form, and differ only, in being less ornamented with sculptures. The entrance into this is by a single gate to the eastern side, guarded by two warders of the same character with those already described [the *dvārapāla* statues at Caṇḍi Sewu], but of inferior size. All the temples of this group, have been pillaged of their images, but a mutilated figure of Buddha, close by, seemed to indicate what the contents of the familiar temples had been" (Crawfurd 1820: 342).

[107]A manuscript in the KITLV library written by van der Vlis and dating from 1841 refers to the pair of *dvarapāla* statues at Lumbung previously mentioned by Mackenzie, which places their disappearance between 1840-1885 (Roy Jordaan, pc 5 Sept. 2012).

"Whereas 14 shrines are turned inward, two shrines of the eastern row face the central secondary shrine of the same row, rather than the main temple. Furthermore, the importance of the central shrine of the eastern row is underlined by the existence of a small stone pathway linking it directly to the main temple.... Due to this organization, it is unlikely that *candi* Lumbung housed an iconography similar to that of *candi* Sewu: the *buddha* would have required an equal treatment – as it is the case at Sewu. At Lumbung, only one shrine faces west and it seems very unlikely that a pantheon would have comprised 5 *buddha* in *varada-mudrā*, 5 in *bhūmisparśa-mudrā*, 5 in *abhaya-mudrā* but only one in *dhyāna-mudrā*. Rather, the architectural composition suggests that the pantheon of Lumbung involved a relation between one main principle (expressed through the main temple) and an inferior but complementary principle (expressed physically through the shrine facing the main temple)" (Degroot 2009: 141).

The Mantrayāna *maṇḍala*-s known to us all have four gateways facing the cardinal directions, whereas Caṇḍi Lumbung's singular entrance is in the east. Based on the *Upadeśa*, it appears that the wrathful divinities of the Akṣobhya *maṇḍala* take up their positions in the east quadrant of the *maṇḍala*. So it is not impossible that the builders of Caṇḍi Lumbung had taken this into account and restricted site access to the east in order to ensure that the temple complex remained protected from malevolent spiritual forces. Malandra (1993: xviii) remarked that "ideal pairings [of objects and text] are seldom found in the history of Indian art" and that maintaining such an orthodox view would at the very least impede an adequate appraisal of the earliest known groups of sculptural representations of esoteric divinities at Ellora, where a number of rock-cut *maṇḍala*-s are also preserved *in situ*. Further details concerning the arrangement of the image emplacements at Caṇḍi Lumbung are presented in Appendix A.

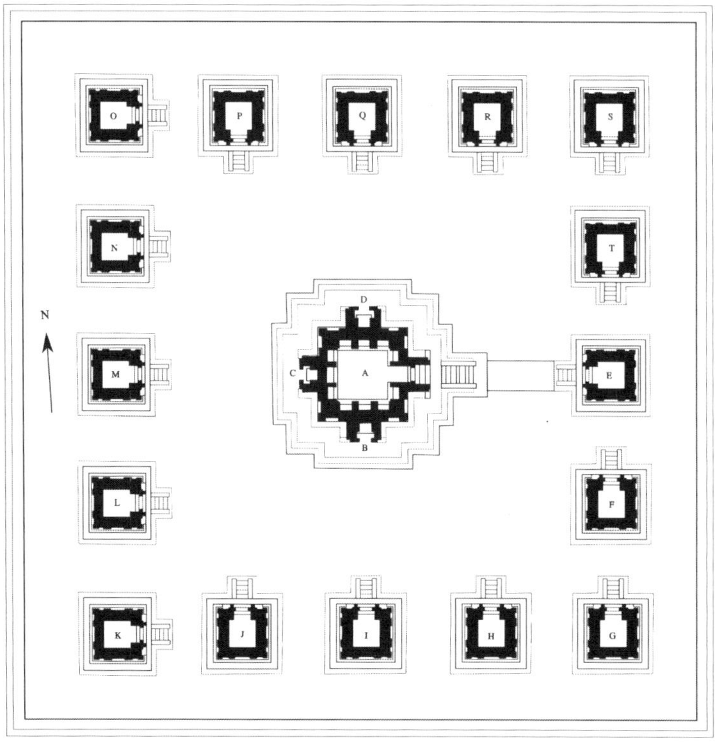

Fig. 3-8. Architectural plan of Caṇḍi Lumbung (after Dumarçay 2007: 140).

IV: The Abhayagirivihāra charter from the Ratu Baka Plateau

The so-called Ratu Baka inscription of 792/3 CE is known today as the Abhayagirivihāra charter because the Sanskrit text refers to the consecration of this 'Buddhist monastery on the fearless mountain' (Monier-Williams *et al.* 2004: 60). Composed in the Siddhamātṛkā ('Matrix of perfection', also known as Siddham) script initially called *prae-nāgarī* by early Dutch epigraphy specialists, this incomplete Sanskrit inscription consists of nine fragments, eight of which were discovered between 1816 and 1954 on the western prominence of Ratu Baka: a wedge-shaped elevated plateau to the east of modern-day Yogyakarta separating the plain of Prambanan in the north from the plain of Saragedug in the south. Moreover, the majority of these fragments were unearthed in close proximity to an ancient structure that the Javanese called the *kraton* ('king's palace') according to the written accounts of van Boeckholtz (*circa* 1790), Reimer (1791), Mackenzie (1814) and Crawfurd (1820).

The archaeological complex known today as Caṇḍi Ratu Boko consists of three distinct terraced compounds located in the western, eastern and southeastern sectors of what is a historical park open to the public. Located 2.3 kilometers to the south of the Caṇḍi Prambanan temple complex, the site that archaeologists associate with the Abhayagirivihāra is the largest structure located within the park's southeastern compound. Surrounded by a high stone wall, the stone platform (*pĕṇḍapa*) consists of a square and a rectangle that are interconnected by a short stone bridge. Crawfurd described the discovery of a fragment of an inscription amidst the ruins of this unusual structure in 1816.

> "The square terrace is constructed of huge blocks of hewn stone, measuring 68 feet to a side, and being four feet high. This terrace is surrounded at the distance of 14 feet, by a wall ascertained from a small portion of it, yet nearly perfect, to have been 11 feet high .... Dr. Tytler who accompanied me in one of my last excursions to Prambanan, discovered in the largest of the two pillars of stone on the terrace, a fragment of a slab of stone on which was a Deva-Nagari inscription" (Crawfurd 1820: 350).

De Casparis conjectured that this initial fragment was probably one of two pieces inscribed with the so-called *prae-nāgarī* script (ultimately cataloged as D.50a and D.50b) subsequently found by IJzerman (1886: 112) beside the outer wall of the so-called *kraton* ('palace', also known as the *kĕraton* or *kaḍatuan*). Two smaller fragments (D.50c and D50.d) belonging to the same charter were subsequently discovered by Rothe near the remains of the stately entrance building in the western compound. According to a communication from E. W. van Orsoy de Flines, fragment D.50e was recovered in Yogyakarta in 1938 or shortly thereafter (de Casparis 1950: 11, n. 10).

D.50e is roughly triangular in shape and reportedly contains extracts from seven different lines; no photograph of this fragment has ever been published. De Casparis (1950: 12) thought it obvious that this particular fragment, which is 13 cm. in height and has a maximum length of 20 cm. at its base, must have fit into the central portion of the charter.

The subsequent discovery of additional fragments from the same inscription has demonstrated that de Casparis' supposition was correct.

Based on the five fragments known to him in 1950 (D.50a–D.50e), de Casparis noted that the inscribed area of the stone was 36 cm. in height and estimated its original length to have been in the 70 cm. range, e.g. about the same height and length as the Kalasan inscription. The text of the Abhayagirivihāra charter consists of 18 lines of unequal height and with the *akṣara*-s being stylistically comparable to those appearing on the Kalasan charter of 778/9 CE. The top of fragment D.50c, which is located in the bottom left corner, connects to the bottom edges of fragments D.50a and D.50b. Hence, these three fragments form an integrated component. By contrast, the precise lateral placement for fragment D.50d—which must have come from the bottom section of the stone—is uncertain given that it does not attach directly to any of the other fragments (see figure 4-2).

A photograph depicting fragments a, b, c and d was published by Bosch (1929a) as an addendum to his lengthy article devoted to the Śrī Saṅgrāmadhanaṃjaya (Kĕlurak) inscription. According to de Casparis, however, the final line from D.50c does not line up with the final line of fragment D.50d, which he thought should be 1 cm. lower than it is positioned in the photo reproduced by Bosch. Figures 4-1 and 4-2 follow de Casparis' suggestion. Though in theory line 18 could have alternatively ended in the gap between D.50c and D.50d, the respective meanings of the transcribed text fragments belonging to the bottom lines of the two pieces suggest they belong to the same stanza.

Fig. 4-1 The photographed segments from the Abhayagirivihāra charter.

In 1954, four more fragments belonging to the same inscription were unearthed in the vicinity of the so-called *kraton*. The largest piece (D.50f3) is depicted separately in photo OD-19382 and also appears in the company of four fragments from an unrelated inscription that displays a different type of script in OD-19377. Two of the smaller pieces (D.50f1 and D.50f2) connect to the top of D.50f3, and with the fourth fragment (D.50f4) connecting to the bottom (see de Casparis 1961: 244; OD-19472; and Pinardi 1984: 38). To maintain continuity with the somewhat misleading statements made by de Casparis in 1956 and 1961 about the discovery of "a new fragment" belonging to the so-called Ratu Baka charter in 1954, the entire far right side of the charter will henceforth be identified as D.50f. "This new fragment, larger and better preserved than the others, makes it possible to re-establish most of the text, although small lacunae still remain" (de Casparis 1961: 241-242).

The unearthing of D.50f helped to clarify the precise location within the mosaic of fragments from whence D.50e had come. "Owing to the long lacunae the exact place of fragment *e* in the inscription had remained uncertain. The discovery of the new fragment now proves that the lines of fragment *e* ought to have been inserted one line below the numbers of the transcription in *Prasasti Indonesia*, I" (1961: 242, n. 11).[1] Additionally, the transcription for strophe 12 published by de Casparis in 1961 establishes that D.50e and D.50f must directly connect to one another at line 13 of the entire text. Based on the dimensions and the placement information given above, the approximate shape and position of D.50e is indicated by the dotted outline shown in the middle of figure 4-2.

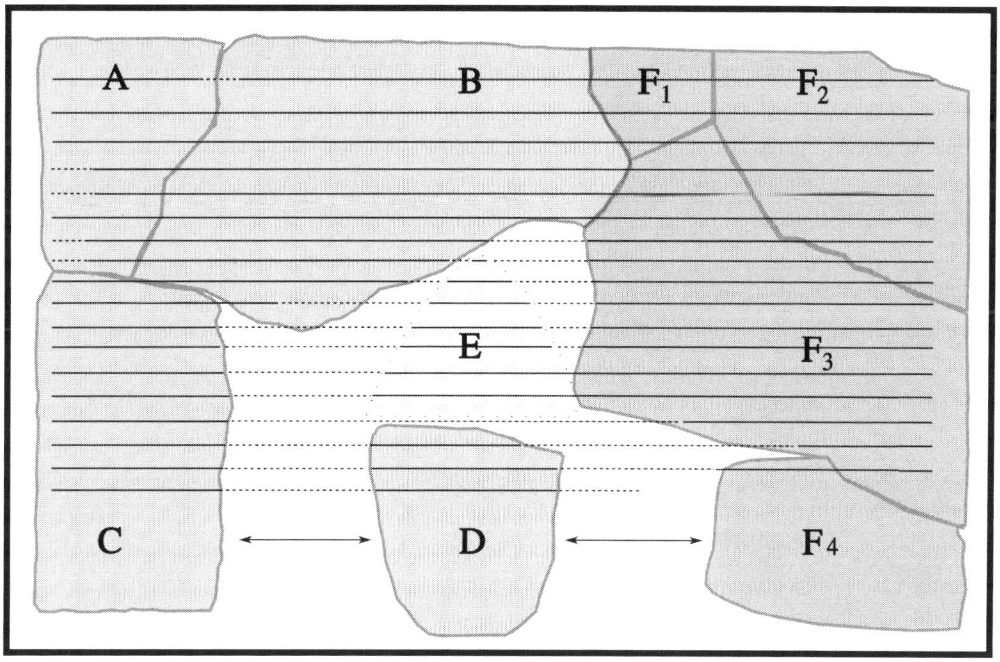

Fig. 4-2. Abhayagirivihāra charter fragments with approximate outline of D.50e shown.

[1]To correct for this error, the revised transcription presented in Appendix C takes into account all of the relevant information published by de Casparis in 1961 and 1981 so that the charter's Sanskrit line segments from the available fragments can be read in the proper sequence. For comparison purposes, the original transcription published by de Casparis in 1950 is reproduced in Appendix B.

The vast archaeological complex on the Ratu Baka Plateau

In advance of presenting an annotated transcription and revised translation for the Abhayagirivihāra charter, it will prove useful to review the historical record concerning the environs in which all but one of the inscription's fragments were recovered. François van Boeckholtz (*circa* 1790: 4) wrote that the ruler of Brambanang (e.g. Prambanan) had resided on a mountain (*berg*) in order to have a wide view over the city and the surrounding lands. He also noted that a cave (*spelonk*) and various other remains testify to this.[2] When C. F. Reimer[3] visited the ruins of Prambanan in 1791, the Javanese told him that the ruins of a former king's palace—together with the remains of temples, buildings, and waterworks—still stood on this range of hills to the south of the area's principal roadway (Bosboom 1902: 586). Mackenzie (1814: IX: 26) and Crawfurd (1820: 350) likewise alluded to the same Javanese folk tradition concerning the existence of an ancient royal palace on the western prominence of the Ratu Baka Plateau.

The selection of a hilltop location for the construction of such a vast man-made complex raises an important question: What relationship had formerly existed between the so-called *kraton* and the numerous temple sites scattered across the plains of Prambanan (north) and Saragedug (south) as well as in the eastern half of the Ratu Baka Plateau? Stutterheim (1926b: 8-9) observed that the ancient path leading south from Caṇḍi Prambanan did not continue to follow the temple complex's north-south axis, as had been previously thought, but rather ran perpendicular to Prambanan's third and outermost enclosure wall, which deviates substantially from the alignment of the two inner yards with the cardinal directions (see figure 4-3 below). Given its south-southwest heading, this path would have passed by two or three *caṇḍi*-s in the vicinity of Prambanan Kidul, the remains of which included the statues of Hindu divinities such as Ganeśa, Śiva accompanied by Nandi, Viṣṇu with Garuḍa, and a sculpture of Guru with his famous kneeling *śiṣya*-s (Stutterheim 1926b: 9).

While exploring the same area south of Prambanan more than a century earlier, Crawfurd (1820: 349) had apparently encountered some of the same images to which Stutterheim subsequently referred: several sculptures of Ganeśa; three mutilated statues of male divinities, each accompanied by his *vāhana* (Nandi, Garuḍa and a third that Crawfurd did not identify) and with a *yoni* that fit the lower part of each image; several typical Buddha images; and a sculpture of Sūrya depicted with his seven-headed horse and the charioteer Aruṇa.

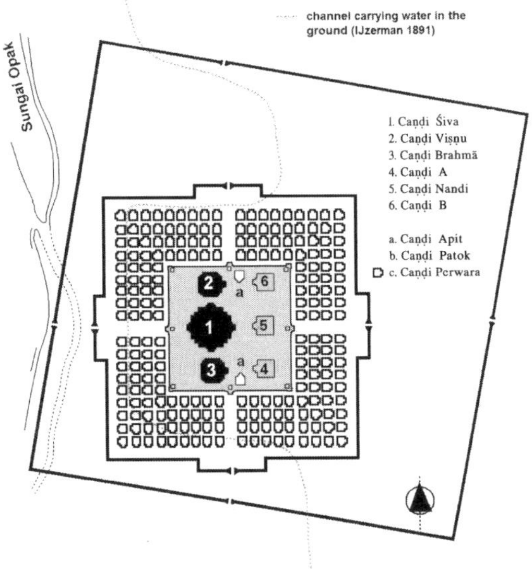

Fig. 4-3. Prambanan ground plan (after Jordaan 1996: 4).

[2]My thanks to Roy Jordaan for supplying a summary of this incomplete manuscript (see the bibliography).
[3]The former director of the fortifications and inspector of waterworks for Batavia and environs.

Crawfurd also encountered a couple of four-handed statues: the first had a skull in his crown, a *pāśa* in one of the four hands and a moon crescent at the back; the second featured a garland of skulls in his crown and with a moon crescent once again displayed in back.

> "This ground is alleged by the natives to have been the site of a town or city and certainly has that appearance. Here the walls of a great square enclosure are still to be traced, particularly to the north and west sides. By measuring these, they are discovered to have been 900 feet to a side. The appearance of the square, is that of a modern Craton, and tradition relates, that it contained the King's palace, but of this there is no vestige; towards the eastern side of the enclosure, are however to be found a number of images of a very interesting and determinate character. The ruins of the temples in which these [sculptures] were contained, form as at Cabon Dalam [e.g. Caṇḍi Sojiwan] the materials of the rude dykes which separate the neighbouring fields and gardens" (Crawfurd 1820: 348-349).

Stutterheim (1926b) surmised that the ancient road connecting Caṇḍi Prambanan with the sprawling Ratu Baka building complex must have taken a bend to the west at the foot of the plateau until reaching the point along the western edge of the prominence where he spied a trail amidst the limestone cliffs that perhaps had formerly been invested with an andesite rock staircase. At the highest point of this path, which was badly worn by water gushing with great intensity along the soft limestone during the island's rainy seasons, Stutterheim found a few actual stairway steps as well as the beginning of another path heading east. Following this steep trail up the hillside, Stutterheim entered the *desa* Dawung (see the 1926 Dutch Army map in the KIT collection). Nearby was the westernmost remnant of a stone clad slope, surmounted by what he surmised to be the remains of a wall in ruinous condition. It extended from the north edge of the hill to behind the *desa*, where it bent at a right angle to the east. Upon approaching this stone-clad slope, Stutterheim encountered another narrow path heading east that climbed less steeply. At the end of this trail he found the remnants of a small temple near the crest of the plateau's western prominence, which has a maximum height of 229 m. above sea level.[4] Previously dubbed Caṇḍi Dawung by IJzerman and covered for the most part with vegetation, the small shrine was found to have a square foundation measuring about 5 m. per side. A Japanese resident of Yogyakarta had absconded with some of the small shrine's ornamental components for placement in his home garden. Stutterheim thought that a reconstruction remained possible — at least on paper. Among other things, the temple had staircase wings featuring lion heads as well as

[4]Mackenzie (1814: IX: 25-27) and IJzerman (1891: 111-113) approached the Ratu Baka Plateau from Caṇḍi Sojiwan, which is located in the *desa* Kabon Dalem to the southeast of Caṇḍi Prambanan (see figure 4-22). IJzerman likewise succeeded in finding an ascending trail at the foot of the plateau directly south of Caṇḍi Sojiwan, whereas Mackenzie's native guide failed to find an upward path at the same point and subsequently led Mackenzie's party along the foot of the plateau for approximately two miles before finding a way to make an ascent. The first structures encountered by Mackenzie and IJzerman were the man-made caves within the eastern compound hewed from the area's limestone strata. By contrast, Crawfurd (1820: 349) reported having approached the so-called *kraton* by proceeding directly south from the temple remnants he had previously discovered on the south side of Caṇḍi Prambanan: "Ascending the range of southerly hills so frequently mentioned, and in a direction nearly due south from the relics just described, we find not above a few hundred yards from the rugged brink of the hills, the remains termed by the Javanese, the Craton or royal residence of Boco" (Crawfurd 1820: 349-350).

makara sculptures of a refined style.

Continuing along the path, Stutterheim encountered two terraces constructed from cleanly chopped andesite blocks that rose in succession at small intervals. These terraces measured approximately ± 15 m. and ± 20 m. per side, respectively.

"Following the path further, we cannot avoid the greatest ruins on the hill, namely those which are regarded as the actual *kĕdaton*. Once again it is a large *pĕṇḍapa* terrace of stout, although not very huge, dimensions, (20x20 m. [whereas the] *pĕṇḍapa* of Mangkunagaran at Surakarta measures 50 m. square!), placed on a low paved square surrounded by a wall. Entrances, which still exist in part, were found in the center of this wall on the north and south sides. The wall there-above had the typical Prambanan crown [consisting] of a series of graceful pinnacles, in form not unlike the bud of a blue lotus.... On the south side of the actual *pĕṇḍapa* terrace (within the wall surrounding it) is also a smaller raised terrace comparable to a *pringgitan* [inner room, or sitting room] but without the contiguous Dalĕm. Finally, at some distance from the aforementioned [enclosure] wall ran a second wall that drained out the rainwater collected in the lower part through very fine *makara* spouts of a nearly East Javanese style. This wall is greatly mangled and dilapidated" (Stutterheim 1926a: 132).

Fig. 4-4. Western compound before the restoration (credit: Collectie Tropen Museum).

The first systematic archaeological campaign to excavate the entire complex did not take place until 1938, when the mammoth *gopura* (alternate spelling: *gapura*) leading into the western compound first came to light (Bernet Kempers 1938: 11-14). Among other things, the initial campaign confirmed that the vast complex actually encompassed three different compounds located in the western, eastern and southeastern sectors. Subsequent campaigns conducted in 1948 (Oudheidkundig Verslag 1950: 33-37), 1954 and 1973 have revealed additional architectural, archaeological and historical details of considerable importance. Beyond the discovery of first-phase (e.g. prior to *circa* 800 CE) pot sherds, for example, the

1973 campaign unearthed "a number of pieces of brick and limestone blocks which appear to be facing stones. There is some reason to believe that both the bricks and the limestone blocks originally came from structures that were destroyed when the surviving andesite-faced structures [were built] at Ratu Baka" (Asmar & Bronson 1973: 59).

Figs. 4-5 & 4-6. Monumental *gopura* fronting the third terrace of the western compound.

Figs. 4-7 & 4-8. Abhayagirivihāra ***pĕṇḍapa*** **enclosure wall** (top) **and map of the entire site** (bottom) **on the western prominence of the Ratu Baka Plateau based on maps drawn by Dumarçay** (1993: 185) **and Degroot** (2006: 57) **plus satellite images from Google Maps.**

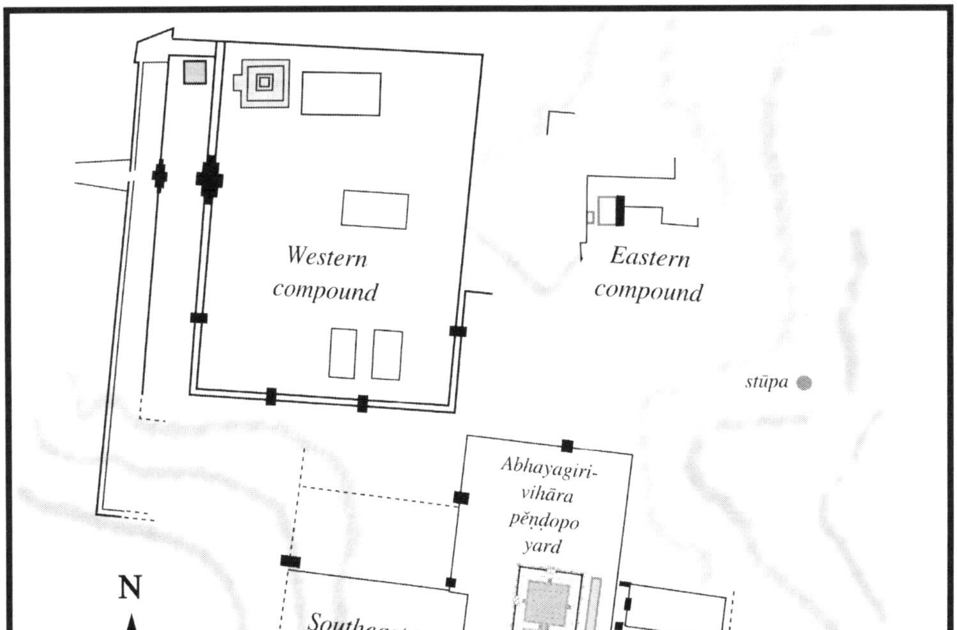

The *western compound* consists of three terraces, the second of which has a stone foundation at its northern extremity that corresponds in size and location to the previously mentioned Caṇḍi Dawung. It is regrettable that the Japanese resident of Yogyakarta who had moved parts of this small temple to his home garden apparently did not return the structure's ornamental stones when restoration activities began at Ratu Baka in 1938, as he had promised Stutterheim he would do.

The entrance to the first terrace appears to have consisted of a singular ramp. The stone retaining wall of the second terrace is interrupted by three staircases followed by a tripartite gateway. Continuing on the other side of the portal, the three staircases lead visitors up to the monumental *gopura* ('town-gate; the ornamental gate of a temple') of the third terracc, which is fronted by a short landing surrounded by a low balustrade with five doorways to the rear, each of which has a corresponding staircase on the far side of the massive walled enclosure. The compound's builders had leveled the limestone bedrock of the third terrace and also had hewed the limestone cliffs to the north and northeast to form the upper part of the third terrace perimeter whereas the lofty walls in the southcast, south and west are all man-made constructions.

Figs. 4-9, 4-10 & 4-11. Stout walls of the third terrace of the western compound (top), **a cave in the eastern compound** (center) **and the *pĕṇḍapa* ruins** (bottom) **in the southeastern compound** (photo credits: Collectie Tropen Museum 1910-1930).

The massive walls enclosing the western compound's third terrace are 5 m. in height. In the northwest corner there is an elevated structure featuring a staircase on its west side that leads up to a large and deep fire pit. Immediately behind this building there is an artificial water tank that was carved directly out of the bedrock. The southern half of the third terrace, which appears to have been segregated from the northern half by a low wall or fence, are several smaller stone platforms as well as two additional man-made water tanks.

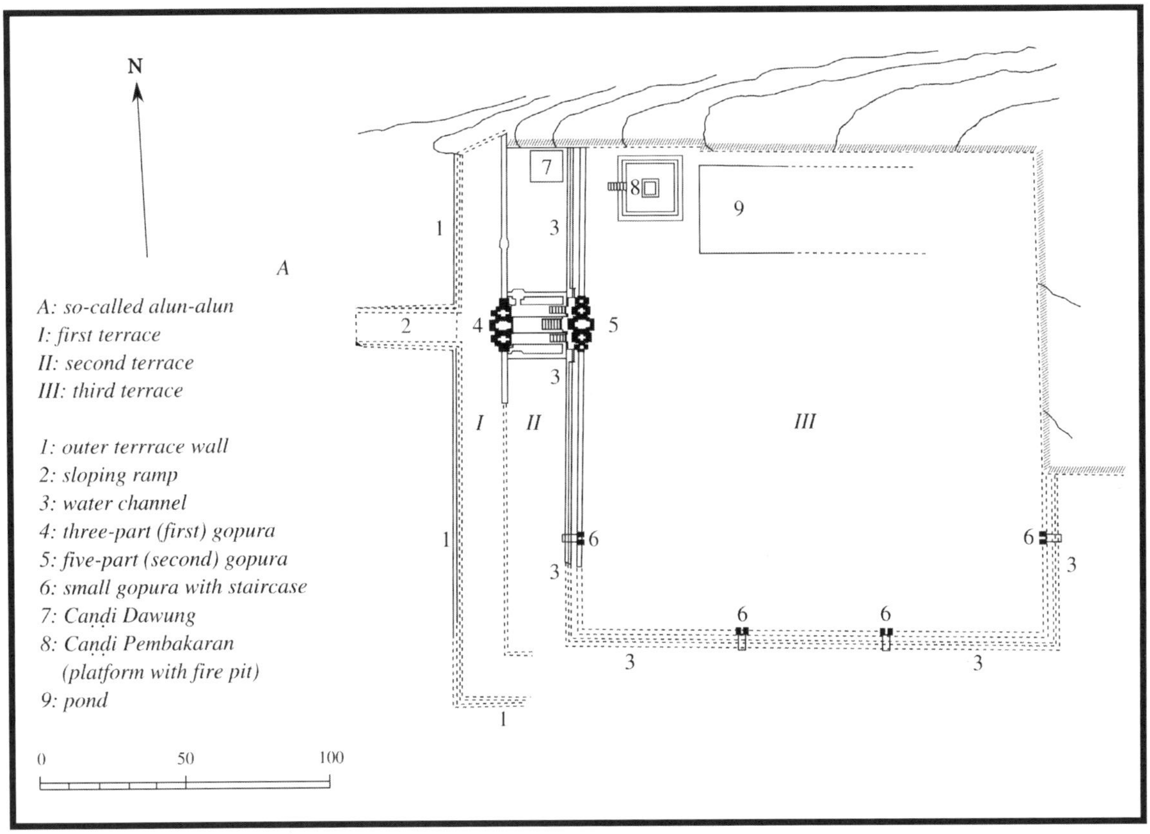

Fig. 4-12. The western compound (after OV 1950: 34 but with updated emplacements for three of the small *gopura* structures).[5]

The *eastern compound* incorporates a long staircase hewed in part from the plateau's limestone bedrock, terraces containing man-made caves dug into the soft, limestone strata and an artificial pool. During his visit to the site in 1812, Mackenzie (1814: IX: 26) found a sculpture seated in a meditative posture, presumably a Buddha image, opposite the smaller cave. This part of the Ratu Baka complex has not yet been fully excavated.

The *southeastern compound* likewise consists of several terraces as well as a total of nine enclosed areas, including an exceptionally large courtyard that originally had been surrounded by a moat. This last mentioned courtyard, which the Javanese guides of Mackenzie (1814: IX: 27) and Crawfurd (1820: 350) identified as the actual *kraton*, contains

[5]More recent architectural drawings submitted by Dumarçay (1993) and Degroot (2006) suggest that the third terrace actually has an even narrower rectangular shape than shown above (see also figures 4-8 and 4-21).

the huge double-platform surrounded by an enclosure wall measuring 34 m. (east-west) by 40 m. (north-south) and with gates on its south, west and north sides (figure 4-13).

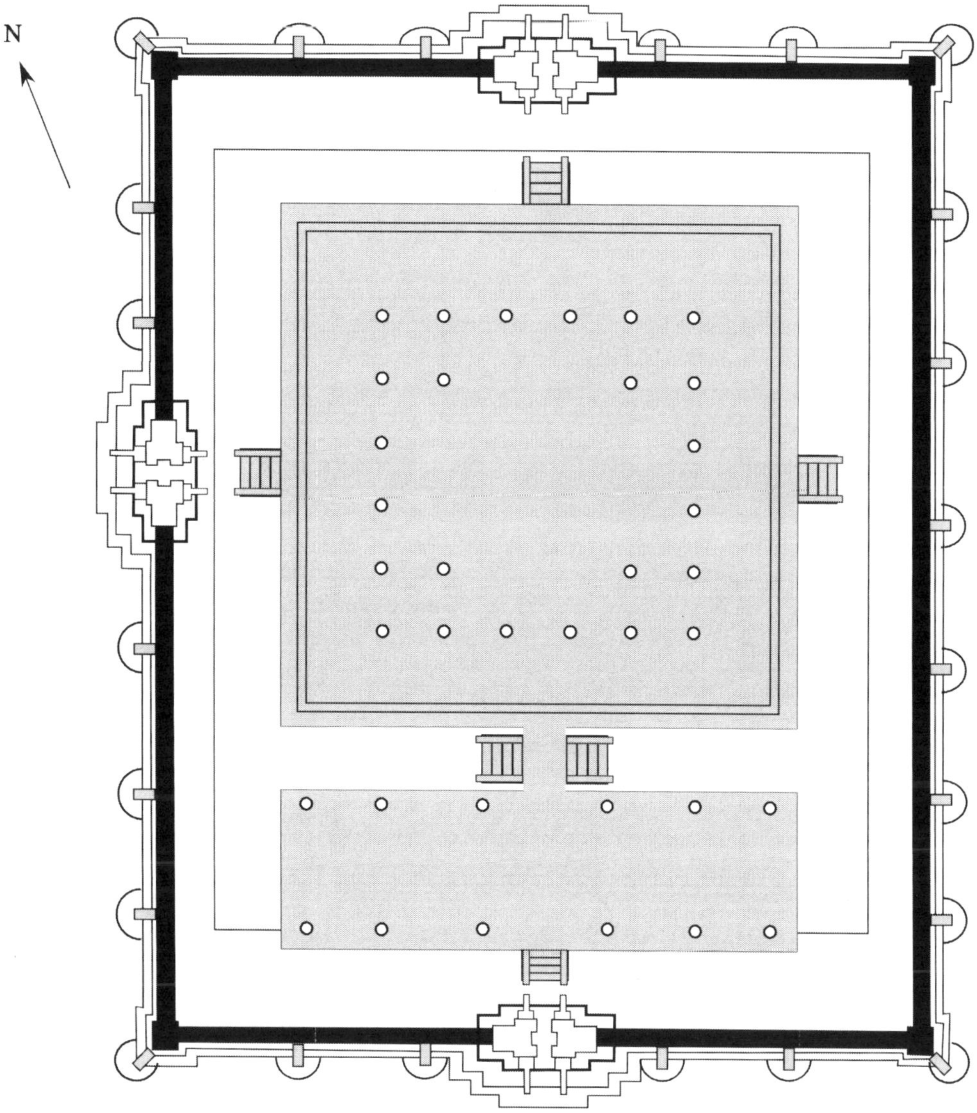

Fig. 4-13. *Pĕṇḍapa* in the southeastern compound at Ratu Baka (after Degroot 2006).

This double-platform, which is 143 cm. in height, is surrounded by a floor paved with flat stones. The square northern platform (20 m. x 20 m.) is accessed by a staircase on the west, north and east sides, whereas the rectangular southern platform (20 m. x 6 m.) has a single staircase on its south side. The two platforms are connected by means of a narrow stone bridge with staircases on the west and east sides that are 250 cm. in length and 190 cm. in width (Pinardi 1984: 37). The majority of the fragments comprising the Abhayagirivihāra charter were recovered in the vicinity of this part of the southeastern compound.[6]

[6]For a satellite view, enter https://www.google.com/maps/place/7°46'16.6"S+110°29'24.3"E in your web

Annotated transcription and revised translation

Bosch (1929a: 63-64) was the first western scholar to publish a partial transcription of the so-called Ratu Baka charter, whilst de Casparis (1950: 21-24) published the first comprehensive treatment in his *Inscripties uit de Śailendra-tijd* (*Praśasti Indonesia*, I). Following the discovery of additional charter fragments in 1954, de Casparis published an updated report that presents his transcriptions, translations and other remarks pertaining to strophes 10, 12, 13, 14 and 15 (de Casparis 1961: 241-248). This was eventually followed by another article that presents his revisions to strophes one, two and three (de Casparis 1981: 73-74). It is regrettable that the transcription and translation of the Abhayagirivihāra charter published by Sarkar (1971/2: I: 41-46) failed to fully account for the contents of de Casparis' 1961 article, which Sarkar had even cited in a footnote (1971/2: I: 46, n. 11). For example, Sarkar perpetuated the erroneous line segment assignments for fragment D50e originally published by de Casparis in 1950 and also left unmentioned the change in the reading of the charter's promulgator from Dharmmatuṅga (de Casparis 1950: 22) to Samaratuṅga (de Casparis 1961: 245).

De Casparis never issued a completely revised transcription for this charter, despite having twice promised to do so (see de Casparis 1956: 341 and 1961: 242). His poor curation of the so-called Ratu Baka inscription is one of the more disappointing episodes in the history of Central Javanese epigraphy. Chandra (1995: 10-21) addressed some of the deficiencies pertaining to the works by de Casparis and Sarkar by publishing revised transcriptions and translations for the strophes to which de Casparis had devoted separate studies in 1961 and 1981. Among other things, Chandra's work includes emendations that help to clarify the meaning of several stanzas. The annotated transcription and revised translation segments to be presented below also include additional suggestions made by Chandra through his personal communications with the author of the current work.

Bosch (1929a: 5-14) has described in detail the close stylistic similarities between the Siddhamātṛkā script style featured in the Abhayagirivihāra (792/3 CE) and Kalasan (778/9 CE) charters. He even thought that both *praśasti*-s might have been carved by the same hand, despite the interval of 14 to 15 years between the two charter dates. By contrast, Bosch observed that the type of Siddhamātṛkā script featured in the Śrī Saṅgrāmadhanaṃjaya (782 CE) and Plaosan (year date unknown) inscriptions displays a stylistic coherency that clearly sets them apart from the Abhayagirivihāra and Kalasan charters.[7] And it is all the more remarkable that the Śrī Saṅgrāmadhanaṃjaya inscription was promulgated just four years after the Kalasan inscription as well as a decade prior to the promulgation of the Abhayagirivihāra charter. Given that both the Śrī Saṅgrāmadhanaṃjaya and Plaosan inscriptions refer to the arrival of religious personages hailing from the Indian subcontinent (Gauḍīdvīpa and Gujara) it is possible that foreign dignitaries had influenced—or were directly involved in—the production of both charters.

browser's URL window, click on the "Earth" tab in Google Maps and then use the zoom tool to view individual compounds within the historical park. Offline readers who have Google Earth installed on their computing devices may also enter the following latitude and longitude coordinates for the Abhayagirivihāra in the Google Earth search window: -7.771288, 110.490095.

[7]For detailed discussions of the stylistic dissimilarities between the Kalasan/Abhayagirivihāra and Śrī Saṅgrāmadhanaṃjaya/Plaosan script types, see Bosch 1929a: 4-11, de Casparis 1950: 12-14 and de Casparis 1956: 176-177.

Bosch viewed these two stylistic variants as representative of the third or final development phase of the Siddhamātṛkā script. Due to the so-called 'nail-heads' that appear at the top of the letter tokens, which act to enclose the tops of many individuals characters, especially in the Kalasan and Abhayagirivihāra charters, the early Dutch epigraphy experts referred to this script type as *prae-nāgarī* as opposed to the later *Devanāgarī* script, which features a running line that encloses the tops of all the characters. Moreover, in some cases these distinctive marks were broadened in the four *praśasti*-s unearthed in Central Java, forming a line across the top of two or more sequential characters in some instances, though the occurrence of this is sporadic rather than consistent (Bosch 1929a: 6).

The number of syllables in lines one to four of the Abhayagirivihāra charter, which encompass the first three strophes, are 43 (1), 49 (2), 48 (3) and 52 (4), respectively. Due to *akṣara* width and height variations,[8] however, the text segments appearing further down the face of the stone had in all probability contained even more syllables per line than at the top, on average. In the hypothetical reconstructions of the meters presented for selected verses below—for which the total syllable count remains an unknown quantity—the repetitive Δ symbol provides readers with a rough estimate for the number of *akṣara*-s missing from one or more line segments containing a strophe. Furthermore, the following designations are used hereunder to identify which portions of a particular strophe come from one of three fragments: D.50d ( ]† †[ ), D.50e ( ]* *[ ) and D.50f ( ]‡ ‡[ ), thereby maintaining continuity with the notation system introduced by de Casparis in 1950 and which he subsequently modified in 1961. A gap in any line of the text for which no fragment has been recovered is indicated by a different set of bracket marks ({ }). Given the poor quality of the existing charter fragment photos as well as the lack of public access to all of the inscription's components, the immediate goal of the following discussion is to set the stage for a renewed investigation of the entire charter, provided that the entire *praśasti* eventually becomes available for public inspection. The ultimate aim, however, is to rekindle enough interest in the Abhayagirivihāra charter to inspire higher resolution photographs, *estampages* and complete transcriptions for all the fragments to be prepared and published so that scholars can undertake a truly comprehensive study of this very important document with respect to our understanding of the history of Central Java during the late eighth century.

Strophes one, two and three (Śārdūlavikrīḍitam meter)

— — — ¦ ⏑ ⏑ — ¦ ⏑ — ⏑ ¦ ⏑ ⏑ —, ¦ — — ⏑ ¦ — — ⏑ ¦ ⏓ ‖

Oṁ.
Dhīgambhīraguh*o* <vara>smṛtiśilaḥ sadvākyadhātūj<j>valo
maitrīprasrava*ṇaḥ* samādhivanavān=alpecchatākandharaḥ /
yo <'>ṣṭābhi*r*=a [2] <pi>lokadharmmapavanair=ugrair=na saṃkampitas=[9]

[8] De Casparis (1950: 23, n. 10), for example, observed that lines six, seven and eight display *askṣara*-s that are significantly smaller than those presented in the charter's preceding lines.
[9] Chandra (1995: 13) emended de Casparis' uncertain reading of *adhi* to *api*.

taṃ saṃvuddhasumerum=ūrjjitaguṇaṃ jñānograśaktin=name // 1 //

1. I pay homage to him, the Perfectly Enlightened One (Sambuddha) who is (verily) the Sumeru, whose mighty power of Awareness is a great virtue, whose deep cave is wisdom, whose rock is the most excellent body of sacred tradition, whose splendor is dwelling in the stratum of the exposition, whose spring is benevolence, whose multitude of forest-groves is profound meditation, and through the inaccessibility of few desires whose great cliff is perfectly unshaken by mighty winds: the eight of the worldly conditions (e.g. of profit and loss, defamation and fame, praise and blame, suffering and joy).

1. **I pay homage to** (name, from √nam)[10] **him** (tam, masc. sing. acc. pronoun), **the Perfectly Enlightened One** (samvuddha = sambuddha) **who is** [verily] **the Sumeru** (Sumerum, sing. acc. of sumeru), **whose mighty** (ugra) **power** (śaktin = śaktiḥ, sing. nom. of śakti) **of Awareness** (jñāna)[11] **is a great** (ūrjjita = ūrjita) **virtue** (guṇam, sing. acc. of guṇa), **whose deep** (gambhīra, said of the navel) **cave** (guho = guhaḥ, sing. nom. of guha) **is wisdom** (dhī), **whose rock** (śilaḥ, read as śilāḥ, sing. nom. of śilā) **is the most excellent** (vara) **body of sacred tradition** (smṛti), **whose splendor** (uj<j>valo = ujjvalaḥ, sing. nom. of ujjvala) **is dwelling in** (sad) **the stratum** (dhātu) **of the exposition** (vākya, 'disputation, speech, words'), **whose spring** (prasrava*ṇaḥ*, read as prasravaṇaṃ, neut. sing. nom. of prasravaṇa) **is benevolence** (maitrī), **whose multitude of forest-groves** (vanavān, read as vana-vāna: vana, 'forest, grove'; vāna, 'multitude of groves') **is profound meditation** (samādhi), **and** (api) **through the inaccessibility** (tā) **of few desires** (alpeccha) **whose** (yo = yas) **great cliff** (kandaraḥ, sing. nom. of kandara) **is perfectly unshaken** (na saṃkampitas) **by mighty** (ugrair = ugraiḥ, pl. instr. of ugra) **winds** (pavanair = pavanaiḥ, pl. instr. of pavana): **the eight** ('ṣṭabhir = aṣṭabhis, pl. instr. of aṣṭan)[12] **of the worldly conditions** (lokadharmma = lokadharma).

Lok<e=carrṣiva>rapravāhisamayān=ākramya [3] yo dīpyate[13]
  vitrastāḥ pratiyānti tīrthyavṛṣabhā yasya prabhāvoddhatāḥ /
nānādṛṣṭi<vi>*śāṅka* vṛndam=api yo bhasmīkaroti kṣaṇāt=
  taṃ sarvvānu [4] <niba>ndha-pradahanaṃ saddharmmavahnin=name // 2 //

2. I pay homage to him who, after having overcome the prevalent doctrines ... (of the most eminent of sages and among the people), shines forth the fires of the Good Law, by whose majesty were agitated the most eminent of the brahmanical mendicants in the proximity to go back in panic, who is causing the cessation of attachments, each and every one in succession, who is (effecting the annihilation) of various wrongful views, and who reduces to ashes immediately a multitude of apprehensions.

---

[10]De Casparis (1981: 74) and Chandra (1995: 17) translate *name* as 'I pay homage', whilst Sarkar (1971/2: I: 48v) renders the term as 'do I offer my homage'.

[11]For the translation of *jñāna* as Awareness see Tribe 1997b: 122 and 129, n. 29. The equating of the Sambuddha with Sumeru establishes the Completely Enlightened One at the symbolic center occupied by Mahāvairocana in the Yogatantra cycles "as the Awareness of the Perfectly Pure Dharma Sphere".

[12]e.g. of profit and loss, defamation and fame, praise and blame, suffering and joy.

[13]Chandra (1995: 13) emended de Casparis' uncertain readings of Lok*air*=<va>ṣṣ*adha*ra to Lok<e=carrṣi-va>ra.

2. **I pay homage to** (name, from √nam) **him** (tam, masc. sing. acc. pronoun) **who** (yo = yas), **after having overcome** (ākramya, the absolutive of √ā-kram, 'to rise, mount, ascend') **the prevalent** (pravāhi, read as pravāhin) **doctrines** (samayān, pl. acc. of samaya) ... [of the most eminent (<va>ra) of sages (<ṛṣi>) and (<ca>)[14] among the people (lok<e>, the sing. locative of loka)], **shines forth** (dīpyate, third pers. sing. present from √dīp) **the fires** (vahnin, read as vahnīn, pl. acc. of vahni) **of the Good Law** (saddharma), **by whose** (yasya) **majesty** (prabhāva) **were agitated** (uddhatāḥ, pl. nom. of uddhata) **the most eminent** (vṛṣabhā = vṛṣabhāḥ, pl. nom. of vṛṣabha) **of the Brahmanical mendicants** (tīrthya)[15] **in the proximity** (anti) **to go back** (pratiyā) **in panic** (vitrastaḥ, from vitrasta, 'frightened'), **who is causing** (prada) **the cessation** (hanam, sing. acc. of hana) **of attachments** (nibandha), **each and every one** (sarva) **in succession** (anu, 'one after another'), **who is** [effecting (prada) the annihilation (hanam)] **of various** (nānā) **wrongful views** (dṛṣṭi), **and** (api) **who** (yo = yas) **reduces** (karoti, third pers. sing. present from √kṛ) **to ashes** (bhasmī) **immediately** (kṣaṇāt, the sing. ablative of kṣaṇa, 'any instantaneous moment in time') **a multitude** (vṛndam, sing acc. of vṛnda) **of apprehensions** (<vi>śāṅka, read as viśaṅkā).[16]

Śaikṣāśaikṣasahasra<n>akramakaro yaḥ śūnyatāni<mitto>[17]
nirmmokṣaikarasaḥ subhāṣitāmahāratnākaro hrīhradaḥ /
[5] <saṃg>*ūḍ*hārthavicāraṇāvaranadivegaiḥ samāpyāyitaṃ
śikṣāvandanavaddhavelam=amalam=vande guṇāgrā<rṇa>vaṃ // 3 //

3. I extol the Supreme ... (Ocean) of Virtues whose (crocodile and) sea-monster (are those) of the thousands of disciples (in training) and Arhats (beyond training), whose teachings are an immaculate shoreline bounded by reverence, who is the voidness ... (and causelessness) relating to the essence of complete liberation, whose great jewel-mine is eloquent discourse, (and) whose deep pool of modesty is invigorated by the rushing currents of most excellent flowing waters: the reflections ... (on esoteric) objectives.

3. **I extol** (vande, first pers. sing. middle present from √vand) **the Supreme** (agra, 'foremost')... [Ocean (a<rṇa>vam, sing acc. of arṇava, 'sea')] **of Virtues** (guṇa) **whose** [crocodile and] **sea-monster** (<n>akramakaro = nakramakaraḥ) **are** [those] **of the thousands** (sahasra) **of disciples** [in training] (śaikṣa, 'a young Brahman pupil studying with his preceptor; in accordance with the right teaching or rule') **and Arhats** [beyond training] (aśaikṣa), **whose teachings** (śikṣā = śikṣāḥ, pl. nom. of śikṣā)[18] **are an immaculate** (amalam, read as amalām, f. sing acc. of amalā, 'spotless, pure, clean') **shoreline** (velam, read as velām, f. sing. acc. of velā) **bounded** (vaddha = baddha, 'bound; embanked [as a river]') **by reverence** (vandana, read as vandanā), **who** (yaḥ = yas) **is the voidness** (śūnyatā) ... [and causelessness (ani<mitto>, read as animittā)] **relating to** (aika)[19] **the essence**

[14]*Carrṣi=carṣi*, the transformation of *ca+ṛṣi* in accordance with the rules of external *sandhi*.

[15]According to Burnouf (2010: 184, 473), *tīrthya* (lit. 'one who has performed a pilgrimage to sacred ponds'), *tīrthika* and *tīrthakara* are synonymous terms used in Buddhist texts to designate all ascetics who are not Buddhists and in particular all Brahmanical mendicants.

[16]Chandra (1995: 13) suggested emending de Casparis' uncertain [f.]reading *<vi>śāṅka* to *<vi>marśa* ('deliberations').

[17]Chandra (1995: 14) proposed *<n>akramakaro* for de Casparis' reading of *cakramakaro* and emended de Casparis' uncertain reading of *śūnyatānisvaro* to *śūnyatānimitto*.

[18]'Training in higher thought' (*adhicittaśikṣā*), 'training in higher morality' (*adhiśīlaśikṣā*) and 'training in higher learning' (*adhiprajñāśikṣā*).

[19]According to external *sandhi* rules, *nirmmokṣa+aika = nirmmokṣaika*.

(rasaḥ) **of complete liberation** (nirmokṣa), **whose great** (mahā in comp. for mahat) **jewel-mine** (ratnakaro, read as ratnākaraḥ, sing. nom. of ratnākara) **is eloquent discourse** (subhāṣitā) [and] **whose deep pool** (hradaḥ, sing. nom. of hrada) **of modesty** (hrī) **is invigorated** (samāpyāyitam, sing. acc. of samāpyāyita) **by the rushing currents** (vegaiḥ, pl. instr. of vega, 'a stream, flood, current; speed, rapidity, quickness, velocity') **of most excellent** (vara, read as varā) **flowing waters** (nadi, read as nadī): **the reflections** (vicāraṇā = vicāraṇāḥ, pl. nom. of vicāraṇā) ... [on esoteric (<saṁg>ūḍha, 'completely hidden or concealed from view')] **objectives** (artha, 'aim, purpose').

Strophe four (Unidentified meter)

Based on the transcription of line six submitted by de Casparis, the meter of the following fragment from the latter part of the fourth stanza cannot be identified. The verse segment transcribed by de Casparis was in all probability preceded by approximately 20 syllables in the latter portion of line five on fragment D.50f following the end of the prior strophe.

]‡ △△△△△△△△△△△△△△△△△△△△ ... ‡[[6] prāptan = tena vuddhatvaṃ samvāsī*m* = *abhavebhave* vuddhatvaṃ // 4 //

△△△△△△△△△△△△△△△△△△△△ ... — — —⏑ — — — — — — —⏑ ⏑ — ⏑ — — — — —//

4\. ... / ... while dwelling in the state of a Buddha as existence in non-existence, by him was attained Buddhahood.

4\. ... **while dwelling in** (samvāsī*m*, read as saṃvāsi, neut. sing. nom. of saṃvāsin) **the state of a Buddha** (vuddhatvaṃ = buddhatvam neut. sing. nom. of buddhatva, 'condition or rank of a buddha') **as existence in non-existence** (abhave-bhave, the sing. locatives of abhava and bhava, respectively),[20] **by him** (tena) **was attained** (prāptan, read as prāptam, sing. acc. of prāpta) **Buddhahood** (vuddhatvaṃ = buddhatvam sing. acc. of buddhatva).

Strophe five (unidentified meter, possibly a variant of the Āryā meter)

With respect to strophe five, only the initial syllables from line six of fragment D.50b were transcribed by de Casparis. The following diagram suggests the possibility that this stanza had been composed in a variant of the Āryā meter. Given that the next verse begins at the start of line seven, the remainder of line six appearing on fragment D.50f must have contained the remainder of this stanza.

adhimuktir = ddhanadevaḥ satatam = a ...[21]]‡ fragment D.50f ‡[

[20]The avoidance of the dualistic positions of permanence (*bhava*) and nihilism (*abhava*). "The only way to tear [the veil of ignorance] asunder and cross the bounds of darkness is through the practicing of 'śūnyatā' in all its aspects—through the practice of bhāva-śūnyatā, abhava-śūnyatā, svabhāva-śūnyatā and parabhāva-śūnyatā" (Śāntideva & Prajñākaramati 1990: 410).

[21]Between line six on D.50b and its continuation on D.50f there is a missing fragment (see figure 4-2) that

| ⏑ ⏑ – | – ⏑ ⏑ | – – || ⏑ ⏑ ⏑ ⏑ | - - - - | - - - - | - - - - | - - - ||
| - - - - - | - - - - | - - - - || - - - - - | - - - - | - - - - | - - - - | - - - || 5 ||

5. With confidence, the lord of wealth is constantly ....

5. **With confidence** (adhimuktir = adhimuktiḥ, sing. nom. of adhimukti),[22] **the lord** (devaḥ, sing. nom. of dhanadeva) **of wealth** (ddhana = dhana) **is constantly** (satatam, sing. acc. of satata) ... / ... // 5 //

Strophe six (Mālinī meter)

⏑ ⏑ ⏑ ¦ ⏑ ⏑ ⏑ ¦ – –, – ¦ – – ⏑ ¦ ⏑ – ⏓ ||

---

[7] ⏑ bhuvanakaranāntaḥ pāti no duḥkhamūlaṃ kṣapaya kamalapāṇe prāṇināṃ kleśajāla*ṃ* </>

Strophe six in Mālinī meter

<tri>[23]	bhu	va	na	ka	ra	nān	taḥ	,	pā	ti	no	duḥ	kha	mū	laṃ	
kṣa	pa	ya	ka	ma	la	pā	ṇe	,	prā	ṇi	nām	kle	śa	jā	laṃ	/
⏑	⏑	⏑	⏑	⏑	⏑	–	–	,	–	⏑	–	–	⏑	–	–	
⏑	⏑	⏑	⏑	⏑	⏑	–	–	,	–	⏑	–	–	⏑	–	–	//

6. He who exhausts the root cause of our suffering in the (three) worlds through the destruction of its agency, O thou the Bearer of the Lotus (please) cause the web of afflictions to burn for (all) living creatures.

6. **He who exhausts** (pāti, third pers. sing. present of √pā) **the root cause** (mūlam, sing. acc. of mūla) **of our** (no) **suffering** (duḥkha) **in the** [three] **worlds** (<tri>bhuvana) **through the destruction** (antaḥ) **of its agency** (karana = karaṇa, 'instrumentality'), **O thou the Bearer of the Lotus** (kamalapāṇe, sing. vocative of kamalapāṇi) [please] **cause the web** (jālam, sing. acc. of jāla) **of afflictions** (kleśa) **to burn** (kṣapaya, read as kṣāpaya, causative derived from √kṣai) **for** [all] **living creatures** (prāṇinām, pl. genitive of prāṇin).

Between the end of strophe six in line seven of fragment D.50b and the beginning of the same line on D.50f there is a gap in the stone for which no fragment has been recovered. It

---

presumably would have contained roughly a half dozen *akṣara*-s. There is also a short gap in the stone at the start of line seven that perhaps had contained one or two syllables as well as perhaps the double *daṇḍa* marking the end of strophe five.

[22]"The Sanskrit word *adhimukti* is composed of the prefix *adhi* and the verbal root *muc*, 'to liberate,' 'to release,' or 'to be free.' As a whole, the word *adhimukti* means 'trust' or 'confidence.' When these meanings are combined, one may take *adhimukti* to indicate 'abiding with confidence in a state of freedom'." (Park 1983: 15-16).

[23]Emendation proposed by de Casparis (1950: 16).

is possible in theory that the *akṣara*-s which originally appeared in this gap plus the ensuing *akṣara*-s in line seven from D.50f had constituted the second *pāda* of a half verse (e.g. two quarters consisting of 15 *akṣara*-s, or 30 in total) of a strophe in Mālinī meter (compare with strophe 12 below). Prior to his realization in 1961 that the insertion of the first line of D.50e must have begun in line eight, de Casparis (1950: 23, n. 12) estimated that this segment would have constituted approximately 29 syllables.[24]

Strophes 'seven, eight and nine' (uncertain meters)

De Casparis (1961) estimated that this portion of the text had originally contained three stanzas, which is indicated by his identification of strophe ten as a verse composed in the Āryā meter. However, the presence of three strophes would only appear to be likely if the half-verse in Mālinī meter presented above had been intended to stand on its own, and with the remainder of line seven having constituted the major part of a separate verse.

The transcribed segments of line eight as well as line nine up to the beginning of D.50e are too fragmentary to enable us to conclusively determine the meters for any strophes therein. The contents of this portion of the text will be covered in the later discussion segment of this chapter, wherein the meter possibilities will be reviewed and in which conjectural translations for the transcribed text fragments will be proposed.

Strophe ten (Āryā meter)

Line nine, from fragment D.50e and the ensuing gap between stones to fragment D.50f:

]* *rā*jyam = alaṃkurvāṇaṃ tejaḥpūrṇṇā *[{ ... gap between stone fragments ... }]‡
<ala>ṅkaraṇaṃ / gurubhiḥ saṅghārāme '*nya*vihāro 'yaṃ kṛtaḥ paścāt ‡[// 10//[25]

Hypothetical diagram in the Āryā meter:

| – ⏑ ⏑ | – – | – – ‖ – – | – – | - - - ⏑ | – ⏑ ⏑ | – ‖
| ⏑ ⏑ – | – – | – – ‖ ⏑ ⏑ – | – – | ⏑ | – – | – ‖ 10 ‖

10. Equal to making the kingdom (an adornment) on account of an abundance of brilliancy, this other vihāra in the monastic complex was later built by the preceptor(s).

10. **Equal to** (alam) **making** (kurvāṇam) **the kingdom** (rājyam) ... [an adornment (<ala>ṅkaraṇam)] **on account of an abundance** (pūrṇṇā<t> = pūrṇāt, sing. ablative of pūrṇa) **of brilliancy** (tejaḥ = tejas, 'effulgence') ... **this** ('yaṃ = ayam) **other** ('nya = anya) **Buddhist monastery** (vihāro =

---

[24]Including *saṅgā* from D.50e, which de Casparis (1961) subsequently realized must belong to line eight.

[25]The speculative reading of *rājyaṃ alaṃkurvāṇaṃ tejaḥpūrṇṇāpa<ṇaṃ panaṃkaraṇam>* initially proposed by de Casparis (1950: 21) was shown to be untenable with the discovery of fragment *f*, as it would not conform with the Āryā meter in which the second hemistich is composed.

vihāraḥ, sing. nom. of vihāra) **was later** (paścāt) **built** (kṛta) **in the monastic complex** (saṅghārāme = saṃghārāme, sing. locative of saṃghārāma) **by the preceptor(s)** (gurubhiḥ, the pl. instr. of guru).[26]

Strophe 11 (unidentified meter)

Suggestions for potential meter possibilities as well as a conjectural translation for the text fragments for this strophe from the beginning of line 10 will be presented in the following discussion segment.

Strophe 12 (Mālinī meter)

]‡ ... Ayam = iha jinasūnoḥ padma ‡[[11] pāṇeḥ[27] kṛpāloḥ
prathita ⏑ ⏑ ⏑ — — —⏑ — —⏑]* pādaiḥ /
Jinavaravina yoktaiḥ śikṣitānāṃ *[ ]‡ <ya>tīnām =
abhayagirivihāraḥ kāritaḥ siṅhalānām //

Strophe 12 in Mālinī meter																	
a	yam	i	ha	ji	na	sū	noḥ	,	pad	ma	pā	ṇeḥ	kṛ	pā	loḥ	
pra	thi	ta	⏑	⏑	⏑	—	—	,	—	⏑	—	—	⏑	pā	daiḥ	/
ji	na	va	ra	vi	na	yok	taiḥ	,	śik	ṣi	tā	nāṃ	<ya>	tī	nām	
a	bha	ya	gi	ri	vi	hā	raḥ	,	kā	ri	taḥ	siṅ	ha	lā	nām	//
⏑	⏑	⏑	⏑	⏑	⏑	—	—	,	—	⏑	—	—	⏑	—	—	

12. Here this Abhayagirivihāra of the son of the Jina Padmapāni the Compassionate has been caused to be made for the sake of Siṅhalese (ascetics) trained in the most excellent *vinaya* of the Buddha by means of the words (uttered) by the celebrated Venerable ... (with the proper name [pluralis majestatis] or names presumably having originally appeared in the strophe's lacuna of ten syllables).

12. **Here** (iha) **this** (ayam, third pers. sing. nom. pronoun) **Abhayagiri vihāra** (vihāraḥ, sing nom. of vihāra) **of the son** (sunoḥ, sing. genitive of sūnu) **of the Jina** (jina) **Padmapāṇi** (padmapāṇe, sing. genitive of padmapāni) **the Compassionate** (kṛpāloḥ sing. genitive of kṛpālu), **which has been caused to be made** (kāritaḥ) **for Siṅhalese** (siṅhalānām = siṃhalānām, pl. genitive of siṃhala) ... [ascetics (<ya>tīnām, pl. genitive of yati)] **trained in** (śikṣitānām, pl. genitive of śikṣita) **the most excellent** (vara) **vinaya** ('rules of discipline for monks') **of the Buddha** (jina) **by means of the words** (uktaiḥ, pl. instr. of ukta) [uttered] **by the venerable** (pādaiḥ, pl. instr. of pāda) ... **celebrated** (prathita) ... .[28]

---

[26]Chandra (pc 11 March 2011) has expressed the opinion that *gurubhiḥ* would refer to the supreme preceptor and is plural out of respect, e.g. *pluralis majestatis* (lit. 'the plural of majesty').
[27]Given as *vāṇaḥ* in de Casparis' original transcription.
[28]According to Chandra (1995: 10), the proper name of the preceptor would have appeared in the strophe's lacuna of ten syllables. He surmised that the plural instrumentals *uktaiḥ* and *pādaiḥ* are examples of *pluralis*

Strophes 13 (unidentified meter) **and 14** (a variant of the Āryā meter)

Meter possibilities and a conjectural translation for the fragmentary contents of strophe 13, which appears to have extended from the beginning of line 12 on D.50c and ended in the middle of line 12 on fragment D.50e, will be presented in the discussion segment. Strophe 14, which appears to have extended from the middle of line 12 on fragment D.50e to the middle of line 13 on fragment D.50e, also shall be reviewed in the discussion segment. As we shall see later on, the latter verse appears to have been composed in a variant of the Āryā meter.

Strophe 15 (Āryā meter)

Śakanṛpakālātī *[ ]‡ tair = varṣṣaśataiḥ saptabhiś = caturdaśabhiḥ /
Varṣṣaiś = cāpy = abhivṛttaiḥ kṛtā pra ‡[[14] tiṣṭhā vihārasya // 15 //

| ⏑ ⏑ ⏑ ⏑ | – – | – – || – ⏑ ⏑ | – – | ⏑ – ⏑ | – ⏑ ⏑ | – ||
| – – | – ⏑ ⏑ | – – || ⏑ – ⏑ | – – | ⏑ | – – | – || 15 ||

15. When seven hundred and fourteen of the years of the era of the Śaka-king had elapsed, and also during the rainy season, the consecration of the *vihāra* was accomplished by means of superior practices.

15. **When seven** (saptabhiś = saptabhiḥ, pl. instr. of sapta) **hundred** (śataiḥ, pl. instr. of śata) **and fourteen** (caturdaśabhiḥ, pl. instr. of carturdaśa) **of the years** (varṣṣa = varṣa) **of the era** (kāla) **of the Śaka-king** (śaka-nṛpa) **had elapsed** (atīta), **and also** (cāpy = ca-api) **during the rainy season** (varṣṣais = varṣaiḥ, the pl. instr. of varṣa, lit. 'together with the rains'), **the consecration** (pratiṣṭhā, sing. nom. of pratiṣṭhā) **of the vihāra** (vihārasya, sing. genitive of vihāra) **was accomplished** (kṛtā) **by means of superior** (abhi-, a prefix to nouns conveying superiority or intensity) **practices** (vṛttaiḥ, pl. instr. of vṛtta).

Strophes 16, 17 and 18 (unidentified meters)

The remaining fragmentary lines of the transcribed Sanskrit text are too sporadic for us to consider any hypothetical translation possibilities. A few key phrases identified therein will be examined in the discussion segment below.

---

majestatis, e.g. references to a single person holding a high office. If the composer had intended to name two preceptors here then he presumably would have used the dual instrumentals *uktau* and *pādau*.

Discussion of the strophes and their potential relationships with the natural and man-made features of the Ratu Baka complex and its environs

In 1981, de Casparis unconvincingly attempted to demonstrate that the Abhayagirivihāra charter represented a 'blueprint' for Barabuḍur. If this inscription was intended to signify a model for anything, then the more plausible hypothesis would be to suggest that the entire contents of the charter directly pertains to the natural and man-made features of the Ratu Baka complex and its environs, such as the area's natural spring and limestone bedrock as well as the caves, forest-groves, artificial pools and great cliffs. Moreover, the initial three strophes, which are all composed in the Śārdūlavikrīḍitam meter, pay homage to the Buddha in his three aspects (*ratnatraya*) of Body (Buddha), Speech (Dharma) and Mind (Saṅgha). The opening stanza is dedicated to the Sambuddha; v.2 to the fires of the noble Dharma; and v.3 to the Saṅgha as the immaculate Ocean of Supreme Virtues whose *nakra* and *makara* are the thousands of disciples (*śaikṣa*) in training (the first seven stages or *bhūmi*) as well as the Arhats (*aśaikṣa*) who are beyond training (beginning with the eighth *bhūmi*).

> "Stages 1 through 7 are devoted to the active pursuit of the bodhisattva ideal; the eighth stage is called 'The Immovable' (*acalā*), and it marks the shift to a qualitatively different aspect of the bodhisattva's career [devoted to] ... the nondualistic knowledge and higher mental faculties (*jñānābhijñānācarya*) indispensable to all buddhas" (Candrakīrti *et al* 1989: 22).

Verse one. Whether any part of this sprawling complex had ever actually served as the king's palace (*kraton*)—as Javanese folklore maintains—continues to be a debatable issue to which we shall return later. If we momentarily entertain the notion that the Śailendra king had resided somewhere on the plateau's western prominence, then the equating of the Sambuddha with Sumeru in the charter's opening strophe would suggest that the elevated site had been considered to be the terrestrial equivalent of the abode of Indra on the summit of the cosmic mountain,[29] and with the charter's opening stanza referring metaphorically to the building complex's more prominent characteristics.

In attempting to justify his hypothesis that the opening strophes of the inscription present a 'blueprint' for Barabuḍur, de Casparis (1981) suggested that the charter's benedictory verse was unique among the Javanese charters in that it invoked the cosmic mountain as the composition's principal divinity. However, Chandra (1995) rightly noted that the composer is only metaphorically comparing the Sambuddha ('Completely Enlightened One') with the cosmic mountain Sumeru.

The man-made caves found in the eastern compound represent this sector's most distinctive aspect. On Sri Lanka, rock caves (*guha*) were located in the general vicinity of the so-called double-platforms constructed for Buddhistic ascetic sects.

> "The presence of numerous cave-dwellings at Riṭigala [to the southeast of Anurādhapura], with early Brāhmī inscriptions including one record of a royal donor,

[29]The summit of Sumeru is also the residence of Mahāvairocana within *maṇḍala*-s described in texts from the Yogatantra cycles.

establishes the antiquity of the site. Of singular relevance, however, is the presence of the double-platform structures at a place associated with the *Paṁsukūlikas*. The double-platform buildings on the hill above the 'Bānda Pokuṇa' are the most substantial architectural remains at Riṭigala" (Bandaranayake 1974: 118)

One of the small man-made caves found on the Ratu Baka Plateau appears to have been associated with a Buddha image seen by Mackenzie (but mistaken for a Jain sculpture) within the immediate environs of its exterior.

"Of the use of these Chambers the Natives could give no information nor form any conjecture.... They say that the Susunan and Sultan, when embarrassed or melancholy, retire to these cells, and shut themselves up for eight days in austere fasting and contemplation. Whatever may be in this, it is extremely probable that they might be intended for some such purpose, which the provision of water in the cell [a square basin cut into the rock] seems to corroborate, and also the contemplative Jain Saniassi [in fact, a Buddha sculpture in all probability], represented in a posture of medi[t]ation directly facing the first cell" (Mackenzie 1814: 238).[30]

Fig. 4-14. Modifications made to the terrain within the eastern compound at Ratu Baka.

[30]Crawfurd likewise believed these man-made caves were hewn into the cliffs to provide retreats for monks. "I have no doubt that these excavations, constituted the retreat of holy devotees, who sought a reputation by the performance of those austerities believed so efficacious, according to the religious system of the Hindus" (Crawfurd 1820: 351).

A considerable amount of the interior support filling for several temples constructed during the ninth century on the Prambanan Plain came from Ratu Baka's white limestone cliffs. The use of this filler of crushed rock might plausibly have been intended to symbolically transfer the perfectly unshakable nature of the Sambuddha-Sumeru to the temples nearby, which were continually subject to the threat of damage from earthquakes and volcanic eruptions.

Verse two. The charter's second strophe refers to the fires of the Good Law (*saddharma*). In the northwest corner of the western compound there is a unique construction consisting of a square base of 22.5 m. per side that incorporated two superimposed levels of which only the second could be reach by the structure's singular staircase in the west. This edifice is known today as Caṇḍi Pembakaran. The top of the higher platform has a square fire pit at the center measuring 4 m. per side and with a depth that extends to ground level (Bernet Kempers 1950: 33). It has been suggested that this fire pit, which is lined with limestone, had served as a crematorium. However, Bernet Kempers noted that the ashes recovered from the bottom of this pit contained no traces of bones. An alternate possibility is that this structure had been used for burning fragrant woods during religious ceremonies or perhaps even for conducting the *homa* rites to which the *Vairocanābhisambodhi-sutra* (VAS) and other Mantrayāna texts refer (see, for example, Wayman and Tajima 1992: 189-208).

Fig. 4-15. One of the man-made caves within the eastern compound at Ratu Baka.

The discovery of Hindu as well as Buddhist statuary and inscriptions on the plateau's western prominence is a good indication that the site's principal religious affiliation had shifted from Buddhism to Śaivism over time. On the other hand, v.2 of the Abhayagirivihāra charter refers to Hindu worshipers (*tīrthyavṛṣabhā*) being in the proximity (*anti*), which suggests that a Hindu religious community also may have resided on the plateau during the late eighth century. Stutterheim (1926a: 134-135) allowed that the small spring in the *desa* Dawung at the western end of the prominence would have been a natural site for attracting indigenous Javanese ascetics during the period preceding the charter's date. Fieldwork conducted on the western part of the plateau in 1973 offers a modicum of support for this view (Pinardi 1984: 43-44).

Verse three. As noted above, the third strophe extols the Supreme Ocean of Virtues whose *nakra*-s and *makara*-s are [those] of the thousands of disciples in training and the Arhats beyond training (de Casparis 1981: 74). This clearly evokes the Saṅgha component of the *ratnatraya.*[31] When viewed as a unified segment of the text, the initial strophes composed in the Śārdūlavikrīḍitam ('Tiger's play') meter[32] have three of the five elements—earth, fire and water—as their principal themes. In the later Javanese Buddhism of the *Sang Hyang Kamahāyānikan Advaya-Sādhana*, the elements earth, fire and air are identified with the Tathāgatas Vairocana, Amitābha and Ratnasambhava and their respective spiritual families (Chandra 1995: 427-428).

Perhaps the *ratnatraya* is symbolized by the tripartite *gopura* fronting the western compound as well as the three staircases leading up to the mammoth *gopura* fronting the main terrace. The unique triad of miniature *caṇḍi*-s discovered within the site's southeastern compound also might be related to the *ratnatraya*. The three structures are situated in the area immediately to the southeast of the double platform where the majority of fragments from the Abhayagirivihāra charter were discovered. To the east of the first four paved terraces is a small stone platform (6.50 x 6.50 m) that has a water trough at its southeast corner. The three miniature temples stand in a row on the eastern side of this trough, with the largest (1.35 x 1.34 m) structure occupying the central position and flanked on either side by smaller (1 m) structures of equal dimensions (see Degroot 2009: 237-238).

> "Before the restoration work carried on in 1981 they were located east of the pendopo enclosure, behind the eastern elongated terrace.... The *candi* were at a lower level than the terrace, facing its wall but were so close to it that it was barely possible to reach them from the front. As their dimensions were similar to the rectangular traces visible on the platform southeast of the pendopo, they were thought to belong to the latter and were moved by the SPSP DIY to the place they now occupy. I can see no objection to their removal, although I think it is important to keep in mind that at a later stage in the occupancy of the Ratu Boko compound they were moved to a secondary localization and were not linked to the water system any longer" (Degroot 2009: 237, n. 126).

---

[31]As we have already seen in the prior chapter, the opening salutation of the Śrī Saṅgrāmadhanaṃjaya inscription (782) is *namo ratnatrayāya*—Homage to the Three Jewels. Chandra (pc 9 Sept. 2010) also had noted that it is possible in theory that the initial three stanzas of the Kayumwuṅan charter (824) were likewise dedicated to the Three Jewels: the hero abiding on the lofty mountain (Buddha), the Good Law (Dharma) and a deity or personage venerated by the venerable (Saṅgha).

[32]A tiger-skin garment tied at the waist is an attribute of Avalokiteśvara images found in peninsular Thailand and Indonesia (Beek & Invernizzi 1991: 78).

A gold strip inscribed with *Oṁ rudra ya namaḥ svaha* was discovered in the pit in front of the miniature *caṇḍi*-s (Setianingsih 2002: BG 1410a), which Degroot (pc 2 Apr. 2012) viewed as a good indication that the ensemble was constructed during a period subsequent to the founding of the Buddhist *vihāra* immediately to the north.[33] On the other hand, it remains possible that the Rudra *mantra* had been deposited within a Buddhist context. Rudra numbers among the 25 *vāstudevatā*-s occupying the standard foundation plan or *caṇḍita* for Mahāyāna Buddhist sites according to the *Vāstuvidyāśāstra,* an architectural treatise discovered in Sri Lanka (Marasinghe 1989: 13 and fig. 7). The plot or square assigned to Rudra—signified by a cow, calf and *mantra*—may also be associated with the monk's dwelling (*munivāsa*) according to this text (Jayasuriya *et al.* 1995: 9, 178). Besides, this ritual deposit may be related to the others found in the vicinity of where the three miniature structures are thought to have been installed originally.

> "In the southeastern compound, near the miniature candi, underneath the water trough were 6 *peripih*. Five of them were earthen pots containing metal fragments and semi-precious stones and were laid according to the cardinal points. The 6th *peripih* was of a slightly different nature: it was a bronze pot. Located south of the other[s] and not in a line, it containcd golden, silver and bronze strips, but also glass beads and seeds (Hambali 1993-1994: 13)" (Degroot 2009: 239).

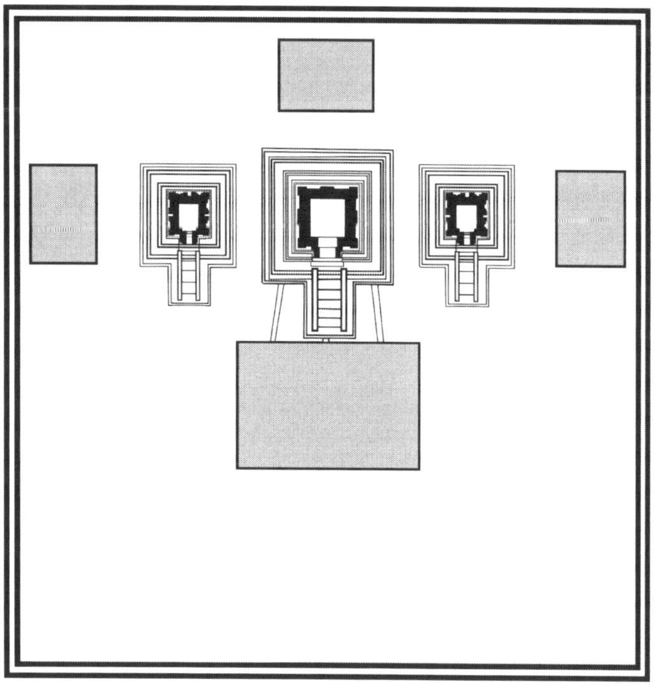

Figs. 4-16 & 4-17. The three miniature *caṇḍi*-s (view from the west side; line drawing after an illustration by Degroot, pc 1 Apr. 2012).

[33]Asmar & Bronson (1973) have proposed that this *mantra* had been deposited in the pit during the ninth century or thereafter, perhaps after the three miniature *caṇḍi*-s had been relocated to the east side of the *pĕṇḍapa* enclosure. In my opinion, however, the question remains open.

Chutiwongs (2010: 786-788) speculated that these *caṇḍi*-s in reduction, together with their accompanying array of water ducts, originally had been designed for the ritual ablution of *dharmaśarīras* and *dharmadhātu,* which "can be translated and understood as 'Word Relics' or 'Teaching Relics'. Of these, the most current tangible forms are sacred texts, extracts of sacred texts, or formulas—written and preserved on all kinds of material [such as] ... inscribed gold sheets, cut in oblong forms to imitate palm-leaf manuscripts, known from many countries including Indonesia". Furthermore, all three structures appear to have played a role in ritual ablutions given that three channels conducted "the sanctified and sanctifying water from the ablution platform through the bases of the triple shrines into the collecting basin placed on the terrace".

Verses four and five. The meters for strophes four and five cannot be identified with certainty from the readable segments. The initial segment of line six is presumably the latter part of strophe four because of the pair of stroke marks immediately after the second appearance of *vuddhatvaṃ* in the same half-verse. Hence, the portion of line six immediately following the double *daṇḍa* is designated as strophe five. It might have been intended to express the outcome of the prior verse, perhaps as the moral of the story.

Verse six. In Mahāyāna Buddhism, the root cause of suffering (*duḥkhamūla*) and the web of moral afflictions (*kleśajāla*) are the prime active causes of samsaric existence in the present life. The root cause of suffering is the desire for selfish gratification whilst the web of afflictions signifies the controlling conditions that lead to the generation of evil *karma*: attachment, aggression, ignorance, pride, false views and doubt (*Abhidharmakośa* 5.lc-d). There is also a passive prime cause of samsaric existence known as *saṃskāra:* the residual forces inherited from prior births. However, *saṃskāra* also has a positive side in that it represents the residual good *karma* that leads to enlightenment, and is represented as such in both the Śrī Saṅgrāmadhanaṃjaya and Plaosan inscriptions.

Verses seven, eight and nine. The numbers that de Casparis assigned to this charter's later strophes in 1961, beginning with v.10, suggests that three strophes had intervened between his original transcription for line seven, which amounts to a half-verse in Mālinī meter. With the discovery of fragment D.50f, however, it is reasonable to think that the remainder of line seven, including the sizable gap between fragments D.50b and D.50f, had presented the rest of the same verse in Mālinī meter. Due to the fragmentary nature of the ensuing segment leading up to the start of what de Casparis had labeled strophe 10 in 1961, his numbering system is maintained herein solely for the sake of maintaining continuity with prior discussions of this charter.

The surviving portions of line eight up to *saṅgā* on fragment D.50e appear to have constituted a verse composed in a variant of the Āryā meter, which limits the placement of an amphibrach (⏑ — ⏑) to the second, fourth and sixth foot of the first hemistich and the second and fourth foot of the second hemistich. However, the reverse would be the case if the verse had been composed in Udgīti meter whilst a verse composed in Āryāgīti meter may have an amphibrach in the second, fourth and sixth foot of either hemistich.

The inclusion of *saṅgā-* near the very end of this strophe is deduced from the shape of fragment D.50e as described by de Casparis. From his translation of strophe 15, it is clear that the base of fragment D.50e must have directly attached to D.50f at line 13. This would place the tip of the triangular-shaped fragment D.50e containing *saṅgā-* in close proximity to the preceding text in line eight of fragment D50.b (see figure 4-2).

The following hypothetical diagram and translation is based on the supposition that this fragmentary strophe had been composed in the Udgīti meter, which is featured in v.2 of the Kalasan charter. The following conjectural translation suggests that Javanese folk tales about kings residing on the Ratu Baka Plateau just might contain a kernel of truth.

Hypothetical diagram in Udgīti meter and conjectural translation:

| ------ | --- – | – – || ⏑ – ⏑ | – --- | ⏑ | ------ | = ||
| ⏑ ⏑ – | ⏑ – ⏑ | ⏑ ⏑ – || ⏑ ⏑ ⏑ ⏑ | – – | ⏑ ≚ ⏑ | – – | = ||

[8] . . .] sa skandhe pravṛddhadhī . . . . abhidhārthyatāgraphalade jayati mahārājaka {small gap between D.50b and D.50e}]* saṅgā *[{gap between D.50e and D.50f}

... in his military wing, the design of which is fully developed ... (for [all] contingencies), through the inviolability of his proper surroundings, the king is victorious in the yielding of the foremost (results).

...[34] **in his military wing**[35] (skandhe = sing. locative of skandha, 'division, esp. a division of an army or a form of military array'), **the design** (dhī = dhī<ḥ>, sing. nom. of dhī)[36] **of which is fully developed** (pravṛddha) ... [for (all) contingencies (<pra>saṅgā<nām>, pl. genitive of prasaṅga)],[37] **through the inviolability** (tā)[38] **of his proper** (arthya) **surroundings** (abhidhā), **the king** (mahārājaka<ḥ>, sing. nom. of mahārājaka) **is victorious** (jayati, third pers. sing. present active of √ji) **in the yielding** (phalade, sing. locative of phalada, 'bearing fruit; bringing profit; giving anything as a reward')[39] **of the foremost** (agra) [results].

With respect to the ensuing strophe, the initial half-verse apparently is presented in line eight of fragment D.50f for which there is no transcription. However, the second half-verse appears at the beginning of line nine. The presence of two potential amphibrachs in this segment of the text suggests that the second half-verse could have been composed in either the Udgīti or Āryāgīti meters. Given the large number of *akṣara*-s estimated for the segment of line eight that comes from fragment D.50f, however, Āryāgīti would seem to be the more probable possibility for us to consider.

---

[34]Perhaps, he (*sa* = *saḥ*, sing. nom. pronoun).

[35]Chandra (pc 8 Aug. 2011) glossed *skandhe* as 'in his military headquarters', though the literal expression for this is *skandhāvāre*, e.g. 'in the king's camp or headquarters; in the royal residence'.

[36]*Dhī* means 'wisdom, intelligence, knowledge, design splendour'. Moreover, this can also be the initial syllable of a Sanskrit term such as *dhīratva*, 'fortitude, courage'.

[37]e.g. in future events or circumstances that are possible but cannot be predicted with certainty.

[38]It is interesting that Abhayagirivihāra also can mean the Buddhist monastery on the mountain of safety.

[39]According to Chandra (pc 8 Aug. 2011), *abhidhā-arthyatā-agra-phala-de* would mean "the appropriate defense which yields superior results".

{gap between D.50e and D.50f}]‡ . . . . ‡[[9] pa . . . . . dharmmadhani . . . . ṇe *karamva*pāṇau gurau dhanurvi . . . .

Below is a hypothetical verse diagram compatible with the Udgīti or Āryāgīti meters, though even in this case the remaining text fragments do not provide us with sufficient context for positing a translation without also having to propose a number of highly speculative emendations.

| ~ ~ ~ ~ ~ ~ | ~ ~ ~ ~ ~ ~ | ~ ~ ~ ~ ~ ~ ‖ ~ ~ ~ ~ ~ ~ | ~ ~ ~ ~ ~ ~ | ~ ~ ~ ~ ~ ~ | ~ ~ ~ ⏓ | ~ ~ ~ ‖
| – ⏑ ⏑ | ⏓ ~ ~ ~ | ~ ~ ~ – ‖ ⏑ – ⏑ | – – | ⏑ – ⏑ | – ⏑ ~ ~ | ~ ~ ~ ‖

Verse ten (Āryā meter). According to de Casparis (1961: 247), the part of the transcription from *gurubhiḥ* onward comes from fragment D.50f, though he did not specify whether *-ṇkaraṇaṃ* also belongs to the same fragment. The above translation assumes this last to have been the case given that de Casparis presents *<ala>ṇkaraṇaṃ* as immediately preceding *gurubhiḥ*. The large gap that de Casparis inserted prior to *-ṇkaraṇaṃ* in his transcription implies that he was unable to read several of the preceding *akṣara*-s. These missing syllables presumably fell within the gap between fragments D.50e and D.50f.

De Casparis interpreted the strophe's use of *anya* ('other') as a reference to the building of a second monastery on the Ratu Baka plateau.

> "Now it may be argued that the use of *anya* could indicate another Abhayagiri Vihāra, in other words, a *vihāra* built on behalf of the monks assumed to have left the Ceylonese Abhayagiri. There is, however, a much simpler explanation: the Javanese monks living in the monastery on the Ratubaka Plateau found that their community had expanded so quickly that they appealed to the Śailendra king to have another monastery built. Their request was granted and the new monastery was given the name Abhayagiri. It is evident that the *gurus* here referred to are not the Sinhalese of strophe XII but the Javanese *gurus* of the Śailendra king. The whole strophe is similar to strophe II of the Kalasan inscription" (de Casparis 1961: 247, n. 22).

Given that strophe 12 states that a *vihāra* was built specifically for Siṅhalese monks, then the reference to the building of another *vihāra* might plausibly apply to the addition of a branch of the Siṅhalese Abhayagirivihāra to a Buddhistic monastic complex that had already existed on the Ratu Baka Plateau prior to 792/3 CE. Miksic (1993/94), Sundberg (2004), Degroot (2006) and Chutiwongs (2010) have already noted the similarities between the unique double-platform construction in the complex's southeastern compound and the double-platforms (*padhanaghara parivenas*) constructed for Siṅhalese Buddhist ascetics living the general vicinity of the famous Abhayagirivihāra at Anurādhapura. On Sri Lanka these double meditation platforms were surrounded by an enclosure wall with three gates, usually in three of the four cardinal directions (north, south and east or west, north and east (Degroot 2006: 61-62). However, the Ratu Baka *pĕṇḍapa* differs from the Siṅhalese examples in that the two interconnected platforms at Ratu Baka are not of equal dimensions and the *makara* water spouts demonstrate that the structure of this *pĕṇḍapa* is more ornate than its Siṅhalese counterparts. Additionally, the three gateways in the enclosure walls surrounding the Javanese Abhayagirivihāra face the north, south and west, whereas their Siṅhalese counterparts typically face the north, south and east. On the other hand, the charter states that the Javanese Abhayagirivihāra had been specifically dedicated to Padmapāṇi, whose *padmakula* is closely associated with the cardinal direction west.

> "[The Siṅhalese double platforms were] especially designed for severe spiritual exertions, concentration and meditation ... [and] consist of one or more double-platform structures with no permanent structural roof, built on rock or rock-like ground within a walled enclosure, and usually surrounded by water or a moat .... [They were] presumably meant for forest-dwelling monks (*arannika*) and dating probably from about the 5th–10th century (Bandaranayake 1974: 130-133; Wijesuriya 1998). The most sophisticated and most accomplished in style and aesthetics are formed of the group called *Tapovana* (=forest of meditation), or the Western Monasteries, situated to the west of the ancient capital Anuradhapura. Considering the positioning of the buildings and stylistic comparison, the double-platform enclosure at Ratu Baka appears to be closest to the group forming the southern compound of the Western Monastery D of the Anuradhapura *Tapovana* (see Bandaranayake 1974: fig. 34), datable from about the 8th–9th century" (Chutiwongs 2010: 784-785).

Verse 11 (unidentified meter). Based on the sizable gaps between fragments as well as the defaced text segment on fragment D.50b, the total number of estimated *akṣara*-s missing from this lacuna-ridden stanza is too great for the verse to have been composed in any variant of the Āryā meter. Hence the following conjectural translation is limited to presenting possible meanings for the surviving text fragments.

[10] punaḥ karttuṃ pari .... { gap between D.50b & D.50e }]* <ava>nipatisa ....
...... tuṅgam = atulavalavegaviva *[{gap between fragments D.50e and D.50f}]‡ ....
....

Given that the following strophe pertains to the Abhayagirivihāra, one naturally has the expectation that v.11 would likewise directly pertain to the same Buddhist monastery constructed for Siṅhalese ascetics. This surmise is supported by the word *punaḥ* (in comp. for *punar*, 'furthermore') whilst *karttuṃ* = *kartum* (lit. 'to do', an indeclinable infinitive from √*kṛ*) seems to refer to that which 'should be done' when used in grants (Kölver & Müller-Luckner 1997: 171). Following a lengthy lacuna, there appears the emended text fragment *<ava>nipatisa-*, of which *avanipati* would mean 'king' and with *sa-* being the first syllable of a compositum ending in *-tuṅgam*. The verse's last Sanskrit text fragment *atulavalavegaviva*°, the fast-flowing (*vega*, 'stream, flood, current; speed, velocity') ... [cleft (*viva<ram>*, 'chasm, slit, cleft, hollow, vacuity')] of the incomparable (*atula*) enclosure (*vala*), perhaps refers to the great ramparts and open water channel surrounding the third terrace of the western compound at Ratu Baka. The duct running along the outer edge of the stone ramparts (figure 4-17) originally was enclosed within a low balustrade attached to the narrow channel (Chutiwongs 2010: 794). The Abhayagirivihāra's double-platform, which was immediately encompassed by a flat paved area followed by high walls, also possessed an extensive waterworks consisting of numerous *makara* spouts, which had disgorged water into the series of stone basins placed below them (Degroot 2006: 67).

> "The third terrace measures roughly 130m (E-W) x 170m (N-S). It is sustained on its western, southern and eastern sides by a wall doubled (at its feet) by a small open duct. This duct is linked to the tank located in the northeastern part of the terrace.
> To the west, the enclosure wall is interrupted by a five-doors *gopura*, linked through a staircase and a pathway to the *gopura* of the second terrace. To the west, the enclosure wall is interrupted by a five-doors *gopura*, linked through a staircase and a pathway to the *gopura* of the second terrace. Four simple *gopura* are located respectively on the western, southern (2) and eastern sides" (Degroot 2009: 235).

Fig. 4-18. View north along the formidable wall surrounding the Ratu Baka 'kraton'.

It is possible that the western compound's exterior balustrade and waterworks are symbolically related to the mountain range encircling the salt water ocean at the outer boundary of the Hindu-Buddhist cosmological world. Perhaps the western compound's balustrade and channel were intended to reinforce the site's symbolic connection with Sumeru. It is significant that the charter's opening stanza metaphorically refers to the Sambuddha Sumeru whose deep pool (*hradaḥ*) of modesty (*hrī*) is invigorated (*samāpyāyitam*) by the rushing currents (*vegaiḥ*) of excellent (*vara*) flowing waters (*nadi* = *nadī*).

Other evidence suggests that the mammoth ramparts and *gopura* of the western compound may date from the reign of Samaratuṅga. Sundberg (2003) has illustrated and described the gold-foil inscription, now presumably lost, that was unearthed in the immediate vicinity of the retaining wall for the *gopura* with five doors during 1948 (Oudheidkundig Verslag 1950: 36). It exhibited the form of two interconnected diamonds incised with a Buddhist *mantra* and a *vajra*. Sundberg has dated this mantra to the reign of Rakai Panaraban (784—803) based on the fact that the text includes the word *panarabwan*, which Sundberg perceived to be a variant orthography for the name of the reigning Javanese king, as well as paleographic considerations.

> "The foil has been inscribed on both the leaves of each side with a short inscription written in a script commonly called Kawi or Palaeojavanese. These four inscriptions repeat the basic mantra *oṃ ṭakī hūṃ jaḥ svāhā* but with a highly significant variant on one side: within the exaggerated bubble which comprises the vowel 'ī' there are a further two cramped lines comprising the characters 'panarabwan' and 'khnipas'." (Sundberg 2003: 164-165).

Sundberg interprets *oṃ ṭakī hūṃ jaḥ svāhā* as a variation of *hūṃ ṭakījjaḥ:* the *mantra* uttered by Vajrapāṇi for the purpose of summoning and subjugating Śiva, Umā and other Hindu divinities, which subsequently were assimilated within a *maṇḍala* on the summit of Mount Sumeru, according to the *Sarva Tathāgata Tattva Saṅgraha* (STTS). However, Sundberg viewed the *Oṃ... svāhā* construction of the gold-foil *mantra* as an indication that it had served as a form of benediction: "it is as though the Javanese inscription is a hearkening to the glory of Vajrapāṇi's triumph rather than a formal attempt to duplicate the feat of summoning using the proven efficacy of his mantra" (Sundberg 2003: 170). Additionally, Sundberg surmised that the promulgator of the Abhayagirivihāra charter had been the Rakai Panaraban cited in the list of Javanese kings presented in the Wanua Tĕngah III charter of 908 CE.

> "Not only does this conclusion accord with the coincidence and contemporality of Panarabwan and Samaratuṅga on the heights of the Ratu Baka in the period around 790, but seems to derive also from the nature of the Great Gate and its endowment. Accepting the manifest Śailendra suzerainty over the plains of Prambanan during this time, how could the king Samaratuṅga allow the king Panarabwan to construct not only the tallest feature of the plateau but also a feature under which the great Śailendra *mahārāja* would have to pass to access the escarpment and his *vihāra*" (Sundberg 2003: 175-176).[40]

Given that *hūṃ ṭakījjaḥ* is a *mantra* for subjugating Hindu divinities, however, Jordaan

[40]More recently, Sundberg (2011) has sought to identify Samaratuṅga with the Raka of Panaraban.

and Colless (2004: 62) argued that it had been placed near the gate of the Ratu Baka complex for the purpose of ensuring that the Raka of Panaraban continued to remain a vassal king subject to the authority of the Śailendra dynasty, with the encircling of the Javanese king's name 'Panarabwan' within the crescent above the '*ī*', intended to "convey the idea of his being caught and tied up with ropes and rendered powerless". As we have previously seen in Chapter II, however, the proposed vassal status for Panaraban's predecessor is a problematic component of the two-kings theory proposed by Jordaan and others for the Kalasan charter. So we naturally wonder whether the circle might rather have been intended to signify a magic circle of protection as is the customary symbolic interpretation of the Sanskrit world for circle (*maṇḍala*), perhaps signifying in this instance that the wealth of the dharm (*dharmadhani*) united (*karamba,* 'intermingled') within the Śailendra preceptor (see v.9 above) also extended protection and defense to 'Panarabwan' out of friendship or mutual regard. One could argue that 'Panarabwan' had sponsored something belonging to the western compound (see Jordaan & Colless 2004: 56) in much the same manner as the kingdom's monarchs and other high dignitaries had contributed to the building of sanctuaries at Caṇḍi Plaosan Lor during the middle of the ninth century. However, Jordaan and Colless (2004: 59-60) observed that the excavation report states that the *mantra* was found amidst the "remains of the big retaining wall in front of the first gate", e.g. in the area occupied by the ramp leading down from it. The lack of any Sanskrit or Javanese title or honorific preceding 'Panarabwan' also casts doubt on Sundberg's identification of this presumed appellation with Rakai Panaraban.

Verse twelve (in Mālinī meter). The transcription for strophe 12 published by de Casparis in 1961 is based on the contents of fragments D.50c, D.50e and D.50f.

> "The text of this Mālinī strophe is scattered over three fragments. Its beginning up to *padma-* is found on the new fragment at the end of line 10; the following eight syllables are on fragment *c* at the beginning of line 11; the two last syllables of the second *pāda* and the third up to *śikṣitānāṃ* inclusive are read on fragment *e*, whereas the remaining part of the third and the entire fourth *pāda* occur in line 11 of the new fragment" (de Casparis 1961: 242).

Noting that the *pĕṇḍapa* and its enclosure walls had undergone several construction phases, Degroot (2006: 72) has proposed that it was only during the third building phase that the site was modified for the use of the Siṅhalese ascetics mentioned in v.12.

- First construction phase (prior to 792/3): a square terrace surrounded by a square enclosure wall;
- Second construction phase (prior to 792/3): the extension of the courtyard to the south, with the square terrace becoming located in the northern part of the enclosure; "an elevated path links it to the southern *gopura*. Some important buildings must have been located south of the *pendopo*. Probably Buddhist."
- Third construction phase (792/3): the addition of a second platform to the south of the square terrace in the north of the enclosure, thereby bringing the site into conformation with the style of the double-platforms found at monastic wilderness sites on Sri Lanka.

- Fourth construction phase (early ninth century): the addition of the ornamental bases depicting the *vāhana* for each of the five Tathāgatas.
- Fifth construction phase (856 CE): addition of three miniature *caṇḍi*-s in the general vicinity of the double platform. The ritual deposits discovered beneath these three small edifices included a foil stamped with a mantra mentioning the Hindu divinity Rudra.
- Sixth construction phase (post 856 CE): The three temples in reduction are moved to a new location south of the double platform.

Nevertheless, many of the time-line elements proposed by Degroot are debatable. Strophe 10 speaks of the building of a *vihāra* by the preceptor or preceptors of the entire temple complex *saṅghārāma*. I can think of no reason why we should not consider the alternate view that the monks from the original Abhayagirivihāra in Sri Lanka had made modifications to the original structure prepared for them at a date subsequent to that of the charter. Degroot's dating of the three miniature *caṇḍi*-s also does not account for the possibility that a Rudra *mantra* can occur within a Siṅhalese Mahāyāna Buddhist context, as previously noted above (see also Dalton 2011: 120). Besides, the fixed dates that Degroot has assigned to the fifth and sixth construction phases appear to have been intended to conform to a speculative theory proposed by de Casparis, which is based in part on his conjectural reading of the Śivagṛha inscription of 856 CE.

I am unaware of any valid grounds for concluding that the *vāhana* of the five Tathāgatas had been unknown to Javanese Buddhists in the late eighth century. And the majority if not all of the Kumbhayoni inscriptions that provide the other principal supporting element for Degroot's time-line were found at locations in the eastern half of the Ratu Baka prominence[41] (for example, at Dawangsan 750 m. to the east of Ratu Baka's southeastern compound and at Pereng near the northeastern foot of Ratu Baka). So the Kumbhayoni inscriptions might not have any direct bearing on the fifth and sixth construction phases as proposed by Degroot.

Verse 13. The meter for strophe 13 as transcribed by de Casparis has not been identified. "The first of the two intervening strophes (XIII), only half of which can be deciphered, appears to inform us about the aim of the foundation; one of the compounds that has remained legible is *sakalajanahitārtham:* 'for the weal of all people'." (de Casparis 1961: 245).[42]

△△△△△△ ... ‡[[12] dānaṃ śāsanaḥ syanti . nānā { gap between fragments D.50c and D.50e }]* prajānāṃ .... matirabhavannaḥ karttuṃ śe *[{small gap between fragments D.50e and D.50f}]‡ sakalajanahitārtham

The Sanskrit word *śāsanaḥ* presumably refers to the monarch's 'royal grant'. However, the meaning of *syanti* remains unclear. The closest Sanskrit parallel would be *syandi*, 'pouring, flowing, running', e.g. 'issuing forth'. Furthermore, *nānā* can mean 'distinctly' and *dānam* 'imparting'. Chandra (pc 11 March 2011) has speculated that a portion of this

[41]Arlo Griffiths, pc 25 March 2012.

[42]The compositum *sakalajanahitārtham* appears on line 12 from fragment D.50f.

verse would refer to the monarch as saying, "'Then it came to our mind [*matirabhavannaḥ* = *matiḥ-abhavat-naḥ*] and to the subjects (*prajānāṃ*) to make (*karttum*) [a donation (*dānaṃ*)] for the benefit of all the people' (*sakala-jana-hitārtham*) ....'"[43] But all of the above suggestions must be viewed with extreme caution given the fragmentary condition of the strophe as well as our inability to establish the meter.

Verse 14. De Casparis initially proposed the emendation *śailendra<vaṅsatilaka>* for this fragmentary strophe. "From the meter it appeared that this word [e.g. *śailendra*] stood at the beginning of the second half of an Āryā strophe, so there is a good chance that the expression used here is *śailendravaṅśatilaka*, which we frequently find used for the Śailendra kings" (de Casparis 1950: 15). Following the discovery of fragment D.50f, however, he simply remarked that strophe 14 "states that the vihāra was erected in the prospering kingdom (*rajye pravarddhamāne*) of the Śailendra king Samaratuṅga" (de Casparis 1961: 245).

]‡ . . . <r>ājye pravarddhamāne . . . . ‡[[13] samaratuṅgadevasya śailendra {gap between fragments D.50c and D.50e }]* . . . .

Given Bosch's surmise that both the Kalasan and Abhayagirivihāra charters had been carved by the same hand, it is also possible that the compositum *śailendra<rājagurubhis>* had been intended here, as we also find to have been the case in v.5 of the Kalasan charter, the identical components of which are underlined below:

> <u>rājye pravarddhamāne</u> rājñaḥ śailendravaṅśatilakasya /
> <u>śailendra</u>rājagurubhis tārābhavanaṃ kṛtaṃ kṛtibhiḥ // (5)

In the following hypothetical diagram of strophe 14, *śailendra<rājagurubhis>* would be a metrically compatible emendation for a verse composed in the Āryā meter, though there is no single *daṇḍa* following *samaratuṅgadevasya*[44] to be seen in the Abhayagirivihāra charter:

Hypothetical diagram of strophe 14 in Āryā meter:

Verse 15 (Āryā meter): De Casparis first transcribed the following compositum from what he thought was line 12 from fragment D.50e in 1950: *śākanṛpakālātī*. After the discovery of fragment D.50f in 1954, however, he realized that *śākanṛpakālātī* belonged one line

[43]The small gap between fragments D.50e and D.50f suggests that the missing word or phrase had consisted of just a few syllables. Through there are a number of possibilities for completing *śe-*, *śe<khare>* ('on the summit of the mountain') provides an interesting potential match based on context.

[44]It is customary for the coronation name of a king to be preceded by an honorific, which may not have been the case here unless it had originally been placed at the end of the prior line. De Casparis gave *Dharmmatuṅga* as the name of the Śailendra king in his 1950 transcription, while noting that only the latter two syllables were certain. He corrected this to Samaratuṅga in his 1961 article.

lower (13) and that the rest of the strophe to which it belongs "is read on line 13 of the new fragment and ends on line 14 of fragment *c*" (de Casparis 1961: 241-242).

I have translated *varṣṣaiś=cāpy* from the second hemistich as 'during the rainy season' (lit. 'together with the rains', e.g. those belonging to the rainy season) for several reasons. The extensive waterworks incorporated into the design of the so-called *kraton* at Ratu Baka obviously must have had a religious purpose, perhaps one pertaining to the collection of holy water. The rainy season is also the time of the year when the *vihāra* becomes a retreat for Buddhist ascetics and thus an appropriate time for the consecration of the Abhayagirivihāra to have taken place in the presence of the entire religious community. Additionally, given that *varṣṣa* (=*varṣa*) already appears in the first hemistich, where it conveys the meaning of year, in my opinion the composition would be more elegant if *varṣaiḥ* (the plural instr. of *varṣa*) had been intended to convey an alternate meaning in the second hemistich, thus avoiding repetition.

Chandra (pc 11 March 2011) translated the second hemistich as follows: the consecration of the *vihāra* and also the years (*varṣaiḥ*) passed victoriously (*abhivṛttaiḥ*). "The surcharged expression abhivṛtta carries a sense of exhilarating victory over the insuperable difficulties encountered during the years of its construction". However, this does not account for the fact that *varṣaiḥ* also appears in the second half of the verse presenting the date in the Sri Sangramadhanamjaya inscription whereas *abhivṛttaiḥ* does not.

Remaining lines of the inscription. With the exception of the final line of the Ratu Baka charter, the remaining verses are too fragmentary for us to translate, though some phrases do stand out. De Casparis (1950: 23) noted that the compositum *vihāraparipālanā* in line 15 of the Abhayagirivihāra charter is comparable to the compositum *vihāraparipālanārtham* ('proper maintenance of the *vihāra*') from the final strophe of the Śrī Saṅgrāmadhanaṃjaya inscription. Moreover, the next segment of the Abhayagirivihāra charter may have pertained to the members of the rural gentry responsible for "monitoring the implementation of the orders of the king, presumably a sort of inspector of public works, also understood under the last to mean works of a religious nature" (Bosch 1952: 114). In line 16 we encounter the phrase *san tavānakādibhiḥ*, which is once again almost identical to *saṅ tavānakādibhiḥ* from v.9 of the Kalasan charter, with the latter being the title of one of the three members of the rural gentry collectively known as the *sang māna katrīṇi*. It is also possible that *saṇ* = *ḍa*- might represent the beginning of a Sanskritized title for another Javanese dignitary, such as the *saṅ ḍa<punta>* associated with Hindu religious duties.

The charter's final strophe must have concluded in the gap between the end of the segment on D.50d and the beginning of D.50f given that there is no line 18 on the latter fragment. So the charter's final stanza apparently had begun in the segment of line 17 from D.50f and had ended on the last line of the inscription.

The cadence of short and long syllables contained in the surviving text fragments that appear on fragments D.50c and D.50d would certainly be compatible with a verse in a variant of the Āryā meter, though the Upendravajrā meter is also a possibility. The two diagrams below the transcription display entirely hypothetical verses in the Upendravajrā and Āryā meters, both of which were also featured in the Kalasan charter. If this is a strophe in Āryā meter, the light syllable *ga* in *jātārthavibhāgavijñāḥ* only fits the metric requirements of the second hemistich as it is displayed below.

]‡ D.50f ‡[[18] -m = anuśāsanajñā bhavanti (gap between fragments)]† ta ... ...
jātārthavibhāgavijñāḥ †[

Upendravajrā meter: | ⏑ – ⏑ ¦ – – ⏑ ¦ ⏑ – ⏑ ¦ – – ||

| - - - - ¦ - - - ⏑ ¦ ⏑ – ⏑ ¦ – – || ⏑ – ⏑ ¦ - - - - ¦ - - - - ¦ - - ||
| - - - - ¦ - - - - ¦ - - - - ¦ - - - - || ⏓ - - - ¦ – – ⏑ ¦ ⏑ – ⏑ ¦ – – ||

Āryā meter:
| - - - - - | - - - - - | - - - - ⏑ || ⏑ – ⏑ | – – | ⏑ – ⏑ | - - - - - | - ||
| - - - - - | - - - - - | ⏓ - - - - || – – | ⏑ ⏑ – | ⏑ | – – | - || 18 ||

Here are the hypothetical translations for the individual text fragments from the final verse from the Abhayagirivihāra charter:

- ... **they are** (bhavanti, third pers. pl. active present from √bhū) **conversant in** (jñā = jñāḥ, pl. acc. of jñā, 'familiar with') ... **this instruction** (anuśāsana) **of the** ... [-m];[45]
- ... [and] **experts** (vijñāḥ, pl. acc. of vijñā) **in the exposition** (vibhāga) **of the meaning** (artha) **of the** ... [(-jāta)].

The above is based on the near duplication of these text fragments in v.11 of the Kalasan charter,[46] which is reproduced below with the near identical components underlined. Hence, one naturally suspects that the Upendravajrā meter selected for use in the Kalasan charter likewise was used for the composition of the Abhayagirivihāra inscription's final verse, which de Casparis labeled strophe 18.

anena puṇyena v<i>hārajena pratītya jātārthavibhāgavijñāḥ /
bhavantu sarve tribhavopapannā janā jinānām anuśāsanajñāḥ // (11)

[45]Sarkar's (1971/2: I: 48) parsing of *m = anuśāsanajñā bhavanti* as *manu-śāsana-jñā-bhavanti* and his attempt to interpret this as a reference to "the codes of Manu" seem spurious to me given the Buddhistic context of the charter.

[46]De Casparis (1950: 24, n. 17) remarked that *jātārthavibhāgavijñāḥ* is found in v.11 of the Kalasan charter.

V. The Kayumwuṅan charter of Central Java's Veṇuvanavihāra

The Kayumwuṅan (also referred to as the Karangtĕngah) charter consists of two distinct texts inscribed in the same type of Palaeojavanese script and with the opening Sanskrit and ensuing Old Javanese segments both citing the same date in 746 Śaka (=824 CE). Only two of the charter's five fragments were sent to the Batavia Museum, where they were cataloged separately as D.27 and D.34. A third fragment was transported to the city of Magelang in Central Java for safekeeping but was subsequently lost. Fortunately an estampage (*afprent* no. 113) and a cast (*afgietsel*) of fragment *C* had already been made and shipped to the Rijksmuseum van Oudheden at Leiden (de Casparis 1950: 24-25; Damais 1955: 111, n. 2).[1] The inscription's remaining two fragments were either lost as well or never recovered in the first place. Based on the script style and stone type characteristics shared by all three of the recovered fragments, it was subsequently noticed that they actually belonged to the same charter. Figure 5-1 shows what de Casparis (1950: 24-26 and fig. 2) presumed to be the original state of the stone. In height, width and thickness, fragment *B* measures 44x37x13 cm., whereas the dimensions of fragment *E* are 39x58x10 cm. (Groeneveldt 1887: 382, no. 27 and 384, no. 34). Two slightly different sets of measurements were given for fragment *C:* 50 cm. at the top versus 46 cm. below, and 21 cm. as well as 45 cm. on the sides; or height 45 cm. and 25 cm., breadth 47 cm. (Sarkar 1971/2: I: 64 and 73, notes 1 & 3). Hence, the height of the original charter would have exceeded 1.0 m. by several cm.

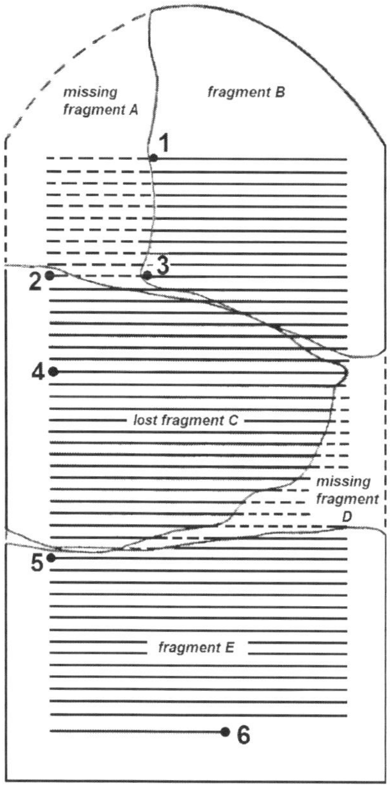

Fig. 5-1. Sketch of the fragments from the Kayumwuṅan charter, with the missing fragments *A* and *D* indicated by line dashes. (1) the beginning point of the charter on fragment *B* (D.27); (2) the start of the first line on the lost fragment *C*; (3) the location where the first line from fragment *C* had ultimately connected with line 11 of fragment *B*; (4) the start of line 19, which is entirely preserved on fragment *C*; (5) the beginning point of the first line (37) on fragment *E* (D.34); and (6) the end of the text (after de Casparis 1950: fig. 2).

[1]The Rijksmuseum voor Volkenkunde ('National Museum of Ethnology') has preserved a number of inscription *abklatches* from Central Java that were originally manufactured *circa* 1880 for the (Rijks)museum van Oudheden ('National Museum of Antiquities') also located in Leiden. According to Sarkar (1971/2: I: 64), the inventory number for fragment *C* was 2994. However, the museum's online database shows a gap between (MVL inventory nos. 1403-) 2992 and 3000 with respect to the *afgietsels* originating from Central Java.

Fig. 5-2. The two fragments of the Kayumwuṅan charter on display at the National Museum in Jakarta (photo credit: Shigehisa Taguchi).

The origin of the Kayumwuṅan charter

De Casparis (1950: 24-25) contended that the only certainty about the origin of the charter's fragments was that they had resided for a long time at the house of a low-ranking Dutch civil servant (*controleur*) in Magelang and claimed that the existing historical record was based on suspect oral communications that could not be trusted. He then attempted to link this inscription with Caṇḍi Barabuḍur in the South Kedu area of Central Java—a hypothesis subsequently adopted by Kandahjaya (2004 and 2009). To show that this had *not* been the case, we shall begin by examining the earliest written references to fragments from the charter, as well as the records referring to the other major archeological remains recovered from the environs of the *desa* Traji, District Parakan, Temanggung Regency.

De Casparis' three-paragraph discussion of the charter's provenance neglected to comment upon a manuscript written by Hoepermans in 1865 and preserved in the Batavia Museum's library thereafter until finally published in 1913. Both Verbeek (1891) and Krom (1914) relied on Hoepermans' *Hindoe-oudheden van Java* as a primary reference. Citing Verbeek (1891: 138), de Casparis (1950: 24) wrote that fragment *C* had been discovered by Hoepermans in a *controleur's* house in Magelang, which is an inaccurate assessment of what both Verbeek and Hoepermans actually had written.

Traji. According to Hoepermans (1913: 168), a sizable inscription fragment was one among a number of antiquities (*yoni*, *liṅgam*, ornamented temple stones) that formerly had stood in front of Traji's Missighit (glossed as 'church', but actually a 'mosque'), which appears to have served as an informal repository where antiquities discovered in the surrounding area were brought for safekeeping. He remarked that this fragment's script, which was small and fine, had suffered a lot of damage and was unclear. This description is comparable to what de Casparis subsequently wrote about the Kayumwuṅan charter's extensive weathering and beautifully executed but relatively small script, which has *akṣara*-s just 0.5 cm. in height, on average.

> "Throughout, however, where the forms are well preserved, it appears that the characters are engraved with the utmost care. The writing is perfectly regular, [with] all *akṣaras* of equal height and written with an equal degree of cursivity. Precisely because of this diligence it has been possible to read the majority of the document .... Small details in the execution of a character frequently prove sufficient to identify it, even if half of these [details] has disappeared" (de Casparis 1950: 25-26).

Hoepermans mentioned that the aforementioned inscription fragment had been transported from Traji to Magelang in October of 1865 and had either stood in front of, or beside, the controleur's house. Hoepermans wrote that it was said at the time that the fragment from Traji was thought to be the missing half of an inscribed stone already kept in the museum at Batavia.

Verbeek (1891: 138, no. 242) repeated Hoepermans' observation that a pedestal, a *liṅga* and temple stones had been found in the vicinity of Traji, as did Krom (1914: 268, no. 967). Moreover, Verbeek and Krom concluded that the partial inscription from Traji described by Hoepermans was actually fragment *C* of the charter from what he identified as the nearby hamlet 'Karangtĕngah', the precise location of which is not known with certainty. A closer examination of this important issue will be reserved for a later discussion segment.

Tĕlaja. According to Hoepermans (1913: 168-169), the architectural remains closest to Traji were discovered in the *desa* Tĕloijo (=Tĕlaja) three kilometers (*twee paal*; one *paal* = 1506 m) to the south of Ngadirejo. The location at which this village had formerly stood, which can be surmised from the 1870, 1891 and 1907 maps[2] preserved in the Royal Tropical Institute (KIT) collection, constitutes the southeastern part of modern-day Karanggedong.[3]

> "In the vicinity of this *desa* is a cemetery in a grove of bamboo and brushwood [wherein] are found fifteen large square blocks of volcanic stone [*brandsteenen*] of 69 cm. [1 el] in height and width; on top of these stones are found raised ledges [*riggels* = *richels*], in the mode of moon crescents [or half-moons]. For the purpose of expiation, guilty ladies sat on these volcanic stones (see temple Selo grio). The locals call this [type of] stone *batu sumpah* [oath stone?]. Stones chiseled into squares such as these, however, are rare. No other traces [of antiquities] are found in this *desa*" (Hoepermans 1913: 168-169).

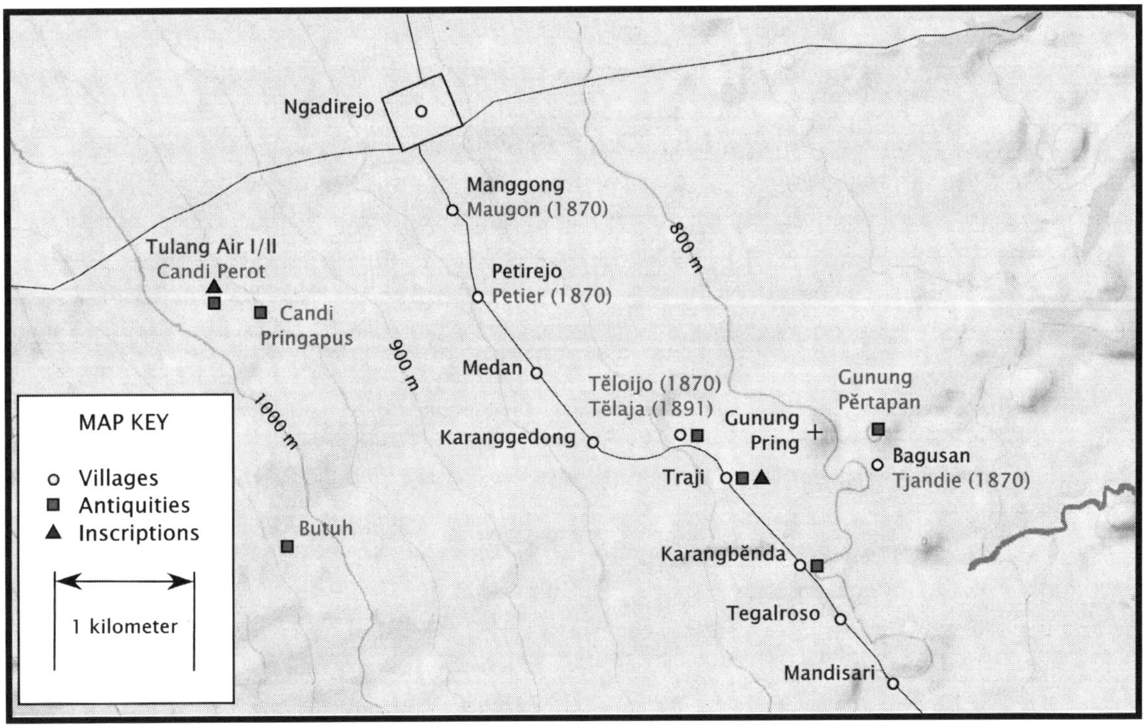

Fig. 5-3. Villages, antiquities, inscriptions and other sites to the south of Ngadirejo.

[2]The distance between the center of Ngadirejo (7.235275 S; 110.060765 E) and the *desa* identified as Tĕloijo on the 1870 map (7.256646 S; 110.078348 E) is 3.067 km, thus consistent with Hoepermans' estimate of two *paal* (=3.012 km). This was calculated through the use of the "distance between pair of latitude/longitude points" tool hosted at: http://movable-type.co.uk/ (accessed 10 May 2014).

[3]Verbeek (1891: 137) equated Tĕloijo with the toponym Tĕlaja, which appears on a Dutch Army map dating from 1907 as the name of a river (Kali Tĕlaja).

Verbeek (1891: 137, no. 241) subsequently recorded that this same set of stone artifacts were located in Tělaja nearby Traji. "Fifteen large square-cut stones, 1 m. long and wide and provided with a curved figure from above, which protrudes above the surface a little".

Gunung Pěrtapan and the hamlet Tjandi. The name of this hill[4] is of considerable interest given that the Old Javanese segment of the Kayumwuṅan charter refers to the Javanese aristocrat Rakaryān Patapān (written as Partapān in the Sang Hyang Wintang inscription), as we shall see later on. Hoepermans was the first to note the former existence of an ancient temple foundation on the Gunung Pěrtapan.

> "Coming from Ngadirejo and approaching this *desa*, namely Traji, you leave the road and walk through a coffee plantation opposite of which is situated the hill Pěrtapan (hermitage or place of prayer), and which belongs to the nearby *desa* Tjandi (=Caṇḍi). On this hill we found traces of former antiquities: a number of stones with and without ornamentation are still in attendance here, likewise also a few segments of a foundation in the ground " (Hoepermans 1913: 168-169; see also Verbeek 1891: 138, no. 244).

Knebel and Krom also provided a few additional details about the ancient temple remnants found on Gunung Pěrtapan, which is located 1.25 km east of Traji and just to the north of the hamlet Bagusan, which was labeled on the 1870 map as 'Tjandie'.

> "On this hill we found a flat area, surrounded by an oval-shaped earthen rampart, of which the longest center-line amounts to 17 m. and the shortest 11.90 m. The area is planted with banyan, *tédjå*, *bendå* and *kanṭil* trees, amidst of which a temple once stood" (Knebel 1911: 275).

The surviving parts of the temple had included pieces of the foundation, three *kala* heads, a crowning element [*topstuk*], the upper parts of some pilasters and stone blocks (Krom 1914: 296, no. 971).

'Karangtěngah'. Hoepermans did not refer to Karangtěngah by name or to the discovery of any additional inscriptions (or fragments thereof) in the vicinity of Traji. Four years after Hoepermans completed his manuscript in 1865, however, an inventory of ancient charters from Central Java's Temanggung Regency (NBG 1869: CVII)—which also refers to the Caṇḍi Perot (Tulang Air) and Ḍang Pu Hawang Gělis (Gåndåsuli I) inscriptions, among others—alludes to an inscription from Karangtěngah. Moreover, an inventory letter listing the *papier mâché* impressions of Javanese inscriptions prepared for, and sent to, the Rijksmuseum van Oudheden in Leiden (NBG 1876: II: III) mentions an inscribed stone from Karangtěngah (presumably fragment *C*) as does an inventory of *papier mâché* impressions still in the possession of the Genootschap (NBG 1876: II: VI), whereas the supplement prepared by J.L.A. Brandes for Groeneveldt's *Catalogus* states that the provenance was unknown for fragments *B* and *E*, which were already in the Museum at Batavia and cataloged as nos. 27 and 34 (Groeneveldt 1887: 382 and 384). By contrast,

[4]Two other Gunung Pěrtapan toponyms are found in Central Java: one is located to the north-northwest of Traji and is shown in figure 5-5 while the other is located further to the east at a location off the map. A *liṅga* 1.1 m. in height and two round stones were found at the latter site, according to Verbeek (1891: 133, no. 224).

Verbeek (1891: 138, no. 243) comments upon three fragments of an inscribed stone from 'Karangtĕngah', one of which was for some time kept next to the *controleur's* house in Magelang, but subsequently was lost (i.e. fragment *C*). "The other two pieces are now in the Museum at Batavia, recorded as stones nos. 27 and 34".

Verbeek considered 'Karangtĕngah' to have been another hamlet located in the general vicinity of Tĕlaja and Traji, although this toponym is unattested elsewhere as pertaining to any location in this specific part of Central Java. On what is presumably his 1891 map, which is preserved in the KIT collection, the entry for 'Kg. tengah' is located to the south-southeast of Traji. Additionally, the site is marked with a plus sign (+) on this map to show that it was an inscription's place of origin.

Krom (1914: 296, nos. 968, 969) likewise identified 'Karangtĕngah' as the discovery place of an inscribed stone commencing with Sanskrit verses, and then [*vervolgens* = next] a *praśasti* from 769.[5] "The stone is broken into five fragments, three of which have been lost (*A*, *C* and *D*) and two (*B* and *E*) incorporated into the Batavia Museum. One of the lost fragments (*C*) was first situated at Traji (no. 967) and later brought to Magelang (no. 679)". In his next entry Krom cited a report by Knebel (1911: 275) concerning the discovery of a small rotund niche containing the figure of a kneeling '*rĕṣi*'[6] in the hamlet Karangbĕnda (*desa* Tegelroso), which occupies the same area as an unnamed hamlet on the south side of Traji on the map from 1870. Karangbĕnda is located beside the road just 1.2 km to the southwest of Gunung Pĕrtapan. This raises the question as to whether Karangtĕngah had been an earlier name for the *desa* Karangbĕnda, or if whoever had initially identified the charter's fragments as having coming from Karangtĕngah had misheard the name of the hamlet.

Given that Krom provided entries for both Karangtĕngah and Karangbĕnda, however, it would seem that he had considered the former to have been a small hamlet located somewhere between Traji and Karangbĕnda. Jordaan (pc 7 Oct. 2012) observed that Karang-tĕngah literally means 'Karang in-between' or 'Karang in the middle', which suggests that a hamlet known as Karangtĕngah could have been located formerly somewhere in between modern-day Karanggedong (identified as Karang Tjaugakan on the 1870 map in the area immediately north of the old *desa* Tĕlaja) and Karangbĕnda. However, this is not the only possibility. The 1907 Dutch Army map displays the additional toponym Karanganom on the west side of Traji. So the location of Karangtĕngah—or even whether a hamlet of that name had ever existed in this area—remains an open question.

The ancient toponyms cited in the Kayumwuṅan charter

Nevertheless, the ancient toponyms cited in this charter and their continuity with toponyms presented several other inscriptions from the Temanggung Regency strongly reinforce the charter's association with this particular region. Van der Meulen (1979) compared the

[5]De Casparis (1950: 30-31) subsequently corrected the cipher dating misread by Goris and Brandes to 746 Śaka, equivalent to 824 CE.

[6]Whether this figure had actually depicted a Brahmanical *rĕṣi* (=*ṛṣi*) or a Buddhistic ascetic is unknown. Recent research suggests that the bearded figures prominently depicted in the reliefs at Barabuḍur and on the lintels of the *caṇḍis* Sewu, Pawon and Ngawen may represent bearded Buddhist ascetics known as *siddhas* (Sundberg & Giebel 2012: 165-168).

village names cited in the Old Javanese segment of the Kayumwuṅan inscription (see the designations presented in bold typeface in Appendix D) with the village names presented in the charters of Sang Hyang Wintang (Gåndåsuli II; *in situ* south of modern-day Parakan Wetan), Tulang Air, Mantyāsiḥ I and Tri Tĕpusan II (Caṇḍi Pĕtung II; origin unknown).

> "That the contents of these *praśasti* concern overlapping territories is evident from the number of names of villages and jurisdictions that are common to all or several of them. These jurisdictions were certainly still coherent geographical entities, because the names (with a few exceptions) are only found in this territorial context and not in inscriptions originating elsewhere" (Van der Meulen 1979: 37-38).

Among other things, a significant number of ancient toponyms are not only duplicated across several charters but in some cases the toponyms can even be correlated with their modern-day counterparts in Central Java's Temanggung Regency. For example, several toponyms from the Old Javanese segment of the Kayumwuṅan charter (see Appendix D) can be linked in theory to contemporary village names: Trihaji with Traji, Ptir with Petir (Petier on the 1870 map) and also Petirrejo (Ptir + *rāja*, according to Van der Meulen), Hajihuma with Juma, and Kanḍaṅan Lamwas with Kandangan. He also observed that the Mantyāsiḥ I (907 CE) charter refers to Kayumwuṅan as well as the volcanoes Sumbing (Sumwing) and Sundoro (Susunḍara).

The Old Javanese segment presented on fragment *E* from the bottom of the Kayumwuṅan charter states that the Rakaryān Patapān pu Palar had donated the income from several irrigated rice fields to support a *vihāra* constructed by king Samaratuṅga's daughter, as designated by the Sanskrit portion of the same charter. The five rice fields Babadan, Kisir, Sāntwi Karung, Kuling and Kaliru<nga>n (see Resiyani 2010: 54-55) had belonged to the villages Luapanḍak, Kayumwuṅan, Ptir and Tri Haji, respectively. The same charter segment also delineates the extent of the grant using the *ha* (=*hamat*), a unit apparently related to a system of measure noted by Wisseman Christie (1996: 150), which is "based upon the quantity of seed or seedlings (*winih*) needed to plant a given area. The units in which this seed was measured– *tū* (abbr.?), *ha* or *hamat* and *wha* (abbr.?)—have been found only in a limited number of early inscriptions connected with the Kedu region of north Central Java, which may have belonged to a single early statelet later annexed by the expanding state of Mataram". Rakaryān Patapān also was the promulgator of the Sang Hyang Wintang (Gåndåsuli II) rock inscription dated by Damais (1952: 28, n. 1) on epigraphical grounds to the same period as the Ḍang Pu Hawang Gĕlis (Gåndåsuli I) inscription of 827 CE. The latter stone was recovered from the vicinity of the *desa* Diwak, 3 kilometers to the west of Parakan (Hoepermans (1913: 167) but subsequently was lost. By contrast, the Sang Hyang Wintang (Gåndåsuli II) boulder inscription found *in situ* near the village of Gondosuli (District Bulu, Temanggung Regency) describes the founding of a Śaiva family shrine by Partapān Siḍa Busu Plār (see de Casparis 1950: 50-73 and Damais 1968: 332-339).[7]

[7] According to the opinion of Damais (1968: 389), the appellation Ratnamaheśvara mentioned in this charter is likely to be the name of the hermitage, though from a strictly grammatical point of view Damais admitted that de Casparis' interpretation of Ratnamaheśvara ('Great lord of wealth') as a designation applicable to Ḍang

Kayum-wuṅan (824)[8]	Sang Hyang Wintang (*circa* 830)[9]	Tri Tĕpusan I/II (842)[10]	Muṇḍuan (807)	Tulang Air I/II (850)	Wanua Tĕngah I/II (863)	Mantyāsiḥ I (907)	Mantyāsiḥ III (907)	Rukam (907)	Wanua Tĕngah III (908)
Kayumwuṅan	Kyu bunngan	Kayumvuṅan		Kayumvuṅan		Kayumvuṅan	Kayumwuṅan		
Ptir		Ptir	Ptir			Ptir			
Tri Haji		Tri Haji							
Tyusan		Tpusan				Tpusan	Tpusan		
Wariṅin		Wariṅin				Waringin			
Kaṇḍaṅan Lamwas		Kaṇḍangingan	Kaṇḍangan	Kaṇḍangan					
Mantyāsih	Mantyāsiḥ	Mantyāsih				Mantyāsiḥ	Mantyāsiḥ	Mantyāsiḥ	
Patapān	Partapān	Patapān	Patapān	Patapān		Patapān	Patapān	Patapān	
Paṇḍakyan		Paṇḍakyan				Paṇḍakyan			
Sukun		Sukun							
Wuatan		Wuattan							
	Bunut	Wunut		Wunut			Wunut	Wunut	
	Praggāluḥ	Praggāluḥ				Praggaluḥ	Praggaluḥ		
		Pamigaran						Pamigaran	
		Puhunnan				Puhunan	Puhun		
		Wunha		Wunha					
		Muṇḍwan	Muṇḍuan			Munduān	Muṇḍuan		
		Kḍu				Kḍu	Kḍu		
			Haji Huma			Haji Huma	Haji Huma		
						Tangkil	Taṅkil	Taṅkil	
						Sumving			
						Susuṇḍara			
	Tarukan								
				Kuñci					
									Pikatan
									Titang
					Wanua Taṅaḥ			Wanua Tnaḥ	Wanua Tĕngah
				Tulang air			Tulang ṅair		
				Air Hulu		Air Hulu	Air Hulu		

Fig. 5-4. Toponyms cited in charters from the Temanggung Regency.

Karayān Partapān Siḍa Busu Plār was theoretically possible.

[8]See Appendix D.

[9]De Casparis (1950: 153) thought that the minor deviations in spelling found below may be attributed to the use of Old Malay in the Sang Hyang Wintang charter.

[10]See de Casparis 1950: 86-87 and 152-155.

Among other things, the ability of the Rakaryān Patapān pu Palar to donate the income from irrigated rice fields belonging to Luapaṇḍak, Kayumwuṅan, Ptir, and Tri Haji, as attested in the Old Javanese segment of the charter, is sufficient evidence that he had exercised administrative power in the region due to "the fact that he allocated revenues from fields owned not by him but by these villages. From such fields he could only allocate the part due to the king. He would not have used his own domain except on behalf of a family foundation for his own ancestry" (Van der Meulen 1979: 36).

The Muṇḍuan charter (from hamlet Toro, village Kertosari, district Jumo, Temanggung Regency) demonstrates that the administrative power of the Rakaryān Patapān had extended even further to the north of Ptir (Petirejo) as early as 807 CE. The personal name of Rakaryān Patapān in the Muṇḍuan (807) and Tulang Air I/II (850) charters of 850 is Pu Manukū, with the latter perhaps having been a grandson. In the Wanua Tĕngah I/II charters of 863 CE, Pu Manukū adopted the title of Rakai i Pikatan (Damais 1949: 24) previously held by Śrī Mahārāja Rakai Pikatan dyaḥ Saladū (847–855 CE).

According to Resiyani (2010: 169), the ten charters listed in figure 5-4 came from the following locations within the Temanggung Regency.

- Kayumwuṅan (824): general vicinity of *desa* Traji, district Parakan.
- Sang Hyang Wintang (*circa* 830): *desa* Gondosuli, district Bulu.
- Tri Tĕpusan (842): origin unknown. Resiyani (2010: 111-112) has proposed *desa* Tepusen, district Kaloran.
- Tulang Air I/II (850): hamlet Candi, *desa* Pringapus, district Ngadirejo.
- Muṇḍuan (807): hamlet Toro, *desa* Kertosari, district Jumo (Wiseman Christie 2002: 20, as cited by Resiyani 2010).
- Wanua Tĕngah I/II (863): *desa* Lempuyang, district Candiroto.
- Mantyāsiḥ I (907): SE of *desa* Mergowati, district Kedu.
- Mantyāsiḥ III (907): North of the village Bojonegoro, district Kedu.
- Wanua Tĕngah III (907): district Kalonan.
- Rukam (908): *desa* Parakan, district Parakan.

Kayumwuṅan is mentioned by name in six of these charters, including the Sang Hyang Wintang (Kyu bunggan) boulder inscription promulgated by Ḍang Karayān Partapān Siḍa Busu Plār.

Sundberg (2006: 114, n. 31) surmised that the Kayumwuṅan inscription had come from the village of Karanggedong just to the north of Traji, with Karangtĕngah being "a mistaken name which has been propagated through the literature". In the absence of any factual basis in the records for supporting his conjecture, however, the icon indicating the location of the Kayumwuṅan charter in figure 5-5 has been placed between Traji and Karangbĕndo. The entry for Karangtĕngah written by Verbeek (1891: 138) immediately followed his comments about Traji, which in turn were preceded by his prior entries for four other sites at latitudes to the north: Kramat, Caṇḍi Perot, Caṇḍi Pringapus and Tĕlaja, which had occupied an area corresponding to part of the southeast quarter of modern-day Karanggendong. As previously mentioned, the location for 'Kg. tengah' south-southeast of Traji is marked with a "+" on the aforementioned 1891 map to indicate that it was associated with an inscription. The next village of any consequence in this direction is

Karangbĕnda (=Karangbĕndo, see the 1907 Dutch Army map in the KIT collection), the site where Krom reported the discovery of a stone niche.

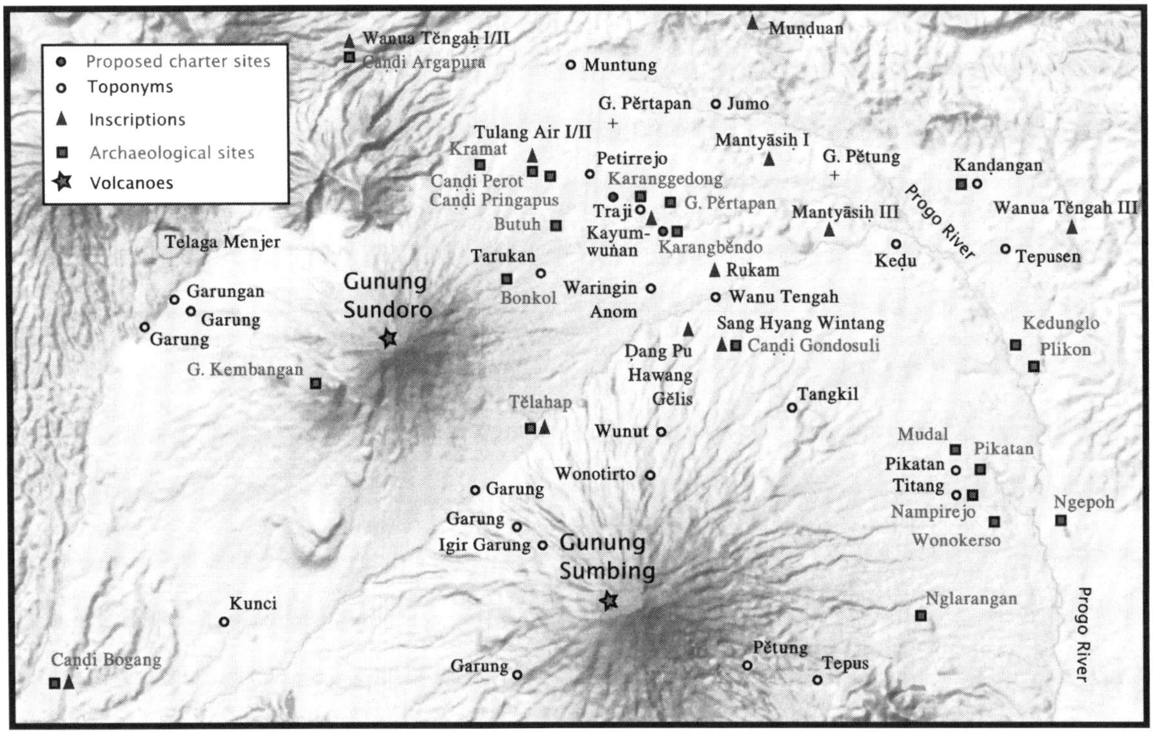

Fig. 5-5. Map of the Gunung Sundoro/Gunung Sumbing region of Central Java.[11]

Figure 5-5 also indicates the locations for the toponyms Garung and Garungan found in the general vicinity of the volcanoes Sundoro and Sumbing. Though variants of this appellation frequently appear as toponyms located in many other parts of Java, the cluster of seven sites shown on the map suggests the possibility that they had belonged to the estate of the Rakarayān i Garung who had enforced royal orders elsewhere in Central Java in 819 CE, according to the Garung inscription (Damais 1955: 26-27, n. 2). Even without knowledge of the dates provided by WT3, Damais nevertheless divined that this Garung was not the king but was nevertheless speaking with royal authority. Damais also thought it possible, though not certain, that the Rakarayān i Garung in 819 CE had subsequently ascended the throne as Śrī Mahārāja Rakai Garung (829–847).[12]

[11]Some of the inscription locations and toponym identifications are those proposed by Resiyani (2010), whereas other are based on GPS data supplied by Degroot (2009) as well as an extensive examination of the Royal Tropical Institute (KIT) maps collection hosted online until budget cuts led to the highly useful web service's regrettable closure in August of 2013. The modern-day Desa Waringin on the southwest slope of Gunung Sumbing is situated beyond the bottom edge of the graphic presented above.

[12]In 1982, Indonesian archaeologists excavated the remains of a Buddhist temple at Selomerto (Wonosobo Regency). Called Caṇḍi Bogong, the remains include Buddhistic images and gold-foil Sanskrit inscriptions displaying the Palaeojavanese script (see Dwiyanto 1984; and Dumarçay 2007: 219). Given his patronage of subsidiary shrines at Caṇḍi Plaosan Lor and his restitution of *sīma* rights for the Buddhist monastery at Pikatan, it is possible that Rakai Garung had also been involved in the construction of Caṇḍi Bogong.

Fig. 5-6. Tri Tĕpusan I (Caṇḍi Pĕtung I) **charter D. 107** (photo credit: Shigehisa Taguchi).

Both de Casparis (1981: 60-63) and Kandahjaya (2004: 256-257; 2009: 13) have argued that the Kayumwuṅan charter featuring Prāmodavarddhanī and the Tri Tĕpusan I/II[13] charters founded by the Javanese aristocrat Śrī Kahulunnan in 842 CE would pertain to Barabuḍur. The Tri Tĕpusan I/II charters (see figure 5-6) refer to a religious foundation (*kamūlān*) at the *bhūmisambhāra* ('the ground for accumulating knowledge and merit'), a designation which Kandahjaya interpreted as signifying a key functional aspect of Barabuḍur and thus supposed by him to have been the official name for Barabuḍur.

Though the hamlet of Kayumwuṅan is cited in six inscriptions known to have come from the Temanggung Regency, including the Tulang Air I/II (also known as Caṇḍi Perot I/II) charters (see figure 5-7), the same toponym is not mentioned in any of the other *praśasti* found elsewhere in Central Java.[14] It is also striking that so many of the toponyms cited in the Kayumwuṅan and Tri Tĕpusan I/II charters are found in other inscriptions discovered in Central Java's Temanggung Regency, which is far removed from the environs of Barabuḍur on the other side of Sumbing. This strongly suggests that the theories postulated by de Casparis (1950) and Kandahjaya (2004) concerning a direct link between the Kayumwuṅan charter and Barabuḍur, or one of its nearby temples, are incorrect.

[13]Damais (1952: 28) gave these two inscriptions the secondary name of Caṇḍi Pĕtung I/II but without identifying the source from which he had extracted this additional information.

[14]De Casparis's rationale for a Barabuḍur-area origin for the Kayumwuṅan charter was founded on the grounds that fragments from this inscription "were first noticed at the Magelang government yard where they were sent for preservation. De Casparis's justification (1956:211) must be rejected, for we know that both the [Tulang Air] inscriptions recovered from Candi Perot, on the eastern slopes of Mount Sindoro Sindoro and thus not many miles from Karang Tengah, were sent to Magelang before being transported to the National Museum in Jakarta" (Sundberg 2006: 114-115).

Fig. 5-7. Tulang Air I charter (photo credit: Shigehisa Taguchi).

Other issues of contention

In advance of presenting an annotated transcription and a revised translation for the Sanskrit segment of the Kayumwuṅan charter we shall briefly review a few other contentious issues still being debated among scholars today. For example, dc Casparis (1950: 37) thought one had to assume there was a special reason why the inscription's composer had devoted considerable attention to the daughter of Samaratuṅga without ever mentioning the king's wife or son.

> "The fact that the inscription dealt with the daughter at such great length—whereas neither the wife nor a son became mentioned anywhere—is so unusual that a special reason must be assumed for this. The explanation is readily available that the king had no son, at least from his principal wife, so that in the first place the future of the dynasty was firmly settled on the princess. The simplest explanation, however, is not necessarily the correct one; through comparison with other documents it appeared that the relationship is more complicated—even if it is also in conformity with the above statement in principle".

However, it appears that the Kayumwuṅan charter actually does contain a reference to Samaratuṅga's queen, as we shall see in the discussion of v.7 below.

Damais (1968: 361) regarded the focus on Prāmodavarddhanī as potentially an indication that Samaratuṅga had died prior to 824 CE. Samaratuṅga is known to have been ruling since 792/3: the date of the Abhayagirivihāra charter. So if he was still living in 824 then he would have already been on the throne for 32 years, or even a few years longer given that the Śrī Saṅgrāmadhanaṃjaya inscription of 782 was the last proclamation known to have been promulgated by Samaratuṅga's presumed father. Gonda (1997: 10) was even stronger in his support for Damais' surmise that Samaratuṅga had died prior to 824 CE, writing "it appears that a Śailendra princess founded a Jina sanctuary in order to ensure for her deceased father and herself the state of a *sugata* (Buddha)". So it would seem that both Damais and Gonda were comfortable with reading the inscription's laudatory verses about Samaratuṅga as having been intended to serve as a eulogy for a deceased monarch.

The significance of the Śrī Ghananātha image mentioned in v.11 of the Kayumwuṅan charter also remains a matter of ongoing debate. De Casparis (1950: 139-140) proposed that the image had depicted Samaratuṅga's father. He also presumed that the monarch who had promulgated the B-side of the Isthmus of Kra stele and the Śrī Saṅgrāmadhanaṃjaya inscription had abdicated the throne prior to 792 CE and had ultimately died in or around 812, that is to say 12 year prior to the date of the Kayumwuṅan charter, based on a single reference to the *śraddhā* held for a king of Majapahit in East Java five centuries later. Damais (1968: 360) rightfully rejected the proposal of twelve years as a standard by which to calculate the duration between the death and interment of a Javanese king.

Though de Casparis (1950: 139) translated the appellation Śrī Ghananātha as the 'Illustrious Lord of the Clouds', *ghana* also can mean 'striker, killer or destroyer'. Still, the death of the Śailendra dynasty's 'Illustrious destroyer of enemy heroes' would have in all probability occurred at some point between 782 and 792. De Casparis (1950: 21) initially proposed that Saṅgrāmadhanaṃjaya had abdicated to allow his son to ascend the throne, based on his speculative emended reading of *<paṇaṃ>karaṇa* in the Abhayagirivihāra charter. But Sundberg (2009: 336) noted that if Śrī Saṅgrāmadhanaṃjaya had actually abdicated to become a monk then he would have assumed a Buddhist consecration name in all probability.

Chandra (1995: 227) surmised that the appellation Śrī Ghananātha had been posthumously awarded to the husband of Prāmodavarddhanī as one who had 'gone to the clouds', e.g. died and gone to heaven. Furthermore, he viewed the presumed images of Ghananātha and Āryya cited in v.11 as representing the husband (*nātha*) and father-in-law (*ārya*) of Prāmodavarddhanī, respectively, based on the use of these two designations in Sanskrit drama. "Ghananātha refers to her lord (*nātha*) or husband who has gone to the clouds, skies or heaven. Departed persons are spoken of in the copperplates of Mantyāsiḥ I as 'rushing through the *ākāśa-patha* or ways of the firmament'..." (Chandra 1995: 228).

More recently, Kandahjaya (2009: 11) has argued that the designation Śrī Ghananātha simply refers to the historical Buddha Śākyamuni without more. His view is based on the use of Śrī Ghana as an epithet for the Buddha in the *Lalitavistara-sūtra* (24.1): "I praise the feet of Śrī Ghana, overspread with a thousand-spoke chariot-wheel, which, having the radiance like the glowing countless-petaled lotuses, are continually rubbed by the tiaras of the gods". Furthermore, Kandahjaya noted that v.8 of the inscription "attests the usage of the word *ara*, being a spoke of a wheel". However, Kandahjaya made no attempt to account for °*nātha*, which appears as part of the consecration names for famous Buddhist devotees such as Buddhanātha and Maitreyanātha. As we shall see below, when we view Śrī Ghana as an alternate expression for indicating 'Buddha', then *śrīghananātha* may actually then be interpreted as meaning 'he who has the Buddha for lord'.

Sanskrit script and compositional meters

Though badly weathered, the Palaeojavanese script of the Kayumwuṅan charter can still be recognized as a type quite similar to that of the Kañjuruhan (Dinoyo) charter of 760 CE discovered in East Java, though the former script is actually neater and more regular.

> "All letters are of precisely the same height with generous interlinear space. They are well aligned with clear, but unobtrusive, serifs. The *virāma* is, as in Dinoyo and Ligor [= Isthmus of Kra stele], expressed by a concave horizontal stroke over the letters of about the width of the average letter. The *akṣaras* are moderately sloping. The script of the many short inscriptions on the reliefs of the concealed foot of Barabuḍur is quite similar to that of Karangtĕngah, from which it differs only in its less formal style" (de Casparis 1975: 32).

From the perspective of the "ornamental and cosmetic formation of the characters", Sundberg (2006: 116) has characterized the Kayumwuṅan and Barabuḍur scripts as "highly ornate and stylistically idiosyncratic standouts" in comparison with other Palaeojavanese inscriptions dating from 760 (Kañjuruhan), 792 (Mañjuśrīgṛha), 807 (Muṇḍuan), 821 (Kamalagi), 822 (Huwung), etc. Sundberg also believed it to be "significant that the Kayumwuṅan script matches to an unprecedented degree the script used to execute some of the short legends on the bases of the small shrines at Plaosan Lor" (Sundberg 2006: 118-119), a point to which we shall return in Chapters VI and VII.

The selective use of different Sanskrit meters in the Kayumwuṅan charter is also worthy of further comment. The skillful narrative organization of the Sanskrit composition, which elegantly pivots from Samaratuṅga to his daughter at the precise mid-point of the text, concludes with a wish for the Buddhist monastery founded by Prāmodavarddhanī to endure for the ages.

Chandra (1995: 228) and Kandahjaya (2004: 132) have surmised that the charter's opening verse pertained to the composition's principal Mahāyāna Buddhist divinity, whereas de Casparis (1950: 32) presumed that the initial three verses in Sragdharā meter had all pertained to the same Buddhist deity. Though the lacunas in verses one, two and three prevent us from reaching any final conclusions, enough content remains to suggest the that they might have been dedicated to the Buddha, Dharma and Saṅgha, respectively (Chandra, pc 15 Sept. 2010). As we have already seen in Chapter IV, the initial three strophes of the Abhayagirivihāra charter, which are all composed in Śārdūlavikrīḍitam meter, appear to have been dedicated to the Buddha, Dharma and Saṅgha, respectively.

Strophes	Meter	Meaning
1, 2 & 3	Sragdharā: four *pāda*-s, each consisting of 21 syllables and with a caesura after every seventh syllable.	'Wearing a garland'
4, 5, 6, 7, 8 & 9	Vasantatilakā: four *pāda*-s, each of which contains 14 syllables	'Spring ornament'
10	The Gīti meter of the Āryā meter[15] class is composed in syllabic instants or measures (*mātrā*).	'Song, singing'
11	Śārdūlavikrīḍitam: four *pāda*-s, each consisting of 19 syllables	'Tiger-sport'
12	Vasantatilakā: four *pāda*-s, each of which contains 14 syllables	'Spring ornament'
13 & 14	Anuṣṭubh: four *pāda*-s, each of which contains eight syllables	'To follow in praise or invocation'
15	Sragdharā: four *pāda*-s, each consisting of 21 syllables and with a caesura after every seventh syllable.	'Wearing a garland'

Fig. 5-8. The Sanskrit meters featured in the Kayumwuṅan charter.

Strophes four through eight appear to pertain to king Samaratuṅga. De Casparis (1950: 32) and Chandra (2008: ix-xi) have adopted this view, though the first mention of Samaratuṅga by name does not occur until the initial half-verse of stanza eight. Strophes four through nine and v.12 are all composed in Vasantatilakā meter (de Casparis 1950: 38-40), which exhibits a pattern of long and short syllables that periodically duplicates the

[15]There are 12 *mātrā*-s (each consisting of four measures, with every heavy, or *guru*, element counting as two measures and every light, or *laghu*, element counting as one measure), in the first and the third *pāda*-s of a verse in Āryā meter, whilst the second *pāda* has 18 *mātrā*-s, and the fourth *pāda* has 15 *mātrā*-s. By contrast, the Gīti meter has 12 *mātrā*-s in the first and third *pāda*-s and 18 *mātrā*-s in the second and fourth *pāda*-s.

cadence of the Śailendra monarch's name in each and every *pāda* as well as that of the family epithet 'ornament of the Śailendra dynasty' (*śailendravaṃśatilaka*). The latter compatibility potentially explains why this specific meter was also selected for use in the single complete verse in the Śrī Saṅgrāmadhanaṃjaya inscription as well as in the Nālandā charter.[16]

The poet's reprise of the cadence of the Vasantatilakā meter in v.12 of the Kayumwuṅan inscription is also interesting because it potentially signals the return of the king. The same type of reversion to metric theme is found in the Nālandā charter of Devapāla, in which the Vasantatilakā meter is featured in vs. 20, 24, 25, 27 and 28 (Shastri 1924: 326). Strophes 24 and 25 pertain to the *śailendravaṃśatilaka* and the Śailendra king of Yavabhūmi. However, the metrical theme switches to Praharṣiṇī in the next stanza, which describes the declining fortunes of the king's opponents: the "crooked ones in the world" who have "ways of moving that are very ingenious in striking others" (Sastri 1942: 101-102). Then the metrical theme reverts to Vasantatilakā meter in vs.27-28, which refer to the son of the Śailendra king of Yavabhūmi as the "foremost warrior in battlefields".

A generally familiar modern analogy would be the musical themes used in motion pictures, with the three *Lord of the Rings* films providing an excellent thematic example. The appearance of the normally peaceful sedate Hobbits from the Shire is signaled by a slow and sweet lyrical theme sounded solely by woodwind instruments, whereas the arrival of the Riders of Rohan is announced by a staccato of marshal trumpet tones and with the theme of Aragorn—heir to the throne of Gondor—beginning and ending with drawn-out full orchestral tones. Moreover, the literal meaning of the meter names may be of assistance in identifying the symbolic theme of each strophe or group of multiple verses composed in the same Sanskrit meter. As we shall see later when examining the contents of the Plaosan inscription, that charter's composer went so far as to incorporate the meter's name into the text of one of the strophes from each block of verses composed in the same meter.

With respect to the Kayumwuṅan charter, the meter used in the strophe mentioning Śrī Ghananātha by name is Śārdūlavikrīḍitam, which means 'Tiger-sport'. In the so-called Kĕlurak inscription, three verses either pertaining to Mañjuśrī or the Śailendra *guru* as Mañjuśrī's terrestrial counterpart (Kumāraghoṣa can mean 'Voice of the Kumāra'), are composed in Śārdūlavikrīḍitam meter. As the famous silver image of Mañjuśrī discovered near Semarang, Central Java demonstrates (see Chapter III, figure 3-5), one of the defining attributes of the Kumārabhūta is a tiger claw necklace. Likewise, the tiger claw necklace is an attribute of the youthful god of war Skanda, who is equally known by the epithet Kumāra. The Śārdūlavikrīḍitam meter is also featured in vs.30-33 of the Nālandā charter (Shastri 1924: 326) referring to the younger Śailendra king Bālaputradeva and his mother Tārā. It is interesting that v.31 evokes the births of Skanda and the son of Śuddhodana (e.g. Buddha) as metaphorical parallels for the birth of Bālaputra.

Likewise, the composer of the Śrī Saṅgrāmadhanaṃjaya inscription employed specific meters to signal a change in the principal figure or theme of a strophe or strophes. The opening stanzas, which pertain to Buddhist divinities, are in Āryāgīti meter; the strophes in which king Śrī Saṅgrāmadhanaṃjaya is the principal figure are composed in Vasantatilakā

---

[16]De Casparis also proposed the emendation of *śai<lendravaṃśatilaka>* for v.5 of the Kayumwuṅan charter, which was composed in the Vasantatilakā meter.

meter (vs. 4, 5, 6 & 19); and the verses devoted to either the Mañjuśrī image or the Śailendra *guru* Kumāraghoṣa, presumably as the proponent of the Mañjuśrī cult on Java, are composed in the Śārdūlavikrīḍitam (vs. 7, 8 & 10) meter.

Annotated transcription and revised translation

The Kayumwuṅan charter (824) is the only surviving Śailendra proclamation to feature both Sanskrit and Old Javanese text segments, and with the dateline from the Sanskrit composition even incorporating the names of the concurrently-running five-day, six-day and seven-day weeks, which is a unique characteristic of the indigenous Javanese calendar. Inscriptions featuring text segments in two different languages are very rare on Java. However, the Kayumwuṅan charter is only bilingual in the sense that it includes an administrative segment in Old Javanese. Only the Wukiran (Pereng) stele of 863 and the so-called Calcutta stele (also known as the Pucangan inscription) of King Erlaṅga are truly bilingual (Damais 1968: 324).

Prior translators of the Kayumwuṅan charter, or portions thereof, include Brandes (1913: 4-6), de Casparis (1950: 24-49), Bosch (1952b), Sarkar (1971/2: I: 67-76), Chandra (1995: 226-230; 2007: ix-xii) and Kandahjaya (2004: 113-142). The Sanskrit transcription that appears below is based on the reading provided by de Casparis (1950: 38-40). Emendations proposed by de Casparis, Sarkar, Chandra, Kandahjaya and the author of the current work have been placed within angle brackets and with their translations also enclosed within square brackets.

The Sanskrit text displayed on fragment *B* is badly weather-beaten, for which reason I shall leave it up to the epigraphy specialists to further evaluate the plausibility of the emendations from various translators that appear in the footnotes for lines eight (*taruṇām* = *<k>aruṇām*); 10 (*<vaśato>*); 12 (*atira* = *a<c>ira* and *ma<tīn>*); and 14 (*<sāsvā>mi*) through direct examination of D.27. Other emendations, such as *saṃkru<sta-bhāvaiḥ>* and *śai<lendravaṃśatilakaḥ>*, fall within a lacuna at the beginning of the following line on the missing fragment *A* or the lost fragment *C* and hence cannot be visually verified.

Sragdharā meter

|– – –|– ⏑ –|–, ⏑ ⏑|⏑ ⏑ ⏑|⏑ –, –|⏑ – –|⏑ – –|

– – – – ⏑ – –, ⏑ ⏑ ⏑ ⏑ lamahāvajraparyyaṅkavaddhaḥ
rakṣatv=ā*m*ūlaṣimho bhavajabhavacarā*t*yantasaṃkru [2] ⏑ – ⏓ /[17]
– – – – ⏑ – –, ⏑ ⏑ matarahitottuṅgaśailasthaśūro
yat=sajjīvāparasmāravalam=akhila – [3] , – ⏑ – – ⏑ – ⏓ // 1 // [18]

---

[17]The lacuna at the beginning of line two is erroneously given an extra syllable in the transcription prepared by Kandahjaya (2004: 117), likewise at the beginning of line four.

[18]According to de Casparis (1950: 41), the relatively small lacuna at the beginning of the first line indicates that a short salutation term must have preceded the first strophe, such as *namaḥ* or *svasti*.

1. ... steadfast in the great adamantine sitting posture ..., may the lion (down) to the root protect (those) caused to be coming into existence and wandering endlessly ..., may the hero abiding on the lofty mountain, which is uninhabited by ... dogma, (guard against) the adverse power belonging to Desire for (the sake of) good beings without exception ... .

1. ... **steadfast** (vaddhaḥ = baddhaḥ, sing. nom. of baddha, 'bound, fixed, fastened; manifested, shown, visible') **in the great adamantine** (mahāvajra) **sitting posture** (paryyaṅka = paryaṅka) ...,[19] **may the lion** (ṣimho, read as siṃho = siṃhaḥ, sing. nom. of siṃha) [down] **to the root** (āmūla, read as āmūlam)[20] **protect** (rakṣatv = rakṣatu, third pers. sing. imperative of √rakṣ, 'to save, protect, guard') [those] **caused to be** (bhav-aja)[21] **coming into existence** (bhava) **and wandering endlessly** (cara-atyanta) ...,[22] **may the hero** (śūro = śūraḥ, sing. nom. of śūra) **abiding** (stha) **on the lofty** (uttuṅga) **mountain** (śaila), **which** (yat, in comp. for yad) **is uninhabited** (rahita, 'deserted') **by** ...[23] **dogma** (mata, 'doctrine'), [guard against (rakṣatu)] **the adverse** (apara, 'opposite') **power** (valam = balam, sing. acc. of bala) **belonging to Desire** (smāra) **for** [the sake of] **good** (saj in comp. for sat) **beings** (jīvā, read as jīvāḥ) **without exception** (akhila, 'without a gap, complete, whole') ....

––––⏑––, ⏑ varavaśavatāsāditādharmmavṛndān
lokānāṃ laukyavuddhair=agaditam = atu<la-> [4] , –⏑––⏑–⏓ /[24]
––––⏑––, cchidam = akhilabhavavyādhibhaiṣajyam=agraṃ
saddharmaṃ yukticittaḥ praṇama<ti> [5] ⏑⏑–, –⏑––⏑–⏓ // 2 //[25]

2. ... extended heaps of injustices like the subjection of the ..., ... which for ordinary persons is not recounted by the Buddhas of worldly mundane existence, ... the prime medicine for all the world's ailments, ... with a conscientious mind, (he pays homage to) the Good Law.

2. ... **extended** (āsādita) **heaps** (vṛndān, read as vṛndāni, pl. acc. of vṛnda) **of injustices** (adharma) **like the subjection** (vaśa-vat) **of** ...,[26] **which for ordinary persons** (lokānām, pl. genitive of loka) **is not recounted** (agaditam, sing. acc. of agadita, 'untold') **by the Buddhas** (vuddhair = buddhaiḥ, pl. instr. of buddha) **of worldly mundane existence** (laukya),[27] ...,[28] ... [(-cchidam)][29] **the prime** (agraṃ

[19]... of boundless strength (*<amitava>la = amitabala*); see de Casparis 1950: 38.
[20]De Casparis was a somewhat uncertain about his reading of āmūla, or *āmūlam* with the *-m* elided for the sake of the meter. The latter is either an adverb or indeclinable meaning 'from the beginning', or an indeclinable meaning 'by the root', 'to the root' or 'entirely'. In my opinion, the translation proposed by Wayman (1981: 150) of 'down to the root' best fits the overall context. See the discussion segment.
[21]"As then *bhu*, or *bhav*, means to be, *bhav-aja* means to cause to be" (Parkhurst 1882: 50).
[22]... through excessively persecuted (*samkru<ṣta>* 'extremely abused') states of existence (<*bhāvaiḥ*>, pl. instr. of *bhāva*). Kandahjaya (2004: 118) proposed the emendation *saṃkru<ṣṭamānaḥ>*.
[23]Perhaps, 'false' (*<ripu>*). For *-matarahito*, Kandahjaya (Ibid.) proposed 'being deserted of thought'.
[24]The first short syllable in the lacuna at the beginning of live five is missing from the transcription prepared by Kandahjaya (2004: 119).
[25]The lacuna at the beginning of line six lacks a short syllable in the fifth place in the transcription prepared by Kandahjaya (2004: 119); likewise de Casparis (1950: 38).
[26]The possibilities include 'ancestors, family' (*<pra>vara*) or 'sovereign, the best of men' (*<nṛ>vara*).
[27]*Laukya* conveys the sense of belonging to the world of mundane existence (see Sarmah 1991: 30).
[28]'Unequaled' (*atu<la->*); see de Casparis 1950: 38.
[29]*Chidam* literally means 'cutting off', though when appearing as part of a compound it may be glossed in different ways depending on the context, such as in *bhīticchida* ('keeping away fear or danger'). In strophe

read as agram, sing. acc. of agra, 'foremost') **medicine** (bhaiṣajyam, sing. accusative of bhaiṣajya) **for all** (akhila, 'complete, whole, without a gap') **the world's ailments** (bhava-vyādhi), ... **with a conscientious** (yukti, read as yukta, 'attentive') **mind** (cittaḥ) [he pays homage to (praṇama<ti>, third pers. sing. present from √praṇam)] **the Good Law** (saddharmam, sing. acc. of saddharma).

Fig. 5-9. Fragment D. 27 of the Kayumwuṅan charter (photo credit: Shigehisa Taguchi).

– – t = kāruṇyam=agrañ=jagati gatiśatānantaduḥkhābhibhūte
bhaktisvīyā ⏑ [6] – –, ⏑ ⏑ ⏑ ⏑ ⏑ ⏑ ⏑ –, – ⏑ – – – ⏑ mānām /
prītyā *rā*jā tale dan , dadharatulamahā , jñānapuṇyapra*sūti*-
[7] – – – – ⏑ – –, ⏑ ⏑ ⏑ ⏑ ⏑ ⏑ ⏑ –, – ⏑ tām = vandyavandyaḥ // 3 //

3. ... the utmost compassion unto a world besought by endless sorrow over hundreds of rebirths, ... through his own devotion ... , with affection, the king on earth equal to Yama is the source of great knowledge and spiritual merit[30] ... one who is to be venerated by the very venerable.

---

two in particular we would not be surprised to encounter a metrically compatible compound for qualifying the 'prime medicine for all the world's ailments', such as along the lines of *duḥkacchidam*, 'sorrow-removing' or *pāpamūlacchidam*, 'sin-root-severing'.

[30]This translation follows those proposed by Sarkar (1971/2: I: 69) and Kandahjaya (2004: 120).

3. ... **the utmost** (agrañ, read as agram, neut. sing. acc. of agra, 'foremost') **compassion** (kāruṇyam, neut. sing. acc. of kāruṇya) **unto a world**[31] (jagati, the sing. locative of jagat) **besought** (abhibhūte, sing. locative of abhibhūta, 'aggrieved, overcome') **by endless** (ananta) **sorrow** (duḥkha) **over** (abhi) **hundreds** (śata) **of rebirths** (gati), ... **through his own** (svīyā) **devotion** (bhakti) ...;[32] **with affection** (prītyā), **the king** (rājā, sing. nom. of rājan) **on earth** (tale, sing. loc. of tala, 'surface') **equal to** (tula, read as tulā) **Yama** (dandhadhara, read as daṇḍhadara) **is the source** (prasūti<m>, sing. acc. of prasūti, 'procreator') **of great knowledge and religious merit** (mahājñānapuṇya)[33] ... **one who is to be venerated** (vandyaḥ, sing. nom. of vandya) **by the very venerable** (vandya).[34]

Vasantatilakā meter

|— — ⏑ ¦ — ⏑ ⏑ ¦ ⏑ — ⏑ ¦ ⏑ — ⏑ ¦ — ⏓ ‖

Śrīmat=samastasugatais=sasutaiḥ parāntyaiḥ
nīrukta- [8] — ⏑ ⏑ ⏑ — ⏑ ⏑ — ⏑ — ⏓ /
— — ⏑ — -tsu taruṇām=atha duḥkhiteṣu[35]
sattveṣu vuddhacariteṣu garīyasīñ=ca // 4 //

4. As elucidated by all the glorious Buddhas together with (their spiritual) sons beyond count ...; whenever among beings in mental distress he is compassionate and among the very honorable in the practices of the Buddha.

4. **As elucidated** (nīrukta, read as nirukta, 'explained') **by all** (samasta) **the glorious** (śrīmat) **Buddhas** (sugatais = sugataiḥ, pl. instr. of sugata) **together with** [their spiritual] **sons** (sasutaiḥ pl. instr. of sasuta) **beyond** (para) **count** (antyaiḥ, pl. instr. of antya, 'the number 1000 billions') ...; **whenever** (atha, 'if, now, then') **among beings** (sattveṣu, pl. locative of sattva) **in mental distress** (duḥkhiteṣu, pl. locative of duḥkhita, 'grieved in mind'), **he is compassionate** (taruṇām, read as karuṇām, sing. acc. of karuṇā)] ... **and** (ca) **among the very honorable** (garīyasīñ, read as garīyasām pl. genitive of garīyas) **in the practices** (cariteṣu, pl. locative of carita) **of the Buddha** (vuddha = buddha).

Śraddhāñ = ca [9] — ⏑ ⏑ ⏑ — ⏑ ⏑ — ⏑ — ⏓
— — ⏑ -lāgraguṇavadgaṇam=atyavāśi /
lebhe vigūḍhamanujendragaṇān=mahiṣyaṃ
śai [10] — ⏑ — ⏑ ⏑ ⏑ — ⏑ ⏑ — ⏑ — ⏓ // 5 //

---

[31]Or, 'among people'.
[32]The case ending *-mānām* is left untranslated.
[33]Chandra (pc 16 June 2010 and pc 15 March 2014) proposed the following alternate translation: '... with joy (*prītyā*, sing. instr. of *prīti*), the king (*rājā*, sing. nom. of *rājan*) who has upheld (*dadhara*, read as *dadhāra*, the third pers. sing. perfect from √*dhṛ*) ... this (*idan*, read as *idam*, neut. sing. acc. pronoun) [utmost compassion (*kāruṇyam=agram*, neut. sing. acc.)] through the generation (*prasūti*) of incomparable (*tula*, read as *atula*) and supreme (*mahā*, in comp. for *mahat*) knowledge (*jñāna*) and religious merit (puṇya)] ...'. In this case, however, he has left unexplained the *tala* from *taledan* (read by him as *tala-idam*).
[34]Here, the declension *-tām* for which the noun is unknown, is left untranslated.
[35]The transcription prepared by Kandahjaya (2004: 121) erroneously includes an extra long syllable in the lacuna at the beginning of strophe three, *pāda c* as well as the same error in the lacuna at the beginning of strophe four, *pāda b*.

5. ... and full of faith,[36] ... [in the circle of his near and distant neighbors] whose assemblage of men is full of lofty qualities; ... from the multitude of the ... kings, ... (he) has obtained (for himself) a queen ... [an ornament of the Śailendra dynasty].

5. ... **and** (ca) **full of faith** (śraddhāñ, read as śraddhām, sing. acc. of śraddhā), ...[37] [in that circle of near and distant neighbors (<tan-maṇḍa>la)][38] **whose assemblage of men** (gaṇam, sing. acc. of gaṇa) **is full of** (vad = vat) **lofty** (agra) **qualities** (guṇa); ... **from the multitude** (gaṇān = gaṇāt, sing. ablative of gaṇa) **of** ... [(vigūḍha)][39] **kings** (manujendra) **he has obtained** [for himself] (lebhe, sing. third pers. middle perfect from √labh) **a queen** (mahiṣyam,[40] derived from mahiṣī: 'any woman of high rank, [esp.] the first or consecrated wife of a king [also pl.] or any queen') ... [an ornament of the Śailendra dynasty (śai<lendravaṅśatilaka>)] ....[41]

Vistīrṇṇasaṅga ⏑ ⏑ — pyananāmvupūrṇṇa-
prauḍhadviṣadvikasitāmvujalocanāni /
[11] tanmaṇḍalā ⏑ ⏑ ⏑ — ⏑ ⏑ — ⏑ — ⏓
nītyasmṛtāni sahasaiva samākucanti // 6 //

6. (Being under the control) of extensive worldly attachment, the expanded lotus-like eyes of proud enemies were filled with tears ... herewith; ... constantly engaged in thoughts of ... (their expanded lotus-like eyes) have suddenly just drawn in.

6. [Being under the control][42] **of extensive** (vistīrṇṇa, read as vistīrṇa) **worldly attachment** (saṅga), **the expanded** (vikasita) **lotus-like** (ambuja) **eyes** (locanāni, pl. nom. of locanā) **of proud** (prauḍha) **enemies** (dviṣad = dviṣat) **were filled with** (pūrṇṇa = pūrṇa) **tears** (amvu = ambu, 'water, liquid') ...[43] **herewith** (anā); ... **constantly engaged in** (nītya, read as nitya) **thoughts of** (smṛtāni; the pl. acc. of smṛta) ...,[44] [their expanded lotus-like eyes] **have suddenly** (sahasā, an adverb) **just** (eva, indecl.) **drawn in** (samākucanti, from sam-ā-√kuñc).[45]

Caṇḍapratāpaparitāpitabhūribhū- [12] paḥ

---

[36]As a Buddhist term, *śraddhā* "denotes the act of sustaining confidence, remaining steadfast, or supporting trust, in the sense of abiding firmly. To convey this sense, Buddhist faith as *śraddhā* is compared to a huge mountain, solid wall, or immovable boulder" (Park 1983: 15).

[37]Following Kandahjaya (2004: 121), I have left *atyavāśi* untranslated (see the discussion segment pertaining to this verse).

[38]Emendation proposed by de Casparis (1950: 42).

[39]F.B.J. Kuiper suggested reading *'vigūḍhamanujendra = avigūḍhamanujendra*, and as meaning "not-obscure (i.e. leading) kings" (Bosch 1952b: 197, n. 12). However, Damais (1955: 43, n. 1) expressed strong doubt about de Casparis' reading of *vigūḍha*, 'proceeding in secret', noting that the *-ḍha* appears to be a *-gha*.

[40]The discussion segment covers Kuiper's parsing of *mahiṣyam* as originally presented in Bosch 1952b: 197.

[41]Emendation proposed by de Casparis (1950: 39).

[42]De Casparis (1950: 142) proposed the emendation of *<vaśato> = vaśataḥ*, sing. nom. of *vaśata*.

[43]Perhaps, 'which were pouring down (<o>pyan, read as opyān, pl. acc. of opya),' though this is by no means the only possibility,

[44]Doubtlessly qualified by something previously expressed in *pāda c*, of which the only remnant is *tanmaṇḍalā*, 'that circle of [the Śailendra monarch's] near and distant neighbors' to which the prior strophe perhaps alludes if de Casparis' emendation is correct.

[45]See the discussion segment for this verse.

santāpapāvanama —⏑ ⏑ —⏑ —⏓ /[46]
—— *guṇ*o 'pi hirapītakaro 'vadātaḥ
sā*cāti*rānubhavatoṣavivi- [13] ktacittaḥ // 7 //

7. Many a king was tormented on account of his fierce prowess, with anguish being present as a means of purifying (the mind) ... ; his mind is judicious out of contentment with recent experience, and notwithstanding his (warlike) character, which is without a blemish, he is (to be compared with) a diamond filled with rays of light.

7. **Many** (bhūri) **a king** (bhūpaḥ, sing. nom. of bhūpa) **was tormented** (tāpita) **on account of** (pari) **his fierce** (caṇḍa) **prowess** (pratāpa), **with anguish** (tāpa, 'mental or physical pain, sorrow, affliction') **being present** (san, in comp. for sat) **as a means of purifying** (pāvana) ... [the mind][47] ...; **his mind** (cittaḥ) **is judicious** (vivikta, read as viviktam) **out of contentment** (toṣa) **from recent** (*atir*a, read as acira) **experience** (anubhava), **and** (ca) **notwithstanding** ('pi = api) **his** ... [warlike (<sūro = sūraḥ>)][48] **character** (guṇo = guṇaḥ, sing. nom. of guṇa, 'quality'), **which is without a blemish** ('vadātaḥ = avadātaḥ, sing. nom. of avadāta, 'blameless, pure, spotless'), **he** (sā, read as saḥ)[49] **is** [to be compared with] **a diamond** (hira, read as hīra) **filled with** (pīta) **rays of light** (karo = karāḥ, pl. nom. of kara).[50]

Śrīmān=asau samaratuṅga iti kṣitī —
——⏑ —⏑ śavidhām=adharo mahīyān /
tasyātivallabhatarā [14] duhiteha cakre
grāme jinālayam=araṃ ⏑ ⏑ —⏑ —⏓ // 8 //

8. He the illustrious (lord) of the earth known as Samaratuṅga ... becomes mightier; his very darling daughter in this world has constructed a Jina abode in the village fitting for ....

8. He (asau) **the illustrious** (śrīmān, sing. nom. of śrīmat) ...[lord][51] **of the earth** (kṣiti) **known as** (iti) **Samaratuṅga,** ...[52] **becomes mightier** (mahīyān, sing. nom. of mahīyas); **his** (tasya, third pers. sing. genitive pronoun, lit. 'of his') **very** (ati) **darling** (vallabhatarā, sing. nom. of vallabhatara) **daughter** (duhitā, sing nom. of duhitṛ) **in this world** (iha) **has constructed** (cakre, third person middle perfect from √kṛ 'to do, to make') **a Jina-abode** (jina-ālayam, sing. acc. of ālaya) **in the village** (grāme, sing. locative of grāma) **fitting for** (aram) ....

—— mibhūpaguṇaśīlavibhūṣanākhyā

[46]The transcription prepared by Kandahjaya (2004: 123) lacks one long syllable in the lacuna at the end of *pāda b* in strophe six.
[47]Sarkar (1971/2: I: 66) proposed the emendation *ma<tiḥ>*, the sing. nom. of *mati,* 'mind', which contrasts nicely with *cittaḥ* in the second half-verse.
[48]Emendation proposed by Chandra (pc 15 Sept. 2010).
[49]The next stanza names the king, so 'she is' (*sā*) would not fit the overall context of v.7.
[50]Or perhaps, 'and (*ca*) notwithstanding (*api*) his [warlike (*sūraḥ*)] character (*guṇaḥ*), he (*sā*, read as *saḥ*) is (to be compared with) a diamond (*hira*, read as *hīra*) filled with (*pīta*) moonbeams (*karāḥ*) of white brilliance (*avādataḥ*)'. Fame, which is the core value of kingliness and the principal concern of *praśasti* discoure, "is invariably white by poetic convention" (Pollock 2006: 143).
[51]De Casparis (1950: 39) proposed the emendation (*kṣitī<ndraḥ>*, the sing. nom. of *kṣitīndra*.
[52]For the problematic *-śavidhām=adharo*, see the later discussion segment for this verse.

strai- [15] ṇāgamāvirahitā karuṇātmikā ca /
rārajyate na ⏑ titārya ⏑ — ⏑ — ⏑
— — ⏑ -rāntaviśayeṣu karo- [16] ti bhaktim // 9 //[53]

9. (She), famed for her adornments of moral conduct and attributes of ... a king, is not bereft of feminine appearance and is compassionate by nature; ... she shines bright ... not ... she devotes (herself) to spheres of activity ....

9. [She (<sā>)], **famed** (ākhyā) **for her adornments** (vibhūṣana, read as vibhūṣaṇa) **of moral conduct** (śīla) **and attributes** (guṇa) **of** ...[54] **a king** (bhūpa), **is not bereft** (avirahitā, 'not separated from') **of feminine** (straiṇa) **appearance** (āgama)[55] **and** (ca) **is compassionate** (karuṇā) **by nature** (ātmikā, 'having the nature of'); **she shines bright** (rārajyate, an intensive verbal form derived from √rañj or √raj) ... **not** (na) ...[56] **she devotes** [herself] (karoti bhaktim) **to spheres of activity** (viśayeṣu, read as viṣayeṣu, the pl. locative of viṣaya) ....[57]

Gīti[58]

Sā kāntiñ = candramaso gatiñ = ca haṅsāt = svarañ = ca kalaviṅkāt
Se ⏓ ⏓ ⏓ ⏓ *ṇāṃ* [17] harati śrīmat = prāmodavarddhanīkhyātā // 10 //

| — — | — — | ⏑ ⏑ — ‖ ⏑ — ⏑ | — — | ⏑ — ⏑ | ⏑ ⏑ — | — ‖ **first hemistich**
| — - - | - - — | ⏑ ⏑ — ‖ — — | — — | ⏑ — ⏑ | — — | — ‖ **second hemistich**

10. She, celebrated as the Illustrious Prāmodavarddhanī, steals ..., the beauty of the moon, gait from the swan, and melody from the *kalaviṅka* (the Indian cuckoo).

10. **She** (sā), **celebrated** (khyātā) **as the Illustrious** (śrīmat) **Prāmodavarddhanī, steals** (harati, third pers. sing. present from √hṛ) ...,[59] **loveliness** (kāntiñ, read as kāntim, sing. acc. of kānti) **from the moon** (candramaso = candramasaḥ, sing. gen. of candramas, which lit. means 'of the moon'), **gait** (gatiñ, read as gatim, sing. acc. of gati) **from the swan** (haṅsāt = haṃsāt, sing. ablative of haṃsa), **and** (ca) **melody** (svarañ, read as svaram, sing. acc. of svara) **from the kalaviṅka** (kalaviṅkāt, sing. ablative of kalaviṅka, 'the Indian cuckoo').

---

53 The transcription prepared by Kandahjaya (2004: 124) erroneously adds one extra long syllable at the end of the lacuna at the beginning of *pāda d* in strophe eight.
54 '... a spiritual preceptor (<*svā*>*mi*) and ... '. Sarkar (1971/2: I: 66) proposed the emendation <*sāsvā*>*mi*.
55 According to Chandra (pc 15 March 2014), "The word *āgama* with the adjective *straiṇa* should mean 'religious observances appropriate to a lady (*strī*)'. It refers to the princess who was devoted to all the sacred rites required of her".
56 The emendation <*pa*>*tita-ārya-* has been proposed by Chandra (pc 15 Sept. 2010).
57 '... of the superior (<*utta*>*ra*)] end-of-life (*anta*)'. The emendation <*utta*>*rānta* was suggested by de Casparis (1950: 43).
58 According to Morgan (2011: 172), the most common meter in the Āryā class is Gīti ('song, singing'), which has 12 measures in the first and third quarters (*pāda*-s) and 18 measures in the second and fourth quarters.
59 Sarkar (1971/2: I: 70) proposed 'the eyes of the doe' (*se*<*kṣane mṛgī*>*ṇāṃ*) but this breaks the meter.

Śārdūlavikrīḍitam meter

|– – –|⏑ ⏑ –|⏑ – ⏑|⏑ ⏑ –,|– – ⏑|– – ⏑|⏓‖

Śāk<e>ndryāṃ rasasāgarakṣitidharair=yyāntyāṃ *sa* mā – ⏑ ⏓
– – – ⏑ [18] ca rāmapakṣavasato kāṣṭātithau tatra ca /
Tuṃlaināma-umānis=ākhyasahite vāre *pu*rāṇād=gu<rau>
– [19] -pte śrīghananātham=āryyasahitaṃ prātiṣṭhipan=mandire // 11 //

11. In (the year of) the king of the Śakas which is passing with savors (six), seas (four) and mountains (seven) [e.g. Śaka 746], ... and ..., and being in the dark fortnight on the best lunar day therein, on the day of the week Tungle by name in association with the (day of the week) called Umanis (and Guru) from ancient times, ... [she] had established the Śrī Ghananātha [image] together with the Ārya at the temple.

11. **In** (the year of) **the king of the Śakas** (śākendryāṃ, read as śākendrāyām, sing. locative of śākendrā),[60] **which is passing** (yyāntyāṃ = yā-antyām) **with savors** (rasa = six), **seas** (sāgara = four) **and mountains** (kṣitidharair = kṣitidharaiḥ, pl. instr. of kṣitidhara = seven) [e.g. Śaka 746], ...,[61] **and** (ca) **being** (vasato) **in the dark fortnight** (rāmapakṣa) **on the best** (kāṣṭā, read as kāṣṭhā, 'the highest limit, top, summit; mark, goal, limit') **lunar day** (tithau, sing. locative of tithi) **therein** (tatra), **on the day of the week** (vāre, sing. loc. of vāra) **Tungle** (tuṃlai) **by name** (nāma) **in association with** (sahite, sing. loc. of sahita) [the day of the week] **called** (ākhya, read as ākhyā) **Umanis** (umānis)[62] ... [and Guru (gu<rau>, sing. loc. of guru)][63] **from ancient times** (*pu*rāṇād = purāṇāt, sing. ablative of purāṇa), ... [she (sa, read as sā)][64] **had established** (prātiṣṭhipan, read as prātiṣṭhāpana, 'fixing, placing') **the Śrī Ghananātha** (ghananātham, sing. acc. of ghananātha) [image] **together** (sahitam) **with the Ārya**[65] (āryya) **at the temple** (mandire, sing loc. of mandira).

---

[60]In place of Śākaindryāṃ in de Casparis' transcription, Damais (1955: 114-115; see also 1968: 327) read *Śākendryāṃ*, which he interpreted in the sense of the king of the Śākas. "The only difficulty would be the use of the feminine. This can be explained by implying a word meaning 'year' which in Sanskrit are feminine like *sama* or *sarad*. There is therefore no difficulty here."

[61]De Casparis (1950: 46, n. 7) submitted the emendation *mā<se-śucau>*, e.g. 'in the month Śuci', which he regarded as a synonym for Jyaiṣṭha; see the discussion segment.

[62]Tungle (Sanskritized as *tuṃlai*) is the name of the first day of the six-day week in the indigenous Javanese calendrical system, whereas Umanis is the name of the first day of the five-day week.

[63]Damais (1955: 115, continuation of n. 2 from p. 114) accepted de Casparis' (1950: 39) restitution of *gurau,* sing. locative of *guru* = Thursday) because *gur-* was still clearly visible on the stone.

[64]Chandra (1995: 227) proposed the emendation *<prā>pte*, which conveys the sense of when something has happened, as in the locative absolutive *kāle śubhe prāpte*: 'an auspicious time having arrived'. Furthermore, Chandra (1995: 227) proposed to read the uncertain syllable *sa* in *pāda a* as *sā*, i.e. 'she'. This approach was likewise adopted by Kandahjaya (2004: 125): "[L]ooking at the context, this suggestion seems reasonable, considering that the last two and half verses all talk about Prāmodavarddhanī...". On the other hand, *sa (=sas)* would properly mean 'he'.

[65]Either a reference to an Āryya image or the title of a Buddhist priest whose complete name had been given in v.8.

Vasantatilakā meter

|— — ⏑ ¦ — ⏑ ⏑ ¦ ⏑ — ⏑ ¦ ⏑ — ⏑ ¦ — ⏓ ‖

Tacchenduvimvaśakalapratimam=vibhāti
rāhor=bhiyā sapa- [20] di sampatitaṃ dharitryāṃ /
tasyānupuṇyam=athaved<a>m=udeti<śu>bh<raḥ>
<bu>ddhais ⏑ — ⏑ *taruṇair*=uṣitaṃ manojña- [21] m // 12 //[66]

12. And that (temple) shines like the piece of the moon's disk just fallen to the earth (as if) in fear of Rāhu; but in accordance with his meritorious deeds, the splendid (Śrī Ghananātha image)[67] nevertheless rises above this charming (temple) inhabited by Buddhas ....

12. **And that** (tacca = tat-ca) [temple] **shines** (vibhāti) **like** (pratimam, read as pratimām, sing. acc. of pratimā) **the piece** (śakala) **of the moon's disk** (induvimva = indubimba, neut.)[68] **just** (sapadi, 'instantly, at once') **fallen** (sam-patitam, sing. acc. of patita) **to the earth** (dharitryām, sing. locative of dharitrī) [as if] **in fear** (bhiyā) **of Rāhu** (rāhoḥ, sing. genitive of rāhu); **but** (atha) **in accordance with** (anu, 'according to') **his meritorious deeds** (puṇyam, masc. sing. acc. of puṇya; tasya, third pers. sing. masc. genitive pronoun) **the splendid** (śubhraḥ, masc. sing. masc. nom. of śubhra) [Śrī Ghananātha (image)] **nevertheless** (vā) **rises above** (udeti, from √ude) **this** (idam, neut. sing. acc. pronoun) **charming** (manojñam, neut. sing. acc. of manojña) [temple] **inhabited** (uṣitam, neut. sing. acc. of uṣita)[69] **by Buddhas** (buddhais = buddhaiḥ, pl. instr. of buddha) ....[70]

Anuṣṭubh meter

|⏓ ⏓ ⏓ ⏓ ¦ ⏑ — — ⏓ ¦ ⏓ ⏓ ⏓ ⏓ ¦ ⏑ — ⏑ ⏓ ‖

Śrīmadveṇuvanābhikhyam = vidhāya jinamandiraṃ /
yat = puṇyam = āptam = etena daśad = āpnotu saugatam // 13 //[71]

13. Whatever spiritual merit has been gained after having established this Jina temple similar to the sacred Veṇuvana, by this (merit) may one obtain the Buddhistic (doctrine) ... !

13. **Whatever** (yat) **spiritual merit** (puṇyam) **gained** (āptam) **after having established** (vidhāya, the absolutive of vi + √dhā) **this Jina-temple** (jina-mandiram) **similar to** (abhikhyam) **the**

---

[66]Transcription corrections submitted by Bosch (1952b: 194); see also the discussion segment.
[67]i.e. Śrī Ghananātha.
[68]On the image consecration date, the waning moon was in its fourth and final quarter of the lunar month, so a part of the lunar disk was still illuminated, and with 'just now completely fallen to the earth' potentially being a reference to this fractionally visible moon having just descended below the western horizon, which might help to establish the time of day in theory.
[69]See Bosch 1952b: 194.
[70]Bosch (Ibid.) characterized de Casparis' reading of *sakṛtya* (in the space marked above as ⏑ — ⏑) as impossible and obliquely expressed reservations concerning de Casparis' reading of *taruṇair.*
[71]De Casparis' transcription does not indicate where line 21 ends and line 22 begins; nor does that of Sarkar (1971/2: I: 67).

illustrious (śrīmad = śrīmat) **Veṇuvana, by this** (etena, sing. instr. pronoun) [merit] **may one obtain** (āpnotu, third pers. sing. imperative from √āp) **the Buddhistic** [doctrine] (saugatam)[72] ....[73]

Padam = atyantaduṣprāpam = anuttaram = agocaram /
tatsutānāṃ mayā yuktaṃ tūrṇṇam = eva labbeya yat // 14 //

14. May that which is extremely difficult to obtain, is unsurpassed and beyond the human senses be obtained by me quickly; so also for the monks who hereby are provided with an abode.

14. **May that which** (yat) **is extremely** (atyanta) **difficult to obtain** (duṣprāpam, sing. acc. of duṣprāpa), **is unsurpassed** (anuttaram, sing. acc. of anuttara) **and beyond human senses** (agocaram, sing. acc. of agocara) **be obtained** (labbeya, read as labheya, first pers. middle optative of √labh) **by me** (mayā, first pers. sing. instr. pronoun) **quickly** (tūrṇam); **so also** (eva) **for the monks** (sutānām, pl. genitive of tatsuta, 'son, child, offspring', i.e. sons of the Buddha) **who hereby** (tat) **are provided with** (yuktam, sing. acc. of yukta) **an abode** (padam, sing. acc. of pada).

Sragdharā meter

|– – –|– ⏑ –|–, ⏑ ⏑|⏑ ⏑ ⏑|⏑ –, –|⏑ – –|⏑ – –|

Aurvvā*gnir*=yā<va> [23] d=uṣṇaśvasanavaśagatākṣanyadam=bodhidṛṣṭyā
yāvat=prāntā dharitrī vivudhagaṇasamākrāntamūrttiś=ca meruḥ /
yāva <t=khe> [24] svān=gabhastīn=daśaśatagaṇanām=ujjhati vyomavṛtraḥ
– – – – ⏑ – –, *suga*taguṇagaṇas=tāvad=āstām=vihāraḥ // 15 //

15. (As long as) Aurva-Agni is feeding upon hot winds, which are under control and sightless owing to *bodhi*-insight;[74] as long as Meru as well as the earth up to its limits are trodden upon by the manifestation of the multitude of the very wise, as long as the sun in heaven emits his own rays a thousand-fold into the sky, so long may this monastery endure as the multitude of the Buddha's virtues ... .

15. [As long as (yā<va>d = yāvat)][75] **Aurva-Agni** (aurvvāgniḥ) **is feeding (**nyadam, read as nyādam, the sing. acc. of nyāda) **upon hot** (uṣṇa) **winds** (śvasana), **which are under control** (vaśa) **and sightless** (gatākṣa) **owing to *bodhi*-insight** (dṛṣṭyā = dṛṣṭyāḥ sing. ablative of dṛṣṭi [dṛś-ti]);[76] **as**

---

[72]Bosch (1952b: 194-195) noted that *saugata* means 'Buddhist' or 'Buddhistic' rather than Sugatahood, as proposed by de Casparis (1950: 46) and adopted by Kandahjaya (2004: 127). On the other hand, one might interpret the use of *saugatam* here as a replacement for *sugatam* made for the sake of the meter.
[73]Though the original transcription has *daśad* (= *daśat*, 'consisting of ten') Bosch (1952b: 195) noted that this makes no sense in the present context; see the discussion segment for this strophe.
[74]*Dṛṣṭi:* 'view, vision, look, eye, notion, perspective; understanding, intelligence; knowledge' (Huet 2012).
[75]See de Casparis 1950: 40.
[76]Aurvāgni is the apocalyptic submarine fire destined to destroy the world at the end of each eon. The second verse of the Old Javanese *Sang Hyang Kamahāyānikan* refers to just such a total annihilation, or *mahāpralaya,* prior to the start of another temporal cycle: '*duvĕg kumirakira paḍĕma niṅ mahāpralaya rike bhuvana*'. The general sense is that Buddha intends for everyone to enter extinction (*nirvāṇa*) through their own efforts, not because of the *mahāpralaya* (Acri, pc 8 March 2014). In another Vajrayāna Buddhist text we

long as (yāvat) **Meru** (meruḥ, sing. nom. of meru) **as well as** (ca) **the earth** (dharitrī, sing. nom.) **up to its limits** (prāntā = pra-antāḥ, pl. nom. of anta) **are trodden upon** (samākrānta) **by the manifestation** (mūrttiś = mūrtiḥ) **of the multitude** (gaṇa) **of the very wise** (vivudha = vibudha), **as long as** (yāvat) **the sun** (vṛtraḥ, sing. nom. of vṛtra)[77] **in heaven** (khe, sing. locative of kha) **emits** (ujjhati, third pers. sing. present of √ujjh) **his own** (svān, pl. acc. of sva) **rays** (gabhastīn, pl. acc. of gabhasti) **a thousand-fold** (gaṇanām, sing. acc. of gaṇanā, 'the enumeration'; daśaśata, 'of a thousand')[78] **into the sky** (vyoma in comp. for vyoman); **so long** (tāvad) **may this monastery** (vihāraḥ, sing. nom. of vihāra) **endure** (āstām, read as āsthām, sing. acc. of āsthā, 'place or means of abiding') **as the multitude** (gaṇas = gaṇaḥ) **of the Buddha's virtues** (sugata-guṇa)[79] .... .

Discussion of the strophes

Verse One. The opening strophe or strophes appearing in the Kalasan and Abhayagirivihāra charters appear to have served as *maṅgalācaraṇa* segments dedicated to the inscription's principal divinity or divinities—a surmise that is likewise applicable here. Kandahjaya (2009) believes that this initial strophe is dedicated to the Buddha Śākyamuni and has proposed the existence of a relationship between the historical Buddha's epithet of Śrī Ghana found in Mahāyāna texts such as the *Lalitavistara-sūtra* and the *Amarakośa* (I,1,1,9), and the image consecration name Śrī Ghananātha supplied in v.11 the Kayumwuṅan charter. Though the compositum *uttuṅgaśailasthaśūro* in the invocation verse is potentially an allusion to this divinity, Damais (1968: 413) and Sarkar (1971/2: I: 73, n. 15) also viewed *uttuṅgaśaila* as an obvious allusion to the Śailendravaṃśa.[80]

Another compound of great interest combines *ṣimho* (read as *siṃha* 'lion', 'prince, king, hero' or 'eminent person') with *āmūla<m>*, which can function as an adverb, and hence *rakṣatu-āmūla-ṣimhaḥ*[81] might mean '(like) a lion (*ṣimho=siṃha*) may He protect (*rakṣatu*) from the start/beginning (*āmūla=āmūlam*) [those] caused to be coming into existence ... ', As an indeclinable, however, *āmūlam* would mean 'to the root', 'from the beginning' or 'entirely'. Wayman (1981: 150-151) translated *rakṣatu-āmūla-ṣimhaḥ* as '[may] the lion down to the root protect'.

---

find *bodhicitta* being likened "to the fire that destroys the world at the end of an eon (*kalpa-uddāha-agni*) because it burns up all bad deeds ... [and] to a region under the earth called Pātāla because it makes an end of all unmeritorious things (perhaps in the sense of swallowing up or consuming them) ..." (Mrozik 2007: 47).

[77]Kandahjaya (2004: 128) remarked that the Balinese *Dvādaśāditya-stava* refers to Indra as the name of the sun during the month of Jyeṣṭha. He also associated *vṛtraḥ* with Indra due to the divinity's assimilation of epithets such as *vṛtrahā*, 'killer of Vṛtra'.

[78]Note that *gabhastīn* is masc. whereas *gaṇanām* and *daśaśata* are fem. in gender.

[79]Kandahjaya (2009: 11) has argued that the compound *sugataguṇagaṇaḥ* has a direct bearing on the poet's use of the image consecration name of Śrī Ghananātha, at least insofar as it pertains to the way the epithet had been rendered in Chinese translations of the *Lalitavistara* and other texts.

[80]Though *-ttuṅga* is a suffix that appears in Śailendra consecration names, the breath pause or caesura between *-matarahito* and *-ttuṅga*, which is inherent in the structure of the Sragdharā meter, suggests that *-ttuṅgaśailasthasuro* is a compositum set apart from the text that precedes it.

[81]De Casparis transcribed rakṣatv=āmūlaṣimho in the middle of the inscription's initial line. Here it is worth noting that the elision (*avagraha*) mark between *rakṣatv* and *āmūlaṣimho* is an addition based solely on a surmise made by de Casparis, who has elsewhere stated that "avagraha marks have not been found in any inscription from Indonesia" (1961: 247, n. 22). Furthermore, de Casparis had italicized the *m* in *āmūla* to express his uncertainly and also transcribed *ṣimho* not *siṃho*. Though Chandra has expressed doubts about the validity of the reading *āmūlaṣimho* he has been unable to suggest an alternate reading.

"[T]he verse reminds us of some lion capitals on bare pillars still remaining in India and said to have been created by Aśoka—the ones by him now proved to have stone platforms at the base or root of the pillar. The [inscription's opening verse] seems to portray the Buddha as the lion upon the pole which is in the center of Mt. Meru, and which pole continues down through the ocean to its base, which, according to the ... Javanese legend, is the Baḍavaṅ Anala".

A sixteenth century Javanese text entitled the *Kauravāśrama* refers to the island of Java being borne by (the turtle) Baḍavaṅ Anala, which the Balinese also identified with the Fiery Mare's Mouth in the ocean (Hooykaas 1964: 103, 109-110). This, of course, is in all probability a reference to the apocalyptic subterranean fire to which the final strophe of the inscription refers.

As noted above, *āmūlam* also conveys the meaning of 'from the beginning'. So *āmūlasiṃha* can be taken to mean '(like) a lion from the beginning', perhaps as a reference to the Buddha Śākyamuni, the lion of the Śākya clan (*śākyasiṃha*) who spoke in a voice like a lion's roar upon taking his initial steps following his birth, according to the *Nidānakatha*.

"At this birth the Buddha took seven steps to the north (*uttara,* lit. 'the upper region'). At his seventh step he stopped and with a voice like a lion's roar cried out, 'I am at the summit of the world, I am the best in the world, I am the eldest in the world; this is my last birth, for me there will never again be another existence'." (Snodgrass 1990: 116).

Returning to the issue of the identity of the principal divinity of the Sanskrit portion of the Kayumwuṅan charter, the kings of South India may have had themselves depicted in temples in the guise of divinities as early as the seventh century. The following inscription found at Tiruchirappalli identifies an image of the Pallava king Mahendra I with Śiva.

"When King Guṇabhara (Mahendra) carved a stone figure (Gaṅgādhara) in the wonderful stone temple on the top of the most splendid mountains, this King entitled *vidhi* (the creator), made '*sthāṇu*' (Śiva) true to the meaning (stationary) and became himself '*sthāṇu*' (fixed immortal) together with him (Śiva) before the eyes of the world" (Poundurai 2005: 27).

So it would not be surprising if similar beliefs about combining the essences of a monarch and a beloved divinity within the same image had made their way to Java by the early ninth century.

Though Bosch (1952b: 194) was apparently the first to identify Śrī Ghana as an epithet for the Buddha, he viewed the use of Śrī Ghananātha in v.11 as a metrically compatible synonym for Buddhanātha, which can mean "He who has the Buddha for lord" or "pious Buddhist". By way of analogy, he drew attention to the comparable meaning to be derived from the appellation Maitreyanātha, either another name for Asaṅga or that of his teacher. We shall discuss the appellation Śrī Ghananātha in more detail later. For the moment we shall maintain that the compositum *-uttuṅgaśailasthaśūro* could apply simultaneously to an image abiding on a lofty (man-made) mountain as well as a Śailendra ancestor or ancestral spirit (Manes) thought to periodically return through rebirth as a member of the Śailendra bloodline, a belief that one can easily imagine making the bodhisattvas of Mahāyāna Buddhism particularly attractive to members of this dynastic line of kings. In her attempt to explain the unusual arrangement and contents of the Gaṇḍhavyūha reliefs at Barabuḍur, for example, Gifford has pursued the following line of argument:

> "If the Śailendra considered the celebrant to be a person who would, in the future, become a bodhisattva capable of sending down *nirmāṇakāyas*, then he would, upon his death, become a particularly powerful ancestor.... It is possible that the ritual celebrant could have been seen as a *nirmāṇakāya* who would, after death, send another *nirmāṇakāya* to benefit all beings, and particularly the people of Java" (Gifford 2004: 338-339).

The opening strophe of the Kayumwuṅan charter specifically alludes to the protective function of the inscription's principal divinity. This is also the principal characteristic associated specifically with deceased Javanese royalty in the imprecation formulas found in a number of later inscriptions from Central Java, such as the Mantyāsiḥ I charter of 907 (Wisseman Christie 2001: 26, 50-51). This protection function is also stressed in other Javanese charters, which summon the spirits of deceased Javanese kings for the purpose of witnessing royal grants, e.g. "all you deities who are known to protect the *kraton* of the illustrious Mahārāja in the country (*bhūmi*) of Matarām ... " (Sarkar 1971/2: I: 149, 232, 253).

De Casparis (1950: 177) proposed to equate the opening stanza's Sanskrit phrase *matara* with Matarām, the name of the kingdom first attested in the Mantyāsiḥ I charter of Balitung. Damais (1968: 412-413) thought this was technically plausible given that the lack of the final *-m* in *matarum* could be for the sake of the meter. However, he also remarked that in the Sanskritization of a Javanese word ending in *-m* such as *tarum*, the word is not rendered as *taru* but as *taruma*. Damais also observed that Matarām is spelled with a long ā when it appears in the later epigraphy of Central Java.

Kandahjaya (2004: 118) interpreted the compound *matarahita* as *mata-rahita*, with *rahita* meaning 'deserted, lonely, solitary, or destitute' and *mata* meaning 'thought, believed, or imagined'. "This might refer to a characteristic of the hero who is 'being deserted of thought' abiding at the lofty mountain (*uttuṅgaśaila*), perhaps Meru.... 'The hero who is being deserted of thought' might be put here in relation or in contrast to 'the unsurpassed power of *smāra*' (*parasmāravalam*)". *Smāra* with the long *ā* actually means 'belonging to desire', though it is also possible that the long *ā* appears here simply for the sake of the meter. Still, *rahita* also can be glossed as either 'unaccompanied' (i.e. 'solitary') or 'unoccupied' (i.e. 'deserted') whereas *mata* can mean 'doctrine'. Including the two syllables following the initial caesura in *pāda c*, a compositum such as *<ripu>matarahito* would potentially mean unaccompanied by (or uninhabited by) false doctrine.[82]

Earlier translators have surmised that *uttuṅgaśaila* meant lofty hill and viewed this as a reference to an image installed at a hill-top location. The temple remains discovered on top

[82]Emendation proposed by the author of the current work.

of the hill to the east of Traji offer a hypothetical geographical locale. However, it is equally plausible to suggest that the 'hero abiding at the lofty mountain which is completely uninhabited by [false] dogma' had applied to the image of Śrī Ghananātha installed at the monastery (*vihāra*).

In place of the emendation *saṁkru<dhyamanā>* tendered by de Casparis (1950: 41), Kandahjaya (2004: 117-118) proposed *saṃkru<ṣṭamānaḥ>* of which *saṃkruṣṭa* is indeed a more plausible suggestion. However, the singular nominative *mānaḥ* does not fit the context, which appears to require a plural form. In my opinion, *saṃkruṣṭa<bhāvaiḥ>*, that is to say wandering endlessly 'through extremely afflicted states of being', is a plausible alternative. However, it is not possible to resolve this issue. Line one of the inscription ends with *saṃkru-* and therefore the remainder of the compositum had appeared in the initial segment of line two on the missing fragment *A*.

Verses two and three. Given that the initial verse appears to refer to the principal divinity of the entire composition, it is notable that the second verse pays homage to the Good Law (*saddharma*) and the third verse refers to one who is to be venerated by the very venerable, e.g. the senior members of the monastic community or Saṅgha. Hence, the poet may have intended these three verses in Sragdharā meter to constitute a discrete segment paying homage to the *ratnatraya*, as was previously seen to be the case in the Abhayagirivihāra charter of 792/3 CE.[83]

For *tale dan dadhara* in v.3, de Casparis (1950: 41-42) proposed reading *tale daṇḍadhara*, presumably then being a reference to the characteristic virtue (*guṇadharma*) of consecrated kings as the administrators of punishment (*daṇḍadhara*) upon the unjust. Though de Casparis noted that the reading of *daṇḍa* can be excluded on paleographic grounds, he believed this might possibly have been a mistake. Kandahjaya (2004: 120) adopted this emended reading, which he interpreted as an epithet of Yama: "... with affection, the King, on earth equal to [with *tula* read as *tulā*] Yama, the source of great *jñāna* and *puṇya* [*sambhāras*]...".

On the other hand, the *Sragdharā* meter requires a breath pause or caesura after the seventh and fourteenth syllable of each *pāda*, so the third *pāda* of strophe three would actually be read as *prītyā-rājā-taledan, dadhara-tula-mahā, jñāna-puṇya-prasūti*. Chandra (pc 16 June 2010) proposed reading *taledan dadhāra*, e.g. with the long ā sign having been omitted from *dadhara* for the sake of the meter. When parsing *taledan dadhara* as inclusive of the verb *dadhāra*, then there is no other option than to read *taledan* as nonstandard *sandhi* for *tala+idam* and with the neut. sing. acc. pronoun *idam* perhaps referring back to the utmost compassion (*kāruṇyam agrañ*) mentioned in the initial half-verse. However, Chandra (pc 15 March 2014) has not explained what *tala* would then mean.

Chandra (2007: x) elected to translate the non-adjacent word *rājā* and compound *vandyavandyaḥ* in verse three as the "monarch who is venerated by the venerable [Buddhist monks]", though he subsequently revised this to the "monarch who venerates the venerable [monks]" (pc 22 July, 2010). Kandahjaya (2004: 120) avoided linking the word *rājā* to *vandyavandyaḥ* and simply translated the latter as "one who is to be venerated by the venerable ones". The lengthy lacuna that precedes *-tām=vandhyavandyaḥ* leaves open the possibility that it had included a reference to a king's donation of—or posthumous

[83]Kandahjaya (2009: 13) mentioned that Ghana can mean 'cube': a number raised to the third power.

identification with—an image, in which case 'one who is to be venerated by the very venerable', e.g. the Veṇuvana monastery's senior Buddhist monks, would be entirely appropriate. But if the poet's intention was for *vandhyavandyaḥ* to apply to the stanza's aforementioned king (*rājā*), then '[one who is] to be saluted reverentially by the very venerable' would seem to be the preferable translation.

Verse four. Chandra (2007: ix) and Kandahjaya (2004: 120) independently suggested that the word *taruṇām* in strophe four would either be an error on the part of the lapicide or a misreading of *karuṇām*. Given the similarities between the *ta* and *ka* tokens the proposed emendation is plausible. Moreover, there really is no reason why we cannot accept *nīrukta* = *nirukta*, as de Casparis and other translators have done for the sake of the meter. Kandahjaya also referred to his difficulty in interpreting the syllable *su* preceding *taruṇām.* However, this is actually *-tsu* in the transcription[84] and therefore can be part of a compound ending in *-tsu.* For example, *vyāptimatsu* ('in extending') is the plural locative of *vyāptimat.*

Chandra (1995: 226) translated *pāda a* as, "All the glorious Sugatas, with their acolytes...", which is incorrect. *Sasutaiḥ* is the plural instrumental of *sasuta*, which means 'together with sons or children' and hence does not mean acolytes. Plus, *sasutaiḥ* is qualified by *parāntyaiḥ*, which is *para*°, 'beyond', plus the plural instrumental of *antya*, which means 'the number 1000 billions', hence the gloss of the phrase as 'beyond count'.

Verse five. Kandahjaya (2004: 121) dismissed *atyavāśi* as unrecognizable. A perusal of the many Sanskrit words that begin with *aty*° shows that when *ati-* is prefixed to nouns and adjectives it often expresses the idea of something being too much or excessive. For example, *atyādara* means excessive (*ati*) deference (*ādara*), whilst *atyabhisṛta* means 'having approached too much, having come too close'. Like Kandahjaya, however, I did not succeed in finding a plausible match for *atyavāśi* and therefore have left it untranslated.[85]

Kandahjaya's translation of this strophe consists of a succession of disjointed phrases. In particular, his tentative interpretation of de Casparis' emendation of <*tanmaṇḍa*>*la* seems to have been motivated by his desire to directly link this inscription with Barabuḍur, which we have already seen is not probable: "... and full of faith ... the multitude of those endowed with good qualities at the top of [that maṇḍala?] ... has obtained the multitude of [the] hidden lord of men ... on a woman of high rank ... an ornament of the Śailendra dynasty ..." (Kandahjaya 2004: 122).

For de Casparis, only *śraddhāñ* (e.g. *śraddhā,* 'faith, trust, confidence, trustfulness, faithfulness, belief in') and *ca* ('and') were clearly legible. Kandahjaya's rendering of *śraddhā ca* as 'and full of faith' has been adopted herein though *śraddhā* also conveys a more nuanced meaning in Buddhist philosophical treatises, as indicated previously.

---

[84]The transcription of verse four provided by Kandahjaya (2004: 121) presents an extra long syllable in the third *pāda* that is not in the original transcription.

[85]Even if one were willing to drop the long ā vowel sign, the theoretical meaning of *atyavaśi* (from *ati+avaśin*) would be 'excessively not independent, or excessively not exercising one's own free will'). Though the meaning of *atyavaśa* (= *ati+avaśa*, 'excessively independent, free') would appear to provide a better contextual fit with respect to promoting the fame of the monarch, there is no declension for *avaśa* that ends in *-i* or *-in*. Hence, the question remains open.

If strophe five does indeed speak about an assemblage of men endowed with lofty qualities from the Śailendra king's circle of near and distant neighbors (*maṇḍala*), this would potentially explain what had enabled the ornament of the Śailendra dynasty to dominate the multitude of kings subsequently mentioned in strophe six. Through the reference to the Śailendra king's circle of near and distant neighbors, the poet also might have been praising the donors of the yields of irrigated rice fields mentioned in the Old Javanese segment of the inscription, including the Rakaryān Patapān pu Palar. The construction of a *vihāra* by Prāmodavarddhanī within a territory under the control of another ruler is comparable to the agreement reached by Bālaputra and Devapāla in the Nālandā charter.

> "As far as I know, land or rent grants by a lower-status personage to a higher one do not exist. They would in any case be contrary to the spirit of a feudal hierarchy. Pu Palar bestows a favor on Prāmodavarddhanī: anyone could erect a shrine, but only the king could make its upkeep a governmental responsibility. It is therefore unthinkable that Pu Palar was in any way subject to Śailendra power" (Van der Meulen 1979: 36, n. 52).

Chandra (1995: 227) initially viewed *mahiṣyam* as a derivative of "*mahiṣa* 'great, powerful, buffalo'" and more recently proposed that *mahiṣyam* would mean 'supremacy' (Chandra, pc 15 Sept. 2010). By contrast, Kandahjaya (2004: 124) translated *mahiṣyam* as 'a woman of high official rank', though *mahiṣī* especially means 'queen' or 'the first wife of a king'.[86] It is in the sense of 'with his queen' or 'by the queen' that the composers of classical Sanskrit texts have often employed *mahiṣyā*. Furthermore, the middle present form (as opposed to active or passive) of the verb 'has obtained' would potentially convey the additional meaning of something obtained for oneself.

Kuiper noted that *mahīṣyaṃ* as the accusative of *mahīṣī* is found in Vedic literature in a few instances, but probably as errors, whilst abnormal forms of *-yam* for *-īm* are unknown in the classical language. "Still, as far as I can see there is no doubt that the poet meant *mahīṣi* (first wife), but the meter demanded a long penultimate. As a construction formation *mahīṣyaṃ* (after *striyam*) is conceivable. *Lebhe* fits well with this" (see Bosch 1952b: 197, n. 12).

Verse six. According to Chandra (pc 12 July 2012), "*samākucanti* is in contrast to *vikasit-ambuja-locanāni*. The lotus eyes of arrogant enemies, which were wide open (*vikasita*) have suddenly shut down (*samākucanti*)". In the opinion of Kandahjaya (2004: 122-123), however, "the word *samākucanti* seems to come from *sam-ā-√kuñc*, meaning 'to draw in, bring to an end, stop,' rather than *saṃ-√kuc* (or *-kunc*), meaning 'to contract, shrink, close,' as suggested by [de] Casparis and Sarkar". However, Kandahjaya's translation of the second half-verse does not make any sense to me: "the *maṇḍala* of that ... they are not traditional and suddenly stop". It is entirely possible that the compound

[86] The potential allusion to Samaratuṅga's queen as having come from the monarch's circle of near and distant neighbors (*maṇḍala*) is of great interest. As previously discussed in Chapter I, the identification of Samaratuṅga with the king described as the 'foremost warrior on battlefields' (*samarāgravīra*) in the Nālandā charter and the accompanying reference to the latter royal personage's queen Tārā, the daughter of king Varmasetu of the lunar lineage, remains debatable. Even if correct, the Nālandā copperplate does not prove that Tārā's father had been a foreign king or that she had been anything other than of Javanese extraction.

tanmaṇḍala in the lacuna-ridden *pāda c* refers to the Śailendra monarch's circle of near and distant neighbors and hence be the object of the thoughts (*smṛtāni*) of the proud enemies whose lotus-like eyes have suddenly just (*sahasaiva* = *sahasā-eva*) drawn in (*samākucanti*).

Verse seven. Kandahjaya (2004: 123) declared the phrase *sācātira* to be unrecognizable and did not account for it in his translation of this strophe. Given that de Casparis was uncertain about his reading of *atira*, the emended reading of *a<c>ira* proposed by Chandra provides us with a plausible means for translating the second half-verse in a way that seems to fit the stanza's overall context: 'out of contentment (*toṣa*) with recent (*acira*) experience (*anubhava*)'.

Verse eight. The meaning of *pāda b* from this strophe (— — ⏑ — ⏑ -śavidhām=adharo mahīyān) has been hotly debated by translators from the very beginning until today. De Casparis (1950: 177) proposed *<bhūmim=vyadhād-da>śavidhām=adharo mahīyān* as potentially being a reference to the king having constructed Barabuḍur as a material expression of the well-known ten stages (*daśabhūmi*) of the bodhisattva's career. De Casparis' speculatively reconstructed initial half verse was rendered as, "He the exalted earth supporter called Samaratuṅga, lower but more powerful, who founded the tenfold terraced sanctuary". However, "lower but more powerful" is an irritable rendering, wrote Bosch (1952b: 192, 193), because it fails to make proper sense and thus calls into question the remainder of de Casparis' reconstruction for *pāda b*. For Damais, the emended text would literally mean "Samaratuṅga ... lower but more powerful had built a land ten-fold". The objection also can be raised that Barabuḍur does not actually incorporate ten levels. In any event, we have already seen that the charter's probable provenance affords no direct link with Barabuḍur.

Kandahjaya (2004: 123-124) hedged his bets by translating the initial half-verse in two different ways: with and without *-śavi*: "He, the Illustrious Samaratuṅga, is the Lord of the Earth, ... <the lower becomes greater ... [ten-] fold> or <the abode becomes greater>.... At this point, both possibilities seem plausible". By contrast, Chandra (pc 15 Sept. 2010) thought that *adharo* (=*adharaḥ*) should be read *metri causa* as *ādhāraḥ* ('support, patronage'),[87] and with *dhāmādhāro mahīyān* then supposedly meaning a 'great builder'. When we enter the realm of speculation, just about anything seems possible, but the addition of two long vowel signs to make a single word comply with the meter is pushing the envelope. Therefore, due to its lengthy lacuna, the meaning of *pāda b* must remain an open question beyond surmising that it had designated something which had caused the king to become greater or more powerful (*mahīyān*). According to Bosch (1952b: 193, n. 4), the more probable solution would be a word ending in ∘*dharo*, in which case it would not be possible to maintain the reading of ∘*śavidhāma*.[88]

With respect to the second half-verse, Kandahjaya (2009: 11) discovered that a stanza from the *Lalitavistara* referring to Śrī Ghana also includes the Sanskrit term *ara*. Hence, he translated v.9 as, "His most beloved daughter made in this village an abode of Jina (*Jinālaya*) being the spoke of an altar formed like a wheel ..." (Kandahjaya 2004: 124). But his interpretation of *ara* in the present context makes no sense to me.

---

[87]The reading of *adharaḥ* as the second pers. sing. active imperfect of √*dhṛ* would seem to be precluded by the presence of the third pers. masc. pronouns *asau* and *tasya* elsewhere in this verse.

[88]When accounting for the presence of *-śavi*, the emendation *<da>śavidhām* becomes possible in theory.

Verse 9. Kandahjaya (2004: 125) accepted the emendation *<sāsvā>mi* submitted by Sarkar (1971/2: I: 66) for filling in the lacuna at the beginning of *pāda a*. Prior translators have presumed that it was the king's daughter who had performed the rite of image consecration later cited in v.11. If correct, this would lends a modicum of support to the speculative suggestion that the poet may have intended to note her possession of the attributes of both a spiritual preceptor (*svāmi*) and a king (*bhūpa*).[89]

Kandahjaya (2004: 124) remarked that the compound *rārajyate* at the beginning of *pāda c* is an intensive verbal form of √*rañj* (or √raj), which means 'to shine brightly' or 'to be greatly excited, exult'. Moreover, this is immediately followed by the particle na, 'not'. Next, Chandra (pc 9 August 2010) proposed the emendation *<pa>tita* ('descended, fallen down, fallen in battle'), which seems plausible in light of the later comparison with the completely fallen (*sampatitaṃ*) crescent moon in v.12. It is also theoretically possible that the poet had employed *patita* in place of *pātita* in order to conform with the strophe's meter, in which case we arrive at a meaning that is even less ambiguous and closer to what Chandra has proposed: 'felled, struck down, overthrown'.

According to Chandra (pc 16 June 2010), stanza nine refers to the conjugal attachment, feminine ethics and compassion of the princess, who was well known for her familial adornments of being dedicated to the moral virtues and 'royal qualities' of her spouse, e.g. with *svāmi* meaning 'husband' from Chandra's point of view. Chandra also viewed his second emendation of *ārya<putra>*, 'husband', in *pāda c* as the natural compliment for the word *āryya* that subsequently appears in v.11 given that the latter word often denotes a father-in-law in the epic literature of India.[90] However, his previously proposed emendation for *ārya* ⏑ — (see Chandra 1995: 228) is inadmissible because *āryaputra* is expressed metrically as *ārya* — ⏑ . Hypothetical emendations for the *ārya* ⏑ — ⏑ — ⏑ segment that do comply with the strophe's meter include Ārya<ka> ('grandfather'),[91] Ārya<kumāra> ('crown prince'; see Pāṇini's *Ashṭādhyāyī:* VI,2,58) or even Ārya<kumārabhūta> ('having become the crown prince', an epithet of Mañjuśrī; see Kalamani 2008: 15). To retain his original theory, Chandra (pc 12 July 2012) has decided to embrace the alternate emendation of *ārya<kumāra>*.

With respect to the *pāda d* segment — — ⏑ *-rāntaviśayeṣu*, a self-inflicted transcription copying error misled Kandahjaya (2004: 125) into believing that *<atik>rānta* or *<abhik>rānta* were potential emendations. When *-rānta* becomes *krānta,* however, the prior syllable automatically becomes heavy, whereas the meter actually requires a light syllable:

[89]Only a few Sanskrit words end in *–mi* for which de Casparis (1950: 43) suggested *<tad bhū>mibhūpa* in light of the appearance of *bhūribhūpaḥ* in verse seven as well as what he viewed as the poet's predilection for alliteration of this sort. In this case, *<sā bhū>mi* perhaps would refer to the royal 'position' or 'status' of Prāmodavarddhanī given that in dramatic terms *bhūmi* can be used to refer to 'the part or personification (played by an actor)'. Other emendations that are metrically acceptable replacements in theory include *<sā jā>mi* as a possible reference to consanguinity or relationship by blood, such as the 'relation of brother and sister'.

[90]In the *Abhijñānaśākuntalam* by Kālidāsa, for example, the heroine Śakuntalā addresses her husband Duṣyanta as Āryaputra, 'son of Ārya/father-in-law' (Jain & Cardona 2003: 54).

[91]Prāmodavarddhanī could have elected to honor a deceased ancestor through the consecration of an image long after the individual's death.

| — — ⏑ ¦ — ⏑ ⏑ ¦ ⏑ — ⏑ ¦ ⏑ — ⏑ ¦ — ⏓ ||
| — — ⏑ ¦ -rā-nta-vi ¦ śa-ye-ṣu ¦ ka-ro-ti ¦ bha-ktim || 9 ||

De Casparis (1950: 43) proposed the emendation *<sā-utta>rānta,*[92] in which case *pāda d* potentially could mean she (*sā*) devotes herself (*karoti bhaktim*) to spheres of activity (*viśayeṣu,* read as *viṣayeṣu*) for the superior (*uttara*) end of life (*anta*). Other potential emendations compatible with the meter include *<pa>rānta* or even *<apa>rānta* if the latter had been immediately preceded by a syllable that ended in -a or -ā, either of which would convey a meaning similar to what has been proposed above.

Verse 10. It is not until this strophe that the beloved daughter of Samaratuṅga is identified by name as the Illustrious Prāmodavarddhanī. Though all other translators have parsed her royal title of *śrīmat* as 'princess', if Prāmodavarddhanī were wed to the king of another royal family prior to 824 CE then her title conceivably could have meant 'queen'. This is potentially relevant to Chandra's theory about the death of her hypothetical spouse, which will be investigated further in the segment of Chapter VIII dedicated to the identity of the aristocrat Śrī Kahulunnan who had sponsored the construction of four shrines at Plaosan Lor and promulgated two copies of the Tri Tĕpusan charter (842) pertaining to the donation of land to a religious foundation known as the *kamūlān i bhūmisambhāra.*[93]

The emendation *se<kṣane mṛgī>ṇāṃ* proposed by Sarkar (1971/2: I: 67), which was subsequently adopted by Kandahjaya (2004: 125), is not compatible with the strophe's meter (see the diagram in the translation segment above). As previously said, this strophe in the Gīti meter deviates from the Āryā meter by duplicating the same number of measures in both half-verses.

Verse 11. Chandra (1995: 227) wrote that *aindrī*[94] designates the lunar mansion Jyeṣṭha and is also the name of the eighth day in the dark fortnight of Mārgaśīrṣa, which accounts for why he subsequently misconstrued the consecration date in another publication (Chandra 2007: xi). In any event, Damais (1955: 114-115) read the verse's opening compound as *śākendryāṃ* instead of *śākaindryāṃ.*[95]

Sarkar (1971/2: I: 74, n. 18) supported de Casparis' emendation <*śucau*> (from *śuci*) as a term for designating the hot summer month of Jyeṣṭha in order to bring this verse into conformance with the dateline provided in the Old Javanese segment of the same charter. Damais (1955: 115) found the restitution of *śucau* very tempting and very satisfactory metrically, but noted that *śuci* would actually mean Aṣāḍha rather that Jyeṣṭha, with the latter month being designated in a more precise manner by *śukra.* "The trouble is that [*śukra*] does not suit the meter. The restitution of *śucau* is better but it is not absolutely sure." On the other hand, *śuci* can convey the meaning of 'a particularly hot month (according to some Jyeṣṭha, according to others Āṣāḍha) or the hot season in general'.

---

[92]After the application of *sandhi* rules, however, *sā+uttara* would become *sottara.*

[93]Van der Meulen (1979: 37-38) observed that several of the villages mentioned in the Kayumwuṅan and Gåndåsuli II charters are also cited in the Tri Tĕpusan inscription promulgated by Śrī Kahulunnan.

[94]In fact, the entry is found under *aindra* in the Monier-Williams Dictionary p. 234, col. 1.

[95]Among other things, *indrya* means 'belonging to Indra', and the *nakṣatra* Jyeṣṭha has Indra as its presiding divinity.

Hence, it is possible that *śucau* had been intended to refer to the hot summer season comprising the months Jyeṣṭha and Āṣāḍha. The indigenous Javanese term Hapit (or [H]apit, see Jordaan 1994:7) awarded to the Indian months Jyeṣṭha and Āṣāḍha, which is attested in the *Arjunawiwāha* (early eleventh century), suggests the possibility that the Javanese had considered these two particular months to form a single unit (see de Casparis 1978: 40).

De Casparis (1950: 46, n. 8) presumed that *kāṣṭā* (read as *kāṣṭhā*)[96] would be a name for the tenth *tithi*, an interpretation subsequently adopted by Kandahjaya (2004: 126). However, I have not been able to locate any literary citations that would substantiate this surmise, which de Casparis (1950: 40) apparently had based on the strophe's reference to the tenth day of the dark fortnight in the ensuing Old Javanese segment of the charter. According to the *Viṣṇu Purāṇa*, 'fifteen twinklings of the eye' constitute one *kāṣṭhā*; 30 *kāṣṭhā*-s, one *kalā*; thirty *kalā*, one *muhūrta*; and one day is equivalent 30 *muhūrta*-s.

Previous translators have assumed that the syllable *sa* in *pāda a* must refer to Prāmodavarddhanī ('she', e.g. *sa*, read as *sā*) given that she is the subject of the prior two and a half strophes. However, de Casparis was uncertain of his reading, which is why it appears in italics in his transcription. This had to have been a short syllable to fit the meter. However, we cannot rule out the possibility that the composer had presented entirely different syllables in the lacuna at the end of *pāda a* than what de Casparis had proposed. For example, another possibility for expressing the name of the month provided in the Old Javanese segment of the text that also would be compatible with the metric requirements of the lengthy lacuna at the end of line 17 is *samā<gamejyeṣṭhāmūla>ca*, e.g. 'and (*ca*) in union with (*samāgame*, sing. locative of *samāgama*) the month of Jyaiṣṭha' (*jyeṣṭhāmūla*).

The consecration of an image or images during the dark fortnight of Jyeṣṭha is noteworthy. When personified as a goddess, Jyeṣṭha is also known as Alakṣmī, the goddess of misfortune whose crow attribute signifies bad luck, famine and death as well as dead ancestors. Tiwari (1985: 7, n. 35) cited Jyeṣṭha as an example of a malevolent *nakṣatra* believed to possess a malignant nature.[97] Furthermore, the charter's promulgation during *Jyeṣṭha* is of interest given that the name of the month also conveys the meaning of 'eldest brother', which in theory could apply to the hypothetical emendation of *Ārya<kumāra>* ('crown prince') previously mentioned above.

The bright half of the lunar month was generally regarded as the auspicious fortnight for performing rituals involving the participation of divinities whereas the rites performed during the dark half were for honoring and benefiting deceased ancestors. So when the Kayumwuṅan inscription states that the consecration ceremony took place on the 'best day of the dark fortnight' this peculiar statement invites further scrutiny.

According to the *Manusmṛti* (1,16), the entire dark fortnight of the lunar month is the equivalent of a 'day' of the ancestors (*pitara*), whereas the bright fortnight is their 'night'. Hence, people presented offerings to the ancestors during the dark fortnight because this

[96]Damais (1955: 115, continuation of n. 2 from 114) confirms that the word was written with a *ta* not a *tha*.

[97]Within the entire corpus of the inscriptions of Central Java, there are only a few examples of charters having been issued during the month of Jyeṣṭha. The only other inscriptions in Damais' list that date from the dark fortnight of Jyeṣṭha are the Wanua Tĕngah I/II charters (863): *jīṣṭamāsa tithi pañcamī kṛṣṇapakṣa*. Damais (1955: 27-28, including n. 2 on p. 28) observed that the composer had substituted Jīṣṭa for Jyeṣṭha as the name of this month. The few other examples from Damais' list were issued during the bright fortnight of Jyeṣṭha.

was when they were 'awake'. The recommended days of the dark fortnight for funeral sacrifices begin with the *tenth*, excepting only the fourteenth (*Manusmṛti* 3,276). "He who performs it on the even (lunar) days and under the even [-numbered] constellations, gains (the fulfillment of) all his wishes" (*Manusmṛti* 3,277). The moon occupicd an even-numbered constellation (Pisces, 12) on the tenth day of the dark fortnight of Jyeṣṭha in 824 CE, whereas the moon occupied an odd-numbered constellation (Aries, 1) during latter half of the eleventh, all of the twelfth and three-quarters of the thirteenth days of the dark fortnight. Given that funeral rites were not permitted on the fourteenth day of the dark fortnight, the tenth conceivably could have been selected as the 'best' day.

Both the Old Javanese segment of the Kayumwuṅan inscription and the Tulang Air charter (Caṇḍi Perot, 850 CE; see de Casparis 1956: 241, n. 180) refer to the presence of astrologers (*wariga*) among the individuals assembled to witness grants. We shall therefore take a moment to examine the charter's astrological details below.

	Celestial Longitude	Nakṣatra	Pāda	Rāśi	Navāṃśa
Lagna	20 Scorpio 52' 46.10"	Jyeṣṭha	2	Scorpio	Capricorn
Sun	1 Gemini 07' 23.81"	Mṛgaśīrās	3	Gemini	Libra
Moon	19 Pisces 07' 25.96"	Revatī	1	Pisces	Sagittarius
Mars	5 Aries 38' 28.42"	Aśvīni	2	Aries	Taurus
Mercury	4 Gemini 24' 22.48"	Mṛgaśīrās	4	Gemini	Scorpio
Jupiter	13 Pisces 40' 36.51"	Uttara Bhādrapadā	4	Pisces	Scorpio
Venus	15 Cancer 53' 57.06"	Puṣyā	4	Cancer	Scorpio
Saturn	28 Taurus 18' 02.93"	Mṛgaśīrās	2	Taurus	Virgo
Rahu	24 Virgo 52' 34.04"	Citra	1	Virgo	Libra
Ketu	24 Pisces 52' 34.04"	Revatī	3	Pisces	Aquarius

Date:	May 30, 824 (Gregorian calendar)[98]
Local Time/Zone:	16:41:04; 7:00:00 (East of GMT)[99]
Sunrise & Sunset:	5:46:21 and 17:22:57
Place:	Karangbĕndo, District Parakan, Temanggung Regency, Central Java
GPS Coordinates:	110° 05' 11" E; 7° 15' 56" S
Lunar Yr-Mo:	Krodhin - Jyeṣṭha
Tithi:	Kṛṣṇa Daśamī (Mo) (100.00% left)
Vedic Weekday:	Thursday (Ju)
Nakṣatra:	Revatī (Me) (81.57% left)

Fig. 5-10. Astrological details pertaining to the dating of the Kayumwuṅan charter.[100]

[98]The date of 26 May 824 supplied by Damais (1955) appears to be based on the Julian calendar.
[99]The local time coincides with the start of *kṛṣṇadaśamī*, which is the *tithi* mentioned in the Old Javanese segment of this charter.
[100]Based on data provided by the South-East Asian Calendars (SEAC) software application developed by J.C.

Varāhamihira has described the various characteristics of lunar mansions as well as the appropriate activities to be conducted when the moon occupies the *nakṣatra* Revatī. "The various ceremonies of purification, religious rites, the practice of austerities...shall be commenced when the Moon passes through the asterisms of Hasta, Revatī, Svātī, Anurādha, Puṣyā and Citra and when Jupiter is in conjunction with Mercury, Venus or the Moon" (*Bṛhat Saṃhita* 98,16). Moreover, the *Upaniṣads* speak of the souls of the deceased being reborn in the dark half of the month, when they descend to the earth in the form of rain, and with the water becoming the food eaten by the people and hence transformed into the seed that gives rise to renewed life. Hence, the date may have been considered appropriate for the bringing to life of an image that signified the combined essence of a Buddhist divinity with a deceased personage who was connected in some way with the Śailendra family: by blood, marriage or even spiritual affiliation (i.e. a beloved *guru*). Furthermore, Varāhamihira states that "on Thursdays shall be done any work or business connected with...the Pitris and the Devas, umbrellas, fans, ornaments, kings, temples, alms-houses, auspicious deeds, science, beautiful objects, fruitful objects, truthful words, the practice of austerities, sacred fire and wealth" (*Bṛhat Saṃhita* 104,62).

Strophe 11 is also significant with respect to its incorporation of the names for the days of the five, six, and seven day weeks running concurrently within the indigenous Javanese calendar, as also proves to be the case with respect to the Mañjuśrīgṛha inscription (792 CE) unearthed in the temple yard at Caṇḍi Sewu (Miksic 2001). The unique combination of the names of the five, six and seven day weeks occurs only once every 210 (5x6x7) days, a cycle known as the Wuku or Pawukon. On Bali, this unique combination of days from the three different 'weeks' forms the basis for determining the temple's anniversary, at which time celebratory rites are performed by the entire community. The *odalan* is "the date on which the temple was first 'activated', on which the gods come down from the heavens to inhabit it" (Geertz 1973: 395).

De Casparis (1950: 46) translated the word *āryya* as the 'noble ones', a surmise subsequently adopted by Kandahjaya (2004: 125). However, Bosch (1952b: 194, n. 6) remarked that this expression (āryya, read as *ārya*) was only used as a title in charters and thus one would expect another word to have been used to refer to a group of relatives or court officials in a general sense. On the other hand, the meaning of *āryyasahitam* in v.11 remained unclear to Bosch.

According to Chandra (pc 16 June 2010), *āryya* in this instance does not connote an honorific prefix (like Mr. Venerable), but an individual himself. In classical Sanskrit drama Ārya can serve as the term used for referring to a father-in-law, e.g. in the sense of an 'honorable man'. Or, in a Buddhist context, Ārya may simply mean the 'master' in the sense of being a term of respect for addressing a venerated Buddhist priest or spiritual preceptor. Given the ample number of spelling deviations found in the Sanskrit segment of the Kayumwuṅan charter, the reference to Ārya in strophe eight and Āryya in v.11 may simply be divergent spellings for a single term intended to apply to the same personage, and with the expression *ārya* in v.8 having been followed by an appellation lost in the ensuing lacuna.

Eade at the Australian National University and Lars Gislén at Lund University, and the Jagannatha Hora software program developed by P. V. R. Narasimha Rao.

Damais (1955: 59) could not detect the presence of a *tha* in *prātiṣṭhipan* in *pāda d* of v.11 when he examined a photograph of the stone's *estampage*. From the paleographic point of view, the *akṣara* exhibited the usual form of the *ta*, e.g. *prātiṣṭipan*. In any event, the composer or the lapicide appears to have committed yet another spelling deviation. The expression one would expect to find here, *prātiṣṭhāpana*, is incompatible with the meter.

With respect to the consecration of the image of Śrī Ghananātha, Damais (1968: 381) also observed that Śrī can be used in Sanskrit texts as an honorific in advance of the name for any divinity, though the Kayumwuṅan charter would then be providing a rare example of the honorific Śrī to precede the name of a Buddhist or Hindu deity in the Sanskrit inscriptions of Central Java, the last known of which was issued in 863 CE. There are a large number of examples from Sanskrit and Old Javanese charters from Central Java and elsewhere in Asia in which the honorifics *śrī, śrīmān* and *śrīmat* served as the royal titles of kings and other high-ranking Javanese aristocrats during the eighth and ninth centuries: Śrī Sañjaya (Canggal, 732), Śrī Mahārāja (B-side of the Isthmus of Kra stele), Śrīmān Kariyāna Paṇaṃkaraṇa (Kalasan, 778/9), Śrī Saṅgrāmadhanaṃjaya (from the former *desa* Kĕlurak, 782), Śrī Nareśvara (Mañjuśrīghṛa, 792), Śrīmān Samaratuṅga and Śrīmat Prāmodavarddhanī (Kayumwuṅan, 824), Śrī Mahārāja (undated votive inscriptions, Plaosan Lor and Kidul), Śrī Kahulunnan (undated Plaosan Lor votive inscriptions and Tri Tĕpusan, 842), Śrī Vīravairimathana (Nālandā, *circa* 843-850), Rakai Pikatan dyaḥ Saladū (Wanua Tĕngah III charter), Śrī Maṇḍaki (Tulang Air, 850), Śrī Kumbhaja (Ratu Baka *liṅga* inscriptions of Rakai Wailang pu Kumbhayoni, 856), Śrī Mahārāja Śrī Bhuvaneśvara Viṣṇusakalatmakadigvijaya Parakramotuṅgadeva Lokapāla (e.g. Rakai Kayuwaṅi; Kañcana, 860), Śrī Mahārāja Rakai Kayuwaṅi (Tunahan, 873), Śrī Mahārāja Rakai Kayuwaṅi Śrī Sajjanotsavatuṅga (Ngabean VI, 882) and Rake Watukura dyaḥ Balitung Śrī Dha[rmodaya Mahāśambu] (Tĕlahap, 899).

Chandra (pc 1 Sept. 2010) thought it possible that Śrī Ghananātha had actually combined the title and personal name belonging to a royal personage. "In India we have such names, e.g. Ghanaśyāme was my brother-in-law". Furthermore, the combination of the Buddhistic epithet *śrīghana*[101] with ◦*nātha*[102] is suggestive of a consecration name. As Gonda has observed, the Sanskrit word *nātha* provides a typical indication of the character of the monarch.

> "The neuter *nātham* is in Vedic texts used to denote the ideas of 'refuge' or 'protection': 'let all the gods be my refuge'; 'they run for help to Prajāpati, seeking refuge'. In post-Vedic texts the masculine *nātha-* is often used to signify the patron, protector of the

[101]Several Khmer inscriptions dating from the eighth to the twelfth centuries refer to *śrīghana*. Jacques (2007: 192) has speculated about the existence of an esoteric '*śrīghana* sect' devoted to a pentad of Buddhas depicted on two lintels at Phimai in northeast Thailand, whereas Sharrock (2013: 43) has proposed Vajrasattva and Hevajra as this cult's supreme divinities at Angkor during the twelfth century. However, the evidence they have gathered to date for associating *śrīghana* with a group of divinities is slim and entirely circumstantial.

[102]The Plaosan inscription refers to another Buddhistic image as *naranātha* ('lord of men'), a designation that also was posthumously applied to king Sañjaya in the Old Javanese Taji Gunung inscription (910). Sarkar (1971/2: II: 125) translated *śrī sañjaya naranattha* as 'the illustrious ruler of men (namely) Sañjaya'. For examples of the use of ◦*nātha* during the East Javanese period as part of the name of a divinity known as the lord of the mountains (e.g. *parwatanātha* and *girinātha*), see Supomo 1972.

helpless: the husband is the *nātha-* of his wife in distress; the lord Kṛṣṇa is the *nātha-* of those who suffer grief and adversity; in battle heroes are *nāthas* of their companions; an army is protected by a heroic *nātha-*; Rāma is the *nātha* of the world. When cattle are said to have the god of rain, Parjanya, as their *nātha-*, this means that they are completely dependent on him" (Gonda 1956: 39).

In the Hindu *pañcarātra* image consecration tradition set forth in the *Kapiñjala-saṃhita,* the rites take place over a three-day period, with the ritual bath and the opening of the eyes taking place on the second day. "The ceremony concludes on the third day with the purification of the temple precincts and the installation of the image in the sanctum sanctorum" (Swearer 2004: 233-234). Buddhist image consecration rites based on the so called 'Vedic' traditions presented in the Purāṇas and other contemporary texts were widely practiced in Burma, Nepal, Sri Lanka, Thailand and Tibet, as well as in Cambodia, where:

"Bizot considers the Buddha image consecration ritual to be an amalgam of the popular belief that the Buddha imbued his image with his ten perfections (*pāramī*) to protect his teaching for 5,000 years coupled with the belief in a cult of guardian figures—heroes killed in battle and deceased-kings—who have become protectors of the religion (*sāsana*). It is these guardian deities who 'take possession of the image during the consecration rites ... [and] receive the food offering made each morning to the central image of the Buddha in the *vihāra*.' Bizot suggests that the cult of the Buddha image incorporates a cult of the gods of the human realm (*devatā manussaloka*) and ancestral deities and, correspondingly, that many Angkor monuments were intended for the worship of the spirits of parents and ancestors" (Swearer 2004: 225-226).

Verse 12. In light of the crucial transcription corrections submitted by Bosch (1952b: 195)[103] that subsequently escaped the attention of Damais (1968), Sarkar (1971/2), Chandra (1995, 2007) and Kandahjaya (2004),[104] the contents of strophe 12 must be closely scrutinized. Both half verses project an operative neutrality concerning their respective

[103]"For *atha vedim* I read: *athavedam* (split into *athavā idam*); for *bhūbhṛt*: *śubhraḥ*; and for *vṛddhais*: *buddhais* (?); while I have no improvements at hand for the impossible *sakṛtya*. Also due to the fact that in the sole reproduction of the inscription which I could examine here (the plaster cast of a *papier mâché* impression of fragment *C*, referred to in Juynboll, Catalogus, p. 233), the part along the right margin is almost unreadable. As for clarity, other parts also leave much to be desired. The reading of the last line of v.12 is too uncertain to allow any translation" (Bosch 1952b: 197, including n. 7 & n. 8).

[104]Based on de Casparis' original transcription, Sarkar (1971/2: I: 70) and Kandahjaya (2004) translated the erroneous term *bhūbhṛt* as meaning 'king', and the entire second half-verse from the viewpoint of Samaratuṅga ascending an equally fallacious *vedi*. "And that (temple), looking like a piece of the orb of the moon suddenly fallen to the earth for fear of Rāhu, shines. Then, according to his meritorious act, the king, together with elders and youths, respectfully goes up the elevated altar, which is brilliant and pleasing to the mind" (Kandahjaya 2004: 127). Here is the original transcription as read by de Casparis:

Tacchenduvimvaśakalapratimam=vibhāti
rāhor=bhiyā sapadi sampatitaṃ dharitryāṃ /
tasyānupuṇyam=atha vedim=udeti bhūbhṛt
vṛddhais=sakṛtyataruṇair=uṣitaṃ manojñam // 12 //

subjects, with the initial half-verse referring to the sheen of something (*tac ca,* 'and that') compared to a piece of the moon just fallen to the earth (*sampatitam*). This is subsequently contrasted with the personage to which the second half-verse refers. For Bosch, the operative neutrality of the first half-verse ('and that') can only pertain to the sanctuary (*mandire*) mentioned at the end of the prior stanza, whilst the operative neutrality of the second half-verse ('but the magnificent') can only pertain to the Śrī Ghananātha image.

According to Bosch (1952b: 194), one possibility is that the Śrī Ghananātha image had been a representation of king Samaratuṅga.

> "Śrīghananātha—used *metri causa* for Buddhanātha—means "He who has the Buddha for lord", "pious Buddhist", and can be none other than the Samaratuṅga profusely glorified in the prior strophes. This would therefore not be the reigning monarch and promulgator of the inscription in 824, more or less as [de Casparis] presumes, but the monarch whose interment and year of death is stated in v.11—not that of Samaratuṅga's predecessor, which would have fallen in the year 812, provided that the aforementioned period of time between death and interment [proposed by de Casparis] is correct".

As circumstantial evidence for supporting this possibility, Bosch cited the absence of any prior references in the charter to another royal personage who conceivably might have been represented, such as Samaratuṅga's father (as proposed by de Casparis) or a hypothetical son-in-law (as proposed by Chandra). Still, there are a sufficient number of large gaps in the initial verse triad to have conceivably allowed the poet to mention another royal personage by name. Moreover, Bosch's theory does not, by itself, negate Kandahjaya's hypothesis that the image of Śrī Ghananātha signified the Buddha and nothing more. On the other hand, there are several factors which suggest that Bosch's interpretation is more probable.

First and foremost, v.12 may be nothing else than an archetypal representation of death and rebirth as a downfall (*sampatita*) and an arising (*udeti*)[105] using classic lunar and solar metaphors. The moon signifies the path of the ancestors associated with death and rebirth (*pitṛyāna*) whilst the sun is the path of the non-returner (*devayāna*). The reference to the eclipse demon Rāhu ('Seizer') is also doubtlessly significant given his close identification with Darkness and Death (Kramrisch 1946: 325). Known as the Ender (*antaka*), Rāhu is the devourer born from Siṃhikā, the lioness otherwise known as Nirṛti (Destruction), and is said to be a son as cruel as Yama (Death) and Kāla (Time). So the poet's allusion to a downfall in fear of Rāhu can be interpreted as a classic reference to the fear of death, and perhaps also to the *vihāra* given Rāhu's close identification in ancient India with the so-called 'face of glory' depicted architecturally on Javanese temples.

Second, v.12 reprises the classic cadence of the expression Śailendravaṅśatilaka through the poet's selection of the Vasantatilakā meter, but without mentioning the king—unless, of course, the Śrī Ghananātha image was intended to be identified with a Śailendra monarch. Besides, the Vasantatilakā meter's name alone ('spring ornament') is sufficient for proclaiming the themes of transformation and regeneration embedded in the verse's text.

---

[105]The verb *udeti* also suggests that this image is the *uttuṅgaśailasthaśūro* to which the opening verse refers.

Third, the Plaosan inscription apparently refers to the lost icons, probably made of metal, that originally had been mounted on the crowning elements of the twin structures at the center of the Plaosan Lor temple complex, as the reader shall see in Chapters VI and VII. Given that the consecration of the Śrī Ghananātha image must have taken place less that a decade before construction began at Plaosan Lor, it is entirely plausible to suggest that the Veṇuvanavihāra likewise had possessed an exterior icon. This is what v.12 of the Kayumwuṅan charter suggests to me. Given the fragmentary nature of the stanza, however, there is certainly room here for other interpretations.

When informed about Bosch's transcription corrections for this stanza, Chandra wrote: "Adopting the revised reading of Bosch and omitting the doubtful (*sakṛtyataruṇair*) the stanza would refer only to the sanctuary. I would like to translate as follows: 'And that (sanctuary) shines like a part of the lunar disc suddenly fallen to the earth in fear of Rāhu, and now (*atha vā*) by virtue of his piety, and because charming with the Buddhist icons it shines in radiance'. The prose order of the second half would be: *athavā tasyānupuṇyam idam buddhair uṣitaṃ manojñaṃ śubbhraṃ udeti.* Instead of <*śu*>*bh*<*raḥ*> the syntax requires <*śu*>bh<*raṃ*>. The contrast is: because of Rāhu its glamour should have been dimmed, but by virtue of his piety and the sanctity of the Buddhist images it rises radiant" (Chandra, pc 11 Feb. 2014). "The entire stanza refers to the sanctuary that arises due to the merit (*puṇya*) of him (*tasya*). I cannot be sure of who 'he' is. *Śubhraḥ* is a nom. sg. masc. adjective without any noun: it hangs in the air. If it were the neut. sg. (*śubhram*) it would qualify *idam*" (Chandra, pc 9 March 2014). Still, one wonders why a temple constructed by Prāmodavarddhanī would be said to arise 'by virtue of his piety'?

Verses 13 and 14. Kandahjaya has proposed that the word *daśad* (= *daśat,* 'consisting of ten') appearing in strophe 13 should be read as an abbreviated form (or perhaps erroneous spelling) of *daśadha*, which means 'ten-fold' or 'in ten parts'. Within the context of the verse, he has interpreted this as a reference to the ten stages of the bodhisattva path to Buddhahood as delineated in the *Daśabhūmika-sūtra*.

> "Whatever merit has been obtained by building the temple of Jina (*jinamandira*), which is similar to the famous Veṇuvana, by means of this [merit] may one attain Sugatahood which is tenfold [13]. May I quickly obtain the place of the sons of the Buddha (Buddhists), which is extremely difficult to obtain, unsurpassable, and beyond perception (i.e., *nirvāṇa*) [14]" (Kandahjaya 2004: 127-128).

However, Bosch (1952b: 195) expressed the opinion that *daśad* does not make any sense in the present context. Chandra has proposed the substitution of *jagad* (=*jagat*) for the Sanskrit word *daśad* on semantic grounds because *ga* and *śa* are similar in the Javanese script, though he would prefer to see the reading *jagad* verified from the inscription's cast if it still exists. The question remains open.[106]

[106]Chandra also viewed strophes 13 and 14 as a set of paired verses and has translated this segment accordingly. "Whatever (*yat*) merit (*puṇyam*) I have gained (*mayā āptam*) by constructing (*vidhāya*) the Jina-temple (*jina-mandiraṃ*) called (*ābhikhyam*) the sacred (*śrīmad*) Veṇuvana, thereby (*etena*) may the world (*daśad,* emended to *jagad*) quickly (*tūrṇam*) attain (*labheya*) the Buddhahood (*saugataṃ padam*) which is very difficult to obtain (*atyanta-duṣprāpam*), is unsurpassed (*anuttaram*) and beyond the human senses (*agocaram*); so also (*eva*) his monks (*tatsutānāṃ*). The prose sequence would be: *śrīmad-veṇuvana-ābhikhyaṃ*

Verse 15. The above translation segment for the initial half-verse of this Sanskrit strophe is substantially different from what Chandra (2007: x) had proposed, given that he had interpreted *bodhi* as applying to the initial part of *pāda b:* 'as long as (*yāvat*) the earth (*dharitrī*) remains bounded (*prāntā*) by the Bodhi'. Aside from the fact that 'remains bounded' is an eccentric interpretation for *prāntā,* Chandra's 2007 translation failed to account for *dṛṣṭyā.* He also viewed *vivudhagaṇa* as pertaining to the multitude of *devas* (as icons) occupying Mount Meru. However, Kandahjaya (2004: 129) has provided a less problematic translation for *vivudhagaṇa* as a reference to the multitude of the very wise. Here the poet is not just referring to Meru, but also to the earth up to its limits (*prāntā=pra-antāḥ*).

Kandahjaya found the compositum *uṣṇaśvasanavaśagatākṣanyadam* in *pāda a* very difficult to parse and his translation ultimately hinges upon his interpretation of *aurvvagnir* as a literal reference to the legend of Aurva, whose wrath produced a flame that threatened to destroy the world, according to the *Mahābhārata* and the *Harivaṃśa.* References to this apocalyptic submarine fire also are found in a number of Old Javanese texts dating from the late ninth or early tenth century onward (see Hooykaas 1964: 109-117).

Based on his interpretation of the legend, Kandahjaya broke down the ensuing compositum as *uṣṇa-śvasana-vaśagata-akṣa-nyad-am* and with the last syllable becoming affixed to the final component of the *pāda*: *ambodhidṛṣṭyā.*

> "Following the legend, the translation takes *akṣa* as the sense organ or eyes, considering that it would be subject to the will of the hot wind, and the fire of Aurvva would consume the world, had the fire not [been] controlled by the ocean.... 'As long as Aurvva, [whose] hot wind subjugates the eyes, [whose] fire [which would] consume [the world] is controlled by the ocean'...." (Kandahjaya 2004: 129).

The *Harivaṃśa* (1, 45, 49-65) describes Aurva as having tongues of fire that towered over heaven even as it spread across the ten quarters. At the behest of Brahmā—the Hindu deity formerly associated with volcanoes on Java—Aurva's father agreed to cast his fiery son into Brahmā's ocean abode where it became the submarine fire.

Sarkar (1971/2: I: 71) translated *pāda a* as, "So long as the underground fire (volcanic fire) breathing hot remains, as the wise see, unsuppressed through the openings which are in its control". However, I follow the lead of Kandahjaya with respect to viewing Aurva-Agni as principally being a reference to the apocalyptic submarine fire, even though the siting of the Veṇuvanavihāra within about 10 km of the caldera at Mount Sundoro could plausibly lead us to view this term as a reference to an active volcano.[107] On the other hand,

jina-mandiram vidhāya mayā yat puṇyam āptam, etena jagad atyanta-duṣprāpam anuttaram agocaram saugataṃ padam tūrṇam eva labheya, tat-sutānāṃ mayā yuktaṃ" (Chandra, pc 22 July 2010).

[107] The historical reports concerning the mountain's volcanic activity include 19 separate incidents over the past 200-plus years, the most recent of which occurred on 6 December 2011. Scientists also estimate that a major eruption in the third century (circa 230 CE) generated a pyroclastic flow that spread its deposits as far away as 13 km from the caldera, and with a second major eruption having taken place circa 470 CE. During the periods between their major eruptions, active volcanoes often emit sulfurous vapors through the caldera as well as via numerous small volcanic vents (called fumarole) spread across their slopes. These sulfurous vapors make an audible hissing sound, which makes it seem as if the volcano is 'breathing'. Hence, *uṣṇa-śvasana* is

I found it easier to read the compositum with which Kandahjaya had struggled as *uṣṇa-śvasana-vaśa-gatākṣa-nyadam* (= *nyādam, metri causa*), and with *bodhidṛṣṭyā* standing alone at the end of the *pāda* based on the presumption that the poet had intended to draw a contrast through the use of *gatākṣa* ('sightless') and *dṛṣṭyā* ('vision').

The initial three *pāda*-s provide us with a literary schematic of the universe from the viewpoint of traditional Hindu-Buddhist cosmography. Aurva-Agni is the legendary submarine fire known as the 'equine-head' (*vaḍavāmukha*) and considered to be the entrance to hell. Said to be located in the southern ocean near the earth's south pole (Kramrisch 1981: 403-404), the submarine fire is the opposing nadir point in comparison with the earth's north pole, above which rises the slopes of the cosmic mountain that mark the beginning of the heavenly realms where the gods reside. 'As long as the earth up to its limits, as well as Meru, is trodden upon by the (divine) manifestation of the multitude of the very wise', also potentially can be correlated with Agni as the external manifestation of the fiery ascetic energy (*tejas*) possessed by Ṛṣis (Mitchiner 1982: 216, 254) as well as other divine beings (see Coomaraswamy 1997: 212; and Snodgrass 1985: 171, 269).

In *pāda c,* the composer continues to build upon the macrocosmic analogy outlined above by referring to the duration of the sun with a thousand spokes. In cosmological terms, this is the great sun-door that leads to the empyrean (see Coomaraswamy 2004), which is the uttermost limit of all that exists and therefore symbolically conceived as occupying the zenith point in relation to the rest of the universe. By contrast, the submarine fire signifies the sun submerged in the primal waters (Kak 2002: 3), below which is the earth-supporting *nāga*. This surmise is supported by the close identification of the solar divinity Viṣṇu with the oceanic equine-head identified with the submarine fire.

The cosmological model briefly sketched above receives a modicum of support from the statement in the opening verse of 'may the lion down to the root protect', as proposed by Wayman (1981: 150-151). Here it is also worth noting that the final stanza reprises the Śārdūlavikrīḍitam meter selected by the poet for the inscription's initial triad of strophes.

The same cosmological model also potentially can be correlated with an ancient tradition in India that pertains to three forms of Agni, the Hindu god of fire, according to Chandra (pc 5 Aug. 2012).

> "The last stanza 15 refers to the three fires: subterranean (*aurvāgni*), the terrestrial and the celestial (sun in the sky). The fire or Agni refers to the might of a monarch, as in the *yūpa* inscription of King Mūlavarman. King Aśvarmā who was like the sun (*aṃśumān*) had three sons resembling the three sacrificial fires. Mūlavarman was the foremost among them. In the India tradition, the three fires were kept aglow in the house by the performer of the *agni-hotra* and his consort throughout their lives, to ensure the cosmic regularity of sunset and sunrise. In our inscription, these three fires have been substituted by the three cosmic fires.... Ṛgveda 10.45.1-3: 'From heaven Agni was born, the second time from us (men), thirdly in the waters'. The order of Agni's abodes is heaven, earth and water (Macdonell 1897: 93)".

---

also suggestive of 'the hissing of heat' or 'hot breathing'.

Hence, strophe 15 potentially alludes to the three cosmic fires, which are correlated as follows: the *aurva* fire with *bodhi-dṛṣṭi*, the terrestrial fire with the manifestation of the multitude of the very wise, on the earth and on Mount Meru, and the celestial fire with the 'Great Sun Door' of the non-returner.[108]

> "The Buddha is the humanized type of Agni, the Sacrificial Fire. At his cremation he is simultaneously the devouring fire and the holocaust. His apparitional, factitious body (*nirmāṇa-kāya*) is burnt away so as to reveal his true Dharma-Body (*dharma-kāya*). The ashes are the visible and remaining traces of his transformation. Their presence in the stūpa testifies that the Buddha has passed through the self-consuming conflagration of Perfect Knowledge" (Snodgrass 1985: 356).

In *pāda a* the composer draws our attention to the contrast between the sightless power of the submarine Agni and the Buddhistic vision of *bodhi*, with the second as the antidote for the destructive power of the first. The full import of this becomes clearer when we notice that the vital life forces within the human body are also identified as forms of *agni*. At the microcosmic level, the submarine fire can perhaps be correlated with the primal human desires associated with the lowest of the psychic energy centers or *cakra*-s.[109] However, Buddhist meditative practices enable the *bodhicitta* to rise above the lower *cakra*-s, both literally and figuratively, by ascending the psychic nerve (*merudaṇḍa*) that parallels the human spinal axis. It is probably not mere coincidence that fire, wind and 'serpent power' (*kuṇḍalinī*) form an essential triad in the root *cakra* identified with the element earth. Thereafter the arising vital life force passes through the remaining *cakra*-s[110] until ultimately emerging from the crown *cakra*, the summit of Mount Meru within the human body, to manifest as the 'sun' of a thousand spokes (*sahasrāra*). The microcosmic analogies set forth here-above enable us to provisionally view the term *bodhidṛṣṭyā* as being closely related to the conventional Buddhistic term *bodhicitta* in this particular instance.

In *pāda d* the inscription's composer inextricably links the macrocosmic axis of the entire universe with the Veṇuvanavihāra, not only as a meditation retreat for monks but also as the monumental embodiment of the Buddha who has pierced the Great Sun Door that leads to the empyrean.

---

[108]For example, the multitude of the very wise can be viewed as a reference to Ṛṣis. "An association between the Ṛṣis and Agni/Fire is evident from the very earliest times. In the *Ṛgveda*, the birth and kindling of Agni is frequently ascribed to Aṅgiras, Bhṛgu, Atharvan and their descendants; it is similarly related that the Seven Ṛṣis kindled and gave birth to Agni—all of which may be associated with the ritual kindling of fire in the context of the sacrificial cult.... Agni is said to 'possess' the Seven Ṛṣis.... In a Brāhmaṇa passage, the Seven Ṛṣis are said to constitute the very essence of Agni" (Mitchiner 1982: 254). Through the performance of *tapas*, the Ṛṣis achieve a self-transformation into fiery heat or *tejas* as the external manifestation of fiery ascetic energy: "for by cursing the *adhārmic* or unrighteous actions of their transgressors, they once again preserve *dharma* and maintain the correct ordering of the universe" (Mitchiner, 1982: 216).

[109]In the *Yama(pūrva)tattva*, an Old Javanese text fragment dealing with care for the dead, the aforementioned fiery turtle or Baḍavaṅ Anala "figures as the first mentioned of a dozen frightening animals, belonging to the macrocosmos—but to be found in the lower part of the human body, that microcosmos, and to be known by his mind, that microcosmos par excellence" (Hooykaas 1964: 116).

[110]For example the *maṇipūra cakra,* e.g. where the 'digestive fire' cooks the food, is located at navel height.

"Hindu and Buddhist thinking assumes the existence of a strict analogy between the macrocosm and the microcosm, that is, between the world constituted by the individual being on the one hand and the total cosmos on the other. The *Tantras* describe a highly complex cosmo-physiology in which the bodily organs and functions are equated with cosmic counterparts .... The gods who dwell in the heavens also abide in the *cakras* of the human body and rule over the senses .... The identity of the body and the cosmos is realized by the practice of meditational techniques.... The cosmic body realized by these meditational means is the Body of the Buddha, which is identified with the total cosmos. It is also the body of the stūpa, since the stūpa is likewise identified with the universe. The stūpa is at one and the same time the body of the whole world and the Body of the Buddha, which is the body of perfected Man, of the Buddha as the universal type or norm of the human" (Snodgrass 1985: 360).

Conclusion

Jordaan and Colless (2009) refer to "certain indications of a diminished political influence of the Śailendras" but without delineating them all in a single place. Perhaps the clearest evidence of this is the replacement of the Chinese designation 'Ho-ling' for the Javanese trade missions sent to China from 768 to 818 with Shê-p'o beginning in 820 and thereafter in 831, 839 and from 860 to 873. Given that this abrupt change occurred just a few years prior to the date of the Kayumwuṅan charter, the death of Samaratuṅga (or perhaps his designated heir) remains a plausible hypothesis worthy of further consideration. Samaratuṅga ascended the throne at some point between the dates of the Śrī Saṅgrāmadhanaṃjaya inscription (782) and Abhayagirivihāra (792/3) charter. Hence, the Śailendra monarch would have been of a relatively advanced age by 824 CE if still among the living at that time. On the other hand, if the inscription's opening verse triad refers to the enlightened body, speech and mind of the preceding Śailendra monarch Śrī Saṅgrāmadhanaṃjaya—presuming that he had undergone an apotheosis as is suspected to have been the case with respect to Rakai Pikatan, based on the contents of the Śivagṛha inscription of 856 CE (see Chapter VIII)—then the Kayumwuṅan charter would present us with a classic example of a Sanskrit *praśasti* covering three generations. The statement concerning 'one who is to be venerated by the venerable' in v.3 would make eminent sense in this context, and with the phrase 'in accordance with his meritorious deeds' (*tasyānupuṇyam*) from v.12 potentially pointing back to the king in v.3 as 'the progenitor (i.e. the source) of supreme knowledge and meritorious acts' (*mahājñānapuṇyaprasūti*).

All we know with any degree of certainty is that something truly momentous must have occurred to cause the charter's composer to say of Prāmodavarddhanī that 'she shines bright ... not'. Radiance is the indispensable and essential condition of kingship that is normally expressed in royal proclamations in one way or another. The relatively recent death of her father or another close family member certainly would qualify as a credible explanation for why the poet would have included such an unusual statement about Prāmodavarddhanī in the Sanskrit portion of the charter. Furthermore, these remarks stand in stark contrast to the contents of the first half of strophe nine, which lauds the very qualities that we would expect to be proclaimed in a charter about a high-ranking member of the royal family.

VI. The lost icons once crowning the twin *vihāra*-s at Plaosan Lor

Insofar as I am aware, the small west-facing niche cut into the *harmikā* and pinnacle for the principal *stūpa* crowning either *vihāra* at Plaosan Lor has not yet received the close attention it deserves.[1] Prior to embarking on a comprehensive discussion of the principal Plaosan inscription, we shall examine the potential applications for these small exterior niches and their possible impact on the translation of specific verses and strophe fragments from what appears to have been the foundation charter for this particular temple complex, which was constructed during the first half of the ninth century.

A short notice concerning the existence of an emplacement for an icon on the superstructure of the main *stūpa* crowning one of the two centrally placed temples at Plaosan Lor was published in *Oudheidkundig Verslag* (1950: 30). According to the opinion of the report's author concerning this peculiar feature, the recess probably had served for the placement of a small statue that had represented the edifice's supreme divinity. The writer also noted that unlike Caṇḍi Sari, which gives the impression of having a flat roof due to the separate but equal treatment of the three superstructures placed above the edifice's three *cellae*, each *vihāra* at Caṇḍi Plaosan Lor has a pyramidal structure at the center of the entire roof that is crowned by a *stūpa* that towers over all other elements atop the building. A reexamination of photos taken in 2004 confirms that the crowning structures for both monastic buildings have identical emplacements for icons (figures 6-2 & 6-3) that formerly had faced the western horizon at roughly the same point of the compass onto which the entire temple complex is oriented.

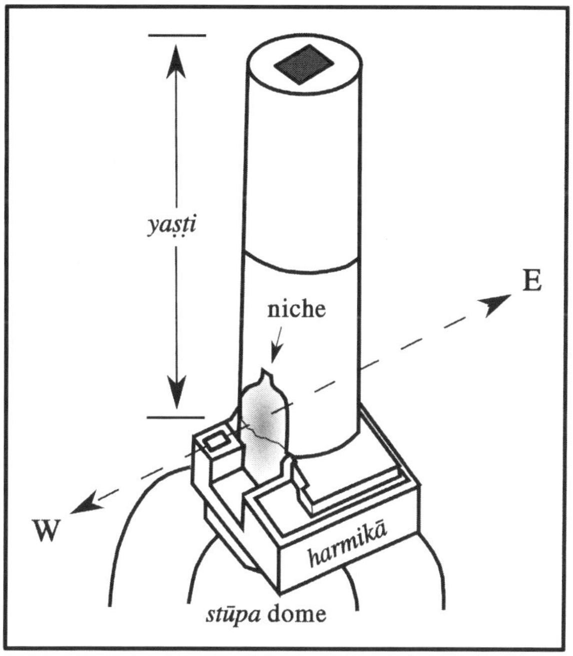

Fig. 6-1. Niche in the *harmikā* and *yaṣṭi* in each of the crowning *stūpas* on the twin *vihāra*-s at Caṇḍi Plaosan Lor (based on the photograph in *Oudheidkundig Verslag* 1950: fig. 17).

[1]The existence of the lost icons originally installed on the principal *stūpa-harmikā* structures crowning the twin *vihāra*-s at Caṇḍi Plaosan Lor may never have come to my attention were it not for the kind and generous efforts made on my behalf by Roy Jordaan, who has been a wellspring of inspiring insights as well as a veritable Kubera bestowing a wealth of crucial data concerning the art, architecture, culture and history of Central Java's Classic Age civilization without which my own research in these areas would have been greatly diminished. I was delighted to present to my 'good friend' (*kalyāṇamitra*) an early draft of this discussion on the occasion of his reaching the Dutch formal age of retirement in June of 2012.

Figs. 6-2 & 6-3. A view from a point to the north of the northern *vihāra* with enlarged details of each crowning *stūpa* (above); **west-facing niche in the *harmikā* and pinnacle above the *stūpa* dome** (right).

The space made available for an icon in each case extends from the middle of the quadrangular stone surmounting the *stūpa* dome to the lower part of either *stūpa* spire. There is also a rectangular notch cut into the pinnacle's west side just above what appears to be the outline of an aureole. This small notch may have accommodated one end of a horizontal bar, the other end of which had terminated in the support nub for a sun shade. Van Kinsbergen, for example, shot three photographs of a bronze image (P-024267, P-024268 and P-024296)[2] of a female Buddhist divinity with the well-known Buddhistic *ye dharmmā hetuprabhavā* text inscribed on its base. This statue incorporates a horizontal arm for the sunshade, which juts out from the top of the statue's aureole. The bar's other end has a conical nub for supporting a parasol.

The ensuing discussion examines two scenarios for what these unique niches at the top of

[2]Groeneveldt (1887: 188, no. 640) appears to describe the same image or one that is closely comparable.

the two buildings originally had contained: either the image of a divinity or another type of icon that had perhaps also served as a reliquary. In either case, it is likely that this statue or icon had been made of bronze, silver or gold so that it would have reflected the rays of the sun and the moon. The value of such an icon's metallic content also would which would explain why not a trace of its former existence has been unearthed at the site given that treasure hunters would have carted away any metal objects and melted them down for their own financial benefit. This likewise would account for the absence of the principal sculpture in each of the three interior chambers of either *vihāra.* The disturbance of the ritual deposits that archaeologists unearthed below the floor of the northern edifice's central chamber in 1993 demonstrates the extent to which looters were willing to go in order to acquire artifacts of material value (see Miksic *et al.* 2001: 324-325).

A brief *stūpa* symbolism review

Before taking up the question of the identity of the lost icons, we shall briefly review the potential symbolic significance of their installation on the rectangular stone block and pinnacle above the dome of the principal *stūpa* for each building. The Sanskrit designations for thc primary components of a *stūpa* are presented in the *Divyāvadāna*, a text with which Javanese Buddhists were familiar during the ninth century, as the Barabuḍur narrative reliefs depicting stories from this early Buddhist compilation clearly indicate. The segment from this text pertaining to the construction of a *stūpa*, which has been translated by Bénisti (1960: 74-78), tells the story of a traveling merchant who, upon returning to his home, had learned that the Buddha Kṣemankara previously residing in the kingdom had entered *parinirvāṇa* and that the king had erected a small *caitya* over this Buddha's physical remains. Despite the objections of the local Brahmins, who wanted the merchant's gold for themselves, the trader obtained the king's permission to use his earnings to construct a more substantial edifice to house the relics of the Buddha Kṣemankara. The text then presents a description of the various architectural components for the *stūpa* that the merchant had constructed, including the four staircases (*sopāna*), three terraces (*medhi*), the dome (*anda*, 'egg'), the little 'summer-house' (*harmikā*) surmounting the dome, the mast (*yūpayaṣṭi*) and the so-called 'rain vessel' (*varṣasthāla*; see Appendix F).

Fig. 6-4. Free-standing *stūpa* installed at ground level within the Plaosan Lor complex.

On each of the four sides of the *stūpa*, the tradesman then constructed four more edifices called the Birth, (*jāti*), the Enlightenment (*abhisambodhi*), the Preaching (*dharmacakra-*

pravartana) and the Total Extinction (*parinirvāṇa*) *mahācaitya*-s.

However, the principal Buddhist edifices constructed in Central Java do not conform to the type of *stūpa* described in the *Divyāvadāna*. Moreover, beginning in the late eighth century it is likely that Javanese Buddhists also had become aware of some of the alternate names for the construction components of *stūpas* through their direct contacts with monks hailing from the original Abhayagirivihāra founded in the Siṅhalese kingdom of Anurādhapura. In the *Mahāvaṃsa* (XXXI,124), for example, the *harmikā* was known as the 'quadrangular building' (*caturassa-caya*) whereas in the later Siṅhalese texts (Gosling, 1996: 131) it was called the 'citadel of the gods' (*deva koṭuvā*).

As Mus (1933: 764, 931) has shown, the *harmikā* signifies the very summit of Mount Meru: the peak of the cosmic mountain and the residence of Indra in the Trāyastriṃśa heaven of the 33 *deva*-s. According to Buddhist cosmography, this is the lowest of the four heavens belonging to the 'World of Desire' (*kāmadhātu*). Beyond identifying several artistic renditions depicting Meru in the form of a *prāsāda*, Mus delineated the parallel relationships between the *stūpa* as the macrocosmic model of the world and with the human body as the microcosmic equivalent.[3] Mus (1933: 618) also noted that the Old Javanese *Sang Hyang Kamahāyānikan* refers to the body of the *yogin* as internally and externally a *stūpa-prāsāda*. For Mus, the dome of the *stūpa* encases the *prāsāda*, excepting only the pavilion symbolizing the summit of Mount Meru's central peak. What the SHK's enigmatic passage also suggests is that the term *stūpa-prāsāda* would likewise be applicable to towering edifices on which the *stūpa* served as the crowning element.

Fig. 6-5. *Harmikā* from Shotorak, Kapisa, Afghanistan (Photo by John C. Huntington courtesy of the Huntington Photographic Archive at The Ohio State University).

Bénisti (1960), Snodgrass (1981), Harvey (1984) and a host of others were able to deduce that the *harmikā* of the *stūpa* corresponds to the crowning element of Hindu temple architecture known as the *śikhara*, 'crested; peak (of a mountain)'. This Sanskrit word is

[3]The Buddha expressed this equivalence in the *Laṅkāvatāra-sūtra* (v.672; see the 1956 translation by D. T. Suzuki) when he said, "Within the body, measuring one *vyāna* [the measure of two outstretched arms] there is a world; the cause of its rising, the attaining of cessation, and the path (*pratipad*) — this I teach to sons of the Victor" (e.g. the bodhisattvas). In the *Saṃyutta Nikāya* (IV,35,166) the Buddha also declared, "That in the world through which one, perceiving the world, arrives at his conception of the world, that in the Order of the Blessed One is called 'the world'."

derived from *śikhā* ('hair-tuft'), and specifically in the sense of the hair-tuft worn by Hindus "to mark the location of the 'aperture of Brahman' (*brahmarandhra*), the point where the axis of the body (*merudaṇḍa*, *brahmadaṇḍa*) emerges from the top of the head. The same associations are connected with the word *stūpa*, which in its literal sense also means 'topknot' or 'crest'; whence its derivative, *stūpika*, which is the topmost finial of a building, the portion of its axis that emerges above the capstone" (Snodgrass 1981: 263).[4]

Figs. 6-6 & 6-7 The *stūpa* in cave 19 at Ajanta (top, photo credit: Mark Kobayashi-Hillary) **and close-up view of the *harmikā*** (bottom, photo credit: Nicolas Revire).

The *stūpa* pinnacle symbolizes the Cosmic Tree that ascends from the summit of Mount Meru. For Buddhists, this *axis mundi* is the 'seat of wisdom' (*bodhimaṇḍa*) at the center of which stands the Bodhi Tree,[5] magically transported to the summit.[6] The huge Bodhi Tree, which the *Mahāvaṃsa* (XXXX,63) describes "as being in the relic chamber of the great *stūpa* at Anurādhapura, is said to have a canopy over it on which are depicted the sun, moon and stars—all said to revolve round Meru. Around the tree are placed statues

[4]The connection between the future Buddha's top-knot and the Trāyastriṃśa heaven is found in an early Pali text entitled the *Introduction to the Jātaka* (i,64-65). When the future Buddha cut off his top-knot, together with his diadem, he tossed it in the air while saying, "If I am to become a Buddha, let them stay in the sky; but if not, let them fall to the ground". The lord of the devas Sakka (= Indra) "received them in an appropriate jewelled casket, and established it in the Heaven of the Thirty-Three Gods as the 'Shrine of the Diadem'" (Zimmer & Campbell 1946: 160-161).

[5]The microcosmic counterpart in the human body is the spinal column, which is called the *merudaṇḍa* (Snodgrass 1981: 360).

[6]Harvey (1984: 75) notes that "in Burma, free-standing parasols are sometimes worshipped as Bodhi tree symbols, and the metal parasols on *stūpas* sometimes have small brass Bodhi leaves hanging from them".

of the Four Great Kings, the gods said to guard the slopes of Meru" (Harvey 1984: 81).

Buddhas were depicted on all four sides of the *stūpa-harmikā* at several sites in India and elsewhere in southern Asia during the centuries preceding the construction of Caṇḍi Plaosan Lor. For example, each of the four sides of a *harmikā* from Shotorak (Kapisa, Afghanistan; *circa* 50—250 CE), which was stolen from the Kabul Museum, depicts a seated Buddha with attendant figures. From the Huntington Archives' photos we can see that the hand gesture made by the Buddha varies depending on which side of the *harmikā* we view.[7] In each case, the Buddha is flanked by one or more attendants (see, for example, figure 6-5).

Other *stūpa-harmikā* examples dating from the third to the fifth centuries display scenes from the life of the historical Buddha Śākyamuni. "The square *harmikā* commonly would have had four narrative panels, one facing each direction, usually showing some variation of the birth, enlightenment, first sermon and Parinirvāṇa" (Behrendt 2003: 123; see also 110, 133-134 and 213). Hence, the four faces had depicted the same events symbolized by the four *mahācaitya* structures mentioned in the *Divyāvadāna*. Moreover, a photo taken in the former Gandharva region of Pakistan's northwestern frontier province shows the image of a Buddha depicted in the Gandharvan style (Kusana period) displaying the *dharmacakra-mudrā* and seated on a *stūpa-harmikā* (see P-011123 by J.E. Lohuizen de Leeuw).

Fig. 6-8. *Harmikā*, cave 26 at Ajanta (Photo credit: Nicolas Revire).

Two cave shrines at Ajanta, which date from the sixth century, also display images of the Buddha on the *harmikā*. In cave 26, for example, the *stūpa-harmikā* depicts three seated Buddhas above and three standing figures below, either a Buddha flanked by an attendant on either side or three standing Buddhas (see figure 6-8). In cave 19, the *harmikā* features a seated Buddha facing the cave's entrance, which apparently displays the *dharmacakra-mudrā*. The figure standing on the top of the *harmikā* may be one of the four *lokapāla* directional guardians, which elsewhere became depicted above the *harmikā* and on the pinnacle of the *stūpa*, whereas the sides of the *harmikā* feature painted images (see figures A-16 and A-17 in Appendix F). Additionally, a small bronze votive *stūpa* found at Ashrafpur (Dacca, Bangladesh), which Bénisti dated to the ninth century, has a *harmikā* on each side of which is depicted a Buddha displaying the *mudrā* associated with the cardinal

[7]The figures depicted on the three sides of this *harmikā* for which there are photographs in the Huntington Archives (http://huntington.wmc.ohio-state.edu/public/) display the *dharmacakra-mudrā*, the *bhūmisparśa-mudrā* and the *dhyāna-mudrā*, respectively.

direction in which he faces (see Banerji 1933: 153, pl. LXXV c; Bénisti 1986: 19; and Bagchi 1993: 117).

In ancient Sri Lanka the *harmikā* of the *stūpa* often displayed an image of the sun, or images of both the sun and the moon. "The courses of the heavenly bodies are governed by Meru. The clockwise passage of the sun around Meru is reflected by the *pradaksiṇā* ritual, which defines or creates sacred space and thereby makes possible the ascent or projection from the plane of mundane life to that of the sacred" (Mabbett 1983: 66-67).

With respect to those instances in which only the sun had been depicted on the *stūpa-harmikā*, one of the potential analogies that can be drawn from Vedic texts is that between the sun and the eye, as noted by Coomaraswamy (1997: 217): "We need hardly say that 'Sun' and 'Eye' are constantly assimilated notions in Vedic mythology, and that is from the same point of view that the Buddha is frequently called the 'Eye in the World' (*cakkumāloke*)".[8] A related Hindu-Buddhist art motif with Vedic roots is the world pillar crowned by a *cakra* symbolizing the sun. Such pillars honoring the Buddha have been erected in India and elsewhere since the time of King Aśoka. Brown has noted the apparent interchangeability of the *stūpa* and the *cakrastambha* forms depicted in the Maha Sarakham plaques unearthed in northeastern Thailand during 1972, though he admits there is not enough evidence to decide the matter unequivocally.

> "[On these plaques] a *cakra* is literally mounted on what is unquestionably a *stūpa*.... A second example is found on a *sema* from Wat Si Thammaram, Ban Tat Thong, Yasonthon Province, with the *cakra* placed on top of a vase-*stūpa*. We have, then, the conflation of the *cakrastambha* and the *stūpa*.... the doctrinal significance was known, and known so well that it allowed an understanding of the appropriateness of the conflation of the *stūpa* and *cakra* imagery [and with the sun often being] visualized as on the *harmikā* of the *stūpa*. Images of the sun and moon were actually placed on the *harmikā* in Sri Lanka..." (Brown 1996: 95, including n. 114).

The use of the sun and moon as paired symbols may have led to the Nepalese custom of painting a pair of eyes on each of the four sides of the *stūpa-harmikā*, though this motif appears to post-date the eleventh century in Nepal and did not come into prevalent usage until the fifteenth century (Starza 1993: 71). Still, the motif can be traced back to the Vedic identification of the sun and the moon as the eyes of the Cosmic Power variously identified as the Skambha, Puruṣa, Prajāpati, etc.[9] The eyes painted on the *harmikā* of the Nepalese *caitya* also help to convey the notion that the *stūpa* is a monumental body modeled on a human figure seated in the posture of meditation.

The shields (Newar = *halapau* or *halipati*) mounted directly above the four faces of the *harmikā* on the Nepalese *stūpa* also depicts "images of the transcendent Buddhas guarding the four directions. Vairochana is represented four times in the upper storey" (Purdy 2001). A Nepalese Buddhist text entitled the *Kriyāsaṃgraha* specifies the area located between the

[8]Snodgrass (1985: 77) refers to a Kampuchean ritual in which the king "thinks of his body as Meru, his right and left eyes as the sun and the moon, his arms and legs as the four directions".

[9]The bodhisattva Avalokiteśvara is described in the same fashion in the *Kāraṇḍavyūha-sūtra* (see Studholme 2002: 40).

top of the *harmikā* and the mid-point of the spire as the proper location for the placement of the four guardians (*lokapāla*) of the cardinal directions (see figures A-14 & A-15 in Appendix F).

Fig. 6-9. Swayambhunath *stūpa* near Kathmandu, Nepal (photo credit: Nancy Collins).

When the sun alone is depicted on the *stūpa-harmikā*, it symbolizes the great Sun Door: the supernal sun considered to signify the passage to liberation in both the Buddhist and Hindu traditions. "Those who have sought the Self by penance, abstinence, faith and knowledge attain the sun by the Northern Path or the path of *devayāna*. From thence they do not return. This is the immortal abode, free from fear, and the highest" (*Praśna Upaniṣad* I,10). Coomaraswamy (1943) noted that "Buddha's powers are greater than [Māra's] because his range is greater; he knows the Brahmaloka as well as the worlds up to the Brahmaloka (i.e., under the Sun), while 'Death's' power extends only up to the Brahmaloka and not beyond the Sun".

Meru and the supernal sun appear on opposite sides of the *kakayon* of Javanese shadow play (*wayang*) performances.[10] One side of this hand-held attribute is entirely engulfed in flames while the other depicts a temple on which the *stūpa-harmikā* is replaced by the head at the base of the Cosmic Tree. This 'face of glory' (*kīrtimukha*) atop the roof of the temple —better known as the 'lord of the forest' (*banaspati*) on Java—is yet another solar symbol for demarcating the passage that leads to the empyrean: the highest heaven, believed to contain the pure element of fire. Furthermore, the Garuḍa half-images on the sides of the temple help to clarify the structure's identification with Mount Meru. "Danielou [1964: 91-92] cites the story in which Narada incited Vayu, the wind, to attempt to break Meru's summit; Vayu drummed up a great storm lasting a year, but Garuḍa protected the mountain" (Mabbett 1983: 71).[11]As for the equivalent structure atop the dome of the Buddhist *stūpa*, "it is certainly not by purely 'practical' considerations that one can explain the position of the *harmikā* or 'little dwelling' or *deva kotuwā* or 'citadel of the gods' immediately above and outside the apex of the *stūpa*; whereas the *raison d'être* of this emplacement becomes immediately evident if we understand that 'immediately above the apex of the dome' is as much as to say 'beyond the Sun'; all that is mortal being contained

[10]The *kakayon* is a multivalent symbol that can, among other things, signify a tree, a temple or a mountain.

[11]For a discussion concerning the symbolic significance of the animal figures appearing on either side of the *kīrtimukha*, see Long 2009: 240-246.

within, and all that is immortal exceeding the structure" (Coomaraswamy 1997: 214).

Fig. 6-10. The Javanese *kakayon* (photo credit: Collectie Tropen Museum).

The short inscriptions on the pinnacle bases of two *stūpa* spires

Overall, the numerous short votive inscriptions found at Caṇḍi Plaosan Lor have enabled scholars to push back the site's construction time-line. Sundberg (2006: 117-118, n. 39), for example, has noted that the shrines bearing short inscriptions must have been erected in the early to mid-830s, based on the observation made by Damais (1968: 504) that none of the Javanese aristocrats mentioned in the Tulang Air inscription (850 CE) are named in the short inscriptions at Plaosan Lor. However, the square bases of just two *stūpa* spires (III-14 & III-15) out of the 116 subsidiary shrines originally erected within the outer courtyard at Caṇḍi Plaosan Lor are known to have displayed short votive inscriptions. According to the *Kriyāsaṃgraha,* the square base of the *stūpa* pinnacle or *yaṣṭi* symbolizes the four *brahmavihāras*. Located near the *gopura* B4 (see de Casparis 1958: Plate I), the *stūpa*-s III-14 & III-15 bear the legends '*anumoda rakai gurunwaṅi dyaḥ salaḍū*' and '*astupa* (or *asthupa*) *śrī mahārāja rakai pikatan*' on opposing sides of each spire's base, locations which are potentially significant with respect to architectural symbolism. All the dozens of other short votive inscriptions for the small *prāsāda* structures in the outer temple yard were installed "on the upper band of the basement coping" (Dumarçay 2007: 212).

A few other *stūpa* constructions, such as II-21, III-24, III-35 and III-56, also had displayed short legends but de Casparis (1958) did not report whether any of these had likewise been incised on the base of a *yaṣṭi*. Of particular interest is *stūpa* III-24, which had displayed the legend '*dharmma śrī mahārāja*', which can be associated with the prior Javanese monarch Rakai Garung (829—847) on the following grounds. Rakai Pikatan's pre-coronation legends as 'Rakai Gurunwaṅi dyaḥ Salaḍū' as well as the legends of his predecessor 'Rakai Gurunwaṅi Dyaḥ Rāṇu' (on the *yaṣṭi* bases from *prāsāda* I-5 and I-6), indicate that both aristocrats must have sponsored shrines that were constructed during the reign of Rakai Garung. Moreover, Kusen (1994: 87) observed that when Rakai Garung reestablished the *sima* at Wanua Tĕngaḥ in November, 829 he was accompanied by the Raka of Sirikan pu Suryya, who also contributed two small shrines at Plaosan Lor (I-15 and I-16). Furthermore, *Śrī Kahulunnan,* who issued the Tri Tĕpusan I/II charters in 842 CE, contributed at least four shrines at Plaosan Lor (I-18, I-19, II-21 and II-22), which were placed in close proximity to other shrines bearing the short legend '*dharmma śrī mahārāja*' (I-17, I-21 and III-24), e.g. those presumably belonging to Rakai Garung. Kusen also has suggested that *Kahulunnan,* which meant 'queen-mother' according to Boechari (1982: 17-18), may have been the mother of Rakai Garung.

De Casparis (1958: 23) had suspected that Rakai Gurunwaṅi dyaḥ Saladū had been the aristocratic name for a future king prior to his ascension to the throne. The Wanua Těngah III inscription unearthed in 1983 demonstrates this by providing the complete name of the future monarch: Śrī Mahārāja Rakai Pikatan dyaḥ Saladū (847—855 CE; see the king's list in Jordaan and Colless 2009: 37). This enables us to deduce that Rakai Gurunwaṅi dyaḥ Saladū had been the aristocratic designation of Rakai Pikatan during the reign of his predecessor Rakai Garung.[12] Presumably at some point after Pikatan had ascended the throne, his regal appellation was inscribed on the bases of the spires belonging to the two *stūpa*-s built during his predecessor's reign (Sundberg 2009: 338 and 2006: 107, n. 16).

Fig. 6-11. Spire belonging to *stūpa* III-14.

One possibility is that the legends of Śrī Mahārāja Rakai Pikatan had been posthumously inscribed on his two *stūpa* spires to signify that the deceased king had ascended to Indra's heaven on the summit of Meru.[13] Out of all the short inscriptions at Plaosan Lor, only Pikatan's begin with *astupa* or *asthupa*; all other legends start with *anumoda* or *dharmma*. As the Buddha himself noted in the *Dīghanikāya* (XVI,5), the erection of a *stūpa* for a deceased universal monarch (*cakravartin*) is entirely appropriate (Govinda 1970: 5). The Śivagṛha inscription of 856 CE, which was issued more than a year after the end of Pikatan's reign, appears to refer to Pikatan through the use of the title Jātininrat, a designation perhaps intended to signify his apotheosis.[14] Though we must keep in mind that

[12]"[E]ither Garung was himself a Śailendra king or else supplanted one in an unexpectedly respectful manner ..." (Sundberg 2006: 107, n. 16).

[13]De Casparis (1958: 10-11) did not indicate whether the short inscriptions on II-21 and II-22 (*anumoda śrī kahulunnan*) as well as III-35 (*anumo<da>..*) had likewise been incised on the *harmikā*-s of these three *stūpa* constructions. He was also uncertain whether the inscription a*numoda sang tumungtung pu baruṇa* belonged to *stūpa* III-56 or to *prāsāda* II-49.

[14]Though de Casparis (1956: 318) translated *jāti-niṅ-rat* as 'Birth of the world', Damais (1968: 477) wondered whether one should interpret *jāti* in the usual sense that it has in Old Javanese: 'origin', 'cause', as the expression can apply to a manifestation of the Deity in a similar way to that of the Sanskrit *bhuvanakṛt*. For a

the other side of the spire's base already had presented Pikatan's former aristocratic title, it remains interesting that the positioning of his legends coincide with the emplacements for the four *lokapāla* guardians above each *harmikā* in cave shrines at Ellora and Ajanta.

As previously noted in Chapter V, the benedictory verse of the Kayumwuṅan charter (824) potentially alludes to a Buddhist divinity—or a deceased Śailendra ancestor honored through the consecration of a Buddha image—described as the 'hero abiding on the lofty mountain' (*uttuṅgaśailasthaśūro*). Furthermore, both the Kayumwuṅan and Plaosan inscriptions refer to a temple or image metaphorically described as having fallen from the sky and with their sheen compared to the light of the sun or the moon. Given that the Kayumwuṅan charter only predates the first part of Rakai Garung's reign by a few years, it is entirely possible that the builders of the Veṇuvanavihāra had likewise installed the image of Śrī Ghananātha on the exterior crowning structure of the Veṇuvanavihāra.

If we logically surmise that the Plaosan Lor temple complex had been constructed from the inside out, then the two *prāsāda* constructions (I-5 and I-6) bearing the short votive inscriptions of Rakai Gurunwaṅi dyaḥ Rāṇu would presumably be those of Pikatan's predecessor, with Rakai being his feudal title and Gurunwaṅi indicating the toponym over which he had authority.[15] As de Casparis (1958: 22-23) remarked, the assignment of these two subsidiary buildings to locations immediately in front of the *gopura* providing access to the inner courtyard of the south *vihāra* is significant. It suggests that Rakai Gurunwaṅi must have been an extremely important feudal principality from a political point of view. He also believed that the *stūpas* (I-14 and I-15) belonging to Rakai Gurunwaṅi dyaḥ Salaḍū (= Rakai Pikatan) had been placed "at either side of one of the two main passages leading into the northern temple (A1) and immediately behind the *gopura* B4 ... to lay particular stress on this relation between the king and the heir apparent" (de Casparis 1958: 22-23). Though his surmise that Rakai Gurunwaṅi dyaḥ Salaḍū and Rakai Gurunwaṅi dyaḥ Rāṇu had been the titles of an aristocrat and his spouse has been shown to be incorrect by Damais (1968: 508-509), de Casparis' remark about the respective locations of I-5/II-6 and III-14/III-15 potentially signifying a "relation between the king and the heir apparent" remains of interest. This would lend a modicum of support to the hypothesis that the designation Rakai Gurunwaṅi had appertained to the incumbent of an important principality during the reign of Rakai Garung, perhaps that of the heir apparent.[16] Whether Pikatan acquired this principality as the result of his familial lineage, as Kusen (1994: 88) supposed, a marriage or other factors remains unknown to us.

---

discussion of those aspects of the Śivagṛha inscription which suggest that Rakai Pikatan was deceased in 856 and that the Javanese had considered him to be a deified royal ancestor, see Jordaan 1991: 169 as well as Jordaan & Wessing 1996: 68-69.

[15]A king who briefly ruled in Central Java during 887 CE was entitled Śrī Mahārāja Rakai Gurunwaṅi dyaḥ Bhadra (see Jordaan & Colless 2009: 37). According to Damais (1970), Gurunwaṅi is found under the title Śrī Mahārāja in Munggu Antan; on Taji Gunung; on Timbanan Wungkul; and in the East Javanese inscription of Sugih Manek of 915 CE (as cited by Sundberg in pc 20 May 2012).

[16]Damais (1968: 506) noted that the Old Javanese suffix *waṅi* means 'scented'. Citing van der Tuuk, Damais further observed that *gurun* pertains to the 'feather of a goose or chicken' and is also a synonym of 'an egg'.

The lost icons and the Plaosan Inscription

Though the presumed Plaosan Lor foundation charter does not specifically refer to the Śailendra dynasty, Bosch (1929a: 8-13) and de Casparis (1956: 176-178) have already written at length about the close affinity that exists between the script styles selected by the respective composers of the Śrī Saṅgrāmadhanaṃjaya and Plaosan inscriptions. De Casparis (1956: 180) also believed that the script similarities alone presented a strong argument in favor of surmising that the Plaosan inscription had been issued by one of the Śailendra kings of Central Java. Additionally, he noted that certain references found in the inscription's fragmentary strophes offer circumstantial support for his theory. Though the question remains open, we shall nevertheless examine the contents of the Plaosan charter and its relation to the Plaosan Lor temple complex below and in the following chapter.

Several stanzas from the incomplete Plaosan inscription—which is missing the first six lines and then followed by 12 additional lines of which only text fragments remain—may refer to a shining image or perhaps another type of metal icon. Hence, the contents of the entire inscription needs to be reexamined and reinterpreted, based on our awareness of the *stūpa-harmikā* emplacement crowning the either *vihāra*. As a complete translation of this inscription appears in the next chapter, the following analysis of the Sanskrit text will be limited to only those segments that potentially pertain to the topic at hand, beginning with the transcription and translation for what de Casparis had designated as verse one:

> Naranāthābhisaṃskārabhāro vibhāti bhāsvaraḥ /
> Dharmmasambhārasamitapratimāprati [14] —⏑⏓ // 1 //

> "Bearing the burden of consecration as the lord of men, he shineth forth, the Brilliant One, as the incomparable sunrise in the form of an image adorned with the equipment of Dharma" (de Casparis 1956: 194, 197).

According to de Casparis, *abhisaṃskārabhāro* would mean "bearing the burden of consecration". *Bhāra* means 'burden, load, weight; a large number, mass, bulk; work, labor, task', whereas it is *bhara* without the long *ā* which conveys the meaning of 'bearing, carrying, bringing; bestowing, granting; maintaining, supporting'. Furthermore, de Casparis' translation of the second half-verse is based on his supposition that the stanza-ending phrase cut short by a lacuna must have pertained to the sun, e.g. "as the incomparable sunrise" (*prati<modayaḥ>*). However, he should have placed this last part in brackets to alert readers that this segment of the translation is speculative.[17] If we wish to engage in a modicum of speculation of our own, there is another plausible emendation at hand. In *pāda d* of v.16, *bhavabhidapratimapratimāmrtaiḥ* means "by the immortal ambrosias (*amrtaiḥ*) of the peerless image (*apratimapratimā*) for breaching [the wall of] (*bhid*) phenomenal existence (*bhava*)".

The alternate emendation of *aprati<māmṛtaiḥ>* is a metrically-compatible replacement for *prati<modayaḥ>* that substantially alters the meaning of strophe one.

---

[17]The translation of strophe one by Sarkar (1971/2: I: 48) is even more unsatisfactory: "He shines forth resplendent with the charge of consecration of a king, representing an image which is an embodiment of all forms of religion".

1. A mass of supernatural facilities shines forth as the Lord of men resplendent ... [with the incomparable immortal ambrosias] in [the form of] an image which is commensurate with the equipment of Dharma.

1. **A mass** (bhāro = bhāraḥ, 'large quantity, mass') **of supernatural facilities** (abhisaṃskāra, which also can mean 'super-preparations; antidotes'; see the discussion below) **shines forth** (vibhāti) **as the Lord of men** (naranātha) **resplendent** (bhāsvaraḥ) ... [with the incomparable immortal ambrosias[18] (aprati<māmṛtaiḥ>)][19] ... [in the form] **of an image** (pratimā) **which is commensurate with** (samita) **the equipment of Dharma**[20] (dharma-sambhāra).[21]

We would not expect the composer of a Buddhistic text to use *abhisaṃskāra* to refer to a 'consecration' given that this Sanskrit term conveys a multiplicity of distinct complex meanings[22] for Buddhists that simply cannot be ignored without good reason, even though those meanings are very difficult to translate. The equivalent word appearing in texts belonging to the Pali Canon is *abhisaṅkhāra*. Among other things, this Pali term can be used to refer to the preparation, accumulation and storage of the deep mental impressions arising as a consequence of one's volitional activities of body, speech and mind. Hence, *abhisaṅkhāra* is the 'motive force' (Matthews 1983: 59-61) inextricably linked with the Buddhistic views of *karma* and rebirth.[23]

One potential cue for unraveling the meaning of *abhisaṃskāra* with respect to its use in the Plaosan Lor *praśasti* comes from the context in which the term *saṃskāra* appears in the final strophe of the Śrī Saṅgrāmadhanaṃjaya inscription, e.g. as a concise way for explaining how the Śailendra monarch had come to encounter his *guru* Kumāraghoṣa. Chandra (1995: 224) has interpreted this as a reference to the king's "noble deeds performed in prior incarnations". However, *saṃskāra* may have been intended to convey an even more

[18]Buddhist texts often refer to the Buddha's wisdom as the *amṛta* and his teachings are said to be equivalent to the sprinkling of the immortal ambrosia. "With the lovely ambrosia of wisdom, he brings satisfaction to beings who are like a fire and cannot be satisfied by anything divine or human" (from Bhāvavikeka's account of the Buddha, v.354; see Eckel 1992: 191). "[A]nd with this Ambrosia that Exalted One sprinkles the world of men and the Worlds of the Gods; and sprinkled with this Ambrosia, both gods and men have obtained deliverance from Birth, Old Age, Disease, Death, and from sorrow, lamentation, suffering dejection, and despair" (*The Questions of King Milinda* vs.335-336).

[19]In ancient India, the moon was believed to be the storehouse of the *amṛta*, which became resplendent on the full moon *tithi* due to the abundance of divine nectar. According to the *Viṣṇu Purāṇa*, the gods drink the nectar of the moon during the waning phase of the month from full moon to new moon, and from this being their food, they are immortal. In tantric *yoga* also, the crown *cakra* (*sahasrāra*) is characterized as "the full Moon without the mark of the hare, resplendent as in a clear sky; it sheds its rays in profusion, and is moist and cool like nectar" (Woodroffe 1919: 428).

[20]In other words, the performance of sacred duties (*puṇya)* and the achievement of excellence in spiritual knowledge (*jñāna)* by means of which the Buddha attained enlightenment and deliverance.

[21]Chandra (pc 24 May 2012) expressed the opinion that it was not the image which was shining, but rather the accomplishments of the king who had donated the image. "The translation would be, 'The plentitude (bhāra) of the supreme (abhi) saṃskāra of the king (naranātha) shines (vibhāti) in all its sheen (bhāsvaraḥ) because of the incomparable (apratima) sanctity (amṛta) of the image (pratimā) illuminated (samita) by his dharmic accumulations (dharma saṃbhāra)'."

[22]See the entry in Edgerton 1953: II: 57.

[23]Additionally, *abhisaṅkhāra* is the designation for the second link in the twelve-fold chain of dependent co-origination (*paṭiccasamuppāda* = Skt. *pratītya-samutpāda*).

complex meaning. According to the *Majjhima Nikāya* (III,99), the Buddha has explained that purposive, aspiring states of mind (*saṅkhārā*) are capable of inducing specific rebirths.[24]

"Monks, here a monk is endowed with faith, is endowed with virtue, is endowed with learning, is endowed with generosity, is endowed with wisdom. It occurs to him: 'Would that I might be reborn in companionship with the rich aristocracy after the disintegration of my body after death'. He fixes his mind on this, concentrates his mind on this, develops his mind on this. These aspirations and this fixation of his, so developed and practiced, will lead to rebirth there. Monks, this way, this method will lead to rebirth there" (Johansson 1981, No. 24).[25]

Through his analysis of the many ways that *saṃskāra* and *abhisaṃskāra* became translated into Chinese over time, Hsing-kong concluded that *saṃskāra* possesses a dynamic aspect as the "forces preparing the consciousness and through it the way both to [the] suffering of Samsara [and the bliss of] Nirvana," which also accords "perfectly with the outlook of the early meditation scriptures in China". It is what makes one "ready to reap the fruits of one's actions, of whatever kind they may be", whether they are the 'preparations' (*saṃskāra*) of a person bound to suffering and mundane existence or the pure activities of liberated sentient beings (Hsing-kong 1995: 294, 297). Besides, the Chinese translators of Buddhist texts clearly believed that *abhisaṃskāra*-s are actually the 'super-preparations' of liberated sentient beings, e.g. the supernatural powers, intentions, or karmic actions determining the functions of body, speech and mind.

"Chinese language seems to be more suitable than English in rendering the meaning of samskaras as both passive [所造] and active [能造] forces. They represent a certain potential in mind [功能，功用] to prepare [造作] the world in accordance with one's karma. When connected with meditation practice [加行，加行方便], they guide the mind to perform feats of supernatural powers [作別故意], or activate the otherwise dormant supernatural faculties [as special creations = *abhisaṃskāra*-s], becoming also the equipment [資糧] for the attainment of the goal of practice" (Hsing-kong 1995: 300).

The *Differentiation of the Middle and the Extremes* (*Madhyāntavibhaṅga;* see Asaṅga and Thrangu Rinpoche 2000: 64-65) delineates five faults pertaining to the practice of meditation (also known elsewhere as the five obstructions to flawless *samādhi*) and their eight antidotes: 1-4) faith, aspiration, exertion and pliancy as the antidotes for laziness; (5) mindfulness as the antidote for forgetting the instruction or meditative object of observation; (6) introspection as the antidote for the non-identification of laxity and excitement; (7) application as the antidote for non-application; and (8) equanimity as the

[24]For more on the relationship between *saṅkhārā* and *abhisaṅkhārā*, see Pali Text Society 1905: 664.

[25]Johansson 1981, No. 24: 'A strong wish may influence rebirth' (*Majjhima Nikaya* III,99f). Johansson also noted that the wish for rebirth is only effective "if the necessary qualifications are present, i.e. faith, virtue, knowledge, intelligence. In this way, the internal causal process can be used, either in order to form a new life of a certain type or in order to avoid another rebirth".

antidote for unnecessary application (Wallace 1995: 205-220). Bodhibhadra (*circa* 1000 CE) —the teacher of Atiśa during the latter's sojourn at Nālandā—used *abhisaṃskāra* (Tibetan = *'du byed pa*, 'deliberate action/application [of remedies]') as a term for collectively referring to these eight antidotes in his 'Chapter on the collection of meditative stabilization' (*samādhisambhāraparivarta;* see Zahler 2009: 22-23, 382).

The shining forth of light in strophe one of the Plaosan inscription suggests that the 'Lord of men' (*naranātha*) possessed awesome powers as an outgrowth of his accumulation of a large number of *abhisaṃskāra*-s, e.g. 'super-preparations' or 'supernatural faculties'. It is also interesting that the use of the alternate emendation *aprati<māmṛtaiḥ>* proposed herein provides a match for the identification of *abhisaṃskāra* as a set of eight antidotes, given that *amṛta* also means 'antidote to poison' and with the immortal ambrosia of the Buddha's wisdom being the ultimate antidote for *saṃsāra*. Plus the statement about the image as being commensurate with, or equal to, the equipment of Dharma matches Hsing-kong's previously cited observation about the *abhisaṃskāra*-s "becoming also the equipment [資糧] for the attainment of the goal of practice".

Either emended version of the refreshed translation for strophe one presented above provides a suitable introduction for what strophe three subsequently communicates.

> ≚ ≚ ḥ sva ≚ ⏑ yāvā ≚ catussugatasaṅgataḥ /
> Prāsādādbhutasaṃbhraṣṭaḥ kim=bhāti tadṛśaś=ciram // 3 //

> "... from the contact with the four sugatas; how is it possible that he continues to shine forth after having fallen into the temple by a miracle" (de Casparis 1956: 194, 198).

On the other hand, it is equally possible to translate this as "after having fallen *onto* the temple".

> 3. ... having united with the Sugatas of the four times ..., why does this apparition shine forth for a long time after having fallen from the sky to the temple (as if) by a miracle?

> 3. **Having united with** (saṅgataḥ = saṃgataḥ) **the Sugatas of the four times** (catussugata) ..., **why** (kim) **does this apparition**[26] (tadṛśaś = ta[d], 'this'; dṛśaḥ, 'appearance, look') **shine forth** (bhāti) **for a long time** (ciram) **after having fallen from the sky** (saṃ-bhraṣṭaḥ) **to the temple** (prāsāda) [as if] **by a miracle** (adbhuta, 'wonderful occurrence')?

De Casparis (1956: 198, n. 100) did not think it probable that the word *saṅgataḥ* (= *saṃgataḥ*)[27] could have meant 'having joined' with the four Sugatas, which he also doubted would be a reference to four Jinas: "why not five?" An obvious answer is that the 'fallen' image could have been envisioned as the centrally placed fifth member of a Buddhistic pentad united with the Jinas of the cardinal directions and four eons (*catursugata*).[28]

[26]i.e. 'the appearance of something remarkable or unexpected, typically an image of this type'.

[27]In the Śrī Saṅgrāmadhanaṃjaya (Kĕlurak) inscription, *saṅgata* appears in a fragmentary strophe (v.3) that is equally difficult to interpret.

[28]Catussugata may refer to the Buddhas of the four cosmic eons, e.g. those of the four orients (Mus 1998: 267), or perhaps to the Sugatas of the four times of past, present, future and utterly transcendent.

Furthermore, de Casparis believed that the fragmentary first half-verse of the third strophe must have explained why the image had fallen to the temple as if by a miracle. Still, it is more logical to presume that the answer to the question posed in strophe three had been provided in the first half of the next verse, of which *bhūbhṛd = iva* ('like a mountain' or 'like a king') is the only readable phrase.[29]

The references to the image shining forth in strophes one and three[30] are potentially related to the contents of strophes eight and 12.

G*a*ha*na*pāraśāsārthavyāhāramañjuśīkaraḥ /
Cāracīvarasāndhyābhradhībhūridalayoja [17] <naḥ> // 8 //

"Making the gentle rain of his discourses, which aim at teaching (the converts) how to cross the depths (of the ocean of Saṃsāra), descend, he is to be compared with a twilight cloud in his dark monk's dress, while he concentrates himself on the manifold petals of his mind" (de Casparis (1956: 194, 200-201).

De Casparis (1956: 200, n. 108) admitted that the phrase 'how to cross the depths (of the ocean of Saṃsāra)' "cannot well be combined with the simile of the 'rain of the discourse' [*vyāhāramañjuśīkaraḥ*] descending out of the 'cloud of the Dharma'...." However, there are alternate meanings for *gahana*—such as 'impenetrable darkness' as well as 'the impenetrable (wilderness)'—that also can serve as metaphors for *saṃsāra*.[31] Moreover, what de Casparis translated as the "gentle rain of his discourses" (*vyāhāra-mañju-śīkaraḥ*) has a microcosmic parallel in the body of the *yogin* seated in meditation: the drops of sweet immortal nectar (*amṛta=bodhicitta*) flowing down the central psychic nerve from the *cakra* at the crown of the head.

8. [To be compared with] an evening thundercloud in a monk's dress of different colors while directing thoughts to a single point on the manifold petals of the mind, may you lead [the faithful] to the other side of impenetrable darkness through the splendid fine rain of your discourses on the objective.

8. [To be compared with] **an evening thundercloud** (sāndhya-abhra) **in a monk's dress** (cīvara) **of different colors** (cāra, read as śāra) **while directing thoughts to a single point** (yoja<naḥ>, read as yojanam, neut. sing. nom. of yojana) **on the manifold** (bhūri) **petals** (dala) **of the mind** (dhī), **may you lead** (śāsa, sec. pers. sing. active imperative from √śās, 'to govern, direct, command') [the faithful] **to the other side** (pāra) **of impenetrable darkness** (gahana) **through the splendid**

[29]Besides, the fragmentary first half of the prior verse contains the syllable *sva* followed by a lacuna of two syllables. Several words that begin with *sva*° pertain to Indra's heaven or celestial light, though it is to be admitted that other possibilities remain. Only a few Sanskrit words fit the meter of the ensuing ⏑ *yāvā* ⏓ construction, of which 'in the abode of prosperity' (<*śri*>*yāvā*<*se*>) or 'dwelling with Śrī' (<*śri*>*yāvā*<*sin*>) seem plausible in the present context.

[30]As we shall see in the next chapter, strophe 19 of the same inscription also refers to an image and/or temple that is "as pure as the disk of the moon" (de Casparis 1956: 206).

[31]In the *Mañjuśrīmūlakalpa,* the Buddha Śākyamuni states, "I have dwelled for a long time in the impenetrable wilderness that is *saṃsāra*. Whenever there are beings to be converted, I act. Just as there are [such] beings, I bestow beneficial rituals" (Wallis 2002: 71, see also 77, 157).

(mañju, 'charming, lovely, beautiful') **fine rain** (śīkaraḥ, sing. nom. of śīkara)[32] **of your discourses** (vyāhāra) **on the objective** (artha, 'aim, purpose').

A thorough discussion of strophe 12 must be postponed until the following chapter. For the moment we shall concentrate on the contents of the first half-verse, which may be provisionally translated in the following manner at this time:

Kanakakokanadodaravisphurad-
ruciradīpaśikhākṛtatāmasaḥ/

12. Doing away with the dark, with the flame of the splendid lamp quivering (like lightning) on the calyx of a lotus (made) of gold ... /

12. **Doing away with the dark** (kṛta-tāmasaḥ),[33] **with the flame** (śikhā) **of the splendid** (rucira) **lamp** (dīpa) **quivering** [like lightning] (visphurad = visphurat, present active participle of visphur)[34] **on the calyx**[35] (udara, 'belly, the thickest part of anything, womb') **of a lotus** (kokanado = kokanadaḥ) [made] **of gold** (kanaka) ... / [36]

The initial half-verse contains several ambiguities that may have been intended to exploit multiple possible meanings. The lamp (*dīpa*) eliminating the darkness is the metaphor *par excellence* for evoking the spiritual light kindled in bodhisattvas in the *Avataṃsaka-sūtra*. "Enlightening beings' lamp disperses darkness so people can see the right road" (Cleary 1993: 1117). "Great enlightening beings wish their bodies to be great bright lamps able to illumine all sentient beings" (*ibid.*, p 610). Bodhisattvas "are lamps for all sentient beings, because they cause them to see clearly the consequences of actions; they are lights for all sentient beings, because they cause the extremely profound wondrous truth to be illuminated; they are a torch for all in all times, because they cause them to clearly understand the truth; they are illumination for all worlds, because they cause them to enter the state of radiant light; they are clarifiers for all realms of being, because they reveal the powers of the enlightened" (*ibid.*, p. 470). Moreover, *śikhā* can mean 'peak, summit, pinnacle' as well as 'crest, top-knot and crown of the head'; and in Sri Lanka the architectural term for the *stūpa* dome is *udara* (*Mahāvaṃsa* XXXV,2). Besides, the doing away with the darkness potentially points back to the theme of crossing the impenetrable darkness, which was presented as a metaphor for *saṃsāra* in strophe eight. In particular, the comparison to an evening thundercloud therein suggests the potentiality of lightning while the stanza's unnamed divinity is directing his thoughts to a single point on the petals of his mind.

Other potential meaning ambiguities found in the initial half-verse of strophe 12 can be

[32]Acri, pc 23 Feb 2014: "There might also be a hidden reference/śleṣa, by assonance, to mañjuśikharaḥ, intended as mañju(śrī)śikhara 'the pinnacle/turret of Mañju(śrī)".
[33]As proposed by Sarkar (1971/2: I: 48(xiii).
[34]The poet's prior reference to an evening thundercloud in v.8 may account for his subsequent use of this word in v.12.
[35]*Udara* is a synonym of *garbha*, which specifically means calyx, among other things.
[36]Kālidāsa refers to lotus-shaped *kanakaka-mala* ear ornaments made of gold in *Meghadhūta* II, 2.

inferred from our knowledge of Buddhist architecture. For example, the base of the *stūpa* dome is often decorated with lotus petals, a motif that likewise applies to the single or double bases (*padmāsana*) for Buddhist sculptures.[37] Any exterior metal sculptures would have appeared to quiver like lightning whenever evening clouds temporarily obscured the rays of the moon. What's more, during the daytime metal icons would have shone forth resplendent and around the time of the sunset, they would have appeared like flames amidst the lengthening shadows cast by the temple complex's subsidiary shrines, gates and courtyard walls.

The Plaosan inscription appears to have been installed in its own small shrine located directly in front of the entire complex at a point in line with the wall that splits the innermost courtyard into two equal halves. The inscription's front-and-center placement potentially would have provided Sanskrit-literate visitors to this Buddhist religious foundation with a poetically elegant explanation for the visual phenomena they must have encountered whenever visiting the temple complex. The inscription's metaphorical allusions also suggest the possibility that the lost icons may even have served as meditative objects. For example, the contemplation of an oil lamp, a flame, or the light of the sun are all methods for applying the antidote for laxity during meditation practice:

> "If the object on which your attention is trained becomes vague, as if a sense of gloom has descended upon the mind, be it slight or dense, as the remedy for that, hold in mind and repeatedly familiarize yourself with images of light such as an oil-lamp, a flame, or sunlight. If you do this, there will arise great mental clarity and limpidity" (Wallace 1995: 214-215).

The lost icons and the temple plan

The second half-verse from strophe five is also potentially relevant to the discussion at hand: "twenty Jinas are shining forth here, accompanied by Bodhisattvas" (de Casparis 1956: 199). If we include the two exterior icons installed on the twin *vihāra* rooftops in our count, there were twenty images which could perhaps have been considered Buddhas in theory: the six, long since vanished, centrally placed images on the six altars along the back walls of the twin *vihāra* buildings together with their accompanying pairs of attendants on either side of each altar, which amounts to eighteen in total. It is possible that the dozen flanking images do not depict bodhisattvas but rather Buddhas in royal attire for signifying the Dharma and Saṅgha elements of the *ratnatraya*, which is suggested by their elevated emplacements on the main altars in each chamber as well as the Plaosan inscription's reference to an abode for the Three Jewels in v.10.[38] The remaining 28 additional sculptures —the four housed in the side-wall niches of the two entrance antechambers and the 24 collectively housed in the side-wall niches of the lower and upper storey in each of the six

[37] The lotus of the heart-mind is also the psychic foundation on which Buddhist deities or their seed syllables (*bīja*) are envisioned as residing on the disc of the moon during meditation (Snodgrass 1985: 204).

[38] "Nobody could, in an adequate Çloka, give a description (of this statue), which is endowed with an abode for the Three Jewels, and shines forth owing to the presence of those jewels that are the complete (transcendent) qualities" (de Casparis 1956: 201). This led de Casparis (1956, 201, n. 113) to speculate that a *mantra* pertaining to the *ratnatraya* might have been inserted into the cavity of the image. However, this could also apply to an external image featuring a lotus base on which a short text had been inscribed.

cellae—can be assigned hypothetically to the 'sons of the Conquerors' (*jinasuta*, e.g. bodhisattvas).

Counting the two lost icons on the *vihāra* rooftops, the sculptures associated with either building would have amounted to 24, or a total of 48. This provides a numerical fit for one of the symbolic cosmic diagrams, called *caṇḍita*, for Buddhist image houses (*garbhagṛha*) delineated in the *Mañjuśrīvāstuvidyaśāstra* (VVS), a medieval Mahāyāna Buddhist treatise discovered in Sri Lanka in 1983.[39] The portion of the text identified in the colophons as the *Citrakarmaśāstra* (CKS) refers to plans incorporating 49, 64, 81 and 225 squares.[40]

Based on the total number of statues encompassed within the two structures, it would appear that the closest numerically applicable *caṇḍita* for the central courtyard at Caṇḍi Plaosan Lor would be the *sthaṇḍila* plan of 49 (7x7) squares described in the CKS. Like all other *caṇḍita* variants, each of the 49 squares of the *sthaṇḍila* plan has a distinct Hindu divinity as its fundament. Nevertheless, only 48 squares are available for permanent assignment to Buddhist divinities. The singular *brāhmikapāda* at the center of the diagram is for "the *Brahma-pīṭha*, the standing place for the *karmārcya*", which is "a subsidiary image meant for use in ritual" (Marasinghe 1991: 33, 192). At Caṇḍi Plaosan Lor, a segment of the floor within each of the three interior chambers of either *vihāra* may have been set aside for ritual purposes. Each chamber is divided into three segments of unequal dimensions. The easternmost part is occupied by the altar, whereas the floor segment immediately in front of the altar is about 4-5 cm higher than the floor in the significantly larger western part (Long 2009: 289-290).

The interconnected double inner courtyard at Plaosan Lor potentially signifies the male and female gender elements of the site's twin image houses: the south *vihāra* only displays male human figures in the reliefs on its interior walls—generally presumed to represent this Buddhist religious foundation's donors—whereas the north *vihāra* only displays female human figures. In theory, the 20 Jinas mentioned in the Plaosan inscription can be assigned to locations within the plan's interior 24 squares: eight Buddhas to the *daivikapāda* (the six formerly occupying the central place on the altars in the three chambers of each *vihāra* plus one in the *harmikā-yaṣṭi* niche above the principal *stūpa* dome on the roof) and the 12 Buddha *parés* flanking the principal image on each altar) in the *mānuṣapāda*. The outermost tier of 24 squares forming the *paiśācapāda* would then be available for assignment to images of the sons of the Buddha (*jinasuta*), e.g. the bodhisattva images. This would leave the remaining four squares of the core area available for assignment to the additional four images within the twin *vihāra* structures: the two pairs of images in the

[39]Written in a Siṁhalese script, the VVS employs the word *caṇḍita* as its all-embracing term for referring to temple plans of various sizes and dimensional shapes. For this reason, I have previously proposed that *caṇḍi*, the Javanese word for temple, may be a derivative of this Mahāyāna Buddhist architectural term (Long 2011). A date anterior to the fourteenth or fifteenth centuries has been proposed for the sole surviving copy of this text, based on the cursive form of its Siṁhalese script, and with the entire text in its fully developed form believed to date from the eleventh to twelfth centuries. However, the initial three chapters discuss certain types of monastic structures only built between the third and ninth centuries, which suggests the VVS has retained data from substantially older texts (see Jayasuriya *et al.* 1995: 16).

[40]In all but name, these so-called cosmograms are comparable to known variants of the Hindu *vāstupuruṣa-maṇḍala*. Both types assign comparable lists of Hindu divinities to one or more squares in each plan, where they collectively serve as the underlying substrate on which the entire temple structure rests.

antechambers. In theory, these four sculptures can be considered as associated with the icons on the *vihāra* rooftops since they were housed in the antechambers closest to the building's exterior. Alternatively, the four corner squares of the outermost tier can be divided in half to enable the outermost group to contain 28 images, though the CKS only mentions this practice of dividing the squares into halves or thirds in reference to images depicting the Buddhist female deities that the text designates as *śakti*-s (Marasinghe 1991: 35). This appears to have been the case with respect to some of the images at Caṇḍi Kalasan, with two or more occupying a single square of the temple plan (see Long 2011: 6, figure 3). In any event, the square *sthaṇḍila* is, like all other known Hindu (*vāstupuruṣa-maṇḍala*) or Buddhist (*caṇḍita*) temple plans, an archetypal cosmogram rather than an architectural blueprint for delineating the temple's specific dimensions or sculptural emplacements. For example, the CKS states that the image house (*garbhagṛha*) can be circular, square, oval, rectangular, octagonal or even sixteen-sided (Marasinghe 1991: 21).

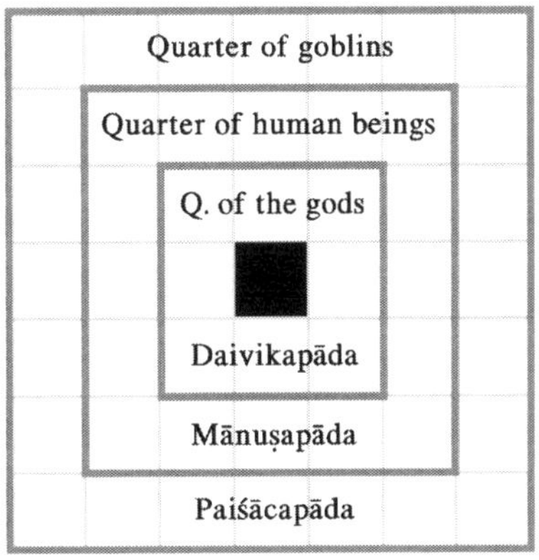

Fig. 6-12. The *sthaṇḍila* plan of 49 (7x7) squares from the CKS, with the central black square representing the *brāhmikapāda*.[41]

Relic deposits for bringing the temple to life

Each of the two exterior image emplacements discussed at the outset of this chapter may even have served a dual purpose: (a) to house a metal icon for symbolically spreading the light of the Dharma and (b) as a reliquary for the deposit of a *mantra* and/or other objects and possibly even placed within the compartments of a special repository constructed for this purpose. Though the VVS does not mention the *harmikā* specifically, the text's translators have surmised that in "all probability, this stanza [3.3.95], and the first line of the next deal with the *harmikā*; the relic casket was probably placed inside this" (Silva *et al.* 1995: 211, n. 11). Here is the translation for the verses from the third chapter of the VVS entitled 'The characteristics of the *caitya*' (*caityalakṣaṇam*):

> "It [the *harmikā*] is coated with white plaster and looks beautiful with rows of leaves. Strings of pearls and gems should be fixed in between rows of lotuses [3.3.95]. After it has been made to look beautiful with various kinds of ornaments, the expert builder should cause it to be firmly fixed. Above it there should be a *stūpi* made of metal (*loha*) [3.3.96]". The *mantra* should be deposited in the middle of it. The relics too should be deposited in it. They should be placed in a copper receptacle four or five *angulas* wide [3.3.97]. One should arrange nine portions in it and install there-in the nine deities beginning with Īśāna; he shall also deposit the eight kinds of grain and the five kinds of metal, in due order [3.3.98]. He shall also deposit there-in the following minerals ... [3.3.99]. In the centre, in the plot of Brahmā, (the following) *mantra* should be deposited by worthy

[41]See the design layout for the roof of Caṇḍi Mendut, which had originally integrated 49 *stūpa*-s (Long 2009: xxxviii, fig. 5).

builders. The material for inscribing the *mantra* should be a leaf of gold, silver or copper [3.3.100]" (Silva *et al.* 1995: 210).[42]

The relics housed within the *harmikā* of the Sinhalese *stūpa* were deposited for the purpose of bringing the entire architectural body to life. "Inseminating the womb (*garbha*) they quicken the dead mass of the masonry. The *Cūlavaṃsa*, describing the Tamil invasions of Sri Lanka, depicts the invaders as disemboweling the *stūpas* and depriving them of life by tearing out the relics. *Jīvita*, 'life', is the term used in the history : the sacred deposit constitutes the life of the construction" (Snodgrass 1985: 354).

Many boxes (*yantragala*) made of stone and brick, together with a few examples made of copper and bronze, have been discovered on Sri Lanka. They are typically subdivided into nine or 25 compartments and provided with a lid.[43] In those cases in which their deposits have not been disturbed they were found to contain the figures of deities, crystals and semi-precious stones, and other auspicious objects made copper, silver or gold foil (O'Connor 1966: 58). In Sri Lanka, however, these ritual depositories were typically placed within the *harmikā* at a location directly above the central axis of the edifice.

O'Connor (1966: 60) also noted that the same types of ritual deposits were placed in the *stūpa*-s constructed in ancient India from the time of King Aśoka. They had typically included buried objects, usually in combination with relics or a text, for the purpose of giving "the *stūpa* its internal vivifying and spiritual force" and hence were part of the essential ritual of consecration or *prāṇapratiṣṭhā*. Later Buddhism, the Mahāyāna and especially the Vajrayāna "codified the ritual of consecration which does without the presence of a relic. Instead it substituted the liturgical imposition of a divine spirit".

In Central Java, many of the older temple superstructures had collapsed in ancient times, which makes it impossible to assess the frequency with which their crowning elements had originally incorporated relic deposits. However, it appears likely that at least some Javanese sanctuaries had relic deposits installed on their rooftops.

> "In the ruins of the roof structure of one of the candis at the Gedong Songo complex a stone top piece was found which contained a bronze box in which there was a gold *lingga* (Krom 1923a I:238). On the Dieng plateau a cylindrical stone top piece on a lotus cushion was discovered near Candi Dwarawati. Under this several inscribed gold plates were found (Krom 1923a I:189). These examples would suggest that [a] *pripih* was placed in the superstructure of a candi" (Soekmono 1995: 31).

A metal statue of Vairocana found in the vicinity of the village Rejoso to the east of Plaosan has the well-known *ye dharma hetuprabhavā* expression of the Buddhist faith inscribed on its base, which was also the case with the previously mentioned bronze image of a female Buddhist divinity photographed by van Kinsbergen. So if metal statues likewise

---

[42]The same text's other translator Marasinghe (1991: 25, 193, 198, 231) characterized the *stūpi* as a type of *adhiṣṭhāna,* which he defined as the base of an edifice, or the base of any structure, such as a pinnacle. Among other things, *adhiṣṭhāna* also means 'a residence, abode, seat' (MWD).

[43]The latter are miniature versions of the Sinhalese plan for laying out entire monasteries called an *upapīṭha*, which consists of a cosmogram containing 5x5 squares (see Marasinghe 1989: figs. 3, 8a, 9-11, 17).

featuring short inscriptions on their bases had been mounted on the twin *vihāra* rooftops they presumably could have accomplished the dual purpose of depicting a divinity as well as depositing a short text at the level of the *harmikā*.

The ritual deposits found beneath the north *vihāra* at Caṇḍi Plaosan Lor

During the systematic demolition of the base of the north *vihāra* at Plaosan Lor during 1993 in preparation for the total restoration of the entire edifice, archaeologists noted the existence of a 3.5 m x 3.5 m. square pit beneath the first floor of the building's central chamber that had previously been disturbed, presumably by treasure hunters (Soekmono 1995: 121-122; Gutomo & Wirasanti 1998: 53-55; and Miksic *et al.* 2001: 323-324). At a depth of 2.5 m. below ground level and directly below the central chamber were discovered four stone relic caskets (*peripih* or *pripih*) with lids, of which three were found empty (see figure 6-13). Only the one occupying the southeast corner of the pit was undisturbed. The interior space of this last relic casket contained inscribed gold and silver foils, fourteen gold coins, a worn bronze scroll, gold and bronze dust mixed with soil as well as a bronze vessel containing the following seed varieties: jambe, Job's tears (*Coix lachrymal*), kemiri (candlenut, *Aleurites moluccana*), nutmeg, pinang (*Areca catechu*), and coffee (Miksic *et al.* 2001: 323). In the vicinity of the one intact *peripih* were found a bronze mirror with handle, a worn bronze scroll, gold and bronze dust mixed with soil, as well as scrolls of gold and silver inscribed with the well-known '*ye dharma hetu...*' expression of the Mahāyāna Buddhist Faith as well as esoteric Buddhist *dhāraṇī*-s.

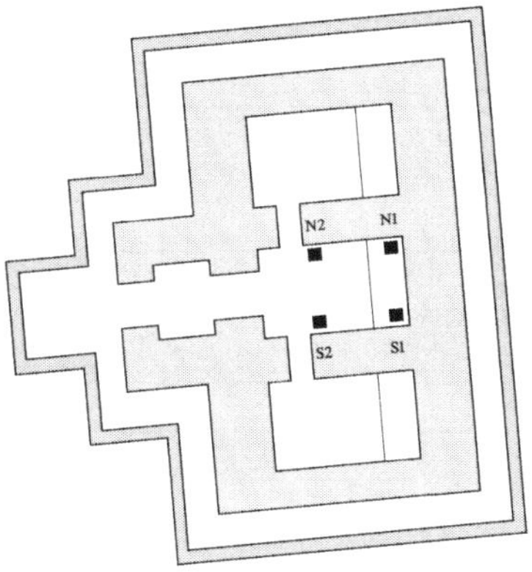

Fig. 6-13. Four *peripih* (N1-N2 and S1-S2) **in the pit beneath the central chamber of the north *vihāra* at Caṇḍi Plaosan Lor.** (See also Soekmono 1995, plate 7).

The discovery of loose gold, silver and bronze artifacts inside the pit is interesting in that it is unlikely that treasure hunters would have discarded these items if they had found them in the three empty *peripih* discovered by archaeologists in 1993. Soekmono (1995: 31) noted that "careful excavations of pits at Candi Ijo and in the Loro Jonggrang complex [have] proved that both pripih caskets and loose pripih were deposited".

Given that the twin *vihāra* structures at Caṇḍi Plaosan Lor occupy the central courtyard, which has a wall in the middle with an interconnecting gate, these two edifices can be considered as comprising the principal *garbhagṛha* unit for the entire temple complex. An undisturbed stone box (*pripih*) for housing consecration deposits also was uncovered beneath the foundation of the northern *vihāra*, but it only contained sand,[44] which suggests

[44]A small bronze image of a bodhisattva thought to be representative of Padmapāṇi—replete with a *dhāraṇī* inscribed on a folded silver plate that had been inserted in the bottom of the image's base—was recovered during the excavation of the northern cella of the south *vihāra* (Oudheidkundig Verslag 1950: 30). However, no indications were given that would lead us to presume that this image had been placed under the floor as a ritual deposit.

that the inscribed gold and silver scrolls as well as other artifacts found beneath the floor of the northern *vihāra* had served as the principal deposits for both buildings.[45]

> "An excavation was carried out in the area beneath the central chamber during thc Japanese period [= of occupation, 1942-1945] but did not yield any results. This time the excavation was done deeper and brought to light at a depth of 170 meter (+/- 0.25 cm) underneath the base of crushed stone the head of a statue, a fragment of stone from the temple's frame and the broken left hand of an image. These findings confirm that this place was already spoiled by treasure-hunters in the past.
> "Below these findings was found a sandstone box measuring 0.5 m, the sides of which had cracked. Considering that the soil around the box was still undisturbed then surely it is in its original place. However, after the box was opened and its contents inspected, it was found to consist of fine sand only.
> "Underneath this stone box there is yet another layer of river-stones of 0.5 meters thick" (Dinas Purbakala 1959: 26).

Two gold-leaf inscriptions discovered underneath the central chamber of the north *vihāra* at Caṇḍi Plaosan Lor were provisionally transcribed by Kusen (Gutomo & Wirasanti 1998: 54; Miksic *et al.* 2001: 323-324). More recently, Griffiths (2014) has published photographs of the inscribed rolls, together with substantially revised transcriptions of what turns out to be several *dhāraṇī* texts.

Griffiths noted that the gold-leaf scroll featuring six inscribed lines is a variant of the *Bodhigarbhālaṃkāralakṣadhāraṇī,* examples of which have been found in India, Afghanistan, China, Tibet and elsewhere on the Asian mainland (Strauch 2009).

> "(1) [siddham] namo bhagavate śākyamuṇaye tathāgatāyarhate samyak◊samvuddhāya tadyathā ∘oṁ vodhi vodhi vodhi satvetathāgata(2)gocare | dhara dhara hara hara prahara prahara mahāvodhicittadhare | culu culu śatasahasrarasmisañcodite (3) sarvvatathāgata bhāṣite | guṇāguṇavati | vuddhaguṇa ∘avabhās(e) mili mili gagamatala-pratiṣṭite (4) sarvvatathāgatathāgatādhiṣṭite | mabhastale | sama sama prasama prasama sarvvapāpaśamaṇe | sarvapāpe (5) viśodhani | hulu hulu | vodhimārgasamprasthite sarvvatathāgatapratiṣṭhite śuddhe śuddhe svāhā || (6) ∘oṁ sarvvatathāgata-vyalokite jaya jaya svāhā || ∘oṁ huru huru jayamukhe svāhā || : || [fleurons]"

> "'Homage to the Lord Śākyamuni, the Tathāgata, the Arhant who is completely awakened. [The dhāraṇī is] like this: OM. Awaken awaken, you (female deity of this dhāraṇī) who belong to the domain of all Tathāgatas! Take take! Steal steal, you who hold the thought of great awakening! CULU CULU, you who are impelled a hundred thousand rays, who have been uttered by all Tathāgatas! O virtue, O you who possess virtue! You who possess the light of the virtues of a Buddha! MILI MILI, you who are established on the vault of the sky, you who are governed by all Tathāgatas, you sky-

[45]*Mayamatam* 12, 1-3a: "A foundation deposit with all the components (prescribed) is a source of success; an incomplete deposit or the absence of any one component leads to failure; this is why the foundation deposit should be set in place with the utmost care and without error" (Dagens 1994: 121).

surface! Calm, calm! Appease, appease, you who appease all evil, you who purify all evil! HULU HULU, you who have set out on the path to great awakening, you who are established by all Tathāgatas, pure one, pure one, SVĀHĀ! OM. You who are observed by all Tathāgatas, win, win, SVĀHĀ! OM. HURU HURU, you who are the face of victory, SVĀHĀ!'" (Griffiths 2014: 162-163).[46]

Among the questions that remain to be answered is why were these three *dhāraṇī* texts selected for use as ritual deposits at this particular site and what relationship, if any, do they have with respect to the lost icons originally installed above them on the *stūpa-harmikā* crowning the central chamber as possibly suggested by the reference to 'you who are established on the vault of the sky' as well as the allusions to 'a hundred thousand rays' and 'the light of the virtues of a Buddha'. Griffiths remarked that the three *dhāraṇī* segments presented above exhibit several variations from the other known examples. Hence one also naturally wonders whether modifications had been made for a particular purpose.

The gold-leaf scroll with four inscribed lines begins with the traditional *ye dharmā hetuprabhavā* formula,[47] which is immediately followed by three distinct segments paying homage (a) to the *samyak-sambuddhas;* (b) to the Blessed Jewel-Peacock (*ratnaśikhine*), the Tathāgata, the Arhat whose *dhāraṇī* is '*oṃ ratna ratna ratnasaṃbhave svāhā*' (presumably Ratnasambhava, whose *vāhana* is the peacock); and (c) to the Blessed Mañjuśrī Kumārabhūta. This leads us to wonder whether this text may pertain to the image triad placed in the south cella of either *vihāra*, where sculptures of Mañjuśrī and a divinity displaying a flaming jewel attribute flank the missing principal image.

"(1) [siddham] ye dharmmā hetuprabhavā hetun teṣān tathāgato hy avadat teṣaṃ ca yo nirodha °evamvādī mahāśramaṇaḥ ‖ namaḥ saptānāṃ (2) samyaksaṃvuddhakoṭīnāṃ tadyathā cala cula cunde svāhā ‖ namo bhagavate ratnaśikhine tathāgatāyārhate samyaksaṃvuddhāya (3) tadyathā °oṃ ratna ratna ratnasaṃbhave svāhā ‖ namo bhagavate mañjuśriye kumāra kumāra(bhū)tāya tadyathā amala amala amalame(4)trāya svā(hā)".

"We have here the ye dharmāḥ formula, followed by a dhāraṇī called the Saptasaptatisamyak-saṃbuddhakoṭibhiruktā 'Proclaimed by seventy-seven crores of completely awakened ones', and two further dhāraṇīs of which the first is attested in transliteration in the Chinese canon (Taishō 1383, 21:904b), while the last (of doubtful reading) remains unidentified" (Griffiths 2014: 164).

[46]Acri, pc 23 Feb. 2014: "Here Griffiths' translation of guṇa as 'virtue' seems to me an edulcorated, 'ethicized' version of a word that in the medieval indic world undoubtedly meant 'magical powers/supernatural qualities' (see Acri 2011: 62). Even a neutral translation, such as 'property', implies that these properties, because they were of the Buddha, were of a supernatural character".

[47]All things proceed from some cause; this cause has been declared by the Tathāgata; all things will cease to exist; this is what is declared by the Great Ascetic.

VII: The Caṇḍi Plaosan inscription

In 1816, Crawfurd discovered an inscription on the west side of Caṇḍi Plaosan Lor at a spot that coincided with the dividing wall separating the temple complex's north and south *vihāra*-s:

> "To the present group of buildings there are two entrances, both to the western side, and each guarded by a pair of the gigantic warders.... About midway between the gates I discovered a slab of black stone with an inscription in the Deva Nagari characters, much effaced and I fear illegible, except in one or two places. The stone is at least a foot thick, and as it bears no marks of the application of blows it seems somewhat difficult to account for its being broken as it is, unless we suppose that it was placed in an elevated situation and fractured in its fall" (Crawfurd as cited by Bernet Kempers 1949: 181).

Fig. 7-1. Caṇḍi Plaosan inscription, inventory No. D.82 (photo credit: Shigehisa Taguchi).

The inscription formerly had been housed in its own separate shrine (see figure 7-2). This special treatment suggests that the presumed Plaosan Lor foundation charter may have been regarded as a holy relic worthy of veneration on its own. The small shrine's location is outside of the outer walled perimeter that surrounds the subsidiary temples and occupies the same north-south line as the *dvārapāla* images, which have a protective function.

Fig. 7-2. The small shrine formerly housing the Plaosan inscription.

Hoepermans (1913: 234) had mentioned the existence of another segment coming from the same inscription, but it was not until 1976 that fragments were recovered from the site (Boechari 1976: 18, n. 13). However, nothing was ever published about the contents of these fragments and indeed it is not even certain that their whereabouts are known today. Hence our discussion of the Plaosan inscription must be limited to the inscribed stone numbered D.82 in the National Museum at Jakarta—the only segment available to J. G. de Casparis for the transcription and translation he published in 1956.

De Casparis (1956: 177-178) thought that the most probable dating for this inscription would be before the mid-ninth century, though the text itself mentions neither a definitive date nor the name of the reigning king. The original inscription contained 23 lines of a Sanskrit text in the Siddham script, but nothing was recovered from the initial four lines. Still, de Casparis remarked that enough trace elements remained to deduce their former existence. Only text fragments were readable from line five through the end of line 13.

De Casparis' abbreviated coverage of the inscription's opening lines, together with a few questionable translations in key strophes, have provided other researchers with a somewhat misleading view about what this document actually states. For example, his assertion that strophe 18 refers to a temple that 'was made different' (i.e. had been renovated) is doubtful. The archaeological record does not support his contention that the twin *vihāra* structures at Plaosan Lor had undergone major modifications over time. The frequently cited remark made by Dumarçay (1986: 50 and 2007: 211, n. 5) about the discovery of an earlier foundation underneath one of the twin buildings in 1951-1952 appears to be based on a misreading of the Indonesian archaeological reports.

De Casparis initially proposed that the compositum *bhūjayottuṅgade<vaḥ>* in line six would be the consecration name for the image of the Śailendra dynasty's supposed founder, presented in the guise of a bodhisattva *cakravartin*, "or, to be more precise, the name attributed by the later Śailendra generations in the ninth century A.D. The name has not been traced in other sources" (de Casparis 1956: 184). As support for his original bodhisattva *cakravartin* theory he cited the composer's use of rain and cloud metaphors in strophe eight, presumably for the purpose of evoking the tenth bodhisattva stage installed on the *dharmameghabhūmi,* which is also known as the *abhiṣekabhūmi* (de Casparis 1956: 183, n. 33). Moreover, de Casparis sought to link *bhūjayottuṅgadeva* with the compositum *varanarādhirājarāja* that appears in the final strophe of the Plaosan inscription.

> "It may be concluded that this supreme king was endowed with powers characteristic of the Bodhisattvas abiding on the very highest *bhūmi*. Therefore, the last strophe of the inscription is very probably an invocation addressed to the same Bhūjayottuṅgadeva conceived of as a Bodhisattva-Cakravartin" (de Casparis 1956: 184-185).

In conformance with an unsubstantiated theory first proposed by Cœdès, de Casparis initially proposed that the Śailendra dynasty had originated in the kingdom of Fu-Nan. This was based on his conjecture that the compositum *varanarādhirājarāja* had pertained to an otherwise unknown sixth-century king from mainland Southeast Asia. His speculations are obviously untenable in the absence of any supporting data and de Casparis himself subsequently abandoned them and endorsed a Javanese origin hypothesis for the Śailendra dynasty. "It now seems more likely that they were purely Javanese.... The Śailendras, probably a local family from the Kedu, possibly from the area just around Borobudur, carved themselves a kingdom in the fertile valleys" (de Casparis 1990: 14).

The inscription's initial line fragments

Given that de Casparis was unable to definitively establish the meter for the verses presented in lines five through 13, he did not publish any full translations for them. However, he surmised that the verse fragments in lines five and nine through thirteen had been composed in Āryā meter and that lines six and seven contain parts of strophes composed in Mālinī meter. We shall more closely examine these points in the following discussion of all of these text fragments, which includes speculative translations that must be viewed with caution given the lack of clarity about the specific meters in play. By contrast, de Casparis fully translated all the remaining lines of the inscription, which contain strophes composed in the Anuṣṭubh (1-10), Dhrutavilambhitam (11-17) and Praharṣiṇī (18-19) meters, respectively.[1]

Lines one through four. The contents of the first four lines of the Plaosan inscription shall forever remain a mystery, unless perhaps missing fragments rediscovered more than 45 years ago one day make a miraculous reappearance.[2] Given that the surviving portion of the

[1]Throughout this chapter we shall refer to the text fragments in the initial part of the inscription according to their line numbers (5-13), whereas the strophes for which de Casparis identified the meter are designated as vs.1-19.

[2]Still, Boechari (2012: 163-164, n. 13) was uncertain whether the fragments from a big stone inscription that he found in a small building on the west side of Plaosan Lor's outer yard actually belonged to D.82 or to a separate inscription. I visited the archaeological station near Caṇḍi Plaosan in April of 2005 to learn where these missing fragments were kept and whether they had ever been transcribed or translated, but the director of the facility declined to comment other than to say that his office was working on a detailed study of the temple complex that would be coming out 'shortly'. We are still awaiting its appearance. Sundberg (2006: 107, n. 16) likewise attempted to locate these crucial fragments without success. "They seem to have tragically disappeared without a trace, the second Śailendra inscription to go missing.... I am indebted to the one individual still alive who examined the inscription with Boechari, Prof. Riboet Darmosoetropo, who

Plaosan inscription does not contain a conventional dateline, one or more of the missing fragments may have supplied the requisite astronomical details. We would also expect the text to have opened with one or more invocatory verses. The Plaosan inscription's reference to an abode for the Three Jewels in strophe 10 suggests the possibility that the text had opened with a triad of verses dedicated to the Buddha, Dharma and Saṅgha, respectively. If composed in a lengthy meter such as Śārdūlavikrīḍitam (Abhayagirivihāra and Kayumwuṅan charters) or Sragdharā (Kayumwuṅan inscription), the benedictory segment of the Plaosan inscription would have occupied three full lines plus a fraction of the fourth. Or, if we apply the model of the Kañjuruhan charter (Griffiths 2011a: 37), the opening verse may have included the date and with the remainder of the missing text having presented a genealogical account of the inscription's promulgator.

Line five. De Casparis believed that the first readable text fragment in the top right corner of the stone presents part of a verse composed in measures (*mātrā*), specifically Āryā meter. However, de Casparis also expressed doubt about his reading of the italicized segments of the transcription.

[5] ... ... vijara*kāya*vibham=vibhāti guṇavi*bhāmalapu*trajananaṃ yais=taruṇavala-
[5] ... ... ⏑ ⏑ ⏑ – ⏑ ⏑ – ⏑ – ⏑ ⏑ ⏑ ⏑ – ⏑ ⏑ – ⏑ ⏑ ⏑ – – ⏑ ⏑ ⏑ ⏑ ⏓ ...

Despite de Casparis' surmise (1956: 178 and 192, n. 67), line five is clearly incompatible with the Āryā meter. The analytical options available to us include supposing that the half-verse or complete strophe had ended with the word *yais*, despite the lack of any *daṇḍa* at this stage of de Casparis' transcription, or presuming that the line is composed in a meter that has not yet been identified. The first option enables the fragment through *yais* to be read as the first hemistich of a strophe in Āryā meter only after one presumes that the uncertain segment <*bhāmalapu*> must contain two errors (◊):

| - - - ⏑ | ⏑ ⏑ – | ⏑ ⏑ – ‖ ⏑ – ⏑ | ⏑ ⏑ ⏑ ◊ | ⏑ ⏑ ◊ ⏑ | ⏑ ⏑ – | – ‖   hypothetical Āryā meter hemistich

Under the second option, the text can only be translated freestyle given that the meter has not been identified. Keeping in mind that any translation of such a problematic verse can only be viewed as speculative—as is likewise the case with the remainder of the text fragments preceding what de Casparis had labeled as 'strophe one' for this inscription—the entire line may be interpreted in the following manner:

L5. He shines forth devoid of delusion in an ageless body through which the splendors of his virtues are coming into existence in a son without blemish; as the power just risen ... .

L5. **He shines forth** (vibhāti, third person sing. present of vi- √bhā) **devoid of delusion** (vibham = vi-, 'without'; bham, sing. acc. of bha) **in an ageless** (vijara) **body** (kāya) **through which** (yais, pl. instr. pronoun) **the splendors** (vibhā) **of his virtues** (guṇa) **are coming into existence** (jananam,

mentioned to me that the fragments were very hard to read. Boechari's notes on this inscription also seem to have disappeared".

sing. acc. of janana) **in a son** (putra) **without blemish** (amala); **as the power** (vala = bala)[3] **just risen** (taruṇa)... .[4]

Line six. The next several lines do indeed appear to contain fragments from multiple verses composed in the Mālinī meter (15 syllables per *pāda*), which begins with six short syllables. However, only *pāda b* and *pāda c* of a complete verse remain to be read in line six. The compound *taruṇavala* at the end of line five also would conform with the Mālinī meter in theory, but the lack of a double *daṇḍa* following *yais* makes this interpretation problematic and so the possibility remains that this may have been the opening syllables of a strophe composed in a completely different meter.

On the posterior part of the stone, the number of syllables per line ranges between 65 and 79 syllables, and with the average count being 73 syllables. Given that the presumed Mālinī half-verse in the latter part of line six only amounts to 30 syllables, there would have been ample space at the beginning of lines six and seven to have accommodated the two quarters missing from this verse. The first half of line seven likewise originally had offered sufficient space in theory for the initial segment from yet another stanza in Mālinī meter.

[6] ... ... svaparahitaguṇasya sva ... ādvitīyaṃ /
smaraharavaravarṣṣad = bhūjayottuṅgade-<vaḥ>

L6. ... (full) of virtue for the well-being of self and others (he is) without a parallel for his own (subjects); producing the rains which are the boons that are desire-destroying, the lofty lord of the arising victory (bhūjayottuṅgade<vaḥ>) ... .

L6. ... [full] **of virtue** (guṇasya, sing genitive of guṇa) **for the well-being** (hita, 'welfare, benefit') **of self** (sva) **and others** (para) [he is] **without a parallel** (advitīyam, sing. acc. of advitīya) **for his own** (sva) ... [subjects (<prajā>)[5]]; **producing the showers** (varṣṣad = varṣat, present active participle of √vṛṣ) **which are the boons** (vara) **that are desire-destroying** (smarahara), **the lofty lord of the arising victory** (bhūjayottuṅgade<vaḥ>) ... .

Though Damais (1968: 438) argued that nothing is stated in line six that would discount the possibility of Bhūjayottuṅgadeva being the consecration name of the reigning king who had promulgated the inscription, one wonders about the absence of a preceding honorific such as Śrī, Śrīmān or Śrīmat.[6] Many of the stand-alone *perwara* and *stūpa* constructions in the temple complex's outer yard originally had displayed short votive inscriptions featuring the honorifics, titles and personal names of their aristocratic donors.

[3]Or, the initial part of a compound having to do with power or strength.
[4]According to Chandra (pc 16 Dec. 2010), *kāya-vibhā* and *guṇa-vibhā* are the binary correlates of the physical and ethical merits of a king.
[5]Emendation proposed by Chandra (pc 3 Dec. 2010).
[6]For example, Rakai Kayuwaṅi was also known as Śrī Bhuvaneśvara Viṣṇusakalatmakadigvijaya Parakramotuṅgadeva Lokapāla lañcana (860) as well as Śrī Sajjanotsavatuṅga (882); Rakai Balitung was Śrī Īśvarakeśavotsavatuṅga; Rake Hino Mpu Siṇḍok was Śrī Īśānavikrama Dharmottuṅgadeva (see Damais 1952). Other Javanese kings for which we lack the corresponding coronation titles may have had similar *abhiṣeka* names.

First half of line six:																
˘	˘	˘	˘	˘	˘	—	—	,	—	˘	—	—	˘	—	—	
Second half of line six:																
sva	pa	ra	hi	ta	gu	ṇa	sya	,	sva	˘	—	ād	vi	tī	yaṃ	/
sma	ra	ha	ra	va	ra	va	rṣṣa	,	dbhū	ja	yo	ttu	ṅga	de	[vaḥ]	
First half of line seven:																
˘	˘	˘	˘	˘	˘	—	—	,	—	˘	—	—	˘	—	—	//
˘	˘	˘	˘	˘	˘	—	—	,	—	˘	—	—	˘	—	—	
Second half of line seven:																
˘	˘	˘	˘	˘	˘	—	—	,	—	˘	—	—	˘	sa	ṅgaṃ	/
˘	˘	ti	ku	śa	la	rā	ge	,	ya	śca	vṛ	ddhi	mvi	bha	rtti	//

Fig. 7-3. Verses that may have been composed in Mālinī[7] meter.

The absence of any honorific immediately in advance of *bhūjayottuṅgade<vaḥ>* leads us to consider whether this compositum may actually be an epithet. The Sanskrit adjective *uttuṅga* means 'lofty, high, tall'. So the entire compositum can literally mean the 'lofty lord (◦*uttungadeva*) of the arising (*bhū*) victory (*jaya*)'.[8] By contrast, de Casparis had surmised that the principal image mentioned in the inscription had depicted a tenth-stage bodhisattva on the threshold of becoming a Jina, which fits the epithet hypothesis proposed above. In any event, *bhūjayottuṅgadevaḥ* would be a highly appropriate designation for any Buddhistic images enshrined on the crowning elements of the twin *vihāra*-s at Plaosan Lor.

Featured in the Old Javanese Kakawin *Smaradahana* ('The burning of Smara, the god of desire'), *smarahara* is a well-known epithet for Śiva that literally means the 'love-destroyer'. Though the phrase *smarahara* is comparable to the Buddha's famous epithet *māra-niṣūdana* ('Slayer of Desire') it would be highly unusual for the poet to have used this as a literal reference to the Buddha. Sarkar (1971/2: I: 48xi) interpreted the use of *smarahara* in line six as follows: "... with virtues for well-being of self and others, he is without a parallel—that Uttuṅgadeva with arms showering boons like the killer of the god of love (i.e. Mahādeva)".[9] And Chandra (pc 3 Dec. 2010) took this one step further by suggesting that *bhūjayottuṅgadeva* had been the consecration name of a Śivaite monarch: "He is the Bhūjayottuṅgadeva (on whom) the Destroyer of Desire (=Śiva) is showering boons". The viewpoints of Sarkar and Chandra cannot be excluded from consideration, especially given that we would expect the composer of any Sanskrit *praśasti* to have devoted ample space to the glorification of the reigning monarch. However, the translation previously submitted above follows de Casparis' lead in presuming that the poet had not intended for *smarahara* to function as a direct reference to the deity Śiva in this particular instance.

[7]According to Huet (2012), Mālinī means 'who wears a garland, crowned, surrounded by'.

[8]Coincidentally, *bhūjaya* as an architectural term for designating a variety of *maṇḍapa* in Gujarat and elsewhere in ancient India. "The maṇḍapa having 32 pillars 8 forming the central octagon and the rest surrounding them is known as Bhūjaya in the canons. The maṇḍapa of the Neminatha temple at Cirnar illustrates this variety" (Sompura 1968: 375).

[9]Aside from the issue of shortening the vowel ū in *bhūjayo*, I do not see the merit in only giving a partial translation for *bhūjayottuṅgade<vaḥ>*.

Line seven. The surviving text fragments in line seven are compatible with an abbreviated half-verse (two quarters) composed in the Mālinī meter (see figure 7-3 above), and with the content also suggesting the possibility that it may have pertained to the reigning monarch.

[7] ... ... saṅgaṃ / ... ... ti kuśalarāge yaś=ca vṛddhim=*vibha*rtti // śara-[10]

L7. [Having a propensity for] ... ... / ... ... and the one who bestows prosperity out of affection for the welfare (of his subjects).

L7. [Having a propensity for (saṅgam)][11] ... ... / ... ... **and** (ca) **the one who** (yaś = yaḥ) **bestows** (vibhartti = bibharti, third person sing. present of √bhṛ) **prosperity** (vṛddhim, sing. acc. of vṛddhi) **out of affection** (rāge = sing. locative of rāga) **for the welfare** (kuśala) ... [of his subjects (<prakṛ>ti)].[12]

Line eight (unidentified meter). Only the first of the two readable text segments in this line is capable of fulfilling the requirements of the Mālinī meter, whereas the second contains one syllable too many (de Casparis 1956: 193, n. 72).[13] However, the latter text segment does meet the requirements in theory for the end of one hemistich composed in the Āryā meter, whereas the first segment does not.

[8] ... ... jamvulakṣmyāḥ / ... ... lolakīrttyā vilokinyāḥ // sa-

L8. ... owing to the loveliness of the rose apple (tree or fruit) ... / on account of the one who is aware of the quivering glory ... ... //

L8. ... **owing to the loveliness** (lakṣmyāḥ, sing. ablative of lakṣmī) **of the rose apple** [tree or fruit] (jamvu = jambu) ... /[14] **on account of the one who is aware** (vilokinyāḥ, f. sing. ablative of vilokin)[15] **of the quivering** (lola)[16] **glory** (kīrttyā = kīrtyā, sing. genitive of kīrti) ... ... //

[10]The final component in line seven, which appears at the beginning of a new verse, is *śara,* which can mean 'an arrow, shaft' or 'to rend, destroy'. Many Sanskrit words beginning with *śara°* pertain to arrows, archery or the autumn, with the latter due to the autumn season's association with the constellation of the Archer Sagittarius (Dhanu, 'Bow'). For example, *smaraśara*, 'arrows of Desire', appears in a later strophe from this inscription. Elsewhere in this inscription, however, we find the word *śaraṇam,* 'place of refuge, shelter'.

[11]This Sanskrit word appears in a fragmentary context in several of the Śailendra inscriptions. Among other things, *saṅga* can mean 'relation to, association with; devotion to, propensity for'. I have placed the above translation in brackets to indicate its speculative nature due to the lack of context.

[12]Emendation proposed by Chandra (pc 3 Dec. 2010).

[13]One might be tempted to dismiss this as a compositional error, but de Casparis (1956: 178) remarked that in all other respects the language of the text is correct and "no grammatical or orthographical errors could be noticed.... The strophes run remarkably well and might even have some poetical merit".

[14]De Casparis (1956: 180) interpreted this text fragment as a reference to a queen from Jambudvīpa (i.e. India), whilst Sarkar (1971/2: I: 48xi) viewed it as naming Lakṣmī, the goddess of fortune and beauty.

[15]Vilokinī ('She who is aware') is the name of one of eight goddesses associated with Padmanartteśvara (Bhattacharyya 1958: 135), a form of Avalokiteśvara mentioned in the *Nāmasaṃgīti* (v.105).

[16]*Lola* is an epithet of Lakṣmī that means 'the fickle or changeable one'. Both the goddess and her consort Viṣṇu display a 'dangling hand gesture' (*lola-hasta-mudrā*) for which the outfacing palm is stretched downwards along the side of the body and with the extended fingers pointing down.

At first blush it would seem that the two segments belong to different strophes. But the two fragments contain expressions that potentially can be interpreted as different allusions to the same goddess Lakṣmī and therefore may also pertain to a royal spouse.[17]

Line nine (unidentified meter). The first of the two text fragments from this line is compatible with a (first) hemistich in Āryā meter, whereas the second fragment immediately preceding the double *daṇḍa* is not.[18]

[9]……… … … satatārthakāriṇī varadā / … bhāryyā tāreva virājati // gatinā kuśala-

L9. A young woman (granting boons) who is bringing about uninterrupted opulence … / … (and) a spouse being eminent like Tāra // … skillful through expedient means …

L9. A young woman [granting boons] (varadā, sing nom. of varadā)[19] **who is bringing about** (kāriṇī, f. sing. nom. of kārin)[20] **uninterrupted** (satata) **opulence** (artha) … / … [and] **a spouse** (bhāryyā = bhāryā, sing. nom. of bhāryā) **being eminent** (virājati, sing. third person present of vi-√rāj)[21] **like Tāra** (tāreva) // … **skillful** (kuśala) **through expedient means** (gatinā)][22] …

The phrase *tāreva,* 'like Tārā', is a comparative allusion to the Buddhist goddess Tārā.[23] "This line highlights the role of the wife who is dignified like Tārā. She is a constant companion and guide in acts that are of advantage to the husband and thus she is a boon. She is intelligent in working out the logistics (*gati*) in moments of need. Gati is help (*kā gatiḥ* 'what help is there', often used in Sanskrit drama). The wife and husband are thus a dynamic bi-unity in the success of grand achievements" (Chandra, pc 3 Dec. 2010).

Line ten. The following Sanskrit text segments comply with the requirements of Āryā meter. However, de Casparis' transcription (1956: 193) indicates the presence of a double *daṇḍa* following *satkāyam*, though it appears at first blush that a only a single *daṇḍa* is warranted.

---

[17]The conception of the queen as the *śrī lakṣmi* or *rājalakṣmi*—"the embodiment of a dynasty's legitimacy, right to political authority and magical religious power"—appears to have been current in Central Java during the mid-ninth century. "Furthermore, the Old Javanese kakawin *Rāmāyaṇa*, dated to this same period, in Canto 24.96 refers, in the context of Wibhiṣana's consecration as ruler of Lāngkā following the death of his brother Rāvaṇa, to the return of the rājalakṣmī to the kingdom of Langkā" (Worsley 2006: 238; see also Acri 2010: 490-491).

[18]The latter text segment in line 9 cannot have been composed in either Udgīti or Āryā meter because an amphibrach (⏑ — ⏑), such as *vi-rā-ja*, cannot fall in the seventh discrete segment of either hemistich.

[19]*Varadā* is an epithet of Lakṣmī as the gracious giver of boons (Coburn 1984: 160).

[20]Perhaps this is a pun on *kariṇī,* ('female elephant'), which can conceivably convey several nuances. First and foremost, there is no such thing as an antisocial female elephant. Her "apparent altruistic behavior" includes frequent interactions with other elephant families, clans, and sub-populations (Sukumar 2003: 185-186).

[21]*Virājati* can express "...the idea of 'being illustrious, conspicuous, eminent' in various contexts dealing with good fortune and prosperity" (Gonda 1966: 119).

[22]Chandra (pc 10 Dec. 2010) interpreted *gatinā* as the sing. instrumental of *gati*. Given that *gati* has the feminine rather than the masculine gender, however, the singular instrumental would properly be *gatyā.*

[23]*Tāreva* also appears in the Nālandā inscription (Sastri 1942: 101) in relation to the consort of 'that king' previously described as 'the foremost warrior on battlefields' (*samarāgravīra*) in the same charter.

According to Chandra (pc 3 Dec. 2010), the stanza refers to the construction of a glorious image (*sat-kāya*) and its associated montane[24] temple (*bhūbhṛtam*).[25] "*Kāya* means a three-dimensional image, in contrast to a two-dimensional painting. This distinction is clear in Tibetan where *sku* '*kāya*' is an icon, and *than-ka* 'plain' is a painting on a flat surface." Though we shall diagram this below as if it were two halves of a single verse in Āryā meter, the double *daṇḍa* following *satkāyam* does suggest that the composer had intended the reader to consider each segment as a stand-alone statement.

[10] ……………… ñjabhṛto ……………… <a>ṣṭapādasatkāyaṃ //
janayām=vabhūva bhū*yo* bhūbhṛtam=adyāṣṭahastāṅśam //

Hypothetical verse diagram in Āryā meter:

| - - - - | - - - - | ⏑ ⏑ — ‖ - - - - | - - - ⏑ | ⏑ — ⏑ | — — | — ‖ first hemistich
| ⏑ ⏑ — | ⏑ — ⏑ | — — ‖ — ⏑ ⏑ | — — | ⏑ | — — | — ‖ second hemistich

L10. ... the venerable image of ... (eight) 'feet' ... // Furthermore, he begat 'the mountain (or king)' ... [see the discussion segment below for speculative translations for the rest of this last text fragment]. //

L10. ...[26] **the venerable** (sat) **image** (kāyam, sing. acc. of kāya, 'body') **of** ... [eight (<a>ṣṭa)] **'feet'** (pāda) ... // **Furthermore** (bhūyo in comp. for bhūyas),[27] **he begat**[28] (janayāṃ-vabhūva = janayām-babhūva, the periphrastic perfects of √jan, 'be born, generate' and √bhū, 'to be', respectively)[29] **'the mountain (or king)'** (bhūbhṛtam, sing. acc. of bhūbhṛt) ... //

According to Chandra (pc 3 Dec. 2010), the compositum *<a>ṣṭapādasatkāyam* pertains to a venerable image, and with *pāda* in this instance signifying the length of a human foot, hence an sculpture with a height of about 1.8 meters (8 *pāda* x 12 *angula*). "This must have

[24]'Pertaining to, growing in, or inhabiting mountainous regions'.

[25]"Many temples show the characteristics of a mountain and may be called Merus in the same way as modern Balinese temple buildings" (Bernet Kempers 1959: 20).

[26]No attempt has been made to translate the fragment ◦*ñjabhṛto* in line 10 above. Bhṛto (= *bhṛtaḥ* or *bhṛtoḥ)* can be derived from either *bhṛt* ('bearing, carrying, bringing, procuring, possessing, wearing, having, nourishing, supporting, maintaining') or *bhṛta* ('borne, carried; gained, acquired; filled, full of'). There are relatively few options for completing *-ñja* as a stand-alone term, such as *gañja* ('treasury; a place where grain is stored; mine'), *piñja* ('moon'), and *raśmipuñja* ('a heap, mass or multitude of rays').

[27]However, de Casparis (1956: 193, n. 75) thought that the alternate reading of *bhūpo* (=*bhūpaḥ*, 'earth-protector ') could not be excluded.

[28]Perhaps a reference to the ritual bringing to life of the image or temple.

[29]Compare with *ārādhayām babhūva*, 'became engaged in paying homage' (*Śrīmad Bhāgavatam* 5,2,2) and *bhāvayām babhūva,* 'he begot' (*Śrīmad Bhāgavatam* 5,1,24).
The ritual insemination of a *stūpa* reliquary is a Siṅhalese practice that was discussed in the previous chapter. "No image can be worshiped before consecration which is done when the entire construction (the temple and its surrounds) is constructed. The temple had been completed" (Chandra, pc 3 January 2011). We also recall that the fragment in line five had previously referred to a person or deity coming into existence (*janana*), though in this earlier instance de Casparis' reading of *kāya* ('body') is not certain.

been the height of the person in whose memory the image was dedicated". Additionally, Chandra proposed to translate *bhūbhṛtam* as 'montane temple'.

De Casparis (1956: 193, n. 75) tentatively interpreted *bhūbhṛtam=adyāṣṭahastāṅśam* as a reference to an image of a deceased king, whose body ? (*aṅśam*) "is 'at present' eight armed". However, *aṅśam* (=*aṃśam*) does not mean 'body' but rather a part, share or portion of something, either tangible or intangible. So it is possible that *adya-aṣṭa-hasta-aṅśam* might mean 'whose allotment is now eight cubits', with the cubit (*hasta*) being the distance between the elbow and middle fingertip, e.g. 40-50 cm (see Wisseman Christie 1998: 149), and with eight cubits ranging from 3.2 meters to 4.0 meters.

De Casparis (1956: 193, n. 7) supposed that the composer had intended to make a pun by contrasting *<a>ṣṭapādasatkāyaṃ* and *aṣṭahastāṅśam,* respectively. If his presumption is correct, we would not expect both *aṣṭapāda* and *aṣṭahasta* to have been intended to serve as references to eight parts of the same body. On the other hand, *aṣṭapāda* and *aṣṭahasta* might refer to an image and a structure, respectively, if we consider that *bhūbhṛtam* could be a metaphorical reference to a ritual insemination of either the four *peripih* placed in the 3.5 x 3.5 meter pit beneath the central chamber of the north *vihāra* (Soekmono 1995: 121-122) or one of the *caṇḍi perwara* or *caṇḍi stūpa* structures in the temple complex's outer yard.[30]

Chandra (pc 5 Dec. 2010) has expressed the opinion that *adya-aṣṭa-hasta-āṅśam* would be an astronomical detail[31] that refers "to an auspicious date in the eighth degree (*aṃśa*) of the thirteenth lunar mansion".[32] The use of 'begat' in the half verse does prompt our contemplation of a possible reference to a birth in an Hindu-Buddhist astrological sense, e.g. with the rite of bringing to life an image or temple coinciding with the position of the moon in one of the 27 lunar mansions (*nakṣatra*),[33] which is considered to be highly

---

[30]The square body of the reconstructed *caṇḍi perwara* in the outer courtyard at Plaosan Lor measures 3.45 x 3.45 m. and also has a height of 3.85 m., whilst the supporting base measures 4.52 x 4.52 m. without the 0.74 x 1.31 m. staircase projection (Patricia 2001). With respect to the reconstructed *caṇḍi stūpa*-s, the diameter of the base that forms the *stūpa* proper is 3.95 m., whilst the supporting ground-level footer measures 4.95 m. per side (see Long 2009: 286-287). It is also worth noting that *aṅśa* is a Sanskrit loan-word adopted by the Javanese for designating a freehold located at a considerable distance from the principal sanctuary that it was intended to support (Boechari 1982c).

[31]*Aṅśam* also can mean 'day'. Since the sun moves about one degree in 24 hours during the days surrounding the equinoxes, one 'day' would be roughly equivalent to one degree of celestial longitude.

[32]The phrase *sthirāṅśavidite* occurs in the first strophe of the Canggal inscription of king Sañjaya (732 CE), which presents the date of the text. Griffiths (2011a) translated this part of the strophe as [on the hill (parvvate)] "known as sthirāṅśa", though he also wrote that it is "not certain at all that sthirāṅśavidite qualifies parvvate rather than the dating formula or a part thereof". De Casparis (1978: 22) translated *sthira-aṅśa-vidite* as 'to be known as a stable sign'. In Hindu-Buddhist astrology, the "fixed signs, Vṛṣabha, Siṃha, Vṛścika and Kumbha, symbolise firmness and stability" (Sivapriyananda 1990: 89). However, *aṅśa* (=*aṃśa*) does not mean 'sign' but rather a 'share, portion, part' or a 'degree of longitude or latitude'. In my opinion, *sthirāṅśa-vidite* qualifies the preceding words *lagne kumbhamaye*, which are likewise in the locative case: 'with Aquarius (*kumbha*) as the ascendant (*lagne*, e.g. the celestial meridian ascending the local horizon) at a known stable degree' or 'part'. This last point perhaps refers to the *nakṣatra* Pūrvabhādrapada (20° 00' Aquarius - 03° 20' Pisces) associated with cosmic stability and fearlessness (Behari & Frawley 2003).

[33]Alternatively, *adyāṣṭahastāṅśam* might be a unique reference to the annual arrival of the sun at the eighth degree of Hasta, e.g. on 18/19 September, which coincided with Java's vernal equinox in the month of Āśvina. On this date annually the sun's celestial longitude coincided with that of the 'Rice Barn' (Lumbung),

influential with respect to an individual's destiny. In light of the fragmentary nature of the first transcribed segment of line 10, however, all three of the speculative interpretations presented here-above are offered with reservations.

Line 11. This line contains what could be the first hemistich of a verse in either the Āryā or Udgīti meters. Moreover, it must have been preceded by yet another entire verse, of which absolutely nothing has survived. The text segment includes a reference to thunder and lightning, "which denote the monsoon rains eagerly awaited by agricultural peasants. Likewise the king was looked up to by the people" (Chandra, pc 3 Dec. 2010). The reference to bringing thunder and lightning also potentially pertains to what becomes stated subsequently in strophe eight, which seems to be comparing a Buddhistic divinity's monastic garments of various colors to an evening thundercloud and his discourses to rain.

[11] .... sajjanataḍitkuliśabhṛt=kuleśaśaraṇaś=ca ......ḥ /valamālā

Hypothetical verse diagram in either Āryā or Udgīti meter:

| ‒ ⏑ ⏑ | ⏑ ‒ ⏑ | ⏑ ⏑ ‒ ‖ ⏑ ‒ ⏑ | ⏑ ⏑ ‒ | ⏑ - - - | - - - - | ‒ ‖ first hemistich
| ⏑ ⏑ ‒ | ‒ - - | - - - - ‖ - - - - | - - - - | - - - - | - - - - | ‒ ‖ second hemistich

L11. ... the bringer of the thunder and lightning for virtuous men who is the lord of the family and a refuge ... /

L11. ... **the bringer** (bhṛt, sing. nom. of bhṛt) **of the thunder** (kuliśa) **and lightning** (taḍit) **for virtuous** (saj = sat) **men** (jana) **who is the lord of the family** (kuleśa) **and** (ca) **a refuge** (śaraṇaś = śaraṇaḥ, sing. nom. of śaraṇa) ... / ... [34] ... //

De Casparis (1956: 193, n. 76) viewed the long fragment in line 11 as potentially a reference to Vajrapāṇi, "whose *vajra* is considered the symbol of the powerful fire that burns the impurities of those good men (*sajjana*) who have attained a high state of perfection". The reference to the lord of the family (*kuleśa*) also potentially suggests the spiritual father of the *vajra-kula* Akṣobhya. On the other hand, this particular text fragment might be referring instead to the royal promulgator of the inscription.

> "Above all the sovereign is indeed responsible for rainfall and this not only through his fitness as a ruler, but also by his presence itself. 'Indra, seeing that all the kṣatriya sovereigns ruled their kingdoms very virtuously, poured down vivifying showers of rain at the proper time and at the proper place, and thus protected all creatures'. Where there is no king rain will not fall. If he sins, that is to say transgresses the dharma in any respect,

the Javanese name for the Southern Cross (Crux) constellation (Hien 1896, 4: 2). According to the indigenous Javanese calendar (*pranatamangsa*; see Long 2009: 254), this is the Labuhan period when the Javanese began making preparations for the inception of the island's next agricultural cycle. Besides, other Javanese inscriptions (879 and 901 CE) mention that the people were required to provide certain sanctuaries with flowers and other offerings "at every equinox in the months of Caitra and Asuji [=Āśvina]" (Boechari 1982c).

[34] Unfortunately we do not know the context of the line-ending compound *valamālā*, which might mean 'garland' or 'crown' (*mālā*) of 'power' or 'strength' (*vala = bala*).

be it 'ritual', 'moral' or otherwise, or if his purohita ('chaplain') makes a mistake, rain can cease. In times of drought the subjects approach the ruler for the much desired water" (Gonda 1956: 42-43).

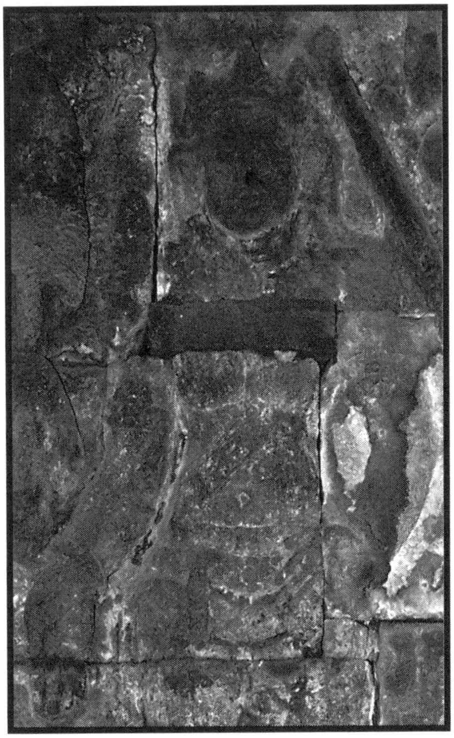

The inscription's references to the rains are also interesting in light of the *mudrā* displayed by standing female (north *vihāra*) and male (south *vihāra*) figures depicted in relief on the interior chamber walls. This boon-bestowing hand gesture is also known in India as *abhaya-hasta or lola-hasta.*

> "Elderly villagers knew the names of those asterisms under which rain was certain to occur, or essential, or both and sometimes the expectations had crystalised into adages. For instance, rains under the asterism hasta were believed to be so certain that they insured the crop from disaster. Appropriately enough, the hasta rains were compared to the abhayahasta (right hand held with the palm outwards and the fingers pointing downwards) of Vishnu. Hastada male raitanige abhaya hasta kottide: hasta rains have given abhayahasta to cultivators" (Srinivas 1976: 120).

Figs. 7-4 & 7-5. Royal figures in relief from the interior of the north and south *vihāra*-s.

According to the folklore of Gujarat—from whence Buddhists had perhaps come to visit the Plaosan temple (see later in v.14)—thunder or lightning in Hasta "foretells good harvests and a prosperous year. Thunder in the same naksatra is believed to muzzle the jaws of serpents and other noxious creatures.... If thunder is not heard during this naksatra, mosquitoes and other insects and vermin are believed to be likely to multiply..." Furthermore, the rains during the fortnight in which the sun occupies Hasta "... are so much esteemed that each drop of them is said to be worth a drop of ghi. People store the harthio varsād or the rain water of Hasta in reservoirs for drinking purposes, believing it to be very pure..." (Enthoven 1914: 34).

Line 12. De Casparis thought that line 12 contains a reference to the waterworks at the greater Plaosan temple complex, which was originally surrounded by a man-made moat featuring a carefully constructed stone foundation.[35]

> "The second pāda deals with something very dear (*priyatama*) which for that very reason (this might have been expressed by *eva*) was surrounded (*pari*° is probably the beginning of one of the various words meaning 'to surround', such as *pari-dhā*) by a ditch (*parikhā*). If we try to establish a relation between the preceding part of the strophe and these words, we might conclude that the bees (*alabhṛt*) are attracted by the scent of the blue lotuses (*utpala*), probably those carried by Bodhisattvas such as Mañjuśrī (?); the bees are not of course held back by the ditch protecting the foundation where the Bodhisattvas are placed" (de Casparis 1956: 194, n. 78).

[12] ... ... takalolatphalotpalālabhṛtaḥ / priyatamam=eva parikhayā pari- ...

Hypothetical verse diagram in Āryā meter:

- - - -	- - - -	- - - - ‖	- - ⏑ ⏑	– –	⏑ – ⏑	– ⏑ ⏑	– ‖	first hemistich
⏑ ⏑ ⏑ ⏑	– ⏑ ⏑	⏑ ⏑ – ‖	⏑ ⏑̲ - -	- - - -	- - - -	- - - -	– ‖	second hemistich

L12. ...(like) the bees among the blue lotuses with the swinging fruits ..., just so is a most beloved ... (surrounded) ... by a moat ... ... //

L12. ...[like] **the bees** (ala-bhṛtaḥ 'bearers of the sting') **among the blue lotuses** (utpala) **with the swinging** (lola) **fruits** (phala) ..., [36] **just so** (eva) **is a most beloved** (priyatamam, sing. acc. of priyatama) ... [surrounded (pari-)] ... **by a moat** (parikhayā, sing. instr. of parikhā) ... ... //

On the other hand, the poetic allusion proposed by de Casparis is unclear. Perhaps the composer had been comparing the nectar-producing lotus that draws the bees to something that is communicated later in the inscription about 'the immortal ambrosias of an incomparable image' (*pratimapratimāmṛtaiḥ*). Given that *amṛta* also means 'nectar', it remains possible that the poet was alluding to the image being surrounded by a moat full of lotus flowers as well as surrounded by a devoted entourage: the subsidiary shrines erected by the members of the royal court as well as the human figures carved in *bas*-relief on the interior walls of the twin *vihāra*-s.

According to the Caṇḍi Canggal inscription, Śiva's pair of lotus feet "...are kissed by the gods, beginning with Lekharṣabha (Indra), who have their crowns bent down, resembling bees; whose reddish petals are his toes; the lightly colored ends of whose filaments are the flashing beams (reflecting) on his toe-nails..." (Griffiths 2011a: 30). A reference to Rāvana, Bāṇa and Arjuna adoring the lotus feet of Great Lakṣmī like honey-making bees

[35]We are unable to determine the symbolic significance of the complex's extensive water works at this time. However, it is notable that great care was taken to connect it with the Prambanan temple complex via underground conduits (Jordaan, pc 16 January 2011).

[36]Here, *-taka* has not been translated.

also appears in a Sanskrit *liṅga* inscription promulgated by Rakai Wailang Pu Kumbhayoni on the Ratu Baka plateau in 856 CE.

> "[T]he bees coming to suck the honey from her lotus-feet are the usual simile for the heroes worshiping the feet of the goddess.... the pollen of Śiva's lotus-feet drops down from [the body of the goddess] and is compared with the drops of water trickling down from a woman who has just come out of the water. The simile expressed in the whole strophe is a rather complex one: the bees, who are the heroes worshiping the goddess, are attracted by the pollen dropping down [from] her, but the pollen itself does not belong to the goddess but is due to her worshiping the feet of Hara" (de Casparis 1956: 278-279, including n. 155 & n. 157).

Line 13. Only the final phrase *jinasutaḥ* remains to be read in line 13. *Jinasutaḥ* means 'son of the Buddha', e.g. a bodhisattva.

Transcriptions and revised translations for strophes 1-19

The Sanskrit script featured in the Kalasan (778/9 CE) and Abhayagirivihāra (792/3 CE) charters is substantially different from the other type of Siddhamātṛkā found in the Plaosan and Śrī Saṅgrāmadhanaṃjaya inscriptions, which "display a number of curious features not yet found together, at least in that very form, in any Pre-Nāgarī inscriptions from India. The latter type, that in which the Kĕlurak and Plaosan inscriptions are written, exhibits no real differences from the script used by some of the Pāla kings in Bengal and Bihar" (de Casparis 1956: 176). Those discrepancies that do exist between the latter two inscriptions amount to:

> "differences in execution rather than in the forms of the akṣaras themselves. Thus the height and breadth of the Plaosan akṣaras amount to about double of those of the Kĕlurak ones. In addition, the latter were executed without much care; as a matter of fact, a considerable number of irregularities may be noticed and there are even some obvious lapses. Nothing of the kind could be noticed in the Plaosan inscription. Wherever the akṣara forms are well preserved, they prove to have been executed with the utmost care" (de Casparis 1956: 176-177).

Strophes 1-10 in Anuṣṭubh meter:

⏓ ⏓ ⏓ ⏓ ⏑ — — ⏓ ⏓ ⏓ ⏓ ⏓ ⏑ — ⏑ ⏓

Naranāthābhisaṃskārabhāro vibhāti bhāsvaraḥ /
Dharmmasambhārasamitapratimāprati [14] — ⏑ ⏓ // 1 //

1. A mass of supernatural facilities shines forth as the Lord of men resplendent ... [37] in (the form) of an incomparable image which is commensurate with the equipment of Dharma.

[37]Proposed emendations: 'with the unequaled (*aprati<mā>*) immortal ambrosias (*<amṛtaiḥ>*) ...' (Chandra, pc 9 Oct. 2010) or 'as an incomparable (*aprati<mā>*) sunrise *<amodayaḥ>* ...' (de Casparis 1956: 194, 197).

1. A **mass** (bhāro = bhāraḥ, sing. nom. of bhāra) **of supernatural facilities** (abhisaṃskāra, which also can mean 'super-preparations; antidotes') **shines forth** (vibhāti, third pers. sing. present of √vibhā) **as the Lord** (nātha) **of men** (nara) **resplendent** (bhāsvaraḥ, sing. nom. of bhāsvara) ... [in the form] **of an image** (pratimā) **which is commensurate with** (samita) **the equipment** (sambhāra) **of Dharma** (dharmma = dharma).

————⏑——⏓⏓⏓⏓⏓⏑—⏑⏓ /
⏓⏓⏓⏓⏑——⏓ nīrajān=varayānagān // 2 //

2. ... those free from passion (and) abiding in the most excellent vehicle.

2. ... **those free from passion** (nīrajān, pl. accusative of nīraja) **and abiding in** (gān, pl. accusative of ga) **the most excellent** (vara) **vehicle** (yāna).

⏓⏓ ḥ sva ⏓⏑ yāvā ⏓ catussugatasaṅgataḥ /[38]
Prāsādādbhutasaṃbhraṣṭaḥ kim=bhāti tadṛśaś=ciram // 3 //

3. ... having united with the Sugatas of the four times ..., why does this apparition shine forth for a (very) long time after having fallen from the sky to the temple (as if) by a miracle.

3. ... **having united with** (saṅgataḥ) **the Sugatas of the four times** (catussugata, e.g. the Jinas of the cardinal directions/four eons) ... , **why** (kim) **does this** (ta, read as tad) **apparition** (dṛśaś = dṛśaḥ, sing nom. of dṛśa, 'appearance, look') **shine forth** (bhāti, third pers. sing. present of √bhā) **for a** (very) **long time** (ciram, indeclinable) **after having fallen from the sky** (saṃ-bhraṣṭaḥ) **to the temple** (prāsāda) [as if] **by a miracle** (adbhuta, 'wonderful occurrence')?

Bhūbhṛd=iva vi- [15] ——⏓⏓⏓⏓⏓⏑—⏑⏓ /
⏓⏓⏓⏓⏑——⏓⏓ *ra*ṇaḥ pā*pabhā* ⏑ naḥ // 4 //

4. ... in the same manner as a king/mountain ... / ... (the destroyer) of evil.

4. ... **in the same manner as** (iva) **a king/mountain** (bhūbhṛd = bhūbhṛt) ... / ... [the destroyer (bhā<ñja>naḥ, sing. nom. of bhāñjana)] **of evil** (pāpa) ... .

Saṃbhavabhramaṇaśrāntaviśrāntavodhim=eṣyati /
Viṃśatīha virājante jinā jinasutānvitāḥ // 5 //

5. Coming to the end of wandering wearied throughout worldly existence, he will attain that Bodhi (which is the eternal repose); indeed, twenty Jinas accompanied by Jina-sons shine forth herein.

---

[38]Just a few complete Sanskrit words are compatible with ⏑ *yāvā* ⏓ but only 'in the abode of fortune or prosperity' (*śriyāvāse*) and 'dwelling with Śrī' (*śriyāvāsin*) seem at all plausible in the present context.

5. **Coming to the end** (viśrānta) **of wandering** (bhramaṇa) **wearied** (śrānta) **throughout worldly existence** (saṃbhava), **he will attain** (eṣyati, third pers. sing. future of √i) **that Bodhi** (vodhim = bodhim, sing. acc. of bodhi) [which is the eternal (aśrānta) repose (viśrānta)]; **indeed** (ha), **twenty** (viṃśatī) **Jinas** (jinā = jināḥ, pl. nom. of jina) **accompanied by** (anvitāḥ, pl. nom. of anvita) **Jina-sons** (jinasutā) **shine forth** (virāj) **herein** (ante, the sing. locative of anta, 'in the inside/proximity').

Analpajanmopajitya viśvāvaraṇavāraṇaḥ /
[16] ⏓ ⏓ ⏓ ⏓ ⏑ — — ⏓ ⏓ ⏓ ⏓ ⏓ ⏑ — ⏑ ⏓ // 6 //

6. After having vanquished numerous births as an (all-resisting) elephant against all obstructions (in the universe) ... .[39]

6. **After having vanquished** (upajitya, the absolutive of upa- √ji) **numerous** (analpa) **re-births** (janma, sing. acc. of janman) **as an** [all-resisting] **elephant** (vāraṇaḥ) **against all** (viśva) **obstructions** (āvaraṇa) [in the universe (viśva)] / ... //

⏓ ⏓ ⏓ ⏓ ⏑ — — ⏓ ⏓ ⏓ ⏓ ⏓ ⏑ — ⏑ ⏓ /
⏓ ⏓ ⏓ ⏓ ⏑ — — ⏓ duḥkhaśamanaśāsanaḥ // 7 //

7. ... whose doctrine is for allaying suffering ... .

7. ... / **whose doctrine** (śāsanaḥ) **is for allaying** (śamana) **suffering** (duḥkha) ... .

*Ga*ha*na*pāraśāsārthavyāhāramañjuśīkaraḥ /
Cāracīvarasāndhyābhradhībhūridalayoja [17] <naḥ> // 8 //

8. [To be compared with] an evening thundercloud in a monk's dress of different colors while directing thoughts to a single point on the manifold petals of the mind, may You lead [the faithful] to the other side of impenetrable darkness through the splendid fine rain of Your discourses on the objective.

8. [To be compared with] **an evening thundercloud** (sāndhya-abhra) **in a monk's dress** (cīvara) **of different colors** (cāra, read as śāra) **while directing thoughts to a single point** (yoja<naḥ>, read as yojanam, neut. sing. nom. of yojana) **on the manifold** (bhūri) **petals** (dala) **of the mind** (dhī), **may You lead** (śāsa, sec. pers. sing. active imperative of √śās, 'to govern, command, direct')[40] [the faithful] **to the other side** (pāra) **of impenetrable darkness** (gahana) **through the splendid** (mañju, 'charming, lovely, beautiful') **fine rain** (śīkaraḥ, sing. nom. of śīkara) **of Your discourses** (vyāhāra) **on the objective** (artha, 'aim, purpose').

⏓ ⏓ ⏓ ⏓ ⏑ — — ⏓ ⏓ ⏓ ⏓ ⏓ ⏑ — ⏑ ⏓ /
⏓ ⏓ ⏓ ⏓ ⏑ — — ⏓ ⏓ kṣaṇārtham=vidīyate // 9 //

[39]In Buddhism, the elephant symbolizes the power to overcome all obstacles.
[40]Chandra (pc 3 Jan. 2011) proposed translating *śāsārthavyāhāra* as, '...discourses, which aim [is] to direct ...', but this would require *ārtha* to be read as *artha*.

De Casparis (1956: 195, n. 86; 201, n. 111) remarked on his "rather uncertain" reading for which he proposed the emendation *<ra>kṣaṇārtham=vidīyate* [read as *vidhīyate*] ("is distributed for protection").

Ratnatrayāśayopetaṃ samastaguṇaratnabhaṃ /
Kaśśin=na vaktuśakto vas=tatpuṇyāyām=anuṣṭubhi // 10 //

10. Nobody would be able to offer to utter (a verse) in praise after an apparition as propitious as that one endowed with an abode for the Three Jewels, whose semblance of jewels is their combined (transcendental) qualities.

10. **Nobody** (na) **would be able** (śakta) **to offer** (vas) **to utter** (vaktu in comp. for vaktum, the indecl. inf. of √vac) [a strophe] **in praise after** (anuṣṭubhi, sing. locative of anuṣṭubh) **an apparition** (kaśśin, read as kāśin, 'shining, appearing, having the semblance of') **as propitious as** (puṇyāyām, sing. locative of puṇyā)[41] **that one** (tat) **endowed with** (upetam, sing. acc. of upeta) **an abode** (āśaya) **for the Three Jewels** (ratnatraya), **whose semblance** (bham, sing. acc. of bha) **of jewels** (ratna) **is their combined** (samasta) [transcendental] **qualities** (guṇa).

Strophes 11-17 in Drutavilambitam[42] meter:

⏑ ⏑ ⏑ — ⏑ ⏑ — ⏑ ⏑ — ⏑ —

Vividhagandhasudigdhavarā[18] ⏑ —
⏑ ⏑ ⏑ — ⏑ ⏑ — ⏑ ⏑ — ⏑ — /
⏑ ⏑ ⏑ — ⏑ ⏑ — ⏑ ⏑ — ⏑ —
⏑ ⏑ ⏑ — ⏑ ⏑ — ⏑ ⏑ — yate[43] // 11 //

11. ... lavishly besmeared with fragrances of various sorts ... .

11. ...[44] **lavishly** (su, 'greatly', adverb) **besmeared** (digdha) **with aromatics** (gandha) **of various sorts** (vividha) ....

Kanakakokanadodaravisphurad-
ruciradīpaśikhākṛtatāmasaḥ /
Śiśiraraśmirucāpravarānvayaḥ
sakalakhādya [19] ⏑ — ⏑ ⏑ — ⏑ — // 12 //

12. Doing away with the dark, with the splendid light of the pinnacle quivering (like lightning) on the calyx of a lotus (made) of gold, (being linked to) an eminent entourage by the luster of the cool-rayed (moon), all kinds of food ... .

---

[41] See de Casparis 1956: 201, n. 112.
[42] Lit. 'fast-slow', which is suggestive of the Latin epigram 'make haste slowly' (Morgan 2011: 121).
[43] De Casparis (1956: 195, n. 88) thought that *-yate* may have been preceded by *dī*, i.e. *dīyate*.
[44] De Casparis (1956: 187 and 195, n. 87) proposed the emendation *varā<ṅgaṇāḥ>*, which is debatable.

12. **Doing away with** (kṛta) **the dark** (tāmasaḥ, sing. nom. of tāmasa), **with the flame** (śikhā) **of the splendid** (rucira) **lamp** (dīpa) **quivering** [like lightning] (visphurad = visphurat, pres. act. participle of visphur) **on the calyx** (udara, 'belly, the thickest part of anything, womb') **of a lotus** (kokanada) [made] **of gold** (kanaka), [being linked to] **an eminent** (pravara, 'eminent; family, race, ancestor') **entourage** (anvayaḥ, sing. nom. of anvaya, 'succession; lineage, descendents, family; being linked to') **by the luster** (rucā) **of the cool-rayed** [moon] (śiśiraraśmi), ... **all kinds of food** (sakala-khādya) ... .

⏑ ⏑ ⏑ – ⏑ ⏑ – ⏑ ⏑ – ⏑ –

pravarasamvaravāravarāṅgaṇāḥ /
Hṛdayanīrajasāndrarasāntaram
harati kāmijanasya samantataḥ // 13 //

13. ... for the eminent women of most excellent forbearance in their appointed places, (he)[45] removes on all sides the (interior) field of intense emotions in the heart-lotuses of lustful people.

13. ... **for the eminent** (vara) **women** (aṅgaṇāḥ) **of most excellent** (pravara) **forbearance** (samvara, read as saṃvara)[46] **in their appointed places** (vāra), [he] **removes** (harati, sing. third person present of √hṛ) **on all sides** (samantataḥ, adverb) **the** [interior] **field** (antaram, sing. acc. of antara)[47] **of intense** (sāndra) **emotions** (rasa, 'sentiment, desire') **in the heart-lotuses** (hṛdaya-nīraja)[48] **of lustful** (kāmi) **people** (janasya, sing. genitive of jana).

Satatagurjaradeśasamāgatais
sugatabhaktibharapraṇatai[20] ⏑ – /
⏑ ⏑ ⏑ – ⏑ ⏑ – ⏑ ⏑ – ⏑ –
⏑ ⏑ ⏑ – *tkri*yate jinamandiram // 14 //

14. By those who arrived nonstop from the region of Gujara bowed by the burden of devotion to the Buddhas, ... a Jina temple is (immediately worshiped).

14. **By those who arrived** (samāgatais = samāgataiḥ, pl. instr. of samāgata) **nonstop** (satata, 'uninterrupted') **from the region of Gujara** (gurjaradeśa) **bowed** (praṇatai<ḥ>, pl. instr. of praṇata) **by the burden** (bhara) **of devotion** (bhakti) **to the Buddha** (sugata), ... **a Jina temple** (jina-mandiram, n. sing. nom. of mandira) ... [is immediately (<sapadi>) worshiped (<sa>tkriyate, third. pers. sing. passive present of sat- √kṛ)].[49]

Kvacid=asaṅkyaśikhāmaṇibhūṣaṇāḥ
praṇayinīprakaṭīkṛtamanmathāḥ /
Sugatavimvavilokananirjita-
smaraśarā*kuśalāḥ* śa [21] ⏑ – ⏑ – // 15 //

---

[45]The subject of the verse is unclear. De Casparis (1956: 202, n. 118) believed this to be the Buddha.
[46]The transcription published by Sarkar (1971/2: I: 48x) has *saṃvara* in place of *samvara*.
[47]Gonda (1938: 488) remarked that °*anta* and °*antara* can mean 'sphere, circle, field'.
[48]*Nīraja* also means 'free from passion'.
[49]Emendations proposed by de Casparis (1956: 195, n. 90).

15. Somewhere (a number of young princes)[50] adorned with innumerable crown pearls whose amorous passions had manifested (themselves) to their beloved ones, after being conquered when gazing intently at the image of the Buddha, ... from the impieties of the arrows of Desire.

15. **Somewhere** (kvacid) [a number of young princes, e.g. 'ornaments'] **adorned with** (bhūṣaṇāḥ, pl. nom. of bhūṣaṇa) **innumerable** (asaṅkya) **crown** (śikhā) **pearls** (maṇi) **whose amorous passions** (manmathāḥ, pl. nom. of manmatha) **had manifested** (prakaṭīkṛta) [themselves] **to their beloved ones** (praṇayinī), **after being conquered** (nirjita, past passive participle of nis- √ji) **by gazing** [intently] (vilokana, 'looking at, contemplating, paying attention to, becoming aware of') **at the image** (vimva = bimba) **of the Buddha** (sugata), ...[51] **from the impieties** (akuśalāḥ, pl. nom. of akuśala, 'sin, demerit') **of the arrows** (śara) **of Desire** (smara).

⏑ ⏑ ⏑ — ⏑ ⏑ — ⏑ ⏑ — ⏑ —

vigataroṣadṛśo 'ntaradṛṣṭiṣu /
Sakalalokam=asāv=api nirvṛto
bhavabhidapratimapratimāmṛtaiḥ // 16 //

16. ... in their inner visions (they become) devoid of the perception of anger; moreover, that one at ease (departed) the material world by means of the immortal ambrosias of the peerless image for breaching (the wall of) phenomenal existence.

16. ... **in their inner** ('ntara = antara) **visions** (dṛṣṭiṣu, pl. locative of dṛṣṭi) [they become] **devoid of** (vigata) **the perception** (dṛśo = dṛśaḥ, 'look, appearance') **of anger** (roṣa); **moreover** (api), **that one** (asāv = asau, sing. nom. pronoun from √adas) **at ease** (nirvṛto = nirvṛtaḥ)[52] [departed (vigata)] **the material** (sakala) **world** (lokam, sing. acc. of loka) **by means of the immortal ambrosias** (amṛtaiḥ, pl. instr. of amṛta) **of the peerless image** (apratima-pratimā) **for breaching** [the wall of] (bhid, 'breaking, piercing, destroying; wall') **phenomenal existence** (bhava).

Vahulamohamahātimirāvṛto
jinavad=astinirodha [22] ⏑ — ⏑ —/
⏑ ⏑ ⏑ — ⏑ ⏑ — ⏑ ⏑ — ⏑ —
drutavilambitasādhanavanditaḥ // 17 //

17. Surrounded by the immense intense limit of deep delusion, he is able to (attain) the destruction (of it) like a Jina ... one who is venerated for empowerments having their fruit delayed and without delay.

---

[50]According to de Casparis (1956: 203, including n. 124), "a number (of young men)" who are "of a very high rank, probably princes".
[51]De Casparis (1956: 203, n. 127) suggested the emendation *śa<raṇāgatāḥ>*, they 'came to seek refuge'.
[52]In addition to 'at ease', *nirvṛta* can mean 'ceased, ended, terminated, extinguished' as well as 'free from care or anxiety'; and like the "Pali nibbuta functioning as ppp. to nirvāṇa and its relatives, *released, entered into nirvāṇa* (oftener pari-nir° ...)" (Edgerton 1953: II: 304).

17. **Surrounded by** (vṛta)[53] **the immense** (mahā) **intense** (ati) **limit** (mirā) **of deep** (vahula = bahula, 'dense, thick') **delusion** (moha), **he is able to** (asti, third pers. sing. present of √as) [attain] **the destruction** (nirodha<m>, sing. acc. of nirodha)[54] [of it] **like** (vad = vat) **a Jina** (jina) ... ; ... **one who is venerated** (vanditaḥ) **for empowerments** (sādhana) **having their fruit delayed** (vilambita) **and without delay** (druta).[55]

Strophes 18-19 in Praharṣiṇī[56] meter:

— — —, ⏑ ⏑ ⏑ ⏑, — ⏑ — ⏑ — —

Saṃsārāvanicaratān=na dharmato 'nya-
    jantūnām=varaśaraṇaṃ triśarmmadhīraiḥ /
Koṣo 'sāv=itarakṛto 'pi pālanīya-
    [23] — — — ⏑ ⏑ ⏑ ⏑ — <praharṣaṇīyaḥ>[57] // 18 //

18. In terms of an essential nature for living beings, there is no other better shelter (than the Dharma), which those roving over the earth undergoing transmigration (obtained) by means of persevering in the Triple-refuge; this treasure, even if cultivated in an unremarkable (manner), should be observed ... .

18. **In terms of an essential nature** (dharmato = dharmatas)[58] **for living beings** (jantūnām, pl. genitive of jantu), **there is no** (na) **other** ('nya = anya) **better** (vara) **shelter** (śaraṇam, sing. acc. of śaraṇa) [than the Dharma], **which those** (tān, pl. acc. pronoun) **roving over the earth** (avanicara) **undergoing transmigration** (saṃsāra) [obtained] **by means of persevering** (dhīraiḥ, pl. instr. of dhīra) **in the Triple-refuge** (triśarmma = triśarma);[59] **this** (asāv = asau) **treasure** (koṣo = koṣaḥ, sing. nom. of koṣa), **even if** (api) **cultivated** (kṛto = kṛtaḥ) **in an unremarkable** [manner] (itara, 'commonplace'; Chandra, pc 10 Dec. 2010, glossed this as 'in an abbreviated manner'), **should be observed** (pālanīya-)[60] ... .

---

[53] This stands in contrast with *nirvṛtaḥ* in the prior stanza.

[54] De Casparis (1956: 196, n. 91) proposed the emendation *nirodha<m=avāpnuyāt>, or ava-āpnuyāt,* the third pers. sing. optative of *ava* + *√āp*.

[55] A *sādhana* is a detailed description of the evocation of an esoteric divinity by means of visualization, *mantra* recitation and the other methods through which the *sādhaka* attains complete liberation or a lesser spiritual fulfillment (*siddhi*). "Around the evocation are described ritual preliminaries that function to orient the sādhaka's state of mind and post-evocatory and concluding acts" (Tribe 1994: 6). The Plaosan inscription's reference to *sādhana*-s contradicts the art-historical view (see, for example, Fontein 2013: 9) that esoteric Buddhism did not spread to Java prior to the tenth century.

[56] 'Joyful'.

[57] Based on the poet's incorporation of a variant of the name of the meter in one strophe from each of the text segments containing vs.1-10 and vs.11-17, respectively, de Casparis (1956: 196, n. 94 and 205-206, n. 136) proposed a highly speculative reconstruction and translation for all of *pāda d.*

[58] See, for example, Harrison 1992: 61 and Tribe 1994:87, n.63.

[59] "*Tri-śarma* refers to *Buddhaṃ śaraṇam gacchāmi, Dharmaṃ śaraṇam gacchāmi, Saṅghaṃ śaraṇam gacchāmi. Śarma = śaraṇa*" (Chandra, pc 10 Dec. 2010).

[60] De Casparis 1956: 190, n. 93: "Presumably, this word ended in a consonant which could be combined into a ligature with the first consonant of pāda d, i.e. either a dental or a palatal sibilant (words beginning in a lingual are extremely rare)".

*Kṛt*vemaṃ śaśadharavimvaśuddham=āpam=
yat=puṇyam=bhajatu jano jinakramasya /
*Asmān=ra*kṣa varanarādhirājarāja
dṛṣṭikleśam=api janā na rāgabaddhāḥ //

19. After having constructing this pure like the disc of the moon, by whatever merit of Buddha's Way I have attained, may the people be participants (in that merit); O supreme lord of human emperors, may You protect us so that men bound to passion do not even have wrong views.

19. **After having constructed** (kṛtvā, absolutive of √kṛt) **this** (imam)[61] **pure** (śuddham, sing. acc. of śuddha) **like the disc** (vimva = bimba) **of the moon** (śaśadhara), **by whatever** (yat) **of the Buddha's Way** (jina-kramasya, sing. genitive of krama) **I have attained** (āpam, first person aortist of √āp), **may the people** (jano = janaḥ, sing. nom. of jana) **be participants in** (bhajatu, third person sing. imperative of √bhaj, 'obtain as one's share') **that merit** (puṇyam, sing. acc. of puṇya); **O most excellent** (vara) **lord** (rāja, sing. vocative of rāja) **of human** (nara) **emperors** (adhirāja), **may You protect** (rakṣa, sec. pers. sing. imperative of √rakṣ) **us** (asmān, first pers. pl. acc. pronoun) **so that men** (janā = janāḥ, pl. nom. of jana) **bound to** (baddhāḥ, pl. nom. of baddha, 'attached to') **passion** (rāga) **do not** (na) **even** (api) **have the affliction** (kleśam, sing. acc. of kleśa) **of wrongful views** (dṛṣṭi).

Discussion of the strophes

Strophes one through 10 are all composed in the Anuṣṭubh meter. In the opinion of de Casparis (1956: 179, 182, n. 30 and 186), the entire segment likely pertains to the principal image being mentioned in the inscription, which is presumably encountered for the first time in the opening verse of the series. Anuṣṭubh, the most common of all Sanskrit meters in classical literature, is an epithet of the goddess of speech that means 'following in praise or invocation'.

Verse One. Translation revisions for this strophe were already discussed extensively in Chapter VI. To the foregoing I would simply add that Edgerton (1953: II: 57) had remarked that *abhisaṃskāra* can signify both 'performance' (of action) and 'accumulation' (of merit or demerit) when appearing in the Mahāyāna literature. Given that the Buddha's wisdom (*jñāna*) is frequently identified as the *amṛta*, the initial verse, as emended by Chandra, can indeed be viewed as presenting all of the essential components comprising the equipment of Dharma (*dharmasambhara*): wisdom (*jñāna*) and meritorious deeds (*puṇya*).

Verse Two. Chandra (pc 24 May 2012) has proposed a different translation for the verse fragment from strophe two: " ... to those who are spotless (i.e. immaculately pure, *nīrajān*), those who follow (◦*gān*) the noble (*vara*) way (*yāna*)".

Verse Three. De Casparis (1956: 186) supposed that the allusion to an image which had fallen into the temple was sufficient evidence that the temple itself had already been in existence for some time prior to the miraculous event. However, no compelling evidence has been discovered at the site to indicate the existence of an earlier structure, which means

[61] A comparable expression involving operative neutrality appears in v.12 of the Kayumwuṅan charter. According to Chandra (pc 3 Jan. 2011), "kṛtvā, 'having constructed', refers to the completion of the image; śaśadhara-bimba-śuddham can mean the pure (śuddha) statue (bimba) with [the aura of the] moon".

the image in question had in all probability been constructed at approximately the same time as the temple to which it belonged.

Verse Four. This stanza is for the greater part lost in lacunas.

Verse Five. According to de Casparis, the composer's use of the future tense in this verse indicates that the divinity (and/or personage) represented by the image is not yet to be considered a Buddha. The next Jina-son poised to attain Buddhahood is Maitreya (figure 7-6), who was depicted twice in each of the twin *vihāra* structures. The duplication of Maitreya and Mañjuśrī—as a member of a triad in the north (Maitreya) and south (Mañjuśrī) chambers of each *vihāra* and again in the sidewall niches of each building's antechamber—is potentially clarified if one considers the images seated on the altars to be Jinas in royal dress (i.e. Buddha-*parés* signifying members of the *ratnatraya*).

> "The mention of twenty Jinas might be important for our knowledge of Tjaṇḍi Plaosan. Twenty is not, of course, a usual number for Jinas and this point makes it probable that the number relates to a definite detail of the foundation: the foundation included already twenty Jina images before the installation of the Bodhisattva [e.g. the principal image presumably described in vs.1-10]. *Buddhasutānvitāḥ*, 'accompanied by Buddha-sons, i.e. Bodhisattvas', probably means that each Jina would be accompanied by two Bodhisattvas. This would bring the original total of Jinas and Bodhisattvas to sixty" (de Casparis 1956: 199, n. 105).

De Casparis did not attempt to explain why we should presume that each Jina sculpture 'probably' had been accompanied by two bodhisattva images. An alternate hypothesis that spreads the total number of images across both buildings was presented in Chapter VI.

Fig. 7-6. Image of the bodhisattva Maitreya from the north niche in the antechamber of one of the *vihāra*-s at Caṇḍi Plaosan Lor.

Verse Six. Sarkar (1971/2: I: 55) translated the initial half-verse as, "Having conquered a number of existences, he has done away with the veil of the universe", whilst de Casparis (1956: 200) proposed, "After having vanquished numerous lives as an elephant breaking through all kinds of obstacles". It is difficult for me to understand why either scholar—short of totally relying on their presumptions about the context alone—had justified to themselves the translation of *vāraṇaḥ* as 'breaking through' or 'has done away with'.

The translation for strophe six proposed by de Casparis also includes an allusion to an elephant (*vāraṇaḥ*). In support of his interpretation, de Casparis (1956: 200, n. 106) maintained that the theme of numerous rebirths as an elephant was intended to signify 'the essence of an elephant' as a prerequisite for aspiring bodhisattvas, which is symbolically expressed in the story of the Buddha's final birth in which the Bodhisattva assumes the form of a white elephant with six tusks while descending into the womb of his mother Māyā.

Verse Seven. Of strophe seven only *duḥkhaśamanaśāsanaḥ* can be read with certainty. De Casparis (1956: 200) translated this as "whose doctrine appeases suffering".

Verse Eight. This strophe has already been discussed in Chapter VI.

Verse Nine. We shall pass by this strophe in silence due to the extensive lacuna and the uncertainty expressed by de Casparis' about his reading, which was cited above.

Verse 10. This stanza refers to an 'abode for the Three Jewels' but in a context that was unclear to de Casparis (1956: 201, n. 113), who envisioned two possibilities: the image either had contained a *mantra* for the Three Jewels or had been installed at a temple dedicated to the *ratnatraya*, e.g. a sanctuary in which the Buddha, Dharma and Saṅgha were represented as a triad. As discussed in Chapter VI, a loose gold-foil scroll discovered in the pit underneath the north *vihāra* appears to allude to the *ratnatraya*. This is likewise the case with the inscribed gold plate discovered in the outer temple yard between two of the *prāsāda*-s founded by Śrī Kahulunnan (de Casparis 1956: 170-172). In my opinion, stanza 10 of the Plaosan inscription alludes to the miraculous appearance of the image previously described in strophe three. In strophe 10, the composer focuses on the highly propitious nature of the image's supernatural arrival, which is indescribable.

Verse 11. De Casparis (1956: 187, 201, n. 115) presumed this verse to be the first in a series containing short vignettes, with each centered upon a significant detail of the temple complex. He applied this theory to all of the verses (11-17) composed in the Drutavilambitam meter. If this had been the case, however, then why are the two stanzas supposedly alluding to a female retinue (v.11 & v.13) separated by an intervening strophe? It is worth keeping in mind that his surmise pertaining to royal women in strophe 11 is based on his emendation of *varā<ṅganāḥ>* (see de Casparis 1956: 187 and 195, n. 87): "The completion is uncertain, but a word meaning 'women' seems to be required by the context". However, Buddhist practices have long included the anointment of images, texts, *bodhi*-trees and other sacred objects.

Verse 12. De Casparis (1956: 201-202, n. 116) thought that the principal subject of this strophe, which he did not see conveyed in the initial half-verse, would be indicated by the compound *pravarānvayaḥ*, which he translated as 'his excellent retinue'. Though Sarkar (1971/2: I: 48.xiii) likewise presumed that *pravarānvayaḥ* would have supplied the verse's principal subject, he translated the same compound as 'the best of the clan' and *śiśira-raśmi-rucā* as 'having the beauty of the moon's rays'. However, the identification of v.12's principal subject (or passive verb construction) remains in doubt due to the presence of a lengthy lacuna at the end of the second half-verse.

De Casparis' translation of *rucira-dīpa-śikhā* as the 'blinding splendour of the crest of his head' supposes that the first half-verse refers to the image of Buddha whilst the second half-verse would refer to bodhisattvas, even though this strophe provides no overt indication of either. In light of what has already been stated in Chapter VI, it becomes possible to view this statement as a reference to the pinnacle of the temple. And if we engage in a modicum of speculation of our own and consider this strophe as a description of how the votive shrines constructed by high-ranking members of the Javanese aristocracy had been illuminated by the reflected luster of the cool-rayed moon.[62]

De Casparis (1956: 188, 202, n. 117) speculated that the stanza's reference to all kinds of food pertains to *pūjā* offerings supposedly dropped in surprise by the bodhisattvas upon encountering "the blinding splendour of the Buddha". However, what remains to be read in the stanza itself provides no clear indication of this. We could just as easily propose that these presumed food offerings were believed to have undergone a transformation upon exposure to the rays of the full-moon (*purṇimasya*), such as is envisioned to occur during the month of Āśvina in India.[63] The relationship between the presentation of food offerings and the light of the moon can be correlated in theory with elements pertaining to ancestor worship, given that *pravarānvayaḥ* also can mean '(being linked to) a succession of ancestors'. Confronted with the lacuna obscuring the final part of strophe 12, however, we are unable to reach any firm conclusions.

The Mañjuśrīgṛha inscription (792 CE) unearthed in the temple yard at Caṇḍi Sewu presents the name of the shrine's deceased founder as Śrī Nareśvara. "This temple is the manifestation of the glorious offering [possessed by] Shri Nareshwara who has incarnated in the realm of the gods" (Miksic 2001). Like the designation Naranātha from the Plaosan inscription, Nareśvara means 'Lord of men'.[64]

The Wuatan Tija inscription (880 CE) invokes "the royal ancestors who protect the palace of the king of the state of Mataram (*kaḍatuan śrī mahārāja i bhumi i mataram*)—an appeal that was to become more frequent in the inscriptions of succeeding decades, as the state entered a period of internal turbulence" (Wisseman Christie 2001: 45). Likewise, the Mantyāsih inscription (907 CE) calls upon "the deified kings of the past at Mḍang Poḥ Pitu" (the site of King Balitung's capital) beginning with Sang Ratu Sañjaya (Ibid: 26, 50-51). Central Java's Mantyāsih inscriptions also "mention several *bhaṭāra* who possibly were connected with the souls of royal ancestors and considered to be protectors of the realm. These were: bhaṭāra i malangkuśeśvara, ing puteśvara, i kutusan, i śilābhedeśvara and i tuleśvara.... An obstacle to this comparison is the existence of a preposition of place separating the word *bhaṭāra* from the names" (Soekmono 1995: 70). On the other hand, the

[62]De Casparis (1956: 177, n. 13) had stated that the Plaosan inscription "does not seem to contain a word about the small temples surrounding the main buildings of the Plaosan complex". On the other hand, we have already seen that line 12 of this inscription refers to something that is surrounded by a moat (*parikhayā*), perhaps a reference to the temple complex as a whole. Given the fragmentary state of this charter, it would be dangerous to presume that the smaller temples had not yet been built at the time the inscription was promulgated.

[63] The full moon heralds the Śārad Pūrṇimā festival night during which Hindus believe the full moon showers the earth with *amṛta*, making newly harvested crops ready for consumption. To absorb the ambrosia, milk thickened with rice and mixed with sugar is left outside to be bathed in the moonbeams all evening long (see Sehgal 1999: 509).

[64]Whenever ◦*iśvara* appellations became used in this manner on the Asian mainland, it was always in relation to a *liṅga* or Śiva image (e.g. Parameśvara for King Jayavarman II). Still, the appearance of an ◦*iśvara* appellation in a strictly Buddhist context (a deceased personage identified as Śrī Nareśvara) is demonstrated by the contents of Central Java's Mañjuśrīgṛha inscription.

'place' where each was thought to reside was likely to have been the image or icon—or during the later East Javanese period, the pedestal on which was installed the image (Weatherbee 2011: 133)—in which the personage's essence was conceived to mingle with that of a beloved deity.

Verse 13. De Casparis (1956: 202, n. 118 and n. 119) mentioned the difficulty he had faced when translating this strophe due to the lacuna obscuring the contents of *pāda a* and the repetitive use of *vara* (or *vāra*) in *pāda b*. Given that the verb *harati* ('removes, takes away, cuts off, severs') is in the third person active singular, whilst *varāṅganāḥ* ('eminent women') is plural, he supposed that the stanza's principal subject would be the Buddha or an image thereof, based on what is subsequently revealed about the divine image mentioned in stanzas 15 and 16, as we shall see below.

The composer's use of *vāra, samantataḥ* and *antaram* in this strophe are noteworthy. The reference in the *pāda b* to 'most excellent forbearance' (*pravara-saṃvara*) suggests that *vāra* ('appointed place') may be glossed as 'harem' given that the word can also mean 'anything which covers, surrounds or restrains', 'anything chosen, choice or exquisite' and 'anything enclosed or circumscribed in space or time'. On the other hand, these additional nuances also potentially pertain to thc enclosed space within the north *vihāra*, where the eminent female figures and female attendants occupy their appointed places. This sense of exclusivity is reinforced by the adverb *samantataḥ* ('on all sides') and the direct object *antaram* ('sphere, circle, field; interior; room, space in general'; see Gonda 1938: 488).

The apparent division of the twin *vihāra*-s into female (north) and male (south) cloisters noted by Moens (1921: 584-585) and other scholars—as potentially indicated by the genders of the images in relief on the interior walls of the two structures—may actually have been the reverse of what until now has commonly been accepted. If the female figures were intended to signify the king's consorts and daughters together with their servants (i.e. a harem), as de Casparis suggested, then the north *vihāra* might have been the king's royal foundation, and the south *vihāra* the royal foundation of the queen. The reference to the annihilation of the field of intense desires in the heart-lotuses of lustful people suggests the possibility that the north *vihāra* had been intended for use by male visitors, if de Casparis' theory is warrantcd. It is also interesting that a parallel statement subsequently is made in strophe 16 about a number of young men (princes, i.e. 'ornaments'), as we shall see below. This suggests that the text's composer may have intended to begin his narrative at the north *vihāra* and only subsequently focused the attention on the south *vihāra*. As previously mentioned in Chapter VI, the *peripih* discovered intact below the undisturbed floor of the south *vihāra* only contained finely granulated sand, which suggests that the inscribed scrolls and other items recovered from the pit beneath the north *vihāra* had served as the principal foundation deposits for both structures.

Verse 14. De Casparis (1956: 189) thought that the 'uninterrupted' (*satata*) arrival of visitors from Gujaradeśa was more attributable to commercial trade relations than to the appearance of religious teachers from India, as made evident in the statement about the *guru* from Gauḍīdvīpa that appears in the Śrī Saṅgrāmadhanaṃjaya inscription. Damais disagreed. "In fact, the two are not mutually exclusive and it is impossible to know what the proportion was of commercial and religious relations" (Damais 1968: 436).

Figs. 7-7 & 7-8. The crowned figures depicted in relief within the south vihāra.

Verse 15. De Casparis (1956: 203, n. 123) suggested that *kvacid* ('somewhere') may have also appeared at the beginning of other strophes in which the initial text has been lost in lacunas. "The term clearly suggests that the descriptions refer to a number of separate scenes. If one presumes that the word had already been used before, one might translate [it as] 'elsewhere'." Along with de Casparis (1956: 190, n. 60), one therefore wonders whether the crowned princes to which stanza 15 alludes are related to the royal figures depicted in relief inside the south *vihāra* (see figures 7-7 & 7-8).

Both de Casparis (1956) and Sarkar (1971/2) had translated *manmathāḥ* ('amorous passions') as if it were a plural accusative instead of a plural nominative. Though de Casparis' reading of *akuśalāḥ* (lit. 'sins, demerits'), which has been glossed above as 'impieties', is not beyond doubt, this expression does seem to fit the reference in the first half-verse to a number of young men whose amorous passions had revealed (*prakaṭīkṛta*, 'manifested, displayed, shown') [themselves] to their beloved ones.

Verse 16. This strophe refers to anger, which "is one of the three poisons of spiritual life: passion (kāma), anger (krodha), and delusion (mohe). Mohe occurs in the following stanza 17", whereas verse 13 alludes to the poison of amorous passion (Chandra, pc 5 Dec. 2010). The verbal element missing from *pāda c* originally must have appeared in the initial half-verse. I have selected *vigata* as the one surviving term from *pāda b* that logically completes the meaning of the second half-strophe based on the close association of *nirvṛta* with *nirvāṇa*.

In stanza 15, the poet refers to a number of royal youths adorned with innumerable crown pearls through the use of the plural nominative *bhūṣaṇāh*, i.e. three or more; and there are three figures in relief to which this can potentially refer. So when the second half of v.16 refers to "that one" it is possible that the poet was actually referring to the solitary personage depicted in figure 7-8.

Verse 17. This stanza refers to a personage who is able to attain the destruction of the dense darkness of deep delusion 'like a Jina'. This compels us to recall the use of the future tense in strophe five to refer to a person or divinity who is destined to attain the ultimate rest in the future. De Casparis saw this as evidence that the principal image he envisioned as being described in vs.1-10 was that of a bodhisattva. However, it is also possible that certain verses in this inscription actually refer to the temple complex's abbot or even a royal patron. Several of the Śailendra inscriptions discussed in prior chapters contain references to royal gurus, chaplains and abbots. For example, the so-called Kĕlurak inscription includes a verse which suggests that the Śailendra monarch may have received an esoteric empowerment from his *guru* Kumāraghoṣa.

Fig. 7-9. Religious figures in relief in the south *vihāra* at Plaosan Lor.

In relation to strophe 17 of the Plaosan inscription, Chandra (pc 10 Dec. 2010) has translated *drutavilambhita* in the following freestyle manner: 'which, though obtained rapidly (*druta*), were extended continuously over a long time (*vilambhita*)'. "The king visualized various *sādhana*-s rapidly due to his *saṃskāra*, and yet he continued to practice them over a long time, to eliminate the dense darkness of passions entirely". On the other hand, *sādhana*-s are manuscripts that delineate the worship of esoteric Buddhist divinities. So the personage to which this stanza refers could have been a royal chaplain, who was venerated for having produced such efficacious methods of worship.[65]

Krom (1923) thought that a pair of figures which appear together in a relief occupying the north-facing wall of the northernmost interior chamber of the south *vihāra* (figure 7-8) may represent the head Buddhist and Śivaite priests of the kingdom, an interpretation which would seem to favor the hypothesis that the inscription had been issued by a Śaivaite king. However, de Casparis (1956: 190, n. 60 and 202-203, n. 120) thought the man with the tall bonnet (figure 7-9) might depict one of the visitors from Gujaradeśa to which strophe 14 alludes.[66] "Everything depends on whether the remarkable headdress could be brought into connection with Gujarat".

Verse 18. De Casparis (1956: 204-205) proposed the following translation, "May this foundation, an excellent refuge for the other creatures who abide on this abode of misery not living according to Dharma (?) be protected by those firm in the Triple-refuge although it was made different". Sarkar (1971/2: I: 48xiii-xiv) weighed in with, "Judged from religious point of view, beings have no other shelter worse than worldly life. Those who are steady in the happiness shown by the Three have viewed this treasure as unworthy. Yet they have to abide by ... ... (and find pleasure therein)". More recently, Chandra (pc 10 Dec. 2010) has provided a clearer expression of what the poet had actually intended to say. "For beings (*jantūnām*) wandering on this earth (*avanica*) of samsaric existence (*saṃsāra*) there is no (*na*) other (*anya*) better refuge (*varaśaraṇaṃ*) than *dharma* (*dharmata*); this (*asau*) treasure (*koṣa*), even if practiced (*kṛto api*) in an abridged manner (*itara*) should be observed (*pālanīya*) by those steadfast (*dhīraiḥ*) in [devotion to] the Triple-refuge (*triśarmma*)...." My personal preference, however, is to refrain from mixing components from two half-verses whenever a sizable lacuna lies in one or the other.

Verse 19. According to de Casparis (1956: 185, n. 39), *varanarādhirājarāja* represents "an unusual way to denote kings in inscriptions from Indonesia". Chandra (pc 3 Jan. 2011) has translated this compositum as the most excellent (*vara°*) lord (*°rāja*) of human emperors (*nara-ādhirāja*). Given that this final verse combines dedication of merit and benedictory elements, one suspects that this epithet refers to the principal Buddhistic deity being honored in the entire charter. Whether this epithet simply had been intended to honor the Buddha as a world sovereign or *cakravartin*, or to signify a deceased ancestor presented in identical symbolic terms, remains an open question.

---

[65]For example, see Schoterman (1986) concerning the *ācārya* Dharmakīrti, who may have been the chief religious minister for the king of Sumatra when Atīśa (980–1054 CE) was residing on the island. Dharmakīrti was the author of two *sādhana*-s that have been preserved in Tibetan translations.

[66]A specific formula featured in the Kalasan inscription that includes the phrases *bhūyo bhūyo yācate* and *kāle kāle bhavadbhiḥ pālaniyaḥ* in relation to the word *dharmasetu* ('bridge to the Dharma') is echoed in the early ninth century inscriptions from India's Gujarat region (see Vyas & Shah 1995: 146 & 155 and Sircar: 1965: 193).

VIII: Suggestions for future research

The final chapter of this book is devoted to examining some of the key issues raised by long-standing hypotheses about the Śailendra dynasty that are in need of a fresh look and renewed research. Moreover, new hypotheses are submitted hereunder for explaining certain aspects of the inscriptions and temple architecture which already have been discussed in earlier chapters.[1] For example, one of the most important questions unanswered by proponents of the two-dynasties theory discussed in Chapter II is why two Śailendra monarchs would have chosen to bestow their patronage upon at least three different religious foundations located in such close proximity to the dominions of the Mahārāja Paṇaṃkaraṇa dyaḥ Pañcapaṇa of the Kalasan charter?[2] Furthermore, if the center of Śailendra power in Central Java was not in the general vicinity of Kalasan, Ratu Baka and the Prambanan Plain, where three of the dynasty's charters have been recovered (see figure 8-1 below), then where was it located and why didn't the Śailendra dynasty elect to build equally impressive religious foundations within its own domain on Java?[3]

As previously discussed in Chapter I, the date of the Isthmus of Kra stele coincides with the anniversary of a significant event in the history of maritime Southeast Asia pertaining to the king of Śrīvijaya who had initiated a *siddhayātra* on *ekādaśī-śuklapakṣa* in the month of Vaiśākha during Śaka 605, according to the Kedukan Bukit inscription. It is therefore highly interesting that Damais (1955: 205) ventured the suggestion that the most probable date to be recovered from the text fragments presented in verse 12 from the Śrī Saṅgrāma-dhanaṃjaya inscription would be the full-moon day in the month of Āśvina (=Asuji) in 704 Śaka. If correct, this would have been the anniversary of the coronation of Rakai Panangkaran, according to the Wanua Tĕngah III charter: "In 668 Śaka, in the month of Asuji, on the 15th day of the light half of the month, [the weekday] Paniruan (in the six-day week), Pahing (in the five-day week), Anggara (in the Indian seven-day week)" (Wisseman Christie 2001: 30, see also 51).

According to the *Viṣṇudharmottara-purāṇa* (2, a.162), "On every anniversary of the first 'coronation' the king should repeat the rites; this leads to welfare, to increase of the country, to the destruction of the enemies and so on. Then the 'inauguration' has become cyclic, annually carrying the ruler and his realm beyond a difficult stage, and recreating the beneficial power inherent in kingship" (Gonda 1966: 143).

---

[1]For a list of the major archaeological and historical hypotheses discussed in this book, see the hypotheses entries in the Index.

[2]Anthropologist Roy Jordaan (2006: 18) considers it plausible that a marital alliance had been arranged between the two families. He has also postulated that king Airlangga had married Śrī Sanggrāmavijaya, presumably a Śailendra princess, during the eastern Javanese period (Jordaan 2007).

[3]The South Kedu area appears to be the most plausible location. The original brick construction housing a triad of impressive Buddhistic images at Caṇḍi Mendut (Brandes 1902: 141-143; Long 2009: xxxii-xxxiii), which was subsequently encased in a stone mantle, may very well date from the same period as the first stage of construction at Caṇḍi Kalasan previously mentioned above. A short inscription in the Palaeojavanese (Early Kawi) script, as well as the remains of a *pĕṇḍapa* and two other brick structures also were unearthed in the immediate vicinity of Caṇḍi Mendut (for an overview, see Long 2009: xxix-xxx, 60-61).

Davidson (2011) has observed that the classical and medieval royal consecration rites of India had directly inspired Buddhist *abhiṣeka* performances, among other things, as a rite of coronation as well as a ritual of renewal.

> "[These] were rites appropriate to overlords or emperors (*rājādhirāja* or *cakravartin*), even if we sometimes encounter local princes arrogating both the rites and the epithets for the purpose of feudal posturing. The difference between the rite of coronation and renewal is that the former was more often referred to as the 'great coronation' (*mahābhiṣeka*) while the latter was designated the 'renewed consecration' (*punarabhiṣeka*), either to be performed on the anniversary of the great coronation or in the winter month of Pauṣa (December—January, *pauṣābhiṣeka*) .... Both coronation and renewal rituals were always associated with *homa* sacrifices and related Brahmanical rites ...."[4] (Davidson 2011: 72; see also Quaritch Wales 1977: 154).

Still, Damais' reading of strophe 12 from the inscription found in the former *desa* Kĕlurak will need to be verified from a fresh reading of the stone before we can apply this data to our analysis of the single-dynasty and two-dynasties theories for the Kalasan charter.

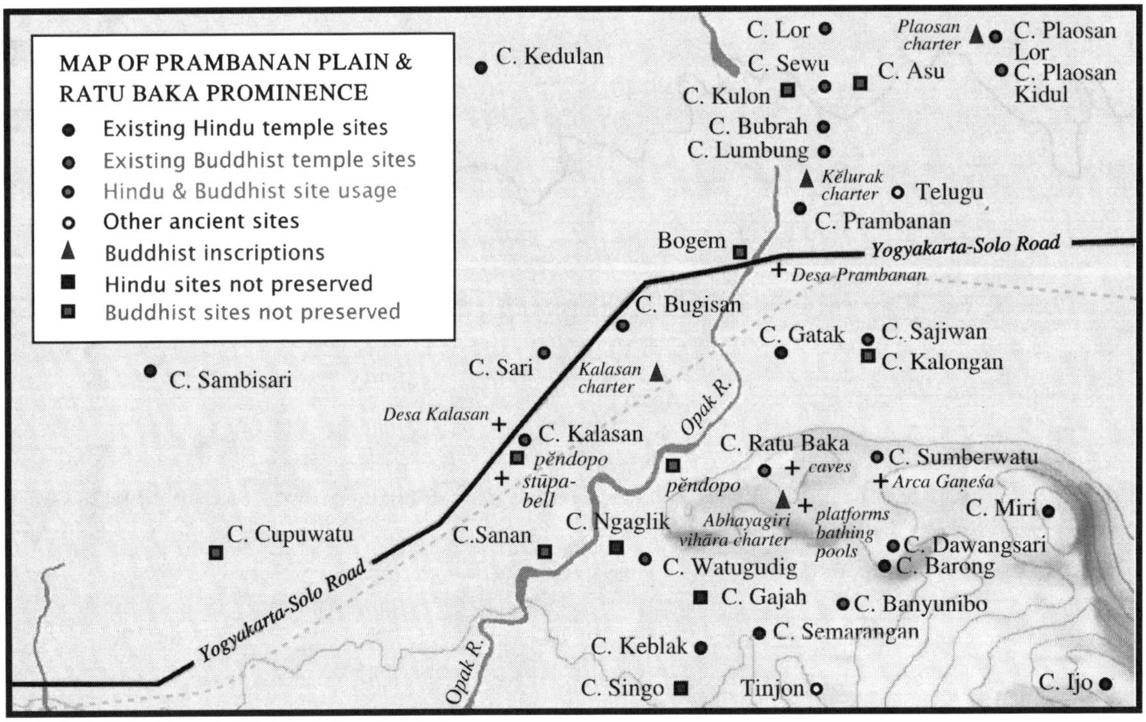

Fig. 8-1. Map of the Prambanan Plain and Ratu Baka prominence.[5]

[4]This would explain why it would have been advantageous for the promulgator of the so-called Kĕlurak inscription to have had a Brahmin from Bengal present as his spiritual *guru*. For a discussion of the importance of *homa* rites in a Vajrayāna context, see Wayman and Tajima 1992: 189-202.

[5]The locations marked for the Kalasan and Śrī Saṅgrāmadhanaṃjaya charters are only rough approximations based on the general nature of the descriptions of their respective finding places as reported in the early Dutch-language literature.

Esoteric Buddhist rites and the Śrī Saṅgrāmadhanaṃjaya inscription

The designation of one or more Buddhist divinities by means of four names or epithets ending in °*īśvara* in v.1, which Bosch remarked are typical designations for the Hindu god Śiva,[6] may have had a specific purpose with respect to the Śailendra king's political relations with other states during the latter half of the eighth century. Furthermore, a similar intent may likewise have inspired the equating of Mañjuśrī with all the Hindu divinities in v.15 of the Śrī Saṅgrāmadhanaṃjaya inscription.

In ancient India, Bhadreśvara ('Lord of Well-Being' = *īśvara*, 'lord'; *bhadra*, 'prosperity, happiness, health, welfare, good fortune') was a well known designation applied to Śiva and Śivaite temples in the *Purāṇa*-s and elsewhere (Gupta 1989: 169-170). However, it was in Southeast Asia that the cult of Bhadreśvara appears to have reached its apogee. During the late fourth or early fifth century, the king Bhadravarman constructed a Bhadreśvara temple at My Son (Central Vietnam). According to Southworth (2001: 165-169), the three surviving Sanskrit steles for the demarcation of this temple's physical boundaries not only confirm the shrine's dedication to Śiva but also mention his consort Umā as well as Brahmā and Viṣṇu. After a fire decimated the original structure, King Śambhuvarman (died 629 CE) rebuilt the temple but changed its name to Śambhubhadreśvara, thereby intermingling the names of the shrine's principal deity, original founder and reigning monarch (Cœdès 1968: 69-71).

The Po-Nagar Stele of the Cam king Satyavarman (inscription no. 2; 1 April 784 CE) refers to a sea raid by pirates that had previously occurred in Śaka 696 (774/5 CE):

> "[F]erocious, pitiless, dark-colored people of other cities, whose food was more horrible than that of the hungry ghosts, and who were vicious and furious like Yama, came in ships, took away the *liṅga* of the God, and set fire to the dwelling-place of the God, as the Daityas furnished with arms did in heaven" (Golzio 2004: 34-35).

Furthermore, the Yang Tikuḥ Stele of the Cam monarch Indravarman I (721 Śaka = 799/800 CE) specifically refers to a raid conducted by forces from maritime Southeast Asia in 787/8 CE, during which the Bhadrādhipatīśvara temple to the west of the capital Vīrapura (modern Phan Rang, Vietnam) was stripped of its icons and destroyed by fire.

> "V. Coming out from the west of the town, worshiped in the three worlds, he shines in the world from afar, with splendour as his ornament.
> VI. He is called Bhadrādhipatīśvara because he is the master of welfare, and maintains, by his splendour, the welfare, the health and the good of the worlds.
> Now, for a long time, having enjoyed treasures, grain-stores, male and female slaves, silver, gold, jewels, etc., he, the dust of whose lotus-like feet is worshiped by the three worlds, became, by his own prowess, the cause of the prosperity of the entire world.
> Then owing to the excess of faults in the Kali age it (i.e. the temple, also called Bhadrādhipatīśvara) was burnt by the army of Java coming by means of ships, and became empty" (Golzio 2004: 43).

[6]Viśveśvara is also potentially applicable as an epithet for Viṣṇu in Hindu religious treatises such as the *Bhagavad Gītā*.

King Indravarman I subsequently reinstalled the temple's principal icon under the name Indrabhadreśvara, which once again intermingles the names of the shrine's principal deity and that of the reigning monarch. However, the plundering of the kingdom's Bhadrādhipatīśvara *liṅga* in 787/8 CE would doubtlessly have been viewed as a devastating event for a political state in which this icon was perceived as the spiritual source of the polity's well-being and stability. A ninth century inscription promulgated by Indravarman II states the following:

> "He who has obtained the position of the head of the gods by means of his extraordinary power and fame, who is called Śambhubhadreśvara, to him I address this hymn out of devotion. Śambhubhadreśvara, shining in the company of a number of gods, is alone fit to be worshiped. He, the very quintessence of purification, protected the city of Campā where all the religions were prevalent. All the kings who have reigned in prosperous Campā, have become famous in the world, as Bhadreśvara there forms the essence of perpetuity and sovereignty...." (Golzio 2004: 70).

According to the Chinese Chronicles, the pre-Angkorian Chenla kingdom in mainland Southeast Asia also venerated a Bhadreśvara liṅga installed at Vat Phu (southern Laos) in the early fifth century. "Near the capital of the kingdom is a mountain named Ling-chia-po-p'o (= Lingaparvat), on the summit of which a temple was constructed, always guarded by a thousand soldiers and consecrated to the spirit named P'o-to-li (viz. Bhadreśvara) to whom human sacrifices are made" (Snellgrove 2004: 16). A significant number of inscriptions dating from the later Angkor period also refer to various temples in which a Bhadreśvara *liṅga* had been enshrined (Lustig 2009: 203-205, 208-209, 218; Soekmono 1995: 42). Hence, the phrase 'Hail to thee, the unchanging intrinsic nature of the *sugatapada* Bhadreśvara' may have held a special significance for the Śailendra king with respect to his wider sovereignty aspirations during the historical period in which Śrī Saṅgrāmadhanaṃjaya had promulgated his inscription.

The Śailendra king's initiation into the cult of the princely youth Mañjuśrī may even have influenced the selection of the *Gaṇḍavyūha* as the crowning tale depicted in the galleries at Barabuḍur, wherein the hero of the tale Sudhana is represented in the garb of a prince replete with a royal retinue—a remarkable divergence from a text in which Sudhana is described as a young boy and identified as the son of a merchant. It suggests the possibility that the monument's architect had intended these reliefs to integrate biographical elements pertaining to one or more of the Śailendra kings. The encounter between Sudhana and Mañjuśrī in the southern segment of the second gallery at Barabuḍur firmly places the pilgrim onto the spiritual path that leads him to Maitreya who, at the snap of his fingers, enables Sudhana to enter the tower of the Buddha Vairocana wherein the young pilgrim experiences an extraordinary visionary revelation of the *dharmadhātu*. Ultimately, however, Samantabhadra and Sudhana became cast in the central roles of *guru* and *sādhaka* in the concluding segment of fourth gallery reliefs, which depict the final chapter of the *Gaṇḍavyūha*, also known as a separate work entitled the *Bhadracarī*—a name that brings our attention back to the reference to Bhadreśvara in v.1 of the Śrī Saṅgrāma-dhanaṃjaya inscription.

In the *Sarva-tathāgata-tattva-saṁgraha* ('Compendium of principles of all the Tathāgatas', hereafter STTS), Brahmā, Viṣṇu, Maheśvara and a host of other Hindu divinities deemed evil criminals in need of taming are involuntarily summoned and subjugated by Samantabhadra-Vajrapāṇi. Maheśvara inquired about the identity of the divinity whose orders he should now obey and Mahāvairocana replied: "You should now know that this is the Supreme Lord of All Tathāgata, the Father of All Tathāgata, who performs the will of All Tathāgata, the highest son of All Tathāgata, the all-virtuous Samantabhadra Vajrapāṇi Mahāsattva Bodhisattva. In order to transform all sentient beings he has received the Mahākrodarāja abhiṣeka consecration" (Linrothe 1999: 184).

When Maheśvara refused to obey the orders of a being which he denigrated as "a mere *yakṣa*", Samantabhadra-Vajrapāṇi slayed the Hindu divinity. At the request of the Tathāgatas, however, Maheśvara was resurrected and eventually tamed, enlightened and consecrated as the Tathāgata of a distant world system. Samantabhadra-Vajrapāṇi (also called Vajrahūṃkāra and Trailokyavijaya in the STTS): "produced the 'Moon-Foot' Symbol of the Thought of Enlightenment (*bodhicitta*) of All the Buddhas through the use of the following *mantra*: 'OM Most Excellent Moon, Light-Ray of Samantabhadra, Great Adamantine One HUM'. As soon as the spell was pronounced, the Buddha Most Excellent Moon came forth from his foot, and having settled in the form of a lunar crescent on the head of Maheśvara, who was trodden on by Vajrapāṇi's foot, he took up his position on Vajrapāṇi's left side.... 'Oho! [T]he peerless wisdom of all the Buddhas, That one should gain buddhahood by the mere touch of this foot'." (Snellgrove 1987: 139-140).

In the wake of the subjugation, taming and conversion to Buddhism of Umā and Maheśvara (= Śiva, the Śivaite 'Lord of the Three Worlds'), the victorious Buddhist divinity known thereafter as Trailokyavijaya had become the new 'Master of the Three Worlds' (*trailokyādhipati*). Hence, this legend presents a well-known precedent for a Buddhist divinity having usurped the name or epithet of a conquered Hindu divinity, and thus potentially applicable to vs. 1 and 15[7] of the Śrī Saṅgrāmadhanaṃjaya inscription.

Though the STTS legend briefly recounted above does not pertain to Mañjuśrī directly, in Mañjuśrīmitra's *Upadeśa* as well as in other NS commentaries we similarly find noxious Hindu divinities and demigods likewise being tamed and converted to Buddhism by a group of divinities belonging to the *vajra-kula-maṇḍala* led by Trailokyavijaya (Wayman 1985: 31). Hindu divinities also become assigned to positions within the *maṇḍala* over which Dharmadhātuvāgīśvara Mañjughoṣa presides.

Mañjuśrī is called Mañjughoṣa when he signifies the Dharmakāya, which is "not other than the variegated items of the *maṇḍala*. The Lord in the center of the *maṇḍala* can also be understood as the central component – the *maṇḍa* – while the surrounding gods and goddesses are the containing element – the *la*; and these are nontwo" (Wayman 1985: 28). So when v.15 of the Śrī Saṅgrāmadhanaṃjaya inscription refers to Mañjuśrī (Mañjuvāk) as the "Lord (*svāmī*) containing all the gods", the statement is entirely consistent with a non-dual interpretation of Mañjughoṣa as both the core and containing elements of the Dharmadhātuvāgīśvara *maṇḍala,* which also integrates a contingent of formerly noxious Hindu divinities at the periphery. In the later prose section of the NS on benefits, the Buddha tells

[7]The reference to 'He the ... Brahmā, Viṣṇu, Maheśvara' in v.15 of the Kĕlurak inscription can be equated in theory with the three major divisions of a *śivaliṅga*: the square base, octagonal mid-section and round head.

Vajrapāṇi (initially designated as Vajradhara and Trilokavijaya in NS v.1) that when he and other worshipers recite the *Nāmasaṃgīti* in its entirety, the benefits they receive include the assimilation of the protective powers of all these Hindu deities.

As stanza 16 from the Śrī Saṅgrāmadhanaṃjaya inscription states, "Situated in this place for welfare and prosperity, this Mañjuśrī who is active and strong shall be the paramount protection of another's property making a steadfast effort for his region." Furthermore, the theme of protection is taken up once again in v.18, where the Tārkṣya (= Mañjuśrī) is called upon to protect the defense [of the region], by destroying all dangers with his gentle roar (*mañjurava*, an epithet of Mañjuśrī). So having learned that the Śailendra king's preceptor —who was, so to say, veritably Mañjughoṣa himself—had bestowed great supernatural powers on the Śailendra monarch, we naturally wonder whether these powers had included the ability to tame and assimilate the Hindu state divinities and divine entourages of rival kingdoms on Java and elsewhere in Southeast Asia. Whether future research on this topic might lead to fruitful results remains an open question.

The Abhayagirivihāra and the temples on the Prambanan Plain

Sundberg (2003: 178) has suggested that the interconnected five gates of the monumental *gopura* of the western compound might have served as a conduit for divinities summoned through the use of a *mantra* to a *maṇḍala* on the summit of Ratu Baka, symbolically considered the Buddhist Sumeru as the opening stanza suggests.[8] This theory demands further investigation. The gold foil inscription unearthed in front of the western compound, which in Sundberg's opinion integrates a variant of the appellation Panaraban—the apanage domain associated with the reigning king between 784 and 803 CE—might have been associated with a movable image (*calanti pratimā*) and pedestal periodically stationed in one of the five doorways. Snellgrove expressed the opinion that this loose *oṃ ṭakī hūṃ jaḥ svāhā mantra* had been associated with a statue rather than a building (see Sundberg 2003: 178, n. 29). The temporary placement of movable Buddhist statuary within open doorways is otherwise unknown on Java, but the same may be also said about the huge *gopura*, for which no other Hindu-Buddhist architectural parallel has been discovered on the island.

In comparison with the doorway at the center of the structure, the conjoined openings on either side become successively narrower in width and shallower in depth. Among other things, these open passageways have walls with slightly recessed sides in their central parts (see the drawing in Oudheidkundige Verslag 1938: 12), which suggests the possible provision of additional maneuvering space when installing images therein. A local resident discovered a knife and sword made of iron in the paddy field close to the structure that the Javanese believe to have been the actual *kraton*.[9] Including the handle, the sword measured 60 cm to 70 cm. in length and displayed the same form as the swords displayed by Hindu

[8]In support of this theory, Sundberg cited the following observation made by Snellgrove (1987: 222-3): "the four door guardians represent the four stages of introducing the divinities into the maṇḍala, which are effected by the mantra Jaḥ Hūṃ Vaṃ Hoḥ! Vajrāṅkuśa (Vajra-Hook) summons them; Vajrapaśa (Vajra-Noose) draws them in; Vajrasphoṭa (Vajra-Fetter) binds them and Vajrāveśa (Vajra-Penetration) alias Vajraghaṇṭā (Vajra-Bell) completes the pervasion of the maṇḍala by wisdom".

[9]*Kraton* is a derivative of the Old Javanese *kĕraton* (*kĕ-ratu-an*), 'the place of the *ratu*', i.e. king (Naerssen & Iongh 1977: 17); the Old Malay equivalent is *kaḍatuan* (*ka-datu-an*), 'the place of the *ḍatu*', i.e. ruler.

and Buddhist divinities in the region's narrative reliefs (Oudheidkundige Verslag 1950: 37), which suggests that this artifact might have served as the attribute for a sizable image.

With the above configuration in mind for Ratu Baka's monumental *gopura*, it is possible to envision the similarities with the image layout in the individual chambers within the twin *vihāra* at Caṇḍi Plaosan Lor. The largest image, presumably a seated Buddha sculpture cast in bronze or another metal, formerly occupied the center of the altar, flanked by a somewhat smaller image to either side plus two even smaller images housed in the pair side-wall niches within each *cella*. If we view the monumental *gopura* at Ratu Baka as having been intended to suggest a similar ordering of images, then it is possible to envision the lengthy spaces on the second terrace to either side of the main entrance staircase as having provided ample room for the congregation. To accommodate human traffic between the second and third terraces there is a second entrance of normal human proportions elsewhere on the west side that is comparable in size to the other small entrances found on the south and east sides of the western compound.

The image procession is a well documented component of early Buddhistic ritual that dates all the way back to the era of the rock edicts of King Aśoka, and with these annual events known to have been held in parts of India, Khotan, China, Sri Lanka and Southeast Asia.[10] According to the biography of Xuanzang (d. 664 CE), for example, the seventh century Chinese Buddhist monk witnessed two different image processions, including one near the Ganges River in which about a thousand monks from the Nālandā monastery had participated (Beal 1911: 177-178). The organization of the personages attending the ceremony at the place of assembly suggests a possible rationale for how the three terraces on the west site of Ratu Baka's western compound might plausibly have been put to use.

> "The procession began at early dawn from the traveling palace (*of the king*). As they drew nigh the gate of the outer court of the place of assembly, each one was directed to dismount whilst they conducted the figure of Buddha within the hall. There they placed it on a precious throne, whilst the king and the Master of the Law [e.g. Xuanzang] in succession, presented it with offerings.
> After this the king ordered the princes of the eighteen countries [in addition to the kings Śīlāditya and Kumāra-rāja, who had ridden on either side of the Buddha image in the guise of Śakra (Indra) and Brahmā, respectively] to enter the Hall; then, of the most renowned priests celebrated for learning he selected about one thousand to enter the hall; of celebrated Brahmans and followers of heretical doctrine he selected five hundred to enter the hall, and about two hundred of the great ministers of the different kingdoms. The unbelievers and secular persons (*who were not able to be admitted*) he ordered to be seated outside the gate of the entrance hall" (Beal 1911: 178).[11]

---

[10]For an overview with an emphasis on image processions in China beginning in the second century, see Lai 1999: 41-75.

[11]The Yang Tikuḥ inscription of Indravarman I suggests that Campā had also made use of a movable image that apparently had served as the mobile counterpart to the fixed *liṅga* that was considered to be the palladium of the kingdom (Golzio 2004: 70). Several seventh century inscriptions unearthed in Sumatra refer to the *devatā* protecting the *kaḍatuan* of Śrīvijaya. Kulke observed that Boechari had translated the relevant entry as "divinities who are the roots [*mūlāña*] of this imprecation formula", from which Kulke suggested "that 'mobile' (*calanti*) images (*pratimā*) as representatives of this *mūla devatā* of the Kraton of Śrīvijaya might

Chapter VIII: Suggestions for future research

The fifth century Chinese monk Faxian wrote an account of the image procession that he had witnessed in the kingdom of Khotan. Among other things, he mentioned that a moveable pavilion decorated with the seven precious substances had been constructed for the procession in which the Buddha image was placed in the middle, flanked on either side by an image of a bodhisattva, which suggests the possibility that this triad had been intended to represent the Three Jewels (*ratnatraya*). Behind this triad were placed statues of the Hindu divinities. Moreover, all of these images were made of gold or silver and also ornamented with precious stones.

> "When (the car) was a hundred paces from the gate, the king put off his crown of state, changed his dress for a fresh suit, and with bare feet, carrying in his hands flowers and incense, and with two rows of attending followers, went out at the gate to meet the image; and, with his head and face (bowed to the ground), he did homage at its feet, and then scattered the flowers and burnt the incense. When the image was entering the gate, the queen and the brilliant ladies with her in the gallery above scattered far and wide all kinds of flowers, which floated about and fell promiscuously to the ground. In this way everything was done to promote the dignity of the occasion. The carriages of the monasteries were all different, and each one had its own day for the procession. (The ceremony) began on the first day of the fourth month, and ended on the fourteenth, after which the king and queen returned to the palace" (Faxian 1886: 19).

Faxian also witnessed the annual procession of the Buddha's tooth relic while visiting Sri Lanka. It is potentially significant that the final destination of the palladium of Anurādhapura had been the original Abhayagirivihāra of this Siṅhalese kingdom.

> "[T]he king exhibits, so as to line both sides of the road, the five hundred different bodily forms in which the Bodhisattva has in the course of his history appeared.... All these figures are brightly coloured and grandly executed, looking as if they were alive. After this the tooth of Buddha is brought forth, and is carried along in the middle of the road. Everywhere on the way offerings are presented to it, and thus it arrives at the hall of Buddha in the Abhayagiri-vihāra. There monks and laics are collected in crowds. They burn incense, light lamps, and perform all the prescribed services, day and night without ceasing, till ninety days have been completed, when (the tooth) is returned to the vihāra within the city. On fast-days the door of that vihāra is opened, and the forms of ceremonial reverence are observed according to the rules" (Faxian 1886: 106-107).

Degroot (2006: 71) has tendered the following speculation. "Could it be that the name Abhayagiri was chosen by the Javanese not only because of religious links with the Sri Lankan monastery but also because Ratu Boko housed the palladium of the Mataram Kingdom? Although there is no mention of this palladium in the inscriptions, we should

---

have been sent to those places where the imprecatory inscriptions were 'posted' in the outer regions...." (Kulke 1993a: 166, n. 30). For a discussion concerning the use of *calantī pratimā* in India, see Kulke 1993b: 356-358.

bear this possibility in mind. It could explain why it was important for Hindu kings to take over the place rather than destroy, abandon or leave it to Buddhism alone".

A variety of practices associated with mobile Buddhist images in maritime Southeast Asia is recounted by the seventh century monk Yijing (1896: 45-46). These included the sculpture's transportation in a cart or palanquin accompanied by the playing of music, the bathing and anointment of the divine image at its temporary location in the courtyard of a house, and the presentation of offerings such as flowers and incense before the icon by the people. So it is hypothetically possible that the five interconnected passages of the monumental *gopura* had been constructed to house reproductions of the principal icons venerated at one or more of the temples located within a 3.5 kilometer radius or so of the Ratu Baka Plateau. Several Buddhist religious foundations were already flourishing within the general vicinity during the late eighth century, such as Kalasan, Lumbung and Sewu and perhaps Sari and Bubrah as well. Furthermore, the image of Padmapāṇi to which the Abhayagirivihāra charter refers also could have been placed within one of the five *gopura* doorways and with a statue of Vajrapāṇi, to which the gold-foil *mantra* discovered in the general vicinity of the huge gateway pertains, housed in one of the other doorways.

Fig. 8-2. The so-called Caṇḍi Pembakaran, which rises above the wall surrounding the third terrace on the north side of the western compound's entrance (photo credit: Masgatotkaca).

In theory, Caṇḍi Pembakaran (figure 8-2) could have functioned as a center for the ritual burning of fragrant woods, and with the terraces as levels for segregating the participants according to a ranking similar what what Xuanzang had described above. The channel running along the base of the third terrace's ramparts might have been constructed to retain the image lustration water, though the validity of this final point can only be ascertained through an intensive study of the western compound's waterworks. With respect to the pavilion or hall described in some of the image procession accounts presented above, it is interesting that column bases for what had perhaps been an open air pavilion were found in the southeastern compound.

IJzerman (1886: 112) noticed the presence of a large number of unusual oval artifacts measuring 65 cm by 50 cm and featuring artistic designs of which the dominant motif was one of the five animals serving as the *vāhana* for the Tathāgatas of the cardinal directions and the zenith (figure 4-19 and OD-8260-63), though at least some of these stones may not have displayed any animal motif (see OD-8264). IJzerman discovered these unusual finds near two stone platforms located on the east side of the compound's numerous bathing pools, which were hewed directly out of the plateau's bedrock. The smaller northern platform, which has a singular staircase on its west side, is 14.0 m. (east-west axis) by 15.56 m. (north-south axis). The larger platform to the south, which has staircases on the east, south and west side, is 22.1 m. (east-west axis) by 21.5 m. (north-south axis).[12] Additionally, about 50 m. directly to the north of these two platforms are the remains of a large *stūpa* (see the map in Dumarçay 1993: 185).

The oval artifacts, which range from 25 to 40 cm in height, have a completely smooth bottoms as well as a smooth top with a square hole carved in the middle. Stutterheim (1930: 304-305) counted three with lions (Vairocana, zenith), six featuring elephants (Akṣobhya, east), three with horses (Ratnasambhava, south), one with peacocks (Amitābha, west), and three with Garuḍa (Amoghasiddhi). He also thought that these stones had served as the pedestals for a series of Buddha statues probably made of bronze, which would account for their total disappearance. However, the square pillars that were also discovered at the same site (see the photos in Degroot 2006: 166) suggest that the oval artifacts had served as their supporting bases. Though discovered in the southeastern compound, it is unclear whether these artifacts had belonged to any of the structures in the immediate vicinity. Just like the triad of miniature temples (figs. 4-16 and 4-17) found near the so-called *kraton*, these oval-shaped stones (fig. 8-3) may have been moved from their original locations to the area wherein they were first spotted by IJzerman. So it is possible that they had belonged to a pavilion set up in the vicinity for use during specific events.

The axial alignment of the north-south axis of the Abhayagiri *pĕṇḍapa* with the entranceways to several temples on the Prambanan Plain to the north (see figures 8-4 & 8-5) provides theoretical support for the image procession hypothesis presented above. The monumental *gopura* of the western compound also faces in the direction of the eastern entrance to the large *pĕṇḍapa* formerly located 130 m. to the south of Caṇḍi Kalasan and guarded by pairs of *dvārapāla* sculptures (see figures 2-7 and 2-8 in Chapter II). These geophysical relationships compel us to recall the axial alignment connecting Barabuḍur with three other structures to the east discovered by van Erp (for a detailed discussion, see Long 2009: 65-68). Barabuḍur originally had a small building on its west side that had been constructed to house one or more bronze images no longer in evidence (Voûte and Long 2007: 113). This unique structure, which was not permanently reconstructed at Barabuḍur, may likewise have been designed for conducting ceremonies involving movable images.

[12]This larger platform shares the same meridian with Prambanan's north-south axis.

Fig. 8-3. Oval stones from Ratu Baka featuring a horse, elephant and Garuḍa (photo credit: Collectie Tropen Museum 1910-1930).

Image processions involving the use of boats are part of the Buddhist ceremonial traditions of Thailand (at Trang on the Isthmus of Kra, for example), Laos and Burma (see, for example, Veidlinger 2007: 181; Kislenko, Arne 2004: 138-139; Scanlon 1985: 125; and Wilder *et al.* 1918: 951). The Kali Opak runs in a southerly direction to the west of the *caṇḍi*-s Prambanan, Lumbung, Bubrah and Sewu, whilst the Kali Borongan/Kali Pereng riverine system (see the 1926 Dutch Army map in the KIT collection and figure 8-6) may have connected the Plaosan temple complex with the western prominence of the Ratu Baka Plateau. The above hypothesis concerning a direct link between the Kalasan and Abhayagiri monasteries is enhanced by an observation made by IJzerman (1891: 15), who reported that the remains of a *pĕṇḍapa* had been discovered on the other side of the Opak River at a distance of 1200 m. from a similar construction formerly located 130 meters south of Caṇḍi Kalasan. Though IJzerman did not supply any directional data, if we use his 1200 m. distance estimate as the radius for drawing a circle that has the former site of the Kalasan *pĕṇḍapa* as its central point, then there is only one place where the circumference intersects with the far bank of the Kali Opak (marked by the + on the circumference of the circle drawn in figure 8-6) in relation to the remnants of the *vihāra* located to the south of Caṇḍi Kalasan.

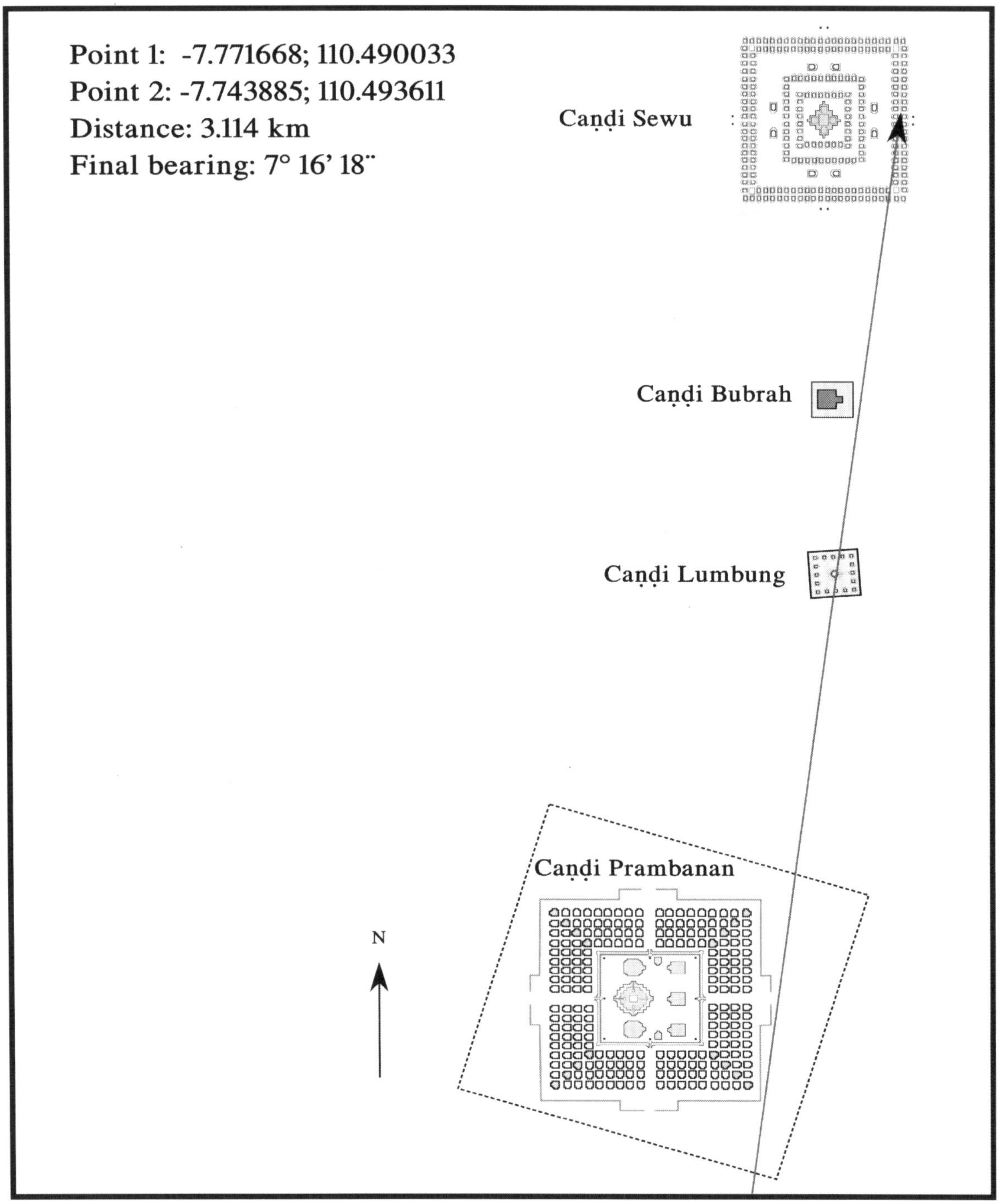

Fig. 8-4. The alignment of the north-south axis of the Abhayagirivihāra enclosure gates and double platform with the center of Caṇḍi Lumbung, and the east entrances to the *caṇḍi*-s Prambanan, Bubrah and Sewu.[13]

[13]The alignments shown in figures 4-20 and 4-21 were calculated using an online software program hosted at http://movable-type.co.uk/scripts/latlong.html (active as of 10 Sept. 2013). This web site displays the results as a satellite view supplied by Google Maps.

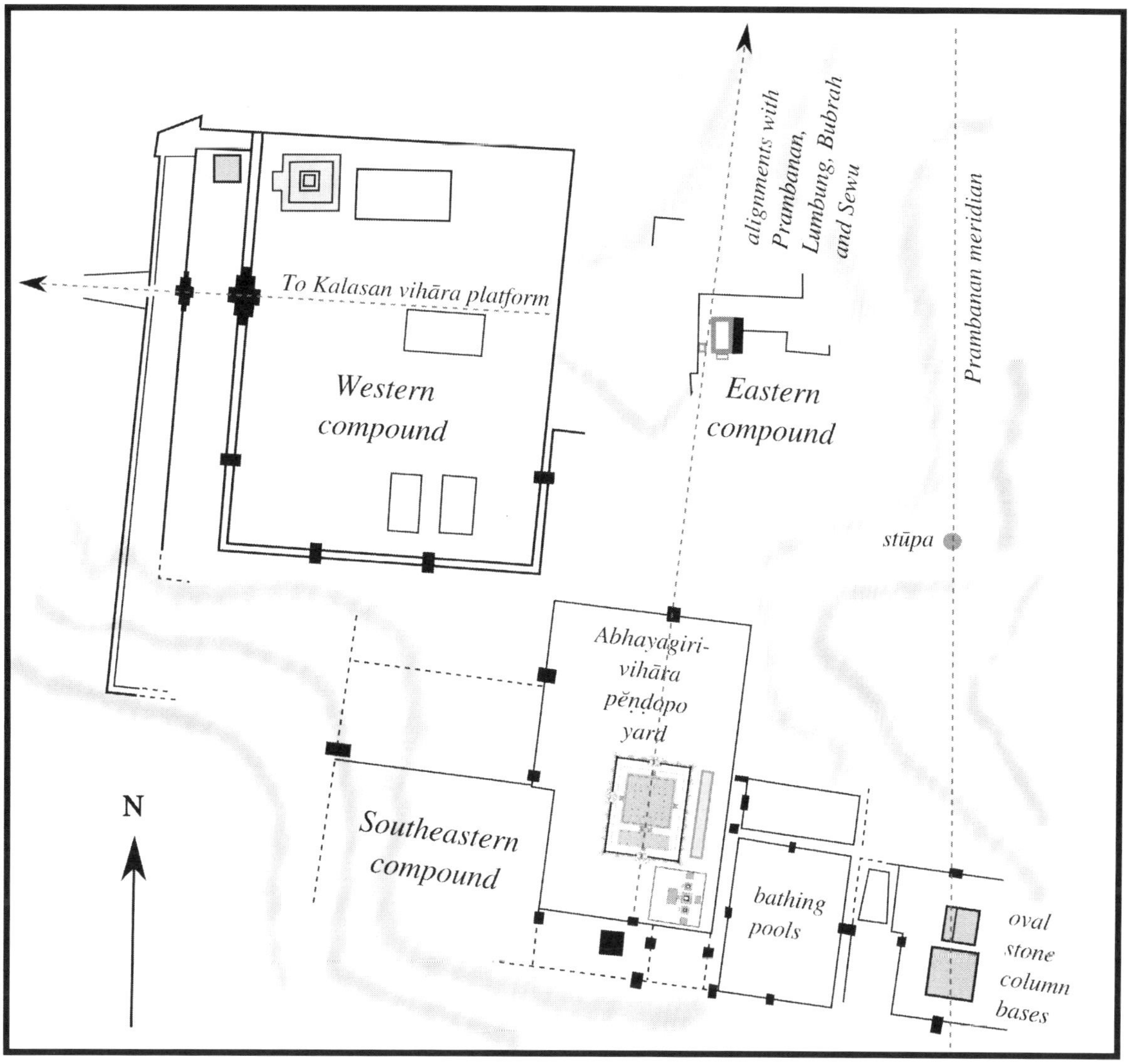

Fig. 8-5. The alignment of the monumental *gopura* of the western compound with the former location of the Kalasan *pĕṇḍapa* (see Long 2011: 7, n. 9) **and the alignment of the north-south axis of the Abhayagirivihāra with the temples depicted in figure 8-4.**

The site, which is approximately due east of the Kalasan *vihāra*, is situated in relatively close proximity to the place where Stutterheim had ascended the steep path in the limestone rock that had several man-made rock steps at the top (see Chapter IV). These stairs as well as the former site of the *pĕṇḍapa* on the far bank of the Progo may have served as elements of the proposed alignment proposed above for connecting the huge *gopura* of Ratu Baka's western compound with the former site of the Kalasan *pĕṇḍapa*. Moreover, the suspected site of the former *pĕṇḍapa* on the far bank of the Opak River would have been relatively close to the Kali Pereng (see the site next to the modern hamlet Modjosari on the 1926 Dutch Army Map in the KIT collection). However, the extent to which these last two interconnected rivers were navigable during ancient times is an important topic in need of further research.

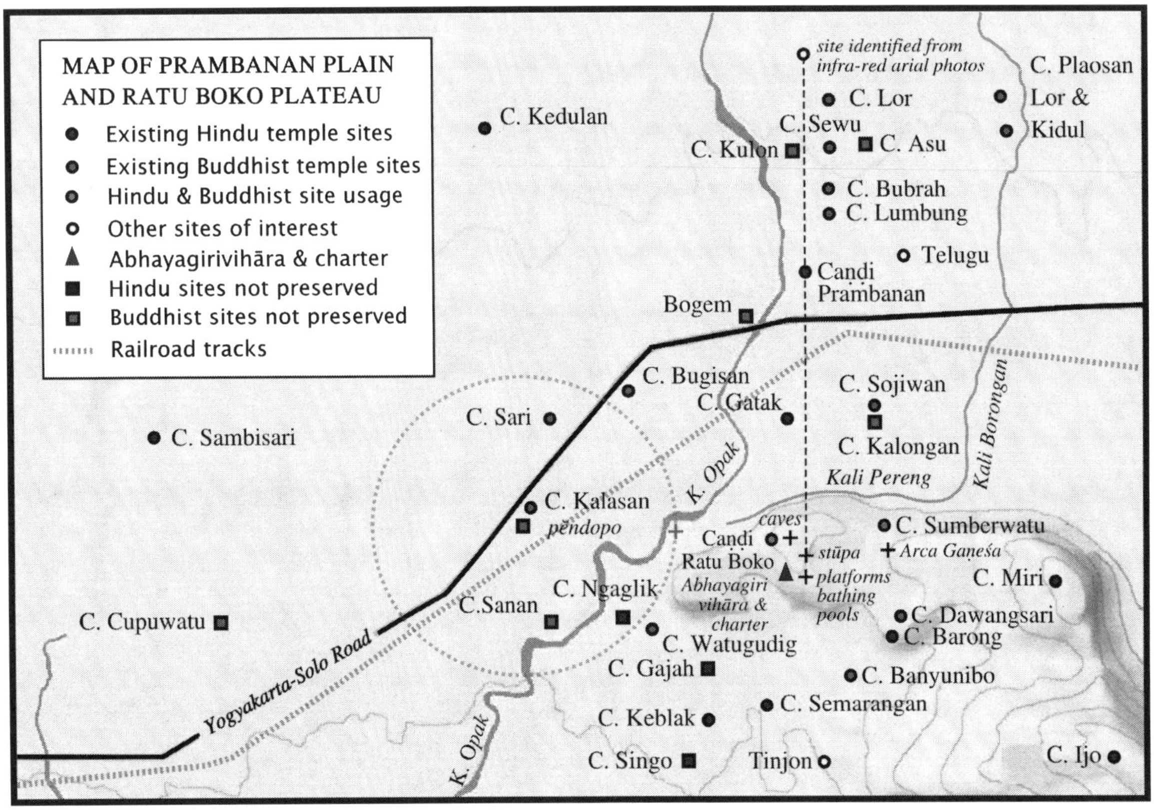

Fig. 8-6. Map of the Prambanan Plain and Ratu Baka Plateau showing a potential location (+) for the platform found by IJzerman on the far bank of the Opak River.[14]

The axial connection between the north-south axis of the Abhayagirivihāra's *pĕṇḍapa* enclosure and the eastern gate of the second enclosure wall at Prambanan might be purely coincidental given that it is generally agreed that the Hindu temple complex was not constructed until the first half of the ninth century, though it is also possible that the site's ninth century builders were well aware of the spatial connections already in place between the Buddhist temples to the north and the *pĕṇḍapa* on the Ratu Baka prominence to the south, and thus took this into account when laying out the new complex. Moreover, due to the uncertainty concerning the finding place of the Śrī Saṅgrāmadhanaṃjaya inscription, it remains possible that the site where Prambanan now stands had been occupied formerly by a Buddhist temple construction.

[14]The Prambanan meridian previously shown in figure 8-5 also intersects with a site located to the north of Caṇḍi Sewu that the late Dr. Caesar Voûte had provisionally identified as a subterranean man-made foundation based on his analysis of infra-red aerial photographs taken of the area (Voûte's drawing was provided by Sundberg, pc 2 Apr. 2012).

"Trying to determine the relationship between Ratu Boko and Hinduism, Bosch (1926: 8–9) suggested that the remains were linked to the largest Hindu temple of the area: Lara Jonggrang. He noticed that the axis of the third enclosure of this temple, if extended southwards, would roughly lead to the western gopura of Ratu Boko. As no conclusive explanation has yet been proposed for the orientation of the outer enclosure of Lara Jonggrang, this hypothesis is worth further examination" (Degroot 2007: 71).[15]

Fig. 8-7. In the eastern compound looking down the rock hewed staircase descending in the direction of the north gate of the enclosure wall surrounding the Abhayagirivihāra.

The later incorporation of Prambanan within the axial relationship between the existing Buddhist sites would be hypothetically possible if Ratu Baka's monumental *gopura* had continued to serve as the ceremonial site for an annual procession of the kingdom's Hindu-Buddhist images. As the short inscriptions on the bases of the small shrines at Caṇḍi Plaosan Lor clearly establish, the kings of Central Java continued to patronize this Buddhist temple complex throughout the reigns of Rakai Garung (829—847) and Rakai Pikatan (847—855). The dating of the ceramics and other artifacts discovered at Ratu Baka demonstrates that the plateau had been continuously occupied for a period of several hundred years (*circa* 700 – 1400 CE; see Pinardi 1984: 43-44). So it is possible that this site had served as a *kraton* for one or more Javanese kings at some later point during the site's lengthy period of occupation, giving rise to the collective Javanese memory concerning its use as a royal palace. During the late eighth and early ninth centuries, however, it is more probable that this extensive complex primarily had a religious focus given that the Abhayagirivihāra charter states that the building constructed for Siṅhalese monks was only an addition to a more extensive Buddhist monastic complex already in existence—perhaps in the western compound facing its sister cloister south of Caṇḍi Kalasan. The Buddhist *mantra* discovered in the vicinity of this compound's monumental *gopura* does suggest a religious purpose for this sector of the site as well.

[15]The 1926 article "Verslag van den Adj.-Oudheidkundige over de ontgravingen op het terrain te Prambanan tusschen den 2den en 3den ringmuur" was written by Stutterheim, not Bosch (see Bernet Kempers 1950: 24).

Rakai Garung and Śrī Kahulunnan

The titles and apanage names for Caṇḍi Plaosan Lor's royal and aristocratic patrons appear in the short votive inscriptions on the basements of the subsidiary shrines at the Plaosan Lor complex and with the majority of these apparently dating from the reign of Rakai Garung (829—847). According to de Casparis (1958: 8-10), 11 of these shrines feature the short votive inscription *dharmma śrī mahārāja* (see, for example, figure 8-8) on their basements and with two more loose stones bearing the same legend having been unearthed at the temple complex but which cannot be attributed to any particular building. Additionally, the same legend appears on the basement of one of the shrines within the site's southern complex, which is known as Plaosan Kidul. All of these legends *sans* any personal name may have been ordered by Rakai Garung given that the two *stūpa* constructions sponsored by Śrī Mahārāja Rakai Pikatan also display his pre-coronation appellation: Rakai Gurunwaṅi dyaḥ Salaḍū (de Casparis 1958: 10).

Fig. 8-8. One of the 13 *'dharmma śrī mahārāja'* legends from Plaosan Lor.

Beyond the 13 legends at Plaosan Lor that we may logically attribute to Rakai Garung, Śrī Kahulunnan was the only Javanese aristocrat found to have sponsored more than two shrines, all of which are located in close proximity (see de Casparis 1958: 9-10, plate I) to those displaying the aforementioned *dharmma śrī mahārāja* legends attributable to Garung. Though the identity of Śrī Kahulunnan remains an open question, there is enough circumstantial evidence to give us a reason to entertain the view of Śrī Kahulunnan as the title of Prāmodavarddhanī[16] as the queen mother and with Rakai Garung having been her son. Hence, one naturally wonders whether Garung's '*dharmma śrī mahārāja*' votive inscriptions were in emulation the promulgator of the B-side of the Isthmus of Kra Stele, who was succinctly declared to be known as Śrī Mahārāja by name. This would make sense if Rakai Garung had indeed been the son of Prāmodavarddhanī and hence the great-grandson of the famed Śailendra monarch known by the epithet 'Destroyer of enemy heroes' and also as 'Śrī Mahārāja by name'.[17]

An Old Javanese charter cataloged by Damais as the Garung inscription bears a date equivalent to 21 March 819 CE—the final year in which the Javanese sent a trade mission to China under the name Ho-ling. This inscription includes the phrase *rakarayān i garung tumurun ājñā*. "In the final analysis, it is very likely that this personage is the Śrī Mahārāja Raka i Garung from the list of 829 Śaka.... The word *ājñā*, as employed in this inscription for the Raka i Garung, seems to have been used in [other] inscriptions in speaking of the sovereigns and therefore means 'royal order'" (Damais 1955: 101).

[16]The name Prāmodavarddhanī can be glossed as 'Increase of joy' or 'Increase of delight' (*pramoda*, 'excessive joy, delight, gladness'; *vardhanīya*, 'to be increased or strengthened, to be made prosperous or happy'). De Casparis (1950:46, n. 5) saw an equivalence between *pramoda* and *pramudita* ('delighted, pleased, glad')—the name of the first *bodhisattva-bhūmi*.

[17]*Śrāddha* rites include the evocation of one's paternal and maternal male ancestors unto the third generation.

Wisseman Christie (2001: 38) has suggested that Rakai Garung's ascent to the throne may have been extraordinary and with the new monarch perhaps even having "forcibly displaced dyah Gula" (827—829), who had "failed to hold onto the throne long enough to be ceremonially installed". Though it is not impossible that Garung had been the son of Rakai Gula, it is certain that Rakai Warak dyaḥ Manara was not Garung's father.[18] Moreover, Rakai Garung demonstrated his political independence from Warak during his first year on the throne by restoring the *sīma* provisions that Warak had vacated for the Buddhist monastery at Pikatan previously endowed with irrigated rice fields by Rakai Panaṅkaran (746—784), who also had donated the village Kalasan to the Tārā temple founded in 778 CE, with the Kalasan charter naming the donor as the Mahārāja dyaḥ Pañcapana Paṇaṃkaraṇa. There is one more bit of information that potentially links Garung with the family of his Śailendra predecessor Samaratuṅga. The Old Javanese segment of the Kayumwuṅan charter refers to the presence of Ḍang Karayān Partapān pu Plār and his wife during the consecration ceremony for the Veṇuvana religious foundation in 824 CE.[19] The same two Javanese aristocrats were subsequently mentioned in the Sang Hyang Wintang inscription (*circa* 832 CE),[20] which mentions that the reigning king (e.g. Rakai Garung) had donated the image for the presumably Śivaite shrine mentioned in this inscription. So it appears that this ally of Samaratuṅga and his daughter had continued to enjoy close relations with the monarch subsequently reigning during 832, which just might be an indication that Rakai Garung had been connected in some way with Samaratuṅga and/or the daughter of the Śailendra monarch.

In addition to supporting the Buddhist religious foundation at Plaosan Lor, Śrī Kahulunnan also had promulgated two copies of the Old Javanese Tri Tĕpusan I/II charters (842)[21] mentioning the donation of land to a (presumably Buddhist) religious foundation called the *kamūlan bhūmisambhara*. These six records demonstrate that Śrī Kahulunnan had been a major supporter of Buddhist religious foundations during the reign of Rakai Garung.

De Casparis (1950: 83-86) was the first to submit a key hypothesis concerning the identity of Śrī Kahulunnan as part of his larger analysis concerning the waning influence of

[18]The Wanua Tĕngah III inscription (Wisseman Christie 2001: 50) states that Rakai Warak was 'interred' (*lumāḥ*) at Kelāsa whereas the father of Garung was 'interred' at Tūk (*anak sang lumāḥ i tūk*), though in both cases *lumāḥ* should be interpreted in the sense of conveying a commemorative function rather than a place for the literal interment of an ancestor's physical remains.

[19]De Casparis (1950: 122-126; 131-133) initially argued that Partapān pu Plār had been the aristocratic name of Rakai Garung. However, the discovery of the Wanua Tĕngah III inscription in 1983 once and for all demonstrated that Rakai Garung was already ruling in 832 CE.

[20]Damais (1950: 28, n. 1) expressed reservations concerning the specific year date.

[21]The date of the Tri Tĕpusan inscription of 11 November 842 comes from identical versions of the same Sanskrit text inscribed on D.107 and D.39 – two inscriptions of unknown origin that eventually were rediscovered in a collection based in Magelang. Both charters, which "very much resemble the Karangtĕngah inscription" (Soekmono 1995: 58), begin with the same eight lines: "Hail! The Śaka year expired, 764, the month of Mārgaśira, fifth day of the bright half of the month, on the weekday Mawulu (six-day week), Wage (five-day week), Saturday (seven-day week) ....[i.e., 11 November 842]. At that time [Śrī Kahulunnan] dedicated the village of Tĕru i Tĕpusan, under the jurisdiction [of Śrī Kahulunnan], as a freehold belonging to the Kamūlān Bhūmisambhāra...." (de Casparis 1950: 91). The name Śrī Kahulunnan has been inserted here twice to replace the mistaken phrases of "Her Majesty the Queen" and "the Queen's" employed by de Casparis.

the Śailendra dynasty on Java, which he attributed to the hypothetical marriage of Samaratuṅga's daughter to a Śivaite Javanese king. His attempt to identify Śrī Kahulunnan with Prāmodavarddhanī appears to have been based on his belief that there were only two possible explanations for why the Śailendra dynasty eventually lost the right to rule on Java: they were either expelled from the island by force or the region's two dynastic powers —the Śailendra and the Sañjaya, according to his interpretation of Central Javanese history —had presumably become united through marriage (de Casparis 1950: 108-109). Of these two choices, he expressed his preference for the latter and centered his attention on Prāmodavarddhanī as the only Śailendra princess known to history for potentially fulfilling the requirements of his theory. However, other scholars have rightfully concluded that it is highly unlikely that Prāmodavarddhanī had been wed to Pikatan. For a summary of the critical analysis de Casparis' initial hypothesis and the evolution thereof, readers are referred to Jordaan and Colless (2009: 36, 38-40). In light of the research conducted by Boechari, however, Jordaan and Colless themselves have proposed that Prāmodavarddhanī had been married to Rakai Garung, which seems doubtful to me.

Boechari (1982a) cited an example from the later literature of East Java in which the title Śrī Kahulunnan was used to refer to the 'Queen Mother', which matched perfectly with the use of the term in later East-Javanese inscriptions. Given that the title Śrī Kahulunnan dates from 842, e.g. during the reign of Rakai Garung (829—847), it is more plausible to provisionally propose that Śrī Kahulunnan had been the king's mother. Presuming for the moment that Prāmodavarddhanī and Śrī Kahulunnan had indeed been one and the same person, then the marriage of the princess to a member of another royal family on Java around the turn of the ninth century, or perhaps even a little earlier, would have allowed her son to have reached maturity prior to ascending the throne in 829 CE.

As highlighted in the prior discussion of the Kayumwuṅan charter, the royal title of *śrīmat* awarded to Prāmodavarddhanī in verse ten of this text from 824 CE has been universally rendered as 'princess' by all translators but also could have signified that she had been the 'queen' of another royal family on Java through marriage. In this respect, Chandra's theory about a potential reference to the death of her husband in the Kayumwuṅan charter is intriguing. On the other hand, the evidence at our disposal is either based on speculative emendations or otherwise entirely circumstantial. As Damais (1968: 352) observed, the aristocratic designation Śrī Kahulunnan provides us with no indication whatsoever whether this personage had been a man or a woman.

De Casparis (1950: 84) identified two possible stems for the Old Javanese appellation *Kahulunnan* based on the term's distinctive *ka-...-an* construction and with either *hulun* or *hulu* serving as the root; the first choice means 'slave' while the second means 'chief'. Damais (1968: 352) allowed that the two dated inscriptions featuring the name Śrī Kahulunnan probably pertain to a personage of royal origin given the addition of the title Śrī, and with the designation *Kahulunnan* almost certainly functioning as a toponym derived from the stem *hulun* rather than *hulu*. This toponym, he wrote, indicates an administrative origin that had also become applied to a proper name, e.g. a 'place where the *hulun* are found'. Even should we be willing to entertain a translation of *Kahulunnan* such as "...'place of the slaves', e.g. housing 'servants' or 'men' in royal service, it is possible that there was originally a function (real or possibly honorary) attached to such a term, and in this case the title of Śrī Kahulunnan could be glossed "...as designating an official having authority over the *Kahulunnan*" (Damais 1968: 347).

However, Teeuw (2001: 530) was unable to subscribe to Damais' interpretation.

"It should be observed that structurally these functions of *ka-an* forms based on a noun should be distinguished from *ka-an* forms based on an adjective, which indicate a quality: from *lituhayu* 'beautiful' comes *kalituhayuwan* means 'beauty'. Damais fails to make this distinction in his discussion of *ka-an* forms". Furthermore, Zoetmulder "mentions a large number of cases of *Kahulunnan* in Old Javanese literature where the word means 'the position (state, attitude) of a *hulun* (servant, follower) in relation to his lord or master, servitude, submission'." (Teeuw 2001: 530).

The *Kawi-Balineesch-Nederlandsch Woordenboek* includes a citation in which Yudhiṣṭira (Udyogaparwa) uses this title to address his own mother, Dewi Kunti, which is "a designation of a function that the Javanese poet has regarded worthy of Dewi Kunti, which evidently means that it is a high function" (Damais 1968: 347). Nevertheless, this particular passage cannot be acccpted as evidence that Śrī Kahulunnan must be a title pertaining to 'Her Majesty the Queen' as de Casparis had claimed. Other Old Javanese words derived from *hulun* were used in the sense of a member of royalty indicating their subject status in relation to others, such as three examples from the Old Javanese *Adiparwa* in which *(ŋ)hulun* is employed "as a substitute for the first person pronoun, even when the user is a king or a *guru*, and with *saŋ hulun* having been employed by a king in addressing priests in the sense of the king being "the servant of the Master" (Damais 1968: 348).

Should Prāmodavarddhanī have adopted the title Kahulunnan on her own initiative, or had been awarded the title,[22] then perhaps it would have been meant in the same sense that the former prince and renowned eighth century Nālandā scholar Śāntideva had submitted the ideas of slavery and servitude in the *Bodhisattvacaryāvatāra*:

"I give my entire self wholly to the Jinas and to their sons. Take possession of me, sublime beings; out of devotion, I am your slave" (2.8). "Now, to propitiate the Tathāgatas, with my entire self I become a servant to the world" (4.125). "May I become a lamp for a being in need of a lamp, a bed for those seeking a bed, and a servant for those requiring a slave" (3.18).

The significantly earlier *Bodhisattvabhūmi* (late fourth or early fifth century) by Asaṅga likewise expresses the idea of bodhisattvas sacrificing their own bodies "by becoming a slave or servant for the sake of others" (Dayal 1970: 175).

---

[22]In the Balinese *Rāmāyaṇa* (XI, 31), Sītā describes herself in a letter to her husband Rāma using the words *kahulun* and *hulun* to indicate that if one day she were reunited with her king, out of love for her husband she would behave as an obedient slave (Damais 1968:350).

The Old Javanese Śivagṛha inscription dating from 856 CE

Outstanding issues pertaining to the presumed activities of the Śailendra dynasty on Java are also raised by the contents of the Old Javanese Śivagṛha inscription of 856 CE (D.28), which provides us with an opportunity to reexamine two long-standing hypotheses. We shall begin by scrutinizing a theory first proposed by de Casparis (1956), who had envisioned that a military conflict had taken place *circa* 855 CE between Rakai Pikatan and prince Bālaputra, a descendant of the Śailendra dynasty whose grandfather had been the king of Java, according to the Nālandā charter. De Casparis' hypothesis raises several questions that demand closer examination. Though we cannot possibly fully address all of the relevant points here,[23] we can at least outline the main issues in need of further research.

Fig. 8- 9. The Śivagṛha inscription of 856 CE (photo credit: Gunkarta Gunawan Kartapranata).

The following discussion focuses on a series of stanzas composed in the Vasantatilakā meter that appears to contain historical data (see figure 8-10).[24] As previously observed, the Vasantatilakā meter featured in the Śrī Saṅgrāmadhanaṃjaya, Kayumwuṅan and Nālandā inscriptions periodically duplicates the cadence of the Sanskrit compositum *śailendravaṅśatilaka* ('ornament of the Śailendra dynasty'). So one could speculate that the Śivagṛha inscription's composer had elected to appropriate the signature meter of a defeated Śailendra monarch in the same manner as Hindu and Buddhist divinities lay claim to the principal attributes of the opponents which they conquer.[25]

Considerable progress has been made in recent years with respect to analyzing and refining de Casparis' translation of various segments of the Śivagṛha inscription. Acri (2010, 2011) has built upon the pioneering work of Aichele (1969) with respect to

[23]One reason why so much remains in doubt is because at least some of the readings proposed by de Casparis (1956: 311-316) may be even more tentative than indicated in his transcription (see Acri 2010: 501, n. 62).

[24]De Casparis also suspected that the preceding stanza five, of which only the fourth quarter remains, had likewise been composed in the Vasantatilakā meter.

[25]The meaning of Vasantatilakā, 'ornament of spring', also may be relevant with respect to the spring season (for locations south of the earth's equator) in which the date of the inscription falls and which also conveys symbolic associations with rebirth and renewed growth.

demonstrating how the allegorical content of the *Rāmāyaṇa Kakawin* can potentially deepen our understanding of the Śivagṛha inscription, while Hunter (2011) has argued that the composer's frequent use of poetic figures of repetition (*yamaka*) enriches the weight and grandeur of the inscription's message. Furthermore, an updated chronological analysis of the regnal years for the Pāla kings (see Jordaan and Colless 2009: 30-34) strongly suggests that the Nālandā charter, which includes a detailed genealogical record for Bālaputra, had been composed between 843 and 850 CE.[26]

Jordaan and Colless (2009: 30) have proposed that Bālaputra could have established friendly relations with Devapāla prior to intervening in Central Java. Among other things, this would eliminate the awkwardness of having to explain how Bālaputra was able to ascend the throne of Suvarṇadvīpa after having been defeated on Java, according to de Casparis' original theory.

> "In view of the prevailing means of communication and the indirect way in which the relation was established (through Balavarman, a Bengal vassal king of Devapāla, who acted as the latter's ambassador), the [Nālandā] inscription could have been issued in 848 at the earliest, 849 or 850 being more probable. Next, Bālaputra had to bide his time waiting for the best opportunity to intervene in Central-Javanese affairs ... [either] on the occasion of Rakai Pikatan's death ... [or] prompted by the imminent abdication by Rakai Pikatan in favor of his probable son and successor Rakai Kayuwangi" (Jordaan & Colless 2009: 49).[27]

Verse 37 of the Nālandā charter designates Bālaputra as the *suvarṇadvīpādhipamahārāja*. In this instance the meaning of 'ruler' for *adhipa* seems superfluous when coupled with *mahārāja*. However, the term also can be used to designate a 'commander', e.g. a person in authority, especially over a body of troops or a military operation.[28] Earlier in the Nālandā charter (v.31) the birth of Bālaputra is compared to that of Skanda, the youthful god of war, and the king of Suvarṇadvīpa is also said to be "expert in crushing the pride of all the rulers of the world and before whose foot-stool (the seat where his lotus feet rested) the groups of princes bowed" (Sastri 1942: 102). Obviously, such all-encompassing declarations of military and political prowess would have been deemed more that an exercise in propaganda if this inscription had been promulgated prior to the defeat of Bālaputra in Central Java—that is, if the Śailendra king had indeed been so bold as to launch an invasion of a more densely populated neighboring kingdom.

---

[26]The previously adopted range of 860 to 870 had compelled de Casparis to dismiss the possibility that Bālaputra had already been the reigning king in Suvarṇadvīpa when he supposedly had launched his attack on Central Java (de Casparis 1956: 297, n. 69). "I do not consider the possibility that Bālaputra would already have been king of Śrīvijaya when he took part in battles in Central Java" (de Casparis 1956: 297, n. 69).

[27]Unfortunately, Jordaan and Colless (2009) do not explain why we should view Rakai Kayuwaṅi as the probable son of Rakai Pikatan.

[28]It also has been suggested that Bālaputra had served as the viceroy of his father in Suvarṇadvīpa (see, for example, Jordaan & Colless 2009: 29-30). *Adhipa* also can mean 'regent', e.g. a person appointed to administer a country because the monarch is a minor or is absent or incapacitated. In this last instance, however, we would not then expect Bālaputra to have been declared the supreme sovereign (*mahārāja*) of Suvarṇadvīpa.

Chapter VIII: Suggestions for future research

The task of landing a huge army on Java's west or north coast and then marching it across hostile territories until reaching the Prambanan Plain would have presented the king of Suvarṇadvīpa—which de Casparis and so many other scholars have interpreted as an alternate designation for Śrīvijaya—with a number of formidable challenges. Though the Tamil monarch Rājendrachōḷa I (1012—1042) was able to mount a successful invasion of Śrīvijayan polities in Sumatra and on the Malay Peninsula during the early eleventh century, his naval and ground forces were able to draw upon the vast resources of a hugely expanded empire on the Indian subcontinent. Besides, the port emporium structure of the Śrīvijayan empire left it extremely vulnerable to attack.

Evidence of hostilities between Java and Śrīvijaya comes from a Song Dynasty record that dates from the end of the tenth century. An envoy to the Chinese emperor's court from Java "'... related that his country was in enmity with San-fo-ts-i [=Śrīvijaya], and that they were always fighting together'" (Sastri 1940: 279). However, the only mid-ninth century activities communicated in the Chinese annals that potentially can be attributed to Suvarṇadvīpa are two trade missions sent to China in 853 and 871 CE.

> "Considering their closeness in time to the revised date of the Nālandā inscription (c. 850), it is reasonable to assume that Bālaputra was responsible for sending these missions, in 853 and 871, from Chan-pei, that is 'Jambi', which is about two hundred kilometers north of Palembang .... The unhappiness of the envoys in 853, as detected by Chinese officials, should not be attributed to diplomatic inexperience of ambassadors of a newly independent state, as Wolters (1966:226) suggested, but perhaps to nervousness over the outcome of Bālaputra's imminent *coup d'etat*" (Jordaan & Colless 2009: 69).

On the other hand, the unhappiness of the Chan-pei envoys in 853 could have been due to the prior defeat of Bālaputra by the Javanese earlier during Pikatan's reign (847—855 CE).

The sole citation from the Śivagṛha inscription that could plausibly be attributed to Śrī Mahārāja Bālaputra is found in the lacuna-ridden seventh verse. Therefore we shall closely examine this stanza's four segments. De Casparis' translation of 7a as "He was a Śaiva in contrast to the queen, the spouse of the hero" was doubtlessly influenced by his flawed hypothesis that Rakai Pikatan had been married to the Śailendra princess Prāmodavarddhanī, who he speculated had subsequently become known as Śrī Kahulunnan —the promulgator of the Tri Těpusan I/II charters and several short votive inscriptions at Plaosan Lor. Jordaan and Chandra subsequently proposed similar translation revisions for this particular verse segment:

> "According to Dr Willem van der Molen, whom I consulted about the matter, the sentence literally reads 'He [the king] was Maheśvara to Īśvari, the spouse of the hero', in which Maheśvara may have three distinct meanings, namely that the King was a 'Great Lord', a 'Śaiva', or even equated with Śiva himself. Obviously the meaning of the designation Īśvari, for his wife, should be changed correspondingly" (Jordaan 1999b: 88, n. 50).
>
> "He was Maheśvara and the consort (*patni*) of this hero (*śūra*) was Īśvari. The royal couple were the veritable divine couple of Umā-Maheśvara" (Chandra (1995: 232).

	Translations by De Casparis (1956: 316-321)	**Translation revisions proposed by others**
6	(a): "The young prince ..., in possession of royal majesty (?)," (b): "protected the country of Java, righteous and with ...," (c): "majestuous in battles and in feasts (?), full of fervour and perfect," (d): "victorious but free from passion, a Great King of excellent devotion."	(b): "sincere and upright (arjawa) he protected the land of Java (jawa)" ... (Hunter 2011: 40).
7	(a): "He was a Śaiva in contrast to the queen, the spouse of the hero;" (b): "exactly a year was the time of the ..... ;" (c): "..... stones heaped up by hundreds for his refuge," (d): "a killer as fast as the wind ..... wālaputra."	(a): "He was Maheśvara to Īśvari, the spouse of the hero" (Jordaan 1999b: 88, n. 50). (c-d): For the conjectural reconstruction of these two verse segments proposed by Aichele (1969: 149), see the discussion segment.
8	(a): "A king, perfect in (this) world, ...," (b): "a protection for his comrades, indeed a hero who knew the duties of his rank;" (c): "he adopted a name proper to a family of honourable Brāhmaṇas (rich in) arts and virtues," (d): "and established his kĕraton at Meḍaṅ situated in the country of Mamrati."	(c): "gifted with art (sense) and virtues as the bearer of a Brahmin family name" (Aichele 1969: 144).
9	(a): "After these (deeds), the king Jātiniṅrat resigned;" (b): "the kingship and the kĕraton were handed over to his successor:" (c): "Dyah Lokapāla, who was equal to a younger brother of the (divine) Lokapālas;" (d): "free were the subjects, divided into the four Aśramas with the Brāhmaṇas ahead."	(b): "The kingdom and the palace were taken by other hands." (c): "Prince Lokapāla, who was regarded (by Rakai Pikatan) as a younger brother [or, the Prince who was regarded as a younger brother of the Lokapāla(s)], was King." (d): "The subjects were safe, divided into the four classes with the Brahmans ahead" (Acri 2010: 490).
10	(a): "A royal order went out to the Patih that he should prepare immaculate funeral ceremonies;" (b): "without hesitation, Rakakai Mamrati gave (grounds) to Wantil:" (c): "he was ashamed for the past, especially for the fact that the village Iwung had been the battlefield (?)," (d): "(and) took the utmost care not to be equaled by him (?)."	(a): "the prime minister began to prepare spotlessly pure royal funerary rites for the king"; (c): "He was ashamed that in the past the battle in Iwung village had been excessive" (Hunter 2011: 41).
11	(a): "All his actions during the time he was here were inspired by a divine majesty;" (b): "there were no enemies anymore: love for his subjects was what he always strived after." (c): "When he could at last dispose of power and riches etc.," (d): "it was only natural that sanctuaries were built by him, the able one."	(a): "All his actions, as long as he (Rakai Pikatan) was here [or, as soon as he (Rakai Kayuwaṅi) was here (that is consecrated king)], were divine blessings." (b): "There were no enemies anymore, love was what was pondered over." (c): "Making use of the availability of an imperishable (store) of wealth, etc." (d): "It is only natural that temples were built by him, the clever one" (Acri 2010: 490).
12	(a): "In addition, he possessed the knowledge, difficult to acquire, of Dharma and Adharma," (b): "but he was unable to conceal the lies of ....." (c): "The wicked ones ceased to act against him, ... (?);" (d): "this was the reason why the Halu, which you see now, was erected."	Acri's comments on this stanza appear in the discussion segment.

Fig. 8-10. Stanzas six through 12 of the Śivagṛha inscription (Vasantatilakā meter).

De Casparis translated the lacuna-ridden verse segment 7b as follows: 'Exactly a year was the time of the (or that he) ...'. He (1956: 293) further hypothesized that this could have referred to "the period in which the main (i.e. the last phase of the ?) struggle took place.... If this inference is correct the decisive battles continued for a year", i.e. in the period of one year between Caitra and Mārgaśīrṣa of the elapsed Śaka year 777 and the same date in the next year when the *liṅga* inscriptions were cut in"; in other words, between 10 March 856 and 27 February 857 (see Damais 1952: 30).

According to the Wanua Tĕngah III charter, however, the coronation of Rakai Kayuwaṅi took place on 8 June 855 (Sundberg 2009: 331). So even if we suppose that a conflict had indeed taken place between Rakai Pikatan and Śrī Mahārāja Bālaputra, the proposed one-year period would need to have begun in the first few months of 854 or perhaps even somewhat earlier.

De Casparis' hypothetical reconstruction of 7c likewise appears to have been heavily influenced by his widely panned hypothesis (see, for example, Damais 1968: 479-481) that Rakai Pikatan had abdicated the throne *circa* 856 CE and thereafter had been known as Rakai Wailaṅ pu Kumbhayoni,[29] the promulgator of multiple *liṅga* inscriptions found on the Ratu Baka Plateau as well as the Sanskrit-Old Javanese Wukiran inscription. De Casparis (1956: 317 and 293) translated 7d in two different ways: "a killer as fast as the wind ... wālaputra" and "killing as fast as the wind ... [he attacked (*a<mri>hi)*] Bālaputra". Damais (1968: 482-483) raised a number of objections with respect to the above translation of 7d: (a) de Casparis did not explain the difficulties inherent in the translation of *awali mwaṅ* ('[on a] level with, as fast as') nor the reasons for the direction he had chosen to adopt; (b) he proposed the emendation *a<mri>hi* based on his predisposition to search for a term that could be glossed as "attacked"; and (c) he applied a meaning for *amrihi* that is not attested elsewhere.[30]

At one point de Casparis asks us to consider the Javanese king to have been the principal subject of this verse, but then he subsequently contradicts his own interpretation by proposing that it was Bālaputra who had built up a stronghold on the Ratu Baka Plateau: "Bālaputra, presumably after a defeat in the open country, retired to a place (this seems to be implied by *ungsyan*) which could be transformed into a stronghold by means of defence works built up with hundreds of stones" (de Casparis 1956: 293) . But if we consider the Javanese king to have been the principal subject of this verse, then it logically would have been Rakai Pikatan who had built up a refuge. In any event, this fragmentary verse provides us with virtually nothing which suggests that any site on the Ratu Baka Plateau had been involved. All we have here is what Chandra (1995: 232-233) has rightly criticized as the stringing together of a large number of "stray elements, arisen out of doubtful readings, into a connected narrative" without considering other plausible alternatives.

---

[29]Rakai Wailaṅ is identified by several alternate names for the *ṛṣi* Agastya (Kalaśaja, Kalaśodbhava, Kumbhaja and Kumbhayoni, respectively) in the *liṅga* inscriptions (see, for example, de Casparis 1956: 244-279, 341-343; and Griffiths 2011b: 133-148).

[30]According to de Casparis, *amrihi* means "directed himself towards" (1956: 293, n. 55) as well as "he strifed after, tried to catch" (1956: 317, n. 11), which he sought to gloss as meaning "attacked, chased".

Aichele (1969: 149) proposed restoring 7c-d based on the *yamaka*-s appearing in this passage (*<giri>sthala, anila, wālaputra*), which he said helped him to define his selection of *a<la>hi* as a substitute for the emendation *ā<mri>hi* proposed by de Casparis.

<(m)āwān giri>ṣṭhala watu n inatus yat uṅsyan
hantāwali[31] mwaṅ anilâ<la>hi wālaputra //

Thus, the plateau (also) was elevated into a refuge with hundreds of stones;
and powerful a killer in league with the wind-god he was,
Bālaputra was vanquished //

Though Aichele's submission is more coherent than what de Casparis had proposed, it needs no saying that the restoration of *(m)āwān giri-* proposed by Aichele is highly speculative.

De Casparis' Rakai Pikatan vs. prince Bālaputra hypothesis appeared to receive a modicum of support from the conclusion reached by Aichele (1969) that the Old Javanese *Rāmāyaṇa Kakawin* not only had been composed during the mid-ninth century but also contains allegorical allusions to birds that were intended to signify the Buddhist agents or dignitaries of Bālaputra. More recently, however, Acri has stated that he has not been able to identify any allegorical elements in the *Rāmāyaṇa Kakawin* which suggest that birds were actually intended to represent Buddhist agents.

> "On the contrary, in various passages of Sarga 24 and 25 we find allusions to tame birds such as parrots which metaphorically link to Buddhists. In spite of the comic and somewhat derisory tone of the stanzas in question, these birds are depicted as neutral characters, often engaged in philosophical debate with their opponents"[32] (Acri 2010: 494).

Rakai Pikatan revoked the tax-exempt status of the Buddhist monastery at Pikatan, which had been restored by Rakai Garung. Rakai Pikatan's known patronage of Buddhist sites is limited to the two *stūpa* constructions which he had sponsored at Plaosan Lor during the reign of his predecessor. Though a short inscription dating from 854 CE pertains to the approval of tax grant for a Buddhist religious foundation called the Abhayānanda-vihāra, Rakai Pikatan played no role in the award.

Wisseman Christie (2001: 41) was somewhat cautious about equating *wālaputra* with Śrī Mahārāja Bālaputradeva, though she thought it quite possible. Given the absence of any allusion to a foreign power or the use of an honorific in front of *wālaputra* ('young son') in the Śivagṛha inscription, however, it is also conceivable that *wālaputra* would be a general reference to a younger son of Rakai Pikatan. One possibility is that his younger son had

[31]Derived from the Sanskrit sing. nom. of *hantṛ*, 'killing, slaying, destroying'; and the Sanskrit adjective *bali*, 'mighty, powerful'.

[32]By contrast, Acri (2011: 82) has argued that "the 'orders' uttered by the *kuvoṅ* [birds] in stanzas 24.112-114", against which the starling warns the other birds, accusing him of deceit, suggests that the character represents a sham ascetic—perhaps an agent disguised as a Śaiva Pasupata sent by a hostile faction to infiltrate Central Java".

mounted an insurrection in the wake of his father's decision to endorse a different successor. Another is that Rakai Kayuwaṅi had actually been a younger son of his predecessor.

> "The wālaputra in this inscription, considered as a personal name by de Casparis, is in our opinion an apposition to the young prince praised in stanzas 6, 7 and 8, who was consecrated king in the kraton of Mĕḍaṅ at Mamratipura. And he was nobody else than Dyah Lokapāla, to whom king Jātininrāt handed over the sovereignty of the kingdom, and who was to be identified with Rakai Kayuwaṅi pu Lokapāla" (Boechari 2012: 130).

Pollock (2006: 143) has argued that fame, "which constitutes a core value of kingliness", is the principal concern of *praśasti* discourse. Considering that the Śivagṛha inscription is the earliest known charter dating from the reign of Rakai Kayuwaṅi pu Lokapāla, and presumably issued at his express order, we would naturally expect the poet to have devoted considerable space to ensuring the enduring nature of his fame. And given that Rakai Kayuwaṅi had reigned for nearly 30 years, it is reasonable to hypothesize that he had been a young prince during the final years of his predecessor's reign. For other reasons, however, I am unable to support Boechari's interpretation. Among other things, poetic discourse promoting the fame of the reigning monarch, Rakai Kayuwaṅi, could have appeared in the initial strophes of the inscription, which have not survived and de Casparis' reading of *yuwanātha* ('young prince') in verse six is uncertain. Besides, the series of verses composed in the Vasantatilakā meter appears to fall into two discrete segments, with the first remark about the establishment of the royal palace (*kĕraton*) of Mĕḍaṅ at Mamratipura[33] appearing in 8d, followed by the death, or perhaps the retirement,[34] of Rakai Pikatan (*saṅ prabhu jātininrat*) in 9a and transference of the kingdom and the royal palace to Rakai Kayuwaṅi in 9b. Given that de Casparis also thought that 5d had been composed in the Vasantatilakā meter, this turning point in the narrative may very well have been intended to fall precisely at the mid-point of this narrative segment, a transition which is is comparable to that from Samaratuṅga to his daughter Prāmodavarddhanī at the mid-point of the Kayumwuṅan charter.[35]

---

[33]Citing the Kañjuruhan charter, Damais (1968: 489) disputed de Casparis' translation of Mamratipura as the 'country of Mamrati' and was all but certain that *-pura* in this case is used in the sense of the king's royal residence.

[34]Aichele (1969: 159) speculated that the reference to the remarkable one-year-old Tañjung tree planted in the neighborhood of the Śiva sanctuary in v.16 would signify that the deified king had died one year prior to the inscription's date: (16b): "its being close to a deity was the reason for its unprecedented growth, there in the eastern quarter (of the temple yard)." (16c): "extraordinary, comparable to a heavenly-corral-tree, its form" (Hunter 2011: 41). For a discussion of the tree as symbolically providing the deified king with the means for making a cosmic descent to the earth, see Jordaan & Wessing 1996: 69.

[35]Unsupportable elements of the young-son theory as proposed by Boechari include his mistaken identification of Rakai Gurunwaṅi dyaḥ Saladū as the eldest sister of Rakai Kayuwaṅi as well as his surmise that Rakai Walaiṅ pu Kumbhayoni had been a member of a Śivaite branch of the Śailendra dynasty who had challenged the ascension to the throne of Kayuwaṅi. Obviously, the so-called 'victory' steles of Pu Kumbhayoni would not have been allowed to stand if they had been launched by a rival royal house and intended to celebrate an insurrection against the reigning king.

The allusion to the king—presumably Rakai Pikatan—as the bearer of a Brahmin family name in 8c has not yet been satisfactorily explained. Damais (1968: 482) objected on the grounds that it would not be proper for a monarch endowed with sovereignty as a *kṣatriya* to have adopted the family name of a *brāhmaṇa*. Given that no inscriptions have been recovered that include a royal consecration name for Rakai Pikatan, the question remains open. Chandra (pc 24 May 2012) thought it possible that Rakai Pikatan's former apanage domain of Gurunwaṅi would perhaps be readable as *guru-nwaṅi*, with *nwaṅ* being the nasalization of *twaṅ* 'reverence, respect', though the "nasal form is not recorded in the dictionary of Zoetmulder". If correct, this might have a bearing on Rakai Pikatan's presumed ecclesiastical title of Jātiniṅrāt as well as why the Javanese considered him to be worthy of apotheosis. However, I shall leave the linguistic issues posed by Chandra's hypothesis for the Old Javanese language experts to debate.[36]

The establishment of a new *kĕraton* by Rakai Pikatan mentioned in 8d suggested to de Casparis (1956: 299) that the old royal palace either had been occupied or destroyed by an enemy, though he admitted that a new one also might have been built to signify the king's increased power and prestige. Wisseman Christie (2001: 40) thought it likely that the relocation of the royal palace by Pikatan had been "designed more to deal with political unease than respond to any locational inconvenience".

The mention of Pikatan's establishment of a *kĕraton* immediately in advance of the remarks concerning the transference of the royal palace and kingdom to Rakai Kayuwaṅi may suggest to the modern reader that this must have been among the last actions of the prior monarch before his death. However, we must be cautious in reading the inscription as if the composer's intention had been to present events in precise chronological order. Pollock (2006: 136-139) has argued that the recording of historical incidents was never one of the primary goals of *praśasti* discourse.

Given that the *liṅga* inscriptions of Rakai Walaiṅ pu Kumbhayoni were all erected between 10 March 856 and 27 February 857, there is a chance that they pertain to the occurrence of an entirely separate conflict over the succession sparked by the coronation of Rakai Kayuwaṅi on 8 June 855. The inscription's singular reference to a battle in verse ten appears to pertain to a village located in the vicinity of the Śivagṛha religious foundation described in vs.14—19.[37]

Stanza nine refers to the transference of sovereignty from *saṅ prabhu jātiniṅrat* to Rakai Kayuwaṅi pu Lokapāla. Aichele (1969: 150) stressed that *uparata* can mean 'passed away, gone' whilst Damais (1968: 477) noted that the term might either mean 'ceased [to exist],

[36]The same aristocratic title not only had been held by a predecessor of Rakai Pikatan, the Rakai Gurunwaṅi dyaḥ Rāṇu, but also by a later king who had briefly ruled in 887 CE: Rakai Gurunwaṅi dyaḥ Bhadra. If Chandra's suggestion is correct, we would perhaps need to suppose that the apanage domain ruled by all of these personages originally would have had a religious function.

[37]For a detailed discussion of the close affinities between the inscription's description of the Śivagṛha religious foundation and prominent features of the Prambanan temple complex, see Jordaan 1991: 170-174. Acri (2010: 484:, n. 17) has speculated that the trace remains of another inscription on the opposite face of the Śivagṛha charter can possibly be interpreted as the defacement of a Śailendra inscription. Still, de Casparis (1956:281) has characterized these so-called Pre-Nāgarī script remnants as somewhat different from those that appear in the known Śailendra inscriptions. Therefore, it would be helpful to have some additional details concerning the few scattered *akṣara*-s that can still be read on the opposite side of the stone to see whether the data would potentially support Acri's conjecture.

died' or 'resigned' (i.e. 'reposed, took a rest') and thought that it would not be impossible that Pikatan had abdicated the throne shortly before he had died. Though Aichele accepted de Casparis' surmise that *jātininrat* must have been the spiritual title of the monarch immediately preceding Rakai Kayuwaṅi pu Lokapāla—based on the subsequent attribution of the identical designation to king Erlaṅga in the *Calon Arang*—he did not agree with de Casparis' theory that *jātiniṅrat* would have been the spiritual title assumed by Rakai Pikatan after his presumed abdication of the throne.

> "... saṅ prabhu Jātiniṅrat ('Earth-born Ruler') cannot [also] be the title of King Pikatan, which he would have carried after his resignation, but either a spiritual title that he assumed when [on the occasion of] exercising religious activities or perhaps an epithet by which the author of the inscription hinted at the impermanence of all human creations—such as in the sense of the *Rāmāyaṇa* verse 3 (31) ... *prakṛti jāti niṅ dadi kabeh matuṅtuṅ pati*. 'According to the Law of Nature all beings end in Death'.... Whether Erlaṅga in memory of the epithet of the deceased King Pikatan held the spiritual title is almost impossible to determine. The meaning associated with it, reminding of *memento mori*, may also have inspired his choice here" (Aichele 1969: 150-151).

Aichele (1969: 146) thought that 9c literally referred to Rakai Kayuwaṅi as the younger brother of Rakai Pikatan, though Acri (2010: 490) has viewed this inscription segment as more of a comparative statement. It is quite possible that 9c contains an Old Javanese adaptation of the Sanskrit *śleṣa* documented by Pollock (2006: 139-141) in his analysis of Sanskrit *praśasti* discourse. As Acri has observed, the third quarter of this verse can be translated in two different ways (see figure 8-9), the second of which may be an allusion to the king's assimilation of the nature of the eight directional guardians of the world, as related in the *Rāmāyaṇa Kakawin*, Sarga 24. "Consequently the king must act according to the *brata* of those eight deities, meaning that he ought to know the good and bad conduct of all his subjects, that he ought to maintain law and order, to be just, rewarding the meritorious and punishing the wrong doers, that he has to cause constant joy, that he must be patient, generous and benevolent, but that he also has to destroy his enemies without delay" (Boechari 2011: 218, see also 227).

De Casparis interpreted the contents of 9d as an allusion to the national liberation of Java from the yoke of Śailendra domination at the outset of Kayuwaṅi's reign. However, Damais (1968: 489) was skeptical about de Casparis' inference, noting that the meaning of *swastha* has nothing to do with anything national. More recently, Acri (2010: 490, n. 27) has noted that "here the term could simply have the more general meaning attested in Old Javanese, namely 'happy, satisfied, safe', etc."

De Casparis (1956: 300) wrote that the expression *rakakai mamrati* that appears in 10b might be another example of a high title derived from the name of a royal residence, or rather, of the region in which this royal residence was situated. Damais (1968: 490) agreed that *rakakai* should be regarded as an honorary designation, but questioned de Casparis' contention that *rakakai mamrati* would very likely be "no other than the retired king himself: the honorific title preceding the name of the *kĕraton* could not well apply to any other person. It is, moreover, the only person whom we should have expected to give grounds" (de Casparis 1956: 319, n. 24). In a later publication, de Casparis (1986: 60) remarked that a royal court official known as the Mamrati hawang Wicakṣaṇa is mentioned in the inscriptions of Pu Siṇḍok, and with *hawang* probably being the title of a religious personage belonging to a specific order. Therefore, *rakakai mamrati* might have been the title of a court official charged with carrying out royal orders pertaining to religious matters.

Acri was unsure whether the principal personage in stanza 11 would be Rakai Pikatan or Rakai Kayuwaṅi.

> "[B]ecause of the absence of any explicit remark as to the identification of the subject of the stanza, and because it occurs just after the mention of Kayuwaṅi's succession in stanza 9 and after the latter king's apparent orders in stanza 10 concerning preparations for Rakai Pikatan's funeral ceremonies, stanza 11 might be understood as referring to Kayuwaṅi himself rather than to his predecessor. In this case, the clause *ni lawasnira ṅke* in 11a may be translated 'as soon as he (Rakai Kayuwaṅi) was here (that is as consecrated King)', pace De Casparis's 'as long as he (Rakai Pikatan) was here', referring to 'the king when he still was a king among his subjccts'." (Acri 2010: 492-493).

It is significant that 11d refers to temples having been built by the king. The coronation of Rakai Kayuwaṅi took place more than 17 months prior to the date of the Śivagṛha inscription. Hence, it is possible that Dyaḥ Lokapāla had initiated construction efforts at the Śivagṛha temple site or elsewhere in Central Java during this early period.[38]

When Acri and Griffiths read stanza 12 directly from the stone, they noticed differences in some important points from de Casparis' transcription. Therefore, the translation published by de Casparis should be read with caution. According to Acri (2010: 501), verse 12 alludes "to the end of the evil perpetrated against Rakai Pikatan (*mantan hale sira*) and to some kind of deceit or lie (*duwa* = *dwa*) associated with that."

We shall now turn our attention to a second long-standing hypothesis that was formulated to shed additional light on the events of 855—856 CE. Damais (1964) had speculated that the Chinese designation of Ho-ling, which was applied to Java in Buddhist texts and the royal court documents of the T'ang dynasty during the seventh, eighth and ninth centuries, would be a transliteration of an Old Javanese toponym. Walaiṅ is prominently featured in the *liṅga* inscriptions promulgated by Rakai Walaiṅ pu Kumbhayoni and recovered from Ratu Baka; it also appears in the Wukiran inscription dating from 25 January 863 CE and recovered from the *desa* Pereng at the northern foot of the same plateau. According to Damais (1964: 125), the use of Ho-ling (or Po-ling) in Chinese source materials between 640 and 818 CE can be interpreted to mean the country of Java if this also had been the name of a royal residence (*kaḍatuan*), in which case it would have designated all of the territory in which the sovereign's power had extended.

[38]It is unfortunate that de Casparis never published his long-promised study pertaining to the short inscriptions in red, white and black paint that were recovered from the *anumoda* buildings at Prambanan (see de Casparis 1958: 7, including n. 22). However, Boechari (2011: 128, including n. 16) refers to the later discovery of the name Kayuwaṅi, which was rendered in red paint within one of the buildings at Plaosan Lor.

Chapter VIII: Suggestions for future research

In 820 CE, after a hiatus of two or more centuries, the more ancient Chinese transliteration Shê-p'o had eclipsed the transliteration Ho-ling as the term for designating Java. Based on this, Damais hypothesized that the power of a rival royal house known locally by the designation Walaiṅ had declined thereafter and had ceased to exist as a political entity on Java in 856 CE.

> "In this case, the expression *walaiṅgajetrā* that is found in the Tryamwaka-liṅga inscription would mean 'by the conqueror of Walaiṅ', that is to say 'by the man who defeated Walaiṅ', and the expression *walaiṅgagoptrā* employed in the Kṛttikawāsa-liṅga inscription would mean 'the protector of Walaiṅ' in the sense of one who, having conquered a country, 'protects' it against new enemies, real or imagined .... Pu Kumbhayoni was not the king himself, which seems certain (it is said once that he 'reigned', *rarāja*, with no royal title given); he was at least of royal descent and since this is his victory he seems to have done away with Walaiṅ as a political entity, so he must belong to the opposing line I call that of 'Jawa' and which vanquished Walaiṅ. I do not conceal the hypothetical nature of this interpretation and others are certainly possible" (Damais 1964: 135-136).

Griffiths (2011b: 136) has noticed that *walaiṅgagoptrā* and *walaiṅgajetrā* may also be interpreted as descriptive determinative compounds meaning 'by the protector [named] Walaiṅ' and 'by the conqueror [named] Walaiṅ', respectively. That these alternative translations for *valaiṅgagoptrā* and *valaiṅgajetrā* are correct is strongly suggested by the most logical reading of 5d from the Wukiran inscription: (a) So long as the Sun and the Moon endure in the sky, (b) so long as the earth is surrounded by the four oceans, (c) so long as the wind (pervades) the ten directions, (d) so long shall (endure) the devotion of him whose name is Walaiṅ.[39] This obviates the need to explain just why Kumbhayoni would have expressed a desire for there to be devotion to what is called Walaiṅ, an interpretation submitted by Damais (1964: 132) that he himself regarded as somewhat enigmatic.[40]

Damais (1964: 132) had observed that the known Javanese inscriptions mentioning Walaiṅ are much later (856, 863, 912 and 912 to 919 CE) than the available Chinese source materials. But he attempted to argue that very few inscriptions of the seventh and eighth centuries Śaka have been recovered, and with the names of countries rarely being mentioned in Javanese charters apart from a more recent period where it appears in the royal titulary.[41] Fifty years later, however, not a shred of evidence has been uncovered that would support viewing Walaiṅ as anything more than as an apanage domain located in the

---

[39] *yāvat khe raviaśinau yāvad dhātrī catussamudravṛtā /*
yāvad daśadiśī vāyus tāvad bhaktir valaiṅnāmnaḥ //

[40] When Damais (1968: 472) subsequently revisited this issue, he argued that *walaiṅgajetrā* could mean one of two things in theory. If Walaiṅ had been the seat of the victorious royal house, then it would potentially mean 'The Savior of Walaiṅ' as in 'He who has dislodged the enemy Walaiṅ' or '... the enemy who attacked Walaiṅ'. By contrast, if Walaiṅ had been the defeated party, the designation could mean 'The Conqueror of Walaiṅ', either 'He who has overcome the country Walaiṅ' or '... the enemy from Walaiṅ'. He also viewed *valaiṅgagoptrā* as equally ambiguous given that it would depend on whether the person who uses this term is the 'protector' or the 'protected'.

environs of the Ratu Baka Plateau during the mid-ninth and early-tenth centuries. Hence, the Ho-ling = Walaiṅ theory proposed by Damais does not appear to provide us with any means for increasing our knowledge of the events that occurred in Central Java *circa* 855 CE.

Based on hints provided by Aichele (1969: 159 and following pages, Griffiths (2011b) has speculated that the references to Langka and Langkapura appearing in two of the *liṅga* inscriptions promulgated by Rakai Walaiṅ pu Kumbhayoni might be allusions to Caṇḍi Prambanan given that the *Rāmāyaṇa Kakawin* describes a very similar temple complex in Rāvaṇa's capital city of Laṅkapura.[42]

> "In fact Acri (2010: 489-93) has tried to suggest a connection, based on his reading of KR 24.95–126 and the Śivagṛha inscription, between Vibhīṣaṇa in the poem and Rakai Kayuvaṅi, both king in Laṅkā, which means that, at the level of worldly realities, that toponym would have to be situated in Central Java".

Wisseman Christie (2001: 44) thought that the original name applied to Caṇḍi Prambanan might have been the *prāsāda i gunung hyang*—or 'sanctuary at the Mountain of the God(s)'—mentioned in a number of inscriptions that date from the reign of Rakai Kayuwaṅi dyaḥ Lokapāla and hail from the Yogyakarta area (see Naerssen & Iongh 1977: 76-81). The inscriptions (see, for example, Sarkar 1971/2: I: 184, 199-201, 215-216; de Casparis 1975: 90; and Wisseman Christie 1993: 196-199) refer to the *rakryān i sirikan*, one of three royal court officials receiving the orders of the king and thought to have been a member of the ruler's immediate family (Boechari 2011: 122, 125). The Jurungan (Polengan III) charter of 876 CE documents the earliest known instance "that an orchard producing fruits with sufficient economic value was changed into a (flower) garden, which certainly offered much less profit, for the benefit of a sanctuary" (Satari 2006-2008: 125), and which also implies that the donation had been made to an existing religious foundation that was already well endowed. However, the relatively late promulgation dates for these inscriptions (872—880) and their place of discovery at Polengan to the south of Yogyakarta argue against the hypothesis that they might pertain to Caṇḍi Prambanan. Though the Jurungan charter presents an extensive list of attendees and gifts, few of the kingdom's highest dignitaries are mentioned. Van Naerssen and Iongh also remarked that the Tunahan (Polengan I) charter refers to the grant of crown lands at Tunahan and Mamali to the Rakryān i Sirikan pu Rakap by Śrī Mahārāja Rakai Kayuwaṅi. Given that the later charters in the same series refer to lands or local dignitaries belonging to Mamali, the *prāsāda i gunung hyang* appears to have been an outgrowth of Kayuwaṅi's initial donation of crown lands in 873 CE. Hence, Wisseman Christie's speculative hypothesis is not sustainable.

Aichele (1969: 159-160) viewed the Śivagṛha inscription as principally pertaining to the dedication of the statue of the deified king and the completion of magnificent Śiva temples,

[41]If Damais' hypothesis was provable, the exclusive use in China of an Old Javanese term to designate the center of the supreme sovereign's power during between 640 and 818 CE would cast doubt on the theory that the Śailendra kings had been members of a dynasty of foreign origin.

[42]It is also noteworthy that the Mantyāsiḥ III charter mentions the toponym Laṅka Tañjung in light of the extensive description of the year-old Tañjung tree in vs.15—16 of the Śivagṛha inscription.

though he also interpreted verses 14 and 25 as possibly pertaining to plans for expanding the complex during one or more later construction phases. For example, Aichele thought that the allusion to the changing of the course of the river in v.25 suggested an undertaking for the express purpose of securing the temple grounds so that additional buildings could become added to the site at a subsequent date. Jordaan (1991) was skeptical that the inscription's composer would have admitted to such a serious defect given its potential to disrupt the magical efficacy of what the poet had otherwise described as the temple's divine splendour. Nevertheless, he saw potential merit in viewing Prambanan as having undergone modifications during the reign of Rakai Kayuwaṅi, and perhaps even thereafter, because it would offer a plausible explanation for the so-called East-Javanese elements of architectural style detected early-on by several archaeologists, which led them to initially assign a tenth-century construction date to the temple complex.

> "Yet to enhance its plausibility, the hypothesis must be elaborated. What needs explanation, for instance, is why only the Śiva temple should have been completed. Does not the inscription itself quite explicitly mention the gateway, the *rankang*, as well as the *anumoda* buildings?" (Jordaan 1991: 174-175).

Developments in East Java

Jordaan and Colless (2009) have attributed the success of the Śailendra dynasty on Java in part to the high degree of isolation from the outside world afforded by the siting of the royal palace in the vicinity of the Prambanan Plain. If Śrī Mahārāja Bālaputra had indeed invaded Central Java during the mid-ninth century, then the loss of the kingdom's previously presumed inviolability may have been one of the contributing factors that had compelled the later kings of the realm to turn their attention to the Brantas Delta region of East Java, as several researchers have proposed (see, for example, de Casparis 1956: 260-261). Therefore, we shall briefly review what is known about the advent of Javanese polities in East Java during the eighth and ninth centuries as well as identify key issues in need of further research.

The Palaeojavanese script similarities displayed by the Hampran and Kañjuruhan inscriptions from Central and East Java, respectively, suggest the possible relevance of a remark preserved in a Notice pertaining to Shê-p'o[43] (Java) from the *T'ang chou Sin,* which states that the king of Java lived in Cheng Shê-p'o ('the town of Java') during the ninth century, but the grandfather of the (current king) *ki-yen*, had transported (the capital) to the east to the city of P'o-lu-chia-ssŭ (Damais 1964: 130; see also Pelliot 1904: 225, n. 2). According to the *Liu Sung of the Six Dynasties,* the earliest recorded trade missions from Shêp'o to China occurred in 433 and 435 CE (Bielenstein 2005: 65). Between 640 and 818 CE, however, Chinese court officials employed the name Ho-ling when recording the

[43]The earliest known use of the designation Shê-p'o appears in the Chinese-language biography of Guṇavarman (367—431 CE), the renowned Buddhist monk from Kashmir who had reportedly converted Java's royal family to Mahāyāna Buddhism (Stache-Rosen 1973). According to his biography, Guṇavarman preached the *Avataṃsakasūtra* and the *Daśabhūmikasūtra* in China, and also translated several Mahāyāna texts into Chinese, such as the *Pu-sha chia ti* ('The stages in the precepts of a bodhisattva') as well as Hīnayāna texts such as the *Dharmagupta-bhikṣuṇī-karman*.

arrival of all Javanese embassies. Thereafter, the Chinese designation for Java reverted to Shê-p'o for the embassies that visited China in 820, 831, 839 and an unspecified year between 860 and 873. These dates correspond to the reigns of Rakai Warak (803—827), Rakai Garung (829—847) and Rakai Kayuwaṅi (855—885), respectively. Consequently, one of these three rulers could hypothetically have been the maternal or paternal grandson of the king who had moved his capital to the city of P'o-lu-chia-ssŭ.

Pelliot (1904) sought to identify P'o-lu-chia-ssŭ with the kingdom P'o-hui-chia-lu that appears in one of two different travel itineraries running from China to India—one by land, the other by sea—prepared by the Chinese cartographer Chia Tan during the Chen-yüan period (785–804). The segment of the itinerary by sea that directly pertains to the discussion at hand began at the capital of the kingdom of Fo-tai (Śrīvijaya), which was said to be located on the branch of a river 360 *li*[44] in length. Having crossed the sea, one arrived in Shêp'o (Java) and after having followed a road for fifteen days, during which travelers passed by two large mountains, they finally arrived in the capital city of Shê-p'o, in which the customs are the same as in Fo-tai (Śrīvijaya) and where the king is called Śrī Mahārāja (*Ssu-li-ho-mo-lo-cho*). Then after eight days on the road heading east, the Pyu embassy arrived in the kingdom of P'o-hui-chia-lu.

> "The country is hot; at intersections and along the roads were planted coconut trees and betel palms. Looking up, we could not see the sun. On the dwelling of the king, the [roof] tiles are made of gold; tiles of silver cover the kitchens. They burn scented woods. The halls are adorned with brilliant pearls. There are two pools whose banks are made of gold; the oars of the boats are fully lined with gold and jewels" (Pelliot 1904: 224-225).

The attention this report devotes to the opulence on display in the kingdom of P'o-hui-chia-lu is interesting given the same report's relatively sparse description of the capital of Shê-p'o.[45] In particular, the reference to the "two pools whose banks are made of gold" brings to mind the report of the mid-ninth century Arab trader Ibn Khurdādhbih about the Mahārāja of Zābag placing a gold brick in a pool or a lagoon each day and saying, "There is my treasure". Abū Zaid later offered an expanded version of the same tale, but with the site of the king's palace and pool or lagoon being located on an estuary. Whenever the level of the water covering the king's virtual reservoir of wealth receded "the bricks appear and shine in the sun" (Tibbetts 1979: 34).

---

[44]*Li* is the Chinese term for a major unit of distance akin to a 'mile' but which was considerably shorter than a kilometer and for which the precise unit length had varied over time.

[45]The Pyu embassy's remarks about Shê-p'o observing the same customs as Śrīvijaya (Fo-tai) and having a king called Śrī Mahārāja led Jordaan and Colless (2009: 59) to think it probable that the embassy had visited the capital of the Buddhist Śailendra king. However, the report designates the capital city as Shê-p'o rather than Ho-ling and the Kalasan charter of 778 CE awards the titles of Śrīmat and Mahārāja to Paṇaṃkaraṇa (= Rakai Panaṅkaran, 746—784). Following Naerrsen (1947), Jordaan and Colless consider Panaṅkaran to have been a vassal of the Śailendra king lauded on side B of the Isthmus of Kra stele. Rakai Panaṅkaran granted the royal irrigated rice fields in Wanua Tĕngah to the Buddhist monastery at *watak* Pikatan in addition to having donated the hamlet Kalasan (Kālasa) to the Buddhist foundation for the goddess Tārā. The founder of the Buddhist monastery at *watak* Pikatan seems to have been the younger brother of Panaṅkaran's royal predecessor Sañjaya.

Chapter VIII: Suggestions for future research

Referring to the *Yinghuan zhilüe* ('A short account of the maritime circuit') penned by the Chinese geographer Xu Jiyu in 1849, Pelliot (1904: 225, n. 2) mentioned that "(the capital) of *Shê-p'o* was moved to the city of P'o-lu-chia-ssŭ"[46] during the T'ien-pao period[47] (742—755 CE). Unfortunately, Xu Jiyu did not identify the source for this additional datum.

Based on the contents of the Kañjuruhan inscription (760 CE), Cœdès (1968: 90) maintained that the "advent of the Buddhist Śailendras seems to have provoked the exodus to the east of Java of conservative elements faithful to the Hindu cults" and that king Devasiṁha and his son Gajayāna—the Śivaite promulgator of the Kañjuruhan charter —"were perhaps related in some way to Sañjaya". Naerssen (1977: 55-56), however, rejected Cœdès' exodus theory insofar as it pertains to the Sañjaya dynasty. "For several reasons I cannot agree with this farfetched hypothesis". Though he did not expressly state his objections, one may surmise that the principal one pertained to his own interpretation of the Kalasan inscription of 778 CE, under which Naerssen (1947) had proposed that the Śailendra and Sañjaya royal families had cooperated in the construction of a temple dedicated to the goddess Tārā.[48]

Archaeologists discovered two of the four fragments comprising the Kañjuruhan[49] inscription in Merjosari village, Malang, East Java. The other fragments from the same charter, which previously had been sent to the museum at Batavia (modern-day Jakarta), reportedly came from the nearby village of Dinoyo. However, the additional archaeological remains found in Merjosari include a stone block displaying the first line of a Prākṛti verse likewise presenting the same variety of Palaeojavanese script as the Kañjuruhan inscription: "The first line displays: ‖ *Svasti āsīd rājā pṛthuśrīh prathitapṛthu* ... i.e. Hail! There was a very successful king, famous, widely..." (Bosch 1924: 282-283). This suggests that the Kañjuruhan charter, which commemorates the founding of an abode for an icon representing the divine sage Agastya, had come from the same site. "Another interesting fact connected with [the Kañjuruhan] inscription is that the cluster of four or five villages surrounding its site contain[s] the scattered remains of small buildings of a distinctly Central Javanese style, which is quite exceptional for East Java" (Van der Meulen 1976: 445-446).

Merjosari is located less than two kilometers away from Caṇḍi Badut. Built entirely in the Central Javanese fashion, Dumarçay (2002) believed Caṇḍi Badut to be in many respects comparable to Gedong Songo—a Śivaite temple complex located about 30 km southeast of

---

[46]Poerbatjaraka (1958: 260) conjectured that the Chinese name for this polity in East Java (P'o-lu-chia-ssŭ) would be a mistaken Chinese transliteration for Pūtikeśvara, a Śivaite designation that appears in the Kañjuruhan charter.

[47]The end of the T'ien-pao period was immediately followed by the An Lu-shan rebellion (755—763 CE), which almost succeeded in overthrowing the T'ang dynasty.

[48]The hypothetical candidates for the grandfather from the Sañjaya lineage are limited to Sañjaya (*circa* 717—746) himself or his successor Rake Panaṅkaran (746—784). Despite Naerssen's objections, it is theoretically possible that either Sañjaya or Panaṅkaran had married a female descendant of Devasiṁha, who Bosch (1924: 282) viewed to be the more probable candidate for the king who had transported his capital to the east. Poerbatjaraka (1958: 260) identified Rakai Balitung (898—?) as the grandson of the king who had moved his *kraton* to the east. However, Chinese court records do not mention the arrival of any embassies from Java during Balitung's reign (see Bielenstein 2005: 65-66; K. Sastri 1940: 268).

[49]De Casparis (1941: 500, 511) proposed to identify the toponym Kañjuruhan mentioned in the charter of the same name with the hamlet Kĕjuron near Caṇḍi Badut to the west of Malang.

Salatiga[50]—and hence proposed a ninth century construction date. Based on the most conspicuous architectural features of Caṇḍi Badut, which consist of the tiered roof as a whole as well as certain ornamental elements (see Jordaan 2012: 65, figs. 1 and 2), Caṇḍi Badut appears to have been constructed somewhat later. Given the ornamental similarities with Central Javanese temples such as Caṇḍi Losari as well as Caṇḍi Kedulan (see Jordaan 2012: 65: figs. 5A & 5b), which was unearthed in Central Java together with two inscriptions that date from the latter half of the ninth century, Jordaan believes that "Candi Badut's location in East Java cannot sensibly be related to mere 'chance.' It should, in my opinion, be explained by the eastward expansion of Matarām at the end of the ninth century and the beginning of the tenth" (Jordaan 2012: 63).

The varieties of Palaeojavanese script displayed by the Hampran (Salatiga)[51] and Kañjuruhan (Malang)[52] charters as well as the aforementioned stone block from Merjosari do seem to suggest that a cultural exchange may have occurred around the time of the T'ien-pao (742—755 CE) period given that the two inscriptions date from 750 and 760 CE, respectively. Unfortunately, we do not know where the capital city of Central Java had been located during this period, or whether there was more than one kingdom in the region at the time.[53] Given that the oldest monuments in the environs of Central Java's Prambanan Plain did not arise until decades later, the capital of Shê-p'o during the mid-eighth century may have been closer to the port town Semarang on Central Java's north coast.[54]

Majumdar (1927: 237) offered the extremely generous estimate of "100 to 150 miles" for the distance that travelers on foot could possibly have traversed during an eight-day road

[50]In 1733, the merchant C.A. Lons wrote a report in which he characterized the small chapels he encountered while visiting Caṇḍi Prambanan as being of similar shape, appearance and height as that seen by him at Salatiga (see Leemans 1855: 11-12). De Graaf (1958: 117-120) concluded that the Salatiga temple had formerly stood to the east of where the modern-day city of the same name is located. In 1746, the Dutch colonial administration demolished the Salatiga temple site and used its stones as building materials for the construction of Fort Hersteller, which ironically means the 'Restorer', the nickname of Governor-General Van Imhoff. The Dutch colonial administration subsequently demolished the fort in 1847. De Graaf concluded that the 'Hersteller' did not arise directly on the site of the ancient temple, which had probably been located to the east of the city, perhaps in or near a hamlet still known in the late nineteenth century as Tjanden.

[51]The stone of Hampran (7° 19' 36" south latitude; 110° 30' 1" east longitude) is located approximately four km to the east of Salatiga and 40 km to the south of Semarang.

[52]With respect to the area in which the inscription fragments were discovered, "The cluster of villages comprises (from east to west): Dinoyo, Merjosari-Merjoyo and Basuki; Badut is located to the south of this triad, while further to the north the spring shrine of Songgoriti should be mentioned as displaying the same style.... The remains found here consist of brick walls and the foundations of *caṇḍis*, parts of whose superstructure (antefixes, stair-heads, ornamented stones, damaged statues, *linggas* and *yonis*) lay scattered all over the site and the surrounding *sawahs*, some even having migrated to the surrounding villages. In addition to our inscription some others, most of them completely illegible, were found here. A systematic excavation would have been impossible [to conduct] without demolishing an important part of the villages and fields and has never been attempted" (Van der Meulen 1976: 446, n. 3; see also Bosch 1924: 282-285).

[53]The use of two very different scripts in the Canggal (Pallava-Grantha, 732 CE) and Hampran (Palaeojavanese, 750 CE) inscriptions suggests that at least two different polities may have existed in Central Java during this period.

[54]The Indonesian historians Budiman and Widodo have proposed that the Bergota hill in the southern sector of modern-day Semarang, which is located six kilometers inland today, actually may have overlooked the old harbor during the eighth century (Voûte & Long 2007: 55-56).

trip between the capitals of the kingdoms of Shê-p'o and P'o-hui-chia-lu during the early ninth century. However, Jordaan (pc 20 Nov. 2013) has argued that the dense forests and jungles carpeting the rugged intervening terrain between either Yogyakarta and Malang (160 miles = 260 km) or Salatiga and Malang (153 miles = 246 km) would have precluded the coverage of such distances on foot in just eight days during the eighth and early ninth centuries. In his opinion, the island's riverine systems would have provided the more practical means for accomplishing any sporadic inter-regional contacts that may have occurred during this period.[55] "It is only after the opening up of roads, primitive no doubt, that larger numbers of people could move from Mataram eastwards, into the Malang area and also southeastwards into the Kediri area". The main roads that existed during the period in question ran north-south and were the same ones as were subsequently used during the period of the United East Indies Company (VOC, 1662–1799; see Jordaan 2013: 3, fig. 1). So the identification of the kingdom delineated in the Kañjuruhan inscription with the kingdom of P'o-hui-chia-lu presented in one of two different Chinese travel itineraries running from China to India appears to be problematic.

[55]A ninth century date initially was proposed on epigraphical grounds for the short inscriptions placed in the four foundation caskets discovered at Caṇḍi Songgoriti, which is located in close proximity to medicinal springs northwest of Malang (Oudheidkundig Verslag 1938: 23; Stutterheim 1956: 70). Caṇḍi Songgoriti also displays certain architectural features (with respect to molding and dentals) known from Central Java that typologically suggest a ninth century construction date (Williams 1981: 45, n. 24). However, the dating of this temple has not yet been the subject of a detailed examination.

Bibliography

BCAI = Bulletin de la Commission Archéologique de l'Indochine
BEFEO = Bulletin de l'École Française d'Extrême-Orient
BKI = Bijdragen tot de Taal-, Land- en Volkenkunde
BSOAS = Bulletin of the School of Oriental and African Studies
EFEO = École Française d'Extrême-Orient
EI = Epigraphia Indica
IHQ = The Indian Historical Quarterly
JAOS = Journal of the American Oriental Society
JGIS = The Journal of the Greater India Society
JIABS = Journal of the International Association of Buddhist Studies
JMBRAS = Journal of the Malaysian Branch of the Royal Asiatic Society
JRAS = Journal of the Royal Asiatic Society
JRASCR = Journal of the Ceylon Branch of the Royal Asiatic Society
JSS = Journal of the Siam Society
NBG = Notulen van de Algemeene en Directievergaderingen van het Bataviaasch Genootschap van Kunsten en Wetenschappen
OV = Oudheidkundig Verslag
ROC = Rapporten van de Commissie in Nederlandsch-Indië voor Oudheidkundig onderzoek op Java en Madura
TBG = Tijdschrift voor Indische Taal-, Land- en Volkenkunde
VBG = Verhandelingen van het Bataviaasch Genootschap van Kunsten en Wetenschappen

Abe, Ryūichi
1999 *The weaving of mantra: Kūkai and the construction of esoteric Buddhist discourse.* New York: Columbia University Press.
Acri, Andrea
2010 'On birds, ascetics, and kings in Central Java, Rāmāyaṇa Kakawin, 24.95–126 and 25', *BKI* 166-4: 475-506.
2011 'More on birds, ascetics, and kings in Central Java: Rāmāyaṇa Kakawin, 24.95–126 and 25', in: Andrea Acri, Helen Creese and Arlo Griffiths (eds), *From Laṅkā eastwards: the Rāmāyaṇa in the literature and visual arts of Indonesia*, pp. 53-91. Leiden: KITLV Press.
2014 "Once more on the 'Ratu Baka mantra': Magic, realpolitik, and Bauddha-Śaiva dynamics in ancient Nusantara" [unpublished draft, to appear in an edited volume entitled *Esoteric Buddhism in Maritime Asia*].
Aichele, Walther von
1969 'Vergessene metaphern als kriterien der datierung des altjavanischen Rāmāyaṇa', *Oriens Extremus* 16: 127-67.
Apte, Vaman Shivaram
1989 *English-Sanskrit dictionary.* New Delhi: Publications India.
1898 *The student's guide to Sanskrit composition: being a treatise on Sanskrit syntax.* Poona: R. A. Sagoon.

Bibliography

Āryāśūra; Jacob S. Speyer (tr)

1895 *Jātakamālā: garland of birth stories by Āryāśūra.* London: Oxford Univ. Press.

Asanga and Thrangu Rinpoche

2000 *Distinguishing the middle from the extremes.* Boulder: Namo Buddha Seminar.

Asiatic Society Of Bengal

1885 *Centenary review of the Asiatic Society of Bengal from 1784-1883.* Calcutta: Thacker, Spink and Co.

Asmar, T. and B. Bronson

1973 *Laporan ekskavasi Ratu Boko 1973.* Jakarta: Lembaga Purbakala dan Peninggalan Nasional/The University of Pennsylvania Museum.

Aśvaghoṣa

1978 'Fifty stanzas of guru-devotion', in: dBaṅ-phyug-rdo-rje, Źva-nag Karma-pa VIIII; Beru Khyentze Rinpoche; and Alexander Berzin, *The Mahāmudrā eliminating the darkness of ignorance: a guide to Ka-gyü Mahāmudrā and Guru-yoga.* Dharamsala: Library of Tibetan Works and Archives.

Atmadi, Parmono

1979 'Beberapa patokan perancangan bangunan candi: suatu penelitian melalui ungkapan bangunan pada relief Candi Borobudur', *Proyek Pelita Pemugaran Candi Borobudur*, Seri C, No. 2, Departemen Pendidikan dan Kebudayaan.

1979 'Study on the height of Candi Borobodur', *Borobudur Reconstruction Committee Pelita* CC/VIII/8, pp. 127-134.

1988 *Some architectural design principals of temples in Java.* Yogyakarta. Gadjah Mada University Press.

Bagchi, Jhunu

1993 *The history and culture of the Pālas of Bengal and Bihar, cir. 750 A.D.—cir. 1200 A.D.* New Delhi: Abhinav Publications.

Bandaranayake, Senake

1974 *Sinhalese monastic architecture: the vihāra of Anurādhapura.* Leiden: Brill.

Banerjee, Radha

1994 *Ashtamahabodhisattva, the eight great bodhisattvas in art and literature.* New Delhi: Abha Prakasha.

Banerji, R.D.

1933 *Eastern Indian school of mediæval sculpture.* New Delhi: [no publisher given].

Baruah, Bibhuti

2000 *Buddhist sects and sectarianism.* New Delhi: Sarup & Sons.

Beal, Samuel

1911 *The life of Hiuen-Tsiang by the shaman Hwui Li with an introduction containing an account of the works of I-Tsing.* London: Trübner.

Beek, Steve van and Luca Invernizzi

1991 *The arts of Thailand.* Hong Kong: Periplus Editions.

BEFEO (anonymous author)

1921 'Péninsule malaise'. *BEFEO* 21: 319-321.

Behari, Bepin and David Frawley

2003 *Myths & symbols of Vedic astrology.* Twin Lakes: Lotus Press.

Behrendt, Kurt A.
2003 *Handbuch der Orientalistik = Handbook of oriental studies, part 2, India. Vol. 17, the Buddhist architecture of Gandhahāra.* Leiden/Boston: Brill.
Bénisti, Mireille
1960 'II. Étude sur le stūpa dans l'Inde ancienne', *BEFEO* 50-1: 37-116.
1986 'Questions suscitées par un stūpa monolithe', *BEFEO* 75: 15-20.
Bernet Kempers, A. J.
1933 *The bronzes of Nālandā and Hindu-Javanese art.* Leiden: Brill.
1938 *Oudheidkundig Verslag*, pp. 1-30.
1949 'Crawfurd's beschrijving van Prambanan in 1816', *TBG* 83: 177-193.
1950 'In Memoriam Dr. W. F. Stutterheim', *Oudheidkundig Verslag* 1941-1947: 15-28.
1959 *Ancient Indonesian art.* Boston: Harvard University Press.
1976 *Ageless Borobudur: Buddhist mystery in stone, decay and restoration, Mendut and Pawon, folklife in ancient Java.* Wassenaar: Servire.
Bernet Kempers, A. J. and R. Soekmono
1954 *Tjandi Kalasan dan Sari.* Djakarta: Dinas Poerbakala.
Bernet Kempers, A. J. *et al.*
1982 *Tjandi Kalasan*, "Legger" samengesteld door A. J. Bernet Kempers, J. Blom, en V.R. van Romondt, c. 1954 (Jakarta). Unpublished manuscript deposited in the library of the Kern Institute, Leiden University [No. I-e-106].
Bhandarkar, R. G.
1889 'A Sanskrit inscription from Central Java', *Journal of the Bombay Branch of the Royal Asiatic Society*, 17: 2-10.
Bhattacharyya, Benoytosh
1958 *Indian Buddhist iconography.* Calcutta: K. L. Mukhopadhyay.
Bhattacharya, Kamaleswar
1972 'Recherches sur le vocabulaire des inscriptions sanskrites du Cambodge', *BEFEO* 52-1: 1-72.
Bielenstein, Hans
2005 *Diplomacy and trade in the Chinese world, 589-1276.* Leiden/Boston: Brill.
Bilimoria, Puruṣottama; Joseph Prabhu; and Renuka M. Sharma
2007 *Indian Ethics: Classical traditions and contemporary challenges*, volume 1. Burlington/Aldershot: Ashgate Publishing.
Boechari
1966 'Preliminary report on the discovery of an Old-Malay inscription at Sodjomerto', *Madjalah Ilmu-Ilmu Sastra Indonesia* III: 283: 241-251.
1976 'Some considerations of the problem of the shift of Mataram's center of government from central to east Java in the 10th century A.D.', *Bulletin of the Research Centre of Archaeology of Indonesia* 10.
1979 'An Old Malay inscription of Srivijaya at Palas Pasemah (South Lampung)', Pra Seminar Penelitian Sriwijaya, Jakarta 1979, pp. 19-40.
1982a 'Aneka catatan epigrafi dan sejarah kuna Indonesia', *Majalah Arkeologi* 5-1/2: 15-38.

1982b 'On the date of the inscription of Ligor B', *Final Report Consultative Workshop on Archaeological and Environmental Studies on Srivijaya*, Appendix 4a, Bangkok: SPAFA.
1982c 'Further remarks on preliminary report on some archaeological finds around the Borobudur temple', *Pelita Borobudur* CC6, 1977.
2012 *Melacak sejarah kuno Indonesia lewat prasasti: tracing ancient Indonesian history through inscriptions.* Jakarta: Kepustakaan Populer Gramedia.

Boeckholtz, François van
c.1790 *Aanteekeningen betreffende Java*, manuscript (incomplete), KITLV library holding DH 457.

Boisselier, Jean
1969 'Recherches archéologiques en Thaïlande', *Arts asiatiques* 20: 47-98.
1979 'Degagement du Phra Chedi de Wat Keo, Chaiya', *JSS* 67-2: 40-46.

Bosboom, H.D.H.
1902 'Een bezoek [van C. F. Reimer] aan eenige tempelruïnen in Midden Java in 1791', *BKI* 54-1: 581-590.

Bosch, F.D.K.
1916 'De Sanskrit inscriptie op den steen van Dinaya', *TBG* 57: 410-444.
1923 'De Sanskrit inscriptie op den steen van Dinaja', *OV* 1923: 29-35.
1924 'Het lingga heiligdom van Dinaya', *TBG* 64: 227-286.
1925 'De oorkonde van het groote klooster te Nālandā', *TBG* 65: 509-588.
1929a 'De inscriptie van Kĕloerak', *TBG* 68: 1-56.
1929b 'Twee belangrijke aanwinsten van het Batavia'sche Museum', *Feestbundel uitgegeven door het Koninklijk Bataviaasch Genootschap van Kunsten en Wetenschappen bij gelegenheid van zijn 150 jarig bestaan 1778-1928*, pp. 39-48. Weltevreden: Kolf.
1930 'Boekbespreking: Dr. W. F. Stutterheim, A Javanese period in Sumatran history, Surakarta 1929', *TBG* 69: 135-155.
1931 'De stichtingsoorkonde van Kalasan', *TBG* 70: 379.
1941 'De inscriptie van Ligor', *TBG* 81: 26-38.
1952a 'Śrīvijaya, de Śailendra- en de Sañjaya-vaṁśa', *BKI* 108-2: 113-123.
1952b 'Boekbespreking. Prasasti Indonesia diterbitkan oleh Djawatan Purbakala Republik Indonesia I. — J. G. de Casparis: Inscripties uit de Śailendra-tijd, A. C. Nix & Co. Bandung, 1950, 204 blz.', *BKI* 108-2: 191-199.
1961 *Selected studies in Indonesian archaeology.* The Hague: Nijhoff.
1968 'Indra's strijd met Vṛtra', *BKI* 124-2: 241-261.

Bowman, John Stewart
2000 *Columbia chronologies of Asian history and culture.* New York: Columbia University Press.

Brandes, J. L. A.
1886 'Een nāgarī-opschrift gevonden tusschen Kalasan en Prambanan', *TBG* 31: 240-260.
1887 Untitled note in *NBG* 24: 25-26.
1902 'Nadere mededeelingen over de Tjandi Mendoet', *NBG* 40: 141-153.

1913 'Oud-Javaansche oorkonden: nagelaten transcripties van wijlen Dr. J. L. A. Brandes', N. J. Krom (ed), *VBG* 13: 1-267.

Brereton, Joel Peter and Madhav Deshpande

1995 *Sense and syntax in Vedic.* Leiden: Brill, 1991.

Briggs, Lawrence Palmer

1950 'The Khmer empire and the Malay peninsula', *The Far Eastern Quarterly* 9: 256-305.

Brown, Robert L.

1996 *The Dvāravatī wheels of the law and the Indianization of South East Asia.* Leiden/New York: Brill.

Burnell, A.C.

1878 *Elements of South-Indian palaeography from the 4th to the 17th century A.D., being an introduction to the study of South-Indian inscriptions and mss.* London: Trübner.

Burnouf, Eugène

2010 *Introduction to the history of Indian Buddhism* (Buddhism and Modernity, Katia Buffetrille, tr). Chicago: University of Chicago Press.

Carman, John Braisted and Frederick J. Streng

1989 *Spoken and unspoken thanks: some comparative soundings.* Boston. Harvard University Press.

Casparis, J. G. de

1941 'Nogmaals de inscriptie van Dinojo', *TBG* 81: 499-513.

1950 *Inscripties uit de Śailendra-tijd.* Bandung: A.C. Nix.

1956 *Selected inscriptions from the 7th to the 9th century A.D.* Bandung: Masa Baru.

1958 *Short inscriptions from Tjaṇḍi Plaosan-lor.* Djakarta: Archaeological service.

1961 'New evidence on cultural relations between Java and Ceylon in ancient times'. *Artibus Asiae* 26: 1961: 242.

1962 'Some notes on relations between central and local government in ancient Java', in: David G. Marr and Anthony Crother Milner (eds), *Southeast Asia in the 9th to 14th centuries*, pp. 49-63. Singapore: Institute of Southeast Asian Studies; Canberra: Research School of Pacific Studies, Australian National Univ.

1975 *Indonesian palaeography: A history of writing in Indonesia from the beginnings to c. A.D. 1500.* Leiden: Brill.

1978 *Indonesian chronology*. Leiden; Köln: Brill.

1981 'Dual nature of Barabudur', in: Luis Gomez and Hiram W. Woodward (eds), *Barabudur: History and significance of a Buddhist Monument*, pp. 47-73. Berkeley: Asian Humanities.

1986 'Central and local government in ancient Java', in: David G. Marr and Anthony Crothers Milner (eds), *Southeast Asia in the 9th to 14th centuries.* Singapore: Institute of Southeast Asian Studies, Canberra, Australia; Research School of Pacific Studies, Australian National Univ.

1990 'Introduction', in: P. Schoppert (ed), *Borobudur, prayer in stone*, pp. 13-7. London: Thames and Hudson.

Chandra, Lokesh

1995 *Cultural horizons of India,* vol. IV. New Delhi: Aditya Prakashan.

2007 'Introduction', in: Voûte, Caesar & Long, Mark. *Borobudur: pyramid of the cosmic Buddha*, pp ix-xi. New Delhi: DK Printworld.
Chandrakīrti
2004 *Introduction to the middle way: Chandrakīrti's Madhyamakavatara with commentary by Jamgön Mipham.* Boston & London: Shambhala.
Chatterjee, Bijan Raj
1926 *An outline of Indo-Javanese history.* Calcutta: Greater India Society.
1933 *India and Java.* Calcutta: Prabasi Press.
Chhabra, Bahadur Chand
1935 'Expansion of Indo-Aryan culture during Pallava rule', *JRAS,* Letters, pp. 1-64.
1965 *Expansion of Indo-Aryan culture during Pallava rule as evidenced by the inscriptions*. Delhi: Munshi Ram Manohar.
Chihara, Daigorō
1996 *Hindu-Buddhist architecture in Southeast Asia*. Leiden/New York: Brill.
Childers, Robert Cæsar
1875 *A dictionary of the Pali language.* London: Trübner.
Chirapravati, M.L. Pattaratorn
2000 'Development of Buddhist traditions in peninsular Thailand: a study based on votive tablets (seventh to eleventh centuries)', in: Stanley J. O'Connor and Nora A. Taylor (eds), *Studies in Southeast Asian art: essays in honor of Stanley J. O'Connor*, pp. 172- 194. Ithaca: Cornell University, Southeast Asia Program.
Cleary, Thomas
1993 *The flower ornament scripture: a translation of the Avatamsaka sutra.* Boston: Shambhala.
Clothey, Fred W. and A.K. Ramanujan
1978 *The many faces of Murukan: the history and meaning of a South Indian god.* The Hague/New York: Mouton.
Chouléan, Ang
1997 'Un point de mémoire collective dans le Cambodge ancien', *BEFEO* 84: 334-339.
Chutiwongs, Nandana
2010 'A visit to Ratu Boko', in: Endang Sri Hardiati; Triwurjani, Rr. (eds), *Pentas ilmu di ranah budaya: sembilan windu Prof. Dr. Edi Sedyawati*, pp. 783-796. Denpasar: Pustaka Larasan.
Claeys, Jean-Yves
1931 'L'archéologie du Siam'. *BEFEO* 31: 361-448.
Coburn, Thomas B.
1984 *Devī-māhātmya: the crystallization of the goddess tradition.* New Delhi: Motilal Banarsidass.
Cœdès, George
1918 'Le royaume de Çrīvijaya'. *BEFEO* 18: 1-36.
1927a 'A propos de la chute du royaume de Śrīvijaya', *BKI* 83: 459-472.
1927b 'Recent archaeological progress in Siam', *Indian Arts and Letters*, New Series 1-1: 57-72.
1930 'Les inscriptions malaises de Çrvijaya', *BEFEO* 30: 29-80.

1948 *Histoire du monde: les états hindouisés d'Indochine et d'Indonésie.* Paris: E. de Boccard.
1950 'Le Śailendra « tueur des héros ennemis »', in: *Bingkisan Budi, een bundel opstellen aan Dr. Philippus Samuel Van Ronkel door vrienden en leerlingen aangeboden op zijn tachtigste verjaardag*, pp. 58-70. Leiden: A. W. Sijthoff's Uitgeversmaatschappij.
1956 'Dhammakāya', *The Adyar Library Bulletin* XX-3 and XX-4. Madras: Theosophical Society, Adyar Library and Research Centre.
1959 'L'inscription de la stèle de Ligor: état présent de son interprétation', *Oriens Extremus* 6-1: 42-48. For the English-language translation, see: Manguin, P.-Y. and M. Sheppard (eds), 1992 *Srivijaya; history, religion and language of an early Malay polity. Collected studies by George Cedes and Louis-Charles Damais*, pp. 105-111. Kuala Lumpur. [Monograph of the Malaysian Branch of the RAS, No. 20].
1961 *Recueil des inscriptions du Siam, deuxième partie: Inscriptions de Dvāravatī, de Śrīvijaya et de Lāvo*. Bangkok: M.C. Piyarangsit Rangsit.
1966 *The making of South East Asia*. Berkeley: University of California Press.
1968 *The Indianized states of Southeast Asia.* Honolulu: East-West Center.
1977 "Śailendra 'Tueur des héros ennemis'", M. J. Richards (trans), in: *Kabar seberang sulating maphilindo* 22. Townsville: James Cook University of North Queensland.
Conze, Edward
1961 *The large sutra on perfect wisdom: With the divisions of the Abhisamayalankara.* London: Luzac.
Coomaraswamy, Ananda Kentish
1943 *Hinduism and Buddhism.* New York: Philosophical Library.
Coomaraswamy, Ananda Kentish and Rama P. Coomaraswamy
1997 *The door in the sky: Coomaraswamy on myth and meaning.* Princeton: Univ. Press.
Crawfurd, John
1820 'The ruins of Prambanan in Java', in: *Asiatick Researches; or, transactions of the society instituted in Bengal, for enquiring into the history and antiquities, the arts, sciences, and literature, of Asia*, XIII: 337-368.
1852 *A grammar and dictionary of the Malay language: with a preliminary dissertation.* London: Smith, Elder and Co. [vol. II].
Daldjoeni, N.
1984 'Pranatamangsa, the Javanese agricultural calendar – its bioclimatological and sociocultural function in developing rural life', *The Environmentalist* 4-7.
Dalton, Jacob P.
2011 *The taming of the demons: Violence and liberation in Tibetan Buddhism.* New Haven: Yale University Press.
Damais, Louis-Charles
1949 'Epigrafische aanteekeningen', *TBG* 83: 1-26.
1952 'I. Études d'épigraphie indonésienne', *BEFEO* 46-1 : 1-106.
1955 'II. Etudes d'épigraphie indonésienne: IV. Discussion de la date des inscriptions', *BEFEO* 47: 7-290.

1964 'Etudes sino-indonésiennes: III. La transcription chinoise Ho-ling comme désignation de Java', *BEFEO* 52: 93-141.
1968 'Bibliographie indonésienne: XI. Les publications épigraphiques du service archéologique de l'Indonésie', *BEFEO* 54: 295-521.
1970 *Répertoire onomastique de l'épigraphie javanaise, jusqu'à Pu Siṇḍok Śrī Īśānawikrama Dharmmotuṅgadewa, étude d'épigraphie indonésienne*. Paris: EFEO.
Daniélou, A.
1964 *Hindu polytheism.* New York: Pantheon.
Davidson, Ronald M.
1981 'The litany of names of Mañjuśrī. Text and translation of the *Mañjuśrīnāma-saṃgīti*', in: *Tantric and Taoist Studies in Honour of R. A. Stein. Mélanges Chinois et Bouddhique*, 20: 1-69.
1995 'The litany of names of Mañjuśrī', in: Donald S. Lopez, Jr. (ed), *Religions of India in practice*, pp. 104-125. Princeton: Princeton University Press.
2004 *Indian esoteric Buddhism social history of the tantric movement.* New Delhi: Motilal Banarsidass.
2011 'Abhiṣeka', in: Charles Orzech, Henrik Sørensen and Richard Payne (eds), *Esoteric Buddhism and the tantras in East Asia*, pp. 71-75, Leiden/Boston: Brill.
Dayal, Har
1970 *The bodhisattva doctrine in Buddhist Sanskrit literature.* New Delhi: Motilal Banarsidass.
Degroot, Véronique
2006 'The archaeological remains of Ratu Boko: From Sri Lankan Buddhism to Hinduism', *Indonesia and the Malay World*, 34-98: 55-74.
2009 *Candi, space and landscape: a study on the distribution, orientation and spatial organization of Central Javanese temple remains.* Leiden: Sidestone Press.
Deussen, Paul
1990 *Sixty Upaniṣads of the Veda 1*. Delhi: Motilal Banarsidass.
Dimmitt, Cornelia and J. A. B. Buitenen
1987 *Classical Hindu mythology: a reader in the Sanskrit Purāṇas*. Philadelphia: Temple University Press.
Dinas Purbakala
1959 *Laporan tahunan 1953.* Jakarta: Departemen Pendidikan dan Kebudayaan.
Diskul, M. C. Subhadradis
1980 'Chedi at Wat Keo, Chaiya, Suratthani', *JMBRAS* 53-2 (238): 1-4.
Donaldson, Thomas E.
2001 *Iconography of the Buddhist sculpture of Orissa.* Abhinav: Indira Gandhi National Centre for the Arts.
Dumarçay, Jacques
1978 *Borobudur.* Oxford/New York: Oxford University Press.
1993 *Histoire de l'architecture de Java.* Paris: EFEO [Memoires Archeologiques 19].
1998 'Note sur le second état du Candi Lumbung et du Candi Bima', in: *Archipel* 56.
1998 'L'horizon nousantarien', in: Denys Lombard; Association Archipel, *Mélanges en hommage à Denys Lombard* (Volume I), pp. 455-464.

2002 'Le Candi Badut', *Archipel* 63: 7-14.
2007 *Candi Sewu and Buddhist architecture of Central Java*. Jakarta/Paris: KPG.
Dumarçay, Jacques and M. Smithies
1986 *The temples of Java*. Singapore; New York: Oxford University Press.
Dupont, Pierre
1943: 'I. La dislocation du Tchen-la et la formation du Cambodge angkorien (VIIe-IXe siècle)', *BEFEO* 43: 17-55.
Dwiyanto, Djoko
1984 'Hasil sementara ekskavasi penyelamatan situs Candi Bogang, Jawa Tengah', *Indonesia Circle* 34: 21-36.
Easwaran, Eknath and Michael N. Nagler
1987 *The Upanishads*. Petaluma: Nilgiri Press.
Eckel, Malcolm David
1992 *To see the Buddha: a philosopher's quest for the meaning of emptiness*. Princeton: University Press.
Edgerton, Franklin
1953 *Buddhist hybrid Sanskrit grammar and dictionary*, vol. 2. New Haven: Yale University Press.
Egenes, Thomas
1995 *Introduction to Sanskrit,* vol. 2. San Diego: Point Loma Publications.
Enthoven, R. E.
1914 *Folklore Notes*. Bombay: British India Press.
Faxian and James Legge
1886 *A record of Buddhistic kingdoms: being an account by the Chinese monk Fa-Hien of his travels in India and Ceylon (A.D. 399-414) in search of the Buddhist books of discipline*. Oxford: Clarendon Press.
Ferlus, Michel
2010 'Localisation, identité et origine du Javā de Jayavarman II', *Aséanie* 26: 65-81.
Finot, Louis
1904 'Notes d'épigraphic: XI. Lcs inscriptions de Mi-Sơn', *BEFEO* 4-4: 897-977.
1910 'Inscriptions du Siam et de la péninsule malaise', *BCAI* II: 147-154.
Fleet, J. F.
1883 'Sanskrit and Old-Cantarese inscriptions', *Indian Antiquary* XII: 156-162.
Fontein, Jan
2013 'Borobudur: A monument of Avataṃsaka Buddhism', in: Marijke J. Klokke and Veronique Degroot, eds, *Materializing Southeast Asia's past: Selected papers from the 12th international conference of the European Association of Southeast Asian Archaeologists, Volume 2*, pp. 3-9. Singapore: NUS Press.
Fontein, Jan; R. Soekmono; Edi Sedyawati
1990 *The sculpture of Indonesia*. Washington, D.C./New York: National Gallery of Art/ H.N. Abrams.
Foucher, A.
1900 *Étude sur l'iconographie bouddhique de l'Inde*. Paris: Leroux.

1918 *L'Art gréco-bouddhique du Gandhâra: Tome II, Les Images, l'histoire, conclusions étude sur les origines de l'influence classique dans l'art bouddhique de l'Inde et de l'Extrême-Orient.* Paris: Leroux.

Geertz, Clifford

1973 *The interpretation of cultures: selected essays.* New York: Basic Books.

Getty, Alice

1914 *The gods of northern Buddhism, their history, iconography and progressive evolution through the northern Buddhist countries.* Oxford: Clarenden Press.

Ghosh, Mallar

1980 *Development of Buddhist iconography in eastern India: A study of Tārā, prajā of five Tathāgatas and Bhrikut.* New Delhi: Munshiran Manoharlal.

Giebel, Rolf W.

2011 'The one hundred and eight names of Mañjuśrī: the Sanskrit version of the Mañjuśrīkumārabhūta-aṣṭottaraśatakanāma based on Sino-Japanese sources', *Indian Logic* 3: 303-346.

Gifford, Julie

2003 *Picturing the path: the visual rhetoric of Barabudur.* Chicago: University [unpublished dissertation].

Golzio, Karl-Heinz

2000 'Considerations on the chronology and history of 9th century Cambodia', *Siksācakr: The Journal of Cambodia Research* No 2.

2004 *Inscriptions of Campā:* based on the editions and translations of Abel Bergaigne, Etienne Aymonier, Louis Finot, Edouard Huber and other French scholars and of the work of R.C. Majumdar: newly presented, with minor corrections of texts and translations, together with calculations of given dates. Aachen: Shaker.

Gonda, Jan

1938 'Altind. °anta-, °antara-, usw.', *BKI* 97: 453-500.

1954 *Aspects of early Viṣṇuism.* Utrecht: Oosthoek.

1956 'Ancient Indian kingship from the religious point of view', *Numen* 3-1: 36-71.

1966 *Ancient Indian kingship from the religious point of view.* Leiden: Brill.

1975 'The Indian religions in pre-Islamic Indonesia and their survival in Bali', *Handbuch der Orientalistik* 3.2.1: 1-54.

1973 *Sanskrit in Indonesia.* New Delhi: International Academy of Indian Culture.

1997 *Religionen.* Leiden: Brill [vol. I].

Goris, R.

1929 'De eenheid der Mataramsche dynastie', *Feestbundel uitgegeven door het Koninklijk Bataviaasche Genootschap van Kunsten en Wetenschappen bij gelegenheid van zijn 150 jarig bestaan, 1778—1928*, pp. 202-206.

Gosling, Betty

1996 *A chronology of religious architecture at Sukhothai, late thirteenth to early fifteenth century.* Ann Arbor: Association for Asian Studies.

Govinda, Lama Anagarika

1970 'The historical and symbolical origin of the chorten', *Bulletin of Tibetology* VII-3: 5-14.

Graaf, H. De

1958 'De verdwenen tjandi te Salatiga', *BKI* 114: 117-120.

Griffiths, Arlo

2011a 'Sanskrit Inscriptions of Southeast Asia'. A reader of inscriptions of Campā, the Malay peninsula, Java and Sumatra compiled on the occasion of the Seventh International Intensive Sanskrit Summer Retreat (August 2011).

2011b 'Imagine Laṅkapura at Prambanan', in: Andrea Acri, Helen Creese and Arlo Griffiths (eds), *From Laṅkā eastwards: the Rāmāyaṇa in the literature and visual arts of Indonesia*, pp. 133-148. Leiden: KITLV Press.

2013a 'The problem of the ancient name Java and the role of Satyavarman in Southeast Asian international relations around the turn of the ninth century CE', *Archipel* 85: 43-81.

2014 'Written traces of the Buddhist past: Mantras and dhāraṇīs in Indonesian inscriptions'. *BSOAS* 77-1: 137-194.

Griswold, A.B. And Buribhand, L. B.

1951 'Sculpture of peninsular Siam in the Ayuthya Period', *JSS* 38: 1-60.

Groeneveldt, Willem Pieter

1877 *Notes on the Malay Archipelago and Malacca compiled from Chinese sources.* Batavia/'s Hage: Bruining; Nijhoff.

Groeneveldt, Willem Pieter and J.L.A. Brandes

1887 *Catalogus der archaeologische verzameling van het Bataviaasch Genootschap van Kunsten en Wetenschappen*. Batavia: Albrecht.

Guenther, Herbert V.

1969 *Treasures on the Tibetan middle way*. Leiden, Brill.

Gupta, Parmanand

1989 *Geography from ancient Indian coins & seals.* New Delhi: Concept Pub.

Gupta, Sanjukta

1972 *Laksmi Tantra, a Pancaratra text.* Leiden: Brill.

Gutomo and Niken Wirasanti (eds)

1998 *Laporan purna pugar Candi Plaosan Lor.* [S.I.]: Suaka Peninggalan Sejarah dan Purbakala Propinsi Jawa Tengah di Prambanan.

Gutschow, Niels and David N. Gellner

1997 *The Nepalese Caitya: 1500 Years of Buddhist votive architecture in the Kathmandu Valley.* Stuttgart: Menges.

Gyatso, Janet

1992 *In the mirror of memory: reflections on mindfulness and remembrance in Indian and Tibetan Buddhism.* Albany: SUNY Press.

Hall, Kenneth R.

2000 'Personal status and ritualized exchange in Majapahit Java', *Archipel* 59:59:51-96.

Hambali, H.

1993-94 *Keraton Ratu Boko in Yogyakarta*. Jakarta: Directorate General for Culture, Department of Education and Culture.

Harrington, Laura

2002 *A View of Mañjuśrī: wisdom and its crown prince in Pāla-period India.* New York: Columbia University [unpublished dissertation].

Harrison, Paul

1992 "Is the Dharma-kāya the real 'phantom body' of the Buddha?", *JIABS* 15-1: 44-94.

2007 'The case of the vanishing poet: new light on Śāntideva and the Śikṣā-samuccaya', in: Michael Hahn, Konrad Klaus and Jens-Uwe Hartmann (eds), *Indica et Tibetica: Festschrift für Michael Hahn*, pp. 215-248. Überreicht: Universitat Wien.

Hartzell, James Francis

1997 *Tantric yoga: a study of the Vedic precursors, historical evolution, literatures, cultures, doctrines, and practices of the 11th century Kaśmīri Śaivaite and Buddhist unexcelled tantric yogas.* Unpublished dissertation, Columbia University.

Harvey, Peter

1984 'The symbolism of the early stūpa', *JIABS* 7-2: 67-94.

Hien, H.A. Van

1896 *De Javaansche geestenwereld, en de betrekking, die tusschen de geesten en de zinnelijke wereld bestaat, verduidelijkt door patangan's of tellingen bij de Javanen in gebruik.* Samarang: Van Dorp.

Higashimoto, Keiki

1965 *An elementary grammar of the Pāli language.* Tokyo: Research Institute of the Pāli Literature, Komazawa University.

Hinze, Oscar Marcel And Bedekar, V. M.

1979 *Tantra vidyā: based on archaic astronomy and tāntric yoga.* New Delhi: Motilal Banarsidass.

Hodge, Stephen

2003 *The Mahā-vairocana-abhisambodhi tantra: with Buddhaguhya's commentary.* London, New York: RoutledgeCurzon.

Hoepermans, N.W.

1913 'Hindoe-oudheden van Java', *ROC* 1913: 73-372.

Hooykaas, C.

1964 *Āgama tīrtha: five studies in Hindu-Balinese Religion.* Amsterdam: N.V. Noord-Hollandsche Uitgevers Maatschappij.

Hopkins, Edward Washburn

1901 *The great epic of India; its character and origin.* New York: C. Scribner's Sons.

Hsing-Kong

1995 'The translation of the term samskara in the Chinese Buddhist literature'. 佛教與 中國文 化國 際學 術會議 論文集上冊 [Buddhism and Chinese culture, the International Conference Proceedings on the texts], pp. 285-302.

Huet, Gérard

2012 *Dictionnaire Français de l'héritage Sanskrit.* http://sanskrit.inria.fr/Dico.pdf.

Hunter, Thomas M.

2011 'Figures of repetition (yamaka) in the Bhaṭṭikāvya, the Raghuvaṃśa, the Śiwagṛha inscription and the Kakawin Rāmāyaṇa', in: Andrea Acri, Helen Creese and Arlo Griffiths (eds), *From Laṅkā eastwards: the Rāmāyaṇa in the literature and visual arts of Indonesia*, pp. 25-52. Leiden: KITLV Press.

Huntington, John C. and Dina Bangdel
2003 *The circle of bliss: Buddhist meditational art.* Chicago: Serindia Publications.
Ichimura, Shohei
1997 'Contemporary significance of Chinese Buddhist philosophy', *Journal of Chinese Philosophy* 24: 75-106.
IJzerman, J. W.
1891 *Beschrijving der oudheden nabij de grens der residentie's Soerakarta en Djogdjakarta.* Batavia: Landsdrukkerij & Nijhoff [text and atlas].
1915 *ROC* no. 1289, p. 112.
Jacq-Hergoualc'h, Michel
2001 'A propos de transferts de formes communs au Campā et au Panpan (Péninsule Malaise) au IXe siècle', *Arts asiatiques* 56: 45-60.
2002 *The Malay peninsula: crossroads of the maritime silk road (100 BC-1300 AD).* Leiden/Boston: Brill.
2004 'La péninsule Malaise au tournant du XIIIe siècle', *Aséanie* 14: 11-27.
Jacques, Claude
1972 'VI. Études d'épigraphie cambodgienne', *BEFEO* 59: 193-220.
2005 'Deux problèmes posés par l'inscription de la stèle de Pra Khan K.908', *Aséanie* 15: 11-31.
Jacques, Claude and Philippe Lafond
2007 *The Khmer empire: cities and sanctuaries, fifth to the thirteenth centuries.* Bangkok: River Books.
Jain, Dhanesh And Cardona, George
2003 *The Indo-Aryan Languages.* London; New York: Routledge.
James, E. O.
1966 *The tree of life. An archaeological study.* Leiden: Brill.
Jamison, Stephanie W.
1983 *Function and form in the -áya-formations of the Rig Veda and Atharva Veda.* Göttingen: Vandenhoeck & Rupre.
Jayasuriya, M.H.F., Leelananda Prematilleke and Roland Silva
1995 *Mañjuśrī vāstuvidyāśāstra.* Sri Lanka: Archaeological Survey of Sri Lanka.
Johansson, Rune E. A.
1981 *Pali Buddhist texts: an introductory reader and grammar.* London: Curzon Press.
Jordaan, Roy Edward
1991 'Text, temple, and tirtha', in: Lokesh Chandra (ed), *The art and culture of South-East Asia*, pp. 165-80, New Delhi: Aditya Prakashan.
1993 *Imagine Buddha in Prambanan: reconsidering the Buddhist background of the Loro Jonggrong temple complex.* Leiden: Vakgroep Talen en Culturen van Zuidoost-Azië en Oceanië, Rijksuniversiteit te Leiden.
1994 *In praise of Prambanan.* Leiden: KITLV Press.
1998 'The Tārā temple of Kalasan in Central Java', *BEFEO* 85: 163-183.
1999a 'Once again the dating of Ligor B'. Paper presented at the 8th Indonesian Archaeological Conference (PIA), Yogyakarta 15-18 February 1999.

1999b *The Śailendras in Central Javanese history: a survey of research from 1950-1999.* Yogyakarta: Universitas Sanata Dharma.

2000 'Coexistence of religions in ancient Central Java', in: Lokesh Chandra (ed) *Society and culture of Southeast Asia: continuities and changes.* New Delhi: Aditya Prakashan.

2006 'Why the Śailendras were not a Javanese dynasty', *Indonesia and the Malay World,* 34-98: 3–22.

2007 'Bĕlahan and the division of Airlangga's realm', *BKI* 163-2/3: 326-355.

2012 'Candi Badut and the trajectory of Hindu-Javanese temple architecture', *Artibus Asiae* 71,1: 55-74.

2013 'The lost gatekeeper statues of Candi Prambanan: a glimpse of the VOC beginnings of Javanese archaeology', *Nalanda-Sriwijaya Center Working Paper Series* No. 14.

Jordaan, Roy and Brian Colless

2004 'The Ratu Boko mantra and the Śailendras', *Berkala Arkeologi* 24(1): 56–65.

2009 *The Mahārājas of the isles: the Śailendras and the problem of Śrīvijaya.* Leiden: University of Leiden.

Jordaan, Roy and Robert Wessing

1996 'Human sacrifice at Prambanan', *BKI* 152-1: 45-73.

Juramie, Anne-Claire

2003 'L'iconographie du temple royal de Caṅgu Nārāyaṇa (vallée de Kâthmându)', *Arts asiatiques* 58: 34-59.

Kak, Subhash

2002 *The Aśvamedha: the rite and its logic.* New Delhi: Motilal Banarsidass.

Kālidāsa

1867 *Śakuntalá; or, Śakuntalá recognized by the ring, the Devanágarí recension, ed. with tr. of the metrical passages, and notes by Sir Monier Monier-Williams.* London: W.H. Allen.

Kandahjaya, Hudaya

2004 *Study on the origin and significance of Borobudur.* Berkeley: Graduate Theological Union [unpublished PhD dissertation].

2009 'The Lord of all virtues', *Pacific World: Journal of the Institute of Buddhistic Studies* 11: 1-24.

Karunaratne, W. S.

1988 *The theory of causality in early Buddhism.* Nugegoda, Sri Lanka: Indumati Karunaratne.

Kern, H.

1906 'Levensbericht van J. L. A. Brandes', *Jaarboek van de Maatschappij der Nederlandse Letterkunde.* Leiden: Brill.

Kislenko, Arne

2004 *Culture and customs of Thailand.* Westport: Greenwood Press.

Klokke, Marijke J.

2006 'The history of Central Javanese architecture', in: Henri Chambert-Loir and Bruno Dagens, eds, *Anamorphoses. Hommage à Jacques Dumarcay*, pp. 49-67. Paris: Les Indes savantes.

2013 'Art historical evidence for the building phases of Borobudur', in: Marijke J. Klokke and Veronique Degroot, eds, *Materializing Southeast Asia's past: Selected papers from the 12th international conference of the European Association of Southeast Asian Archaeologists, Volume 2*, pp. 10-26. Singapore: NUS Press.

Knebel, J.

1911 'Beschrijving der Hindoe-oudheden in de residentie Kedoe', *ROC* 1911: 138-341.

Kölver, Bernhard and Elisabeth Müller-Luckner

1997 *Recht, staat und verwaltung im klassischen Indien = The state, the law, and administration in classical India*. München: Oldenbourg.

Kramrisch, Stella

1946 *The Hindu temple*. Calcutta: University.

1981 *The presence of Śiva*. Princeton: University Press.

Krom, N.J.

1914 'Inventaris der Hindoe-oudheden op den grondslag van Dr. R.D.M. Verbeek's Oudheden van Java. Eerste deel', *ROC* 1914: 1-358.

1920 *Barabudur: archeologische beschrijving*. 's-Gravenhage: Nijhof.

1923 *Inleiding tot de Hindoe-Javaansche kunst*, 3 vols. 's-Gravenhage: Nijhoff.

1927 *Barabudur: an archaeological description*. The Hague: Nijhoff.

1931 *Hindoe-javaansche geschiedenis*. 's-Gravenhage: Nijhoff.

Kuladatta and Tadeusz Skorupski

2002 *Kriyāsaṃgraha: compendium of Buddhist rituals, an abridged version*. Tring: Institute of Buddhist Studies.

Kulke, Hermann

1993a 'Kadātuan Śrīvijaya - empire or kraton of Śrīvijaya? A resassessment of the epigraphical evidence', *BEFEO* 80: 159-180.

1993b *Kings and cults: State formation and legitimization in India and Southeast Asia*. New Delhi: Manohar.

Kundu, Rama

2008 *Intertext: a study of the dialogue between texts*. New Delhi: Sarup.

Kusen

1994 'Raja-raja Mataram kuna dari Sanjaya sampai Balitung; Sebuah rekonstruksi berdasarkan prasasti Wanua Tengah III', *Berkala Arkeologi* 14: 82-94.

Lai, Ming-Chiu

1999 'On the image procession in China from the second to the sixth centuries A.D.: an interpretation of an elephant sculpture at the Kongwangshan site', in: Frederick Hok-Ming Cheung and Ming-Chiu Lai, eds, *Politics and religion in ancient and medieval Europe and China*, pp. 41-75. Leiden: Brill.

Lamotte, Etienne and Sara Boin-Webb

1998 *Śūraṃgamasamādhisūtra: the concentration of heroic progress: an early Mahāyāna Buddhist scripture*. Surrey: Curzon.

Laughlin, J.

2000 'Other people's rituals: ritual eclecticism in early medieval Indian religions', *Journal of Indian philosophy* 28-4: 399-424.

Leemans, C.

1855 'Javaansche tempels bij Prambanan', *BKI* 3-1: 1-26.
Lévi, Sylvain
1905 *Le Népal.* Paris: Ernest Leroux.
Lingpa, Jigme
2007 *Deity, mantra, and wisdom: development stage meditation in Tibetan Buddhist tantra.* Lanham: Snow Lion.
Linrothe, Robert N.
1999 *Ruthless compassion: wrathful deities in early Indo-Tibetan esoteric Buddhist art.* Boston: Shambhala.
Lohuizen-de Leeuw, J.E. van
1981 'The dvārapāla of Barabudur', in: Luis Gomez and Hiram W. Woodward (eds), *Barabudur: History and significance of a Buddhist Monument,* pp. 15-24. Berkeley: Asian Humanities.
Long, Mark Earl
2009 *Caṇḍi Mendut: Womb of the Tathāgata.* New Delhi: Aditya Prakashan.
2011 'Candi Kalasan's Mahāyāna Buddhist pantheon: a comparative analysis based on design principles presented in the Manjuśrī Vāstuvidyāśāstra', in: ManjuShree (ed), *From beyond the eastern horizon: Essays in honor of Professor Lokesh Chandra*, pp. 2-18. New Delhi: Aditya Prakashan.
Lunet De Lajonquière, Edmond
1909 'Le domaine archéologique du Siam', *BCAI* I: 200-237.
1912 'Essai d'inventaire archéologique du Siam', *BCAI* IV: 100-127.
Lustig, Eileen
2009 *Power and pragmatism in the political economy of Angkor*. Sydney: University of Sydney [unpublished PhD Thesis].
Mabbett, I. W.
1983 'The symbolism of Mount Meru', *History of Religions* 23-1: 64-83.
Macauliffe, Max Arthur
1909 *The Sikh religion: its gurus, sacred writings and authors*. Oxford: Clarendon Press.
MacDonald, Ariane
1962 *Le mandala du Mañjuśrīmūlakalpa.* Paris: A. Maisonneuve.
Macdonell, Arthur Anthony
1886 *A Sanskrit grammar for beginners*. London: Longmans, Green.
1893 *A Sanskrit-English dictionary: being a practical handbook with transliteration, accentuation, and etymological analysis throughout.* London/New York: Longmans, Green.
Mackenzie, C.
1814 'Narrative of a journey to examine the remains of an ancient city and temples at Brambana in Java', *Verhandelingen Bataviaasch Genootschap* 7:1-54.
Majumdar, R. C.
1927 *Suvarṇadvīpa: ancient Indian colonies in the Far East.* Calcutta: Modern Pub. Syndicate.
1933 'Les rois Śailendra de Suvarṇadvīpa', *BEFEO* 33: 121-141.

Makransky, John J.
1997 *Buddhahood embodied: sources of controversy in India and Tibet.* Albany: SUNY Press.
Malalasekera, Gunapala Piyasena and Laṅkā Bauddha Maṇḍalaya
1961 *Encyclopaedia of Buddhism: pt. 2. Kāśya-pīya.* Columbo: Government of Ceylon.
Malandra, Geri Hockfield
1993 *Unfolding a maṇḍala: the Buddhist cave temples at Ellora.* Albany: SUNY Press.
Mallmann, Marie-Thérèse de
1964 *Étude sur a du iconographique Mañjuśrī.* Paris: EFEO.
Mañjuśrīmitra; Kunpal Tulku (tr)
1995 *Bodhicittabhāvana.* Dharma Fellowship of His Holiness the Gyalwa Karmapa (http://www.dharmafellowship.org/library/texts/cultivation-of-enlightened-mind.htm accessed 26 July 2014).
Mañjuśrīmitra; Norbu, Namkahi and Kennard Lipman (trs)
2001 *Primordial experience: an introduction to rDzogs-chen meditation.* Boston, London: Shambala.
Marasinghe, E.W. (tr)
1989 *The vāstuvidyāśāstra ascribed to Mañjuśrī.* New Delhi: Sri Satguru.
1991 *The citrakarmaśāstra.* New Delhi: Sri Satguru.
Matthews, Bruce
1983 *Craving and salvation: a study in Buddhist soteriology.* Waterloo: Wilfrid Laurier University Press.
Meulen, W. van der
1976 'The Purī Pūtikeśvarapāvita and the Pura Kañjuruhan', *BKI* 132: 445-462.
1979 'King Sañjaya and his successors', *Indonesia* 28: 17-54.
Miksic John N.
1989 'Urbanization and social change: the case of Sumatra', *Archipel,* Volume 37. Villes d'Insulinde (II), pp. 3-29.
1993/4 'Double meditation platforms at Anurādhapura and the pĕṇḍopo of Ratu Boko', *Saraswati Esai-esai Arkeologi.* Jakarta: Departmen Pendidikan dan Kebudayaan.
2001 'The Manjusrigrha inscription of Candi Sewu, Saka 714/A.D. 792'. Paper presented to the Conference on Texts and Contexts in Southeast Asia, Yangon.
Miksic, John N., Widya Nayati and Tjahjono.
2001 'Recent archaeological research at Candi Plaosan', in: Marijke Klokke and Karel R. van Kooij (eds), *Fruits of Inspiration: Studies in Honour of Professor J.G. de Casparis,* pp. 319-332. Groningen: Egbert Forsten.
Mitchiner, John E.
1982 *Traditions of the seven ṛṣis.* New Delhi: Motilal Banarsidass.
Mitra, Madusudan
1977 *Metres of Kālidāsa.* New Delhi: Tara Prakashan.
Moens, J. L.
1921 'De Tjandi Mendut', *TBG* 59: 529-600.
1940 'Srīvijaya, Yāva and Katāha', *Journal Malaysian Branch Royal Asiatic Society* 27-2: 1-108.

Monier-Williams, Sir Monier; Ernst Leumann; and Carl Cappeller
1899 *A Sanskrit-English dictionary etymologically and philologically arranged with special reference to cognate Indo-European languages.* Oxford: Clarendon.
Morgan, Les
2011 *Croaking frogs: a guide to Sanskrit metrics and figures of speech.* [Los Angeles]: Mahodara Press.
Mrozik, Susanne
2007 *Virtuous bodies: the physical dimensions of morality in Buddhist ethics.* Oxford; New York: Oxford University Press.
Müller, Johannes
1865 *Ueber alterthuemer [altertümer] des Ostindischen archipels, insbesondere die Hindu-alterthuemer und tempelruinen auf Java, Madura und Bali.* Berlin: Gross.
Mullin, Glen H.
2006 *The practice of the six yogas of Naropa.* Ithaca: Snow Lion Publications.
Mus, Paul
1928 '[Book review] W. F. Stutterheim: een belangrijke oorkonde uit de Kedoe; W. F. Stutterheim: A Javanese period in Sumatran history; F. D. K. Bosch: De inscriptie van Kĕloerak', *BEFEO* 28: 515-528.
1929 'G. Coedès : Recueil des Inscriptions du Siam, 2e partie. Inscriptions de Dvāravatī, de Çrīvijaya et de Lăvo', *BEFEO* 29: 446-450.
1933 'Barabudur. Les origines du stūpa et la transmigration. Essai d'archéologie religieuse comparée (suite). 5e partie, La valeur cosmique du stûpa. Cosmogrammes et géomancie dans la croyance commune de l'Asie. Appendice. Les sept pas du Buddha et la doctrine des Terres pures', *BEFEO* 33: 577-980.
1998 *Barabuḍur: sketch of a history of Buddhism based on archaeological criticism of the texts.* New Delhi: Indira Gandhi National Centre for the Arts.
Naerssen, Frits Herman van
1947 'The Śailendra interregnum', in: *India antiqua, a volume of oriental studies presented by his friends and pupils to Jean Phillippe Vogel on the occasion of the 50th anniversary of his doctorate*, pp. 249-253. Leiden: Brill.
Naerrsen, F. H. van and R. C. De Iongh
1977 *The economic and administrative history of early Indonesia.* Leiden: Brill.
Nagao, Gaji and Leslie S.N. Kawamura
1991 *Madhyamika and Yogacara: a study of Mahayana philosophies: collected papers of G. M. Nagao.* Albany: SUNY Press.
Nagao, Gajin M. and Jonathan A. Silk
2000 *Wisdom, compassion, and the search for understanding: the Buddhist studies legacy of Gadjin M. Nagao.* Honolulu: University of Hawai'i Press.
NBG
1868 Untitled note appearing in *NBG* 6: 60.
Nguyeñ, The´Anh And Yoshiaki Ishizawa
1999 *Commerce et navigation en Asie du Sud-Est, XIVe-XIXe siècle.* Montréal: Harmattan.
Nihom, Max

1994 *Studies in Indian and Indo-Indonesian tantrism; The Kuñjarakarnadharmakathana and the Yogatantra*. Vienna: Gerold.

O'Connor, Stanley J.

1966 'Ritual deposit boxes in South East Asian sanctuaries', *Artibus Aṣiae* 28-1: 53-60.

1972 *Hindu gods of peninsular Thailand*, Ascona: Artibus Asiae.

Olivelle, Patrick

1998 *The Early Upaniṣads: annotated Text and Translation.* New York: Oxford University Press.

Oudheidkundig Verslag

1928 *OV* 1927. Batavia: Albrecht, pp. 106-108.

1929 *OV* 1928. Batavia: Albrecht, pp. 12-13, 88.

1938 *OV*. Weltevreden/'s-Gravenhage: Albrecht/Nijhoff.

1950 *OV* 1948. Weltevreden/'s-Gravenhage: Albrecht/Nijhoff, pp. 27-31.

Pali Text Society

1921-5 *The Pali Text Society's Pali–English dictionary,* T. W. Rhys Davids and William Stede (eds). Chipstead: Pali Text Society.

Paranavitana, Senarat

1957 'Perimiyankulama rock inscription of Vasabha', *JRASCR - New Series* 5-2: 129-137.

1970 'Some dues from lands in ancient Ceylon', *The Ceylon Historical Journal,* 19: 61-62.

Park, Sung Bae

1983 *Buddhist faith and sudden enlightenment*. New Albany: SUNY Press.

Parkhurst, Charles H.

1882 *Analysis or the Latin verb illustrated by the forms of the Sanskrit.* Boston: Ginn Brothers.

Parmentier, Henri

1925 'Origine commune des architectures hindoues dans l'Inde et en Extrême-Orient', *Etudes Asiatiques* II: 199-251.

Patricia, Bernadettha

2001 *Peripih komplex Candi Plaosan Lor* [unpublished M.A. thesis]. Fakultas Sastra, University of Indonesia.

Payne, Richard Karl and Kenneth K. Tanaka

2004 *Approaching the land of bliss: religious praxis in the cult of Amitābha*. Honolulu: University of Hawai'i Press.

Pelliot, Paul

1904 'Deux itinéraires de Chine en Inde à la fin du VIIIe siècle', *BEFEO* 4: 131-413.

Petzold, Bruno and Shinshō Hanayama

1995 *The classification of Buddhism: comprising the classification of Buddhist doctrines in India, China and Japan = Bukkyō-kyōhan.* Wiesbaden: Harrassowitz.

Phalgunadi, I Gusti Putu

2000 *The Indonesian Brahmāṇḍapurāṇa: translated from the original classical Kawi text.* New Delhi : Sundeep Prakashan.

Pinardi, S.

1984 'Data sementara bangunan kompleks pendapa kraton Ratu Boko', *Berkala Arkeologi* 5(2): 36-50.

Poerbatjaraka, R. Ng.

1926 'De Calon-Arang', *BKI* 82: 110-180.

1958 'Śrivijaya, de Śailendra- en de Sañjaya-vaṁśa', *BKI* 114: 254-264.

Pollock, Sheldon

2006 *The language of the gods in the world of men: Sanskrit, culture, and power in premodern India.* Berkeley and Los Angeles: University of California Press.

Potter, Karl H., Larson, Gerald James & Bhattacharya, Ram Shankar

1987 *The encyclopedia of Indian philosophies: Sāṃkhya, a dualist tradition in Indian philosophy.* Princeton: University Press.

Poundurai, Raju

2005 'Cultural contrast of South India and South-East Asia: an exploration of the phenomenon of the Devaraja cult', in: Arpurtha Rani Sengupta (ed), *God and king: the Devaraja cult in South Asian art & architecture.* National Museum Institute [New Delhi] monograph series no. 2. New York: Regency Publications.

Prapandvidya, Chirapat

1990 'The Sab Bāk inscription: evidence of an early Vajrayāna Buddhist presence in Thailand', *JSS* 78-2: 11-14 with illustration.

2007 'Phimai (Vimāya) temple in Thailand: The greatest Mahāyāna Buddhist centre during 9th to 12th century CE and its linkage with India'. Paper presented at the *Conference on Buddhism and 21st Century* organized by the government of India at Bodh Gaya from February 3 to 6, 2007.

Premila, M.S.

2006 *Ayurvedic herbs: a clinical guide to the healing plants of traditional Indian medicine.* New York: Haworth Press.

Purdy, Richard

2001 *The stūpa: environment of the vertical horizon.* [unpublished Ph.D thesis, Université du Québec à Montréal].

Quaritch Wales, H. G.

1937 *Towards Angkor in the footsteps of the Indian invaders.* London/Toronto/Bombay/ Sydney: George G. Harrap.

1976 *The Malay peninsula in Hindu times.* London: Quaritch.

1977 *The universe around them: cosmology and cosmic renewal in South-east Asia.* London: A. Probsthain.

Raffles, Thomas Stamford

1817 *History of Java.* London: Black, Padbury and Allen [2 volumes].

1844 *Antiquarian, architectural, and landscape illustrations of the History of Java.* London: Henry G. Bohn.

Rajani, M.C. Chand Chiraya

1974 'Review article: Background to the Sri Vijaya story Part II', *JSS* 62-2: 285-324

Ramachandran, Amirthalingam

1998 *The cultural history of Lower Kṛṣṇa Valley: its contacts with Southeast Asia.* Jaipur: Publication Scheme.

Resiyani, Wulun
2010 *Toponim Masa kini berasal dari sumber prasasti abad IX-X masehi yang ditemukan di kabupaten Temanggung, Jawa Tengah.* Yogyakarta: Universitas Gadjah Mada.
Rhodes, Constantina Eleni
2010 *Invoking Lakshmi: the goddess of wealth in song and ceremony.* Albany: SUNY Press.
Riccardi Jr., Theodore
1989 'The inscription of King Mānadeva at Changu Narayan', *JAOS* 109-4: 611-620.
Richardson, Hugh and Aditya Pal
1983 *Art of Tibet: a catalogue of the Los Angeles County Museum of Art collection.* Berkeley: University of California Press.
Rubinstein, Raechelle
2000 *Beyond the realm of the senses: the Balinese ritual of kakawin composition.* Leiden: KITLV Press.
Sala, Arya Vaidya
1996 *Indian medicinal plants: a compendium of 500 species*, vol. 5. Madras: Orient Longman.
Salomon, Richard
1998 *Indian epigraphy: a guide to the study of inscriptions in Sanskrit, Prakrit, and the other Indo-Aryan languages.* New York: Oxford University Press.
Sanderson, Alexis
2003/4 'The Śaiva religion among the Khmers (part I)', *BEFEO* 90-91: 349-462.
Śāntideva, Parmananda Sharma and Prajñākaramati
1990 *Śāntideva's Bodhicharyāvatāra: original Sanskrit text with English translation and exposition based on Prajñākarmati's Pañjikā.* New Delhi: Aditya Prakashan.
Santiko, Hariani
2010 'Agama Hindu pada masa kerajaan Mataram (abad VII - X masehi)', in: Endang Sri Hardiati and Rr. Triwurjani, eds, *Pentas ilmu di ranah Budaya: Sembilan windu Prof. Dr. Edi Sedyawati*. Denpasar: Pustaka Larasan.
Sarkar, H.
1970 *Some contribution[s] of India to the ancient civilisation of Indonesia and Malaysia.* Calcutta: Punthi Pustak.
1971/2 *Corpus of the inscriptions of Java*, 2 vols. Calcutta: Firma KLM.
1977/8 'The philosophical matrix and content of the Vajrayāna system as practiced by the Śailendra-rulers of Central Java (c. 775-856 A. D.): a search for its origin (a literary and inscriptional approach)', *Annals of the Bhandarkar Oriental Research Institut*e 58/59: 921-938.
1986 'A note on Atīśa Dīpaṅkara, Dharmakīrti and the geographical personality of Survarṇadvīpa', *Bulletin of Tibetology* 1-3: 36-42.
2001 *Glimpses of early Indo-Indonesian culture: Collected papers of Himansu Bhusan Sarkar.* New Delhi: Indira Gandhi National Centre for the Arts.
Sarmah, Thaneswar
1991 *The Bharadvājas in ancient India.* New Delhi: Motilal Banarsidass.
Śaśibālā

1986 *Comparative iconography of the Vajradhātu-Maṇḍala and the Tattva-Saṅgraha.* New Delhi: Sharada Rani.

Sastri, Hirnanda

1942 *Nalanda and its epigraphic materials.* New Delhi: Archeological Survey of India.

Sastri K. A. Nilakanta

1937 'Siddhayātrā', *JGIS* 4: 128-136.

1940 'Śrī Vijaya', *BEFEO* 40: 239-313.

1949 'History of Sri Vijaya', *Sir William Meyer Lectures, 1946–1947.* Madras: University of Madras.

1949 *South Indian influences in the Far East.* Bombay: Hind Kitabs.

Sastri, Mahamahopadhyay Haraprasad

1905 *Catalogue of palm leaf and selected paper MSS. belonging to the Durbar library, Nepal.* Calcutta: Baptist Mission Press.

Satari, Sri Soejatmi

2006/8 'Ancient gardens and Hindu-Buddhist architecture in Java', in: Elisabeth A Bacus; Ian Glover; Vincent C. Pigott, eds, *Selected Papers from the 10th International Conference of the European Association of Southeast Asian archaeologists.* Singapore: NUS Press.

Scanlon, Phil

1985 *Southeast Asia: a cultural study through celebration.* Detroit: Northern Illinois University, Center for Southeast Asian Studies.

Schlegel, G.

1903 'Geographic notes, XVII, Java', *T'oung pao*, 4-3: 228-250.

Schoterman, J.A.

1986 *Indonesische sporen in Tibet: lezing gehouden voor het Oosters Genootschap in Nederland te Leiden op 18 Maart 1985.* Leiden: Brill.

Schweyer, Anne-Valerie

2005 'Po Nagar de Nha Trang (seconde partie). Le dossier épigraphique', in: *Aséanie* 15: 87-119.

Sehgal, Sunil

1999 *Encyclopaedia of Hinduism*, vol. 5. New Delhi: Sarup.

Setianingsih, Rita Margaretha and Sri Hartini

2002 *Prasasti koleksi Museum Negeri Propinsi Sumatera Utara.* Medan: Museum Negeri Provinsi Sumatera Utara.

Shanbhag, Arun

2007 *Prarthana: a book of Hindu psalms with commentary.* Arlington: A. Shanbhag.

Sharma, Ram Sharan

1968 *Aspects of political ideas and institutions in ancient India.* New Delhi: Motilal Banarsidass.

2001 *Early medieval Indian society: a study in feudalisation.* Kolkata: Orient Longman.

Sharrock, Peter D.

2013 'The tantric roots of the Buddhist pantheon of Jayavarman VII', in: Marijke J. Klokke and Veronique Degroot, eds, Materializing Southeast Asia's past: Selected papers from the 12th international conference of the European Association of Southeast Asian Archaeologists, Volume 2, pp. 41-55. Singapore: NUS Press.

Shastri, Hirananda

1924 'No. 17 — The Nālandā copper-plate of Devapāladeva', *EI* XVII: 310-327.

Shaw, Miranda Eberle

2006 *Buddhist goddesses of India*. Princeton: University Press.

Sibeth, Achim

1990 *Les Batak: des hommes en Indonésie, un peuple de l'île de Sumatra*. Genève: Olizane.

Singh, G.P.

2008 *Researches into the history and civilization of the Kirātas*. New Delhi: Gyan.

Singh, Nagendra Kumar

2001 *Encyclopaedia of Jainism*. New Delhi: Anmol.

Sircar, Dineschandra

1965 *Indian epigraphy*. New Delhi: Motilal Banarsidass.

1966 *Indian epigraphical glossary*. New Delhi: Motilal Banarsidass.

Sivapriyananda

1990 *Astrology and religion in Indian art*. New Delhi: Abhinav.

Ślączka, Anna A.

2007 *Temple consecration rituals in ancient India: text and archaeology*. Leiden/Boston: Brill.

Snellgrove, David L.

1987 *Indo-Tibetan Buddhism: Indian Buddhists and their Tibetan successors*. Boston: Shambhala.

2004 *Angkor-before and after: a cultural history of the Khmers*. Trumbull: Weatherhill.

Snodgrass, Adrian

1985 *The symbolism of the stūpa*. New Delhi: Motilal Banarsidass.

1990 *Architecture, time and eternity: studies in the stellar and temporal symbolism of traditional buildings*, volume 1. New Delhi: Aditya Prakashan.

Soedjatmoko *et al.*

1965 *An introduction to Indonesian historiography*. Ithaca: Cornell University Press.

Soekmono, R.

1995 *The Javanese candi: function and meaning*. Leiden/New York: Brill.

Sompura, Kantilal F.

1968 *The structural temples of Gujarat, up to 1600 A.D.* Ahmedabad: Gujarat University.

Southworth, William

2001 *The origins of Campa in Central Vietnam: a preliminary view*. London: School of Oriental and African Studies, University College London [unpublished PhD Thesis].

2004 'Chenla', in: Keat Gin Ooi (ed), *Southeast Asia: a historical encyclopedia, from Angkor Wat to East Timor*, pp. 324-326, Santa Barbara: ABC-CLIO.

Srinivas, Mysore Narasimhachar

1976 *The remembered village*. Berkeley: University of California Center for South and Southeast Asia Studies.

Stache-Rosen, Valentina
1973 'Gunavarman', *Bulletin of Tibetology* 10: 5-54.
Starza, O. M.
1993 *The Jagannatha temple at Puri: its architecture, art, and cult.* Leiden/New York: Brill.
Strauch, Ingo
2009 'Two stamps with the Bodhigarbhālaṁkāralakṣa Dhāraṇī from Afghanistan and some further remarks on the classification of objects with the ye dharmā formula', in: Gerd J. R. Mevissen and Arundhati Banerji, eds, *Prajñādhara: Essays on Asian art hisory epigraphy and culture in honour of Gouriswar Bhattacharya*, pp. 37-56. New Delhi: Kaveri.
Studholme, Alexander
2001 *The origins of oṃ maṇipadme hūṃ: a study of the Kāraṇḍavyūha sūtra.* Albany: SUNY Press.
Stuart-Fox, Martin
2003 *A short history of China and Southeast Asia: tribute, trade and influence.* London: Allen & Unwin.
Stutterheim, Willem F.
1926a 'De bouwvallen op den heuvel van Ratoe Baka bij Prambanan', *Djåwå*, 6: 129–35.
1926b *OV*, pp. 8-10.
1929 *A Javanese period in Sumatran history*. Surakarta: De Bliksem.
1930 'Oudheidkundige aanteekeningen IX: de zogenaamde zuil van Ratoe Baka', *BKI* 86: 301-305.
1935 *Indian influences in old-Balinese art.* London: The India Society.
1956 *Studies in Indonesian archaeology.* The Hague: Nijhoff.
Śubhagupta and N.A. Sastri
1967 'The Bāhyārthasiddhikārikā by Śubhagupta', *Bulletin of Tibetology* 2: 1-96.
Sukumar, R.
2003 *The living elephants: evolutionary ecology, behavior, and conservation.* New York: Oxford University Press.
Sumio, Fukami
2006 'The rise of Tambralinga and the Southeast Asian commercial boom in the thirteenth century'. Paper presented at the *XIV International Economic History Congress, Helsinki 2006*, Session 72.
Sundberg, Jeffrey Roger
2003 'A Buddhist mantra recovered from the Ratu Boko plateau: A preliminary study of its implications for Śailendra-era Java', *BKI* 159-1: 163-188.
2004 'The wilderness monks of the Abhayagirivihāra and the origins of Sino-Javanese esoteric Buddhism', *BKI* 160-1: 95-123.
2006 'Considerations on the dating of the Barabudur stūpa', *BKI* 162-1: 95-132.
2009 'The state of Old Mataram', in: Long, Mark E. *Caṇḍi Mendut: womb of the Tathāgata.* New Delhi: Aditya Prakashan, pp. 329-358.
2011 'The Old Sundanese Carita Parahyangan, king Warak, and the fracturing of the Javanese polity, c. 803 A.D.', in: ManjuShree (ed), *From beyond the eastern*

horizon: essays in honor of Professor Lokesh Chandra, pp. 143-157. New Delhi: Aditya Prakashan.
Sundberg, Jeffrey and Rolf Giebel
2011 'The life of the Tang Court monk Vajrabodhi as chronicled by Lü Xiang (呂向): South Indian and Śrī Laṅkān antecedents to the arrival of the Buddhist Vajrayāna in eighth-century Java and China', *Pacific World* 3-13: 129-222.
Supomo, S.
1972 '"Lord of the mountains" in the fourteenth century "Kakawin"', *BKI* 128-2/3: 281-297.
Suryanarayana, Kolluru
1993 *Inscriptions of the minor Chalukya dynasties of Andhra Pradesh.* New Delhi: Mittal.
Suzuki, D. T.
1956 *The Laṅkāvatāra sūtra; a Mahāyāna text, translated for the first time from the original Sanskrit.* London: Routledge.
Swearer, Donald K.
2004 *Becoming the Buddha: the ritual of image consecration in Thailand.* Princeton: University Press.
Tarling, Nicholas
2003 *The Cambridge history of Southeast Asia, from early times to circa 1500.* Cambridge: Cambridge University Press.
Taylor, Keith Weller
1983 *The birth of Vietnam.* Berkeley: University of California Press.
Teeuw, A.
2001 'Kahulunnan and Sri Kahulunnan', in: Marijke J. Klokke & Karel R. van Kooij, eds, *Fruits of inspiration. Studies in honour of Prof. J.G. de Casparis*. Groningen: Forsten, pp. 525-538.
Theodor, Ithamar
2010 *Exploring the Bhagavad Gitā: philosophy, structure, and meaning*. Farnham; Burlington: Ashgate Publishing.
Tibbetts, Gerald Randall
1979 *A Study of the Arabic texts containing material on South-East Asia.* Leiden: Brill.
Tiwari, Jagdish Narain
1985 *Goddess cults in ancient India: with special reference to the first seven centuries A. D.* New Delhi: Sundeep Prakashan.
Tribe, Anthony
1994 *The names of wisdom: a critical edition and annotated translation of chapters 1-5 of Vilāsavajra's commentary on the Nāmasaṃgīti, with introduction and textual notes.* Unpublished Ph.D. thesis. Wolfson College, University of Oxford.
1997a 'Mañjusri: origins, role and significance', *Western Buddhist Review* 2.
1997b 'Mañjuśrī and 'the chanting of names' (Nāmasaṃgīti): wisdom and its embodiment in an Indian Mahāyāna Buddhist text', in: Peter Connolly and Sue Hamilton, eds, *Indian insights: Buddhism, Brahmanism and Bhakti: papers from the annual Spalding Symposium on Indian religions*. London: Luzac.

Tsoṅ-Kha-Pa Blo-Bzaṅ-Grags-Pa, Joshua W. C. Cutler and Guy Newland
2002 *The great treatise on the stages of the path to enlightenment, volume 2*. Ithaca: Snow Lion.
Tsoṅ-Kha-Pa Blo-Bzaṅ-Grags-Pa and Alex Wayman
1991 *Ethics of Tibet: bodhisattva section of Tsong-kha-pa's Lam rim chen mo*. Albany: SUNY Press.
Underhill, Muriel Marion
1921 *The Hindu religious year.* London: Oxford University Press.
Varaha Mihira and N. Chidambaram Iyer
1884 *The Brihat Samhita of Varaha Mihira* (two volumes). Madura: South Indian Press.
Varāhamihira and M. Ramakrishna Bhat
1981/2 *Varāhamihira's Bṛhat Saṁhitā* (two volumes). New Delhi: Motilal Banarsidass.
Veidlinger, Daniel M.
2007 *Spreading the Dhamma: writing, orality, and textual transmission in Buddhist Northern Thailand.* Honolulu: University of Hawai'i Press.
Veeraprajak, Kongkaew
1986 'Inscriptions from South Thailand', *SPAFA Digest* 7-1: 7-20.
Verbeek, Rogier Diederik Marius
1891 *Oudheden van Java: lijst der voornaamste overblijfselen uit den hindoetijd op Java met eene oudheidkundige kaart.* 's Gravenhage: Nijhoff, Batavia: Landsdrukkerij.
Vickery, Michael
1986 'Some remarks on early state formation in Cambodia', in: David G. Marr, Anthony Crothers Milner (eds), *Southeast Asia in the 9th to 14th centuries*, pp. 86-115, Singapore: Institute of Southeast Asian Studies.
1998 *Society, economics, and politics in pre-Angkor Cambodia: the 7th-8th centuries.* Tokyo: The Center for East Asian Cultural Studies for UNESCO, Toyo Bunko.
2001 'Resolving the Chronology and History of 9th Century Cambodia', *Siksācakr: The Journal of Cambodia Research* No. 3.
2003 'Funan reviewed: deconstructing the ancients', *BEFEO* 90-91: 101-143.
Vi Sītārāmayya
1971 *Purandaradasa*. New Delhi, National Book Trust, India.
Voûte, Caesar and Long, Mark
2007 *Borobudur: Pyramid of the cosmic Buddha.* New Delhi: DK Printworld.
Vogel, Jean Philippe and Chhabra, B. C.
1911 *Antiquities of Chamba State: inscriptions of the pre-Muhammadan period.* Calcutta: Supt. Govt. Printing, India.
Vyas, R. T. and U. P. Shah
1995 *Studies in Jaina art and iconography and allied subjects in honour of Dr. U.P. Shah.* New Delhi: Abhinav.
Wallace, Bruce Allen
1995 *The cultivation of sustained voluntary attention in Indo-Tibetan Buddhism.* [unpublished dissertation, Stanford: Stanford University].
Wallis, Glenn

2002 *Mediating the power of Buddhas: ritual in the Mañjuśrīmūlakalpa.* Albany: SUNY Press.

Wayman, Alex

1981 'Reflections on the theory of Barabuḍur as a maṇḍala', in: Luis Gomez and Hiram W. Woodward (eds), *Barabudur: History and significance of a Buddhist Monument.* Berkeley: Asian Humanities Press, pp. 139-172.

1985 *Chanting the names of Mañjuśrī: the Mañjuśrīnāmasaṃgīti.* Boulder: Shambala.

1997 *Untying the knots in Buddhism: selected essays.* New Delhi: Motilal Banarsidass.

Wayman, Alex, Ferdinand Lessing and Mkhas-Grub Dge-Legs-Dpal-Bzaṅ-Po.

1978 *Introduction to the Buddhist tantric systems, vol. 20.* New Delhi: Motilal Banarsidass.

Wayman, Alex and R. Tajima

1992 *The enlightenment of Vairocana.* New Delhi: Motilal Banarsidass.

Werner, Karel

1990 *Symbols in art and religion: the Indian and the comparative perspectives.* London: Curzon.

Weatherbee, Donald E.

2011 'Majapahit's Śrī Mahārāja Jayanagara and an Old Javanese temple model of politics', in: ManjuShree (ed), *From beyond the eastern horizon: essays in honor of Professor Lokesh Chandra*, pp. 131-141. New Delhi: Aditya Prakashan.

White, David Gordon

2000 *Tantra in practice.* Princeton: University Press.

Whitney, William Dwight

1885 *The roots, verb-forms, and primary derivatives of the Sanskrit Language: a supplement to his Sanskrit grammar.* Leipzig: Breitkopf and Härtell.

Wijesuriya, G.

1988 *Buddhist meditation monasteries of ancient Sri Lanka.* Memoirs of the Archaeological Survey of Sri Lanka 10. Colombo: Department of archaeology, government of Sri Lanka.

Wilder, Royal Gould, Delavan Leonard Pierson and Arthur Tappan Pierson

1918 *The missionary review of the world*, vol. 41. London; New York: Missionary Review Pub.

Wilkins, W.J.

1900 *Hindu mythology: Vedic and Puranic.* Calcutta; London: Thacker.

Willis, Janice Dean

1995 *Enlightened beings: life stories from the Ganden oral tradition.* Boston: Wisdom Publications.

Williams, Joanna

1981 'The dating of Barabudur', in: Luis Gomez and Hiram W. Woodward Jr. (eds), *Barabudur: history and significance of a Buddhist monument.* Berkeley: Berkeley Buddhist studies series.

Williams, Paul

1989 *Mahāyāna Buddhism: the doctrinal foundations.* London; New York: Routledge.

Willson, Martin

1986 *In praise of Tara: songs to the saviouress.* London: Wisdom Publications.

Wilson, H. H.

1850 *Rigveda-saṁhitā* [Vol.1]. London: Allen.

Wisseman Christie, J.

1993 "Texts and Textiles in 'Medieval' Java", *BEFEO* 80: 181-211.

1996 'Weights and measures in early Javanese states'. Paper presented at the *Sixth International Conference of the European Association of Southeast Asian Archaeologists* held in Leiden from 2 to 6 September 1996.

2001 'Revisiting early Mataram', in Klokke and Kooij (eds), *Fruits of inspiration: studies in honour of Prof. J. G. de Casparis*, pp. 25-56. Groningen: Egbert Forsten.

2002 *Register of the inscriptions of Java (from 732 to 1060 A. D.).* Consultation draft, II, no. 54 [unpublished].

Wolters, O.J. and Craig J. Reynolds

2008 *Early Southeast Asia: selected essays.* Ithaca: Cornell University, Southeast Asia Program.

Woodroffe, Sir John George

1919 *The serpent power: being the Ṣaṭ-chakra-nirūpaṇa and Pādukā-panchaka: two works on tantrik yoga.* London: Luzac.

Woodward, Hiram W.

2002 'Tāmbraliṅga', in: Vladimir I. Braginski (ed), *Classical civilizations of South East Asia: an anthology of articles published in The Bulletin of the School of Oriental and African Studies*, pp. 587-607. New York: Routledge-Curzon.

2003 *The art and architecture of Thailand: from prehistoric times through the thirteenth century*. Leiden/Boston: Brill.

2010 'Dvaravati, Si Thep, and Wenden'. *Bulletin of the Indo-Pacific Prehistory Assn.* 30.

Worsley, Peter

2006 'Cosmopolitan vernacular culture and illustrations of the Rama Story at Candi Loro Jonggrang, Prambanan. Part 2: The marriage of the crown prince and the succession in polygamous royal households', in: H. Chambert-Loir and B. Dagens (eds), *Anamorphoses; Hommage à Jacques Dumarçay*, pp 227-39. Paris: Les Indes Savantes.

Yijing; (I-tsing; J. Takakusu translator)

1896 *A record of the Buddhist religion as practiced in India and the Malay archipelago.* Oxford: Clarendon.

Zakharov, Anton O.

2012 'The Śailendras reconsidered'. *Nalanda-Sriwijaya Center Working Paper Series No. 12*. Singapore: Institute of Southeast Asian Studies.

Zahler, Leah

2009 *Study and practice of meditation: Tibetan interpretations of the concentrations and formless absorptions.* Ithaca: Snow Lion.

Zimmer, Heinrich Robert and Joseph Campbell

1946 *Myths and symbols in Indian art and civilization.* New York: Pantheon Books.

Zoetmulder, P. J.

1982 *Old Javanese-English dictionary* [two volumes]. 's-Gravenhage: Nijhoff.

Appendix A: The Caṇḍi Lumbung temple complex

At Caṇḍi Lumbung, the reconstructed subsidiary shrines (*perwara*) all have square internal chambers measuring 1.75 m per side, but otherwise are not entirely identical. Brumund observed that the second temple on the north side of the complex had three niches in the back-wall as well as two small niches without ornamentation in the left and right sidewalls. Moreover, the third shrine had the same three niches located high up the back-wall, as well as the pedestal below, which occupied the whole width of the wall.

> "Three statues seem to have been placed thereon; the one in the middle was undoubtedly seated as is clear from the oval slot in the pedestal wherein it was anchored. Some caṇḍis only have a small niche in the right and left wall; but the three [niches] in the back-wall are a recurrent feature. It is probable that the other [caṇḍis] also had pedestals. But they have disappeared along with the statues [they carried]" (Brumund 1854: 3).

Figs. A-1 & A-2. Image emplacements within a *perwara* at Caṇḍi Lumbung.

Still, two important caveats must be kept in mind: (a) no *perwara* on the east and south sides of the temple complex have been reconstructed and (b) some of their smaller unadorned niches could have been used to house lamps.

The main shrine at the center of the temple complex has a total of 14 niches for images: 11 within the interior chamber, which is 3.15 m square, and one each on the structure's exterior facades facing the south, west and north (see figure A-3). Furthermore, the total number of deity images collectively housed within the 16 *perwara* constructions could have amounted to more than 140. Even when accounting for the lack of pedestals in some structures and the placement of lamps in one or more niches per building, the available image emplacements still would have exceeded 100. Hence, it is possible that the complex as a whole had originally enshrined as many as 150 images in niches and on pedestals.

Fig. A-3. The main shrine at Caṇḍi Lumbung.

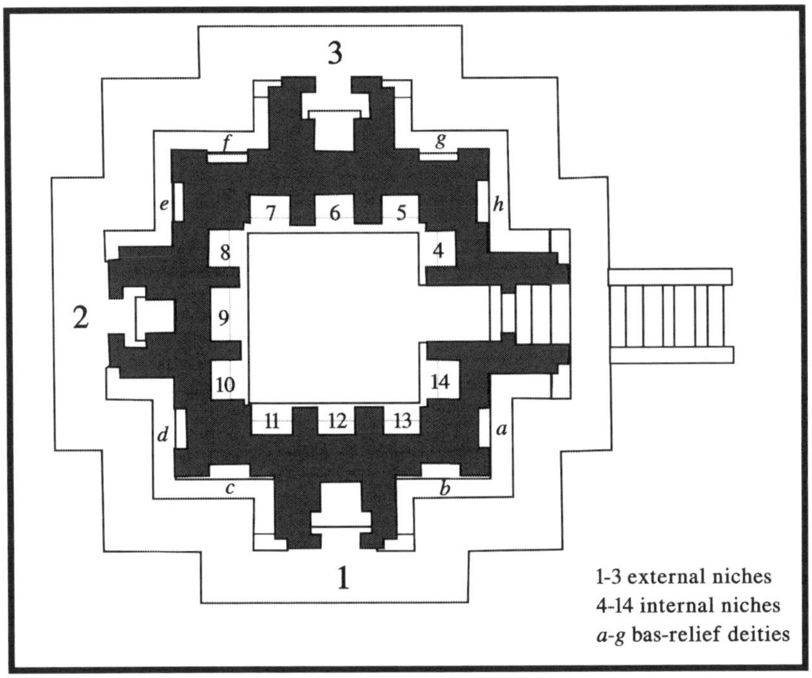

The large number of image emplacements available at this temple complex provides us with another opportunity to consider whether it might have been devoted to representing a Mantrayāna Buddhist *maṇḍala* in which a form of Mañjuśrī had played a major, if not the principal, role. The *maṇḍala* we seek would also need to be inclusive of a substantial number of Hindu as well as Buddhist divinities, as the Śrī Saṅgrāmadhanaṃjaya inscription suggests.

The *Mañjuśrīmūlakalpa* (MMK) describes an elaborate *maṇḍala* in which Mañjuśrī plays a major role and in which a large number of Hindu and Buddhist divinities are present. A detailed description of the MMK published by MacDonald (1962) notes that the principal figure of the text's core *maṇḍala* is the Buddha Śākyamuni, who is depicted directly opposite Mañjuśrī in the central yard. At Caṇḍi Lumbung, the principal image faced the central image of the *perwara* connected by a paved path to the main shrine. Also residing within the central yard of the MMK *maṇḍala* are Avalokiteśvara and his attending six goddesses;[1] Vajrapāṇi and his attending four goddesses;[2] Yamāntaka, Lokatikrantagāmī and the *mahābodhisattva* Ajitañjaya; 16 bodhisattvas (see Donaldson 2001: 165); and other divine beings. Hence, the limited number of emplacements offered within and without the central shrine could not have accommodated all of these divinities, though an alternate distribution of at least some of them—such as the sixteen bodhisattvas, for example—within the sixteen *perwara* constructions at Caṇḍi Lumbung remains a possibility.

The aforementioned four-faced, eight-armed variant of Dharmadhātu-Vāgīśvara Mañjughoṣa bearing the image of Amitābha in his coiffure also remains a possibility in

[1]Tārā ('savioress'), Paṇḍaravāsinī ('white-clad'), Bhrkuṭī ('frowning'), Prajñāpāramitā ('perfection of wisdom'), Tathāgatalocanā ('buddha eye') and Uṣṇīṣarājā ('lady of the wisdom bump').

[2]Vajrāṇkuśī ('lady of the *vajra* hook'), Vajraśṛṅkhalā ('lady of the *vajra* fetter'), Subāhu ('strong-armed one') and Vajrasenā ('lady of the *vajra* army').

theory. The principal interior niche in the back wall of the *cella* is broader than the others and is also surmounted by a far smaller niche. "What the small niche above the Buddha can have contained remains uncertain in any event; it is open to question, however, whether it was a figurine and not rather a lamp or bouquet of flowers" (Krom 1923: 273).[3]

Based on what is found in the cave temples of the western Gnats, Krom submitted the hypothesis that the temple principal niche would have contained a Buddha image, flanked by two bodhisattvas in the back wall's remaining two niches. He assigned the six remaining members of the Eight Great Bodhisattvas to the three niches of either sidewall and for the niches flanked the doorway he proposed images of Hāritī and her *yakṣa* consort. Lacking any surviving statuary, however, this is no more than a conjecture.

Figs. A-4 & A-5. Niches 12, 11, 10 (left) **and nine** (right) **inside the main shrine.**

The small niche above the head of the principal image within the main *cella* at Caṇḍi Lumbung (figure A-5) could in theory have housed a small metal figure of Amitābha. As Donaldson (2001: 161-162) has observed, two standing Mañjuśrī images have been preserved at Ratnagiri (Jajpur, Orissa, India). The first depicts a small figure of Amitābha seated on a lotus blossom directly above the missing head of the principal statue (late eighth to early ninth century). Besides, a second standing Mañjuśrī image (see figure A-6), which has been stylistically dated to the ninth century, displays a single lotus stalk rising beside it, with the lotus blossoms on either side of the head supporting small figures of Akṣobhya and Amitābha. With the book being a typical Buddhistic symbol for the Dharma, we wonder whether this triad had been intended to symbolically identify Mañjuśrī with the Dharma aspect of the *ratnatraya* as well as with the Three Jewels overall.

[3]However, Dumarçay (1974: 47) believed that the contents of the smaller niche had been hidden from view. "This was probably hidden by the ceiling which rested on the cornice and concealed the inner sanctuary of the vault above".

As previously outlined above, *sādhana* 46 from the *Sādhanamālā* describes Dharmadhātuvāgīśvara Mañjughoṣa as being surrounded by 12 other Buddhist divinities, whereas there are only 11 emplacements inside the main cella at Caṇḍi Lumbung, or 12 if we count the small niche above the emplacement for the principal image. The paved path originally connecting the central temple with the middle *perwara* in the east might provide the means for potentially explaining where the outstanding image for completing the core *maṇḍala* had been located.

As Wayman (1985: 23-24) observed, the later commentators on the *Nāmasaṃgīti* maintained that the ritual recitation of the NS text segments previously recounted from Mañjuśrīmitra's *Upadeśa* were intended to produce six or seven discrete *maṇḍala*-s, though only the ritual elements for three *maṇḍala*-s are expressly stipulated in the surviving commentaries. Of these, the later NS commentator Smṛtijñānakīrti believed that the Dharmadhātuvāgīśvara *maṇḍala* of Mañjughoṣa and the Vajradhātu *maṇḍala* of Vairocana were separate domains.[4]

Figs. A-6. Image of standing Mañjuśrī from Ratnagiri (photo credit: Prithwiraj Dhang).

[4]According to the *Niṣpannayogāvalī*, Mañjughoṣa resides in the central shrine of the Dharmadhātuvāgīśvara *maṇḍala*, surrounded by four distinct circles or 'quarters' containing a large number of additional divinities:

(a) With respect to proximity, the first group contains a total of 21 divinities: eight *Uṣṇīṣa* goddesses; Akṣobhya, Ratnasambhava, Amitābha and Amoghasiddhi on mounts in the cardinal directions and their consorts Locanā, Māmakī, Pāṇḍarā and Tārā in the intermediate directions; and four *vajra* gate keepers.

(b) The second group, which has 56 divinities, contains personifications of 12 *Bhūmi* ('spiritual stages') in the east; the 12 *Pāramitā* ('perfections') in the south; the 12 *Vaśitā* ('spiritual disciples') in the west; 12 *Dhāraṇī* deities in the north [which appear to be depicted in the Buddhist cave shrines at Ellora (Malandra 1993: 87-88)]; plus four *Pratisamvit* divinities (representing the four 'branches of logical analysis') and the four 'secret goddesses' Lāsyā, Mālā, Gītā and Nṛtya (see Wayman 1985: 28).

(c) The third group contains a total of 34 divinities: the ten 'wrathful' *Krodha* deities of the eight points of the compass, zenith and nadir; eight offering goddesses; and sixteen bodhisattvas (Bhattacharyya 1958: 83-93): Samantabhadra, Akṣayamati, Kṣitigarbha, Ākāśagarbha (Akṣobhya family, east); Ganganagañja, Ratnapāṇi, Sāgaramati, Vajragarbha (Ratnasambhava family, south); Avalokiteśvara, Mahāsthāmaprāpta, Candraprabha, Jālinīprabha (Amitābha family, west); Amitaprabha, Pratibhānakūṭa, Sarvaśokatamonirghātamati, Sarvanivaraṇaviṣkambhin (Amoghasiddhi family, north).

(d) The outermost group is inhabited by a large number of divinities, including personifications of the 28 asterisms and nine planets; the same eight directional guardians (*lokapāla*) that appear on the central shrine at Prambanan; Brahmā, Viṣṇu, Maheśvara and twelve other Hindu divinities; and four groups representing the eight kings of the *yakṣa*-s, *nāga*-s, *kinnara*-s and *gandharva*-s, respectively (see Wayman 1985: 28).

Appendix B: Original transcription for the Abhayagirivihāra charter published by de Casparis (1950)

]† †[= fragment D50d]* *[= fragment D.50e

[1] Oṃ. Dhīgambhīraguhā ⏑ — smṛtiçilaḥ sadvākyadhātūjjvalo
Maitrīprasravaṇe [⏑ — ⏑ ⏑ — — — ⏑ — — ⏑ ⏓ /
— — — ⏑ [2]] dhilokadharmmapavanair = ugrair = na saṃkampitas =
Taṃ saṃvaddhasumerum = ūrjitaguṇaṃ jñānograça — ⏑ ⏓ // 1 //
— — — ⏑ ⏑ — ⏑ ⏑ ⏑ ⏑ — — — [3]] *mī* dīpyate
Vikrāntāḥ pratiyānti tīrthyavṛṣabhā yasya prabhāvoddhatāḥ /
— — — ⏑ ⏑ — ⏑ — ⏑ ⏑ ⏑ — — — ⏑ ⏓
— — — ⏑ ⏑ — [4]] ndhanapradahanaṃ saddharmavahnin = name // 2 //
Çaikṣāçaikṣasahasracakramakaro yaḥ çunyatānirmmalo
*N*i — — ⏑ ⏑ — ⏑ — ⏑ ⏑ ⏑ — — — ⏑ — — ⏑ ⏓ /
[5] <Saṃgū> ḍhārthavicāraṇāvaranadivegaiḥ samāpyāyitaṃ
Çikṣāvandanavaddhavelam = amalam = vande guṇā — ⏑ — // 3 //
[6] prāptan = tena vuddhatvaṃ samvā*sim* = *abhavebhave* vuddhatvaṃ //
adhimuktir = *ddhana*devaḥ satatam = a [
[7] <tri> bhuvanakaranāntaḥ pāti no duḥkhamūlaṃ kṣapaya kamalapāṇe
prāṇināṃ kleçajāla*m* [ ]* saṅgā *[
[8]] sa*sk*andhe pravṛddhadhī .... abhidhārthyatāgraphalade
jayati mahārājaka [ ]* rājyam = alaṃkurvāṇaṃ
tejaḥpūrṇṇā *[
[9] pa .... dharmmadhani .... [ ] ṇe *karamva*pāṇau gurau dha-
nur = vi [ ]* < ava >nipatisa .... tuṅgam = atu
lavalavegaviva *[
[10] punaḥ karttuṃ pari .... [ ]* .... pādaiḥ . jinavaravina-
yoktaiḥ çikṣitānā *[
[11] vāṇaḥ kṛpaloḥ praçita [ ]* prajānāṃ ....
matirabhava*nna*ḥ karttuṃ śe *[
[12] dānaṃ çāsa*na*ḥ syanti . nānā [ ]* .... ça-
kanṛpakālātī *[
[13] dharmatuṅgadevasya çailendra [ ]* .... pā-
da .... *[
[14] tiṣṭhā*m* vihārasya // sarva [
[15] .... vihāraparipālanā [
[16] san = tavānakādibhiḥ saṇ = ḍa- [ ]† nyam
.... † [
[17] tābhir = viçeṣā .... [ ]† ....
ni çriyam = avadhā †[
[18] m = anuçāsanajñā bha*va*nti [ ]† ta ...... jātārthavi-bhāgavi*jñā*ḥ †[

Appendix C: Emended transcription for the Abhayagirivihāra charter based on remarks by de Casparis (1961, 1981) and Chandra (1995)

]† †[= fragment D.50d
]* *[= fragment D.50e
]‡ ‡[= fragment D.50f
{gap} = unrecovered segment between fragments

[1] Oṃ. Dhīgambhīraguho<vara>smṛtiśilaḥ sadvākyadhātūj<j>valo maitrīprasravaṇaḥ]‡ samādhivanavān = alpecchatākandharaḥ / Yo <′>ṣṭābhir=a ‡[
[2] <pi>lokadharmmapavanair = ugrair = na saṃkampitas = tam samvuddhasumerum = ūrjjitaguṇaṃ jñānograśa]‡ ktin = name // 1 // Lok<e carrṣiva>rapravāhisamayān = ākramya ‡[
[3] yo dīpyate vitrastāḥ pratiyānti tīrthyavṛṣabhā yasya prabhāvoddhatāḥ /]‡ Nānā-dṛṣṭi<vimarśā>vṛndam = api yo bhasmikaroti kṣaṇāt = sam sarvvānu ‡[
[4] <niba>ndhapradahanaṃ sadharmmavhanin = name // 2 // Śaikṣāśaikṣasahasra<n>akra-makaro yaḥ śūnyatāni<mito> ni-]‡ rmokṣaikarasaḥ subhāsitāmahāratnākaro hrihradhaḥ / ‡[
[5] <Saṃgū>ḍhārthavicāraṇāvaranad<i>vegaiḥ samāpyāyitaṃ śikṣāvandanāvaddha-velam = amalam = vande guṇāgrā<rṇa>vam // 3 //]‡ .... ‡[
[6] prāptan = tena vuddhatvaṃ samvāsim = abhavebhave vuddhatvaṃ // 4 // adhimuktir = ddhanadevaḥ satatam = a {gap}]‡ .... // 5 // ‡[
[7] <Tri>bhuvanakaranāntaḥ pāti no duḥkhamūlaṃ kṣapaya kamalapāṇe prāṇināṃ kleśajālaṃ {gap}]‡ .... // 6 // ‡[
[8] . . . saskandhe pravṛddhadhī . . . . abhidhārthyatāgraphalade jayati mahārājaka {gap}]* ... saṅgā ... // 7 // *[{gap}]‡ .... ‡[
[9] pa . . . . dharmmadhani . . . . ṇe karamvapāṇau gurau dhanur = vi {gap // 8-9 //}]* Rājyam = alaṃkurvāṇaṃ tejaḥpūrṇṇā *[{gap}]‡ -ṇkaraṇaṃ / Gurubhiḥ saṅghārāme ′nyavihāro ′yaṃ kṛtaḥ paścāt // 10 // ‡[
[10] punaḥ karttuṃ pari .... {gap }]* <ava>nipatisa . . . . . . tuṅgam = atulavalavega-viva *[{gap}]‡ .... // 11 // Ayam iha jinasūnoḥ padma ‡[
[11] pāneḥ kṛpāloḥ prathita ⏑ ⏑ ⏑ — — — ⏑ — — ⏑]* pādaiḥ / Jinavaravinayoktaiḥ śikṣitānāṃ *[{gap}]‡ <ya>tīnām abhayagirivihāraḥ kāritaḥsiṅhalānāṃ // 12 // ... ‡[
[12] dānaṃ śāsanaḥ syanti . nānā [{gap}]* prajānāṃ . . . . matirabhavannaḥ karttuṃ śe *[{gap}]‡ .... sakalajanahitārtham //13// <R>ājye pravarddamāne .... ‡[
[13] samaratungadevasya śailendra{gap}]* .... //14// śakanṛpakālātī *[ ]‡ tair = varṣṣaśataiḥ saptabhiś = caturdaśabhiḥ / varṣṣaiś = cāpy = abhivṛttaiḥ kṛtā pra ‡[
[14] tiṣṭhā vihārasya //15// sarva {gap}]* ...... pāda ..... *[{gap}]‡ ....‡[
[15] .... vihāraparipālanā { gap}]‡ .... ‡[
[16] san = tavānakādibhiḥ saṇ = ḍa- [{gap}]† nyam .... †[{gap}]‡ .... ‡[
[17] tābhir = viśeṣā .... [{gap}]† .... ni śriyam = avadhā †[{gap}]‡ .... ‡[
[18] m = anuśāsanajñā bhavanti [{gap}]† ta ...... jātārthavi-bhāgavijṅāḥ †[

Appendix D: The Old Javanese segment of the Kayumwuṅan Charter[5]

Fig. A-7. Fragment D.34 of the Kayumwuṅan charter (photo credit: Shigehisa Taguchi).

[25] swasti śakawarṣātīta 746 jyeṣṭamāsa daśamī krĕṣṇapakṣa tunglai umanis wrĕhaspatiwāra tatkāla rakaray*ān* <patapā->
[26] n pu palar sang laki-laki pu palar anakabi mawaiḥ sawaḥ sīma arikiwa luang ing **babadan** lmaḥ ri ... ...
[27] k winiḥnya ha 3 i **kisir** lmaḥ ri **kayumwuṅan** winiḥnya ha 1 wha 1 i sāntwi karung lmaḥ ri **ptir** winiḥnya ha 6 ing **kalir*u*** ... ...
[28] n winiḥnya ha 3 ing kuling winiḥnya ha 3 lmaḥ ri **tri haji** ekapiṇḍa winiḥnya ha 16 wha 1 tatra sākṣī si rawan si ... ...
[29] siḥ winaiḥ takurang yu 1 sisim 1 suhan-suhan 1 si maṇḍakṣa sang **lua paṇḍak** anakbanua i *ji* ... ...
[30] takurang yu 1 simsim 1 ta*s*inta*n*amu sang kaniryyan anakbanwa i **walingbing** watak *s*i ... ...

[5]De Casparis 1950: 40-41; 47-48. The phrases in a bold typeface above are the toponyms listed in figure 5-4.

[31] 1 wadwā sang makudur kinon umadagga saṅ=anakbanwa magawai ri hawuryyan *ra* ...
... ...
[32] karhyang winaiḥ takurang yu 1 si bahas rama ni *mai* ... ... wi ... ...
[33] ... ... kalima si habak ... ...
[34] ... ...
[35] ... ... hlai 1 kalamwi 1 punukan 1 su-
[36] ... ... mañjan rama ni pagar winaiḥ takurang yu 1 juru si jati rama ni swara winaiḥ
[37] takurang yu 1 i **sukun** si madhawa rama ni bhawana winaiḥ takurang yu 1 i **wariṅin** juru si lañcang rama
[38] ni nari winaiḥ takurang yu 1 i **wuatan** kalima si maṅga rama ni napal winaiḥ takurang yu 1 i **paṇḍa-**
[39] **kyan** juru si rindang rama ni gunung winaiḥ takurang yu 1 i **ptir** juru si wikrama rama ni dhara winaiḥ takurang
[40] yu 1 rama si piṅul rama ni ambari winaiḥ takurang yu 1 kalima si kunwurama rama ni taji winaiḥ takurang yu
[41] 1 putiḥ hlai 1 kalambi 1 punukan 1 suhan-suhan 1 i **lupaṇḍak** kalima si kalap rama ni nanta wi-
[42] naiḥ takurang yu 1 putiḥ hlai 1 kalamwi 1 punukan 1 suhan-suhan 1 juru si danaka rama ni dara winaiḥ
[43] takurang yu 1 parwuwus si hrĕm rama nyawak winaiḥ takuramg yu 1 i **tri haji** rama si pañca rama ni tīrtha winaiḥ takurang yu 1 si-
[44] liḥ juru si śaṅkara rama ni carmi winaiḥ takurang yu 1 parwuwus si gunung rama ni rasal winaiḥ takurang yu 1 parwuwus
[45] si katil rama ni buwi winaiḥ takurang yu 1 wariga si sumbut rama ni siddha winaiḥ takurang yu 1 juru matuha syawit rama
[46] ni ayat winaiḥ takurang yu 1 kalima si sampū rama ni bamung winaiḥ takurang yu 1 si pañca rama ni hrĕng winaiḥ takurang yu 1
[47] putiḥ hlai 1 kalamwi 1 lukai 1 punukan 1 wadung 1 patuk krĕs 1 parwuwus sang **kayumvuṅan** si haras rama ni
[48] wikrami anakbanwa i **tyusan** winaiḥ takurang yu 1 parwuwus sang **mantyāsih** sang kīrti punta ni nabha anakbanwa ri
[49] **tri haji** winaiḥ takurang yu 1 parwuwus sang lwa **paṇḍak** si kbal rama ni jamin anakbanwa ri **tri haji** winaiḥ takurang
[50] yu 1 tuhalas ri **hulu luwas** = si silpa rama ni yada winaiḥ takurang yu 1 tuhalas ri **kaṇḍaṅan lamwas** = si
[51] saruḥ rama ni kuting winaiḥ takurang yu 1 kinon **rakai patapān** ... ...

Appendix E: Stūpa constructions in Central Java during the eighth and ninth centuries

The *stūpa* types exhibited at the ancient Buddhist sites in Central Java can be generally categorized as (a) free-standing, as either the principal structure at a site or as a subsidiary structure at a temple complex; (b) the crowning elements for the principal shrine and/or the auxiliary shrines of a temple complex; and (c) the symbolic adornments for Buddhist buildings. The principal examples of the free-standing type in Central Java are known from the remnants found at Buddhist temple sites such as Banyunibo, Cupuwatu, Dawangsari, Mendut, Kalasan, Kalongan, Plaosan Kidul and Plaosan Lor, Ratu Baka, Sojiwan, (Sewu) Lor and the brick *stūpa* bases unearthed at the eastern foot of the hill upon which Barabuḍur rests (Bernet Kempers 1976: 17). Though Barabuḍur is the best known example of a monument that makes extensive use of small *stūpa* forms as symbolic adornments for niches, these are likewise found in abundance elsewhere, such as on the rooftops of the central and/or subsidiary shrines at the *caṇḍi*-s Lumbung, Sojiwan and Sewu.

Free-standing stūpa types. The *stūpa* found at Cupuwatu (Tjoepoe Watoe; see P-044199 and P-044200 by van Kinsbergen) that was later moved to the resident's house in Yogyakarta (IJzerman 1891: 12; P-044585 by Cephas) provides us with an example of the free-standing type.

> "Cupuwatu stūpa, now in front of Gedung Agung, is explicitly likened to a candle-stick by the local population in the alternative name 'Tugu Lilin'. Cupu-watu, a cupu made of stone. A cupu = cepu = cembul is a protrusion, such as on a lid. When the stūpa was discovered in the village bearing the same name it was found buried with only the top element being visible. The locals likened the crowning element of this artifact to the small knob that is commonly found on the porcelain lids of Javanese coffee or tea cups, hence cupu made of stone" (Jordaan, pc 13 July 2012).

The Cupuwatu *stūpa* has a base ornamented with reliefs but is not surmounted by a conventional *yaṣṭi*. The crowning element is a little flame-shaped pillar, which is what gives the *stūpa* the appearance of a tall candle-stick. A comparable motif was used for the antefixes mounted atop the enclosure wall surrounding the Abhayagirivihāra's double-platform on the western prominence of the Ratu Baka Plateau. The dome of the *stūpa* is in the form of a tall cylinder that instead of being smooth is divided into narrow vertical panels and with an ornamental band decorating the mid-point of this structural element. The base of the entire edifice is an octagon. There are four relief bands on the octagonal structure above the multi-petaled lotus symbolizing the primordial waters from whence unfold all possibilities inherent in the stone base (*ādhāraśīlā*)—the "omphalos or nābhi of the temple" as the "concrete form (*mūrti*) of universal manifestation" (Kramrisch 1946: 111-112).

The series of tortoises within the first band evoke the world tortoise believed to support the earth. The largest panels within the second band (the earth-world) depict seated or prancing lions flanked on either side by a standing male figure. The third band (the air-world) is entirely filled with the images of birds with spread and closed wings, whilst the fourth band (heaven) consists of a series of panels in which are depicted a *tricola* motif or seated figures. Additionally the *stūpa-harmikā* has columns at the corners adorned with scrolls of vegetation in relief (Krom 1923 I: 255-257).

Fig. A-8. Freestanding *stūpa* constructions at Caṇḍi Sojiwan. (Photo credit: Roy Jordaan).

Small freestanding *stūpa* designs were also found at Caṇḍi Mendut, either within the temple yard itself or in the general vicinity. Though these structures also possess domes that are cylindrical in form, they do not have a *padmāsana* at the base nor any ornamentation, which suggests that these small *stūpa* constructions were intended to serve as commemorative reliquaries for the venerable monks who had formerly resided at this temple complex, back when the temple complex was still a living religious institution. The lack of any surviving *yaṣṭi* suggests that the *stūpa* spires had been made of metal or perishable materials.

Fig. A-9. The small freestanding *stūpa* constructions at Caṇḍi Mendut.

Figs. A-10 & A-11 Stūpa-harmikā constructions on the roof of a *perwara* at Caṇḍi Lumbung and on the roof of a subsidiary shrine at Caṇḍi Sewu.

Dawangsari is one of the few sites in Central Java where a large free-standing *stūpa* has been unearthed that was not found in close proximity to a far larger building of the *prāsāda* type. Unfortunately, the *stūpa* near the Hindu temple of Caṇḍi Barong in the middle of the Ratu Baka Plateau, approximately 700 meters to the east of the ruins of the Javanese branch of the Abhayagirivihāra, has only been partially restored and appears to be missing the *harmikā* and spire. Degroot (2009: 253) suggests that the site may contain the remains of two *stūpa* constructions.[6] With respect to the 52 small freestanding *stūpa* buildings formerly surrounding Caṇḍi Kalasan, I have already summarized what is known about them elsewhere (Long 2011: 15). Additionally, Degroot (2009: 234) notes the existence of six *stūpa* constructions at Banyunibo that appear to have been placed independent of the site's principal shrine.

Stūpa crowning a prāsāda. At the Sewu and Lumbung temple complexes, the *harmikā* is sandwiched between three narrow horizontal ledges of ascending (top) and/or descending (bottom) dimensions, with the overall effect being that it diminishes the importance of the actual *harmikā* from a visual perspective.[7] Similar ledges appear at the top of the *harmikā*-s in cave shrines 19 and 26 at Ajanta, but not within the space below these structures, which directly rest on bell-shaped *stūpa*-domes. A comparable example is found atop the dome crowning one of the subsidiary shrines at Caṇḍi Sewu (figure A-11). The ascending ledges

[6]For a more detailed survey of the *stūpa* remnants in Central Java, see Degroot 2009.

[7]This suggests that Lumbung and Sewu date from roughly the same period. By contrast, the square *harmikā*-s adorning many of the *stūpa* constructions on the summit of Barabuḍur are stylistically closer to those found at Plaosan Lor and Sojiwan. Based on art-historical considerations, Klokke (2013: 26) has proposed that Rakai Garung had restored the fourth balustrade at Barabuḍur as well as portions of other preexisting Buddhist monuments during the first part of his reign, prior to constructing Plaosan Lor and Plaosan Kidul.

above the *harmikā* appear in many younger representations of Meru found in Buddhist caves as well as on Chinese tapestries and Tibetan *tanka* paintings.

The potential symbolic significance of the number of *stūpa* forms adorning the top tiers of a Javanese Buddhist *caṇḍi* such as Barabuḍur (72) and Mendut (49) have long been the subject of heightened scrutiny and speculation. By contrast, there only appear to be 40 smaller *stūpa* forms surrounding the crowning *stūpa* at Candi Sojiwan (see fig. A-14), though the addition of eight roof-tier niches potentially bring the symbolic numerical count once again to 49 (40+8+1).

At Plaosan Lor, the highest roof level on either reconstructed *vihāra* supports a total of 37 *stūpa* constructions,[8] a symbolic number embedded into the architectural designs of the Kalasan and Mendut temples (see Long 2011: 3-4) that potentially is related to the 37 *bodhipakṣika-dharma*-s. Furthermore, the core area of the *vajradhātu-maṇḍala* features Vairocana surrounded by 36 divinities (Snodgrass 1985: 149-150). Or, if we consider the twin *vihāra*-s at Plaosan Lor as a pair, there are a total of 72 *stūpa* constructions surrounding the principal crowning structures at their summits.

Figs. A-12 and A-13. The dome and icon atop the Kalasan *stūpa* bell.

[8]For a reconstruction on paper of the west-facing facade of a Plaosan Lor *vihāra*, see Atmadi 1979: Lampiran XIV-1.17, fig. 6-2 or Atmadi 1988: 370, Appendix: XIV.1-17, which provide a view of the north side of a *vihāra* roof. The main *stūpa* crowning either *vihāra* is immediately surrounded by two lower tiers of eight *stūpas* each, or 16 in total. Moreover there are five medium-sized *stūpas* on pedestals on the north (3 + 2) and south (2 + 3) sides of the roof, and also five more on the east (2 + 1 + 2) and west (2 + 1 + 2) sides. Additionally, each building's false third level beneath the roof integrates a total of 16 niches (five facing east, three facing south, five facing west and three facing north) as well as a *stūpa* at each of its four corners. It is also interesting that the central tower of either *vihāra* is flanked by two medium-sized *stūpa* constructions on the north and south sides, which collectively may symbolize the five peaks of the cosmic mountain Meru.

A Central Javanese artifact unearthed in the *desa* Kalasan during 1927 is also worthy of our close attention. A Javanese laborer discovered this bronze *stūpa*-shaped bell,[9] which is 57.5 cm. in height and has a maximum diameter of 42 cm., at a depth of about two feet below the surface of a sugarcane field located about 400 meters to the southwest of Caṇḍi Kalasan. A vase with a greenish-colored glaze and a height of 64.5 cm. also was found next to the bell. This second artifact may have served as a holy water vessel (Oudheidkundig Verslag 1927: 106).

Bosch (1929: 47-48) believed that the Kalasan bell was substantially more than a religious implement for producing sonorous sounds in the general vicinity of the Kalasan monastery, the remains of which were discovered by Baker about 200 meters to the south of the Kalasan temple. Given the bell's *stūpa* form, silver patina and lack of a clapper, Bosch viewed this particular example of Central Javanese art as having itself been an object of veneration. The principal point in favor of his hypothesis is the double lotus cushion on which the dome of the bell in the shape of a *stūpa* rests, which is likewise the case with the bell-shaped *stūpa* form of Central Javanese architecture. The *padmāsana* is only found beneath *stūpa* constructions, sculptures of deities or other objects of veneration—a point which leads us to focus on the iconic depiction of a crouching lion atop the double *harmikā,* stylized as yet another *padmāsana*, resting on the dome of the *stūpa* bell.

Bosch suggested that this bronze *stūpa* bell had been given a silver patina so that it would shine forth in the sunlight whenever carried in solemn religious processions. He also observed that the symbolic importance of the lion surmounting the bell's dome becomes clarified when we take note of the connection between the bell as the enclosure for producing sonorous tones and the *stūpa* as the enclosure for the Dharma-preaching Buddha, whose speech (*vāc*) is compared to the roar of a lion.

> "The historical Buddha was known as the lion of the Śākya clan, and the lion's roar is a metaphor for the first sermon, the Buddha's message to the world. Also, the lion's yawn (Skt. *simhavijrmbhita*) is sometimes used as a metaphor for the enlightened conduct of bodhisattvas and saints. Each time a bell was struck, these symbolic messages were made known to the world" (Fontein *et al.* 1990).

The lion is also the *vāhana* of Vairocana, the Tathāgata of the zenith whose family (*kula*) symbol is the *stūpa*. The discovery of oval column-supports near the Abhayagirivihāra on the Ratu Baka Plateau (Degroot 2006: 65-66), each of which displays the *vāhana* of one of the five Tathāgatas, shows that Javanese Buddhists were aware of the lion's link with Vairocana by the first half of the ninth century, if not earlier. Moreover, the ringed hole on the lion's back (not visible in the photograph above), which was for supporting the wooden rod from which this bell hung during processions, may also be considered a symbol for the supernal sun.

---

[9]Other examples of *stūpa*-shaped bells were found in Western Java (P-044790; Claire Holt) and Eastern Java (OD-1628; Leydie Melville). See also the photo by Cephas (P-044606) of a collection of predominantly East Javanese bells.

Fig. A-14. *Stūpa-harmikā* constructions adorning the roof of Caṇḍi Sojiwan (Photo credit: Roy Jordaan).

Appendix F: *Stūpa* components according to the *Kriyāsaṃgraha*

The *Kriyāsaṃgraha* compiled by Kuladatta[10] contains a segment that delineates the structural components of the *stūpa* and equates them with specific elements from Mahāyāna Buddhist doctrine (see Snodgrass 1985: 368, fig. 281). Estimates for the age of this Nepalese text have varied from the ninth to the twelfth century, though Skorupski (Kuladatta & Skorupski 2002: 15) remarked that the copy "preserved in the Kaishar Library in Nepal is dated Samvat 336, which corresponds to A.D. 1216. This is the only firm date that is available to us, and confirms the existence of the *Kriyāsaṃgraha* at the beginning of the thirteenth century". Whether this Buddhist treatise had been written shortly before 1216 CE, or several decades, or even a century prior to that date, remains a matter of conjecture. Nevertheless, just like the VVS this Nepalese Buddhist text clearly contains material of greater antiquity.

Figs. A-15 & A-16. *Harmikā* designs, caves 19 and 26 at Ajanta (photo credits: Nicolas Revire).

As Bénisti's transcription and translation (1960: 89-108) demonstrate, the *Kriyāsaṃgraha* refers to the *stūpa* using the term *dharmadhātu*. In the following discussion, however, we shall emulate Bénisti and continue to use the

[10]It is evident that Kuladatta had compiled his text by drawing upon a large number of sources. For example, Wayman notes that Kuladatta cited 18 verses from the *Vairocanābhisambodhi-tantra* in his own work (Wayman & Tajima (1998: 18).

more universal term *stūpa* when citing the structural elements set forth in this Nepalese compendium of Buddhist rituals. The base of the *stūpa*, which is said to consist of twelve measurement modules that correspond with the twelve-fold chain of Dependent Co-origination (*pratītya-samutpāda*), and can be made round, four sided, have twelve elements or even twenty angles, e.g. with the last platforms having cusps. Above the base are the so-called six platform 'legs', which correspond with the exact count of the six types of awareness.

"This term *janghāvedi*, 'platform legs', is highly significant. It reflects the anthropomorphic symbolism of the *stūpa*. It represents a body, that of the Mahāpuruṣa, the Universal Man, the Buddha. The lower part of the *stūpa* is identified with the lower body and is designated by the same term: *janghā* or 'leg'. We shall see that the dome represents the trunk and the superstructure the head. But the *stūpa* represents not only the body of Buddha; all the references (terms, measures) to the very principles of Buddhism in this text show that the monument is also the body of the Law" (Bénisti 1960: 97).

The *Kriyāsaṃgraha* presents four acceptable forms for the dome that are called (a) like a heap of rice grains (*dhānyakaṭaka*), (b) an alms bowl (*khakkhara*), (c) vase (*kumbha*) and (d) victory-banner (*dhvaja*), and with this last form divided into two subcategories described as vase-like or bell-shaped (Dorjee 1996: 50). At Plaosan Lor, the free-standing *stūpas* in the courtyard—and on the crowning *stūpa*-s on the *vihāra* rooftops as well—exhibit a vase-like form that is distinctly different from the 72 bell-shaped *stūpa* constructions on the summit of Barabuḍur, for example.

Citing Burnouf, Bénisti (1960: 98) explains the term *kumbha* as having its origin in antiquity with respect to the urns that originally had received the cremated remains of the Buddha's mortal body. Beyond simply being a container of relics, however, the *stūpa* dome is also "an analogical representative of the relics. The use of the term *kumbha* for the *stūpa* dome may well have further symbolic meaning. It may relate to the *pūrṇa-ghaṭa* (or *pūrṇa-kumbha*), or vase of plenty.... The *pūrṇa-ghaṭa* is also an auspicious symbol in Hinduism, where it is probably equivalent to the golden *kumbha*, containing *amṛta*" (Harvey 1984: 71-72). The *kumbha* type of dome consists of six measurement modules that precisely correspond with the six super knowledges (*abhijñā*) of the body of the Dharma (*dharmakāya*).[11] The text further states that "above the dome, according to the exact count of the triad of the Means of progress (*yāna*), the *harmikā* is of three modules to the pinnacle, but its width, according to the exact count of the four Noble Truths (*āryasatya*), [is] of four modules. Some increase in the dimensions must be made on each side" (Bénisti 1960: 99). In the opinion of Bénisti (1960: 99), this increase in size (*mānādhika*) must apply to the parts "in addition" to the supplementary reliefs, e.g the extension of the borders at the corners of the *harmikā*. The *Kriyāsaṃgraha* also refers to the *harmikā*, or pavilion, as consisting of two-thirds of the overall height, with the other third presumably consisting of ledges of increasing size, based on the known archaeological remains.

[11]In this respect, Bénisti (1960: 98) notes that the *Dhammakāya*, a Pāli text published by Cœdès (1956), likewise provides undeniable testimony to the equivalence between the *stūpa*, the Buddha and his Dharma.

Figs. A-17 & A-18. Painted deities on the sides of the *harmikā*, Ajanta cave 19
(photo credits: Nicolas Revire).

The square base and spire above the *harmikā* is called the *yaṣṭi,* which is said to be square in correspondence with the exact count of the four *brahmavihāra*-s (loving-kindness, compassion, empathetic joy and equanimity). The text also identifies the space between the top of the *harmikā* and the mid-point of the *yaṣṭi* as the proper location for depicting the guardians of the world (*lokapāla*) and this is where the *lokapāla*-s were installed in cave shrines 19 (figure A-14) and 26 (figure A-15) at Ajanta, as well as on a small *stūpa*-shaped shrine discovered in Sri Lanka (Bénisti 1960: 101). With respect to the lost icons from Caṇḍi Plaosan Lor, however, only a single sculpture or icon had straddled this space.

The spire of the *stūpa* should be adorned with 13 parasols, hence corresponding in number with the 13 *bhūmi*-s,[12] and a *varṣasthālī,* or 'pot in the rain', was placed atop the string of umbrellas. The *Divyāvadāna* refers to the same structural component (*varṣasthāla*) as being that element of the spire "in which large jewels were deposited" (Bénisti 1960: 101). In the opinion of Bénisti, the *varṣasthālī* was likely a type of flaring for receiving the rainwater believed to undergo a transubstantiation into the 'divine ambrosia'.

None of the *stūpa* forms at the principal Buddhist temples of Central Java exhibit umbrellas on the *yaṣṭi*, with the *yaṣṭi* of the main *stūpa* at Barabuḍur being the only potential exception. Van Erp's reconstruction on paper of the main *stūpa* spire at Barabuḍur shows the rudimentary indications of three sun-shades, and with a jewel motif having been mounted at the top of the shaft (see, for example, the illustration in Voûte and Long 2007: 172). On the other hand, the top part of each *stūpa-yaṣṭi* crowning either *vihāra* at Caṇḍi Plaosan Lor has a hole at the center (see figure 6-1), which could have supported a mast made of metal to reflect the rays of the sun and moon, or been made of wood or other perishable materials onto which parasols had been affixed.[13]

> "It seems that the ancient representations give us the images of umbrellas made of light materials (fabric, bamboo, etc.), which had been brought as offerings to the *stūpa* and which were affixed to the pole. But on the monolithic *stūpas* of the Gupta and post-Gupta eras—as well as those illustrated in Nepalese manuscripts—the umbrellas are disc-shaped, arranged one over the other, are firmly attached to the pole, and diminish in size. The ensemble of this overlapping of disks assumes the form of a cone, but sometimes ends up taking on—such as for the Bodh Nath in Nepal, for example—the appearance of a quadrangular pyramid" (Bénisti 1960: 101; see also figure 6-9).

The term *yaṣṭi* denotes the center post in its entirety, including the interior part entering the *harmikā* and the dome. With all measurements having been made on the post and equated with the principles of the Dharma, the *yaṣṭi* is in fact the pivotal component of the *stūpa* and by extension the symbolic axis of the world (Bénisti 1960: 103-104).

---

[12]This datum is important because it allows us to determine that the text in its current form must be several centuries younger the Buddhist temples erected in Central Java during the eighth and ninth centuries, when the available Mahāyāna Buddhists texts and commentaries predominantly discuss 10 *bhūmi*-s.

[13]A proportional measurement study following the method employed by Atmadi (1979: 127-134) for deducing the original height of Barabuḍur may provide us with an estimate of the original height of either *vihāra* at Plaosan Lor.

Index

Index